MARLOWE'S COUNTERFEIT PROFESSION:
OVID, SPENSER, COUNTER-NATIONHOOD

PATRICK CHENEY

Marlowe's Counterfeit Profession

OVID, SPENSER, COUNTER-NATIONHOOD

UNIVERSITY OF TORONTO PRESS
Toronto Buffalo London

© University of Toronto Press Incorporated 1997
Toronto Buffalo London
Printed in Canada

ISBN 0-8020-0971-9

Printed on acid-free paper

Canadian Cataloguing in Publication Data

Cheney, Patrick Gerard, 1949–
   Marlowe's counterfeit profession

   Includes bibliographical references and index.
   ISBN 0-8020-0971-9

   1. Marlowe, Christopher, 1564–1593 –
   Criticism and interpretation.   I. Title.

PR2673.C43 1997   822'.3   C97-930940-9

University of Toronto Press acknowledges the financial assistance to its
publishing program of the Canada Council and the Ontario Arts Council.

University of Toronto Press also acknowledges the financial assistance of the
College of Liberal Arts in The Pennsylvania State University.

For my mother, Marion I. Cheney
and
In memory of my father, Thomas M. Cheney

Contents

Acknowledgments

In a book primarily about literary relations, I am joyfully conscious of professional and personal relations informing my work.

Thanks first to those individuals who have read portions of the manuscript: Emily C. Bartels, Georgia Brown, Margaret P. Hannay, Jeffrey Knapp, Constance B. Kuriyama, the late Walter N. King, and Linda Woodbridge. Thanks also to those who talked with me about my project or otherwise provided encouragement along the way: Judith H. Anderson, Joe Black, John D.C. Buck, Thomas Bulger, Lisa A. Celovsky, Christopher Clausen, Frederick A. de Armas, Elizabeth Fowler, Mark Golden, Roland Greene, Matthew Greenfield, Emily Grosholz, Ronald Harris, Wendell V. Harris, Richard C. McCoy, David Lee Miller, John W. Moore, Jr, Jennifer Morrison, Jeffrey T. Nealon, Charles Nicholl, Anne Lake Prescott, Frank Romany, Michael C. Schoenfeldt, Sanford Schwartz, Lauren Silberman, Donald Stump, Garrett Sullivan, Jeffrey Walker, and Stephen Wheeler. Journal or book editors who have edited articles that eventually formed the nuclei of individual chapters include Evelyn J. Hinz, from *Mosaic* (on *Doctor Faustus*); Paul Whitfield White, from *Marlowe, History, and Sexuality* (on *Tamburlaine*); and Ronald Paulson, from *ELH* (on 'The Passionate Shepherd to His Love'); I am grateful for permission to reproduce material published in their pages. Also, I am grateful to both Maurice Charney and an anonymous reader for the University of Toronto Press for their help with the revisions.

Several students, past and present, have also contributed to the study: Dominic Delli Carpini, Colin Fewer, Laura Getty, Chad Hayton, Heather Hayton, Javier Lorenzo, Jessica K. Nassau, and Michael C. Vennera. Throughout, I have benefited from the thorough and patient scholarship of intrepid research assistants: at the outset, Jeffrey B. Morris; during the middle, Richard Cunningham; and, at the end, Gregory Semenza, who heroically checked all my citations and quotations, proof-read the entire book, and compiled the index (in the process outwrestling that Antaeüs of post-modern publishing, Microsoft Word's terrorizing 'index function').

Through support and funding from several administrators, I have been able to bear the considerable financial cost of this project: Robert A. Secor, my former English Department head; above all, Don Bialostosky, my current English Department head; Caroline D. Eckhardt, my Comparative Literature Department head; Raymond F. Lombra, Associate Dean of Research and Graduate Studies in the College of Liberal Arts; and both George A. Mauner and Robert R. Edwards, past and present directors of the Institute for the Arts and Humanistic Studies. In the Department of English, Nancy Royer, Melissa Price, and Steve Seebart provided valuable computer support.

At the University of Toronto Press, I should like to thank Suzanne Rancourt, who has generously presided over the entire publication process; Barb Porter, who has courteously helped with the printing phase; and Beverley Beetham Endersby, who has meticulously copy-edited the manuscript.

At Corpus Christi College, Cambridge University, I would like to thank the Master and Fellows (as well as Mrs Cannell) for access to the Marlowe materials in the Parker Library.

In the profession at large, I owe special debts to the late Millar MacLure, to whom I can trace my interest in the relation between Marlowe and Spenser; Robert B. Johnstone, who has served as my mentor for twenty-five years; Richard Helgerson, who has written about the English Renaissance with the force of something like magic for me; David Riggs, who carefully read the MS for the University of Toronto Press and provided a constant source of encouragement and insight; Laura Lunger Knoppers, who read parts of the MS and has provided conversation and collegiality in the Renaissance program at Penn State; and Robert R. Edwards, who also read parts of the MS, encouraged me to send my chapter on 'The Passionate Shepherd' to *ELH*, and has guided me throughout in this and in so much else – professional, personal, familial.

Finally, I would like to thank my wife, Debora, and our young sons, Evan and Kelton, for contributing – during our warm family years – the care, commitment, and loving inspiration so vital to the wintry process of research and writing.

PATRICK CHENEY

Texts and Abbreviations

Quotations from Marlowe's plays, with the exception of *Doctor Faustus*, come from *The Plays of Christopher Marlowe*, ed. Roma Gill (London: Oxford UP, 1971), except where noted. Quotations from *Doctor Faustus* come from *'Doctor Faustus': A- and B-texts (1604, 1616)*, ed. David Bevington and Eric Rasmussen (Manchester: Manchester UP, 1993). All quotations from Marlowe's verse come from *Christopher Marlowe: The Complete Poems and Translations*, ed. Stephen Orgel (Harmondsworth: Penguin, 1971). All quotations from Marlowe's *Dedicatory Epistle* of Thomas Watson's *Amintae Gaudia* to Mary Sidney come from *Christopher Marlowe: Complete Plays and Poems*, ed. E.D. Pendry, Everyman's Library (1909; London: Dent, 1976).

All quotations from Spenser's poetry come from *The Poetical Works of Edmund Spenser*, ed. J.C. Smith and Ernest De Sélincourt (Oxford: Clarendon, 1909–10). In abbreviating the titles of Spenser's works, I follow *The Spenser Encyclopedia*, gen. ed. A.C. Hamilton (Toronto: U of Toronto P; London: Routledge, 1990).

All quotations from Ovid come from *Ovid in Six Volumes*, Loeb Classical Library, trans. Grant Showerman, 2d ed., rev. G.P. Goold, 6 vols. (Cambridge, MA: Harvard UP; and London: Heinemann, 1977–89), with the exception of the *Amores*, for which I use Marlowe's translation (*Ovid's Elegies*), unless otherwise noted. The numbering of the *Amores* elegies in the Loeb volume differs from that in Marlowe's translation, because the Loeb prints III.v on Ovid's dream vision, which Marlowe does not translate, since it did not appear in the edition he was using. Thus those poems in *Ovid's Elegies* after III.iv differ in numbering from the Loeb volume, and I indicate the difference in the following way, unless the context is otherwise clear: *Ovid's Elegies* III.xiv(xv). Similarly, the line numbering in the Orgel edition of *Ovid's Elegies*, which begins with the four-line prologue to the work, differs from that in the Loeb edition, which begins with I.i. This difference, however, affects the line numbering of only the first elegy, but even so I try to clarify which edition I am citing.

All quotations and translations from other classical authors – including Lucretius, Virgil, Seneca, Lucan, and Musaeus – come from the Loeb Classical Library, unless noted otherwise. Major exceptions include Homer's *Iliad* and *Odyssey*, for which I rely on the translations of Richmond Lattimore; Plato's dialogues, for which I rely on the edition of Edith Hamilton and Huntington Cairns; Aristotle's works, for which I rely on the edition of Richard McKeon; and the Bible, for which I rely on a facsimile of the Geneva edition of 1560 published by the University of Wisconsin Press. In 'Works Cited,' I identify other editions and translations under a given author's name.

Finally, all quotations from Machiavelli come from *Niccolò Machiavelli: 'The Prince,'* ed. and trans. Robert M. Adams, 2d ed. (New York: Norton, 1992), while all quotations from Chapman come from *The Works of George Chapman*, ed. Richard Herne Shepherd, 3 vols. (London: Chatto, 1911–24), unless otherwise noted.

For the purpose of economy, I include the original text of non–English language sources only when my argument depends on it. Throughout, I modernize the archaic i-j and u-v of Renaissance texts, as well as other obsolete typographical conventions such as the italicizing of names and places.

For formatting and citation, I rely on *The MLA Style Manual* (1985), although occasionally I veer from it in order to emphasize a particular point – as when I include either the title of a work or an abbreviation of it when not absolutely required. The University of Toronto Press has also brought certain features of the text into conformity with house style.

MARLOWE'S COUNTERFEIT PROFESSION:
OVID, SPENSER, COUNTER-NATIONHOOD

A counterfeit profession is better
Than unseen hypocrisy.

Marlowe, *The Jew of Malta*

He affirmeth ... That he has as good Right to Coine as the queene of England.

Richard Baines, Deposition against Marlowe, 1593

Christofer Marly, by his profession a scholar, ... taken here for coining, ... being examined apart never denied anything, only protesting that what was done was only to see the goldsmith's cunning.

Robert Sidney, Letter to Lord Burleigh, Flushing, The Netherlands, 26 January, 1592

I, Ovid, poet of my wantonness,
Born at Peligny, to write more address.

Christopher Marlowe, born at Canterbury

Like to an Almond tree ymounted hye
On top of greene Selinis all alone.

Spenser, *The Faerie Queene*

Like to an almond tree y-mounted high
Upon the lofty and celestial mount
Of ever-green Selinus, quaintly decked.

Marlowe, 2 *Tamburlaine*

Spenser and Marlowe are ... mighty opposites, poised in antagonism ... And even as we are struck by the radical difference, we are haunted by the vertiginous possibility of an underlying sameness. What if Arthur and Tamburlaine are two faces of the same thing ...?

Stephen Greenblatt, *Renaissance Self-Fashioning*

Marlowe is ... an Ovidian poet ... a poet of Ovidian eros ... Marlowe is not Spenser.

Harold Bloom, 'Introduction,' *Christopher Marlowe*

Introduction:

Marlowe's Ovidian Career, Spenser, and the Writing of Counter-Nationhood

From jigging veins of rhyming mother-wits,
And such conceits as clownage keeps in pay,
We'll lead you to the stately tent of war,
Where you shall hear the Scythian Tamburlaine
Threat'ning the world with high astounding terms,
And scourging kingdoms with his conquering sword.

1 Tamburlaine

In this study, I attempt a comprehensive reading of the Marlowe canon.[1] The occasion for my rereading is the discovery of an interlock of three issues, largely neglected in Marlowe studies, that I shall argue preoccupied their author a good deal: the idea of a literary career; the practice of professional rivalry; and the writing of nationhood. The *Tamburlaine* epigraph above, which comes from the prologue to the only work of Marlowe's printed in his lifetime, succinctly interlocks these issues in a way that is programmatic for the following study.

In this prologue, the playwright announces a career turn from the 'jigging veins' of 'clownage' to the 'stately tent of war' – usually understood as Marlowe's rejection of the boorish popular drama of his time in favour of a new drama of high seriousness, of which he will be the inaugural author. However, the playwright superimposes onto this personalized career turn from staged drama his repetition of an actual 'career' text from printed poetry: the programmatic *October* eclogue of *The Shepheardes Calender* (1579), where Marlowe's famous older contemporary, the self-styled 'new Poete,' had predicted his Virgilian progression from pastoral to epic: 'Aban-

don then the base and viler clowne, ... / And sing of bloody ... wars' (37–
40).[2] By superimposing his professional rivalry with Spenser onto his own
idea of a literary career, Marlowe dramatizes the precise programmatic
interlock between the first two issues: he is to manage his literary career in
terms of his rivalry with England's New Poet. The remainder of the
Tamburlaine epigraph reveals what Marlowe's career rivalry is to serve: the
third issue, the writing of nationhood, as his terms 'world' and 'kingdoms'
hint. Yet Tamburlaine's voicing of 'high astounding terms' to '[t]hreat'n ...
the world' and his wielding of a 'conquering sword' to 'scourg[e] ... kingdoms' reveals a strangely subversive writing of nationhood that has not yet
shown up in our taxonomies. This 'form of nationhood' traces to the
Roman author whom Marlowe chose to translate for his own inaugural poem, *Ovid's Elegies*, and from whom I derive the term counter-
nationhood.[3] By interlocking *literary career, professional rivalry*, and
counter-nationhood in a tripartite equation, I thus consolidate the general
thesis organizing the following study: Marlowe manages a complex,
multigenre idea of a literary career, in direct professional rivalry with England's great national poet, in order to pen a poetics of counter-nationhood.

Let us unlock the interlock.

Did Marlowe even have an idea of a literary career?

To my knowledge, no one has ever asked this question, let alone tried to
respond to it. Throughout the twentieth century, scholars have assumed
that Marlowe's works – *Ovid's Elegies*; his lyric poem 'The Passionate
Shepherd to His Love'; his seven tragedies (*Dido, Queen of Carthage*;
Tamburlaine, Parts 1 and 2; *The Jew of Malta*; *Edward II*; *The Massacre at
Paris*; and *Doctor Faustus*); his translation of Book I of Lucan's *Pharsalia*,
known as *Lucan's First Book*; and his Ovidian narrative poem *Hero and
Leander* – belong to no conscious or coherent plan. Rather, they are the
spontaneous product of a wide-ranging, passionate, and revolutionary genius working somewhat randomly towards maturity. This genius, we have
learned, experimented through translation, paraphrase, and creative imitation in genres that Roman authors during the Republic and Empire had
popularized, but that in late sixteenth-century England were again coming
into vogue. Occasionally, we have also learned, the brilliant young man
rode the coat-tails of a cultural trend, such as the Senecan movement in
drama, to construct tragedies of violence, or he reacted to a cultural event,
such as the closing of the theatres in 1592–3, to produce an Ovidian narrative poem.

Spontaneity, opportunism, recklessness – these are what we have come to
expect from an individual whose former roommate, the playwright Thomas

Kyd, accused him of being 'intemperate & of a cruel hart.'[4] Not surprisingly, critics have written relatively few books covering the whole of Marlowe's canon; indeed, most books focus exclusively on the plays. When books do include the poetry, they almost always privilege *Hero and Leander*, neglecting *Ovid's Elegies* and *Lucan's First Book*. The standard biographies are an exception, but what these studies gain in biographical comprehensiveness they lose in vocational insight; in structuring their studies around the chronology of a 'life,' they neglect what Lawrence Lipking identifies as so important in his ground-breaking study of 'poetic careers' – 'the poet's need to shape some sort of career, some sense of destiny or vocation' (xii): 'no poet becomes himself without inheriting an idea of what it means to be a poet ... [E]very major Western poet after Homer ... has left some work that records the principles of his own poetic development ... [G]enres are not collections of laws and precepts but possible ways of solving his [career] problems ... [Major Western poets] share, for all their differences, a common creed: a faith in greatness. Their ambition is less to write individual great verses than to become great poets by achieving great poetic careers' (viii–xi). Marlowe critics, by traditionally tying themselves to the exigencies of a life's haphazard chronology, end up neglecting the 'idea,' the 'creed,' the 'faith' that defines and directs a 'great poetic career.' Consequently, here at century's end, we appear content to view Marlowe in terms of a critical genre we might call 'the imagined intellectual biography.'[5]

To structure Marlowe's intellectual biography, most studies typically work from a popular three-phase model:

1 / during his Cambridge years (1580–7), Marlowe writes 'apprentice' work: his translations of Ovid's *Amores* and Lucan's *Pharsalia*, and then his 'paraphrase' of Books I, II, and IV of Virgil's *Aeneid* in his first tragedy, *Dido, Queen of Carthage*;
2 / during his London theatre years (1587–92), he moves beyond the youthful work produced at Cambridge to mature drama in the form of the six remaining tragedies: *Tamburlaine 1 and 2*, *The Jew of Malta*, *Edward II*, *The Massacre at Paris*, and *Doctor Faustus*;
3 / then, during the London plague years (1592–3), when the theatres close, he concludes his (interrupted) career with an Ovidian narrative poem whose 'raptures,' wrote Michael Drayton, were '[a]ll Ayre, and fire,' the product of a genius that '[h]ad in him those brave translunary things, / That the first Poets had' ('To my Most Dearely-Loved Friend Henry Reynolds ... ,' rpt. in MacLure, ed., *Marlowe* 47): *Hero and Leander*.[6]

The three-phase model of Marlowe's 'life' records the main story that Marlowe critics have told. As a result, we have produced no synthetic view that takes its fire specifically from the shape, context, and goal of Marlowe's literary career.

Evidently, the peculiarities of Marlowe's literary career have presented problems substantial enough to have prohibited research on the topic. The problems begin with dating the works, and thus with forming a stable chronology of composition and publication (from the *Elegies* to *Faustus* to *Hero and Leander*), since only the *Tamburlaine* plays were in print during Marlowe's lifetime – and they without his name on the title page. But the problems also include trying to deal with apparently fragmentary works, and thus with establishing a reasonable degree of authorial plan (*The Massacre at Paris, Lucan, Hero and Leander*), as well as dealing with the prodigious yet interrupted production of a brilliant writer who met his death at the tender age of twenty-nine. These problems are magnified by yet another: scant authorial licence sanctioning any idea about the larger project, since Marlowe communicated little information, leaving only a few prologues (as in *Tamburlaine*), only one non-fictional document in the first person (his Latin *Dedicatory Epistle* of Thomas Watson's *Amintae Gaudia* to Mary Sidney), and only a single fictional work in the first person (*Hero and Leander*).[7]

Confronting these problems, anyone wishing to excavate Marlowe's 'idea' of a literary career is at a distinct disadvantage. Unlike with Spenser, or Jonson, or Milton – or even Daniel, Drayton, and Chapman – what we find with Marlowe is not a complete cultural artefact – 'a Renaissance idea of a literary career' – but simply a shard or series of shards buried deeply beneath layers of artistic and biographical debris.

This predicament, however, is intriguing, even cheerfully challenging, and it is the initial task of this study to excavate the fragmentary site that constitutes Marlowe's literary career.

My primary argument is that Marlowe did have an 'idea' of a literary career, and that he lived long enough to establish its contours. Thus the primary purpose of this book is to describe Marlowe's career idea and to argue for its significance in the reading of his works and in the evaluation of his place in the profession of English letters.[8]

To excavate the site of Marlowe's career idea, I reconstruct the general instrument of a literary career that was of such great importance to early modern poets, including Elizabethan ones: inherited, traditional career patterns. Among available patterns, the most authoritative and dominant remained 'the commonplace of Renaissance criticism – the [Virgilian] progression from pastoral to epic' (Webb 8). Among Marlowe's contemporaries, one poet in particular was just then advertising himself as the 'Virgil of England' – to use a phrase supplied in 1592 for Spenser by Marlowe's friend Thomas Nashe (*Pierce Penilesse* in McKerrow 1: 299). Back in 1579, the year before Marlowe left his home in Canterbury to attend Corpus Christi College, Cambridge, on a Matthew Parker scholarship, Spenser, himself a recent Cambridge graduate just down Trumpington Street at Pembroke College (BA 1573; MA 1576), inaugurated his Virgilian career by publishing his pastoral, *The Shepheardes Calender*; and then in 1590 he began more fully to circumscribe that career by publishing the first instalment of his epic, *The Faerie Queene*. As Spenser writes to open his epic (relying on a theatrical metaphor that turns out to be of interest to Marlowe), he is 'the man, whose Muse whilome did *maske*, / As time her taught, in lowly Shepheards weeds' but who now must 'chaunge' his '[o]aten reeds' for 'trumpets sterne' in order to 'sing of Knights and Ladies gentle deeds' (I.Pr.1; emphasis added).

Our tacit critical practice, then, which assumes that Marlowe worked from no conscious 'idea of a literary career,' belies the practice of and the criticism on many of his contemporaries, especially those, like Spenser, who had assumed the role of literary leadership.[9]

That Marlowe himself understood the Renaissance Virgilian progression from pastoral to epic is clear from *Tamburlaine*, which, within months of the publication of *The Faerie Queene*, advertises itself as a 'tragicall discourse' about a 'Scythian shepherd ... that became ... a monarque' (Jones, *Dedicatory Epistle*, in Gill, ed., *Plays*), and which, as we have already intimated, imitates Spenser repeatedly – often in passages about the Virgilian progression. The most famous among these passages dramatizes Tamburlaine's first action, performed for the benefit of his future wife, the princess of the East, Zenocrate: he exchanges shepherd's 'weeds' for a warrior-king's 'armour,' the oaten reed for the 'curtle-axe' (*1 Tamb* I.ii.41–3), and he even cites an authoritative precedent – not just a deity, but also a reigning poet: 'Jove sometime *masked* in a shepherd's weed' (199; emphasis added).[10] As we shall also see, Tamburlaine's exchange of social garments is metadramatically a change of theatrical costume; this change, in turn, is charged with generic, political, religious, and even sexual significance; and the complete metatheatrical action responds to Spenser.

Probably, however, Marlowe's earliest representation of the Renaissance Virgilian progression appears in his translation of the *Amores*. In Elegy xv of Book I, Ovid had fully represented the tripartite Virgilian progression from the *Eclogues* to the *Georgics* to the *Aeneid* in its proper order; he had dutifully situated the generic progression within a political context, the Empire of Augustan Rome; he had astutely identified the high imperialist *telos* of this model, *fama*; and he had even sublimated an erotic, sexual, or gendered dimension to the program by presenting the idea of a male poet singing the praise of a female city: 'Tityrus et segetes Aeneiaque arma legentur, / Roma triumphati dum caput orbis erit' (25–6: 'Tityrus and the harvest, and the arms of Aeneas, will be read as long as Rome shall be capital of the world she triumphs o'er' [Loeb trans.]). This representation identifies the four primary elements of a career model embedded in Tamburlaine's exchange of costume: a progression of genres, a political context, a poetic *telos*, and a gender dynamics. For Ovid, Virgil's model of pastoral, georgic, and epic serves the feminized Empire in order to secure her fame and that of her male poet.

In his translation of Ovid, however, Marlowe collapses the Virgilian triad into pastoral and epic, eliding the georgic; he scrambles the sacred generic order, putting epic before pastoral; he minimizes the high ring of poetic fame designed to valorize the poet of Empire; and, perhaps not surprisingly, he neuters the principals, as if to deauthorize Virgil even as Ovid had celebrated him: 'Aeneas' war, and Tityrus shall be read, / While Rome of all the conquered world is head.'[11] The motive driving Marlowe's (mis-)translation here may appear lost, but it is not difficult to relocate: he is identifying with Ovid, and he is critiquing 'the Virgil of England.' Both Marlowe's elision and his implied disrespect are what Jonson erases in his own translation (published alongside Marlowe's in the early editions of *Ovid's Elegies*), proving that the shortness of the English heroic couplet in comparison with the Latin elegiac couplet was no excuse for the erasure: 'Tityrus, Tillage, Aeney shall be read, / Whilst Rome of all the conquered world is head' (25–6).[12]

While critics have long understood the importance of traditional, inherited career patterns to the practices of early modern poets, our primary map of English Renaissance literary careers remains Richard Helgerson's 1983 *Self-Crowned Laureates*, which divides English Renaissance poets into three classes: the laureates (Spenser, Jonson, Milton), who modelled themselves largely on either Virgil or (in the case of Jonson) Horace, thereby pursuing a serious and sustained career in which literature served the nation; the amateurs (Lyly, Sidney, Donne), who modelled themselves largely on Ovid (or his Renaissance successor, the Petrarch of the *Canzoniere*), writing poetry only during their youth, and then repenting in their maturity, thereby serving the state through non-literary or diplomatic or ecclesiastical channels; and the professionals (Kyd, Dekker, Shakespeare), who modelled themselves on no one in particular (Helgerson never mentions Seneca), thereby relying on drama simply to make a living.

Within this classification, Helgerson mentions Marlowe only five times in passing (36, 112, 147, 167 [n. 62], 217), almost always in a list of poets who 'made play writing a part of an amateur career' (36). As the title of his book indicates, Helgerson privileges the laureate poet, but he argues that the one great laureate writing during Marlowe's lifetime, Spenser, fashioned his career in direct response to that of the amateurs, noting that in 'its Spenserian phase, laureate self-fashioning was ... largely confined to the amateurs and laureates' (25) – that is, it did not include the professionals. Only with Jonson, Helgerson argues, do we find a writer who struggles against the 'amateur assimilation' of youthful poetry and playwriting to use 'drama as a main vehicle for his laureate career' (36).

Helgerson's analysis is important, but it has at least one unfortunate consequence for Marlowe studies: it makes us forget some salient features of Marlowe's career. First, Marlowe was the first amateur/professional who organized his work in vigorous response to the reigning laureate, Spenser. Second, many of Marlowe's works, as *Ovid's Elegies, Dido*, and *Lucan* alone testify, derive from Roman writers of the Empire – Ovid, Seneca, and Lucan – who shared a goal of responding to Spenser's great classical model, Virgil.[13] And third, Jonson's widely acknowledged debt to Marlowe indicates (but of course does not prove) that Marlowe might qualify as a proto-national poet in the Jonsonian vein. Whereas Jonson, however, mined the satiric lode (Helgerson, *Self-Crowned Laureates* 122–44), Marlowe mined Aristotle's mother-lode: the tragic.[14]

We can never know for certain what the complete artefact of Marlowe's literary career would have looked like had the young poet survived to full maturity, as did the laureates Spenser, Jonson, and Milton. But we do have, I believe, enough evidence to speculate along reasonable lines.

In the chapters that follow, I particularize my primary argument about Marlowe's idea of a literary career by suggesting that Marlowe was in the process of constructing a career model distinctly counter-Virgilian in its forms and goals. This model consists of a brilliant fusing of the careers of three Roman counter-Virgilian poets – Ovid, Seneca, and Lucan – a fusion animated by the genius of a powerful influence on all three Roman writers, Lucretius, with his materialist philosophy.[15] Even though in his writings Marlowe combines Ovidian erotic poetry, Senecan tragedy, and Lucanic epic, all animated by Lucretian materialism, I designate his literary career idea as 'Ovidian.' I do so not simply because that career can be seen to begin and end in the Ovidian mode (*Ovid's Elegies* and *Hero and Leander* [Ellis-

Fermor 11–13]), and not simply because Ovid so profusely informs all of Marlowe's work. More particularly, I call Marlowe's literary career 'Ovidian' because Ovid dramatizes an 'Ovidian career idea' in the very document that Marlowe himself translates.

As we shall see in chapter 1, in the *Amores* Marlowe could have found Ovid responding to the Virgilian progression in the four domains of a career model already identified (literary, political, religious, and sexual). Most important to single out here, Marlowe could have found Ovid replacing the Virgilian triad of genres (pastoral, georgic, and epic) with an Ovidian triad: amatory poetry, tragedy, and epic. Thus the *Amores* begins with an announced plan to write epic (I.i.7–8); it swiftly abandons the Apollonian laurel bough for the 'sea-bank myrtle sprays' of Venus (32–4); it recurrently broods over the conflict between the lower erotic genre and the higher ones of epic (II.i) and tragedy (II.xviii, III.i); and then it appropriately concludes with a formal plan to move into the first of the highest genres, the tragedy of 'Horned Bacchus' (III.xiv[xv].17–20). In fact, the five so-called programmatic poems (I.i, II.i, II.xviii, III.i, and III.xv[xiv]) highlight the drama of Ovid's turn from elegy to the 'area maior' (III.xv.18) of tragedy and epic.[16] This three-genre *cursus* predicts fairly accurately the three genres that Ovid went on to pen before his exile: the series of elegiac poems, including the *Amores*, the *Ars amatoria*, the *Heroides*, and the *Fasti*; his one known tragedy, *Medea*; and his epic, the *Metamorphoses* (see chapter 1).

What is remarkable is that Marlowe is the first Western writer to translate this Ovidian *cursus*, and thus the first to make it literally his own. Equally remarkable, Marlowe produced a series of works that, however spontaneous they have appeared to generations of Marlowe scholars, in fact form a career pattern which conforms to the Ovidian model. Acknowledging that we are peering at shards rather than at a complete artefact, we may construct the following generic-based *cursus* for Marlowe's career:

Phase 1. Amatory poetry: *Ovid's Elegies* and 'The Passionate Shepherd to His Love'
Phase 2a. Tragedy: *Dido, Queen of Carthage*; *Tamburlaine, Parts 1 and 2*; *The Jew of Malta*; *Edward II*; *The Massacre at Paris*; and *Doctor Faustus*
Phase 2b. Epic (pre-mature): *Lucan's First Book* and *Hero and Leander*.[17]

According to this *cursus*, Marlowe's literary career begins where Ovid's did – with a youthful phase of amatory poetry or what Harry Levin usefully terms 'the pastoral fields of Ovidian lyricism' (32). Quite literally, Marlowe's career begins where Ovid's did, since Marlowe inaugurates his career by translating Ovid's inaugural poem. As our discussion has anticipated, Marlowe, in his translation of the Virgilian distich in *Amores* I.xv, reinscribes the Virgilian progression from pastoral to epic in Renaissance terms and contextualizes his (mis-)translation as a counter to Spenser's self-presentation.

In addition to *Ovid's Elegies*, Marlowe's amatory phase includes 'The Passionate Shepherd to His Love.' Unlike Spenser's inaugural phase, which produced a monumental document in the genre of pastoral, *The Shepheardes Calender*, Marlowe's inaugural phase in the genre of the pastoral Ovidian lyric is fragmentary and elusive. 'The Passionate Shepherd' can hardly stand up to the elaborate structure of Spenser's twelve-eclogue 'Calender for every yeare' ('Envoy' 1). Yet, in a modest way Marlowe's pastoral had its own meteoric effect during the period, producing a spate of replies, most famously 'The Nymph's Reply,' written by Sir Walter Ralegh. As we shall see in chapter 3, Marlowe's complex network of diachronic intertextuality – the pastorals of Theocritus and Virgil, a pastoral within Ovid's epic *Metamorphoses* – combined with his synchronic repetition of Spenser's progression from pastoral to epic, reveals that in this lovely lyric Marlowe is contesting the Virgilian progression and countering it with an Ovidian one.

After experimentation with the 'apprentice' phase of amatory poetry, Marlowe's literary *cursus* moves to a mature or 'master' phase that mixes Senecan tragedy with Ovidian and Lucanic epic. The experiments in tragedy remain the most substantial part of the extant record, and thus have received an enormous amount of attention. What the plays have not received is an analysis within the Ovidian *cursus*. Marlowe's seven tragedies divide into three groups – two triads and a single separate play. The first group, which critics place earliest, consists of the triad *Dido* and *Tamburlaine 1 and 2*; the second group, which critics place after the first, consists of the 'plays of policy,' the triadic *Jew of Malta*, *Edward II*, and *Massacre at Paris*; and the single or separate play, which critics see as either a continuation of or a 'return' to the spirit of the first triad, is *Doctor Faustus*: 'O lente, lente currite noctis equi!' (V.ii.74) – a deft rewriting of *Amores* I.xiii.40 ('"lente currite, noctis equi!"').[18]

It is in the tragedy phase of his career that Marlowe most radically rewrites the Ovidian *cursus* for Western culture. He needs to do so because, in the first place, Ovid had failed to write it. In the *Amores*, Ovid had relied on great fanfare to advertise his turn from love elegy to tragedy; but, by the beginning of the Christian era, Ovidian tragedy had fallen into the void – except as a slender and therefore vulnerable linguistic projection or reference by the poet himself and as an equally vulnerable series of isolated references in subsequent writers (see chapter 1). It appears to me that Marlowe accepts Ovid's career model without accepting Ovid's fate; he aims to complete the career that Ovid had failed to complete. And he relies not simply on Seneca and the English Senecan movement, but also on the English Machiavellian movement, to transact that completion. In effect, Marlowe turns to, and depends heavily on, a figure he names 'Machevill' in the prologue to *The Jew of Malta* in order to advance his literary authority as a writer of tragedy in early modern culture.[19]

In the last phase of Marlowe's Ovidian *cursus*, during a lull in the phase of tragedy caused by the closing of the theatres, his career moves into epic: he translates Book I of Lucan's epic *Pharsalia*; and he writes the Ovidian *epyllion Hero and Leander*. The appearance of these two 'pre-epics' in the Stationers' Register together (28 September 1593) may record posthumously Marlowe's plan to complement his work in tragedy with another 'high' genre in the Renaissance hierarchy of genres. Marlowe's epic production is brief, as well as tragically abbreviated, but we should not therefore blind ourselves to its existence. What intrigue me are the ways in which Marlowe's translation of a classical epic and his venture in a 'minor epic' prefigure – train him for – future work in the genre.[20]

By recognizing an 'Ovidian *cursus*' for Marlowe's literary career, we can free ourselves from the arch-spectre of Marlowe scholarship: the problem of constructing an accurate chronology for the canon.[21] None the less, the three generic divisions of Marlowe's Ovidian *cursus* coincide with three of the main conclusions about the dating of Marlowe's canon: first, that Marlowe wrote *Ovid's Elegies* during the Cambridge years (1580–7); second, that he wrote all of the tragedies except *Dido* (and perhaps *Tamburlaine*) after the Cambridge years (1587–92); and, third, that he wrote *Hero and Leander* late in his career. The only work that proves controversial within this broad pattern – that is, that veers from the conventional dating chronology – is crucial to my argument: *Lucan's First Book*. While most critics assign the translation to the Cambridge years as a companion piece to the *Elegies* and *Dido*, such scholars as C.S. Lewis (*English Literature* 486) and recently James Shapiro ('"Lucan"' 323–4) assign a late date, noting that the translation was entered in the Stationers' Register immediately before *Hero and Leander*. In a curious way for such a seemingly marginal work, Marlowe's translation functions as a key to the structure of Marlowe's career idea. Perhaps critics have not seen this structure because they have depended on the scholarly tradition that dates the translation early. As we shall see, this tradition obscures what the Stationers' Register communicates: in 1593,

Marlowe is ready to present himself as beginning work on a new 'epic' phase of his career.

Once freed from the spectre of 'chronology,' we can further excavate the fragmentary site of Marlowe's literary career by dusting off what does remain tangible: the *fiction* that Marlowe creates about his career *within his works*. Marlowe's works may not show him presenting himself through the strategies that Helgerson emphasizes in Spenser, Jonson, and the other 'laureates' (*Self-Crowned Laureates* 23–5), all of whom had the good fortune to get out of their twenties alive. For instance, we cannot locate in the Marlowe canon an authorized persona such as Spenser's Colin Clout or Jonson's Horace in *The Poetaster* (or even Milton's Attendant Spirit in *Comus*). Similarly, we cannot find any Marlowe text ordered by the elaborate humanist apparatus that characterizes Spenser's *Shepheardes Calender* and 1590 *Faerie Queene* or Jonson's 1616 folio edition of his *Works*. Indeed, critics cannot agree on Marlowe's attitude towards the protagonist of the only work published in his lifetime, *Tamburlaine*. Characteristically, we are even forced to acknowledge that the one work which has achieved great international renown as a 'masterpiece,' *Doctor Faustus*, exists in *two* versions and is so plagued by textual problems as to threaten the concept of authorship altogether. Rather than discovering here a rationale for abandoning authorship, however, I see a challenge precisely to test it.[22] To reduce 'Marlowe' to a 'Marlowe effect' is to erase the historicity of Marlowe's achievement, for, as we shall see, he is the first playwright on the new European stage to *author* himself forcibly into his plays.

While the young Marlowe secretes away his intentions as an artist within the Elizabethan literary system more than do the laureates, we can still follow him, for he has left tracks. The most obvious of these include the four prologues he has left us (*1 Tamburlaine, 2 Tamburlaine, The Jew of Malta, Doctor Faustus*) and the two prologue-like scenes in *Dido* and *Edward II*, in all of which Marlowe presents himself and his literary career: 'Not marching now in fields of Trasimene ... / Intends our muse to daunt his heavenly verse' (*Doctor Faustus* Prologue 1–6). Nearly as obvious, but much more rare, are the passages in which Marlowe employs the authorial first-person voice. Thus, in the Mary Sidney *Dedication* he uses the non-fictional 'I': 'I believe that I can achieve more than my unripe natural talents are accustomed to bring forth.' And in *Hero and Leander*, he uses the fictional 'I': 'I could tell ye / ... but my rude pen / Can hardly blazon forth the loves of men' (I.65–70). Most famously, of course, we need to include Marlowe's portraits of his major protagonists (Tamburlaine, Barabas, Edward II, the Guise, Faustus), where critics still regularly find Marlowe, albeit in more intriguing ways than did the Romantics and their heirs.[23] We can include as well Marlowe's portraits of certain minor characters (Ithamore, Gaveston, Lightborn, Baldock, Spencer, Ramus), where critics also find Marlowe lurking – 'live with me and be my love,' sings Ithamore (*Jew* IV.ii.93), quoting 'The Passionate Shepherd to His Love' (1). As we shall see especially in chapter 4, Marlowe's well-documented self-quotation here on the newly formed Elizabethan stage looks to be one of Marlowe's singular inventions for revealing his *authorship* in an otherwise anonymous medium.[24]

We can also find Marlowe's tracks in three other textual sites. The first is his recurrent and extensive metadiscourse, such as Tamburlaine's speech on 'all the pens that ever poets held' (*1 Tamb* V.i.161). The second is his equally recurrent and extensive metatheatre, such as appears in the Guise's report to the Queen-Mother, Catherine, that his men 'shall be actors in this massacre' (*Massacre at Paris* iv.29). The third site is Marlowe's imitation of and intertextuality with the writers we have seen situated within the fiction of his career idea: Lucretius, Virgil, Ovid, Seneca, Lucan, Machiavelli, and Spenser. Sifted and finally reconstructed, all such evidence helps us piece together the artefact of Marlowe's Ovidian career within the Elizabethan literary system.

As my references to Spenser indicate, the secondary purpose of this study is to contextualize Marlowe's Ovidian career idea synchronically, within its immediate literary environment, including its generic, religious, political, and sexual dimensions. Hence, my secondary argument is that Marlowe was constructing his revolutionary career model, not simply as part of the larger Renaissance recovery and assimilation of classical authors, but more particularly to contest the Virgilian-based model of his first great rival, Spenser.[25] Thus Marlowe's well-known diachronic scholarship on classical authors is not strictly 'scholarly,' but a covert strategy for transacting a synchronic rivalry with England's great national poet. In this way, Marlowe's idea of a literary career seeks to establish his authority within the Elizabethan literary system and his artistic fame beyond that system.

In the chapters that follow, I particularize my secondary argument by suggesting that what Marlowe contests are the four main dimensions of Spenser's career model: his generic Christianizing of the Virgilian progression; his political mechanism of reconstructing the Empire of Augustus in Queen Elizabeth's English yard; his *telos* of intimately relating poetic fame to Christian glory; and his gender dynamics relating male to female in the mutual desire of marriage. As alternatives, Marlowe introduces an Ovidian *cursus* championing the genres of amatory poetry, tragedy, and epic; a political goal of challenging the authority of his sovereign through an assertion of his own authority as a writer; an Ovidian goal of poetic fame; and an erotic goal of carving out a new 'homoerotic' space for the artist.[26]

To stage his contestation, Marlowe resurrects and integrates the works of one Roman writer whom he would have known to have committed suicide after taking a love potion, and three Roman writers who all died, at least officially, for their rebellion against the Empire.[27] Marlowe's career model contests Spenser's, and in doing so offers a (secret) critique of what Spenser's literary career serves: the literary, political, religious, and sexual ideals of Queen Elizabeth's nascent Empire.[28]

In critiquing Spenser's four-dimension Virgilian career model, Marlowe is attempting to rewrite Spenser's England. 'Spenser's England,' of course, is not a monolith, for the best recent criticism on Spenser, like that on Virgil, discovers an 'ambivalence' in Spenser's attitude towards his sovereign and the project of empire, revealing him to be protective of the Queen's authority and simultaneously willing to critique its misuses. The problem we confront with Marlowe's rewriting of Spenser's England is thus very much like the one we confront with Ovid's or Lucan's rewriting of Virgil's Rome. Even though in the late twentieth century we can spy the father-poet's ambivalence and resistance to authority, evidently their immediate offspring either could not or would not. Marlowe's Spenser, like Ovid's or Lucan's Virgil, remains largely monolithic. Like Lucan and Ovid with Virgil, Marlowe objects not so much to Spenser (of whom there is little trace in Marlowe) as to what we might call the 'official' Spenser: that part of Spenser consonant with the Crown. If we wish to accuse Marlowe of being a 'bad' reader of Spenser, we need to recall that the company he keeps is good, for both Ovid and Lucan were equally 'bad' readers of Virgil. More profitably, we can concentrate on what Marlowe finds so objectionable about 'Spenser' and push to exfoliate its complexities, psychological as well as literary.

To trace Marlowe's critique of Spenser's writing of England, I rely on Marlowe's repeated 'borrowings' from Spenser. We still lack a detailed analysis of this topic, but critics have long brooded over the problem of 'plagiarism' in the curious conjunction of the two, whom Stephen Greenblatt famously labels 'mighty opposites, poised in antagonism' (*Renaissance Self-Fashioning* 222). In 1793, for instance, Steevens expressed surprise at finding a 1590 simile of Spenser's (*FQ* I.vii.32: 'Lyke to an Almond tree ... / On top of greene Selinus') in a 1587–8 play of Marlowe's (*2 Tamb* IV.iii.115–24) (qtd. in *Variorum Edition* 1: 252–3). In 1805, however, Todd explained that Marlowe had access to Spenser's manuscript and was thus the 'plagiarist' (qtd. in *Variorum Edition* 1: 252–3). Until the mid-twentieth century, critics agreed with Todd, including the two most detailed analyses – by Charles

Crawford (1901) and Georg Schoeneich (1907), both of whom introduced numerous borrowings, ranging from clear 'plagiarism' to skilled *imitatio* and (in the case, especially, of Schoeneich) to close conjunctions, intriguing echoes, and less intriguing parallels. In 1942, however, T.W. Baldwin argued that Spenser was the plagiarist ('Genesis [I]'), only to be countered forcefully in 1944 by W.B.C. Watkins, who largely closed the discussion down (see Baldwin's brief response, 'Genesis [II]'). For readers today, Roma Gill states the consensus in her article on Marlowe in *The Spenser Encyclopedia*, which agrees with Watkins and Todd: Marlowe imitated Spenser ('Marlowe').[29]

Over the last two hundred years, critics have identified numerous textual sites in which Marlowe responds to Spenser's poetry. To these sites, I shall introduce a significant number of my own. Altogether, we shall discover a substantial textual base from which to work – in what remains arguably one of the most remarkable unexamined cases of literary relations in sixteenth-century England.[30]

The case of Marlowe's response to Spenser is important only in part because it identifies Marlowe as the first great, verifiable reader of Spenser's poetry extant (his reading of *The Faerie Queene* began even before *The Faerie Queene* was printed). By peering into Marlowe's response to Spenser, we may better understand the New Poet's reception between the mid-1580s and the mid-1590s, when Spenser himself was most active. What we discover immediately is the enormous power that Spenser's poetry held for his generation; Marlowe read that poetry, as did many others, and he responded with great energy, as many did as well. Yet I wish to show that Marlowe disagreed radically with the judgment of many members of this generation – Sir Walter Ralegh, for instance, who wrote generously of Spenser: 'Of me no lines are lov'd, nor letters are of price, / Of all which speake our English tongue, but those of thy device' (*Commendatory Verse* to 1590 *FQ* 2: 13–14). Like Ralegh, Marlowe understood Spenser's great 'price,' but unlike Ralegh he could not brook Spenser's 'device.'[31]

Marlowe is instrumental in inaugurating a counter-Spenserian movement that reaches its most immediate achievement in Donne and Jonson.[32] The difference between Marlowe and these two counter-Spenserian heirs is that only Marlowe chose to practise in a sustained and daringly precise way the deconstructive strategy articulated four hundred years later by Derrida: 'The movements of deconstruction do not destroy structures from the outside. They are not possible and effective, nor can they take accurate aim, except by inhabiting those structures' (24).[33] As we shall see in chapter 5, Marlowe's famous 'plagiarism' of the 'almond tree' simile from *Faerie Queene*

I is not plagiarism at all, but a quite careful deconstructive strategy, through which Marlowe repeats his rival, but with controlled difference:

> Whose tender locks do tremble every one
> At every little breath, that *under* heaven is blowne.
> > (*The Faerie Queene* I.vii.32; emphasis added)

> Whose tender blossoms tremble every one
> At every little breath that *thorough* heaven is blown.
> > (*2 Tamburlaine* IV.iii.123–4; emphasis added)

In Marlowe's change of Spenser's 'under' to 'thorough,' we discover a pristine window through which to view his deconstructive dismantling of Spenser's hierarchical poetics. Marlowe targets the privileged half of Spenser's binary opposition of faith, which uses the word 'under' to represent God's providential care, and he *deconstructs* it by inserting the word 'thorough' – a splendid spatial conflation of 'heaven' with earth. This is not a hermeneutic of deconstruction so much as a poetics of deconstruction.

To get at this poetics, I fuse two principles hitherto kept largely separate in current critical practice: the principle of imitation and intertextuality from the discourse of literary relations; and the principle of contextualization from the discourse of the New Historicism. The most influential theories of literary relations that have entered Renaissance studies – Harold Bloom's Freudian-based theory of 'the anxiety of influence' and Thomas M. Greene's 'humanist'-based taxonomy of literary 'imitation,' together with an increasingly influential theory, Linda Hutcheon's modernist theory of literary 'parody' – all emphasize a diachronic dimension to the relations between poet and literary source, ephebe and precursor, text and pre-text, text and context. As such, these critics cannot help us understand very much the features specific to the synchronic dimension of such relations – the special requirements a poet must meet when in rivalry with a contemporary or colleague. For instance, their methodologies have little access to the neglected rivalry between Spenser and Marlowe, because these two poets, in their clear 'opposition' to each other, violate a major principle in these theories: that literary rivalry with the Other is characterized, in Hutcheon's terms, by simultaneous intimacy and difference: '*para* in Greek can also mean "beside," and therefore there is a suggestion of an accord or intimacy instead of a contrast ... Parody, then, ... is repetition with difference' (32).[34] Spenser and Marlowe share little of such intimacy. If it is still true, as Hutcheon remarked in 1985, that 'intertextuality and auto-representation ...

dominate critical attention' (2), it is remarkable that we still lack a relatively simple taxonomy that permits us to distinguish between such a popular literary relation as that between Shakespeare and Marlowe and such a less-well-known relation as that between Spenser and Marlowe.

While the most influential New Historicists – Greenblatt, Louis Adrian Montrose, Jonathan Goldberg, Helgerson, and Leah Marcus – have recuperated the authority of synchronic literary studies, all but Helgerson contextualize Renaissance literature by turning away from specifically canonical literary contexts. In fact, most New Historicists situate the literary text within a decidedly non-literary or 'political' context; they are preoccupied with *relations* but not literary relations – relations of power, especially between writer and members of the power structure such as Elizabeth and James.[35]

By contrast, my critical method consists precisely in *contextualizing literary relations* between Marlowe and Spenser. While examining many of the documented 'borrowings' and introducing some of my own, I shall put forward a specific deconstructive strategy that I call the 'typology of intertextuality.' According to this typology, Marlowe uses a clear imitation of a classical text (such as that of Ovid or Virgil) in order to veil his rivalry with a living colleague (such as Spenser).[36]

Nowhere is Marlowe's deconstructive typology more visible than in his repeated occupation of Spenser's deepest originary career structure: the Virgilian persona of the 'shepherd,' as this figure functions to signal the poet's preparation for epic.[37] As we have seen, Marlowe stages this persona in the Scythian shepherd Tamburlaine, but it reappears equally memorably in 'The Passionate Shepherd to His Love,' and then it keeps recurring in innovative ways: in the Virgilian epic matrix of both *Ovid's Elegies* and *Lucan's First Book*; in the recurrent voicings of the passionate shepherd's 'Come live with me' in the plays, especially *Dido*, *The Jew of Malta*, and *Edward II*; in repeated borrowings from and echoes of *The Shepheardes Calender*, as in Iarbus's pastoral utterance 'And all the woods "Eliza" to resound!' (*Dido* IV.ii.10); and in the pastoral matrix of the Virgilian epic 'paraphrase' in *Dido*: 'Silvanus' dwellings' (III.ii.91). This last work, critics have determined, even goes so far as to dramatize the pastoral-epic structure in the formal division of the stage into epic city (Carthage) and pastoral countryside. Less visibly, the strategy resurfaces in a striking way in *Edward II* through the Marlovian Gaveston, who repeatedly imitates and echoes the passionate shepherd (e.g., I.i.1–5), who rises from base 'peasant' to 'earl' (I.ii.11, 30), who often entertains the idea of his own kingship (I.i.171–2, iv.27), and who specifically imitates Spenser from the *Calender* (Steane 208): 'The Shepherd nip't with biting winters rage / Frolics not more to see the painted spring' (II.ii.61–2). We can even detect the strategy underlying Faustus's passionate identification with Paris, the original shepherd-king figure (Virgil, Eclogue II.60–1; Ovid, *Heroides* V.9–32, XVI.49–59; see chapter 9, esp. n. 54). No wonder Marlowe's second great rival identified him in terms of his Virgilian/Spenserian persona: '"Dead shepherd, now I find thy saw of might, / Who ever lov'd that lov'd not at first sight?"' (*As You Like It* III.v.81–2). As Shakespeare permits, we can add *Hero and Leander* to the pastoral-epic matrix, for the 'saw of might' from that Ovidian poem is uttered by the Virgilian/Spenserian 'shepherd.' Indeed, it is remarkable to discover that the Marlovian shepherd is palpably alive throughout the Marlowe canon: in six of the seven plays; and in all three of the extant English poems.[38] Perhaps most significant for Marlowe scholars, even the Mary Sidney *Dedication* relies on the pastoral-epic persona, thereby strengthening the case for Marlowe's authorship: 'rudi calamo ... elati furoris' ('rude quill ... lofty rage').

Consequently, the third purpose of this study is to identify what I take to be the ultimate goal of Marlowe's Ovidian career rivalry with the Virgilian Spenser: its cultural function within the Elizabethan literary system. My tertiary argument is that Marlowe rewrites Spenser's England with a poetics of counter-nationhood: 'scourging kingdoms.'

Probably not by coincidence, our primary map of English nationhood derives from the same critic who gives us our primary map of English literary careers. In *Forms of Nationhood: The Elizabethan Writing of England*, Helgerson emphasizes Spenser and his generation's 'larger project of English self-representation': 'To remake it ['the very linguistic system, and perhaps more generally the whole cultural system'], and presumably themselves as well, according to some ideal pattern' (3). '[I]n most of that writing [about nationhood],' Helgerson continues, 'some other interest or cultural formation – the nobility, the law, the land, the economy, the common people, the church – rivals the monarch as the fundamental source of national identity. In seeking to establish their own authority and the authority of the different groups they represented, the younger Elizabethans were often guilty of an involuntary (and sometimes not so involuntary) lèse-majesté. They pushed claims that subverted the absolute claim of the crown' (10). For Helgerson, the six 'cultural formations' he introduces are oppositional to a seventh, royal absolutism, and together these are the 'forms of nationhood' organizing his study. Thus, in each of his six chapters he shows the relation between a nationhood of royal absolutism and one of the six oppositional forms by focusing on a writer or small group of writers, with Shakespeare chief among them as a staunch supporter of royal absolutism (244).[39]

For the present argument, the two most important contours of Helgerson's map are Spenser's nationhood of the nobility and the Henslowe playwrights' nationhood of the common people. According to Helgerson, Spenser lines up with Henslowe's playwrights against Shakespeare and royal absolutism; however, Helgerson acknowledges Spenser's 'ambivalence' towards absolutism (55, 57), even though he emphasizes that 'central' to the New Poet's 'discipline, as Spenser teaches it, is an aristocratic independence that would make a Leicester or an Essex a dangerous figure in the Tudor-Cecil state' (57): 'Spenser's poem ... serves a ... Gothic ideology of renascent aristocratic power' (59).

If Spenser opposed monarchic power with aristocratic power, Henslowe's playwrights opposed monarchic power with the power of the common people. In the new 'authors' theatre' (199), playwrights 'transgress[ed] ... hierarchy' (200) with 'a strong counterdiscourse ... of ... popular power' (206) – 'a radically subversive peasant, or more generally commoner, ideology' (210).

It is into the nationhood of common people that Helgerson periodically situates Marlowe as a founding father (1, 197, 199–200, 204, 225, 242, 243). Hence, for Helgerson, both Marlowe and Spenser line up against Shakespeare, Elizabeth, and royal absolutism, with each writing a different but equally subversive form of nationhood: Spenser, a nationhood of 'the nobility' or 'aristocratic power'; Marlowe, a nationhood of 'the common people' or 'popular power.'

Spenser may well have written a nationhood of the nobility, but Marlowe almost certainly did not write a nationhood of the common people:

> The sight of London to my exil'd eyes
> Is as Elysium to a new-come soul:
> Not that I love the city or the men,
> But that it harbours him I hold so dear,
> The King, upon whose bosom let me die,
> And with the world be still at enmity.
> ...
> Farewell base stooping to the lordly peers.
> My knee shall bow to none but to the King.
> As for the multitude, that are but sparks
> Rak'd up in embers of their poverty.
>
> (*Edward II* I.i.10–21)

Today, informed critics still identify Gaveston as a voice for Marlowe – and not without a good deal of evidence (Cartelli 131). While we must await chapter 7 to place Gaveston's speech in context, here I wish to observe how Marlowe writes nationhood through nearly half of Helgerson's 'cultural formations.'

Contrary to Helgerson's argument, Gaveston ridicules the Henslowe playwrights' nationhood of common people: 'Not that I love the city or the men ... / And with the world be still at enmity ... / ... the multitude ... are but sparks / Rak'd up in embers of their poverty.' With less rigour but no less rancour, Gaveston also ridicules Spenser's nationhood of the nobility: 'Farewell base stooping to the lordly peers.' Only superficially does Gaveston voice Shakespeare's nationhood of royal absolutism: 'My knee shall bow to none but to the King.' For in fact Gaveston rewrites absolutism with a cultural formation not present in Helgerson's list: *amor* – 'of the erotically charged Ovidian variety' (Cartelli 131). Gaveston loves London because 'it harbours him I hold so dear, / The King, upon whose bosom let me die.' This is absolutism – erotic absolutism, of a totally private order, in which the subject is free to 'love' his sovereign dearly. As the conclusion to Gaveston's speech only hints, however, *amor* is simply one dimension of a larger form of nationhood that is also not present in Helgerson's list, which Marlowe could have found in Ovid's literary heir in that other poem Marlowe translates, the *Pharsalia* – what Lucan calls simply *libertas*: 'I'll fawn first on the wind / That glanceth at my lips, and flieth away' (22–3).[40] As Marlowe had put it as early as *1 Tamburlaine*: 'He that with shepherds and a little spoil / Durst, in disdain of wrong and tyranny, / Defend his freedom 'gainst a monarchy' (II.i.54–6).

In defending freedom against a monarchy, Marlowe forges a tragic poetics of counter-nationhood. In its negative formulation, this poetics foregrounds a bitter objection to the power structure's tyrannical, deterministic suppression of individual freedom; in its positive formulation, however, this poetics foregrounds a cry for freedom from this suppression. For Marlowe, as to some extent for Lucan and Ovid, *libertas* means, above all, freedom of expression: in thought, word, action, and (for some Elizabethans) print.[41] While *Ovid's Elegies*, 'The Passionate Shepherd to His Love,' and *Tamburlaine, Parts 1 and 2* all dramatize the innocence and exuberance (at times the pain and horror) of this freedom, most of Marlowe's other works follow a narrative pattern that clearly mattered a good deal to their author: in *The Jew of Malta*, *Edward II*, *The Massacre at Paris*, *Doctor Faustus*, *Lucan's First Book*, and even *Hero and Leander*, the power structure (whether represented by a corrupt government or by the angry gods, or finally by both) oppresses the individual, always to annihilation.[42]

Marlowe's tragic poetics of counter-nationhood is complex, perhaps all the more so because it is the product of a man writing as a young adult, not as a mature writer, such as we find in Helgerson's men, all of whom had the good fortune to survive into aged adulthood. In Marlowe's writing of counter-nationhood, then, as in his writing of a literary career, we cannot find a completely finished Marlovian artefact – what Helgerson calls with respect to Spenser 'a form of political organization' (54). The best indicator of Marlowe's form of political organization may then be *Lucan's First Book* – not 'Lucan's Ten Books' (itself a fragment of at least a planned twelve). Like his literary career, Marlowe's writing of *libertas* as his signature form of counter-nationhood remains a horribly fragmented shard.

In addition to his youth, Marlowe's dangerous position within Elizabethan culture likely prevented him from producing more than a shard of counter-nationhood. The young man had the bad fortune to be born before his time, for his alleged beliefs were fundamentally transgressive: his so-called atheism; his homoeroticism; his anti-monarchical politics; even his commitment to the popular stage. In our own culture, these are all accepted tenets of ideology. In Elizabethan culture, however, they were not, and not surprisingly critics still see Marlowe as 'Plato's first kind of madman, whose fury arises not from divinity, but from alcohol, lechery, or mental disturbance' (Hulse 100). Marlowe's 'madness' contributed to his short life, but also to his failure to leave behind the kind of clear 'political organization' left by Marlowe's luckier contemporaries, such as Spenser.[43]

As grave as it may have been, Marlowe's predicament could not compare with that of his one great Roman hero who also did not get out of his twenties alive. Lucan wrote, and he wrote furiously, but, as W.R. Johnson reveals (*Momentary Monsters* 11), Lucan lost control of his own language, and in the process lost an edifice amid the ruins: 'Lucan's poem, his wild and sardonic lamentation for the loss of freedom and the end of Rome, gives to our common, universal fear of losing freedom and facing annihilation not only a permanent and more than memorable form but also one that is suitably elusive, fragmentary, disturbing, and uncanny – like the nightmare that summoned it forth' (133). With the mad Emperor Nero at his throat – with hands that in fact embraced childhood friendship but that in the end commanded early adult annihilation – the frenzied author of the fragmentary *Pharsalia* had good reason to fail in the project of finalizing a well-formed counter-nationhood.

Marlowe had the luxury of no such reason; Elizabeth was not Nero. But you could not tell him that. Witness his final image of Faustus, which looks

to be an accurate description of the circumstances under which Marlowe felt
he was writing:

My God, my God, look not so fierce on me!
Adders and serpents, let me breathe awhile!

(*Doctor Faustus* V.ii.120–1)

Let me breathe awhile. That horrific request to the authorities alerts us to
the terms of Marlovian authorship and its project of counter-nationhood.
With God himself showing up at the close, adders and serpents in his
pocket, revealed suddenly and shockingly, and applied to the transgressor's
neck, who could have done more than Marlowe did? who could not have
left the artefact horribly fragmented?[44]

If we choose to identify an institution for Marlovian *libertas* as a cultural
formation, perhaps we can do no better than select another form not present
in Helgerson's list: the university. This institution shows up as the primary
cultural formation in *Doctor Faustus*, but it also emerges through such
figures as the scholar Baldock in *Edward II*, the scholar Ramus in *The
Massacre at Paris*, and even Mercury in *Hero and Leander*: 'And to this day
is every scholar poor' (I.471). That last phrase supplies us with a term for
what we might more accurately call Marlowe's particular cultural formation
– not the government- and church-directed university, but individual and
private scholarship itself – what Marlowe calls simply 'Learning' (*Hero and
Leander* I.465, 482).[45] Marlowe's counter-nationhood of *libertas* is a counter-nationhood of free scholarship, and it is under the cultural formation of
learning that I wish to examine each of Marlowe's works. Marlowe's writing of counter-nationhood, then, is a kind of meta–counter-nationhood,
preoccupied with the private institution of scholarship that gives his writing
birth, form, and direction. This 'scholarly' configuration helps explain the
need to connect Marlowe's writing of counter-nationhood to his poetic
rivalry with Spenser, and thus to his idea of a literary career, with its
foregrounded network of classical writers.[46]

We need, then, to call Marlowe's version of nationhood a 'counter-
nationhood' to distinguish it from the forms that Helgerson privileges in his
book. The term that Helgerson applies to Hakluyt, Camden, and Drayton
applies equally well to his other chief writers, whether, like Spenser and
Coke, they resisted royal absolutism, or, like Shakespeare and Hooker, they
supported it: 'patriotism' (152). Hakluyt speaks for all of Helgerson's men
when he refers to '"the ardent love of my country"' (qtd. 152). As such, all

of Helgerson's writers who contested royal authority did so within the larger cultural formation of national loyalty or patriotism.[47]

Marlowe was no patriot. Not merely was he under house arrest at the time of his death, but, as Charles Nicholl ably shows, he chose a political profession notorious precisely for its ambiguous patriotism: 'The typical Elizabethan spy' is one whose 'motivations, in the most part, boiled down to greed or fear, or a mix of the two, with the question of patriotism coming a poor third ... These agents constantly played both ends against the middle, and fed information to both sides [Protestantism and Catholicism]. In a sense they did not even know which side they were really working for ... The spy kept a foot in both camps, and was ready to jump either way. His commitment to Mr Secretary, to Protestantism, to Queen and Country would be cast off in a moment' (108, 113). We thus need a term like counter-nationhood to distinguish Marlowe's 'subversion' from the subversion of the 'patriots' Spenser, Coke, Hakluyt, and the rest. What Leo Braudy says of Ovid we can apply to Marlowe: 'the poet begins to assert himself as the true nation' (135).[48]

As the *Tamburlaine* epigraph quoted at the outset intimates, Marlowe formally stages counter-nationhood through a recurrent theatrical event: a Marlowe-sounding figure scourges the kingdom of a sovereign or other political leader. Thus, Tamburlaine usurps the thrones of Mycetes, Cosroe, Bajazeth, and many others; Barabas overtakes Ferneze as Governor of Malta (momentarily); and Lightborn assassinates Edward II. Variations appear when an unnamed friar kills King Henry III in *The Massacre at Paris*, and when a damned magician performs demonic magic before a joyful German emperor in *Doctor Faustus*. The most remarkable staging of counter-nationhood, however, occurs in Act V of *Dido*, when Aeneas enters *'with a paper in his hand, drawing the platform of the city'* (i.s.d.), only to break into the exuberant Marlovian rhetoric – or what T.S. Eliot terms 'huffe-snuffe bombast' (59) – for the first time in the play: 'For I will grace them [the walls] with a fairer frame, / And clad her in a crystal livery ...' (5–6). This Marlowe-sounding speaker receives what Leah S. Marcus would call a 'localizing' rebuke from Hermes: 'Why cousin, stand you building cities here, / And beautifying the empire of this Queen' (27–8). In this writing and utterance by a Marlovian figure who goes on to betray, not simply beautify, the empire of a queen, we can detect a momentary rupture of the Virgilian story that suddenly models the Marlovian writing of English counter-nationhood.

What, more specifically, *is* 'counter-nationhood'? An initial reply might resort to what Walter Bagehot said of nation-building in 1887: 'We know what it is when you do not ask us, but we cannot very quickly explain or define it' (qtd. in Hobsbawm 1; cf. B. Anderson 12–16). A more accurate reply would not be more satisfying: counter-nationhood is what Marlowe wrote – what we read in his enigmatic writings. Whatever counter-nationhood is, enigma is central to it. Even though the writer of counter-nationhood speaks of the individual's suppression by royal power, he reveals its oppositional idea, freedom, only obliquely. As the term implies, counter-nationhood is less concerned with the health of the nation than with the illness of the individual. This is what makes the writer of counter-nationhood so trouble and darken the idea of patriotism. He finds himself trapped between an intellectual loathing of state oppression and an instinctual desire for freedom; his habitation of this site is what prevents him from being able, at least as a young writer, to articulate a 'political organization' – a concept of public or private freedom. In this context, Marlowe's works are historically significant, *not because they show the way out*, but *because they do not*. More accurately, they conceal the fact that they do not, for Marlowe superimposes onto his narratives of political oppression a second, hidden story: the (Ovidian) story of the poet's assertion that, despite the oppression of kings, he is free through poetic immortality: 'Verse is immortal, and shall ne'er decay. / To verse let kings give place, and kingly shows' (*Ovid's Elegies* I.xv.32–3).[49]

This argument, coupled with our knowledge of Jonson's subsequent dramatic debt to Marlowe, encourages us to revise our understanding of Marlowe's haphazard and fragmentary canon: to see in outline a counter-laureate career happily in the making – or, perhaps, tragically in the unmaking. Marlowe is not a national poet comparable to Spenser, Jonson, and Milton, or even to Daniel, Drayton, and Chapman; his premature death prohibits that conclusion. The fragmentary site of Marlowe's canon, however, does bear the imprint of a national poet, and our assessment of Marlowe may require a corresponding adjustment.

Thus I have selected as the main title of my book the phrase 'counterfeit profession,' which comes from a passage in *The Jew of Malta*: 'A counterfeit profession is better / Than unseen hypocrisy' (I.ii.289–90). In chapter 6, I read this phrase in context, but for now I wish only to suggest why I find it so programmatic for the interlock of Marlowe's literary career, his rivalry with Spenser, and his writing of counter-nationhood. The phrase evokes a series of interrelated phenomena, biographical and literary, within the Marlovian record: Marlowe's arrest on counterfeiting in The Netherlands (Letter from R. Sidney to Burleigh); his secret profession as a spy; his public profession as a 'scholar' or writer; his use of his writings as a mimetic counterfeit of both drama itself and life, including his life as a spy; his fame as 'an Ovidian poet ... a poet of Ovidian eros'; and even his infamous 'plagiarizing' of Spenser. Marlowe's Ovidian career of counter-Spenserian nationhood is indeed a multifaceted (and fascinating) counterfeit profession.

To structure my study, I devote one part to each of the three generic phases of Marlowe's Ovidian career. In Part I, on the 'sea-bank myrtle sprays' (*Ovid's Elegies* I.i.34), I devote three chapters to Marlowe's amatory poetry. In chapter 1, I examine Ovid's *Amores* in detail, arguing that Ovid inscribes the three-genre *cursus* of amatory poetry, tragedy, and epic in order to contest the authority of the Virgilian *cursus*. In chapter 2, I turn to Marlowe's translation of the *Amores* in order to introduce a new Renaissance Ovid – not the superficial poet of *amor*, but the national poet with a literary career – arguing that Marlowe makes Ovid's *cursus* his own and that he hints at his future project of contextualizing that *cursus* in terms of Spenser's Virgilian one. In chapter 3, I examine 'The Passionate Shepherd' in order to display my full argument in miniature, focusing on a neglected myth of counter-nationhood alertly discovered by Ralegh embedded in Marlowe's lovely lyric: the myth of Philomela.

In Part II, on 'sceptres and high buskins' (*Ovid's Elegies* III.i.63), I devote six chapters to Marlowe's 'master' phase of tragedy. In chapter 4, I examine *Dido*, Marlowe's first 'Ovidian tragedy,' in order to glimpse his initial dramatic experiment of contextualizing his Ovidian *cursus* in terms of his rivalry with the Virgilian Spenser and the writing of counter-nationhood. In chapter 5, I examine the two *Tamburlaine* plays in order to look at Marlowe's fullest attempt to counter Spenser's Virgilian authority. In chapters 6–8, on 'the plays of policy' – *The Jew of Malta*, *Edward II*, and *The Massacre at Paris* – I show how Marlowe inserts 'Machiavelli' into his Ovidian/Spenserian equation in order to flesh out the genre of a nationally significant Ovidian tragedy. In chapter 9, I examine *Doctor Faustus* in order to show how Marlowe uses his Spenserian contextualizing of Ovid to 'unscript(ure)' the genre of Christian tragedy through exploding a specific Spenserian linkage: love, magic, and glory. In the process, I also show, Marlowe manages to inscribe an affirmative poetics, reworking this linkage in Ovidian terms.

In Part III, on 'Trumpets and drums' (*Lucan's First Book* 6), I devote two chapters to Marlowe's 'master' phase of (pre-mature) epic. In chapter 10, I examine Marlowe's translation of Book I of Lucan's epic *Pharsalia* as an attempt to construct what I call a counter-epic of empire. In chapter 11, I read Marlowe's imitation of Musaeus in the 'minor epic' *Hero and Leander*, including Chapman's 'continuation,' against the concept of Spenserian nationhood.

In the afterword, I speculate on the significance (and shortcoming) of my own counterfeiting of the profession within the context of Renaissance studies today. Here, I respond to the dominant critical lens through which we have viewed Marlowe since the seventeenth century – the Shakespearean paradigm, with its privileging of drama over poetry and its neglect of scholarly translation, a genre that lets Marlowe, at long last, counterfeit his profession freely.

PART I

SEA-BANK MYRTLE SPRAYS: AMATORY POETRY

Marlowe contributes to Western poetics by inscribing an Ovidian career model of counter-Spenserian nationhood in late sixteenth-century England.

Marlowe's Ovidian model, like other career models available at this time, is genre-based. In general, it moves from an apprentice phase of lower or youthful genres to a master phase of higher or mature genres. In particular, it unfolds its two-phase progression via a three-genre structure that moves from amatory poetry to tragedy and epic. Rather than solidifying this progressive structure through typology, however, the Ovidian *cursus* renders the structure playfully fluid – non-progressive and non-typological: it sets up a sacred generic order only to scramble it. In this generic play, oscillation infiltrates, contaminates, and finally orders progression. Thus genre progression and genre itself remain vital to the Ovidian poet, but he delights in a series of deft manoeuvres that explode the developmental idea of a career (literary or civic) so important to Roman and Elizabethan culture, even as he clearly develops himself.[1]

The Ovidian poet does not simply generalize his generic-based explosion of culture; he specifies it in terms of the reigning national poet of his day, whether originally Virgil or later the Virgilian Spenser. By rivalling the reigning national poet to manage his multigenre career, the Ovidian poet seeks to pen a poetics of counter-nationhood as the mark of his cultural authority.

Marlowe first inscribes the Ovidian *cursus* of counter-Spenserian nationhood in his line-by-line translation of the *Amores*, known as *Ovid's Elegies*. About this translation, we know only that it was published posthumously and that it was publicly banned and officially burned by episcopal order in 1599, along with its companion poem in the same volume, Sir John Davies's *Epigrams*.[2] Unfortunately, we do not know when Marlowe penned his translation, although critics agree that he penned it during his Cambridge years (around 1585), and most believe that it circulated in manuscript thereafter.[3] While critics have long debated whether Marlowe prepared his translation for publication – either the complete version or the selected one, or both – recent critics believe strongly that the texts of both versions show, not simply a careful hand, but a Marlovian one.[4]

The textual origins of *Ovid's Elegies* may remain obscure, the intentions of its author in doubt, and even its burning a question of guilt by association, but the Bishops' ban supplies a stabilizing cultural event that even its project of censorship could not totally erase: the inaugural, counter-Virgilian poem of the amatory poet's career shows up in the public record as a marked text. Marked by the joint Elizabethan authorities of Church and State, *Ovid's Elegies* is officially burned as a document of counter-nationhood:

> Of me Peligny's *nation* boasts alone,
> Whom *liberty* to honest arms compelled,
> When careful Rome in doubt their prowess held.[5]
>
> > (*Ovid's Elegies* III.xiv.8–10; emphasis added)

1

Ovid's Counter-Virgilian *Cursus* in the *Amores*

The *Amores* is a complex document in and of itself, but two additional features of Ovid's ostensibly inaugural collection of love elegies make discussion of it even more problematic: its perplexing publishing history and its paradoxical relation to Ovid's subsequent poetry. The publishing history is perplexing because Ovid opens by revealing that the text he is presenting is a second edition, because the first edition is not extant, and because we cannot identify the composition or publication dates of either edition.[1] The relation of the second edition to Ovid's subsequent poetry is paradoxical because Ovid combines in a single volume a clear prophecy of poetry to be written in the higher genres of tragedy and epic, and actual descriptive references of works in these genres that are supposed to exist only in the future.

To explore this disorienting 'Ovidian' *cursus*, to contrast it with Virgil's, and to infer Marlowe's attraction to it, we may proceed in three primary stages: first, by identifying the prophetic strain of the generic *cursus*; second, by identifying the rhetorical strain that problematizes that *cursus*; and, third, by examining Ovid's fulfilment of the prophecy in his subsequent poetry.

The Ovidian *Cursus*: Prophecy

In the *Amores*, Marlowe could have found Ovid projecting a literary career that begins with love elegy and that then moves into the *area maior* of tragedy and epic.[2] The primary evidence of this career pattern lies in the five 'programmatic poems': I.i, II.i, II.xviii, III.i, and III.xv. By examining these poems, we may approach the significance of the *Amores* in Ovid's literary career.[3]

In *'Fictus Adulter': Poet as Actor in the 'Amores,'* John T. Davis exemplifies the received wisdom about Ovid's inaugural poem when he identifies 'three essential aspects to the character Ovid creates for himself in the *Amores*': 'Two involve caricature and burlesque ... The third aspect is the protean quality of the protagonist' (37). Davis's primary thesis about Ovid as a role-player with a keen commitment to 'performance' and 'drama' (see 1–35) has three primary limitations. First, Davis's Ovidian persona is primarily sexual: 'shamelessly promiscuous' (37). Second, when Davis does see Ovid's persona in literary terms, he follows a long (and misleading) tradition that limits the persona's 'mockery' to the 'professed *fides*' of the 'elegists,' whom he identifies as 'Catullus, Propertius and Tibullus' (37). And third, Davis's Ovidian persona is never serious, straightforward, or stable: he is committed to 'caricature,' 'burlesque,' and emotional or erotic shape-shifting.[4]

To these three 'essential aspects' of Ovid's self-presentation, we may add a *fourth*: the poet with a literary career. A crucial literary context for understanding this 'aspect' is not simply the 'professed *fides*' of the elegists, but the multigenre career pattern of the non-elegiac Virgil. Ovid may present the playfulness of his persona as he constructs a multigenre career pattern, but he is careful to assert, if not his dead seriousness, at least his professional earnestness.[5]

Primarily, we need to take Ovid's playful, counter-Virgilian earnestness seriously for at least one (neglected) reason.[6] Among the non-Virgilian Roman poets who followed Callimachus in relying on the topos of the *recusatio* – literally, the objection to epic in favour of the lower genres – *Ovid alone went on to write an epic*. He broke free from the elegiac couplet to mine the dactylic hexameter. This fact demands that we distinguish carefully between his often-discussed use of the *recusatio* in the programmatic poems and the uses to which he is clearly indebted (the Callimachean list includes Propertius, Tibullus, and even Horace). We must, that is, interpret Ovid's *recusatio* along the lines that at least some (including Spenser) interpret Virgil's *recusatio* in the *Eclogues* (VI.1–10): as an advertisement for the *area maior*.

To open Eclogue VI, Virgil writes:

My Muse first deigned to sport in Sicilian strains, and blushed not to dwell in the woods. When I was fain to sing of kings and battles, the Cynthian plucked my ear and warned me: 'A shepherd, Tityrus, should feed sheep that are fat, but sing a lay fine-spun.' And now – for enough, and more, wilt thou find eager to sing thy praises, Varus, and build the story of grim war – now will I woo the rustic Muse on slender reed. Unbidden strains I sing not [non iniussa cano]. (Virgil, *Eclogues* VI.1–9)

Critics debate whether this *recusatio* predicts or rejects Virgil's epic, but in a recent and detailed analysis Joseph Farrell concludes: 'it is difficult to resist Cartault's suggestion that in this shifting, tantalizing sequence of allusive artistry, Vergil is "dreaming of his poetic future"' (*Virgil's 'Georgics'* 314; see 291–314). Alertly, Farrell adds: 'If *Eclogue 6* really was conceived as a kind of prospectus [for Vergil's epic], it turned out to be a very misleading one' (314).[7]

This conclusion suggests that in his famous *recusatio* Virgil is projecting his epic but failing to predict the actual form that the *Aeneid* took. For an analogue, we can turn to the *June* eclogue of *The Shepheardes Calender*, where Spenser attempts to project the genre of the love lyric within his Virgilian career (Cheney, *Spenser's Famous Flight* 96–8); this attempt serves as a specific instance of the method of prophecy identified by critics for Spenser and Western poets, 'in which the prophetic poet's utterance is only "partially predictive"' (Cheney 43, quoting A. Fletcher 5). Whether Virgil himself is predicting his epic or not, a Renaissance poet like Spenser probably understood the Virgilian *recusatio* as a device of prophecy. Thus, in *June*, Spenser imitates the Eclogue VI passage when Colin Clout refuses to sing Virgilian epic by asserting his fitness only to write pastoral, in the process imitating line 9 of Virgil ('non iniussa cano'): 'Of Muses Hobbinol, I conne no skill ...: / I never lyst presume to Parnasse hyll, / But pyping lowe in shade of lowly grove, / I play to please my selfe, all be it ill' (65–72).[8] Like Virgil's *recusatio* in the *Eclogues*, Spenser's *recusatio* works the opposite of that concluding the *Odes*, where Horace imitates the opening of Eclogue VI: 'When I wished to sing of fights and cities won, Apollo checked me, striking loud his lyre, and forbade my spreading tiny sails upon the Tuscan Sea' (IV.xv.1–4). Whereas Horace defends his practice of writing in the non-epic genre, Spenser's Virgil (perhaps Virgil himself), Spenser, and – we may add – Ovid are all predicting their writing of epic.[9] Thus the Callimachean lens, so popular in Ovid criticism, is not the best lens for viewing the significance of the *Amores*; it is, as it were, a veil for the most vital: the Virgilian.

Thus the *Amores* – and Marlowe's translation – begins with a four-line prologue marked by its Virgilian matrix:

> We which were Ovid's five books now are three,
> For these before the rest preferreth he;
> If reading five thou plain'st of tediousness,
> Two ta'en away, thy labour will be less.

> (*Ovid's Elegies* [Pr.] 1–4)

As Gian Biagio Conte notes, these lines imitate the four-line pseudo-Virgilian verses prefacing the *Aeneid* (84–7): 'I am he who once composed a song on a slender pipe; then, having left the woods, I made the fields nearby obey the settler even if he was very greedy, and the work pleased the farmers; now, however, (I sing of) the fearful (arms) of Mars (and the man)' (trans. Conte 85). Most students of the Renaissance know that these lines were 'prefixed to the opening lines of Renaissance editions of Virgil's *Aeneid*,' as well as that Spenser famously imitates them in the Proem to Book I of *The Faerie Queene* (Hamilton, ed., *FQ* 27). Yet, as Conte reminds us, the lines 'must have been published no later than the age of Tiberius' (A.D. 14–37), and Ovid's imitation of the lines reveals that by the time he wrote the prologue to the second edition of the *Amores* the verses 'must have ... [existed] in a contemporary edition of the *Aeneid*' (85, 87; cf. Austin).

The pseudo-Virgilian verses are the first evidence we possess of a Virgilian *cursus*. They are, in other words, the oldest evidence we possess of 'a Roman idea of a literary career.' In the introduction, we saw that Ovid is the first poet on record to inscribe the three-genre Virgilian progression clearly (*Amores* I.xv.25–6), and we observed that the inscription traces a wider career model containing not just a vocational or generic dimension but also a philosophical, a political, and even a sexual dimension: 'Tityrus and the harvest, and the arms of Aeneas, will be read as long as Rome shall be capital of the world she triumphs o'er' (25–6; Loeb trans.).[10] From the Virgilian distich in *Amores* I.xv, in other words, we know that Ovid had access to and acute knowledge of Virgil's idea of a literary career (a point Conte overlooks). As far as we can tell, however, the prologue to the *Amores* is the first inscription to alert us to Ovid's interest in the Virgilian *cursus*. And the fact that he both inscribes the *cursus* and parodies it reveals that he was in command of the idea of a literary career.[11]

Both prologues, Virgilian and Ovidian, represent a vocational pattern. Whereas the Virgilian inscribes a pattern of progression for a multigenre literary career, the Ovidian inscribes a pattern of subtraction within a single genre. The difference between the two may not look good for Ovid, but we need not construe it as so. In the pseudo-Virgilian verses, Virgil appears as the poet who had the power to turn from the lower to the higher genres; in his prologue, Ovid displays his own form of power, which appears, not as Virgilian progression (a pattern of quantity), but as Ovidian intensification (a pattern of quality). Ovid's subtraction of five books to three shows his artistic judgment accurately meeting the needs of his audience's judgment. With fewer books to read, they will have to exercise less labour and so can indulge more freely in the poet's entertainment. The witty paradox, however, is that, while the poet's emphasis on elegiac dalliance (see III.i.24) inscribes the amatory genre exactly, his imitation of the Virgilian progression anticipates freedom from this inscription. By its definition, elegy must dally, but Ovid's dalliance proves to be a training ground for the *area maior*. This paradox is not merely the topic of the volume's final poem; it is prepared for throughout: 'Long hast thou loitered,' Dame Tragedy tells the poet in III.i: 'greater works compile' (24). The prologue is simply the first version of the paradoxical definition of the elegiac genre that Ovid, alone among the Latin elegists, will supply as a strategy for competing with Virgil for national authority.

In short, by imitating the Virgilian pattern of multigenre progression, Ovid's pattern of single-genre subtraction can only be two things at once: the poet's announcement of his plan to expand the elegy to a drama in which the poet turns from elegy to the *area maior*; and (therefore) the poet's projection of his plan to define elegy as a training ground for the greater ground of epic.

Accordingly, the *Amores* proper opens with a plan to write Virgilian epic: 'With Muse prepared I meant to sing of arms, / Choosing a subject fit for fierce alarms' (I.i.5–6). Suddenly, however, the poet finds his plan blocked: 'Love ... / Began to smile and took one foot away' (7–8). In objection to this aggression, the poet delivers a hapless complaint to the god for transgressing social and literary decorum: 'What if thy mother take Diana's bow ... / Then scarce can Phoebus say, "This harp is mine." / When in this work's first verse I trod aloft, / Love slacked my muse, and made my numbers soft' (11–22). In the end, however, the poet is compelled to bid 'stern war' farewell, since poetry in that high genre is 'for blunter poets meet' (32): 'Elegian muse, that warblest amorous lays, / Girt my shine brow with sea-bank myrtle sprays' (33–4). In this opening poem, then, the poet announces his abandonment of the Apollonian laurel bough of epic for the myrtle branch of love elegy.

While needing to acknowledge the poet's playfulness in these manoeuvres – he *is* a kind of genetically programmed elegiac poet victimized by desire, a failed Virgilian or national poet, and so another Callimachean elegist – we also need to recall the literal *telos* that these manoeuvres serve. In the end, Ovid will free himself from Amor; he will break the Callimachean bond; he will write an epic that can compete with the *Aeneid*. Rather than closing down the idea of a Virgilian progression, then, the opening poem keeps that idea literally at the forefront of our attention; it announces that Ovid will distinguish himself from the other elegists by meeting Virgil on his own 'area' – that he will compete equally with Virgil and that he is dead serious in his witty attempt to defeat him.[12]

Opening Book II on a symmetrical note, the poet recalls his attempt to write poetry in a higher vein, but by this point he appears happier to admit and more confident to enforce his amatory dalliance: 'I, Ovid, poet of my wantonness, / Born at Peligny, to write more address ... / Let maids whom hot desire to husbands lead, / And rude boys touched with unknown love, me read' (I.i.1–6). The poet's inscription of his elegiac signature – 'poet of my wantonness' ('nequitiae ... poeta meae') – and his identification of his primary readers as inexperienced boys and promiscuous maids prompt him to recall again, in more generically precise detail than in I.i, the epic genesis to his amatory enterprise: 'I durst the great celestial battles tell, / Hundred-hand Gyges, and had done it well, ... / My wench her door shut, Jove's affairs I left ... / Toys and light elegies, my darts, I took' (11–21). Ovid scholars have written very little on this important passage, but J.C. McKeown assumes that it supplies detail to the genesis given in the collection's opening poem: 'the subject of Ovid's abortive martial epic remains unspecified in 1.1 and 2.18; at 2.1.11ff., it is the Gigantomachia' (1: 25; see 87, 93).[13]

Generically, the Gigantomachy is a form of epic poem on Jove's victory over the Giants. According to the myth, the Giants revolted against Jove's authority, and the great god used his awful weapon, the thunderbolt, to achieve mastery over them. Appropriately, Ovid inserts this myth into his description of the war in heaven during the Iron Age near the opening of his epic poem, the *Metamorphoses*, and in terms nearly identical to those in *Amores* II.i (*Met* I.151–60). The appearance of the Gigantomachy in the opening book of Ovid's epic warrants a pause. While the sketch in the *Metamorphoses* may well be a 'compression' of the Gigantomachy in the *Amores*, we might wonder why Ovid would choose to include the sketch in the first place. Since the Gigantomachy in the *Metamorphoses* usually leads critics to recall the Gigantomachy in the *Amores*, we may ask whether the epic sketch serves as a career marker. Does it not in some sense identify the *Metamorphoses* as the epic announced in the earlier volume? Does it not therefore announce Ovid's success in fulfilling the *cursus* projected in the *Amores*?[14]

Unbeknownst to Ovid himself at the outset of his career, the Gigantomachy myth will turn out to be crucial later, for he will repeatedly use Jove's thunderbolt as the arch-trope of his exile, with himself in the role of punished usurper, and Augustus in the role of thundering Jupiter. 'My fate,' he says to Augustus in the *Tristia*, 'has given thee the means of mercy. If at every human error Jupiter should hurl his thunderbolts, he would in a brief space be weaponless ... Do thou also, seeing thou art called ruler' (II.27–39). In the long, autobiographical second book of the *Tristia*, he actually inscribes the Gigantomachy twice (63–72; 331–41). In the second instance, when Ovid explains why he never wrote a (Virgilian) epic (317–20), he refers to the Gigantomachy long ago inscribed in *Amores* II.i: 'Perhaps (but even this I doubt) I am well enough suited to lighter verse, capable of humble measures; but if thou shouldst bid me sing of the Giants conquered by Jove's lightning, the burden will weaken me in the attempt. Only a rich mind can tell the tale of Caesar's mighty deeds if the theme is not to surpass the work. Even so I made the venture, but methought I impaired the theme and – an impious thing – wrought injury to thy might. I returned once more to my light task, the songs of youth, stimulating my breast with fictitious love' (331–41). The *Tristia* representations of the Gigantomachy reveal that Ovid understands the genre to function as an epic poem on a political theme emphasizing Augustus's judgment of the impious.[15] In fact, the exile representations serve as a final career marker, this time making explicit the device already identified in the elegiac and epic phases of Ovid's career. From the vantage point of the Exile Poetry, we can identify three phases of that career, as we shall see shortly.

Back in the *Amores*, however, Ovid is making predictions, but hardly of his exile. Rather, he is presenting himself just as Charles Segal describes him in the *Metamorphoses* – anxious but confident that he can compete with Virgil (*Orpheus* 94). Like the representation of epic in *Amores* I.i, the representation in II.i presents the persona as a poet with a career pattern who in his youth is unable to write in the *area maior* of a nationally significant Virgilian art. This is the fundamental drama of the *Amores*, and at the beginning of Book II it is far from over.

Thus, in the second part of II.i the young poet remains confident in choosing the 'great reward' (35: 'magna ... merces') of a quite different kind – not the Homeric fame of Virgil, but the immediate sexual gratification with his mistress:

> What helps it me of fierce Achill to sing?
> ...
> But when I praise a pretty wench's face,
> She in requital doth me oft embrace.
> A great reward: heroes, O famous names,
> Farewell; your favour nought my mind inflames.

> (*Ovid's Elegies* II.i.29–36)

In bidding farewell to Homer and the rest, the poet is locating a new source for poetic inspiration: not the poetry of a *dead white male*, but the flesh and blood of a living female.[16]

Ovid's elision of the link between his representation of epic as a Gigantomachy in the first part of II.i and his representation of epic as a Homeric poem imitating the *Iliad* and the *Odyssey* in the second part may appear peculiar, but it identifies the Gigantomachy *as* an epic form. From the vantage point of the present study, the elision defines the elegiac poet as a failed national poet and wittily keeps the dramatic prospect of his metamorphosis into a national poet before us.

In the penultimate poem of Book II, the central elegy among the five programmatic poems, the poet actually inscribes the three genres together that form the counter-Virgilian or Ovidian triad: elegy, tragedy, and epic.[17] In lines 1–12, the poet repeats the *recusatio* pattern relating epic and elegy. Addressing his friend Macer, who himself is trying to write Homeric/Virgilian epic (1–3), the poet laments that he 'sit[s] in Venus' slothful shade' and that 'Love' interferes with his composition of 'great things' ('ausuros grandia') (3–4) – the military theme of Virgilian epic, as the echo of the opening line of the *Aeneid* reveals: 'I yield, and back my wit from battles bring, / Domestic acts, and mine own wars to sing' (11–12). In lines 13–18, however, he succeeds in writing tragedy:

> Yet tragedies and sceptres filled my lines,
> But though I apt were for such high designs,
> Love laughèd at my cloak, and buskins painted,
> And rule so soon with private hands acquainted.
> My mistress' deity also drew me fro it,
> And Love triumpheth o'er his buskined poet.
>
> (*Ovid's Elegies* II.xviii.13–18)

The series of parallelisms here is striking – with the opening of the elegy itself (II.xviii.1–12), with the opening elegy of the present book (II.i), and with the opening elegy of the collection as a whole (I.i). In all three, 'Love' interrupts the poet's plan to move into the *area maior*. The effect of the parallelisms is to identify epic and tragedy as the greater ground the poet aspires to pen but cannot because Amor pens him in the elegiac genre. From the standpoint of the present argument, the parallelisms also have the effect of placing before us for the first time the three genres that form the Ovidian triad.[18]

While the first two programmatic poems display Ovid failing to write epic and simultaneously projecting his (future) success in it, this third programmatic poem establishes a similar paradigm for the genre of tragedy, but it also sets up the last two programmatic poems, both of which will also deal with tragedy. Elegy II.xviii is *central* precisely because it serves as the programmatic hinge for the entire volume. Whereas I.i and II.i establish a career relation between elegy and epic, and whereas III.i and III.xv establish a relation between elegy and tragedy, II.xviii brings elegy, epic, and tragedy together in a dynamic career pattern that will turn out to resemble the actual *oeuvre* of Ovid's canon at the time of his exile. Critics make much of the 'drama' of the *Amores*, but the great drama weaving the collection together is the poet's attempt and final ability to make the generic turn from the lower genre of love elegy to the *area maior* of tragedy and epic – in other words, to overcome the traditional *recusatio* by reversing its generic pattern. This is the protean metamorphosis that the *Amores* is finally about. Whereas I.i and II.i formally introduce this topic, and III.i and III.xv carry it to dramatic closure, II.xviii brings it to centre stage.

Thus the poet opens Book III by narrating what Davis calls 'perhaps the best place to see Ovid the actor,' in which the poet 'attends a dramatic reading by the two "goddesses" who lay claim to his talents, Tragedy and Elegy' (108–9). Ovid narrates how 'Elegia' and 'Tragedy' both visit him while he is walking beside a 'stoned-paved sacred spring' (3). The site of the 'fons sacer' is the *locus poeticus* itself. Alertly, Ovid interprets this site as the zone of generic dialogue, the crossroads of lower and higher genres, the very intersection from which the poet is to organize his career. Fittingly, Dame Elegy visits the poet first, since he just happens to be penning her genre: 'Elegia came with hairs perfumèd sweet, / And one, I think, was longer of her feet; / A decent form, thin robe, a lover's look, / By her foot's blemish greater grace she took' (7–10). Although metrically lame below, Elegy looks (and smells) great above; that enticing gown ('vestis tenuissima') is a precise dressing of the genre and makes the lady worth the aesthetic sacrifice – a sacrifice the poet will blissfully need to make if he chooses to favour her. Dame Tragedy, however, interrupts the delicious rendezvous, revealing that three cannot keep company: 'Then with huge steps came violent Tragedy: / Stern was her front, her cloak on ground did lie; / Her left hand held abroad a regal sceptre, / The Lydian buskin in fit paces kept her' (11–14). Heavily dressed, but hardly burdened by it, Dame Tragedy inverts Elegy's erotic paradigm: metrically sound, she overpowers through austerity. You must listen to her, but you could never love her. Dame Tragedy compels favour (rather than enticing it) simply through her threat of violence. Will she muffle you in that long cloak, beat you with that regal sceptre, kick you with those buskined boots? Tragedy demands sacrifice of a different *kind*.

Not surprisingly, Dame Tragedy is the 'first' to speak (15). Who would

dare to have it otherwise? The iron lady's interrogation is enough to motivate even the most elegiac of poets to tragic action: 'A laughing-stock thou
art to all the city' (21). Criticizing him for spending his great talent in
'lewdness' ditty,' she commands him with something like the coercion of
literary law itself: ''Tis time to move grave things in lofty style ... / ... greater
works compile ... / Now give the Roman Tragedy a name, / To fill my laws
thy wanton spirit frame' (22–30).

Remarkably, Dame Elegy is not moved by the threat of tragic violence.
Gifted rhetorician that she is, she engages the poet with the only strategy of
audience accommodation that could counter Tragedy's thundering bombast.
She smiles secretly to him, 'with wanton eyes' (33), and uses the magic of
her gaze to reveal her (previously hidden) trump card: 'Err I?,' the poet asks,
'or myrtle in her right hand lies' (33–4). Elegy, too, has high, coercive
authority – the myrtle branch of the goddess Venus. Thus she accuses 'stout
Tragedy' of trying to 'tread' her 'down' when only she has the power to
make Ovid's mistress, Corinna, 'learn' (35–49). For it is Elegy, not Tragedy,
who possesses the key to unlock the coveted 'door' (40), the golden 'gift' of
Corinna's sweet 'gate' (60, 45).

Caught in this dialogue of genres, at the crossroads of his career, the poet
tactfully insists on the benefits of both love elegy and tragedy in his quest to
achieve fame: if Tragedy will give him 'bright renown' through 'the world,'
Elegy will give his 'love' a 'conquering name' (61–5). In the end, therefore,
he promises, 'Some greater work [grandius ... opus] will urge me on at last'
(70).

Thus, in III.xv the poet concludes the *Amores* with a plan to turn from
love elegy to tragedy:

> Horned Bacchus greater fury doth distil,
> A greater ground [area maior] with great horse is to till.
> Weak elegies, delightful Muse, farewell;
> A work that after my death here shall dwell.
>
> (*Ovid's Elegies* III.xiv[xv].17–20)

With this projected 'meta' (2) or chariot turn from lower to higher genres,
the poet ends his collection.

Ovid's careful *threshold* positioning of the five programmatic poems
reveals the importance he attaches to the generic program. The 'drama' these
poems enact is the most important in the *Amores*: it is the drama of the
Ovidian poet's metamorphosis – his maturation from apprentice to master,
his generic progression from irresponsible neophyte to dutiful counter-

national poet. In this we can discover Ovid's distinction from the Latin elegists indebted to Callimachus. Unlike the elegists, but like Virgil, Ovid tries to inaugurate a career; that we have to take this projection seriously, despite the poet's signature irony and wit, is clear from subsequent publications, especially those in tragedy and epic.

The Ovidian *Cursus*: Problematization

From *Ovid's Elegies*, we *can* extract a relatively stable and coherent Ovidian career model. This model differs from its Virgilian counterpart in terms of the four dimensions discussed earlier. First, the Ovidian model replaces the Virgilian triad of genres with an Ovidian triad. Second, the Ovidian model rejects Virgilian political poetry designed to serve Augustus and the Empire by absenting the poet from Roman politics, and by subtly presenting him as a counter-Augustan poet whose critique of the Empire aims to usurp the Emperor's own cultural authority: 'Verse is immortal, and shall ne'er decay. / To verse let kings give place, and kingly shows' (I.xv.32–3).[19] Third, the Ovidian model rejects the Virgilian program of securing the *telos* of fame for the poet and the Augustan regime, inserting a private, erotic poetry designed to secure the *telos* of fame either for the poet's mistress or, more often, for himself as a poet: 'Thy scope[, Envy,] is mortal, mine eternal fame, / That all the world may ever chant my name' (I.xv.7–8).[20] And fourth, the Ovidian model complicates the Virgilian eternizing of the feminine city of Roma by emphasizing the poet's dalliance with a mistress, usually the famed Corinna: 'In verse to praise kind wenches 'tis my part, / And whom I like eternize by mine art' (I.x.59–60).

Controlling all four changes is what we might term the Ovidian 'career keystone': Marlowe could have found Ovid replacing Virgil's unified, coherent, and progressive pattern that moves typologically through a three-genre model with a disunified, incoherent, and non-progressive pattern that oscillates in a disorienting fashion through an alternative three-genre pattern.[21] Ovid's oscillating, counter-Virgilian, non-typological pattern explains why, on the one hand, he uses an inaugural volume to advertise his (future) progression from amatory poetry to tragedy and epic, but then, on the other, refers to amatory poetry, a tragedy, and at least the beginning of an epic that he has already written.

Ovidian critics have not seen Ovid responding to the generic coherence of the Virgilian progression. Instead, they have debated the problem of canon 'chronology' that Ovid's numerous references, both in the *Amores* and in other poems such as the *Tristia*, create.[22] Is it possible, however, that

Ovid might be exploding the Virgilian notion of a generically progressive career chronology – inventing the problem of career chronology itself?

The four-line prologue to the *Amores* may begin the invention with its technique of explosion, for Ovid's poem speaks in its own voice with a kind of editorial sleight of hand (now you see it, now you don't). What in the first edition the reader knew in 'five books,' we are to read now as metamorphosed into 'three.' Wittily, Ovid's reduction from five elegiac books to three itself functions as a model for his impending turn from epic to elegy, for in the second edition we need to 'labour ... less.' From the outset, Ovid constructs his work in terms of a *deficit* poetics: 'ta'en away' ('demptis').²³

The main example of Ovid's superimposition of a pattern of oscillation onto his Virgilian pattern of progression, however, appears in Book II, Elegy xviii, a poem that critics cannot agree upon as originally slotted into the first edition or inserted for the second (cf. Cameron, 'First Edition' 331– 2, versus Booth 11, 87). Such a *textual* approach, however, obscures the rhetorical strategy of an exploded prophecy. In an ostensibly inaugural project that prophesies future poetry, Ovid refers to poems as having been written that are supposed to exist – according to the *cursus* right then in the process being advertised – only in the future.²⁴ Lines 19–26 refer to two poems in the inaugural phase of Ovid's career, that of amatory poetry. First, lines 19–20 appear to refer to the *Ars amatoria*: 'What lawful is, or we profess love's art [profitemur Amoris], / (Alas, my precepts turn myself to smart!).'²⁵ If the lines do refer to the *Ars*, as critics usually believe, then the reader can only trip into a significant temporal and career fault line. For, as Alan Cameron remarks, 'the *Ars* was written when Ovid was 40 and at the height of his fame: the first books of the *Amores* when he was an unknown in his teens' ('First Edition' 327). Similarly, lines 21–8 clearly refer to the 'first series' of letters in the *Heroides* (I–XII) as well as to the response to them by Ovid's friend Sabinus: 'We write, or what Penelope sends Ulysses, ... / And what poor Dido with her drawn sword sharp' (21, 26).²⁶

What we cannot see in Marlowe's translation is that in the original Ovid also refers to his one known tragedy, *Medea*. Lines 13–14 read in the Loeb translation: 'None the less, I did begin to sing of sceptres, and through my effort tragedy grew in favour' (see Cameron, 'First Edition' 332). That last phrase, 'curaque tragoedia nostra crevit,' gets omitted in Marlowe's translation, and we can only speculate why. Perhaps he could not fit it into his line-by-line translation. Perhaps he could not understand it, ignorant of Ovid's lost tragedy – an alternative we should probably find untenable, in part because Ovid himself refers to *Medea* again in the *Tristia*, in part because Renaissance writers knew about the tragedy.²⁷ Perhaps – and this is worth emphasizing – Marlowe had not written a tragedy yet (his translation is always dated before his first tragedy, *Dido*) – and therefore he was unable to participate fully in Ovid's disorienting system. But, as we shall see in more detail in chapter 2, in most other ways Marlowe does participate – to the max.[28]

Ovid's manoeuvrings and the effect they create are indeed arresting. He writes the first edition of the *Amores*; he begins work on a second edition; but then, in this (still) inaugural collection, he enfolds references both to other subsequent poetry in the elegiac genre (*Ars amatoria*, *Heroides*) and to other subsequent works in the *area maior* (the epic *Metamorphoses* and the tragedy *Medea*). Such career oscillation has as its most immediate effect Ovidian play. Paradoxically, however, the oscillation also compels us to take the play seriously. For, in the strategy of referring to actual works that are supposed to exist only in the future, Ovid constructs something like a mathematical proof of his own ability to turn from the lower to the higher genres: we need to take his play seriously because *in fact he has already made the career turn*. In other words, the strategy of superimposing oscillation onto progression works both to project that turn and to demonstrate the poet's success in fulfilling it.

A variation on this strategy thus emerges in Ovid's program of generic mixing – a program naturally designed in response to the typological program of generic relation established by Virgil, or at least imposed on him by the pseudo-Virgilian verses. At the end of II.xviii, for example, Ovid aims to legitimize love elegy for Macer by observing that even this friend enfolds love elegy into his epic: 'Nor of thee, Macer, that resound'st forth arms, / Is golden love hid in Mars' mid-alarms' (35–6). After citing the examples of Paris, Helen, and Laodamia, Ovid concludes: 'Unless I err, to these [lovers] thou more incline / Than wars, and from thy tents wilt come to mine' (39–40). Whereas, at least from Spenser's perspective, Virgil in the *Eclogues* enfolds epic topoi in order to predict typologically his (future) epic, Ovid here enfolds epic in his love elegy in order to demonstrate the superiority of the inferior genre over epic, but more precisely to represent a kind of pre-Freudian erotic determinism, in which even the epic poet writing of 'great things' (4) cannot escape his appetite. As Ovid candidly admits earlier in Book II, 'I cannot rule myself, but where love please / Am driven like a ship upon rough seas' (iv.7–8). Ovid's generic mixing is Virgilian typology in reverse – the inscription, not simply of the will imprisoned by eros, but of the multiplicity of literary forms collapsed into a single erotic genre.[29]

Ovid's typological generic scrambling within a work translates into a severe problem of generic scrambling within the chronology of the career pattern as a whole. The 'perplexed and obscure' chronology that E.J. Kenney identifies for 'Ovid's early poetry' ('Ovid' 2: 421) is not accidental, nor is it confined to the early poetry. It is something like the signature of the Ovidian *cursus* itself.

The Ovidian *Cursus*: Fulfilment

Thus, if Marlowe found in the *Amores* the paradox of a disorienting system – an unsystematic system – he could have found more of the same in Ovid's fulfilment of the prophecy – the other poems in the Ovidian canon. Conventionally, scholars divide the chronology of Ovid's canon into three phases:

1 / Youthful works: 19 B.C.–A.D. 1: *Amores* (1st ed.); *Medea*; *Heroides*; *Ars amatoria*; *Remedia amoris*; *Medicamina faciei femineae*; *Amores* (2d ed.)
2 / Mature works (interrupted): A.D. 2–8: *Metamorphoses*; *Fasti*
3 / Exile works: A.D. 8–17 or 18: *Ibis*; *Tristia*; *Epistulae ex Ponto*.[30]

In a general way, it looks as if Ovid is well on his way to fulfilling the tripartite generic pattern projected in the *Amores* when he suffers exile. Ovid has completed a number of erotic poems; he has finished one tragedy; he has completed half of an elegiac calendar poem having both political overtones and epic intimations; and he has finished but not polished one epic.[31] Ovid's exile of course demands a new career phase that even Ovid himself was not wise enough to anticipate.

Along these generically patterned lines, then, we need to reconstruct the complete and actual shape of Ovid's literary career. This 'official' career pattern differs from the Ovidian *cursus* projected in the *Amores*. It is the official one that we are most familiar with today and the one on which most medieval and Renaissance readers before Marlowe based their assessments of Ovid:

1 / Amatory poetry: *Amores, Heroides, Ars amatoria, Remedia amoris, Medicamina faciei femineae*
2 / Poetry in the higher genres (*area maior* [*Amores* III.xv.18]):
    2a. Tragedy: *Medea* (not extant)
    2b. 'Epic': *Metamorphoses, Fasti*
3 / Exile poetry: *Ibis, Tristia, Epistulae ex Ponto*.

In Book II of the *Tristia*, Ovid helps us understand the only phase here that readers might find controversial – the phase of *area maior* – for Ovid presents the *Medea*, the *Fasti*, and the *Metamorphoses* as distinct from the earlier amatory phase and part of the same 'grand' phase: 'Yet think not all my work trivial; oft have I set grand sails [grandia vela] upon my bark. Six books of *Fasti* and as many more have I written, each containing its own month. This work did I recently ... dedicate ... to thee [Augustus] but my fate has broken it off. I have also given to the kings of tragedy their royal sceptre and speech suited to the buskin's dignity [Loeb ed. note: 'The *Medea*, a tragedy, not extant' (6: 97, n. 2)]. I sang also, though my attempt lacked the final touch, of bodies changed into new forms [the *Metamorphoses*]' (547–56). The order here of the three 'grand sails' of Ovid's 'bark' – *Fasti*, *Medea*, *Metamorphoses* – may suggest that Ovid intends the *Fasti* to function as a transitional poem into the higher genres of tragedy and epic, thus explaining why he wrote the 'poem' in elegiac metre. However we assemble individual works, we need to acknowledge that Ovid here presents himself as moving from 'trivial work' ('opus ... remissum') to 'grand sails' ('grandia vela').[32]

Moreover, in the opening poem of the *Tristia*, Ovid identifies three phases to his 'official' career when he addresses the *Tristia* itself: 'when you find refuge in my sanctuary, ... the round book-cases, you will behold there brothers arranged in order ... The rest of the band will display their titles openly, ... but three at some distance will strive to hide themselves in a dark place, ... as everybody knows, they teach how to love [the three books of the *Ars amatoria*] ... There are also thrice five rolls about changing forms [the fifteen books of the *Metamorphoses*]' (I.i.105–17). Here, Ovid imagines three spaces on his bookshelf back in Rome – one for his amatory poetry; one for poetry in a higher vein; and one for his exile poetry. Similarly, in the epilogue to Book III of the *Tristia* Ovid divides his career into three phases: 'Three of my children [the three books of the *Ars amatoria*] have caught pollution from me ... There are also thrice five books on changing forms, verses snatched from the funeral of their master. That work, had I not perished beforehand, might have gained a more secure name from my finishing hand ... Add to my books this humble bit also [Book III of the *Tristia*], which comes to you dispatched from a far-distant world' (xiv.17–26). These are the two most detailed 'career maps' in the Ovidian canon. Both, however, are retrospective; they look back on the actual shape of Ovid's career. Both have three phases; both have the same three phases (amatory poetry, poetry in the *area maior*, and exile poetry); and both lament the amatory phase. The second map especially represents Ovid's career as that of a sabotaged national poet.

While evidence like the *Tristia* exists to classify Ovid's career in these terms, he sets out to complicate the issue. For instance, in his autobiography in IV.x of the *Tristia* he cuts the *area maior* phase out of his literary career entirely. Here he refers to his earlier poetry simply as amatory, under the inspiration of Thalia, muse of comedy and light poetry (56), with himself 'fourth in order of time' in the great Augustan tradition of elegists, after Propertius, Gallus, and Tibullus (43–4). That is, he says nothing about the *Medea*, the *Fasti*, or the *Metamorphoses*. In fact, in the Exile Poetry, Ovid repeatedly identifies himself only as an elegiac poet, even when he is trying to repent of that identity (*Tristia* V.i.15–20). Similarly, in the opening poem of *Tristia* V, Ovid identifies his career as one that turns simply from elegy to exile poetry: 'For the future I have diverted my elegies to bashful poems' (23–4).[33] No wonder the Middle Ages and the Renaissance understood Ovid as an elegiac poet concerned largely with the folly of love. Ovid himself goes out of his way to construct precisely this 'Ovid.'

Moreover, while, according to the Elder Seneca (*Suasoriae* III.7), Quintilian (*Institutio oratoria* VII.v.6, X.i.98), and Tacitus (*Dialogus de oratoribus* 12), Ovid composed one tragedy, *Medea*, that play is not extant, and, to complicate the matter, the testimony of Seneca, Quintilian, and Tacitus is contradicted by Ovid's own claim in the *Tristia*: 'I have ... composed nothing ... for the theatre' (V.vii.25–30). It is difficult to say what Ovid was up to; but that is the point we need to emphasize. Just as Ovid makes it too easy to reduce his career to that of the elegist, so he makes it too easy to forget that he excelled in the genre of tragedy, to the extent that he deeply influenced Seneca.[34]

Late in his career, however, Ovid does leave at least three pieces of evidence that he is turning from amatory poetry to the *area maior*. First, in the *Ex Ponto* he appears to refer to his role as a poet of both tragedy and epic when he tells Salanus, 'The thyrsus and laurel tasted by me are foreign to you' (II.v.67: 'thyrsus abest a te gustata et laurea nobis'). The thyrsus and the laurel are the emblems of tragedy and epic, respectively: the Ovidian genres of the *area maior*.

Second, in the opening four lines of the *Metamorphoses* Ovid emphasizes, writes Kenney, that 'he was coming before the public in a totally new guise' ('Ovid' 2: 433): 'My mind is bent to tell of bodies changed into new forms. Ye gods, for you yourselves have wrought the changes, breathe on these my undertakings, and bring down my song in unbroken strains from the world's very beginning even unto the present time' (I.1–4). 'The obvious sense,'

Kenney continues, 'is that Ovid has been metamorphosed from elegist into epicist' (2: 433). As such, in this crucial passage opening his epic Ovid announces the primary *meta* of his counter-Virgilian *cursus*.

Third, in a passage from the opening of Book IV of the *Fasti*, composed during his exile, Ovid reveals that he is trying to present himself as he had done back in the *Amores*; he has succeeded in turning from amatory poetry to the higher genres: 'Thou [Venus], thou hast ever been the task I set myself. In my young years I toyed with themes to match, and gave offence to none; now my *steeds* treat a *larger field*. I sing the seasons, and their causes, and the starry signs that set beneath the earth and rise again, drawing my lore from annals old' (8–12; emphasis added). Ovid here actually quotes from the final passage of the *Amores*, reproducing the metaphor of the poet as charioteer in order to announce his turn to the higher genres: 'pulsanda est magnis *area maior equis*' (*Amores* III.xv.18; emphasis added: 'I must smite the earth with mighty *steeds* on a *mightier course*' [Loeb trans.]). Ovid quotes himself in order to announce that in the *Fasti* he is fulfilling his career projection of turning from amatory poetry to poetry in the *area maior*.[35]

Two 'Ovidian' Career Models

From this analysis, we can say that at least two 'Ovidian' career models were available to Marlowe. The first, or 'official,' model is the one that Ovid completed but did not project. This model is structured around the triad of amatory poetry, higher poetry, and exile poetry; it acknowledges Ovid the poet of *area maior* but heavily favours Ovid the Callimachean, elegiac poet who repents of his amatory poetry, and in the end it reduces the poet's role to that of a hapless 'amateur.' The second model is the unofficial career model that Ovid projected in the *Amores* but left incomplete. This model is structured around amatory poetry, tragedy, and epic; it exfoliates Ovid's maturation into the higher genres; and it asserts the poet's role as a counter-national poet in competition with Virgil.

Marlowe appears to have understood Ovid's official or completed career to be a failure – a consolation prize for the idealized career projected in the *Amores*. Like Spenser, Marlowe presumably knew Ovid's exile poetry, especially the *Tristia* (trans. Churchyard 1572), in which Ovid reflects on his sabotaged career. Thus, just as Spenser aims to 'overgo' Virgil by Christianizing him (Harvey, Spenser-Harvey Letters IV, rpt. in G.G. Smith, ed. 1: 116), so Marlowe aims to 'overgo' Ovid. Rather than Christianizing Ovid, however, Marlowe aims to complete the original or unofficial Ovidian career model that Ovid himself had failed to complete.

Most likely, the notion of a system that is disorienting is what fundamentally attracted Marlowe to the Ovidian *cursus*. Such a system contrasts sharply with those of Virgil and Spenser. Dynamism, not stasis; fluidity, not solidarity; interruption, not completion; oscillation, not pure progression: these become the hallmarks of the Ovidian career model that Marlowe inherits, inscribes, and finally champions in late sixteenth-century culture.

Marlowe's New Renaissance Ovid: *'Area maior'* in *Ovid's Elegies*

Marlowe's inscription of the Ovidian *cursus* in *Ovid's Elegies* is significant initially because it is the very first by any writer out of the Latin into any vernacular language. In fact, it is remarkable to discover that Marlowe is the first Western poet in any language to make Ovid's career pattern *literally* his own. This he achieves by virtue of translating the only poem in the Ovidian canon that inscribes a projected career pattern. For this quite technical reason, Marlowe alone among his contemporaries – English or Continental – deserves the first garland as *Ovidianus poeta*.[1]

Marlowe and the Renaissance Ovid

The *Amores* is unique in the Ovid canon not simply because it projects a career pattern, but also because it alone acquired the dubious distinction of a cultural taboo. Unlike the other poems in the canon, the *Amores* proved invulnerable to the strong medieval and Renaissance penchant for allegorizing and/or moralizing Ovid. Consequently, the poem did not merely go untranslated (again, unlike the other poems in the canon); it failed to find its way into any school curriculum before the seventeenth century. As Eric Jacobsen puts it, both England and Europe established 'an official conspiracy of silence against this particular work' (154).[2]

In Renaissance England, the conspiracy against the *Amores* took a 'monumental' form. All the other translations of Ovid appeared in humanist-looking documents designed to achieve the status of cultural monuments; all have a 'humanist' apparatus.[3] This apparatus usually includes such items as an elaborate or carefully prepared title page; a dedicatory epistle; an address to the reader; a prefatory poem; commendatory verses; etchings, woodcuts, engravings; a frontispiece and sometimes an explanation; pithy translations of Continental humanist writers on Ovid (such as Poliziano and Scaliger); arguments before books or poems in the work; a life of Ovid or other explanation of a given work within Ovid's career; marginal glosses; and an index. While the most elaborate of these monuments are the Golding and Sandys translations of the *Metamorphoses*, Turbervile's translation of the *Heroides* represents the document as monument characteristic of Englishings of Ovid in the period. This translation contains a title page; a dedicatory epistle to Thomas Howard, in which Turbervile sees his translation as a fit way to return Howard's great gifts to him; a seven-line poem titled 'The Translator to his Muse'; an address 'To the Reader'; a verse argument prefacing each letter in the *Heroides*; and a concluding poem, 'The Translator to the captious sort of Sycophantes.' Like the other documents, the Turbervile volume celebrates Ovid as a learned and sweet writer cohering with humanist goals for using poetry within the governance of the state.[4]

By contrast, the first translation of the *Amores* in the history of the West is totally stark. *Ovid's Elegies* appears with a title page, but it is sparse in its own right, including only the title, the author (Marlowe), a spurious place of publication (Middlebourgh); and a small and plain floral design in the middle. It has *no* prefatory material whatsoever. Immediately after the title page, we are surprised to discover the first poem of the translation. The only embellishment is a brief Latin description of each elegy. As if to signify the unique principle ordering the document, Davies's *Epigrams* begins on the same page on which *Ovid's Elegies* ends. As we shall see when we discuss the translation's actual phrasing for both its title and its author, this is uniqueness writ strange.

We can interpret the monumental difference between the document of Marlowe's translation and the other Ovid translations along an obvious line. As a tabooed work, the *Amores* required a transgressive form in order to reach the shady light of day. This line, however, leads us away from the paradox that is so important to Marlowe's use of the *Amores*: the only document in the Ovid canon projecting a *cursus* is the only work achieving the status of a taboo. This paradox helps explain why medieval, Renaissance, and therefore modern commentators fail to identify, name, and examine an Ovidian *cursus* or triad in competition with the Virgilian *cursus*.

Perhaps not by accident, Marlowe enters his inscription of a career 'meta' from amatory poetry to the 'area maior' of tragedy and epic into history at a crucial juncture in the Roman poet's influence on Western literature and culture: 'This last end to my elegies is set, ... / A greater ground with great horse is to till' (*Ovid's Elegies* III.xiv[xv].2, 18).[5] For at this time the 'Renaissance Ovid' was vying for authority with the 'medieval Ovid.' That is, like Shakespeare, Marlowe 'lived during a period in which ways of reading Ovid underwent radical transformation, as a newly unapologetic delight in the poetic and erotic qualities of the *Metamorphoses* came to compete with the predominant medieval practice of moralizing and even Christianizing them' (J. Bate 25).[6]

While Renaissance writers such as Golding and Shakespeare busied themselves with either the moralized or the eroticized Ovid, Marlowe arrived with an Ovid that transcends this dichotomy. Marlowe's new Ovid is an Ovid with a 'literary career' – a poet who presents himself with a multigenre career pattern, a political ideology, a sexual orientation, and a vision of the poet's vocation and sense of destiny. Significantly, in the passage closing the *Amores* quoted above, Ovid relies on the metaphor of chariot-racing to inscribe his version of the literary *cursus honorum*. Marlowe's new Renaissance Ovid is a 'national' poet of 'laureate' status. Since 'in the poems of Ovid the poet begins to assert himself as the true nation' (Braudy 135), Marlowe's Ovid is precisely a counter-national poet.

Marlowe's Ovidian *cursus* makes available an alternative career path fully competitive with the *cursus* privileged by English and Continental culture: the Virgilian *cursus*, as practised variously by the sixteenth-century heirs of Dante and Petrarch, but most importantly for Marlowe by England's reigning national poet, Spenser, who, for all his achievements, followed Virgil in eschewing the stage. Like the Virgilian model before Spenser, the Ovidian model had its practitioners before Marlowe, but the two great Ovidian poets of the late Middle Ages, Jean de Meun and Chaucer (Rand, *Ovid and His Influence* 145), had not followed the Ovidian career path per se. Neither, for instance, had produced a stage tragedy – nor could they, for the Western theatre would remain closed between the end of antiquity and the opening of 'the permanent, public, commercial theaters' in sixteenth-century England and Spain (W. Cohen 17). Chaucer had come close to inscribing the Ovidian *cursus* by beginning his career in the Ovidian mode with the dream visions (*The Book of the Duchess, The House of Fame, The Parlement of Foules*) and proceeding to the higher genres of verse 'tragedy' in *Troilus and Criseyde* and 'epic' in *The Canterbury Tales*. But Chaucer had ended his career with 'Chaucer's Retraction,' a Christianized or Augustinian repentance for past literary sins, and thus had ended by following the course that approximated the exiled Ovid of the *Tristia* (see Cheney, *Spenser's Famous Flight* 60–2).[7]

Unlike earlier Ovidian poets such as Chaucer and Jean de Meun, and unlike earlier translators of Ovid, Marlowe is the first poet to capitalize on the late sixteenth-century formation of the theatre by presenting himself as the new Ovidian poet of his age. Not simply is he the penman of amatory poetry and the writer of (pre-)epic; he is also the stager of tragedy. Translating the *Amores* within a decade of the 1576 building of what is arguably Europe's first playhouse since antiquity (The Theatre), Marlowe positions himself to inscribe the Ovidian *cursus* in a way that few individuals in the history of the West were able to do and that no individual before him had succeeded in doing.[8]

Ovid's Elegies as a Counter-Spenserian Text

Missing in most accounts of the *Amores* and *Ovid's Elegies* are three underlying and interlocked motives: the poet's desire to establish a generic program leading to maturation; his attempt to contextualize this program in terms of the careers of other poets, from whom he could derive inspiration; and his goal of writing a nationally significant art.[9] To the usual motives of wit, sex, prosody, and subversion, we need to add the tripartite foundations of Marlowe's literary career: genre patterning, professional rivalry, and counter-nationhood.

In translating the *Amores* line by line, Marlowe literally inscribes the three-genre, counter-Virgilian *cursus* that Ovid uses to organize the *Amores*. But Marlowe does not simply *repeat* Ovid; he Englishes him in a way that proves original among his contemporaries. According to J.B. Steane, 'Marlowe enters his text with sufficient spirit to make it part of his own poetic life' (282).[10] We can add that Marlowe accommodates Ovid's counter-Virgilian *cursus* to his own counter-Spenserian *cursus*. If in the ten-poem edition of *Ovid's Elegies* Marlowe creates a 'Pythagorean' structure that 'direct[s] us to its central feature, the triumph of poetry over kings' (Pearcy 27), we can witness tangibly the way in which Marlowe uses his translation to write an Ovidian counter-nationhood. By assuming the Ovidian mantle so fully, Marlowe begins a process of contextualization that leads directly from Ovid's Roman rivalry with Virgil to his own rivalry with England's Virgil, and from there to a nationally significant poetics.

Perhaps the most remarkable instance of Marlowe's appropriation of Ovid appears in the stark textual apparatus identified earlier: the title page. The title page for the complete translation reads: '*ALL OVIDS ELEGIES: 3. Bookes By C.M. Epigrams by J.D.*' In the history of English Renaissance translations of Ovid, this inscription is unique. For the title does not identify the work as a translation at all: '*ALL OVIDS ELEGIES.*' Nor does the authorship line present Marlowe as a translator: '*3. Bookes By C.M.*' If we know the volume at hand to be a translation, the capitalized word 'By' is alarming. If we do not, we are presumably deceived into thinking that '*ALL OVIDS ELEGIES*' consists of '*3. Bookes*' of original (Ovidian) verse written '*By C.M.*' The occlusion of the idea of translation also emerges in the following phrase, '*Epigrams by J.D.*' – epigrams by Sir John Davies – which, unlike the three books by C.M., *are* original verse. The title page, then, appears to encourage us to read the volume as original verse written by Christopher Marlowe.[11]

We should not be surprised, therefore, to discover 'C.M.' identifying his intent to translate Ovid by metamorphosing him. In the opening poem, during the first programmatic statement, Marlowe writes:

> With Muse prepared I meant to sing of arms,
> Choosing a subject fit for fierce alarms.
> Both verses were alike till Love (men say)
> Began to smile and took one foot away.
> Rash boy, who gave thee power to *change a line*?
>
> (*Ovid's Elegies* I.i.5–9; emphasis added)

The original Latin for the last line reads, '"Quis tibi, saeve puer, dedit hoc in carmina iuris?,"' translated by the Loeb as '"Who gave thee, cruel boy, this right over poesy?"' The original, in other words, does not mention 'change,' nor does it specify the concept of 'a [poetic] line.' Marlowe *changes* Ovid's original verb for 'give,' 'dedit,' to 'change' itself; he eliminates the legal resonance of 'iurus' (right, jurisdiction) by inserting the more neutral word 'power'; and he converts the generalized literary form, 'carmina' (song, poetry), into the synecdochic 'line.' Marlowe's 'change' to the original self-consciously identifies his program of *changing* the lines he inherits. Since the original verse of the *Amores* was penned by a poet who is himself famous for his *changes* – his *metamorphoses* – 'carmina mutatas hominum dicentia formas' (*Tristia* I.vii.13: 'the verses that tell of the changed forms of men') – he is participating in the play of programmatic metamorphosis itself. The 'rash boy' who has such 'power' is literally the god Amor; but even Ovid would have understood that god to be the rash boy within: 'agitante calescimus illo' (*Fasti* VI.5: 'There is a god within us'). As the spirit of eros metamorphosing the poet from within, the rash boy is thus also the youth who turned out to be so fond of 'rashnes in attempting soden pryvie injuries to men' (Kyd, Letter to Puckering, rpt. in MacLure, ed., *Marlowe* 36). What the rash boy contains in his 'change[d] ... line' is 'power': the power of translation as change, metamorphosis, perhaps homoerotic force, ultimately artistic violence.

We can also witness Marlowe's appropriation of Ovid in his translation of the literary *cursus* itself. At the end of the collection, in lines 8–10, he treats a relative pronoun with functional ambiguity: 'Of me Peligny's nation boasts alone, / Whom liberty to honest arms compelled, / When careful Rome in doubt their prowess held' (*Ovid's Elegies* III.xiv[xv].8–10). In the original, Ovid makes clear just who puts on the arms honourably: it is the Paelignians, the race or 'gentis' of the Paelignians, for Ovid is referring to the 'Social War, 90–89 B.C., by which Rome was compelled to grant citizenship to the Italians' and in which the 'Paeligni were leaders' (Loeb ed., 1: 511, n. a). In Marlowe's translation, however, the antecedent of 'Whom' ('quam') is ambiguous, referring either to 'me' or to 'Peligny's nation.' If understood as referring to 'me,' the lines subtly rewrite Ovid the love poet to construct Marlowe the poet of war. In this case, it is the poet who has donned the armour. Through this ambiguity, Marlowe playfully puns on 'honest arms,' meaning both martial armour and the erotic arms of the beloved – which is exactly where Ovid (and Marlowe) had begun the collection, with a pun on the opening of the *Aeneid*: 'Arma gravi numero violentaque bella parabam edere' (I.i.1: 'Arms, and the violent deeds of war' [Loeb trans.]). Hence, in this concluding elegy the poet mentions Virgil in the very next line: 'In Virgil Mantua joys' (11). Indeed, the point of this elegy is to announce the poet's turn from arms to arms – from elegy to the *area maior* of tragedy and epic.

Such 'changes' to Ovid's 'line' catch Marlowe in the act of making Ovid his own. What he makes in this last elegy, as in the collection as a whole, is the Ovidian *cursus* that is to be the primary *meta* of his career: the Ovidian counter to the Renaissance Virgilian progression from pastoral to epic within the context of counter-nationhood.[12]

Alone among Marlowe's works, *Ovid's Elegies* has not been found to contain an imitation, recollection, or echo of Spenser.[13] In Elegy III.vi[vii], on the poet's impotence, however, Marlowe writes,

> What, waste my limbs through some Thessalian charms?
> May spells and drugs do silly souls such harms?
> With *virgin wax* hath some imbased my joints,
> And pierced my liver with sharp needles' points?
> (*Ovid's Elegies* III.vi[vii].27–30; emphasis added)

Since Ovid's Latin reads '*poenicea ... cera,*' both L.C. Martin and Millar MacLure pause for a gloss. In MacLure's phrasing, 'the reference is to an image of wax made to work spells on the victim. Like Martin, I have found no satisfying explanation of Marlowe's "virgin wax" for "poenicea ... cera," Phoenician (i.e., red) wax' (ed., *Poems* 198).

One explanation produces some satisfaction. In Book III, canto viii, of *The Faerie Queene*, Spenser narrates the unnamed witch's creation of the False Florimell:

> The substance, whereof she the bodie made,
> Was purest snow in massie mould congeald,
>
> ...
>
> And *virgin wex*, that never yet was seald.
>
>   (*The Faerie Queene* III.viii.6; emphasis added)

Spenser's image of 'virgin wex' has a mysterious genealogy. In his edition of *The Faerie Queene*, A.C. Hamilton (376) refers to Sidney's line in a poem originally included in the *Old Arcadia* (Book III, ed. Robertson 240) and then relocated in the *New Arcadia*. During a stunning blason, the hero Pyrochles repeats a song that Philisides (Sidney's persona) had originally sung to his beloved, Mira, in order to praise his own beloved, the princess Philoclea:

> her navel doth unite,
> In curious circle, busie sight:
> A daintie seale of *virgin-waxe*,
> Where nothing but impression lackes.
>
>   ('What toong' in Sidney, *Poems* 62.73–6: 88; emphasis added)

According to William A. Ringler, Jr, 'Sidney worked over this poem more carefully than he did any of his other pieces, for the considerable variations among the 13 substantive texts show that he added to or revised it on at least four different occasions' (410). Ringler adds that the poem 'became a favourite with his contemporaries, who copied or quoted it more frequently than any of his other verses – it was transcribed in at least eight manuscript anthologies, was printed in *Englands Parnassus*, and was quoted or imitated by Puttenham, Marston, Weever, Burton, and others' (410). To this list, we can add (following Hamilton) Spenser and (now) Marlowe.

Since Sidney wrote the *Old Arcadia* between 1577 and 1580, we most likely need to assign the originality of the phrase 'virgin-waxe' to him, rather than to either Spenser or Marlowe. Yet the intertextual conjunction is more complicated than a simple Marlowe–Sidney borrowing. For Sidney's famous song itself imitates parts of Spenser, and thirteen lines after our passage Sidney refers to Ovid: 'Yet never shall my song omitte / Those thighes, for Ovid's song more fitte; / Which flanked with two sugred flankes, / Lift up their stately swelling bankes' (Ringler 62.87–90: 88). In her edition of the *Old Arcadia*, Jean Robertson glosses 'Ovid's song' as follows: 'Cf. Elegy. I.v (Marlowe's translation),' and she quotes lines 19–22 of *Ovid's Elegies* to confirm the idea that Sidney is indeed thinking of Ovid's *Amores* (in Sidney, *Old Arcadia* 460). The poem Robertson cites is the famous elegy on Corinna's noontime visit to Ovid's room, since this poem functions as an Augustan counterpart to Sidney's equally famous Elizabethan erotic representation. Yet it is also possible that Sidney's Ovidian 'thigh' passage derives from and refers to the elegy we are considering – that on the poet's impotence: 'And eagerly she kissed me with her tongue, / And under mine her wanton thigh she flung' (9–10). This possibility emerges because the preceding line reads: 'Her arms far whiter than the Scythian snow' (8). And Spenser, in his imitation of Sidney's 'virgin-waxe' during the False Florimell passage, relies on the Ovidian trope – and in the very same stanza: 'purest snow ... of the Riphaean hils.'[14]

In Elegy III.vi[vii], Marlowe may translate Ovid via both Sidney and Spenser. Here the repetition of Spenser is most important. Hence, in the 'virgin wax' line Marlowe uses the word 'imbased,' meaning 'enfeebled.' Possibly, Marlowe remembered two lines earlier in the story of Florimell, where Spenser uses the words 'Virgin' and 'embace' together: 'But the faire *Virgin* was so meeke and mild, / That she to them vouchsafed to *embace* / Her goodly port' (III.vii.15; emphasis added). Both Marlowe's Ovidian elegy and Spenser's epic narrative deal with witchcraft and sexuality. Only their wax images pertain to magic; Sidney's pertains to royal seals. Yet we need to include Sidney in the intertextual exchange because presumably he was the first to use the image and to identify its Ovidian origin.

Thus, when Marlowe has his Ovidian persona ask whether 'Thessalian charms ... / With virgin wax hath some imbased my joints,' he is indicating that the Ovidian poet's impotence here is not strictly sexual but textual as well, for magic and witchcraft function during the period as a metaphor for poetry (Cheney, 'Two Florimells'). That the wax used is 'virgin' introduces a curious yet unsurprising Marlovian gender twist to the intertextuality. Marlowe succeeds in clarifying what Ovid is *also* talking about: the topic of artistic impotence, as revealed in his references (ll. 59–61) to the two ancient bards, Phemios, the great minstrel in the manor of Odysseus (*Odyssey* I.154), and Thamyris, the legendary poet who competed against the Muses (*Iliad* II.594–600). Evidently, the references to the epics of Homer transcribe artistic potency; they hint that the elegiac poet is preparing for a 'greater ground.'[15]

Finally, 'virgin wax' has political resonance for a nation governed by a Virgin Queen. Maurice Evans remarks of Spenser's 'virgin wax' passage: 'It is the art of make-up that Spenser is describing ... [T]he picture is an unpleasant one, coming painfully near the bone in the way it brings to mind the image of the ageing Virgin Queen Elizabeth' (171). Later, Evans sees the old fisher's attempt to rape Florimell (viii.20–31) as an Elizabeth allegory: 'The old man is the embodiment of the repressed sexual passions in the aged virgin herself' (173). This fisher, of course, is modelled on Ariosto's impotent hermit in the *Orlando Furioso* (II–III, VIII); as Hamilton observes, Spenser here 'seeks to outdo Ariosto's bawdy play on the Hermit's fallen steed (*Orl. Fur* viii. 48–50)' (ed., *FQ* 379). While the topic of sexual impotence identifies one further conjunction between the Marlowe and Spenser passages, it also alerts us to the political significance encoded in the phrase 'virgin wax.' Ovid and Marlowe ask whether 'some[one]' has used virgin wax to 'embase' their 'joints.' The phrase 'virgin wax' suggests that the Ovidian Marlowe is encoding his charge against Spenser, Elizabeth, and their artful cult of chastity for threatening the potency of his art.[16]

By adding these 'changes' to the commentary on *Ovid's Elegies*, we can see more palpably how Marlowe appropriates the Ovidian *cursus* as his own, contextualizes that *cursus* in terms of his rivalry with Spenser, and thereby constructs the origins of counter-nationhood. The appropriation of Spenser's Virgilian epic within a translation of Ovid's elegies functions as a model for Marlowe's program in the translation as a whole. Marlowe is fit to pursue the Ovidian *cursus* and to vie with England's Virgil for national authority.

Marlowe and Ovid

Even if we agree that Marlowe deserves the garland as the West's great *Ovidianus poeta*, we confront an immediate contradiction: the self-avowedly homoerotic Marlowe identifies with 'the West's first champion of true, normal, even conjugal love' (Otis 277).[17] Unlike fellow Augustan poets Virgil, Horace, Propertius, Tibullus, and Gallus, Ovid took little interest in boys, insisting throughout his career that he write only about women: 'I hate embraces which leave not each outworn; that is why a boy's love appeals to me but little' (*Ars amatoria* II.683–4).[18]

Not surprisingly, Ovid left behind a remarkable commitment to marriage and family life. As he reveals in his autobiography (*Tristia* IV.x), he married three times (69–74); he proudly fathered one daughter (75–6), probably with his first or second wife; he inherited a second daughter (whom he calls 'Perilla') through his beloved third wife; he was grandfather to two children (75–6); and after his exile he wrote a poignant series of verse letters to his third wife (*Tristia* I.vi, III.iii, IV.iii, V.ii, v, xi, xiv; *Ex Ponto* I.iv, III.i). The first of these letters sets the tone for the rest: 'Not so great was the love of the Clarian bard [Antimachus] for Lyde or that of her own Coan [Philetas] for Bittis as the love that clings in my heart for thee, my wife, for thee who art worthy of a less wretched, not a better, husband' (*Tristia* I.vi.1–4). The last letter in the *Tristia* is equally remarkable, because Ovid identifies the entire collection as a memorial to this virtuous young woman: 'What a memorial I have reared to thee in my books, O my wife, dearer to me than myself, thou seest ... As long as men read me thy fame shall be read along with me ... for my voice is never silent about thee' (V.xiv.1–17). That we have to believe Ovid when he speaks of his deep love for his wife is clear in a final poignant moment worth recording – his voicing of his wife's name during a fit of delirium: 'All things steal into my mind, yet above all, you, my wife, and you hold more than half my heart. You I address though you are absent, you alone my voice names; no night comes to me without you, no day. Nay more, they say that when I talked strange things, 'twas so that your name was on my delirious lips' (*Tristia* III.iii.15–20).

Ovid even wrote one letter to his stepdaughter, 'Perilla' (*Tristia* III.vii), with whom he shared a priceless bond, the love of poetry. Additionally, he left a heartbreaking recollection on the death of his beloved older brother, with whom he shared the same birthday: 'I was not the first born, for my birth befell after that of a brother, thrice four months my senior. The same day-star beheld the birth of us both: one birthday was celebrated by the offering of our two cakes' (*Tristia* IV.x.9–12). Equally memorable is Ovid's breathtaking address to the spirits of his deceased mother and father: 'Happy both! and laid to rest in good season! since they passed away before the day of my punishment' (81–2). Ovid's representation of himself as a husband, father, stepfather, grandfather, younger brother, and son remains one of the most enduring legacies he has bequeathed to us.[19]

By contrast, Marlowe never married or left any record of an erotic relation with an actual Elizabethan woman, let alone (illegitimate) children.[20] In fact, the only female beloved in the Marlowe record does not appear until 1691, when Anthony à Wood embroiders a detail that first appeared in 1598, when Francis Meres reported that 'Christopher Marlow was stabbed to death by a bawdy serving man, a rivall of his in his lewde love' (rpt. in MacLure, ed., *Marlowe* 46): 'For so it fell out,' à Wood reports, 'that he being deeply in love with a certain woman, had for his rival a bawdy serving-man, one rather fit to be a pimp, than an ingenious amoretto as Marlow conceived himself to be' (rpt. in MacLure 54). As Charles Nicholl reveals, however, à Wood mistakenly romanticizes Meres's account, which probably referred to a homoerotic rivalry (67–8, 82–3).[21]

Finally, Marlowe left no record of his relation with his parents or siblings – unless we find such a record imprinted in his plays, where critics find the playwright repeatedly betraying his Oedipal identity.[22]

By such a sexual profile, then, Marlowe differs radically from Ovid: in the extant record, he never presents himself as a husband, a father, a sibling, or a son.

Marlowe and Ovid differ in other ways as well. Ovid was a son from an established family of old equestrian rank (*Tristia* IV.x.7–8), and he appears to have had a fairly happy home life (1–40). Marlowe, by contrast, was the son of a shoemaker and grew up in a rather troubled family noted around Canterbury for its blasphemy.[23] Moreover, the two writers differ in the contribution each makes to the state through non-literary channels. As a young man, Ovid served Rome by holding minor offices: he was a *triumvir capitalis* or member of a board presiding over prisons; a member of a centrumviral court presiding over questions of inheritance; and a judge in private lawsuits (*Tristia* IV.x.33–5). By contrast, Marlowe served England only through espionage, a semi-legal practice of ambiguous patriotism that repeatedly led him into the seediest parts of his culture, such as Deptford. Finally, Marlowe and Ovid differ right down to the bone. Repeatedly, Ovid emphasizes his physical frailty and distaste for a life of action (*Tristia* IV.x.37–41). By contrast, Marlowe is notorious for engaging in the life of (deadly) action – at Hog Lane (Bakeless 1: 98–100), in Holywell Street, Shoreditch (Bakeless 1: 104–5), in Canterbury itself (Urry 65–8), and finally at Deptford (Nicholl).

Despite the obvious differences, we need not look too far to discover what Marlowe could have found attractive in Ovid and his literary career, and we must assume that in the Elizabethan writer's mind the attractions were sufficient to outweigh the differences. The two writers had a remarkably similar literary genesis. As Ovid records in his autobiography, he was training for the Senate when he broke to become a poet, despite his father's rebuke (*Tristia* IV.x.15–26). Marlowe, as is well known, went to Corpus Christi College, Cambridge, as a Matthew Parker scholar in order to prepare for holy orders, but along the way he broke from that paternal training to become a playwright, poet, and translator. What both paternal turncoats found in their profession of poetry was remarkably similar: a deep personal centre in eros. In the opening line of his autobiography, Ovid identifies his erotic centre: 'That thou mayst know who I was, I that playful poet of tender love' (*Tristia* IV.x.1). Similarly, Marlowe finds his most 'matur[e]' voice in his 'love of beauty' (Ellis-Fermor 123–4), as in Faustus's impassioned cry 'Was this the face that launched a thousand ships' (*Doctor Faustus* V.i.91).

Both poets could find their centre in the flesh because they failed to find their faith in the deity. Thus, Marlowe lets Ovid's participation in Lucretian materialism represent his own 'atheism': 'What, are there gods? ... / God is a name, no substance, feared in vain, / And doth the world in fond belief detain, / Or if there be a God, he loves fine wenches' (*Ovid's Elegies* III.iii.1, 23–5).[24] Allied with their 'atheism,' both poets are noted for their dissident writing. Ovid's relation with Augustus and Rome is complex, but most critics agree that one of his great achievements is his construction of an artistic identity set over and against that of the Emperor, and nowhere does this achievement reach greater defiance than in the very document Ovid designed to placate Caesar: 'my mind is nevertheless my comrade and my joy; over this Caesar could have no right' (*Tristia* III.vii.47–8). Marlowe's subversive stance towards the state requires little documentation here (see esp. Greenblatt, *Renaissance Self-Fashioning*; Dollimore; Sinfield); suffice it to say that he was repeatedly arrested by his own government and that he was probably assassinated by it (Nicholl).

Accordingly, Marlowe could have found his own commitment to secrecy and counterfeiting in Ovid, who repeatedly emphasizes the individual's need for deception, in matters of love as well as in art: 'As for me I recount even true amours but sparely, and a solid secrecy hides my dark intrigues' (*Ars amatoria* II.639–40; see II.313–14, III.155). Of course, we can turn the counterfeited coin over to see that Ovid and Marlowe shared a personality trait of humour and jest – a dark commitment, for it got both poets into trouble. In the *Tristia*, for instance, Ovid defends himself against the charges inscribed in the *Ars amatoria* before an unnamed friend: 'you know that with those arts their author's character had no connexion; you know that this poem was written long ago, an amusement of my youth, and that those jests, though not deserving praise, were still mere jests [iocos]' (I.ix.59–62). Ovid even uses the word *jests* (*iocos*) as a metaphor for his amatory poetry: 'Beguiled by such as these I wrote verse lacking in seriousness, but a serious penalty has befallen my jests [iocos]' (II.493–4).[25] Similarly, Marlowe was famous among his contemporaries for his jesting, which often took the form of scoffing. Our very first report, by Greene, calls Marlowe a 'mad and scoffing poet' (rpt. in MacLure, ed., *Marlowe* 30), and Kyd reports that 'in table talk or otherwise' Marlowe would 'jest at the devine scriptures[,] gybe at praiers' (rpt. in MacLure 35).[26]

Finally, the two poets had a passion for drama. According to J.C. McKeown, Ovid had a 'natural gift for drama' (1: 65; see 63–73; and Davis). Marlowe's natural gift for drama requires little documentation, but we may emphasize what has generally escaped notice: he could have found a precursor for his gift in Ovid.

In short, it appears that Marlowe was able to overcome his difference of opinion about matters of sexual orientation in order to present himself as England's Ovid. What he found in Ovid that he could not have found in any other Western writer was a poet with a counter-Virgilian *cursus* that included amatory verse and work in the *area maior*, especially tragedy.

Marlowe's Ovidian *Cursus*: Elizabethan Origins and Jacobean Repetitions

The Elizabethans appear to have understood the Ovidian *cursus* as an alternative to the Virgilian *cursus*. Marlowe may be the first Renaissance writer in any language to inscribe and adopt this *cursus* clearly, but he is not the first to inscribe it at all.

In the programmatic *October* eclogue to *The Shepheardes Calender*, Spenser does not simply create a dialogue between two shepherds on 'the state of Poet' (97). More important, he creates a dialogue between two competing career models, the Virgilian and the Ovidian, as they pertain to the Christian poet in England during the late 1570s.[27] The eclogue divides in two. Lines 1–36 identify the problem: the young poet who writes 'dapper ditties' (13) merely to delight the youth suffers from artistic impotence, because by penning this lower form he cannot attract patronage from those in positions of power. Then lines 37–120 introduce the solution: the young poet who moves beyond the lower form to the higher genres exercises artistic power, because he aims to fashion and actually save, not merely the youth, but also those wielding the 'awful crowne' (40).

Within this second part, Spenser presents two competing career models as alternative solutions to the poet's problem. In lines 37–96, he presents the older and more sanguine Piers introducing a Christianized, four-genre version of the Virgilian triad of pastoral, georgic, and epic: pastoral, epic, love lyric, and hymn.[28] In lines 97–120, and in 'Cuddie's Embleme' following, Spenser presents the younger and more melancholic Cuddie introducing a three-genre Ovidian *cursus* of amatory poetry, tragedy, and epic. Significant for Marlowe, Spenser emphasizes the genre of tragedy:

> All otherwise the state of Poet stands,
> For lordly love is such a Tyranne fell:
>
> ...
>
> Who ever casts to compasse weightye prise,
> And thinks to throwe out thondring words of threate:
> Let powre in lavish cups and thriftie bitts of meate,
> For Bacchus fruite is frend to Phoebus wise.
> And when with Wine the braine begins to sweate,
> The nombers flowe as fast as spring doth ryse.
>
> Thou kenst not Percie howe the ryme should rage.
> O if my temples were distaind with wine,
> And girt in girlonds of wild Yvie twine,
> How I could reare the Muse on stately stage,
> And teache her tread aloft in bus-kin fine,
> With queint Bellona in her equipage.
>
> But ah my corage cooles ere it be warme,
> For thy, content us in thys humble shade:
> Where no such troublous tydes han us assayde,
> Here we our slender pipes may safely charme.
>
> ...
>
> > Cuddies Embleme.
> > *Agitante calescimus illo &*
>
> > > (*October* 97–122)

Cuddie's speech begins and ends with Ovidian representations. At the beginning, in line 98 – 'For lordly love is such a Tyranne fell' – Spenser inscribes an 'Ovidian conceit' regularly used by 'Elizabethan sonneteers': 'love is an arbitrary tyrant, whose dictates the lover is powerless to resist' (Maclean and Prescott 528, n. 9). At the end, in line 118 – 'Here we our slender pipes may safely charme' – Spenser inscribes a second Ovidian conceit, as E.K. reveals in his gloss: 'For Charmes were wont to be made by verses as Ovid sayth. *Aut si carminibus* ['or if in songs']' [276–7]). The phrase that E.K. quotes is 'not in Ovid' (Oram et al. 183), but Hugh Maclean and Anne Lake Prescott follow W.L. Renwick in speculating that it may be *Amores* III.vii.27–30 – Ovid's elegy on his impotence, which we have already discussed with reference to 'virgin wax': 'Was my body listless under the spell of Thessalian drugs? Was I the wretched victim of charms and herbs, or did a witch curse my name upon a red wax image and stick fine pins into the middle of the liver' (Loeb trans.).[29] Whether Spenser had the *Amores* passage in mind, he clearly writes Cuddie's speech along Ovidian lines, as confirmed by a third and final Ovidian inscription, which immediately follows the last. Cuddie's Emblem reads: '*Agitante calescimus illo &.*' As critics regularly observe, this quotation comes from *Fasti* VI.5: 'agitante calescimus illo' ('There is a god within us'; see Oram et al. 176). Spenser's '&' encourages us to peer more closely at the rest of Ovid's text.

Within the context of the *Fasti*, the passage is crucial, because Ovid narrates how the goddess Juno appeared to him in a vision and then addressed him in career-resounding terms: 'O poet, minstrel of the Roman year, thou who hast dared to chronicle great things in slender couplets, thou hast won for thyself the right to look upon a celestial divinity by undertaking to celebrate the festivals in thy numbers' (21–4). *Great things in slender couplets*: this is Ovid's version of the classical phrase 'to compare great things with small' that John S. Coolidge identifies as a Virgilian strategy of generic progression (2).[30] As such, Ovid uses the Virgilian phrase in a crucial generic moment in order to define the epic dimension of his elegiac work. By quoting this moment, Spenser compels us to read a reversal into Cuddie's turn from the higher genres to the lower – to see a turn from the lower back to the higher. Spenser himself dares to chronicle great things in slender verse. If that lower verse is indeed amatory, as critics agree, then it remains to identify more particularly the *area maior* itself.

The 'greater ground' can only be tragedy and epic – tragedy in its relation to epic. Most critics do not link the *October* passage with tragedy but identify Cuddie as a Bacchic reveller whose bathetic interest in intoxication comically undercuts his poetic authority.[31] Early readers, however, found genuine inspiration. Jonson, for instance, told Drummond of Hawthornden that he 'hath by heart some verses of Spenser's Calender, about wyne, between Coline [Cuddie] and Percye,' and Coleridge remarks passionately, 'how often have I repeated in my own name the sweet stanza of Edmund Spenser' beginning 'Thou kenst not Percie how the ryme should rage' (rpt. in *Variorum Edition* 7: 389, 390).

Two truths are told. Is Spenser parodying the writing of tragedy here or promoting it? We may account for the question by identifying Spenser's rhetorical strategy: the topos of inability. Thus we may apply to Cuddie what Thomas M. Cain says about Colin's refusal to write epic in *June*: 'this topos of inability or affected modesty is in effect an indirect tactic of self-assertion' (Oram et al. 108).[32] In *October*, Spenser indirectly asserts his ability to write tragedy, at the same time that he admits his ambivalence about the prospect. Ultimately, Spenser issues a challenge – to himself and to his colleagues: 'Who ever casts to compasse weightye prise' must 'reare the Muse on stately stage.' In *October*, the New Poet identifies tragedy as the Elizabethan writer's 'weightye prise' – hence the programmatic ring of line 106: 'For Bacchus fruite is frend of Phoebus wise.' Spenser calls on himself and on his colleagues to yoke Apollonian and Dionysian genres in a professional 'frend[ship].'

Spenser's passage is priceless also because of its 1579 troping of Senecan tragedy. Line 104 – 'And thinks to throwe out thondring words of threate' – tropes the fusion of writing and acting Senecan tragedy within a rival poetics: the tragedian translates thought into verbal action – here Senecan divine vengeance and political tyranny; the actor *performs* the declamation bombastically; and the audience, the aspiring tragedian, receives the challenge.[33] The next line – 'Let powre in lavish cups and thriftie bitts of meate' – specifies the source of divine inspiration and the violently appetitive form the threat takes, perhaps grimly alluding to Seneca's *Thyestes*, in which the intoxicated hero eats his sons' flesh.[34] Finally, the famous line 'Thou kenst not Percie how the ryme should rage' contains the word that Gordon Braden identifies as 'the all-consuming subject of Senecan tragedy': the 'voice of a style' that he terms 'rage' (2).[35] Spenser's inscription of such technical terms indicates that in 1579 the New Poet envisions a central role for Senecan stage tragedy within 'the perfecte paterne of a Poete' (*October*, Arg.).[36] What appears to have been particularly important to Marlowe is Spenser's situating of Senecan tragedy within an inscription of the Ovidian *cursus* that functions as an alternative to the Virgilian progression.[37]

Among Spenserian disciples qualifying as laureate poets, Michael Drayton follows Spenser down the Virgilian path, while Samuel Daniel, for all his deep connection with his master, chooses the Ovidian path.[38] In particular, Daniel works from an Ovidian model that moves from love lyric (as opposed to pastoral) to the higher genres of tragedy and historical epic (as opposed to mythological epic) in a spectacular imping of Petrarch (*Delia* and *The Complaint of Rosamond* [1592]), Seneca (*The Tragedie of Cleopatra* [1594]), and Lucan (*The Civil Wars* [1595, 1609]). Hence, in the 1592 edition of *Delia*, Daniel selects as his career motto a passage from Ovid's elegiac precursor, Propertius: 'Aetas prima canat veneres / postrema tumultus' (Let the poet's first age sing of love, his last of war).[39]

The example of Daniel reveals that a Spenserian imitator could move with laureate licence from love lyric to the higher genres, including tragedy and epic. Thus, Daniel legitimizes a career progression that we might be tempted to criticize, as did the playwrights writing *The Pilgrimage to Parnassus*. Their play, notes Harry Levin, allegorizes 'the undergraduates' journey through the arts, hinting that their sojourn in the land of poetry might be a preparation for the ill-famed theatrical district of London' (8):

> Here are entisinge pandars, subtile baudes,
> Catullus, Ovid, wantone Martiall.
> Heare them whilest a lascivious tale they tell,
> Theile make thee fitt in Shorditche for to dwell.
>
> (*The Pilgrimage to Parnassus* 514–17)

As the case of Daniel testifies, however, and as the later example of Jonson confirms, we need not construe Marlowe's move from Cambridge to Shoreditch as simple pandering; his contestation of Spenser encourages us to think otherwise. Marlowe's Ovidian career path may have been disreputable because it led to the theatre, but the paradox served him well: in the theatre alone could he powerfully display his Ovidian *meta* to the *area maior*.[40]

Ovid and Marlowe in the Elizabethan Literary System: A Critical Career Model

While Daniel's career helps us understand what an English Renaissance Ovidian *cursus* looks like in its entirety, Marlowe preceded Daniel down the Ovidian path – and of course to very different effect.[41] In the career fiction we have been examining, Marlowe presents himself as the arch-Ovidian poet of his culture, and he sets himself up as the rival and heir of Spenser, the arch-Virgilian poet. Viewed from this vantage point, Marlowe and Spenser replay for Elizabethan culture the contest that Ovid once played with Virgil in Augustan culture. If we take Jonson's cue and add him to this network of poetic rivalry, we can see something of great import: in front of the Elizabethan literary audience, Spenser, Marlowe, and Jonson replay the Augustan rivalry of Virgil, Ovid, and Horace.

This is not quite the story that Richard Helgerson tells in *Self-Crowned Laureates*. Helgerson privileges Virgil and Horace as the primary models for the Elizabethan laureates, but he subordinates Petrarch (or 'the Petrarch of the *Canzoniere*') and Ovid as the primary models for the amateurs (26). Helgerson mentions Ovid only six times (his interest is 'synchronic,' not 'diachronic' [17–18]), but it is clear that he is thinking of the 'official' Ovid identified in chapter 1: 'the Ovid of the *Tristia*, abandoned by his friends for his *carmen et error*' (86; see 35, 110–13, 116, 194). Accordingly, just as Helgerson identifies Spenser as a Virgilian laureate and Jonson as a Horatian laureate, so he identifies Marlowe (only in passing) as an Ovidian amateur.

As we saw in the introduction, it is within an 'assimilation' of the dramatist to the amateur that Helgerson locates Marlowe: like Greene, 'Marlowe, Peele, Lodge, Nashe, Marston, and Beaumont all made play writing a part of an amateur career ... It was against this amateur assimilation ... that Jonson had to struggle in using drama as a main vehicle for his laureate career' (36). In Helgerson's story, then, Ovid is reduced to the love elegist and the exile poet, leaving no trace of his achievement as tragedian or epic poet, and Marlowe gets lost in a classification crossfire that apparently only Jonson has the critical mass to extricate himself from.

Thus, during his discussion of Jonson, Helgerson brings the three Augustan writers and their Elizabethan heirs into alignment. In the *Poetaster*, Jonson puts Horace, Virgil, and Ovid on stage in order to work out his professional advertisement as a national artist: 'By identifying himself with Horace and positioning himself with respect to the other two, Jonson performs perhaps his most elaborate act of self-presentation. It is here that he most fully defines his relation to the two prime models of a poetic career, the amateur and the laureate, the first represented by Ovid, the second by Virgil' (111). In Jonson's definition, Ovid and Virgil acquire place and dignity (both were '"amorous poets"' [116]), but Jonson's master, Horace, overwrites both competitors (111–16), for Horace alone is a satirist (116) capable of helping Jonson accommodate 'the new, astringent realism of the 1590s' (117). This realism requires Jonson to turn from Spenser's (Neoplatonic) inspiration towards 'learning and hard, slow work' (120) and thus eventually to repudiate erotic poetry (122–8). While Helgerson clearly sees Jonson the Horatian laureate responding to Spenser the Virgilian laureate, he blurs the key middle poet, the English Ovid: 'But while approving him, the play reveals Ovid to be a poet of a quite particular and readily recognizable sort. Like Peele, Marlowe, Lyly, Lodge, and Greene (who called himself "a second Ovid"), he is a prodigal poet' (112).

While accepting Helgerson's identification of Spenser as a Virgilian poet and of Jonson as a Horatian poet, and even his discussion of the relation between the two, we may question his identifications of Ovid as an amateur and of Marlowe as a professional/amateur. Helgerson may be right that the poets he elsewhere terms the 'Elizabethan prodigals' selected Ovid as their prototype.[42] The Elizabethans, however, had two Ovids to choose from – or two Ovidian careers on which they could model themselves. Only one of these models qualifies as 'amateur.' As the translator of the *Amores*, Marlowe could see that Ovid originally inscribed and planned to follow a career model that could compete with the 'laureate' models of Virgil and Horace because it is a counter-version. While each of the other University Wits may vie for the title of England's Ovid, it is Marlowe who deserves the first garland, because it is he, not they, who first inscribes the *cursus* of the 'unofficial' Ovid in his line-by-line translation of the *Amores* and then survives long enough to inscribe its contours.[43]

One reason we need to extricate both Ovid and Marlowe from the model of the amateur poet is that neither inscribes 'the mark of an amateur's career': 'repentance' (*Self-Crowned Laureates* 40; see 30, 51). Perhaps the former Matthew Parker scholar, or the tragedian who staged such scenes as the exile of Gaveston, the murder of Edward, and the punishment of Faustus, or even the poet who penned the shame of Hero, would in the end have turned to a repentant poetry of exile, as Helgerson believes Ovid did.[44] The fact remains: Marlowe did not pen this final (unplanned) stage to Ovid's career, and the contemporary portraits of him (scurrilous though they be) supply little evidence that he ever would have penned it – Kyd's, for instance, or Baines's, or (more enticingly), Beard's: 'The manner of his death being so terrible (for hee even cursed and blasphemed to his last gaspe, and togither with his breath an oath flew out of his mouth) that it was not only a manifest signe of Gods judgement, but also an horrible and fearefull terrour to all that beheld him' (rpt. in MacLure, ed., *Marlowe* 42; cf. Nicholl 65–8). 'Repentance? *Spurca!*' (*Jew of Malta* III.iv.6).

The last time we see Marlowe writing in the first person, he is hardly repenting; rather, he is projecting a career move from amatory poetry to the *area maior* of epic: 'wretch as I am, I believe that I can achieve more than my unripe natural talents are accustomed to bring forth ... I, whose scanty riches are but the shore-myrtle of Venus and the evergreen tresses of the Peneian nymph [Daphne], call you to my aid on the first page of every poem' (*Dedicatory Epistle* to Mary Sidney). Marlowe's reference to the Ovidian *cursus* here – his *meta* from the 'shore-myrtle of Venus' to the 'more' of the *area maior* – indicates that we may need to revise our understanding both of the Renaissance Ovid and of Marlowe as the West's premier *Ovidianus poeta*.

Career Rivalry, Counter-Nationhood, and Philomela in 'The Passionate Shepherd to His Love'

Marlowe's lovely pastoral lyric, 'The Passionate Shepherd to His Love,' occupies a special place in the canon of English poetry. Ever since Izaak Walton referred to 'that smooth song which was made by Kit Marlow, now at least fifty years ago,' critics have eulogized 'The Passionate Shepherd' as 'one of the most beautiful lyrics in English literature.'[1] In accord with such a famous poem, critics have long emphasized a wide array of topics: the complex history of the manuscript; the problem of dating the poem; the maze of classical and Renaissance sources from which Marlowe drew; his recurrent use of the poem in his plays; subsequent writers' repeated imitations of Marlowe; the version of pastoral he pens; the philosophy of sexuality he expounds; and, most recently, the 'political aspects of the Marlovian invitation as mode.'[2] This extensive commentary prepares us well to turn to a contextualizing model that can help us organize the disparate topics and extend the fruitful scholarship on them: the interlock between Marlowe's idea of a literary career; his professional rivalry with Spenser; and his writing of counter-nationhood.

Specifically, we shall see, 'The Passionate Shepherd' fits within the amatory phase of Marlowe's Ovidian career and thus, within its contemporary context, of Spenser's Virgilian career. Marlowe's poem qualifies as an Ovidian amatory lyric preparing the poet to move into the *area maior* of tragedy and epic; and thus it contests Spenser's move from pastoral to epic, including the four principal dimensions of his Virgilian career model: the generic, the political, the philosophical, and the sexual. Consequently, Marlowe rewrites Spenser's England with a poetics of counter-nationhood. One myth in particular, which Sir Walter Ralegh alertly discovered embedded in 'The Passionate Shepherd,' and which is common to Ovid and Spenser as a self-reflexive myth of the poet, metonymically renders Marlowe's career project of counter-nationhood in this lovely lyric: the myth of Philomela. To pursue this argument, we need to turn to another myth, which critics find undergirding Marlowe's smooth song.

The Polyphemus–Galatea Myth: Theocritus, Virgil, Ovid

The Ovidian myth of Polyphemus and Galatea in Book XIII of the *Metamorphoses* (738–897) *invites* the reader to see 'The Passionate Shepherd' as part of an Ovidian *cursus* – in particular, its amatory phase as it prepares the poet for tragedy and epic.[3]

Ovid's situating of the Polyphemus–Galatea myth is generically complex. Within his 'epic' *Metamorphoses*, Ovid tells of Aeneas's wanderings (XIII.623–968), pausing when the Virgilian hero reaches Sicily to narrate the sea nymph Galatea's complaint to her companion, Scylla: 'I was not allowed to shun the Cyclops' love without grievous consequence' (744–5). Galatea tells how she found her life measured equally between her sweet love of Acis, a son of Faunus, and the 'endless wooing' (755) by Polyphemus (750–8). One day, while she lay in Acis's arms, she heard Polyphemus play his reed pipe and sing a song; having heard it, she remembers it now (782–8), and so she feels compelled to repeat it for her friend Scylla (789–869). In this detailed pastoral lyric within a counter-Virgilian epic, Polyphemus presents himself as a passionate shepherd to his love, offering Galatea gifts of nature if she will come live with him: 'Chestnuts also shall be yours and the fruit of the arbute-tree, if you will take me for your husband' (819–20). In the end, however, Polyphemus spies Galatea in Acis's arms; she bolts; and Polyphemus crushes his hapless rival with a piece of the mountainside (874–84).

Writing on Ovid's placement of the Polyphemus–Galatea myth within the Virgilian story of Aeneas's wanderings, Brooks Otis remarks: 'his use of the *Aeneid* (as a frame for rather light, erotic episodes or for unmistakable parodies) is a sure indication of his perfunctoriness, his indifference to his ostensibly serious Augustan purpose' (286). Otis identifies Galatea's 'story' as only 'ostensibly tragic: actually it is Ovid's version of the comic courtship of Polyphemus in Theocritus' eleventh and sixth idylls, a subject that Virgil had partially imitated in his second and seventh Eclogues' (287). Yet the Virgilian context of the tragically light comedy alerts us to a political context that Ovid appears at pains to defuse; for at this time the Emperor Augustus was legislating chastity into marriage, and Ovid would be sacrificed to the legislation.[4] This complex, four-eclogue Theocritean and Virgilian intertextuality for the epic story of Ovid underlying Marlowe's pastoral lyric surely merits further critical attention.

The Theocritean intertextuality is complex because, as David M. Halperin notes, 'Idyll 11 ... has the same subject as Idyll 6 – the courtship of Galatea by Polyphemus; both Idylls 6 and 11, moreover, begin as poetic epistles addressed, respectively, to Aratus and Nicias' (126). In Idyll VI, Theocritus tells his friend Aratus of the singing contest between the shepherds Daphnis and Damoetas, with the topic being Galatea's pelting of Polyphemus's flock (sung by Daphnis) and Polyphemus's game of indifference in response (sung in response by Damoetas). The frame concludes when 'Damoetas ... kissed Daphnis ... And as for the victory, that fell to neither one' (42–6). More important for Marlowe's lyric, in Idyll XI Theocritus tells his friend Nicias how he has learned that only 'the Pierian Maids' offer a 'medicine for love' (1–2), citing Polyphemus's song to Galatea as an example, in which the one-eyed Cyclops falls in love with the sea nymph at first sight and woos her with his pipe: 'And O, there's gifts in store for thee, ... / And come ye away to me' (40–3).

What characterizes both idylls is the combination of a self-reflexive frame in which the male poet addresses a male companion, and an erotic song of an ill-fated heterosexual love between a mountainous beast and a watery beauty. As rewritings of the Polyphemus episode in Book IX of Homer's *Odyssey*, both idylls function as part of 'Theocritus' subversion of epic themes,' and in fact Idyll XI qualifies as the 'most famous of Theocritean subversions,' through which the pastoral poet aims 'to convert the Homeric episode to a comic purpose' (Halperin 232–3). In its inception, in other words, the myth of erotic invitation that will give Marlowe his lyric centre carries with it not simply pastoral beauty and natural bounty, but also poetic rivalry and epic subversion, politics and patronage, ill-fated heterosexual desire and homoeroticism, and the rewards of poetry in the lover's life.[5]

The Virgilian intertextuality is equally complex, although critics find it less influential on Marlowe's reworking of the Ovidian myth. Probably, however, it would be unwise to cut Virgil out of Marlowe's Ovidian game. Indebted to Theocritus's idylls, both Eclogue II and Eclogue VII provide details for the invitation-to-love theme, and E.V. Rieu even celebrates the similarity between Eclogue II and Marlowe's poem by titling his translation 'The Passionate Shepherd to His Love' (31). As Corydon sings to an Alexis who remains absent, 'If only you could bring yourself to live with me' (28; trans. Rieu). The invitation motif has distinct political resonance, as it does in Theocritus, since, as Ian M. Le M. Du Quesnay emphasizes, Virgil wrote the *Eclogues* within the 'patronage' system and the poet's need to perform 'a service to the state' ('From Polyphemus to Corydon' 36). Du Quesnay further contextualizes Eclogue II in terms of Virgil's relation with his bisexual friend, poet, and patron, Gallus (60–3). Not surprisingly, Virgil's homoerotic eclogue held a special interest for Marlowe, for Thomas Kyd tells Sir John Puckering that Marlowe 'wold report St John to be our saviour Christes Alexis' (rpt. in MacLure, ed., *Marlowe* 35).[6] Only Eclogue VII, however, refers to the Polyphemus–Galatea myth directly, when Corydon sings, 'Galatea, ... if thou hast any love for thy Corydon, come hither' (37–40). In Virgil, as in Theocritus, we find pastoral beauty and bounty laced with poetic self-reflexivity and genre mixing, politics and patronage, homoeroticism and heterosexual love, and even the prospect of poetic fame: 'I sing as Amphion of Dirce used to sing' (II.23).[7]

In retelling the Polyphemus–Galatea myth in the *Metamorphoses*, then, Ovid rewrites Virgilian and Theocritean pastoral as an 'Ovidian' amatory poem within an 'Ovidian epic.' In effect, he creates a new genre that we might term 'Ovidian pastoral epic.' Crucial to Ovid's account (as well as to Homer's and to Marlowe's, but not to Virgil's or Theocritus's) is Polyphemus's role as an 'atheist' blaspheming against the gods: he 'despises great Olympus and its gods' (*Metamorphoses* XIII.761; cf. *Odyssey* IX. 273–80). Allied with this emphasis is another Ovidian feature that likely influenced Marlowe: Ovid's emphasis on violence (see Bruster 51, 67–8).

By evoking this intertextual network within a lyric, Marlowe invites us to read 'The Passionate Shepherd' as a self-reflexive amatory subversion of both the state and the state genre, Virgilian epic, within his Ovidian *cursus*. The evocations encourage us to see beneath the 'cosmopolitan' wooing of a nymph by a shepherd a complex generic configuration, a politic plea for patronage, a concern for the *telos* of poetry, fame, and a sexual configuration mixing heterosexual with homoerotic desire.[8]

Marlowe/Ovid/Spenser: A Typology of Intertextuality

Marlowe's intertextuality does not target simply the dead Ovid, the dead Virgil, or the dead Theocritus, but England's living Virgil. Marlowe contextualizes his diachronic imitation of classical poets in a synchronic imitation of a contemporary. He constructs a complex typology of intertextuality. By foregrounding this typology, we can attend to the literary construct that Marlowe's typology serves: Renaissance ideas of a literary career. We can then view 'The Passionate Shepherd' as a site in which Marlowe manages career rivalry and writes a form of nationhood.

Critics have found Spenser in 'The Passionate Shepherd,' to the extent that Harry Morris can conclude that 'Marlowe's lyric poem ... shows more clearly than anything else in the Marlowe canon the nature of the pastoral influence as it comes to him from Spenser' (137). Spenser's influence on Marlowe divides among the four dimensions of career nationhood already identified: the generic, the political, the philosophical, and the sexual.

In reference to Morris's generalized 'pastoral influence,' we may specify a vocational and generic borrowing in lines 7–8, when the shepherd promises the nymph a particular pastoral vision. Together, they will '[s]ee ... the shepherds feed their flocks / By shallow rivers, to whose falls / Melodious birds sing madrigals.' Four times in *The Shepheardes Calender* Spenser presents Colin Clout singing his song beside a spring (*Aprill* 33–6; *June* 7–8; *August* 153–6; *December* 1–4; see also woodcuts to *Aprill* and *December*), and he twice depicts his persona perched beside a waterfall amid birdsong (*June* and *August*). Critics have found origins for Spenser's water trope in Theocritus (*Idylls* I.1–8), Virgil (*Eclogues* I.52–9), and Marot (*Lamentation for Madame Louise of Savoy* 1–4, 17–20).[9] Of these three origins, only the Virgil and the Marot represent the shepherd-poet resting beside a stream where birds sing, and only the Marot represents the shepherd-poet resting beside a waterfall, listening to birdsong. In none of these origins, however, do the birds sing their song in concert with the waterfall itself.

To approximate such an origin, we can turn to a poet totally overlooked in the conversation. Opening Elegy III.i of the *Amores*, Ovid recalls the *locus poeticus* at the generic crossroads of his literary career, the intersection of elegy and tragedy:

> An old wood stands uncut, of long years' space,
> 'Tis credible some godhead haunts the place.
> In midst thereof a stone-paved sacred spring,
> Where round about small birds most sweetly sing.
>
> (*Ovid's Elegies* III.i.1–4)

Perhaps imitating the pastoral setting of Theocritus, but especially Virgil (who alone includes both water and birds), Ovid imagines a sacred spring overseen by birds singing their songs.

Given that Marlowe had translated the Ovidian passage in *Ovid's Elegies*, it is likely that he is imitating it in the water–bird trope of 'The Passionate Shepherd.' What is the significance of this imitation? Most immediately, it expresses what Ovid himself had used the *locus poeticus* to display: generic dialogue – between lower and higher literary forms. In *Amores* III.i, we will recall, Ovid visits the avian-controlled 'fons sacer' only to be confronted by Dame Elegia and Dame Tragedy, and the outcome of the confrontation is Ovid's negotiation between the two: he will continue to serve Dame Elegia so long as he promises to serve Dame Tragedy. Together, both generic ladies will secure his 'renown' (64; see 65). The *fons sacer*, then, is a precise version of the traditional *locus amoenus* functioning as a *locus poeticus*; not simply a fount of inspiration for poetry in general, it is a fount for an 'Ovidian' or counter-Virgilian *cursus* that turns from the lower to the higher genres, from verse to drama, from elegy to tragedy: 'She [Dame Elegy] gave me leave, ... / Some greater work [grandius opus] will urge me on at last' (III.i.69–70). By imitating this career passage, Marlowe is clarifying what we have discovered in the intertextual linkage of Theocritus, Virgil, and the Ovid of the *Metamorphoses*: that 'The Passionate Shepherd' inscribes a generic dialogue between lower and higher forms. We can then profitably identify this dialogue along two parallel diachronic tracks: the Virgilian turn from pastoral to epic; and the Ovidian turn from verse to drama, elegy to tragedy.

Douglas Bruster alerts us to the dramatic dimension of 'The Passionate Shepherd': 'it is unclear whether the speaker in Marlowe's lyric is actually a passionate shepherd or merely intends to watch them: the title of the poem, the authority of which is questionable, remains the only evidence of the former. The lyric voice belongs to one who will remain separate from the shepherds ... ; more importantly, a form of theatrical servitude is promised: "The Shepherd's swains shall dance & sing, / For thy delight each May morning"' (51–2; see also Mirollo 164–5). As we would expect in such a light-hearted poem, Marlowe largely elides his tragic dimension, but he still leaves traces of it – and near the exact centre: in the arresting image of '[a] gown made of the finest wool / Which from our pretty lambs we pull' (13–14), and then in the recognition of winter in '[f]air linèd slippers for the cold' (15). The tragic dimension also remains lodged in Marlowe's subtexts, where Theocritus, Virgil, and the Ovid of the *Metamorphoses* all treat the myth of Polyphemus and Galatea as a 'tragic' myth, ending in separation, and (in the case of Ovid) even in death. In the *Satires*, Horace playfully links the pastoral myth of the Cyclops with the genre of stage tragedy: 'Then he asks him to perform Cyclops' shepherd dance: / with those looks he'd need no tragic mask or heavy boots' (I.v.63–4, trans. Fuchs). For the Romans, evidently, the Polyphemus–Galatea myth functioned as something of a comic tragedy, and it stood ready to be deployed into either pastoral (Virgil) or epic (Ovid). In the genre of a 'comic tragedy,' critics may recognize a staple of the Marlowe canon.

Given Marlowe's generic manoeuvres within the context of his rivalry with Spenser, we may need to read 'The Passionate Shepherd' as two things simultaneously: as an advertisement for Marlowe's own Ovidian *cursus* and as a critique of the *cursus* of England's Virgil. Marlowe's intertextual strategy again anticipates the deconstructive strategy articulated by Derrida (see introduction): 'The movements of deconstruction do not destroy structures from the outside. They are not possible and effective, nor can they take accurate aim, except by inhabiting those structures' (24).

The editors of the *Variorum Edition* were alert to the Spenserian signature coded in the waterfall trope: 'To his contemporaries this was a peculiarly "Spenserian" phrase,' and they cite *The Return from Parnassus*, 'where, in characterizing Spenser, the author wrote: "the waters fall he tun'd for fame, / And in each barke engrav'd Elizaes name"' (7: 279–80). Other contemporaries who imitated Spenser's personal waterfall trope include Drayton and William Browne (*Variorum Edition* 7: 279, 311). To this list, we may add Marlowe.[10]

While Marlowe certainly had access to all four of Spenser's pastoral water-tropes, he appears to have had the *June* passage in mind, since it most closely matches the trope in 'The Passionate Shepherd': 'The Bramble bush, where Byrds of every kynde, / To the waters fall their tunes attemper right' (7–8). In both instances, a poet depicts shepherds beside a waterfall with birds singing to the fall of the water.[11] As we have seen in chapter 1, Spenser's *June locus poeticus* offers Colin Clout a literary crossroads, directly imitated from Virgil's *recusatio* in Eclogue VI.1–10, but also therefore the Ovidian crossroads of elegy and tragedy in *Amores* III.i, which responds to Virgil's *recusatio*: Hobbinol tempts Colin to turn from pastoral to epic (49–64). Given both Spenser's practice of using the water trope as a signature, as well as his contemporaries' understanding of his practice, there can be little doubt that Marlowe is using Ovid to conjoin with his Virgilian rival.

Marlowe is contesting not simply Spenser's Virgilian pastoral, but its very origin: its fount of inspiration. We know that Spenser criticized the Ovidian *fons sacer* in Book I of *The Faerie Queene*, when he describes the site of the enchanter Archimago's hermitage: 'Thereby a Christall streame did gently play, / Which from a sacred fountaine welled forth alway' (i.34). As A.C. Hamilton notes, 'the "sacred fountaine" suggests ... the *fons sacer* of the grove in which Ovid's Muse encourages him to treat of love rather than war (*Amores* III. i 3)' (ed., *FQ* 38). Thus both Marlowe and Spenser translate the *fons sacer* of the *Amores*; yet they judge the Ovidian fountain of poetic inspiration differently. Whereas Marlowe drinks heartily, Spenser does not.

That Marlowe is thinking of Spenser's waterfall and bird trope in lines 7–8 of 'The Passionate Shepherd' may be confirmed by Ralegh, who responds to Marlowe's generalized 'Melodious byrds' in line 8 with a very specific species:

But Time drives flocks from field to fold,
When rivers rage and rocks grow cold,
And Philomel becometh dumb;
The rest complain, of cares to come.

                                        ('The Nymph's Reply' 5–8)

Ralegh interprets Marlowe's 'melodious birds' as nightingales – a species that sings its harmonious song in the spring but ceases in the fall. Yet Ralegh is doing more than writing ornithology or troping the deadening cycle of nature. He is writing literary imitation itself. Probably, he inserts 'Philomel' into his dialogue with Marlowe for two principal reasons. First, Ovid had been the great mythologizer of the Philomela myth (*Metamorphoses* VI.401–674), and he had repeatedly used the myth throughout his poetry (e.g., *Remedia amoris* 61–2, *Fasti* II.629, *Tristia* II.389–90), including in the inaugural poem of his career translated by Marlowe (*Amores* II.vi.7–10, III.xii.32). Second, in *The Shepheardes Calender* Spenser had selected the Philomela myth as his arch-myth of pastoral poetry as it prepares the young poet to write epic, and he had taken Ovid's cue: 'As they [Philomela and Procne] fly from him [Tereus] you would think that the bodies of the two Athenians [Cecropidum] were poised on wings: they were poised on wings! One flies to the woods, the other rises to the roof' (*Metamorphoses* VI.667–9).[12]

The Philomela myth fuses the generic dimension of the poet's career with the political, erotic, and philosophical dimensions. Philomela is not merely a powerful singer; before her transformation into a nightingale, she was a princess, daughter to the King of Athens, Pandion, and thus a descendent of Cecrops, founder of Athens – a genealogy so important that she became known by this political title: 'Cecropis ales' (*Amores* III.xii.32).[13] Typically, poets fuse Philomela's political status with her vocational talent, as when Spenser identifies Colin Clout as 'The Nightingale ... sovereigne of song' (*November* 25). In addition to being a singer and a princess, however, Philomela is also a feminine victim of masculine rape and silencing, figured gruesomely when Tereus cuts out her tongue to prevent her from decrying her abused chastity: 'The mangled root quivers, while the severed tongue lies palpitating on the dark earth, faintly murmuring' (*Metamorphoses* VI. 557–8). Finally, Philomela receives the only consolation available after suffering the brutality of rape and silencing: as the nightingale, the sweetest singer of an elegiac complaint against the prick of masculine violence, she becomes a figure for poetic immortality or fame: the 'mistress of melody.'[14] Because Philomela is such a multidimensional myth, and was deployed by Ovid, Spenser, and other poets as such, it can function graphically as a figure for a poet's particular writing of nationhood. Whereas Spenser had written nationhood by eliding the horror of the myth, Ovid had written counter-nationhood precisely by emphasizing that horror.

By inserting 'Philomel' into Marlowe's imitation of Spenser's bird–water trope, Ralegh is raising these issues, but he is also self-reflexively identifying Spenser's influence on himself. As he reveals in his own epic, *Ocean to Cynthia*, he uses Spenser's pastoral trope to complain of Queen Elizabeth's erotic cruelty and to identify his own rejection of poetic fame: 'under thos healthless trees I sytt a lone / Wher joyfull byrdds singe neather lovely layes / Nor phillomen recounts her direfull mone' (*Ocean to Cynthia* 26–8).[15] Ralegh's alert reading of the Philomela myth in Marlowe's poem, and then his own writing of the myth into his dialogue with Marlowe, self-consciously directs us to the larger career concern of both 'The Passionate Shepherd' and 'The Nymph's Reply': the question of the poet's *voice* – his cultural authority, his credentials for the job of England's national poet.

In the bird–water trope from 'The Passionate Shepherd,' four words particularly show Marlowe questioning Spenser's authority as England's national poet: 'shallow'; 'rivers'; 'falls'; and 'madrigals.' As the passionate shepherd tells his love, together they will 'see' the 'shepherds feed their flocks / By shallow rivers.' On the surface, the shepherd's reference to the river's depth does not appear alarming, but Shakespeare for one had no trouble peering beneath the surface. In *The Merry Wives of Windsor* (1597, 1600–1), Sir Hugh Evans sings a garbled version of 'The Passionate Shepherd,' singling out the 'shallow rivers' line by repeating it no fewer than three times, the last serving as a stage cue to the actor playing Robert Shallow, the country justice (III.i.28–31).[16] We can then profitably take Shakespeare's cue. Since Marlowe in the 'shallow rivers' line is imitating Spenser's Ovidian trope of the birds singing to the waterfall, is he not also criticizing the depth of Spenser's inspiration?[17] Marlowe's change of Spenser's small, serene, and private waterfall to the public 'rivers' appears striking, and probably we should not pass it off only as Marlovian hyperbole. Para-doxically, Marlowe increases the width of the body of water (a river is wider than a 'stream'), but he then flattens the river out by calling it 'shallow.' If the *fons sacer* of Spenser's inspiration is indeed 'shallow,' it is therefore subject to easy evaporation.

Similarly, the word ending the 'shallow rivers' line, 'falls,' nominally refers to a set of waterfalls on the river. Its emphatic position in the line, however, inescapably evokes the idea of falling, as if Marlowe were predict-ing – or hoping for – his rival's fall from poetic power.[18]

Finally, the word 'madrigals' is also striking, being a precise artistic term during the period. The *OED* notes the obscure origin of the word, but speculates that it may trace to the Italian word *mandria*, meaning 'herd,' as well as to a Greek word meaning 'fold': 'the primitive sense according to this view would be "pastoral song"' (headnote). Within a pastoral song such as 'The Passionate Shepherd,' the word 'madrigals' thus looks innocuous enough. Yet the *OED* goes on to identify three definitions, and all three look pertinent to Marlowe's usage: (1) 'A short lyrical poem of amatory character'; (2) in music, 'a kind of part song for three or more voices (usually, five or six) characterized by adherence to an ecclesiastical mode, elaborate contrapuntal imitation, and the absence of instrumental accompaniment'; and (3) the second definition used figuratively as a 'song, ditty.' The *OED* lists 'The Passionate Shepherd' only under the third definition. If defined thus, Marlowe's word suggests that the birds sing a ditty to the 'falls' on the 'shallow rivers.' Within the context of Marlowe's rivalry with Spenser, then, the poet appears to be delimiting Spenser's achievement. For, in the *October* eclogue Spenser had proclaimed that the successful poet must go beyond 'dapper ditties' (13) by writing Virgilian epic (37–48, 55–60) if he wishes to achieve the goal of 'glory' (20).

Spenser himself uses the word 'madrigal' only once in his entire career, and it appears in his *Dedicatory Sonnet* to Ralegh prefacing the 1590 *Faerie Queene* – a Petrarchan sonnet that curiously identifies Ralegh as himself a type of Philomela:

> To thee that art the sommers Nightingale,
>   Thy soveraine Goddesses most deare delight,
>   Why doe I send this rusticke Madrigale,
>   That may thy tunefull eare unseason quite?
>
> (*Dedicatory Sonnet* to Ralegh 15: 1–4)

Here Spenser rewrites the Philomela myth in a striking way. He cross-dresses the male poet as the female 'sovereigne of song,' and he cross-dresses the brutal King Tereus as Queen Elizabeth herself. In the process, he elides the tragedy in Ovid's myth by constructing a myth of 'sommer,' in which the male 'Nightingale' happily receives the love he desires from his 'soveraine Goddess.' At the same time, Spenser inserts himself into his reworking of Ovid's Philomela myth, evidently identifying himself as a friendly correlate to the tactfully eroticized Queen. Anticipating his designation of Ralegh as the 'Shepherd of the Ocean' in *Colin Clouts Come Home Againe* (1591,

1595), Spenser identifies his dedicatory sonnet as a pastoral song – a 'rusticke Madrigale' – which he fears may 'unseason' Ralegh's 'tunefull eare' – destroy the 'sommer' myth he has just constructed.

In the remainder of the sonnet, Spenser uses his water trope from the *Calender*, alludes somewhat dangerously to the Ovidian myth of Jove and Danae, generously refers to Ralegh's own epic 'Poeme,' *Ocean to Cynthia*, and thus politicizes both his own and Ralegh's art in terms of the Virgin Queen's erotic cult (8–14), 'Thy soveraine Goddesses most deare delight.' Spenser here is tactful when subordinating his own epic about Elizabeth to Ralegh's allied project on the Queen's behalf, but he is not without his manoeuvres. The first is his inscription of a generic paradigm relating Ovidian pastoral – the 'rusticke Madrigal' of the sonnet – to the 'thonder[ing] Martial, stowre' of (Ralegh's) epic (11), and then, paradoxically, his attempt to pastoralize his own epic: 'faire Cinthias praises ... rudely showne' (14). Could an unsympathetic observer not characterize Spenser's river here as shallow?[19] The second manoeuvre, to which we shall return, might have attracted the eye of the homoerotic Marlowe: Spenser is addressing his own Virgilian/Ovidian/Petrarchan 'rusticke Madrigale' to another man. The appearance of two key programmatic words from Spenser's sonnet to Ralegh within the Marlowe/Ralegh exchange – madrigal and nightingale – further confirms the need to insert Spenser into the network of intertextuality.

The intertextuality compels us to read Marlowe's 'madrigals' doubly. He is imitating Spenser's 'song or ditty' in order to expose what Harry Berger, Jr, calls in another context Spenser's 'conventionally hyperbolic and ... blatant ... patron-seeking' ('Spenser's *Prothalamion*' 520). But Marlowe is also enfolding both the Italian etymology of 'madrigals' and the other two definitions in order to construct a metonym for his own project and so to distance himself from Spenser. For 'The Passionate Shepherd to His Love' is an Italianate pastoral song in its form, an 'elaborate contrapuntal imitation' of several 'voices' in its technique, a non-'ecclesiastical mode' in its *telos*, and a lyric of amatory character in its topic. The discrepancy at play between the two senses of the term 'madrigal' – the Spenserian 'song or ditty' and the Marlovian amatory pastoral poem in the Italian intertextual tradition – further permits Marlowe to discredit his rival at his rival's expense.

The Politics of Mirth

Marlowe's career rivalry with Spenser is also evident in the other three dimensions of his Ovidian *cursus* at work in 'The Passionate Shepherd.' At stake in Marlowe's waterfall trope, for instance, is a political representation as it relates to the vocational. As we might expect from those alert readers of the Elizabethan literary system, the authors of *The Return from Parnassus* have got it right. Spenser, they suggest, has tapped 'the waters fall' in order to 'engrav[e] ... Elizaes name.'

Among critics, Bruster alerts us to the 'Elizabethan' significance of Marlowe's poem, but he confines himself to a brief statement about 'the political aspects of Marlovian invitation': 'With Elizabeth's status and political power providing one model for a rhetorical grammar which acknowledged – however implicitly – constructed (over biological) gender, "The Passionate Shepherd" ... functioned as a particularly Elizabethan reservoir of cultural energy and ambition' (68).

Bruster's Bakhtinian reading takes us to the right critic, but we can also profitably contextualize Marlowe's lyric in terms of the Bakhtinian concept of the carnivalesque. The first to see that 'The Passionate Shepherd' might be related to festival rites was Louis H. Leiter, who identifies the shepherd's nymph as 'Flora–Venus' (447), and who sees this archetypal figure enacting an 'adornment ritual' (447) derived from 'the festival of Flora in Rome' – 'the yearly May ceremonies of songs and dance' (446). He does not, however, attempt to contextualize Marlowe's festival representation in terms of 'the politics of mirth' later traced by Leah S. Marcus for seventeenth-century culture.[20]

Marcus identifies three critical 'models' for 'how festival "liberty" functions,' and she acknowledges her 'bias' towards the third: 'the dominant "escape-valve" theory'; the Bakhtinian model of 'subversiveness'; and the 'more recent' model, which argues 'for festival's inclusion of both normative and revisionary impulses,' in which festival's 'seemingly lawless topsy-turvydom can both undermine and reinforce' (7). She also pauses to observe that 'Queen Elizabeth I had reportedly liked to see her people "merry" and had been keenly aware of the potential link between public ceremony and the maintenance of order ... [However,] when it came to the promotion and regulation of traditional pastimes, Queen Elizabeth allowed her policy to remain ambiguous' (4).

We can explain a good deal of the cultural energy of Marlowe's lyric by contextualizing it in terms of Elizabethan policy on the politics of mirth. In fact, 'The Passionate Shepherd' looks to be a quite clever model for and response to Elizabeth's 'ambiguous' policy itself. On the one hand, Marlowe constructs a light-hearted, festive ritual of adornment that is attractively normative; on the other, as Ralegh hints, Marlowe transacts a 'festival "liberty"' with its own subversive program. What has not been noticed is that the liberating program of Marlovian festival appears to involve the

Queen herself. While Marlowe writes an Elizabethan carnivalesque poem in the May Day tradition tracing to the Roman Floralia, he superimposes onto this 'Elizabethan' political program an 'Elizabethan' intertextual one. The Spenserian imitation afoot in the poem coerces us to contextualize the politics of mirth further in terms of Spenser's pastoral of 'Elizabethan' courtship in *The Shepheardes Calender*.

Marlowe's imitators appear to have been alert to the significance of his poem for an audience that included – was governed by – a virgin queen. The anonymous poet of 'Another of the Same Nature,' which followed Ralegh's 'Nymph's Reply' in the 1600 *England's Helicon*, is explicit in identifying the shepherd's nymph as 'my summer's queen' (8), and at one point he even refers to her 'majesty' (32). But it is J. Paulin who makes the most of the political resonance – not surprisingly perhaps, since he composed his imitation on the threshold of the English Civil War (Orgel 260): 'For if Contentment wears a crown / Which never tyrant could assail, / How many monarchs put we down / In our Utopian commonweal?' ('Love's Contentment' in Orgel 5–8). Paulin's poem opens and closes with political resonance. The last word of the first stanza is 'state' (4); the last word of the poem is '*Queen*' (32; his emphasis). Paulin even has his lover and beloved appropriate the role of sovereigns in a self-reflexive carnivalesque gesture of *libertas*: their epitaph 'In golden letters may be read, / *Here lie Content's late King and Queen*' (31–2). In *The Merry Wives*, Shakespeare may be revealing a political reading of Marlowe's poem, for we think the play was originally performed for the Queen, and a theatrical tradition tracing to 1702 suggests that he wrote the play at the request of Elizabeth, who wanted to see Falstaff in love (*Riverside Shakespeare* 286).[21]

The political resonance of 'The Passionate Shepherd' traces most immediately to Ralegh himself – Marlowe's most famous imitator: 'A honey tongue, a heart of gall / Is fancy's spring, but sorrow's fall' ('The Nymph's Reply' 11–12). Of this couplet, S.K. Heninger remarks: 'Perhaps the nymph takes her cue from the love-smitten Thomalin in Spenser's *Shepheardes Calender*, who concludes the March eclogue with this emblem' (66): 'Of Hony and of Gaule in love there is store: / The Honye is much, but the Gaule is more' (*March* 122–3). In his gloss on the word 'Gaule,' Thomas H. Cain notes that the unusual spelling of 'gall' should direct us to 'an apparent warning about the queen's impending French marriage' (Oram et al. 62).[22]

If Ralegh does follow his friend Spenser in encoding the Queen's potential marriage to Alençon in the word 'gall,' he appears to be reading 'The Passionate Shepherd' as a French-marriage poem and to be offering a triple warning. Within the narrative, he uses the voice of the nymph to warn the shepherd – and the reader generally – about the decay of pastoral beauty as a result of the turning of the seasons – an idea that obsessed Ralegh throughout his verse (Greenblatt, *Ralegh* 129). Outside the narrative, Ralegh warns Marlowe himself about the dangers of rivalling England's Virgil: because Marlowe speaks with 'a honey tongue' animated by 'a heart of gall,' he is destined to 'fall' in the competition during the 'spring' of his life. Also outside the narrative, Ralegh warns the Queen about the dangers of the French marriage: because Alençon speaks with 'a honey tongue' motivated by 'a heart of gall,' her marriage to the foreigner is doomed.[23]

We need not, however, go to Marlowe's imitators to find the political resonance of 'Come live with me, and be my love.' For Marlowe himself echoes, imitates, and even quotes his own famous invitation in dramatic contexts that are either overtly or covertly political.[24] Several of the self-repetitions display a male character inviting an imperial female to be his love – and almost always in an ironic light. Thus, Tamburlaine responds to the death of Zenocrate, the 'Queen of Persia' (*1 Tamb* V.i.492, 505): 'And if thou pitiest Tamburlaine the Great, / Come down from heaven and live with me again!' (*2 Tamb* II.iv.117–18; on Zenocrate as Elizabeth here, see Zunder 18, 24–5). But Marlowe can also dress the wooer as the female herself. Thus, Queen Dido entreats Aeneas to remain in Carthage with her: 'Conditionally that thou wilt stay with me ... / ... it may be thou shalt be my love' (*Dido* III.i.114, 170). In other instances, the wooer is a male sovereign, as when Gaveston reads Edward's letter, '"come Gaveston, / And share the kingdom with thy dearest friend,"' to which Gaveston responds, 'What greater bliss can hap to Gaveston / Than live and be the favourite of a king?' (*Edward II* I.i.1–5). At times, the politics of the invitation are not simply cross-dressed but cross-signified beneath a mythological veil, as when Jupiter opens *Dido, Queen of Carthage*: 'Come, gentle Ganymede, and play with me ... / And shall have, Ganymede, if thou wilt be my love' (I.i.1, 49). Marlowe here does not simply parody himself; he deploys the carnivalesque to its theatrical best.

Marlowe's practice of placing his own poem in dramatic political contexts, coupled with the similar practice of his imitators, compels us to see political significance in his invitation-to-love motif. As Ralegh and others appear to have recognized, Marlowe uses his motif to invite his sovereign to come live with him and be his love. That is to say, he sues for her patronage. Yet it is difficult to eliminate the potential of a sexual innuendo here, and so we can witness Marlowe's carnival participation in the cult of the Virgin proceeding at its own peril. Perhaps this explains why, in his poem alone among all the versions of 'The Passionate Shepherd' that we possess, we can find no overt political or 'Elizabethan' imagery. Philomel remaineth dumb; the rest complains of cares to come.

As several of Marlowe's self-repetitions hint, Marlowe also understands his invitation to have philosophical resonance. At stake in the communication is the *telos* of the poet's life identified again by the alert authors of *The Return from Parnassus*: 'fame.'

In 'The Passionate Shepherd,' Marlowe's genius, to which Ralegh objects, lies in his ability to capture powerfully for his generation – or for any generation – what Shakespeare calls the mythos of 'boy eternal.' As Polixenes puts it to Hermione in *The Winter's Tale*, 'We were, fair queen, / Two lads that thought there was no more behind / But such a day to-morrow as to-day, / And to be boy eternal' (I.ii.62–5). Through his pastoral voice, Marlowe catches the springtime splendour of boy eternal withdrawing into the crystalline moment of the physical, the material, the concrete. Paradoxically, the boy eternal's totalizing entry into time evaporates the sense of time, congealing the exciting ecstasy into an eternal present – or what Bruster calls 'an eternizing conceit never made fully explicit' (52):

> Come live with me, and be my love,
> And we will all the pleasures prove
> That valleys, groves, hills and fields,
> Woods, or steepy mountain yields.
>
> ('The Passionate Shepherd to His Love' 1–4)

To enter time passionately, that is, is precisely to create the illusion of transcending time. As the illusion indicates, however, the creation is of eternal immanence. This is precisely the deep desire of Dr Faustus, who rejects the major bodies of Western learning because they cannot 'make man to live eternally' (*Doctor Faustus* I.i.24). What is so revolutionary in this play is Marlowe's fabrication of what he clearly considers a post-Christian ideal that he lodges inside the Reformation itself, right at Luther's university, where Faustus teaches. If, as Leo Braudy argues, classical culture postulated earthly fame as life's only long-standing reward, crystallized in Ovid, and if Christian culture reconfigured classical fame as eternal glory, following the lead of St Augustine (and later championed in Spenser), Marlowe appears to be filtering Christian glory back through classical fame to produce a new and striking version of the concept – *of an eternal life within time*.[25] If for Dr Faustus magic is the new 'book' (48) that can bring about this 'greater miracle' (9), for the passionate shepherd it is the discourse of boy eternal.

Because time orders the universe, boy eternal pursues 'pleasure' within nature as the *telos* of the hedonist life. Marlowe's naturalist imagery (valleys, groves, hills, fields, woods, mountain), together with his scientific-sounding discourse – 'prove,' 'yields' – moves his view of pleasure into the philosophical domain. Harry Levin has recognized the philosophy; it is the Epicurean hedonism of *De rerum natura* (70). Thus, Marlowe is, says U.M. Ellis-Fermor, 'the Lucretius of the English language' (xi), and the opening stanza of 'The Passionate Shepherd' brilliantly accommodates Lucretian materialism to Ovidian *amor* – an accommodation for which Ovid himself is famous.[26] In a universe in which the only reality is Lucretian materialism, Ovidian *amor* proves the greater miracle. *Carpe diem.*

Yet Marlowe knows a further paradox: the concretions *yielded* and *proved* are in fact idealized:

> I will make thee beds of roses,
> And a thousand fragrant posies,
> A cap of flowers, and a kirtle,
> Embroidered all with leaves of myrtle.
>
> ('The Passionate Shepherd to His Love' 9–12)

As the shepherd's use of 'make' here betrays, and as the hyperbole of 'thousand' confirms, the gifts are fabricated. What is fabricated is material reality itself: nature. Not just nature in any state, however, but Venerean nature, embroidered all with leaves of myrtle. Herein lies the power of boy eternal: he sings the eros of eternal youth. Marlowe's shepherd thus deploys what Berger isolates as an early modern 'technique of the mind ... the idea of the *second world*': 'The second world is the playground, laboratory, theater or battlefield of the mind, a model or construct the mind constructs, a time or place it clears in order to withdraw from the actual environment.'[27]

Accordingly, Marlowe's fabrication of eternal song is also intertextual. Commenting on the 'bed of roses' stanza, Heninger writes of Ralegh's Nymph: 'She realizes that the shepherd's "wanton fields" lie perilously close to the Bower of Bliss, where pleasures are contrived by the artificial exaggeration of nature' (67). We can indeed specify a potential Marlovian quotation from Spenser, for Acrasia lies upon 'a bed of Roses' (*FQ* II.xii.77), and just previous to this an unnamed voice (it is really Tasso's) sings the famous Rose Song: 'Gather the Rose of love, whilest yet is time' (75). Marlowe's repetition is significant because it catches him in his revisionary project of deconstructing Spenser in order to reconstruct the sexual practices of English Renaissance women, including the Queen: they are to abandon the ideals of Gloriana, Una, or Britomart to embrace the exquisite posture and erotic dress of Acrasia: 'Upon a bed of Roses she was layd, / As faint through heat, or dight to pleasant sin, / And was arayd, or rather disarayd, / All in a vele of silke and silver thin' (77).

According to Leiter, the word 'madrigal' 'literally means "an everlasting"' (446), and he nicely alerts us to the complex troping of poetic fame in the waterfall and birdsong image first clarified by the authors of *The Return from Parnassus*: 'If "falls" with its double "l" implies the possibility of the passing of love, the living birds sing in counter-action a song of permanence. At the same time, "madrigal" with its "l" defines all lovers singing in harmony of the durability of love or the eternal return of the celebration of passion like that suggested in the yearly May ceremonies of songs and dance of the Goddess Flora in stanza six' (446). In depicting the birds singing a madrigal to the waterfall, then, Marlowe is constructing a genealogy not merely of erotic desire, but also of poetic fame. From the mutability literally tumbling in the waterfall, the poet sings his counter-song of temporal permanence.

Ralegh recognizes that the song cannot be permanent, that the spring will never last, that the eros driving the boy's eternal song is an ecstatic dupe. Philomel becometh dumb. He sees Marlowe's 'counterfeit profession' (*Jew of Malta* I.ii.289): counter-fete profession. Boy eternal meets boy eternal. Shepherds create pastoral fictions; the pastoral myth of eternal *otium* is a lie:

> If all the world and love were young,
> And truth in every shepherd's tongue,
> These pretty pleasures might me move
> To live with thee and be thy love.
>
> ('The Nymph's Reply' 1–4)

The gifts are not concrete actualities but mental constructions, the product of the masculine mind as it appears to offer the paradise within, happier far, but as in fact it reaches for the fall. Thus the gifts look suspiciously like the masculine intellect itself:

> Thy gowns, thy shoes, thy beds of roses,
> Thy cap, thy kirtle, and thy posies,
> Soon break, soon wither, soon forgotten –
> In *folly* ripe, in *reason* rotten.[28]
>
> ('The Nymph's Reply' 13–16; emphasis added)

Ralegh's objection to Marlowe's artificially rotten eternity and his emphasis on the 'date' placed upon all such 'joys' (22) have led Hallett Smith to situate the dialogue between the two poets within Spenser's missing Ovidian emblem to the *December* eclogue, explained by E.K. as follows: 'The meaning wherof is that all thinges perish and come to theyr last end, but workes of learned wits and monuments of Poetry abide for ever,' misquoting *Metamorphoses* XV.871–2: 'I have built a great work which neither Jove's wrath nor fire nor sword nor eroding time can efface' (233–4; Oram et al. 212). According to Smith, 'this is clearly the implication of the whole eclogue and, as summary, of the whole *Shepheardes Calender*. Shakespeare found in Ovid the same commonplace and developed it in a non-pastoral setting in his sonnets. The pastoral handling of the theme enjoys an added richness, for, as the reply to Marlowe's "Passionate Shepherd" shows, time is the answer to the pastoral idea. But what if, in poetry, there is an answer to the answer?' (41). At stake in the philosophical dialogue between Raleghan time and Marlovian immortality, in other words, is the idea of poetic fame itself: 'thy posies, / Soon break, soon wither, soon forgotten.'[29]

Finally, 'The Passionate Shepherd' has a sexual or homoerotic dimension. The first to participate in this drama is Marlowe himself, who, as we have seen, imitates 'Come live with me' in the homoerotic Jupiter–Ganymede scene opening *Dido*. But the next to participate in this drama is again Ralegh, who boldly cross-dresses his masculine voice in the garb of a 'nymph.' Consequently, the nymph's reply to the passionate shepherd does not accurately measure the 'different voice' discussed in recent studies of feminine modes of decision making. Women may be concerned with time, the concrete, and the actual, rather than the eternal, the abstract, and the ideal, but they are also committed to affiliation, attachment, and an ethic of care, which Ralegh's female unsurprisingly fails to voice.[30] The Nymph's obsession with time, then, does not so much represent the female's enduring commitment to the realities of femininity as betray Ralegh's obsession with last things. The dialogue is finally between Marlowe and Ralegh; the facing-off, male to male; the voicing, fundamentally masculine.

Once we see Ralegh and Marlowe gazing at each other in the mirror of their texts, we can see what Ralegh appears to have seen in the shepherd's heterosexual discourse: Marlowe's concealed homoeroticism. R.S. Forsythe was the first to cite the 'invitation passage' in the *Januarye* eclogue in *The Shepheardes Calender* as an antecedent to Marlowe's poem, and he found Spenser himself imitating Virgil's Eclogue II (696).[31] Yet the first to link Spenser's passage with Virgil's homoerotic eclogue was the glossarist E.K.:

Hobbinol's gifts 'imitateth Virgils verse, Rusticus es Corydon, nec munera curat Alexis' (98–9). None the less, Spenser does more than simply repeat the homoerotic version of Virgilian invitation; dangerously, he uses his persona, Colin Clout, to distance himself from Virgil through representing the erotic version of the invitation voiced in Theocritus, and especially Ovid:

> It is not Hobbinol, wherefore I plaine,
> Albee my love he seeke with dayly suit:
> His clownish gifts and curtsies I disdaine,
> His kiddes, his cracknelles, and his early fruit.
> Ah foolish Hobbinol, thy gyfts bene vayne:
> Colin them gives to Rosalind againe.
>
> (*Januarye* 55–60)

E.K.'s subsequent gloss on this passage is telling: 'In thys place seemeth to be some savour of disorderly love, which the learned call paederastice ... But yet let no man thinke, that herein I stand with Lucian ..., in defence of execrable and horrible sinnes of forbidden and unlawful fleshliness' (103–14). Given that critics now believe Spenser himself to be E.K., we can here witness the New Poet acknowledging the problem of pederasty; locating the problem in his best friend, Master Harvey; and then trying to distance himself from the problem through a bold declaration: 'let no *man* thinke ...'[32]

What is new in the *Januarye* passage (it is not in Theocritus, Virgil, or Ovid) is the economic transfer of gifts in the gender system: Hobbinol gives the gifts to Colin, but Colin gives them to Rosalinde 'againe.' Spenser uses the transfer to clarify his sexual orientation, but also perhaps to facilitate a cultural wide rechannelling of homoerotic desire into heterosexual desire. Marlowe's apparent recollection of this moment of transfer reveals that he resists his rival's rechannelling project.[33] The gaze, then, is not merely between the passionate shepherd and his love, and not simply between Marlowe and Elizabeth, nor even between Marlowe and Ralegh; it is, as Ralegh himself appears to have recognized, between Marlowe and Spenser.

We need, then, to read Ralegh's decision to reply to Marlowe not just along the usual lines of philosophical difference, but also along the lines of vocational, political, and sexual difference. Ralegh's famous reply to Marlowe indeed qualifies as an apologia for both Elizabeth and Spenser – for the virtues of chastity and friendship that the New Poet was then championing in his epic addressed to the Queen. In 'The Nymph's Reply,' in other words,

Ralegh defends Spenserian poesy, and he does so by counter-textualizing Marlowe's defence of Marlovian poesy in 'The Passionate Shepherd.'

That Smooth Song

By recalling both the classical or diachronic origins of Marlowe's 'smooth song' and its Spenserian or synchronic origins, we can reconstruct the complex ground-plot of Marlowe's famous creation: career rivalry and the writing of counter-nationhood. Marlowe transacts a covert intertextual rivalry with Spenser through an overt intertextual rivalry with Ovid that traces to Virgil and Theocritus. This complex career typology of inter-textuality permits Marlowe to exfoliate a good deal of cultural energy, spread among and interrelating the four principal dimensions of a literary career as Marlowe, Spenser, and other Elizabethans inherited it from Virgil, Ovid, and the Augustans. At heart, what Marlowe criticizes is Spenser's writing of Elizabethan England, with its vision of the poet as an élitist figure of cultural authority penning the aristocratic genres of pastoral and epic; its service to a virgin queen and her regime's imperialist projects; its hypocritical advocacy for a mutual marriage between men and women; and its large claims for poetic fame as a mediator for Christian glory. With respect to Spenser's writing of nationhood, Marlowe 'counters' with a new form of nationhood founded on the kind of *libertas* that he could have learned by translating the Empire's two great counter-Virgilian poets: Ovid and Lucan. 'The Passionate Shepherd' is thus a multifaceted carnival of national liberty. Before the gaze of culture, Marlowe playfully, passionately transacts the freedom of poetic voice, political choice, personal destiny, and sexual orientation on which a new state could be founded.

Marlowe's imitators, especially Ralegh, were alert to the generic, political, philosophical, and sexual dimensions of Marlowe's poem, and thereby they permit us to extend the typology of intertextuality in yet another direction, towards an ever-unfolding future. In the centre of this complex historical trajectory, 'The Passionate Shepherd' functions as a gossamer hinge, so exquisite in its expression that it forges powerful links among past, present, and future – among Ovid, Spenser, and Ralegh, and even the rest who complain of cares to come. The remarkable career matrix of counter-nationhood ordering the origins and repetitions of Marlowe's smooth song helps to register 'The Passionate Shepherd to His Love' as indeed one of the special poems in the canon of English poetry.

PART II

SCEPTRES AND HIGH BUSKINS: TRAGEDY

Marlowe also contributes to Western poetics by situating the genre of tragedy dead in the centre of his counter-Spenserian, Ovidian *cursus*: amatory poetry–*tragedy*–epic.

By centralizing 'Ovidian tragedy,' Marlowe lays claim to the first garland in the Western literary competition for the title of *Ovidianus poeta*. As we saw in chapter 1, in the *Amores* Ovid had advertised himself as a tragedian, but paradoxically he had failed to produce a substantial body of 'Ovidian tragedy.' As far as a Renaissance tragedian could be concerned, Ovid had failed to produce any visible tragedy whatsoever. Ovid may have created the form, but he had failed to fill it. Within just a few years of the West's reopening of the public theatres since their closing in antiquity, Marlowe fills the form. He 'overgoes' Ovid by entering the Ovidian paradox: he becomes the *Ovidianus tragoedus*.

But this is not all. For, as we have seen, Spenser had followed in Ovid's footsteps to use an inaugural poem to advertise himself as a tragedian: 'Who ever casts to compasse weightye prise' must 'reare the Muse on stately stage' (*October* 103–12). Like Ovid as well, Spenser had failed to produce a stage tragedy. Despite evidence that he penned *Nine Comedies*, he eschewed the popular stage, selecting a verse form he later calls the 'Tragick plaint' (*Colin Clouts Come Home Againe* 427).[1] Not merely does Marlowe overgo Ovid; he overgoes Spenser, the would-be *Ovidianus tragoedus*.

As Ovidian tragedians, Marlowe and Spenser agree that the genre is to be a form of nationhood. Spenser's 'stately stage' is both the grand or 'stately' genre in the Renaissance hierarchy of genres and the stage of state itself.[2] Marlowe repeats the dual significance of Spenser's 'stately' in the prologue to *1 Tamburlaine*, but he clarifies the national significance of tragedy, which Spenser had merely hinted at, by adding the word *kingdoms*: 'We'll lead you to the stately tent of war, / Where you shall hear the Scythian Tamburlaine / Threat'ning the world with high astounding terms, / And scourging kingdoms with his conquering sword' (3–6). Spenser was to have reared his muse on a stage that remains patriotic to the state: 'And teache her tread aloft in bus-kin fine, / With queint Bellona in her equipage' (*October* 113–14). Thus, what Spenser will say of tragedy's sister genre, epic, we can apply to his tragedy: 'Fierce warres ... shall moralize my song' (*FQ* I.Pr.1). His is to be a tragedy of nationhood. By contrast, Marlowe's 'stately tent of war' is to be a tragedy of counter-nationhood: 'Threat'ning the world ... / ... scourging kingdoms.' As with his amatory poetry, Marlowe manages Ovidian tragedy through his rivalry with Spenser to advance a poetics of counter-nationhood.

To accomplish this daring goal – to fill the form that Spenser and Ovid had failed to fill – Marlowe needs precedents, alternatives. The most important to this study are three cultural forms fully consonant with Ovidian ideology: Senecan tragedy, Machiavellian political philosophy, and (somewhat paradoxically) 'Christian tragedy.' Marlowe's power lies in his fusion of these forms through the vital animation of two others, Lucretian materialism and Ovidian mythology, the last of which Marlowe could have found penned in the Lucretian-based *Metamorphoses*, the mythographer's bible. From Marlowe's fusion comes a tragic ideology of counter-Spenserian nationhood that requires some patience to demarcate, but this will be the goal in Part II of this study.

Suffice it to say here that Marlowe finds his tragic ideology inscribed in Ovidian myths of daring, contestation, and rivalry. The most important of these myths for our purposes are those of Phaethon, Icarus, Actaeon, and Orpheus. As we shall see, these myths figure prominently in all of Marlowe's 'Ovidian tragedies' except perhaps *The Jew of Malta*, where the playwright appears to let his preoccupation with Ovid give way to a preoccupation with Machiavelli (or the figure of the Machiavel).[3] Phaethon is prominent in the *Tamburlaine* plays; Icarus, in *Dido, The Massacre at Paris*, and *Doctor Faustus*; Actaeon, in *Edward II* and *Doctor Faustus*; and Orpheus, in *The Massacre at Paris*.

At one point, Marlowe even pauses to encapsulate his reinvention of 'Ovidian tragedy':

I'll have Italian masques by night,
Sweet speeches, comedies, and pleasing shows;
...

One like Actaeon peeping through the grove,
Shall by the angry goddess be transform'd,

...

By yelping hounds pull'd down, and seem to die.
Such things as these best please his majesty.

(Edward II I.1.54–70)

We shall await chapter 7 to read this passage in context, but here we can note that Marlowe specifies his idea of a literary career through the genre of tragedy ('Italian masques by night'), relying on the tragic myth of Actaeon in the *Metamorphoses*: 'By yelping hounds pull'd down, and seem to die.' However, Marlowe inscribes Ovidian tragedy through a typology of intertextuality, by which he alludes to Ovid in order to veil his rivalry with Spenser. Thus critics see Marlowe rewriting Ovid's 'Actaeon' through Spenser's Acrasia in Book II of *The Faerie Queene* (Godshalk 62; Zucker 169). What Spenser had derided, Marlowe vaunts. The Actaeon myth is not just any myth, but one that veils the suppression of individual freedom by imperial power (see chapter 7). That the suppressor happens to be the 'angry goddess,' Diana, another name for Marlowe's imperial Queen, should alert us to an inscription with a sharp political edge. Hence, Marlowe presents his counter-Spenserian 'masque' as a form of nationhood, addressed to a sovereign: 'Such things as these best please his majesty.'

Before turning to Marlowe's first 'Ovidian tragedy,' we might consider the idea of an Ovidian tragedy itself. Such an idea comes as close to forming a non-idea as we can imagine, for no Ovidian tragedy exists – or did exist for Marlowe to consult.[4] What Marlowe could have consulted was a series of dispersed fragments: Ovid's own verse representations of his one known tragedy, the lost *Medea*; the classical reports of this tragedy, including two preserved lines, in the Elder Seneca, Tacitus, and Quintilian; and Ovid's numerous references to the Roman theatre, in general, and to both Greek and Roman tragedy (that is, pre-Senecan tragedy), in particular.

To date, Ovid scholars have not examined the idea of an Ovidian tragedy in any detail.[5] Yet the numerous Ovidian representations of and references to tragedy indicate that such a topic merits discussion. Although a book on Marlowe is hardly the place for a detailed analysis, we may sketch out what Marlowe could have known about Ovidian tragedy.

That such a topic could have existed for Marlowe is clear from the dramatic scholarship of that writer whom T.S. Eliot called 'the legitimate heir of Marlowe' (75). Within a few years after Marlowe's death, Jonson puts 'Ovid' on the stage. In *The Poetaster*, Jonson first refers to Ovid as the amatory poet of the elegiac *Amores*, when Ovid's servant, Luscus, opens the play: 'Young master, master Ovid, doe you heare? gods a mee! away with your songs, and sonnets' (I.i.4–5). This 'young,' elegiac Ovid, however, presents himself by first mouthing the genre of tragedy: 'What, hast thou buskins on, Luscus, that thou swear'st so tragically, and high?' (18–19). In fact, Jonson chooses to open his play with precisely that mysterious professional interstice in Ovid's literary career – that which fuses the elegiac *Amores* to the tragic *Medea* (see chapter 1). For, on this very 'morning' Jonson's Ovid has completed an elegy that we know as *Amores* I.xv, the great paean to poetic fame, and Ovid even recites the 'hastie errours' of his 'morning muse' in Jonson's own translation (published alongside Marlowe's in the Mason text of *Ovid's Elegies*): 'My name shall live, and my best part aspire' (83–4). As soon as Ovid finishes his recitation, his father accosts him with a paternal tirade: 'Ovid, whom I thought to see the pleader, become Ovid the play-maker?': 'I hear of a tragoedie of yours comming foorth for the common players there, call'd Medea' (I.ii.8–11). As the historical Ovid had done in the *Tristia* (V.vii.25–30), Jonson's Ovid defends himself against the charge of writing a stage tragedy, in the process introducing verse into the play. Thus, Jonson self-consciously forces to the surface another great Ovidian contradiction, which Jonson himself impressively tries to unwind. In 'Ovid' 's own words,

> I am not knowne unto the open stage,
> Nor doe I traffique in their theaters.
> Indeed, I doe acknowledge, at request
> Of some neere friends, and honorable Romanes,
> I have begunne a poeme of that nature [i.e., *Medea*].
>
> (Jonson, *The Poetaster* I.ii.63–7)

From this scene, we can infer Jonson's own understanding of some of the problems we examined in chapter 1: (1) Ovid wrote the *Amores* and the *Medea* simultaneously, intertwining his composition of elegy and tragedy, the lower and the greater genres; (2) Ovid wrote his tragedy for his personal friends and select countrymen, not for the public theatre, producing thereby a tragedy he calls a 'poem'; and (3) perhaps Ovid only *began* the play, leaving it unpublished and incomplete ('I have begun a poem of that nature'), which appears to be Jonson's explanation as to how the *Medea* got lost.

We can support the first two of Jonson's conclusions by citing Ovid himself. For Ovid's reference to *Medea* in *Amores* II.xviii reveals that he is working on both elegy and tragedy: 'None the less, I did begin to sing of sceptres, and through my effort tragedy grew in favour, and for that task no one more fit than I. But Love laughed at my pall and painted buskins, and at the sceptre I had so promptly grasped in my unkinglike hand' (13–16; Loeb trans.). Similarly, Ovid's reference in the *Tristia* flatly denies that he wrote *Medea* for the theatre: 'As for your news that my songs are being presented with dancing in a crowded theatre, my friend, and that my verses are applauded – I have indeed composed nothing (you yourself know this) for the theatre; my Muse is not ambitious for hand-clappings' (V.vii.25–8). As for Jonson's third conclusion, we have only Ovid's single hint, that he has 'begun to sing' the work – but evidently not finished it (Fränkel 46).[6]

Yet the reports of the Elder Seneca, Tacitus, and Quintilian belie the second and third of Jonson's conclusions.[7] Tacitus indicates that Ovid's *Medea* was not merely complete, but published and celebrated for its achievement in the genre: 'And to-day you will find a larger number of critics ready to disparage Cicero's reputation than Virgil's; while there is no *published* oration of Asinius or Messalla *so celebrated as the "Medea" of Ovid*' (*Dialogus de oratoribus* 12; emphasis added). Quintilian also testifies to the genius of Ovid's tragedy: 'the Medea of Ovid shows, in my opinion, to what heights that poet might have risen if he had been ready to curb his talents instead of indulging them' (*Institutio oratoria* X.i.98). Both the Elder Seneca and Quintilian even reproduce lines from the play:

'I am carried hither and thither, alas, full of the god.'

(Elder Seneca, *Suasoriae* III.7)

'I had the power to save, and ask you then
If I have power to ruin?'

(Quintilian, *Institutio oratoria* VIII.v.6)

Presumably, these extant lines are utterances of Medea herself: both begin with 'I,' and both emphasize the individual's divine power – whether to 'save' or to 'ruin.' These fragments are striking as instances of Ovid's well-known subversion of the masculine-based Roman culture and religion: they represent a woman as the figure of omnipotence – 'full of the god.'

That last phrase has particular significance for the present argument. For the context of the quotation is Seneca's discussion of, first, Fuscus's imitation of Virgil, then Gallio's imitation of Virgil, and finally Ovid's imitation of Virgil. According to Seneca, 'the Virgilian *plena deo*, "she full of the

God,"' originally came from Virgil (5), and Fuscus was fond of imitating the phrase in order 'to win favour for it with Maecenas' (5).[8] Similarly, 'Gallio often brings this phrase in very nicely' (6). And finally, 'Gallio said that his friend Ovid had very much liked the phrase: and that as a result the poet did something he had done with many other lines of Virgil – with no thought of plagiarism, but meaning that his piece of open borrowing should be noticed. And in his tragedy [Loeb ed. note: *Medea* (2: 544, n. 1)] you may read: "I am carried hither and thither, alas, full of the god"' (III.7). We learn a good deal here.

First, we learn that Ovid was attracted to the Virgilian phrase 'full of the god' – that it held a certain fascination for him, most likely because it located the deity inside the individual. We also learn that Ovid imitated Virgil widely, and in this case in particular, in order to establish his own literary fame – an intertextual manoeuvre that renders 'the Virgilian *plena deo*' as a kind of Ovidian metonym for poetic power and artistic divinity. Quite literally, Ovid is full of the Virgilian god. Finally, we learn that Ovid imitated the Virgilian line in a 'tragedy.' That is to say, he imitated a line from a national epic featuring an ultimately comedic male hero within a tragedy featuring a tragic female heroine who herself appropriates the role of the deity.[9] In short, we learn from Seneca that Ovid constructed the idea of Ovidian tragedy out of the idea of Virgilian epic, and that this idea found its centre in the nature and fate of human subjectivity within the context of the Empire.

From Ovid himself, we also learn that he considered the *Medea* one of the three 'grand sails' ('grandia vela') of his literary career, along with the *Fasti* and the *Metamorphoses* (*Tristia* II.547–56): 'I have also given to the kings of tragedy their royal sceptre and speech suited to the buskin's dignity' (*Tristia* II.553–4). From this reference, we also learn that Ovid understands tragedy to focus on a political topic of the highest and most dignified order: that of 'kings' and 'their royal sceptre' – in short, political power and the writing of Roman nationhood. But even here Ovid's reference to his own role in the representation of tragedy hints at a self-reflexivity and subversion that marks a staple in the Ovidian *cursus* as a whole – his counter-Roman nationhood: 'I have also given to the kings of tragedy.' *He* has given *them*.

In this light, Ovid's representation of his confrontation with Dame Tragedy and Dame Elegy in *Amores* III.i may function as a representation of the very interstice in Ovid's career that Jonson chooses for the opening of *The Poetaster* – the interstice that Ovid himself evokes in his earlier reference to the *Medea* in the *Amores* (II.xviii.18): the moment when Love and his mistress interfere with his penning of tragedy. As such, Dame Tragedy becomes a figure for Ovidian tragedy – and probably for the *Medea* itself.[10] The feminine gender of the genre may prove little, but it is at least consistent with Ovid's decision to follow Euripides in boldly making the tragic figure a woman. In the *Amores* elegy, Ovid's career pauses in order to solve a dispute about which feminine figure to serve: Tragedy or Elegy.

Ovid's description of Dame Tragedy may be our fullest and most authentic indication of what Ovidian Tragedy originally looked like: 'There came, too, raging Tragedy, with mighty stride: her locks o'erhung a darkling brow, her pall trailed on the ground; her left hand swayed wide a kingly sceptre, and on her foot was the high-bound Lydian buskin' (III.i.11–14; Loeb trans.). Tragedy's dress, gait, and glance all portray a generalized idea of the genre; but, given that the portrait predates Seneca, it has real historical significance. For Ovid, tragedy is a literary genre written in a style that is serious, dignified, and elevated; it focuses on a political topic pertaining to kings; it is reticent in its eroticism; and it is violent through its emphasis on divine revenge.

When Dame Tragedy herself speaks, she ridicules the poet for his commitment to Dame Elegy and her theme of love (15–22), commanding him to be '"stirred by the stroke of a greater thyrsus"' (23): 'thou hast dallied enough – enter on greater work! Thy theme obscures thy genius. Sing deeds of heroes. "This," thou wilt say, "is the race for my soul to run!" Thy Muse has been but playing – with matter for tender maiden's song – and thy first youth has been given to numbers that belong to youth. Now, let me, Roman Tragedy, win through thee renown! Thou hast the inspiration which will fulfil my needs' (24–30; Loeb trans.). From Tragedy, we learn that the higher genre opposes the lower genre, elegy: Ovid understands tragedy as part of a generic hierarchy, in which love elegy is always in danger of interfering with the poet's need to turn to the higher form. But Tragedy also situates her generic contest with Elegy inside the pattern of a professional literary career: young men write elegies; mature men write tragedies. And she even uses the metaphor from the Virgilian *cursus* to make the point: '"haec animo ... *area facta* meo est!"' By making the *meta* from elegy to tragedy, the mature poet can secure poetic fame ('nomen'). Dame Tragedy considers Ovid ideally suited for the project. In this, we can witness a good deal of self-advertising.

During the dialogue, Ovid applies several 'personality traits' to Tragedy. She walks 'stately' in her 'painted buskins' (31: 'movit pictis innixa cothurnis'); she speaks in 'heavy words' (35: 'gravibus verbis'); she inhabits a 'queenly hall' (40: 'regia ... fores') – a fine inscription of tragedy's metre (see ll. 37–40) and form; she wears an 'austere buskin' (45: 'duro ... cothurno'); and she bears a 'haughty brow' (48: 'supercilio'). These traits emphasize the 'austere' topic and elevated style of tragedy, the formidable task the genre presents to the would-be tragedian, and the topic of nationhood itself. Indeed, the phrase 'regia fores' is a superb metonym for tragedy as a form of nationhood: 'queenly hall.'

At the end of the elegy, Ovid may reveal that we are to read Dame Tragedy as a dramatic representation of *Medea*: 'One honours me with sceptre and lofty buskin; my tongue already feels thy touch, and mighty speech is on my lips' (63–4; Loeb trans.). The present tense working of line 64 recalls Ovid's earlier reference to his tragedy: 'curaque tragoedia nostra / crevit' (II.xviii.13–14). When Ovid concludes the dialogue with Tragedy's agreement to let him finish the *Amores* and with his own acknowledgment that 'close after me presses a greater task' (70), he accurately inscribes the intimate relation between the *Amores* and the *Medea* that we believe existed – that Jonson astutely dramatizes.

Ovidian tragedy has nearly fallen into the void, but scholars believe that Ovid's experiment greatly influenced the one Roman tragedian who succeeded in circumscribing the genre – that figure who became the model of tragedy for the Elizabethans: the Younger Seneca. According to R.J. Tarrant, Seneca's *Medea* was 'undoubtedly shaped by the corresponding play ... by Ovid' (261). Tarrant goes on to call Ovid's *Medea* a 'document ... of central importance for the development of Latin drama in general and of Senecan drama in particular' (263).[11] Consequently, we need to understand Senecan tragedy – and the English Senecan movement of the sixteenth century – as itself infused with Ovidian tragedy. In Marlowe's case, Senecan tragedy *is* in large part Ovidian tragedy.

While, at the beginning of the English Renaissance tragedy movement, Spenser implies a link between these two Roman masters of the genre (see chapter 2), at the height of the movement, Thomas Heywood, later responsible for publishing Marlowe's *Jew of Malta*, makes the link explicit.[12] In his magnificent *Apology for Actors* (1612), Heywood writes a dream vision in which the tragic muse, Melpomene, presents herself to him in order to defend her tragic integrity. Not merely does Heywood set his dream vision with a Latin quotation from *Amores* III.v.1 ('*Nox erat et somnus lassos submisit ocellos*': 'It was night and sleep overcame my tired eyes'), but he describes Melpomene in Ovidian terms – and from the very elegy we have been emphasizing – *Amores* III.i:

– *animosa Tragaedia* [III.i.35: 'Spirited Tragedy']
– *et movit pictis innixa cothurnis*
Densum cesarie terque quaterque caput [III.i.32: 'Standing in her embroidered
    buskins she moved thrice and four times her head thick with hair']

(Apology for Actors, rpt. in Gilbert 553)

Not surprisingly, when Melpomene speaks, she quotes only Ovid – and
no fewer than three times.[13] Given Ovid's dominating presence both in
Melpomene's speech and in Heywood's own prefatory description of the
dream vision, the subsequent reference to Seneca may come as an arrest, but
Heywood softens it by immediately mentioning Ovid himself:

> Oh! Seneca,
> Thou tragic poet, hadst thou lived to see
> This outrage done to sad Melpomene,
> With such sharp lines thou wouldst revenge my blot
> As armed Ovid against Ibis wrot.[14]

(rpt. in Gilbert 555)

Like Spenser in that earlier rendering of tragedy, the *October* eclogue of
The Shepheardes Calender, Heywood here emphasizes the role of tragedy
in the formation of nationhood, and along Spenser's patriotic lines: 'Am I
Melpomene, the buskined Muse, / That held in awe the tyrants of the world
/ And played their lives in public theaters, / Making them fear to sin, since
fearless I / Prepared to write their lives in crimson ink / And act their
shames in eye of all the world?' (rpt. in Gilbert 554). As Alan H. Gilbert
reveals, Heywood presents 'Tragedy [as] a moral teacher' (554). As such,
Heywood joins Spenser as part of the medieval and Renaissance movement
that seeks to 'moralize' Ovid's 'song' – a tradition in which, we have seen
(chapter 2), Marlowe himself refused to play a part.

While Marlowe joins Ovid in using his art to subvert imperial power, he
does not remain slavish to Ovid. He reinvents the form, including its
immediate offspring, Seneca's Ovidian tragedy. For instance, while selecting the sovereign as a principal character in *Dido*, *Edward II*, and *The
Massacre at Paris*, he veers from this pattern in *The Jew of Malta* and *Doctor
Faustus*, while in the *Tamburlaine* plays he stamps the sovereign with a
decidedly non-imperial seal: a shepherd who becomes a king. Similarly,
Marlowe sometimes veers from the *gravitas* of Ovidian and Senecan tragedy, as he does especially in *The Jew of Malta*, with its grim, undignified

Machiavellianism: 'Here have I purs'd their paltry silverlings. / Fie, what a trouble 'tis to count this trash' (I.i.6–7). *Gravitas? Spurca.*

Marlowe's reinvention of Ovidian tragedy becomes another sign of his success in overgoing his great original, whether understood as Ovid himself or the Ovidian Spenser, or typologically both at once.

4

Dido, Queen of Carthage and the Coining of '"Eliza"'

He affirmeth ... That he has as good Right to Coine as the queene of England.

Richard Baines, 1593 Deposition against Marlowe

In *Dido, Queen of Carthage*, Marlowe asserts his 'Right to Coine ... the queene of England.' In Act IV, he clarifies the topical significance of his Virgilian drama for an Elizabethan audience:

> O hear Iarbas' plaining prayers,
> Whose hideous echoes make the welkin howl,
> And all the woods 'Eliza' to resound!
>
> (*Dido, Queen of Carthage* IV.ii.8–10)

In this passage, Marlowe evokes 'Eliza' as a cult name for England's Queen. In establishing an analogy between Queen Elizabeth and Queen Dido, he localizes not just a politics of the queen, but a poetics of the queen. For one poet in particular had made the name 'Eliza' famous in his 1579 *Shepheardes Calender*: 'fayre Eliza, Queene of shepheardes all' (*Aprill* 34). In *Dido*, Marlowe writes his sovereign through with an inscription that 're[-]sounds' an inscription of a professional rival. '"Eliza"' is not simply Elizabeth, but Spenser's Elizabeth – a fictive, not a real queen.[1] As the passage indicates, Marlowe evokes his rival's name for Elizabeth in order to critique Spenser's royal form of nationhood. Thus he repositions a series of Spenserian tropes and their distinct 'Spenserian' discourse, so that the name Eliza 'resound[s]' with 'hideous echoes' that 'make the welkin howl.' By writing himself, his queen, and her principal poet into his tragedy, Marlowe reinvents the traditional 'subject' of tragedy, the sovereign. In reinventing the high literary genre itself, Marlowe situates his self-reflexive, counter-national tragedy along the oscillating continuum of his Ovidian *cursus*.[2]

Critical Contexts

Dido, Queen of Carthage occupies a unique position in criticism on the Marlowe canon: we believe it to be Marlowe's first experiment in tragedy. For most critics, the play forms the artistic bridge between his 'apprentice' work at Cambridge (the earlier verse translations of both Ovid's *Amores* and Book I of Lucan's *Pharsalia*) and his mature work (his London debut in *Tamburlaine, Parts 1 and 2*). Usually, critics note that in *Dido*, alone among all his plays, Marlowe focuses on the erotic relationship between a man and a woman; that he achieves this focus by paraphrasing, translating, and even quoting an episode in Virgil's national epic, the story of Aeneas and Dido in Books I, II, and IV of the *Aeneid*; that he follows Virgil in presenting his central theme (whether identified as the conflict between love and honour, Dido's destructive love, Aeneas's commitment to destiny and empire, the limits of human power within an unjust cosmos, or the fatal danger of divine love); but that, in the process of adapting Virgil to the English stage, he rewrites Virgil. If earlier critics tended to agree with Anthony Trollope that *Dido* is a 'burlesque on Dido's story as treated by Vergil' and therefore 'pretty quaint, and painful' (qtd. in Oliver xix), recent critics tend to agree with T.S. Eliot that the play is 'underrated' (63). For the current generation of Marlowe readers, Jackson Cope sets the pace: 'we have relegated what is perhaps Marlowe's best piece of total theater to the status of apprentice work' (63).[3]

While critics now tend to agree about *Dido*'s uniqueness, its basic features, and its historical importance, they are divided over Marlowe's attitude towards his primary source. By 1986, the central question had become 'whether the young Marlowe was dramatizing Vergil in the right or in a dissident spirit.'[4] In the current climate of the New Historicism, the scales are tipped in favour of Marlowe the dissident, and in the most significant essay published since Leech's account, Emily C. Bartels sees Marlowe taking on Virgil's 'classical, colonialist myth,' giving Dido 'a voice of her own,' and offering 'a pointed critique of imperialism' (37). According to Bartels, 'the play neither silences nor reduces Dido's voice, but sets it beside his [Aeneas's] as a competing alternative' (44): 'the conflict between Dido and Aeneas stands nonetheless as an important protest against the ways that voice was being silenced ... The conflict between these voices creates a problematic indeterminacy ... That indeterminacy, however, is finally the point and not the problem of Marlowe's play' (46, 51).

We may agree with Bartels that both the 'imperializing exploits' narrated by Hakluyt and others and the 'classical past' told by Virgil in his story of Dido, 'which itself is preoccupied with imperialism and the conflicts it produces' (34), form twin 'contexts' for Marlowe's *Dido* and that their intersection stages a dialogic 'conflict' between competing 'voices' – what Bartels calls 'the uncertainties between self and other' (52). None the less, neither the synchronic English political context of colonization nor the diachronic classical literary context of Virgil, or even their intersection, satisfactorily focuses the project of the play. Neither, for instance, accounts for a feature of the text that is marked enough to have become a staple in the editorial tradition of annotating the play.

For in the '"Eliza"' line in Act IV, Marlowe identifies a synchronic literary context as the mediator for both the synchronic political context and the diachronic literary context. According to Bartels, 'what makes Marlowe's plays stand out within this context is that their foreign worlds are not only "Englished"; they make a point of that Englishing. *Dido* ... announces the resemblance between its African landscape and England: Iarbas, in a complaint to Jove, makes "all the woods Eliza to resound" (4.2.10) – a phrase that Edmund Spenser will canonize as part of the English literary tradition – bringing out an embedded parallel between Carthage's queen (whose Phoenician name was "Elissa") and England's' (15–16). For Bartels, the Marlovian line about '"Eliza"' establishes a politically oriented analogy between the fictive and the real queen, and it does so through a 'phrase' that Spenser 'will canonize.' Evidently, Bartels is drawing on a tradition of annotating this intertextual moment and its literary and political resonance. This tradition, however, turns out to be inaccurate, for Spenser does not canonize the phrase 'all the woods "Eliza" to resound.' If anyone canonizes this phrase, it is Marlowe, who alone pens it, makes it famous. Yet, Bartels and the annotation tradition do direct us to an unexamined collision between Marlowe and Spenser.

As we shall see, this collision, and the critical confusion surrounding it, help contextualize Marlowe's rewriting of Virgilian nationhood. In *Dido*, Marlowe transacts an Ovidian career change, from love elegy to tragedy, and this is the most primary thing we can say about the play – the starting-point for criticism. More specifically, Marlowe imitates Ovid's own movement from the *Amores* to *Medea* via the two models of tragedy that he had available to him: the elegiac Ovid of the *Heroides* and Seneca. Marlowe understands this career move as a challenge to Spenser's advertised *cursus* from pastoral to epic, and he rewrites Virgil via Ovid and Seneca in order to challenge Spenser's Virgilian authority as a national poet serving the empire of Eliza.

By focusing on Marlowe's literary career, his rivalry with Spenser, and his writing of counter-nationhood, we will be able to further our understanding of how Marlowe helps form English tragedy. We will then be able to see *Dido* as a first draft of a much larger project, witnessed more substantially in the two remaining plays of Marlowe's first triad, *Tamburlaine, Parts 1 and 2.*[5]

'And all the woods "Eliza" to resound'

In 1885, A.H. Bullen succinctly glossed Marlowe's use of '"Eliza"' in the Spenserian line from Act IV: 'Elissa (Dido)' (2: 350). Then in his 1904 *Works of Thomas Nashe*, Ronald B. McKerrow expanded: 'The two names were regarded as equivalent, and G. Harvey and many others refer to the Queen as Elissa' (4: 300). Next, in 1930, C.F. Tucker Brooke found 'an intentional echo of the many praises of Queen Elizabeth under the title of Eliza,' quoted McKerrow, and added: 'Compare Spenser, *Shepherds' Calendar* [*sic*], April, 39–40 [*sic*], "Then will I sing his [Colin Clout's] lay / Of fayre *Eliza*, Queene of Shepheards all." For the common idea, *all the woods resound*, compare the refrain of Spenser's *Epithalamion* and note on line 18 of that poem in Van Winkle's ed.' (ed., *Life ... and 'Dido'* 194–5). Brooke's phrasing remains elusive, but he implies that Marlowe 'intentional[ly] echoes' Spenser in both *Aprill* and *Epithalamion*; such an implication may underlie the confusion that follows.

For, from these early, tentative identifications come the later, assertive ones. In his 1968 Revels Play edition, H.J. Oliver states openly that 'Marlowe is echoing Spenser's *Epithalamion*, in word and in spirit. Spenser calls on the Muses to help him "resound" his "own loves prayses" and rings the changes on the refrain "The woods shall to me answer, and my Eccho ring." Marlowe makes Iarbas similarly wish the woods to resound with the praises of his love Elissa (Dido's original name and one by which she addresses herself in both Virgil, *Aeneid*, IV. 610, and Ovid, *Heroides*, VII. 193), but in addition he perhaps takes advantage of the interchangeability of "Elissa" and "Eliza" (the name under which Elizabethan poets often flattered Queen Elizabeth) to turn the single line into a passing complimentary reference to the living Queen's fame' (60). Then, in his 1981 edition of *The Complete Works*, Fredson Bowers summarized the issue: 'This is *Elissa*, Dido's original name, forming a parallel, of course, to Spenser's *Epithalamium* and its references to Queen Elizabeth' (1: 62). Finally, in her 1987 Oxford edition, Roma Gill authorizes the following annotation: 'In his misery, Iarbus echoes the words and the movement of the happy lover's song in Spenser's "Epithalamion": "So I unto my selfe alone will sing, / The woods shall to me answer, and my Eccho ring." Dido's original name, by which she addresses herself in *Aeneid*, iv. 610, was "Elissa," of which a variant spelling is "Eliza" (the name frequently used by flattering poets to address Elizabeth I)' (*Complete Works*, ed. 1: 285).

Despite the peculiar evolution of this annotation history – from a simple identification of Dido's alternative name, Elissa, to both Virgil's and Ovid's use of that name, to its political ramification for sixteenth-century readers subject to a queen named Elizabeth, to the final stubborn fixation on the literary precedent of the political significance formed by Spenser's *Epithalamion* – no one seems to have noticed the problems here.[6]

First, Spenser did not publish *Epithalamion* until 1595 – two years after Marlowe's death and one year after the (posthumous) publication of his play. How, then, could Marlowe be imitating *Epithalamion*? The facts as we know them are these. Marlowe met his end on 30 May 1593. Sometime before 22 April 1594 (Bowers, ed. 1: 3), Thomas Nashe published *Dido* on his dead friend's behalf. A few months *later*, after St Barnabas' Day, 11 June 1594, the day of his marriage to another Eliza, Elizabeth Boyle (see *Amoretti* 74), Spenser wrote his marriage ode, *Epithalamion*.[7] Given these facts, we can conclude with some confidence that Marlowe did *not* know Spenser's *Epithalamion*, and therefore that he could not be 'echoing' it in *Dido, Queen of Carthage*. Second, Spenser does not 'canonize' Marlowe's line, because no such line appears in Spenser's poetry. Nor does Spenser direct his woods-resounding formula in his marriage ode to Elizabeth Tudor. Spenser may allude to the Queen in his marriage ode (see line 158), but he directs his Orphic formula exclusively to Elizabeth Boyle. Finally, Marlowe is not offering 'a passing complimentary reference to the living Queen's fame.' The context of the speech indicates otherwise; it is spoken by the abject Iarbus. Moreover, as most recent commentary confirms, Marlowe's attitude towards empire is hardly consonant with Spenserian encomium. Thus Marlowe is not simply repeating Spenser in his politicized use of the Virgilian 'Eliza.'

Long ago, Tucker Brooke recognized that Marlowe may be imitating the *Aprill* eclogue in *The Shepheardes Calender*. The lines Brooke cites – 'then will I singe his laye / Of fayre Eliza, Queene of shepheardes all' – do supply an origin for two features of Marlowe's line: his use of the name 'Eliza,' and his representation of an individual using language to address a queen. The

Aprill lines, however, do not supply the origin for two other features: Marlowe's use of the Orphic formula of the woods resounding, and his wonderfully succinct representation of pastoral complaint as a generic mode.

To locate this twofold origin, we can turn to another eclogue in the *Calender*, where Spenser does use both the Orphic formula and the pastoral complaint together three different times with respect to Colin Clout's song. In *August*, Spenser uses the word 'resound' as one of six words repeated in the elaborate pattern of the sestina, in which Colin complains of his beloved Rosalinde's 'misdeede' (186) – her faithless love of the rival shepherd Menalcas (see *June* 102–4). Of the six uses, three are pertinent to Marlowe's passage (151–2, 159–60, 165–6), but the last most closely anticipates his line: 'More meete to wayle my woe, / Bene the wild woddes my sorrowes to resound.'

Very likely, then, Marlowe forms his Spenserian line by conflating the *Aprill* lines about Colin's 'laye' of 'fayre Elisa' with the *August* formula of the woods resounding and its generic construction of a pastoral complaint. Significantly, Marlowe assigns his Spenserian line to an abject and frustrated lover whom Virgil barely mentions but whom Marlowe dresses out in full costume, and who is on his way to a suicide that critics find ludicrous. The full significance of this remains to be seen.

For now, we may note that Marlowe's insertion of a single line that evokes Spenser, the genre of pastoral, and Queen Elizabeth provides a clue as to how he wishes the audience to view *The Tragedie of Dido Queene of Carthage: Played by the Children of her Majesties Chappell* (title page, 1594 ed.): as an artist's self-conscious generic representation of a political problem within the pattern of an ambitious literary career. We are to understand the play paradoxically as a 'tragedy' of 'humour' about Queen Elizabeth's misguided relation with her suitors within an Ovidian career model.[8]

These suitors are not simply members of European royalty vying for Elizabeth's hand in marriage, principally the Duc d'Alençon of France – since by the mid-1580s, and certainly by the early 1590s, the marriage question had faded in significance.[9] More specifically, Marlowe's suitors may figure those *writers* who argued against the Queen's marriage, with the principal suitor being England's Virgil himself, who, as we have seen with respect to 'The Passionate Shepherd to His Love' (chapter 3), had made the Queen's marriage a topic in *The Shepheardes Calender*. The dialogic principle of 'alternative' and competing 'voices' that critics situate within dramatic characters pertains as well to artists like Spenser. Marlowe's dramatic representation of Iarbus's woody echoing of Eliza is a metatheatrical staging of Marlowe's own imitative project carried out along generic, political, and ultimately career lines. These lines are not simply anti-Virgilian or anticolonialist; they are counter-Spenserian: a critique of England's Virgilian and colonialist national poet. Quite literally, in *Dido, Queen of Carthage* Marlowe *re-sounds* Spenser's pastoral resounding of Eliza, queen of shepherds all.

Ovid, Spenser, Elizabeth

Critics agree that Marlowe relies on Ovid as his most recurrent strategy for rewriting Virgil. In the words of Douglas Cole, 'though the matter is Virgilian, the spirit is Ovid's' (*Suffering and Evil* 85).[10] As critics remark, Ovid had rewritten the Virgilian story of Aeneas and Dido in Letter VII of the *Heroides*, creating the most influential 'alternative' version for medieval and Renaissance culture. We may add that Ovid situated his rewriting of Dido within a career pattern of amatory poetry, tragedy, and epic; he then organized his *cursus* as a response to the Virgilian pattern of pastoral, georgic, and epic. Not simply does Ovid object to Virgil's treatment of Dido, a female victim of the masculine machine of empire, but he removes the African queen from her lowly status as a tragic victim in a national epic, elevating her to the status of a strong and wise 'heroine' occupying her own protected space in an elegiac, erotic genre. Ovid rewrites Virgil along generic as well as ideological lines. In Ovid, unlike in Virgil, Dido does not *die*; she *complains*, she *writes*. Whereas Virgil terminates Dido's plea by reducing her to bitter silence in the afterlife, Ovid eternizes her voice with memorable vigour resonating through the centuries: 'I write, and the Trojan's blade is ready in my lap' (*Heroides* VII.184).[11]

In the most detailed account of the 'political overtones' of the play, William Godshalk observes that the 'tragedy of love points to the tragedy of empire,' and he contextualizes this tragedy in terms of 'Sidney's "Discourse ... to the Queenes Majesty Touching Hir Mariage with Monsieur,"' which opposed the French marriage: 'Such a union ... would lead to the disaffection of a great number of her subjects, and might result in social and political disorders. Certainly there is an analogy here between the two queens ... For [Sidney and Marlowe] ... , romantic love is not an ultimate value to be pursued at all costs' (57).[12]

While endorsing this 'political' context, we may question whether Marlowe's play joins the Leicester–Sidney circle as part of the anti-marriage campaign. Most likely, Marlowe wrote the play initially in 1585–6 – five or six years *after* the Leicester–Sidney circle mounted its attack on the marriage and well after the debate had faded from such intense public interest (Bednarz). Marlowe's 'humour' in *Dido* contrasts with the seriousness of

Sidney's letter to the Queen or John Stubbs's *Gaping Gulf*: Sidney was banished from court, and Stubbs lost his left hand. Marlowe is reticent in his address to the Queen, as we should expect from a future (or training) government agent. Translating an authorized patriotic poet, he relies on a superb dramatic vehicle: a low comedy featuring boy actors voicing the high Virgilian tragedy of erotic desire. With the Queen as a likely auditor of a play performed by her Children of the Chapel, Marlowe has good reason to be on his best political guard.

In the *November* eclogue, the chief poet of the Leicester–Sidney circle had presented his persona, Colin Clout, singing a funeral elegy on a figure whom E.K. mysteriously identifies as 'some mayden of greate bloud, whom he calleth Dido' (Arg.). As Barbara J. Bono observes, 'numerous similarities link this dead heroine to the Elisa/Eliza of *Aprill*: both are daughters of great shepherds, intimately associated with flowers, and beloved of the Muses and shepherds' ('Dido' 218). Both figures also have a clear relation to Virgil's story of Dido and Aeneas. And *Aprill* closes with two emblems – both quotations from Virgil's Dido story: '*O quam te memorem virgo?*' (*Aprill* 163; *Aen* I.327) and '*O dea certe*' (*Aprill* 165; *Aen* I.328). Moreover, both *Aprill* and *November* have a special relation to Queen Elizabeth. In the Argument to *Aprill*, E.K. says that '[t]his Aeglogue is purposely intended to the honor and prayse of our most gracious sovereigne, Queene Elizabeth,' and the most compelling criticism on the eclogue emphasizes its political or 'Elizabethan' significance (Montrose, '"Eliza"'). If in *Aprill* Spenser openly presents Eliza as Elizabeth, in *November* he is more mysterious. Yet many critics now believe that 'the mysterious Dido is most probably designed to embody the prophetic fears of the group around Leicester who were strongly opposing the French marriage' (McLane 60).[13]

Not simply do Spenser's *November* and *Aprill* eclogues and Marlowe's play share an 'analogy' between 'Dido' and 'Eliza,' but they have been identified as doing such.[14] Both poets are representing Elizabeth, and both are evoking the Queen's marriage with Alençon, but neither Spenser nor Marlowe is praising the Queen, or even evoking the Alençon marriage, in the same way. After Monsieur's death, evidently, Marlowe evokes the French marriage in order to divorce Spenser.

Dido's Counter-Spenserian Career

Spenser infiltrates annotation of *Dido* as early as Brooke's 1930 edition, but back in 1919 T.S. Eliot provided a clue for later critics when he identified one of the major 'verse accomplishments of *Tamburlaine*': 'Marlowe gets into blank verse the melody of Spenser' (62). In 1963, Harry Morris adds that 'Spenser's influence on *Dido* is at least as noticeable and perhaps more so': 'the predominant style of *Dido* is of Spenserian melody' (136–7).[15]

To construct the Spenserian context of *Dido* further, we can examine the four dimensions of Marlowe's career model: the literary, the erotic, the theological, and the political. To probe the literary dimension, we should recall that, when Marlowe was likely writing *Dido*, Spenser was caught in the career interstice between Virgilian pastoral (the 1579 *Shepheardes Calender*) and Virgilian epic (the 1590 *Faerie Queene*).[16] What is striking is that Marlowe should compose a Spenserian-sounding play on a Spenserian topic during what must have been a most anxious time for the New Poet. In *Dido*, Marlowe dramatically occupies the deep structure of Spenser's own generic interstice.

In *Aprill*, Spenser had tacitly situated the Dido story within the pattern of pastoral and epic by quoting the two lines from the epic *Aeneid* within his pastoral eclogue (already identified). In the *Aeneid*, Virgil inaugurates the Dido story when Aeneas lands on the coast of Carthage and enters 'the forest' (I.314: 'silva'), encountering Venus disguised as a 'huntress' (319: 'venetrix'). She claims that she is no goddess, but a maid, that she and other 'Tyrian maids are wont to wear the quiver, and bind their ankles high with the purple buskin': ''Tis the Punic realm thou seest, a Tyrian people, and the city of Agenor ... Dido wields the sceptre' (I.336–401). When we first meet Dido, in other words, we discover the paradigm that Spenser interprets as pastoral-epic.

Similarly, when Dido and Aeneas return to the forest during the cave scene, Marlowe describes the locale in pastoral terms: 'Silvanus' dwellings' (III.ii.91). Indeed, critics have long recognized pastoral and epic topoi within the landscape of *Dido*. Edmund Chambers even speculated 'that one side of the stage was arranged *en pastoralle*, and represented the wood between the sea-shore and Carthage, where the shipwrecked Trojans land and where later Aeneas and Dido hunt. Here was the cave where they take shelter from the storm ... The other side of the stage represents Carthage. Possibly a wall with a gate in it was built across the stage, dividing off the two regions' (3: 35–6).[17] If Chambers is correct, the stage for the 'tragedy' spatially creates the paradigm of pastoral and epic, including the interstice between the two that we have been tracking: the 'wall with a gate in it.'

At the end, Dido refers to this theatrical space when she confronts Aeneas: 'Wast thou not wrack'd upon this Libyan shore, / And cam'st to Dido like a fisher swain? / Rapair'd not I thy ships, made thee a king' (V.i.161–3). Dido claims to have transformed Aeneas from a 'fisher swain' into a 'king.' The idea of the 'fisher swain' is Marlowe's, for in the passage he is translating Virgil uses the words 'eiectum' and 'egentum': 'eiectum litore, egentem / excepi et regni demens in parte locavi' (IV.373–4: 'A castaway on the shore, a beggar, / I welcomed him and madly gave him a share in my throne'). The *OED* has no entry for 'fisher swain,' but the fourth and fifth definitions of *swain* identify a pastoral connotation: 'freq. a shepherd' (Def. 4, citing Spenser, *FQ* III.vi.15: 'shepheard swaynes' – a frequent phrase in Spenser); and 'gen. a lover, ... esp. in pastoral poetry' (Def. 5). For Spenser, as for Marlowe, the word 'swain' likely had pastoral resonance, but the link with 'fisher' is a curious one.

Dido may characterize Aeneas as a 'fisher swain' because he has just come from the sea to assume a lowly social status, but her phrasing recalls a subgenre practised by Dante and made famous by Sannazaro, who wrote five complete and one fragmentary *Piscatorial Eclogues* – about fisher swains. The genre was popular in late sixteenth-century and early seventeenth-century England, when Drayton and Phineas Fletcher both worked in it. Fletcher even refers to Sannazaro as 'th'Italian fisher-swain' (*Purple Island* I.xiii.1).[18] To the usual contours of the piscatorial tradition, we may add that Ovid composed a fragmentary poem on fishing, *Halieutica* (Sea-Fishing), now considered spurious, of which only 134 lines remain, and in which the authorial voice is indeed that of a fisher swain: 'Yet I would not bid you go to the mid-most regions of the sea, or try the depths of the vast ocean; between either extreme will you guide your line more profitably' (83–5; Loeb *Ovid*, vol. 2).[19] In *Dido*, then, Marlowe appears to anticipate Elizabethan colleagues who insert Ovid into the piscatorial tradition.

Thus, back in Act II, Dido changes Aeneas from a fisher swain into a king: 'Warlike Aeneas, and in these base robes! / Go fetch the garment which Sichaeus ware' (i.79–80).[20] By contrast, Aeneas gets Dido to change from a queen into a huntress; in the hunting scene of Act III, she tells Aeneas, 'My princely robes thou see'st are laid aside, / Whose glittering pomp Diana's shrouds supplies' (iii.3–4). Marlowe's text may be Virgilian, but in isolating the Dido story from its epic narrative he reconfigures Virgil as a literary form about the conflict between lower and higher genres, pastoral and epic. Generically speaking, Marlowe's Aeneas is moving up; Dido, down. As a couple, they are incompatible because their *careers* meet at the generic crossroads of tragically opposing metamorphoses.

Dido changes from a queen to a huntress, but, as her imitation of Venus's earlier change from goddess to huntress indicates, she eventually changes from frustrated lover to tragic heroine. Deftly, Marlowe switches generic paradigms, and precisely at the generic crossroads identified earlier. As

Aeneas departs along the Virgilian path from pastoral to epic ('fisher swain' to 'king'), Dido turns tragically down the Ovidian path from amatory poetry to tragedy: 'Now Dido, with these relics burn thyself, / And make Aeneas famous through the world / For perjury and slaughter of a queen. / Here lie the sword that in the darksome cave / He drew ... / These letters, lines, and perjur'd papers all / Shall burn to cinders in this precious flame' (V.i.292–301). The 'relics' and the 'sword' come from Virgil, but the 'letters, lines, and perjur'd papers' appear to be Marlowe's invention, although they have their origin where we should expect. In *Heroides* VII ('Dido to Aeneas'), Ovid *rewrites* Virgil by emphasizing the process of authorship, inscription, letter writing – from Dido's magnificent opening swan image ('Thus ... sings the white swan' [1–3]), to her clear articulation of her project ('I write' [183]), to her final 'inscription' ('inscribar') of her epitaph (193–6). For Marlowe, as perhaps for Ovid himself, the conflict between Dido and Aeneas dramatizes a competition between Ovidian and Virgilian career models. And just as Ovid had contextualized his writing of the story in terms of his rivalry with Virgil, so Marlowe contextualizes his rewriting in terms of his Ovidian rivalry with the Virgilian Spenser.

As to be expected, Marlowe emphasizes the second or erotic dimension. Thus we should probably contextualize his presentation of the relation between the sexes within Spenser's program of mutual, romantic love. Although this program does not get fully articulated until the 1590 *Faerie Queene*, its intimations emerge in the *Calender* (e.g., *October* 91–4). Marlowe's emphasis on the tragic love of Dido and Aeneas undermines Spenser's erotic idealism, which in Book III is also modelled on the Virgilian story (canto ix). But Marlowe's mining project also emerges in Anna's love for Iarbas.

In Act IV, several lines after Iarbas complains about his beloved 'Eliza,' Anna addresses her own beloved, the pagan king himself: 'Away with Dido! Anna *be* thy *song*' (ii.45; emphasis added). The origin of this line may lie in *Aprill*, a few lines after Spenser's 'Eliza' line, when Colin Clout addresses the 'Virgins': 'Of fayre Elisa *be* your silver *song*' (46; emphasis added). The syntactical construction of the two passages is identical; both use the imperative voice. The elements from the domain of logic are the same: a *female* is to 'be' the subject of a 'song.' Both female subjects are of royal blood. Spenser's line also contains one of Marlowe's favourite Spenserian words: 'silver' (H. Morris 138–9). Significantly, too, Spenser also names 'Elisa.' In effect, Marlowe's Anna rewrites Spenser's Colin by relocating the subject of the song from the sovereign other to the self. In context, however, Anna implores Iarbas to choose her as the subject of his song. Here, we can detect what we should suspect in Iarbas's earlier imitation of *Aprill*: Marlowe establishes an analogy not simply between Dido and Elizabeth, but also between Iarbas and Spenser, with Anna functioning as an alter-Eliza. In this intertextuality of erotic 'song,' Marlowe fuses the literary dimension to the erotic one.[21]

Similarly, the third or theological dimension has counter-Spenserian resonance. Critics agree that in *Dido* Marlowe critiques orthodox Christian theology. Nowhere is this clearer than in the opening conversation between Jupiter and Ganymede: 'Come, gentle Ganymede, and play with me; ... / And shall have, Ganymede, if thou wilt be my love' (I.i.1, 49; see Gill, 'Marlowe's Virgil' 143–4). As critics widely recognize, Marlowe here quotes 'The Passionate Shepherd to His Love.' Marlowe's self-quotation is significant initially because it is Marlowe's *very first utterance in the genre of tragedy* – the first line of his first tragedy. By writing himself into his tragedy right from the start, he constructs a self-reflexive lens for viewing his play as a whole. Specifically, he uses a strategy of self-authorship to advance his theological critique, for the great deity of the Olympic pantheon voices the famous erotic invitation of Christopher Marlowe. The playwright does not merely reverse the traditional process advocated in Scripture, in which the individual imitates God or Christ; he reconfigures the central hierarchy of culture, divesting the deity of divine power. Anticipating Faustus's attempt to 'gain a deity' (I.i.65), Marlowe follows Ovid in reserving godhead for himself.

Marlowe's self-authorizing theological critique deauthorizes Spenser's providential poetics.[22] Later in the opening scene, Jupiter tells Venus: 'Aeneas' wandering *fate* is *firm*' (I.i.83; emphasis added). In Book III of *The Faerie Queene*, the magician Merlin clarifies the providential significance of the chaste Britomart's glimpse of the Achilles-like Artegall in Merlin's magic mirror: 'Indeed the *fates* are *firm*' (iii.25:6; emphasis added). John Bakeless sees Marlowe's 'fate is firm' as a translation of one of 'the most famous lines' in the *Aeneid* (2: 62–3): 'manent *immota* tuorum / *Fata* tibi' (I.257–8; emphasis added). Twentieth-century translators have produced no stable rendering of these lines.[23] Moreover, Marlowe's two Elizabethan predecessors in the translation of Virgil do not approximate his translation. In 1573, Thomas Phaer translates the line as 'Feare not ... thy mens good hap, for none their fortune breaks' (sig. A.4ᵛ); in 1582, Richard Stanyhurst translates the line as 'on thy syde destenye runneth' (sig. D.18). Significantly, however, two early-modern translators writing after Marlowe do approximate his line: in 1632, George Sandys translates the line almost verbatim: '*fates* are *firme*' (538); and in 1672 Dryden translates it as 'the *fates* are *fix'd.*' Since Marlowe's phrasing is by no means standard, it may have influenced both seventeenth-century translators. Peculiar to Marlowe's translation, however, is the change of Virgil's plural *Fata* to the singular 'fate.'

Similarly, A.C. Hamilton glosses lines 4–5 of stanza 25, Book III, canto iii (ed., *FQ* 330) – the two lines preceding Spenser's 'fate is firm' line – with another famous passage in the *Aeneid*: '*fates* can make / *Way* for themselves' (*FQ* III.iii.25; emphasis added); '*Fata viam invenient*' (*Aeneid* III.395; emphasis added). Hamilton, however, does not gloss line 4, 'the fates are firm.' In this stanza as a whole, however, Spenser is likely translating two passages from the *Aeneid* that are typologically related. In Book I of the classical epic, Jupiter tells Venus that the fates are firm with respect to Aeneas's destiny; in Book III, the Apollonian prophet Helenus prophesies to Aeneas the firmness of his fate. This typology strengthens the central principle of Virgilian epic, the ordained *telos* of history (Quint 30).

Marlowe repeats Spenser, but with a difference: the fate of Aeneas that is 'firm' is paradoxically 'wandering.' At first reading, the line seems both Spenserian and Virgilian in its orthodoxy. Jupiter is explaining to his anxious daughter, Venus, that Aeneas merely *seems* to be 'wandering.' In fact, Aeneas's 'fate is firm.' But Jupiter's phrasing is contradictory: how can a 'wandering fate' be 'firm'? The contradiction, as well as the emergent humour, is consistent with Marlowe's portrait of Jupiter, which is 'both undignified and frivolous' (Summers, *Christopher Marlowe* 22). Marlowe's use of one line representing both unorthodox and orthodox constructions of fate is characteristic of much else in the play. In a single utterance, Marlowe suggests that Aeneas's wandering is part of a larger providential plan for the founding of Rome, but that this plan constitutes a 'wandering' from what should form Aeneas's true fate, his marriage to Dido. The fates may be firm, but they wander from the truth.[24]

For Marlowe, the theological dimension is closely linked with the fourth or political dimension. At the end of the play, Marlowe may echo Spenser when he has Dido hallucinate the image of Aeneas's apotheosis – in actuality, his escape by ship at sea: '*See, see*, the billows heave him up to *heaven*' (V.i.252; emphasis added). In *November*, Spenser says of Colin, who witnesses the actual apotheosis of Queen Dido, 'I *see* thee blessed soule, I *see*, / Walke in *Elisian fieldes* so free' (178–9; emphasis added). Colin's epiphany of Dido entering the Elisian fields typologically fulfils his earlier sight of Queen Eliza in *Aprill*. Hence, Colin's description of the Elisian fields, with its 'grasse ay greene' (*November* 189), echoes his earlier description: 'See, where she sits upon the grassie greene' (*Aprill* 55). As critics observe,

Spenser's 'Elisian fieldes' puns on Dido's alternate name, Elissa (Montrose, '"The perfecte paterne"' 50–1).

Marlowe's reconfiguring of the *Aprill/November* or Eliza/Dido typology of earth/heaven, politics/salvation is spectacular. For Dido's Spenserian utterance takes a new form: 'Look, sister, look! Lovely Aeneas' ships! / See, see, the billows heave him up to heaven' (V.i.251–2).[25] Whereas Colin witnesses the truth about salvation, Dido witnesses the falsehood of a mental image, Aeneas's raising up to 'heaven' by his ships that ride the 'billows.' For Marlowe, unlike for Spenser, 'Dido' remains mentally trapped in Aeneas's betrayal by a universe bent on destroying her.

'Hideous Echoes': The Forms of Counter-Nationhood

Marlowe's use of Ovid to rewrite the Virgilian Spenser alerts us to the national project of *Dido, Queen of Carthage*. Nowhere is this project more vibrant than in Iarbas's Spenserian prayer to Jove in Act IV, scene ii, which we may now contextualize:

> Hear, hear, O hear Iarbas' plaining prayers,
> Whose hideous echoes make the welkin howl,
> And all the woods 'Eliza' to resound!
> The woman that thou will'd us entertain,
> Where, straying in our borders up and down,
> She crav'd a hide of ground to build a town,
> With whom we did divide both laws and land,
> And all the fruits that plenty else sends forth,
> Scorning our loves and royal marriage-rites,
> Yields up her beauty to a stranger's bed;
> Who, having wrought her shame, is straightway fled.
> Now, if thou be'st a pitying god of power,
> On whom ruth and compassion ever waits
> Redress these wrongs.
>
> (*Dido, Queen of Carthage* IV.ii.8–21)

Set in the 'pastoral' half of the stage, fit for the ritual 'sacrifice' Iarbas performs (1–3), the king's 'plaining prayers' to 'Eternal Jove' (4) shadow what E.K. calls one of the 'three formes or ranckes' of the pastoral genre: the 'Plaintive' (*The general argument* 31–2). Marlowe stages a Spenserian plaintive eclogue by reproducing not simply the woods-resounding formula from *August*, but also Colin's plaining prayer to the gods from *Januarye*:

Ye Gods of love, that pitie lovers payne,
(If any gods the paine of lovers pitie:)
Looke from above, where you in joyes remaine,
And bowe your eares unto my dolefull dittie.
And Pan thou shepheards God, that once didst love,
Pitie the paines, that thou thy selfe didst prove.

(Januarye 13–18)

Like Colin, Iarbas speaks as a male lover betrayed by a female whom he thinks has been unfaithful to him; he addresses his plaint to a deity; and he asks his deity to show him 'pity' as the just way to redress wrongs he thinks have been committed against him. Unlike Spenser, however, Marlowe has let us glimpse his god in action, and by recalling the opening scene with Jupiter we recognize the futility of Iarbas's prayer – a futility dramatized when Iarbas commits suicide at the end of the play. In other words, unlike Spenser, Marlowe does not show his praying speaker to be under the protection of grace.[26]

Marlowe's line 9 is also laden with Spenserian riches: 'hideous echoes make the welkin howl.' This line recalls Spenser's *August* formula for the woods resounding: 'The forest wide is fitter to resound / The hollow Echo of my carefull cryes' (159–60). Marlowe's splendid echo of Spenser's 'hollow Echo' is fine metadiscourse, for echo is itself a trope for poetic fame (Cheney, *Spenser's Famous Flight* 284, n. 32). Marlowe's voicing of Spenser registers a process of fame, by which one poet 'overgoes' another to achieve renown, but it also critiques Spenser's fame – his echo – as 'hideous,' and simultaneously it exults in its own hideousness. Moreover, the word 'welkin' is a well-known favourite of Spenser's throughout the *Calender*, appearing in *Januarye*, when the narrator responds to the eclogue's climactic event, Colin's breaking of his pastoral pipe: 'By that, the welked Phoebus gan availe' (73). What for Spenser is a quaint term for the sky is for Marlowe a metaphysical term for the structure of the cosmos. Like King Lear in the storm, Marlowe's fretful elements *howl*.

The reason Marlowe's elements howl may interest us: Iarbas's hideous echoes resound '"Eliza"' through all the woods. Spenser's Queen is the topic of the echo – the subject of the hideousness. Iarbas's 'plaining prayers' are a counter-mimesis of Spenser's royal form of nationhood.[27] Marlowe's appropriation of Spenser both extends and specifies the critique: it is the New Poet's courtly reign to which Marlowe finally objects. Iarbas's subsequent references to Dido's empire-building – 'borders ... build a town ... divide both laws and land' – make the critique less than subtle, and Marlowe's belated evocation of the French marriage in lines 16–17 borders on the excruciating: 'Scorning our loves and royal marriage-rites, / Yields up her beauty to a stranger's bed.'

The '"Eliza"' passage reveals that Marlowe responds to Spenser's nationhood of 'absolute royal power' (Helgerson, *Forms of Nationhood* 55). Helgerson may be correct that 'many individual passages of *The Faerie Queene* reveal ... ambivalence concerning absolute royal power,' and that Spenser champions a nationhood of 'aristocratic power' (55, 59). But, writing in the mid-1580s, Marlowe is evidently not able to see – or he wishes to occlude – his great rival's ambivalence.

In *Dido, Queen of Carthage*, Marlowe re-sounds Queen Eliza's Spenserian woods in order to echo the hideous literary oppression of Elizabethan royal absolutism. At the outset of his dramatic career, England's new *Ovidianus tragoedus* learns to make the welkin howl.

'Thondring words of threate': Spenser in *Tamburlaine, Parts 1 and 2*

The phrase 'thondring words of threate' does not come from Marlowe, the *Tamburlaine* plays, or Marlowe's dramatic experiments in tragedy; it comes from Spenser, *The Shepheardes Calender*, and Spenser's poetic representation of tragedy in his pastoral. By situating the Marlovian tragedy of *Tamburlaine* within Spenser's *October* eclogue, we may find an important but neglected origin of Marlowe's project: Spenser's mapping of Renaissance ideas of a literary career.

Like *Dido*, the *Tamburlaine* plays have their uniqueness in the Marlowe canon: they are the only works published during the author's lifetime (1590; first staged 1587–8). Consequently, critics believe that the text represents Marlowe's intentions more closely than most of the other works.[1] Not surprisingly, the two plays contain the most substantial conjunction with Marlowe's Virgilian rival; indeed, the imitations, echoes, recollections, and parallels are practically countless (see Crawford; and esp. Schoeneich). Thus, what we have seen to be present in *Ovid's Elegies*, 'The Passionate Shepherd to His Love,' and *Dido* becomes in *Tamburlaine* something like a topic.

In an important analysis of the conjunction, Stephen Greenblatt concludes that 'Spenser and Marlowe are ... mighty opposites, poised in antagonism' (*Renaissance Self-Fashioning* 222). Beginning with the poets' modes of constructing identity, Greenblatt remarks: 'If Spenser sees human identity as conferred by loving service to legitimate authority, to the yoked power of God and the state, Marlowe sees identity established at those moments in which order ... is violated' (222). Moving to the poets' translation of identity into types of heroes, Greenblatt observes: 'If Spenser's heroes strive for balance and control, Marlowe's strive to shatter the restraints upon their desires' (222). Finally, specifying his argument with one famous example, Greenblatt compares Spenser's representation of Arthur's helmet with Marlowe's representation of Tamburlaine's crown: 'What is sung by Spenser in praise of Arthur is sung by Tamburlaine in praise of himself ... Marlowe's scene is self-consciously emblematic, as if it were a theatrical improvisation in the Spenserean manner, but now with the hero's place taken by a character who, in his sadistic excess, most closely resembles Orgoglio' (224).

Greenblatt's analysis inspires further investigation. What, for instance, do we make of Marlowe's manoeuvre through which Tamburlaine sings what Spenser himself has sung? What would motivate Marlowe to stage an 'improvisation' of 'the Spenserean manner'? And why would the dramatist rewrite Prince Arthur as the sadistically excessive Scythian shepherd? Given the might of the opposition between the two poets, why have *we* not scrutinized that opposition in more detail? Remarkably, we have not discovered a lens that can bring the two contemporaries into significant alignment.

One reason may be that only recently have critics like Greenblatt and Richard Helgerson made available a powerful lens for viewing rivals within a literary system. Accommodating to the Elizabethan literary system Greenblatt's principle that 'self-fashioning is achieved in relation to something perceived as alien' and that this 'threatening Other ... must be ... attacked and destroyed' (9), Helgerson argues that Spenser fashions his identity as a 'laureate' poet out of the practices of, and ultimately at the expense of, the Elizabethan 'amateurs' – a class of poets, Helgerson says in passing, that includes Marlowe. What Helgerson does not say is that an amateur like Marlowe, who also becomes a 'professional' dramatist like Shakespeare, fashions his identity out of a laureate like Spenser.

To bring the mighty opposition into significant alignment, we may view the *Tamburlaine* plays through the one lens critics neglect: the Virgilian progression from pastoral to epic. In the 'two tragical discourses' of *Tamburlaine* (Jones, 'To the Gentlemen Readers' in Gill, ed., *Plays*), Marlowe matches his authority as *Ovidianus trogoedus* against Spenser's authority as England's Virgil in the generational project of writing the nation.

The Ovidian *Cursus* in the *Tamburlaine* Plays

In *2 Tamburlaine*, Marlowe pointedly refers to his principal diachronic precursor when the shepherd-king eulogizes the dying Zenocrate, whose 'sacred beauty hath enchanted heaven' (II.iv.85). The reference brings the three genres of the Ovidian *cursus* – amatory poetry, tragedy, epic – into play:

> had she liv'd before the siege of Troy,
> Helen, whose beauty summon'd Greece to arms,
> ...
> Had not been nam'd in Homer's Iliads:
> ...
> Or had those wanton poets, for whose birth
> Old Rome was proud, but gaz'd a while on her,
> Nor Lesbia nor Corinna had been nam'd: *The music sounds and she dies.*
> What, is she dead? Techelles, draw thy sword,
> ...
> And we descend into th' infernal vaults,
> To hale the Fatal Sisters by the hair,
> And throw them in the triple moat of hell.
>
> (*2 Tamburlaine* II.iv.86–100)

Through the initial comparison between Helen and Zenocrate, Marlowe's speech compels us to align the epic genre of the *Iliad* with the tragic genre of *Tamburlaine*. Yet the subsequent conjoining of Ovid's mistress, Corinna, with Tamburlaine's wife appears arresting. Soon as Tamburlaine *names* 'Corinna,' Zenocrate '*dies*.' This arresting conjunction appears to manage a 'career' moment, as if Marlowe were announcing an Ovidian metamorphosis of amatory poetry into tragedy. Such an announcement, we may recall, concludes the collection of elegies featuring Corinna: 'Tender Love's mother, a new poet get; / ... / Horned Bacchus greater fury doth distil, / A greater ground with great horse is to till. / Weak elegies, delightful Muse, farewell' (*Ovid's Elegies* III.xiv[xv].1, 17–19).

Thus the appearance of the Ovidian Corinna, the Homeric Helen, and the Marlovian Zenocrate within a single speech suggests a conjunction of elegy, tragedy, and epic. This conjunction bids us to be suspicious of Tamburlaine's reduction of Ovid to his conventional pose – and his Elizabethan reputation – as a 'wanton poet.' As we saw in chapter 1, Ovid complicates this identity for posterity in the *Tristia* by constructing two 'Ovids': Ovid the wanton poet of elegy, and Ovid the poet of the *grandia vela*. Marlowe's passage contains this complication. That he has his eye on *Amores* III.xv may be confirmed by his inclusion of Catullus, who appears in line 7 of that elegy: 'in Catull Verone [joys].' Since this line also mentions Virgil ('in Virgil Mantua joys'), we may need to under-read Marlowe's Zenocrate passage with this great 'Rom[an]' epicist, especially Marlowe's lines on Homeric epic – a strategy Ovid himself had deployed (*Amores* II.i.29–36, xviii.1–2). Similarly, we probably need to under-read the concluding lines of the passage with the great Roman tragedian, Seneca, as Marlowe's references to 'infernal vaults,' 'Fatal Sisters,' and 'triple moat of hell' suggest, and as the action of violence expressive of rage confirms ('descend,' 'hale ... by the hair,' 'throw').[2]

The two subsequent lines concluding Tamburlaine's speech suggest that Marlowe is indeed staging his own *cursus*, for they anticipate or imitate the author's own lyric voice in 'The Passionate Shepherd to His Love': 'And if thou pitiest Tamburlaine the Great, / Come down from heaven and live with me again' (117–18). As in *Dido*, in *Tamburlaine* Marlowe advertises his own authoring of tragedy.

Final evidence of this project appears through the image underlying the Latin word *cursus*: the chariot. Marlowe's most famous use of this image occurs in *2 Tamburlaine*, where it tracks the rise and fall of the Phaethon-like protagonist. As Timothy J. Reiss argues, Marlowe uses the Phaethon-chariot to metaphorize 'discourse as power' (116; see 107, 130–1). Thus, when Tamburlaine drives his chariot most famously – 'Holla, ye pamper'd jades of Asia' (IV.iii.1) – he stages Christopher Marlowe making the 'ultima meta' from Ovidian amatory poetry to the 'area maior' of Senecan tragedy.

It is during the 'pamper'd jades' scene that Marlowe includes his most famous 'borrowing' from Spenser: the 'almond tree' simile describing Tamburlaine's Arthurian crown.[3] Indeed, Marlowe includes the simile when describing how Tamburlaine drives his chariot into Samarcanda: 'Thorough the streets, ... / I'll ride in golden armour like the sun ... / Then in my coach, like Saturn's royal son / Mounted his shining chariot gilt with fire, ... / So will I ride through Samarcanda streets' (114–30). Through this staging strategy, Marlowe contextualizes his Ovidian *cursus* in terms of Spenser's Virgilian *cursus*.

Scourging Kingdoms

As we have seen, Marlowe constructs the interlock of literary career, professional rivalry, and counter-nationhood in the prologue to *1 Tamburlaine*, which we may look at now in some detail:

From jigging veins of rhyming mother-wits,
And such conceits as clownage keeps in pay,
We'll lead you to the stately tent of war,
Where you shall hear the Scythian Tamburlaine

Threat'ning the world with high astounding terms,
And scourging kingdoms with his conquering sword.

(1 Tamburlaine Prologue 1–6)

Most critics observe that Marlowe here is expressing 'his contempt for the popular theatre of the day' and 'his preference for a serious and elevated theme.'[4] A few critics, however, do acknowledge that Marlowe is also imitating Spenser's projected Virgilian turn from pastoral to epic in the *October* eclogue:

Abandon then the base and viler clowne,
Lyft up thy selfe out of the lowly dust:
And sing of bloody Mars, of wars, of giusts,
Turne thee to those, that weld the awful crowne.
To doubted Knights, whose woundlesse armour rusts,
And helmes unbruzed wexen dayly browne.[5]

(October 37–42)

In both passages, writers advertise their progression from a lower to a higher genre. Both represent this progression through identical images: clownage to war. Both identify similar paradigms to trace the progression: Marlowe represents comedic pastoral as a low-cost and subservient jig, with epic as a martial theatre of state; Spenser represents pastoral as a low-based heap of dust from which the young poet must arise, with epic as a military display of royal awe and courtly courage. And both situate the poet's career within the patronage system: Marlowe, cynically ('keeps in pay'; see Leech, *Christopher Marlowe* 42); Spenser, hopefully ('Turne thee to those').

The differences between the two passages are also striking. For instance, Spenser weds the 'crowne' of the sovereign with the 'helmes' of her 'knights' as a synecdoche for epic – a wedding that Marlowe may rewrite when he appropriates Prince Arthur's martial helmet through Tamburlaine's plundered crown. Similarly, Marlowe changes Spenser's self-reflexive, lyrical, 'sing[ing]' poet to his own, equally self-reflexive, dramatic, listening audience ('you shall hear'). Finally, in the last two lines quoted above, Marlowe redraws an important equation between language and action, poetry and empire, when he conjoins 'high astounding terms, / And ... conquering sword.'[6]

At the end of the prologue, Marlowe relies on the conventional trope for the poem, the 'glass' or mirror, to contest Spenser's prophetic poetics: 'View but his picture in this tragic glass, / And then applaud his fortunes as you please' (7–8).⁷ In *The Faerie Queene*, Spenser repeatedly relies on the mirror to represent the specular power of his Virgilian epic. In the Proem to Book II, for instance, he instructs Queen Elizabeth: 'In this faire mirrhour maist behold thy face, / And thine owne realmes in lond of Faery' (4).⁸ Spenser's Queen is to view his poem as a mirror reflecting both her own beauty and her own country, and her sight is to motivate her to the 'great rule of Temp'raunce' (5). Spenser's poetic glass is ultimately comedic and romantic.

Marlowe's 'glass' is 'tragic.' Yet initially Marlowe follows Spenser in holding up his work as a mirror into which the audience can gaze: 'View but his picture.' Like Spenser again, Marlowe wants his audience to respond: 'applaud his fortunes.' But, unlike Spenser, Marlowe grants the audience freedom to applaud Tamburlaine 'as you please.' While Marlowe's strategy relating playwright and audience is within keeping of Elizabethan theatrical convention, it subtly manages an unjudgmental poetics designed to contest the New Poet's poetics of judgment.⁹

By recalling Greenblatt and Helgerson, we may speculate that Marlowe in his prologue is fashioning his amateur identity as an Elizabethan professional dramatist out of Spenser's laureate art. In *his* inaugural work, Marlowe presents himself as a serious rival to the New Poet.

This thesis explains many features of *Tamburlaine 1 and 2*, but it also entreats us to observe Marlowe here forging a place for himself out of and within the Elizabethan literary system. The four relevant features highlight the 'high astounding terms' through which Marlowe situates himself in this system. Strikingly, the terms are of action, ambition, metamorphosis, and power. They are naturally the main terms by which Spenser advertises himself in *The Shepheardes Calender* and the 1590 *Faerie Queene*. What characterizes the conjunction is what Greenblatt observes in only one example: Marlowe transfers to Tamburlaine the terms Spenser selects for himself.

First, whereas Spenser presents himself turning from pastoral to epic, Marlowe presents Tamburlaine as a shepherd usurping the title of a king. Second, whereas Spenser confidently advertises himself as the poet of *translatio imperii*, Marlowe shows Tamburlaine brutally migrating his empire from east to west. Third, whereas Spenser introduces himself as the new Protestant poet of wedded love, Marlowe depicts his king's wooing of and marriage to the Egyptian princess Zenocrate as an 'offensive rape' (*1 Tamb* III.ii.6; see Shepard 749). And fourth, whereas Spenser vaunts the *telos* of his verse to be an intimate relation between poetic and martial fame and Christian glory, Marlowe presents Tamburlaine exploding this relation.

Marlowe's appropriation of Spenser's self-reflexive terms and actions permits us to characterize the interchange between the two poets as 'metadiscursive' – as discourse about discourse (see Berger, *Revisionary Play* 462). In its most comprehensive form, the intertextual discourse between the mighty opposites *is* career-oriented. This is quite precisely the case, since the documented borrowings permit us to witness Marlowe imitating Spenser in the four discursive domains that the New Poet fuses in his idea of a literary career: artistic, political, erotic, and theological. Read from this perspective, the *Tamburlaine* plays, which often hint at Tamburlaine's poetic powers, function as Marlowe's critically charged, metadiscursive project – his public and dramatic attempt to overgo Spenser as England's new national poet. As Zenocrate inscribes Tamburlaine's powerful sense of metadiscursive competition, '[h]is talk [is] much sweeter than the Muses' song' (*1 Tamb* III.ii.50). Thus a treasured commonplace of Marlowe criticism – 'Tamburlaine is a poet' (Hope 53) – has a special historical context. The many documented borrowings from Spenser in the two plays insist that much of what we say about Tamburlaine we see as Marlowe's competitive rewriting of Spenser.[10]

'Underlying Sameness'

Critics have not pursued the significance of Greenblatt's observation that what Spenser assigns to himself Marlowe assigns to Tamburlaine. For the most part, they have pursued the other side of the coin: the significance of Marlowe's assigning to Tamburlaine the speeches he does. In relating author to protagonist, critics divide into two camps.

The first, the 'romantic,' draws an equation between Marlowe and Tamburlaine, as represented by G.K. Hunter: 'The creative daring of *Tamburlaine*'s author, his clear intention to defy theatrical orthodoxy, mirrors exactly the creative daring of his hero.'[11] This impulse emerges from Marlowe's contemporary antagonists, for in 1588 Robert Greene criticizes Marlowe for 'daring God out of heaven with that Atheist Tamburlan' (rpt. in MacLure, ed., *Marlowe* 29), while in 1593 Gabriel Harvey criticizes the dramatist for his 'tamberlaine contempt' (rpt. in MacLure 40).[12] If we agree that Marlowe establishes an equation between himself and his protagonist, we can, from the perspective of the present argument, read the two plays as an advertisement for himself as the shepherd who becomes a king, the rival to the New Poet, who was advertising himself in similarly 'high astounding terms.'

The second camp of critics, the 'ironic,' denies an equation between Marlowe and Tamburlaine, as represented by Roy W. Battenhouse: 'Certainly, ... there is no very good reason for identifying Marlowe with his stage-character Tamburlaine.'[13] If we agree that Marlowe distances himself from Tamburlaine, we can, from the perspective of the present argument, assume that Marlowe is criticizing the shepherd who becomes a king.

While Battenhouse's 'ironic' reading has the limitations that most critics now assign to it, we may wish to pause a little more over his argument than recent critics have done. In particular, we may wish to follow his lead in order to link Marlowe's detachment from Tamburlaine with Marlowe's imitation of Spenser. We may do so to reverse and then revise his formulation.

Specifically, we may align the division between the two camps of critics with a strategy identified by Greenblatt, in which Marlowe's genius resides in his power to construct a single narrative having both an orthodox and an unorthodox significance: Marlowe condemns Tamburlaine as an anti-Christian villain who succumbs to Christian authority; simultaneously, Marlowe exults in Tamburlaine as an anti-Christian hero who challenges Christian authority.[14] We may then superimpose Marlowe's dramatic strategy in representing Tamburlaine – what Charles Nicholl calls 'these ambidextrous responses' (170) – onto the topic of Marlowe's imitation of Spenser.

Who is the shepherd who becomes a king?

Literally, he is 'Tamburlaine.'

In Marlowe's evocation of Tamburlaine as an anti-Christian hero who challenges the orthodoxy, the Scythian Shepherd inscribes Christopher Marlowe, a serious rival in the Virgilian program to England's New Poet. But in Marlowe's evocation of Tamburlaine as an anti-Christian villain who succumbs to Christian authority, he inscribes Edmund Spenser, the 'masked' pretender to Christian authority. The *Tamburlaine* plays are simultaneously an advertisement for Marlowe as England's new poet and a critique of Spenser as the old poet.

Marlowe's strategy resituates the Virgilian progression within a 'tragical discourse,' and his professional goal is to deauthorize the medium of published verse in order to construct a new zone of authority for the (disreputable) Elizabethan stage.

What renders Marlowe's new zoning project – his rival poetics – unique in the history of poetic rivalry is his strategy of relying on *one* dramatic figure – Tamburlaine – to represent 'the figure of the rival poet' – *both* the writerly self and the artistic Other: both himself and Spenser.[15] Greenblatt appears on the verge of discovering this strategy when analysing Marlowe's 'borrowing' of Spenser's Arthurian plume: 'even as we are struck by the radical difference, we are haunted by the vertiginous possibility of an underlying sameness. What if Arthur and Tamburlaine are not separate and opposed? What if they are two faces of the same thing, embodiments of the identical power?' (*Renaissance Self-Fashioning* 224).

Two faces of the same thing ... What if? Greenblatt is not the first to propose a haunting similarity between the mighty opposites. Our very first comparison – by Leigh Hunt in 1844 – is eloquent on the possibility of an 'underlying sameness': Marlowe's 'imagination, like Spenser's, haunted those purely poetic regions of ancient fabling and modern rapture, of beautiful forms and passionate expressions, which they were the first to render the common property of inspiration, and whence their language drew "empyreal air." Marlowe and Spenser are the first of our poets who perceived the beauty of words' (rpt. in MacLure, ed., *Marlowe* 91). Most likely, Spenser would be horrified. He worked hard to dissociate his art from the kind Marlowe popularized, but it is striking that some of his original readers – Lord Burleigh, for instance – mistook the one for the other (*FQ* IV.Pr.1; see Hamilton, ed., *FQ* 426). In the *Tamburlaine* plays, Marlowe succeeds in challenging Spenser's authority precisely by representing their underlying sameness.[16]

Masked in a Shepherd's Weed

Marlowe's counter-Spenserian inscription of Tamburlaine is clear in the first or artistic dimension: his imitation of the Proem to Book I of *The Faerie Queene*. As we have seen, Spenser here announces his typological fulfilment of his *October* advertisement: 'Lo I the man, whose Muse whilome did maske, ... in lowly Shepheards weeds, / Am now enforst ... / For trumpets sterne to chaunge mine Oaten reeds' (1). In this passage, Spenser identifies himself as the author of *The Shepheardes Calender* and announces his generic turn from Virgilian pastoral to Virgilian epic. He does so through the theatrical image of the 'maske.'

Repeatedly, Marlowe reminds us that his hero is a shepherd who becomes a king. We first encounter the idea on the title page of the 1590 edition: 'Tamburlaine the Great. Who, from a Scythian Shepheard by his rare and woonderfull Conquests, became a most puissant and mightye Monarque.' We encounter the idea again in Richard Jones's *Dedicatory Epistle*: 'I have here published in print for your sakes the two tragical discourses of the Scythian shepherd Tamburlaine, that became so great a conqueror and so mighty a monarch.' Both prefatory advertisements alert us to the central feature of Marlowe's ensuing narrative.

In his first appearance, Tamburlaine thus inscribes his identity to Zenocrate in Spenserian terms: 'I am a lord, for so my deeds shall prove, / And yet a shepherd by my parentage' (*1 Tamb* I.ii.34–5). Then, in his first act, Tamburlaine exchanges attire with Spenserian precedent: 'Lie here, ye weeds that I disdain to wear! / This complete armour and this curtle-axe / Are adjuncts more beseeming Tamburlaine' (41–3). As critics observe, in exchanging shepherd's 'weeds' for a warrior-king's 'armour,' the oaten reed for the 'curtle-axe,' Marlowe repeats Spenser's 'chaunge' from pastoral to epic in the Proem to *Faerie Queene* I. Applying the dramatic strategy of *ambidexterity* identified by Nicholl, we can say that Marlowe is boldly advertising his own generic progression ('Lie here, ye weeds'), yet criticizing Spenser for arrogance in advertising his ('disdain to wear ... more becoming').

Subsequently, Tamburlaine's presumptive leap in status is what galls a real king, Cosroe:

> What means this devilish shepherd to aspire
> With such a giantly presumption,
> To cast up hills against the face of heaven,
> And dare the force of angry Jupiter?
>
> (*1 Tamburlaine* II.vi.1–4)

These lines are especially fraught with Spenserian freight. Cosroe identifies Tamburlaine in terms and metaphors identical to those with which Spenser represents Orgoglio – a 'Geant' (*FQ* I.vii.8) of 'presumption' (10) who uses his oak club to 'cast ... up a mount of clay' (viii.9).[17] Marlowe rewrites Spenser's presentation of himself as a shepherd who becomes a king. For Marlowe, Spenser is a 'devilish shepherd' who becomes a proud 'giant.' Contrary to Spenser's presentation of himself, Marlowe's Spenser uses artistic 'force' to antagonize the deity.

Marlowe's word for Tamburlaine's presumption, 'dare,' recalls a famous line: 'His looks do menace heaven and dare the gods.' The line is famous because our first reference to Marlowe imitates it – Greene's 'daring God out of heaven with that Atheist Tamburlan.' In his extant writings, Marlowe uses the word 'dare' and its derivatives a total of forty-seven times, to the extent that the word functions as something of a Marlovian code word for 'atheism.'

The word 'dare' suggests aggressive verbal competition, but it also suggests competition within a social, political, or theological hierarchy: an individual lower in status challenges one higher in status. The linguistic competition between lower and higher alerts us to a generic significance: the

Virgilian progression from the lowly genre of pastoral to the higher genre of epic. For Marlowe, the word 'dare' can function as a metonym for his rivalry with Spenser (cf. Daiches 79; and Bentson 209, 217–18).

In his poetry, Spenser uses the word 'dare' a total of eighty-five times. In *The Shepheardes Calender,* for instance, he most often uses the word to designate pastoral competition. In *August,* Willye asks Perigot, 'what shalbe the game, / Wherefore with myne thou dare thy musick matche?' (1–2). Later, Willye antagonizes Perigot by repeating the challenge: 'if in rymes with me thou dare strive, / Such fond fantsies shall soone be put to flight' (21–2). This time Perigot meets the challenge: 'Never shall be sayde that Perigot was dared' (24; see *December* 43–8, and 'Envoy' 9).

In presenting Cosroe criticizing Tamburlaine as a 'devilish shepherd' with 'giantly presumption' who '*dare[s]* the force of angry Jupiter,' Marlowe is both implicating Spenser for his arrogant, aristocratic progression from pastoral to epic and making way for himself as a new counter-Virgilian artist.

We can see this implication even more concretely in one of the most intriguing instances of the typology of intertextuality. Pausing with his crown, Cosroe's brother, the weak king Mycetes, remarks:

Accurs'd be he that first invented war!
They knew not, ah, they knew not, simple men,
How those were hit by pelting cannon-shot
Stand staggering like a quivering aspen-leaf
Fearing the force of Boreas' boist'rous blasts.

(1 Tamburlaine II.iv.1–5; emphasis added)

Critics find the origin of the 'aspen-leaf' simile in Golding's 1567 translation of the *Metamorphoses*: 'trembling like an Aspen leaf' (III.46). Thus they find a dual origin for a similar line in *Titus Andronicus*: 'Tremble like aspen leaves upon a lute' (II.iv.45).[18] The origin of both Shakespeare's and Marlowe's lines, however, probably lies in Spenser, who in turn probably owes it to Golding: 'And tremble like a leaf of Aspin greene' (*FQ* I.ix.51).[19] The likelihood of Marlowe's borrowing increases when we realize that the line following the 'aspen-leaf' simile, 'Fearing the force of Boreas' boist'rous blasts,' probably derives from Spenser as well.[20]

Marlowe's 'aspen-leaf' line forms an engaging variation of the typology of intertextuality, for the diachronic intertext is not Ovid, but Golding's Ovid. Marlowe's use of Golding to target Spenser displays an acute reading of the Legend of Holiness, since Spenser's 'aspen leaf' line occurs in the climactic stanza of Book I of *The Faerie Queene* – when the Redcrosse Knight, succumbing to Despayre, reaches for the villain's knife; the simile captures Redcrosse's fear of death, and in the next stanza Spenser's figure of Christian truth, Una, will intervene.[21] Marlowe's repositioning of the simile with respect to Mycetes suggests that the playwright is indeed 'clout[ing]' (II.iv.8) the 'sovereign of song' (*November* 25).

In *1 Tamburlaine*, as critics note (Crawford 204), the Scythian Shepherd targets Spenser again in order to justify his own self-metamorphosis and quest for fame: 'Jove sometime masked in a shepherd's weed, / And by those steps that he hath scal'd the heavens / May we become immortal like the gods' (I.ii.199–201). The lines reproduce the process of competitive imitation that Marlowe is enacting. Not simply does Tamburlaine become immortal by imitating Jove the masking shepherd, but Marlowe achieves fame by imitating the masking shepherd Spenser.[22]

Marlowe's metadiscursive inscription of his hero as a rewriting of Spenser is also clear in the second or political dimension: his imitation of Spenser's program of *translatio imperii*.[23] Not merely is Marlowe's hero a shepherd who becomes a king, but repeatedly he is 'the monarch of the East' (*1 Tamb* I.i.43, I.ii.185; *2 Tamb* III.ii.22; see *1 Tamb* II.vii.62) who brutally moves his empire westward. In *1 Tamburlaine*, for instance, the king proclaims,

> Those walled garrisons will I subdue,
> And write myself great lord of Africa.
> So from the East unto the furthest West
> Shall Tamburlaine extend his puissant arm.
>
> (*1 Tamburlaine* III.iii.244–7)

Critics have glossed this passage – and the similar one in *2 Tamburlaine* ('Stretching your conquering arms from east to west' [I.iii.97]) – by turning to Spenser's description of the Church of England in *Faerie Queene* I, where the sovereign 'scepters' of Una's ancestors 'stretcht from East to Westerne shore' (I.i.5; see Bakeless 1: 207). But Spenser's line is a religious and political version of the translation of empire that he personalizes in *October* and that is the most direct origin, especially of the second *Tamburlaine* passage, as the nearly identical phrasing implies. Continuing his description of the 'awful crown' of epic, Spenser writes: 'There may thy Muse display her fluttryng wing, / And stretch her selfe at large from East to West' (*October* 43–4). Spenser's advertisement for *translatio imperii* helps explain Marlowe's otherwise peculiar notion that Tamburlaine *writes* empire through kingly action.

That Marlowe's paradigm for 'east to west' has specifically Spenserian evocations is clear immediately before Tamburlaine changes his pastoral costume for that of epic and tragedy:

> I am a lord, for so my deeds shall prove,
> And yet a shepherd by my parentage.
> But lady, this fair face and heavenly hue
> Must grace his bed that conquers Asia,
> And means to be a terror to the world,
> Measuring the limits of his empery
> By east and west, as Phoebus doth his course.
>
> (*1 Tamburlaine* I.ii.34–40)

In this speech, Tamburlaine identifies himself to his future wife as a shepherd who has become a king; he dramatically enacts the announced 'chaunge' by exchanging shepherd's weeds for the armour of a 'lord'; and he inscribes the arc of his 'empery' from 'east to west.' Marlowe both advertises himself as the new poet of empire and criticizes Spenser as the false poet of empire.

As the above episode anticipates, Marlowe's metadiscursive inscription of his hero as a rewriting of Spenser is clear in the third or erotic dimension: his imitation of Spenser's Protestant representation of erotic desire.[24] In addition to Tamburlaine's turn from shepherd to king and his translation of empire from east to west, Marlowe's hero woos Zenocrate as an act of male mastery – a critique of Spenser's falsely imitated Ariostan claims to sympathy for the female sex (*FQ* I.iii.1–2) and his equally hypocritical Chaucerian assertions about the mutuality between the sexes (*FQ* III.i.25).

The New Poet opens the 1590 *Faerie Queene* by saying that he will 'sing of Knights and Ladies gentle deeds,' that 'Fierce warres and faithfull loves shall moralize my song,' and that therefore he depends on inspiration from both Venus and Cupid to write his national epic praising Gloriana (I.Pr.1–4). Battenhouse notes that 'it is probable that the captured Zenocrate's distress in *Tamburlaine* owes something to distressed damsels in the *Faerie Queene*,' and he has followed up on Schoeneich's work (60–9) to argue that 'Spenser's description of Duessa's history in *F.Q.* I.2 ... is an important source for Marlowe's story of Zenocrate' (190). The most obvious parallel is that Zenocrate and Duessa occupy the same regal position; both are the Queen of Persia. Duessa wears a crown 'like a Persian mitre' (I.ii.13), while Zenocrate, as wife to the 'King of Persia' (*1 Tamb* II.vii.56), is 'Queen of Persia' (V.i. 492). As Marlowe's seventy-one references to Persia in the two plays indicate, he identifies Tamburlaine and Zenocrate as the King and

Queen of Persia in part to contest Spenser's Protestant project – especially its amatory dimension, as the foregrounding of the marital relationship indicates.

Tamburlaine's soliloquy in *1 Tamburlaine*, in which he debates whether to abide by his humanist-based code of manly reason or to listen to his new romantic-based code of feminine passion, seems deeply indebted to Spenser. 'Ah, fair Zenocrate, divine Zenocrate,' he begins, 'Where Beauty, mother to the Muses, sits, / And comments volumes with her ivory pen' (V.i.135, 144–5):

> What is beauty, saith my sufferings, then?
> If all the pens that ever poets held
> Had fed the feeling of their masters' thoughts,
> And every sweetness that inspir'd their hearts,
> Their *minds*, and muses on *admired* themes;
> If all the heavenly quintessence they still
> From their *immortal* flowers of poesy,
> Wherein as in a *mirror* we perceive
> The *highest* reaches of a human wit;
> ...
> But how unseemly is it for my sex,
> My discipline of arms and chivalry,
> ...
> To harbour thoughts effeminate and faint!
>
> (*1 Tamburlaine* V.i.160–77; emphasis added)

The 'mirror' image here recalls the passage in *October* in which Piers explains to Cuddie about the Neoplatonic power of Colin Clout's love:

> for love does teach him climbe so *hie*,
> And lyftes him up out of the loathsome myre:
> Such *immortall mirrhor*, as he doth *admire*,
> Would rayse ones *mynd* above the starry skie.[25]
>
> (*October* 91–6; emphasis added)

Whereas Piers imagines the male's mental admiration of the female's immortally beautiful mirror as the vehicle for Neoplatonic inspiration and transcendence, Tamburlaine problematizes the process, fearing its effeminizing violation of his martial code. The lines with which Tamburlaine's soliloquy concludes – 'The most obscure passage in the text of the play'

(Harper 77) – appear to imitate Spenser's passage on his turn from pastoral to epic, as William Baldwin's analysis suggests ('Genesis [I]'), but the language is more widely Spenserian, as is the basic thought, which the play is at pains to explode: that 'love and honour ... can never be incompatible, since love of beauty provides the inspiration necessary to the heroism of the warrior' (Harper 77).

Tamburlaine concludes his soliloquy by recording that he feels

> the lovely warmth of shepherds' flames
> And march [or mask]²⁶ in cottages of strowed reeds
> Shall give the world to note, for all my birth,
> That virtue solely is the sum of glory,
> And fashions men with true nobility.
>
> (*1 Tamburlaine* V.i.186–90)

Assimilating claims for the virtue of eros to the career model of shepherd and king, Marlowe relies on key words from Spenser's epic: 'virtue,' 'fashions,' and 'true nobility.' For, in *The Letter to Ralegh*, Spenser states that the 'generall end ... of all the booke is to *fashion* a gentleman or *noble* person in *vertuous* and gentle discipline' (3: 485; emphasis added). Marlowe echoes the word 'discipline' earlier in the soliloquy when Tamburlaine refers to 'My discipline of arms and chivalry,' a euphonious parody of Una's 'discipline of faith and veritie' (*FQ* I.vi.31). In *Tamburlaine*, Marlowe presents his protagonist as the lover and husband of Zenocrate to criticize Spenser's advertisement of himself as the national poet of love and marriage, and thereby to map out the domain of homoeroticism lying latent in the play (*pace* Kuriyama). For Marlowe, love of female beauty inspires masculine violence, both sexual and social, as Tamburlaine's initial 'lawless rapine from a silly maid' reveals (*1 Tamb* I.ii.10), and as his final response to Zenocrate's death confirms: 'This cursed town will I consume with fire, / Because this place bereft me of my love' (*2 Tamb* II.iv.137–8).²⁷

Tamburlaine's soliloquy also introduces us to our last 'high astounding term' through which Marlowe relies on metadiscourse to rewrite Spenser: 'glory.' The idea of fame and glory runs powerfully throughout the *Tamburlaine* plays – to the extent that the idea dominates the text like perhaps no other. Cosroe calls Tamburlaine 'the man of fame, / The man that in the forehead of his fortune / Bears figures of renown and miracle' (*1 Tamb* II.i.2–4), and Tamburlaine himself claims that his goal is to 'spread ... [his] fame through hell and up to heaven' (V.i.465).²⁸

In *October*, as the already quoted image of the winged imperial Muse indicates, Spenser relies on an avian image of fame to represent his Virgilian career model: 'For Colin fittes such famous flight to scanne' (88; see *Spenser's Famous Flight* 14–18, 3–37). Avian imagery runs as a strong current throughout the *Tamburlaine* plays. Often, Marlowe represents fame as winged. In the passage in which he imitates Spenser's masking as a shepherd and in which he claims immortality for his own shepherd, Tamburlaine asks Theridamus and others to join with him in his 'mean estate,' for his 'name and honour shall be spread / As far as Boreas claps his brazen wings' (*1 Tamb* I.ii.202–6). Repeatedly, Marlowe stages the career process of a shepherd becoming a king in order to critique the terms and actions organizing Spenser's career.[29]

But Marlowe's most arresting rewriting of Spenser's 'famous flight' occurs when Cosroe tells Tamburlaine to 'whet' his 'winged sword, / And lift thy lofty arm into the clouds' (*1 Tamb* II.iii.51–2), with this response from Tamburlaine:

> See where it is, the keenest curtle-axe
> That e'er made passage thorough Persian arms!
> These are the wings shall make it fly as swift
> As doth the lightning or the breath of heaven,
> And kill as sure as it swiftly flies.
>
> (*1 Tamburlaine* II.iii.55–9)

The representation of a winged curtle-axe appears curious, if not arresting: a *winged* curtle-axe? Marlowe may be accommodating the topos of the winged arrow (*Odyssey* XXI.404–11) to the armory of his Scythian hero; but the topos had become a standard figure for discourse – a military version of Homer's 'winged words' (Cheney, *Spenser's Famous Flight* 271, n. 23). In this context, Tamburlaine's quest for fame as an act of violence appropriates the authority of 'heaven.' This appropriation reverses Spenser's program in which the quest for earthly fame coheres with Christian glory.

Furthermore, we should probably understand Marlowe's passage in light of the instrument by which Spenser makes his famous flight, the avian based *quill* or *pen*, advertised throughout the *Calender* and Spenser's poetry generally (Cheney, *Spenser's Famous Flight* 265, n. 45). By rewriting Spenser's winged pastoral quill as Tamburlaine's winged epic curtle-axe, Marlowe identifies his art as an epic drama of violent infamy – hence, Tamburlaine's graphic hawking metaphor in which the 'Legions of spirits ... / Direct our bullets ..., / And make your strokes to wound the senseless air,' so that

'Victory begins to take her flight' to their stately tents of war (*1 Tamb* III.iii.156–60).

But Marlowe's clearest response to Spenser's famous flight occurs when Theridamus tells Olympia of Tamburlaine's project:

And eagle's wings join'd to her feather'd breast,
Fame hovereth, sounding of her golden trump,
That to the adverse poles of that straight line
Which measureth the glorious frame of heaven
The name of mighty Tamburlaine is spread.

(*2 Tamburlaine* III.iv.62–6)

Here Marlowe reduces the famous flight to the perfect bliss and sole felicity of an earthly crown. Earthly fame is irreconcilable with Christian glory.

In this career context, not simply Greenblatt's generalized context of heroic and artistic 'identity,' may we read Tamburlaine's appropriation of Arthur's helmet – Marlowe's master-trope for a tragedy of violent infamy. Spenser had represented Arthur's 'haughtie helmet' (I.vii.31) as topped by a 'loftie crest' with a 'bunch of haires discolourd diversly,' which 'shake' and 'daunce for jollity' (32),

Like to an Almond tree ymounted hye
On top of greene Selinis all alone,
With blossomes brave bedecked daintily;
Whose tender locks do tremble every one
At every little breath, that under heaven is blowne.

(*Faerie Queene* I.vii.32)

In the 'Almond tree,' Spenser alludes to Numbers 17: 5–8, in which Aaron's rod blossoms and bears ripe almonds, revealing him to be ordained by God for glory; in 'greene Selinis,' Spenser alludes to Virgil's *palmosa Selinus* in the *Aeneid* (III.705), signifying the town of the victor's palm – a representation for military victory and its reward, the palm or fame (Hamilton, ed., *FQ* 103). While 'ymounted hye' and 'all alone' both suggest pride and individuality, 'jollity,' 'daunce,' 'tender,' and 'tremble' all suggest a playful humility – a paradigm of individual virtue that Spenser calls in *Epithalamion* 'proud humility' (306). Moreover, Spenser locates the Christian almond tree on 'top' of the classical hill – a fusing of classical and Christian, as well as an accurate model of the hierarchical relation between the two (Christian on top, classical on bottom). By fusing Scripture with Virgil, Spenser can use his 'greene Selinis' simile as a trope for the cohesion between Arthur's military fame and his Christian glory.

By contrast, Marlowe describes Tamburlaine's crown this way:

> And in my helm a triple *plume* shall spring,
> Spangled with diamonds, dancing in the air,
> To *note* me emperor of the three-fold world:
> Like to an almond tree y-mounted high
> Upon the lofty and celestial mount
> Of *ever-green* Selinus, quaintly deck'd
> With blooms more white than Erycina's brows,
> Whose tender blossoms tremble every one
> At every little breath that thorough heaven is blown.
>
> (*2 Tamburlaine* IV.iii.116–24; emphasis added)

This is close to 'plagiarism'; but, as critics note, Marlowe *is* 'imitating' in the Renaissance sense: borrowing and transforming. Greenblatt writes: 'Lines that for Spenser belong to the supreme figure of civility, the chief upholder of the Order of Maidenhead, the worshipful servant of Gloriana, for Marlowe belong to the fantasy life of the Scythian Scourge of God' (224). As noted in the introduction, however, it is Derrida who best demarcates Marlowe's deconstructive strategy, for Marlowe does not 'destroy from the outside' but 'take[s] accurate aim' by 'inhabiting' Spenser's deep 'structures' (24).[30]

In his display of deconstructive metadiscourse ('note me'), Marlowe inhabits Spenser's structures through four deft changes. First, he adds the word 'ever' to Spenser's simple 'green,' creating the phrase 'ever-green,' perhaps to clarify the *laurel* greening of Selinus – a trope for the poet's art. Second, Marlowe inserts the line comparing the blossoms on the almond tree to 'Erycina's brows' (the brows of Venus); this insertion overwrites Spenser's fusion of Virgil and Scripture with an Ovidian-based trope that eroticizes the entire simile.[31] Third, Marlowe replaces Spenser's orthodox troping of the hierarchical Christian cosmos '*under* heaven' with the non-hierarchical troping '*thorough* heaven,' further deconstructing Spenser's Christian ideology. Finally, Marlowe clarifies the avian base of the crown image, 'plume' (as opposed to Spenser's non-avian 'crest' and 'haires'). Tamburlaine's 'triple plume' has more than the obvious military significance. The plume is a bird's feather – a quill: the poet's writing implement. Thus, Tamburlaine's 'plume' functions as a metonym for the equation between words and action, 'high astounding terms' and 'conquering sword.'

In *Edward II*, Marlowe will unpack the metadiscursive significance of the military plume in a speech by Mortimer, who interrogates Edward darkly: 'When wert thou in the field with banner spread? / But once! And then thy soldiers marched like players, / ... ; and thyself, ... / Nodding and shaking of thy spangled crest, / Where women's favours hung like labels down' (II.ii.181–6). The metadiscursive significance of the plume emerges even more powerfully when we recall, as Hamlet does, that tragic actors wore not simply the buskins on their feet, but a 'forest of feathers' on their head.[32] Thus inscribed, Tamburlaine invents his return flight to his origin – not Spenser's New Jerusalem (*FQ* I.x.61), but Samarcanda, an eastern House of Pride, as Marlowe's documented borrowing here reveals (2 *Tamb* IV.iii.107 and *FQ* I.iv.4; see Gill, 'Marlowe'); not by the wings of Christian glory, but, as another documented borrowing reveals, on the martial chariot of Lucifera – 'drawn with princely eagles' (127 and *FQ* I.iv.17; see Crawford 261–2). Tamburlaine's motive? To '[b]e famous' (110).

The metadiscourse ordering the plume here throws into high relief the comment by Paul Alpers, who singles out the Selinus stanza as 'one of the most admired in *The Faerie Queene*' and suggests, 'following Eliot's acute observation ... , that Marlowe's "mighty line" owes as much to the additive, formulaic verse of *The Faerie Queene* as to any earlier blank verse' ('Style' 675). Alpers anticipates a salient point. In Tamburlaine's plume, Marlowe mimetically inscripts his Spenserian origin. But the dramatist rewrites that origin: *vertically, materially, tragically* – on the stage, on earth, in time: in a forest of feathers. This is *Marlowe's* famous flight.

Making the Rhyme Rage

We may conclude, then, by recalling the passage in *October* from which this chapter takes its title and in which Marlowe may formally find the genesis of his tragic art. Indeed, if Marlowe's two plays are about a shepherd who becomes a king, we can expect the imitative system in *Tamburlaine 1 and 2* to derive from both *The Shepheardes Calender* and *The Faerie Queene*. As we saw in chapter 2, the bulk of *October* shows Spenser revising the Virgilian career model of pastoral and epic with a four-genre model: Virgilian pastoral, Virgilian epic, Petrarchan love lyric, and the Augustinian-based hymn. We saw further that at least one of Spenser's major disciples, Michael Drayton, follows Spenser in shaping his literary career around this model. At the end of the eclogue, we also observed, Spenser appears to introduce an alternative, and even separate, model, which another disciple, Samuel Daniel, follows. In this model, the poet moves from Ovidian verse to tragedy and epic:

Who ever casts to compasse weightye prise,
And thinks to throwe out thondring words of threate:
Let powre in lavish cups and thriftie bitts of meate,
For Bacchus fruite is frend to Phoebus wise.
...
Thou kenst not Percie howe the ryme should rage.
O if my temples were distained with wine,
And girt in girlonds of wild Yvie twine,
How I could reare the Muse on stately stage,
And teache her tread aloft in bus-kin fine,
With queint Bellona in her equipage.

(October 103–14)

Is Marlowe in essence not born here, and with him Elizabethan tragedy? That alert analyst of the Elizabethan literary scene, Joseph Hall, implies as much when he echoes Spenser's phrasing to describe Marlowe in *Virgidemiae*: Marlowe 'vaunts his voyce' in 'thundring threats' (rpt. in MacLure, ed., *Marlowe* 41). Richard Levin believes that Marlowe is the Rival Poet of Shakespeare's *Sonnets*, and now Maurice Charney, James Shapiro, and Thomas Cartelli have brought the two dramatists into significant alignment.[33] But we must not forget that, in the Elizabethan literary system, Marlowe initially found his artistic genesis not in the plays of a fellow professional, but in the non-dramatic works of the 'Brytanne Orpheus' (R.S., *Commendatory Verse* to 1590 *FQ* 4:4).

In *Tamburlaine*, Marlowe drinks the Bacchic fruit, girts his head with the ever-green garland of wild Selinus, and rears the muse on stately stage. But unlike the gentle Daniel, he does not teach the muse to tread aloft in buskin *fine*, with Bellona *queint* in her equipage. Instead, he relies on alcohol to stage a metadiscursive poetics of violent infamy that powerfully contests the art of England's New Poet. What Marlowe contests *is* the famous flight, with its élitist artistic progression through the aristocratic Virgilian genres, its tyrannical political program of *translatio imperii*, its hypocritical Protestant doctrine of wedded love, and its huge claim to link poetic and martial fame with Christian glory. As Clarke Hulse says, Marlowe qualifies as 'an inspired poet' (96) in the Platonic tradition indebted to Orpheus, but 'Marlowe's inspiration appears to be of a dark kind; he is one of those whom Cicero feared would be made dangerous by their eloquence. One may wonder, in fact, if Marlowe is not Plato's first kind of madman, whose fury arises not from divinity, but from alcohol, lechery, or mental disturbance' (100).

In Tamburlaine's 'Threat'ning the world with high astounding terms,' Marlowe throws back to Spenser his 'thondring words of threate.' But in the process Marlowe teaches Elizabethan culture, including his great dramatic successor, the plumed swan of Avon, what Spenser had failed to teach, when he chose not to publish his now oblivious *Nine Comedies* or take the fiery Cuddie's advice to let the buskin walk on the Elizabethan stage, choosing instead to follow 'the olde famous Poete Chaucer' (E.K., *Dedicatory Epistle to SC* 1–2) in relocating dramatic tragedy within the lyric genre of the complaint: just how, when staging the stately tent of war, the Ovidian dramatist could make Bacchus a friend to Phoebus – and make the rhyme rage.

Machiavelli and the Play of Policy in *The Jew of Malta*

In the second triad, or 'plays of policy,' Marlowe appears to turn, at least in part, away from Spenser and Ovid towards 'Machiavelli' in order to flesh out the genre of tragedy. Una M. Ellis-Fermor's title for *The Jew of Malta*, *Edward II*, and *The Massacre at Paris*, 'the plays of policy,' identifies a conceptual common denominator in three quite different plays – the concept of 'policy' – and an archival common denominator in 'those methods and principles which, to Marlowe and his contemporaries, went under the name of Machiavellianism' (88). Such a grouping participates in a certain straining of the facts; the plays preceding this triad, *Tamburlaine 1 and 2*, writes Irving Ribner, constitute 'about as close an approximation of Machiavelli's central premises and conclusions as anywhere in Elizabethan writings' ('Marlowe and Machiavelli' 351).[1] Despite this caveat, the triadic grouping has an advantage in Marlowe studies because it isolates a distinct phase of Marlowe's dramatic career.

Indeed, the apparent shifts away from Spenser and Ovid provide a valuable clue as to how we are to respond to *The Jew of Malta*, *Edward II*, and *The Massacre at Paris*.[2] Given that the shifts are distinctly *literary* – away from dominant origins of intertextual rivalry – we may wish to characterize the change as career-oriented. We may then regroup the three works under a slightly revised heading: not 'plays of policy,' but 'the play of policy.' This heading draws attention to the metadiscursive way in which Marlowe transacts a career change, and it recalls what Stephen Greenblatt discovers as so dominant in *The Jew of Malta* – 'the will to play': 'The will to play flaunts society's cherished orthodoxies, embraces what the culture finds loathsome or frightening, transforms the serious into the joke and then unsettles the category of the joke by taking it seriously. For Barabas, as for Marlowe himself, this is play on the brink of an abyss, *absolute* play' ('Marlowe, Marx' 53).

Marlowe may turn to Machiavellianism in the second triad for his primary energy, but he does not absent either Ovid or Spenser from his felicity. In *The Jew of Malta*, he situates the genre of tragedy further within his counter-Spenserian Ovidian *cursus*. Now, however, he fleshes out 'Ovidian tragedy' by creating a new brand of European tragedy – the Machiavellian play of policy. As we shall see, he uses this 'play' to dramatize his own subjection and final resistance to the tyranny not simply of orthodox Christian culture, but more precisely of orthodox Christian 'letters' (Prologue 23). The letters he feels subjected to and finally resists are in part those of England's New Virgilian Poet. Consequently, we need to view *The Jew of Malta* within the typology of Marlowe's Ovidian *cursus*; to find in the story of a father using his daughter to combat orthodox authority a Spenserian intertext; and to sift through the play's recurrent metadrama for an imaginative record of Marlowe's own relation to the power structure of his time, especially Queen Elizabeth.[3] Quite impressively, *The Jew of Malta* records its own historicity, its own contextual production, as Heywood's 'Prologue to the Stage at the Cock-Pit' entreats: 'We know not how our play may pass this stage, / But by the best of poets in that age / *The Malta Jew* had being and was made' (1–3).[4]

'The tragedy of a Jew, / Who smiles': The Prologue, Machiavelli, Ovid

The first documented appearance of Machiavelli on the English stage constitutes a breathtaking career announcement. By presenting 'Machevill' speaking the part of the prologue, Marlowe inaugurates a new metadrama *about* the Machiavellian play of policy.

Given that critics place *The Jew of Malta* after both *Dido* and the *Tamburlaine* plays, we may indeed witness here a representational advertisement for a significant career modulation. In this play, unlike in the previous three, Marlowe continues the larger phase of 'tragedy' in the Ovidian *cursus* by relying on the English Machiavellian movement. As Machevill himself puts it:

> I come not, I,
> To read a lecture here in Britanie,
> But to present the tragedy of a Jew,
> Who smiles to see how full his bags are cramm'd;
> Which money was not got without my means.
>
> *(The Jew of Malta* Prologue 29–33)

If, as we think, Machevill concludes his prologue by drawing a curtain to

reveal Barabas in his counting-house (Bawcutt, ed. 199), we can see Machevill
as something like the very *mechanism* of 'the play of policy' itself – encapsu-
lating the roles of actor, director, and even stage-hand, all under the ordi-
nance of the author himself. Machevill's language *is* the language of the
author; he *does* what Marlowe does, as the auto-reflexive language of generic form reveals: 'I ... present the tragedy of a Jew.' Machevill is not simply
a prologue to a play, a spokesman for Barabas, or the ideological progenitor
of the play's energy; 'Machevill' is a linguistic and dramatic model for the
genre of play that Marlowe is penning: a Machiavellian 'tragedy' – a play of
'policy.'[5]

Thus, Heywood's 'Prologue Spoken at Court,' also prefacing his 1633
edition, supplies an interpretive clue: 'you shall find him still, / In all his
projects, a sound Machevill; / And that's his character' (7–9). This prologue's point is that Marlowe transmutes the real Machiavelli into a dramatic
paradigm. The dramatist converts the man into an artistic archetype – 'a
sound Machevill' – a dramatic 'character'; he metamorphoses Machiavellian
political philosophy into a dramatic *action* ('all his projects'); and he places
this character-as-actor within the theatrical medium, through which an
audience views a play: 'you shall find him still.' This is our first authoritative
indicator that Marlowe is inventing a new genre.[6]

Thus we should probably understand Marlowe's generic reinvention in
terms of his own programmatic statement: 'I ... / ... present the *tragedy* of
a Jew, / Who *smiles*.' Marlowe's reinvention does not simply fuse tragedy
and comedy (Eliot's original phrase is 'savage comic humour' [64]); he
reconfigures tragedy *as play* – theatrical play. He insists that tragedy is not
simply 'an imitation of an action' (Aristotle, *Poetics* 1449b.24), but a playwright's theatrical representation of his own personalized project, as
Ithamore's imitation of Marlowe hints: 'Shalt live with me and be my love'
(IV.ii.93).[7]

The Jew of Malta opens with a 'character' who misadvertises himself as
the product of Christian resurrection, or, to use Faustus's classical principle,
'Pythagoras' *metempsychosis*' (V.ii.107):

> Albeit the world think Machevill is dead,
> Yet was his soul but flown beyond the Alps,
> And now the Guise is dead, is come from France
> To view this land, and frolic with his friends.
>
> (*The Jew of Malta* Prologue 1–4)

Machevill opens with a corrective ('Albeit ... Yet') consistent with the fundamental truth of Christian culture: even though people think Machevill is dead, in fact only his body has died; his 'soul' survives. Yet this 'soul' does not ascend to heaven vertically, spiritually, in a Christian apotheosis; it migrates horizontally, materially, in an international beeline: out of Italy, 'beyond the Alps,' into 'France,' and finally into 'this land,' identified later as 'Britanie' (29). From the outset, Marlowe foils orthodox expectations about essentialist transcendence; he emphasizes Machevill's materialist immanence.[8]

Yet, as Machevill subsequently reveals, what is immanent is not the 'soul' at all:

> To some perhaps my *name* is odious;
> But such as love me, guard me from their *tongues*,
> And let them know that I am Machevill,
> And weigh not men, and therefore not men's *words*.
>
> (*The Jew of Malta* Prologue 5–8; emphasis added)

If earlier Machevill identified himself as a 'soul,' here he speaks in terms of his 'name.' Thus he changes his mode of self-presentation from one kind of *succession* to the next – from what appears as Christian spiritual apotheosis to international immortality through reputation or fame. His constriction of 'soul' to 'name' is decidedly linguistic.[9] Thus Machevill's 'name' is 'odious' only in the 'tongues' of such as hate him, which leads him to identify himself *by name* ('I am Machevill'), in terms of 'men' and 'men's words.' By 'Machevill,' Marlowe means a 'name' for a figure who carves out a linguistic space for himself by refusing to grant substance or authority ('weigh') to the language of his enemies.

The linguistic fame Machevill represents is what he goes on to call the fame of 'books' (10). Machevill's materialist immanence is not spiritual but *textual*; his fame, not strictly cultural but literary: 'they read me ...' (11). Like the word 'me' here, Machevill's other personal pronouns appear as signs of textual identity. It is not Machevill who has 'flown beyond the Alps,' but his texts; it is not the man who is 'odious,' but his 'name'; it is not a living form at all against whom 'some speak openly' (10), but rather his documents. The 'they' who 'know' Machevill can therefore only 'read' him.[10]

This process of international textual migration secures the reader's most sought-after earthly achievement: the 'attain[ment of] / ... Peter's chair' (11–12). This *seat* is certainly the papacy (Van Fossen 8), but it is also the textual site of earthly fame, inscribed sardonically in Christian cloth.[11]

Thus, Machevill reveals that death emerges when his reader 'cast[s]' off his 'books' (12); unprotected by Machevill's literary power, the reader is easily 'poison'd' by his 'climbing followers' (13) – those who continue to read Machevill. Safety, position in Peter's chair – power itself – depends on the individual's ability to 'read' Machevill and to inscribe his 'name' through political action parading as religious truth.

The migration of Machevill's 'books' from Italy to France to England represents the process by which *translatio studii* translates into *translatio imperii*: empire gets written from East to West by those who 'read' Machevill's books. This notion runs counter to the official propaganda of the Tudor regime, which insists on the providential migration of the British Empire.[12]

In the next lines of the prologue, Machevill introduces his three main 'political' principles, none of which can be found in Machiavelli himself (Kocher, *Christopher Marlowe* 196–200): 'religion' is 'but a childish toy ... / ... there is no sin but ignorance' (14–15); 'Might first made kings' (20); and 'a strong built citadel / Commands much more than letters can import' (22–3). The usual inference, that Marlowe is presenting not the 'serious exposition of [Machiavelli's] ... actual philosophy,' but the 'popular stage burlesque' of Machiavelli (Ribner, 'Marlowe and Machiavelli' 355), leads us to a salient point: we are to understand Machevill and his philosophy in terms of Marlovian theatricality.

In the concluding lines of the prologue, Machevill encourages us to approach Barabas in terms of this theatricality: 'I crave but this: grace him as he deserves, / And let him not be entertain'd the worse / Because he favours me' (33–5). Machevill's 'I crave but this' is a superb theatrical directive; it shows him defining himself in theatrical terms; he defines his will in terms of audience reception. The word 'crave' even intensifies his will to *addiction*: Machevill's identity exists to 'crave' the response of the audience. Thus, as an audience, we are to 'grace' Barabas 'as he deserves'; we are to 'entertain' him because he has *entertained* us, even though he 'favours' Machevill. The *even though* in Machevill's logic is decisive, because it entreats us to separate Barabas's *evil* ('Mache*vill*ian) policy from *good* theatre; we are to clap – applaud – Barabas for his *performance* even though he is committed to Machevill's malevolent machinations.[13] If we take Machevill's directive – grant him his craving – we are constructed by the playwright in a new Machevillian theatre of evil – the play of policy. Marlowe anticipates this theatrical production by slyly reassigning the art of entertainment to the audience: 'let him not be entertain'd the worse.' Suddenly, we find ourselves the active agents of Machevill's policy; this is the 'play' of *our* lives – absolute play.

By approaching Barabas in terms of his theatricality, we are, in effect, agreeing with Harold Bloom: 'Barabas is Marlowe' (ed. 2).[14] Marlowe's identification with Barabas helps explain the rift of realism created in the lineage of the three Machiavellians identified: Machevill of Italy, the Guise of France, and Barabas of Malta. Whereas both Machevill and the Guise have recent, historical referents, Barabas is Marlowe's creation.[15] The rift in realism crafts a precise interstice between history and literature, context and text, the real and the fictive, and Machevill invites us to view Barabas precisely within this sacred theatrical space.

The prologue, then, constructs the theatrical lens through which we are to view the play. The machinations of Malta are not strictly 'theological' or 'political,' but theatrical. To the extent that we are to comment on theology and politics, we are to place them under the rubric of theatre. In practice, this means abandoning a commitment to 'character analysis.'[16] Instead, we are to attend with consistency to what critics often isolate in Ithamore's repeated references to Barabas's 'nose': the theatrical mask of character itself: 'O, brave, master, I worship your nose for this' (II.iii.171); 'God-a-mercy, nose; come, let's begone' (IV.i.23). Barabas's fake nose is not simply a detail in the text or a lone costume item in the repertoire of an acting company (see MacLure, ed. *Marlowe* 93); it is a kind of synecdoche for theatricality itself, foregrounding the play of policy: 'O mistress, I have the bravest, gravest, secret, subtle, bottle-nosed knave to my master, that ever gentleman had!' (III.iii.9–10).

Barabas's nose appears to derive from an Ovidian gene. In Marlowe's theatrical *nose*, we can detect a secret, subtle allusion to his own bottle-nosed knave of a master, Publius Ovidius Naso, whose last name means 'nose,' as Marlowe's colleagues could not avoid pointing out: 'Nosd like to Naso,' Harvey writes to Spenser (Letter IV in G.G. Smith, ed. 1: 108). The most famous version, however, comes from Shakespeare in *Loves Labour Lost*: 'Ovidius Naso was the man. And why indeed "Naso," but for smelling out the odoriferous flowers of fancy, the jerks of invention? *Imitari* is nothing' (IV.ii.123–6; see J. Bate 2). Nosed like to Naso, Barabas is thus an Ovidian persona – a figure for the comedy of Ovidian tragedy. *Imitari* is something![17]

As the prologue anticipates, in *The Jew of Malta* Marlowe's Ovidian metadrama constructs an imaginative record of how his play of policy comes into being and of how it meets its cultural fate. This argument sheds light on the threefold process of development in Barabas that Greenblatt describes – from 'wealth' as 'the *exclusive* object of his concern,' to 'revenge, at any cost, upon the Christians,' to 'deception virtually for its own sake':

'As Barabas, hammer in hand, constructs the machinery for this climactic falsehood, it is difficult not to equate him with the playwright himself, constructing the plot, and Marlowe appears consciously to encourage this perception' ('Marlowe, Marx' 52).[18] Barabas's shift from 'wealth' to 'revenge' to 'deception' is not ancillary to the play, but its primary action. By following the threefold process of Barabas's 'career' (Greenblatt's term), we can discover a cultural process by which the playwright himself has come to write *The Jew of Malta*. The play is not simply a critique of England's hypocritical Protestantism or its imperialist politics, but a register of how these theological and political ideologies help construct the dramatist and his products – 'help construct' because Marlowe's controlled representation of the process by which institutions construct the individual, made famous by Foucault, registers Marlowe's awareness of this process and presents him as a combatant against it.[19]

'Infinite riches in a little room': Barabas and Spenser

In Barabas's opening soliloquy, we do not see simply 'a highly successful businessman' (Friedman 157) or 'the Renaissance merchant-prince' (Sanders 56); we also see a highly successful Ovidian artist: the English Renaissance playwright-prince (see *Ovid's Elegies* I.xv.31–2). Barabas does not suddenly become a 'playwright' hammering out his 'plot' once Ferneze subjects him to the hypocritical tyranny of Christian authority; the Jew has always been a playwright. Later, when Barabas tells his daughter Abigail, 'A counterfeit profession is better / Than unseen hypocrisy' (I.ii.289–90), he fuses the economic and the political – the mercantile and the Machiavellian – into a professional trope for theatricality itself. Thus, what changes is not Barabas's 'profession,' but the precise minting of his coin.

In watching Machevill draw the curtain on 'Barabas *in his Counting-house, with heaps of gold before him*' (s.d.), we have been too quick to identify the gold and its intensely diligent counter in mercantile terms. As expressed by the counter himself, the inert gold miraculously gives its possessor the animating power of *voice* – language, narration, storytelling:

Well fare the Arabians, who so richly pay
The things they traffic for with wedge of gold,
Whereof a man may easily in a day
Tell that which may maintain him all his life.
(The Jew of Malta I.i.8–11; emphasis added)

Barabas does not simply praise the Arabians because they pay their debts in pure gold; he articulates an ideal in which this refined process of economic exchange permits the Arabians 'easily in a day' to 'tell' others about the material substance that gives them their foundational maintenance. Possession of gold and transaction of it are the first parts of a process that culminates in the individual's articulation of his achievement – his use of language to enfame the self. Marlowe metadramatizes this process by presenting Barabas *telling* of the Arabians' telling.

The metadramatizing of *economic telling* continues in the next part of Barabas's speech (12–18). If Barabas admires the Arabian process by which the individual 'easily' converts gold into discourse, and discourse into fame, he criticizes two groups that pervert the process: the 'needy groom' (12) and a figure we might term the tired miser. The needy groom, if able to 'finger' such 'coin,' would use language ('make') to misunderstand the process, falsifying it into a religious 'miracle' (12–13) – the product not of his own energy, but of some divine power. Such falsification the experienced miser would not commit, for he has spent his youth 'telling' of his economic achievement, and in his old age he knows better than to 'labour' so, choosing to keep silent as the best means for cherishing the privately owned 'steel-barr'd coffers ... cramm'd full' (14–17). Although the tired miser has more experience than the needy groom, he has wasted his youth on 'sweat' and ended his life in inaction (18).

Barabas's review of those who pervert the process of economic telling leads him to identify two groups that can join the Arabians in their purifying of the process: 'merchants of the Indian mines' and the 'wealthy Moor' (19–21). Only the Moor, however, fully replaces the Arabians' conversion of gold into linguistic fame with what appears to be a more practical path to cultural power (19–24). Barabas admires the Indian mine merchants because they rarify their economic practice through trading only in pure metal, but he admires the Moor because he can freely manipulate his riches and 'rate' a costly stone 'indifferently' (29). The Moor can use language to judge mercantile worth without regard, thought, or labour in order to achieve the end of one of culture's most daring rescue operations: in 'peril of calamity,' he can 'ransom great kings,' who themselves have become subjected to tyrannical political forces (31–2). Paradoxically, the Moor's political service to the captive kings hinges on a detached, carefree use of language.

In the famous conclusion to this part of the speech, Barabas takes a cue from and indeed finds his model in the 'wealthy Moor' and his service to 'great kings':

This is the ware wherein consists my wealth;
And thus methinks should men of judgement frame
Their means of traffic from the vulgar trade,
And as their wealth increaseth, so inclose
Infinite riches in a little room.

(*The Jew of Malta* I.i.33–7)

Barabas defends his practice of economic enclosure not strictly by political expediency, but more precisely by political power. By confining the world's massive wealth in his little counting-house, he primes himself for the opportunity of his life – the occasion to ransom a great king.[20]

For Barabas, such an economic and political practice constitutes the highest form of cultural wisdom – what 'men of judgment frame.' This practice is imperative for him because it reconfigures class hierarchy. By framing his 'means of traffic from the vulgar trade,' he acquires so great a lucre that he vaults from his medial economic position in the emerging merchant class of early modern culture, as well as from his lowly social position in the class of Jews, right over the top of the king himself. In effect, by enclosing infinite riches in a little room, Barabas *makes* himself the king of culture. Economic compression results in political inflation. In being able to 'ransom' great kings, Barabas positions himself to function as a cultural saviour – an economic messiah. He is the king of kings.[21]

In this part of his opening speech, then, Barabas presents an *apologia* for his enterprise. He is not simply describing a megalomaniac vision of an idealized role for the downtrodden Jew at the centre of cultural power; he is 'telling' the audience of this vision. In presenting Barabas 'telling it,' Marlowe is modelling a linguistic ideal that forms the genesis of a new dramatic genre.

That this ideal discovers its 'traffic' in kingship should alert us to the 'subject' of tragedy in general and to the role of tragedy in Marlowe's Ovidian career in particular. But before pursuing this idea, we may pick up the remaining 'riches' of Barabas's soliloquy – its opening lines: 'So that of thus much that return was made; ... / Fie, what a trouble 'tis to count this trash!' (1, 7). Barabas does not have access to the ease of the Arabians, the purity of the Indian mine merchants, or the indifferent ratings of the Moor. He must manage his returns with care; he must 'sum' and 'satisf[y]' his 'venture'; he must 'purs[e]' the 'paltry silverlings' of his competitors (3, 6). As Barabas curses his trouble in counting his trash, however, presumably he follows Machevill's directive in the prologue, 'smil[ing]' to see how full his bags are crammed. If so, we witness the dissonance between Barabas's bitter speech and its smiling orifice; we see what the play's 'humour' dramatizes: the primacy of theatricality.

Theatricality also emerges in the strain of metadrama infiltrating Barabas's speech. The key word is the last: 'room.' According to the *OED*, a *room* can be a 'place or seat in the theatre' (Def. III.11.c), citing the 1599 *Every Man Out of His Humour* as its earliest example. But we can cite another 1599 play that *reads* Marlowe's 'room' metadramatically: 'Thus far, with rough and all un-able pen, / Our bending author hath pursu'd the story, / In little room confining mighty men' (*Henry V* Epilogue 1–3).[22] Presumably, even back in the early 1590s the actor playing Barabas would gesture with his hand as he speaks the 'infinite' line, thereby identifying the room of the counting-house with the room of the theatre.[23] The famous line permits the actor to identify the 'infinite riches' as the discourse of the theatre itself and to call attention to 'the place of the stage.' Thus one of the earliest imitations of this line links it with Ovid and Ovidian performance. In *Ovid's Banquet of Sense* (1595), Chapman presents 'Ovid' seeing Corinna/Julia in economically erotic terms: 'He saw th' extraction of all fairest dames: / The fair of beauty, as whole countries come / And *show* their riches in a little room' (2: 29; emphasis added).[24]

Marlowe's economic metadrama helps explain Barabas's *representation of* literary imitation itself: 'As for those Samnites, and the men of Uz, / That bought my Spanish oils and wines of Greece, / Here have I purs'd their paltry silverlings' (4–6). As G.K. Hunter points out, '"Uzz" is ... a country only known from the opening verse of Job: "There was a man in the land of Uz, called Job"' ('Theology' 189). By counterfeiting Scripture, Barabas presents himself as a playwright-prince right from the start: *he* is participating in the system of literary imitation. By pursing the paltry silverlings of the men of Uz, Barabas establishes the superiority of his own literary venture over that of the Bible. Marlowe stages a rival poetics, through which he contests the authority of Western culture's most sacred document.[25]

Marlowe's rival poetics extends to those texts originally composed within his own professional environment. For one of the probable sources for some of the play's plot, idea, and energy is a recently published story of another rich man and his daughter: Spenser's episode of Mammon and Philotime in Book II, canto vii, of *The Faerie Queene*.[26]

In his Revels Play edition of *The Jew*, N.W. Bawcutt cites Spenser three times, and all three come from the Mammon episode.[27] First, on Marlowe's line 108 later in the opening scene, 'Ripping the bowels of the earth for them,' Bawcutt compares *Faerie Queene* II.vii.17: 1–4 and Kyd's *Spanish*

Tragedy III.xii.71 (ed. 73). Kyd's phrasing – 'I'll rip the bowels of the earth' – is closer to Marlowe's, but the context is only metaphorically mercantile. Spenser's phrasing – 'Then gan a cursed hand the quiet wombe / Of his great Grandmother with steele to wound, / And the hid treasures in her sacred tombe / With Sacriledge to dig' – more closely fits Marlowe's context.[28]

In his edition of *The Faerie Queene*, A.C. Hamilton glosses Spenser's passage with Ovid's *Metamorphoses* I.135–40, in which 'mining marks the iron age; his *viscera terrae* suggests S.'s "wombe" (1)' (ed., *FQ* 227): 'And the ground ... the careful surveyor now marked out with long-drawn boundary-line ... [M]en ... delved ... into the very bowels of the earth; and the wealth which the creator had hidden away and buried deep amidst the very Stygian shades, was brought to light, wealth that pricks men on to crime.' To this Ovidian intertext, we may add a Senecan one: 'But those base sons / Spared not to *rifle their own mother's body [Earth] / For gold*, and that dread iron whence ere long / They fashioned arms to fit their murderous hands' (*Octavia* 417–19; emphasis added; trans. Watling: 'sed in parentis viscera intravit suae, deterior aetas; eruit ferrum grave / aurumque, saevas mox et armavit manus'). These lines are uttered by the character 'Seneca' himself – on the four ages of man. Not simply a philosopher's set piece, the speech is an intertextual set piece, in which 'Seneca' presents himself in his own tragedy imitating Ovid, converting 'viscera terrae' into 'parentis viscera.' Thus, Marlowe's line has two classical origins (Ovid and Seneca) and two contemporary origins (Spenser and Kyd). This is the typology of intertextuality at its richest.

Second, on Barabas's phrase 'juice of hebon' in line 101 of Act III, scene iv, Bawcutt cites *Faerie Queene* II.vii.51–2 (ed. 140). Spenser includes the 'Heben sad' (52) when describing the deadly 'hearbes and fruits' (II.vii.51) in Mammon's 'Gardin of Proserpina' (53). As Hamilton again notes (ed., *FQ* 233), the origins of the trees in the Garden are classical (Homer, Claudian, Virgil). But Spenser may also have had Ovid's Orphic catalogue of trees in mind (*Metamorphoses* X.86–106), which the New Poet imitates earlier (I.i.8–9; see Hamilton ed., *FQ* 32).

Third, on Barabas's phrase 'Cocytus' breath,' also in line 101, Bawcutt compares *Faerie Queene* II.vii.56 (ed. 140). In describing Mammon's Garden of Proserpina, just a few stanzas after mentioning the 'Heben sad,' Spenser includes 'Cocytus deepe' (56). As with Bawcutt's first gloss, the other two may not look particularly significant, but they do indicate the tip of a Spenserian iceberg.[29]

Marlowe's and Spenser's narratives conjoin in the father–daughter relationship. Moreover, both Barabas and Mammon are wealthy fathers who attempt to prostitute their daughters to potential suitors; and both do so as part of a strategy of dark deception. Barabas prostitutes Abigail to Lodowick in order to transact revenge on Lodowick's father, Ferneze; Mammon prostitutes Philotime to Guyon in order to secure the knight's damnation. Both fathers work through 'deceiptfull sleight' (*FQ* II.vii.64); and both work through plots conjoining economics with theatre: 'art and counterfetted shew' (*FQ* II.vii.45).

Spenser's Mammon is not a Jew, but he is a demon (vii.8), and Elizabethan England 'had turned its Jews into usurers and its usurers into devils' (Bartels 83). Spenser associates the devil Mammon with usury ('usaunce' [7; see Hamilton, ed., *FQ* 224]), and his only reference to the biblical Barabbas occurs in the Mammon episode: the 'murdrer felonous' of the Pilate episode (62).

One other similarity between Barabas and Mammon is striking. Greenblatt remarks, 'For Marlowe ..., the dominant mode of perceiving the world, in a society hagridden by the power of money and given over to the slave market, is *contempt*, contempt aroused in the beholders of such a society and, as important, governing the behavior of those who bring it into being and function within it. This is Barabas' constant attitude, virtually his signature' ('Marlowe, Marx' 46). Like Marlowe, Spenser detected a grim link between an individual's commitment to money and his contemptful mode of perceiving the world, the result of which is what the Renaissance called 'atheism,' the progenitor of civic violence. Thus, Mammon has stationed as a 'fitting porter of the court of Philotime' (Hamilton, ed., *FQ* 231) a statue-figure made of 'golden mould' (40) who looks decidedly Marlovian: 'A sturdy villein, striding stiffe and bold, / As if that highest God defie he would; ... / Disdayne he called was' (40–1).[30]

Beyond these similarities, Marlowe's *Jew* and Spenser's Mammon episode share actual linguistic representation. The opening descriptions of these two rich figures are distinctly similar, and we can count four hitherto uncited conjunctions in Barabas's opening soliloquy alone. First, the opening stage direction to *The Jew of Malta* shows Barabas in his counting-house 'with *heaps of gold* before him.' Spenser's opening description of Mammon reads: 'And round about him lay on every side / Great *heapes of gold*' (II.vii.5). Second, Barabas describes the Arabians who traffic with '*wedge* of gold' (I.i.9); four lines after Spenser's 'heapes of gold' phrase we learn that Mammon's gold is 'driven, and distent, / Into great Ingoes, and to *wedges* square' (5). Third, Barabas refers to the tired miser 'whose steel-*barr'd coffers* are cramm'd full' (14) – which recalls Mammon's '*coffers* strong, / All *bard* with double bends' (30). Finally, Barabas's famous line, 'inclose / Infinite riches in a little room,' rewords Spenser's reiterated description of Mammon's gold:

> What *secret place* ... can safely hold
> So *huge a masse*.
>
> (*Faerie Queene* II.vii.20)

> In all that *rowme* was nothing to be seene,
> But *huge great yron chests and coffers strong*.
>
> (*Faerie Queene* II.vii.30)

As A. Bartlett Giamatti notes, 'the small space, or the container, rammed with life's plenitude and energy, is the basic image of *The Faerie Queene*' (*Play* 93).[31] If Marlowe is feeding his eye on Spenser's treasury, we can watch him enclosing his rival's infinite riches in his own little room.[32]

Spenser's Mammon episode qualifies as a subtext for *The Jew of Malta*. All of the repetitions identify Marlowe's hero with Spenser's villain – Barabas with Mammon. Thus, Marlowe continues a larger career project of critiquing England's New Poet. His critique is not simply of English Christian culture, but of a rival who was making himself famous as a servant of this culture. What Marlowe critiques through Barabas is Spenser's victimization of such an *inventive* showman as Mammon. In this first phase of his portrait, Marlowe uses Spenser to gather sympathy for his hero; as critics insist, Barabas does not begin the play as an evil man – an evil artist. He is transacting his art within the rules of culture and becomes thereby its most successful venturer. At this point in the play, Barabas understands the opposition – the hypocrisy of the Christian authorities – but he remains content to purse the paltry silverlings of the system rather than to seek revenge upon it.

Counterfeit Succession

In the remainder of the play, Marlowe pursues his Ovidian, counter-Spenserian project to a staged quintessence. What we witness is the paradigm with which we began: the playwright dramatizes his own fate within the Elizabethan literary system – suppression by the power structure. This is the tragic *telos* that gives birth to the playwright's art.

According to Foucault, 'in the darkest region of the political field, the condemned man represents the symmetrical, inverted figure of the king' (rpt. in *The Foucault Reader* 176). Barabas's remarks on kingship later in the opening scene thereby acquire force:

I must confess we come not to be kings:
That's not our fault: alas, our number's few,
And crowns come either by succession,
Or urg'd by force; and nothing violent,
Oft have I heard tell, can be permanent.
Give us a peaceful rule; make Christians kings,
That thirst so much for principality.
I have no charge, nor many children,
But one sole daughter, whom I hold as dear
As Agamemnon did his Iphigen;
And all I have is hers.

(*The Jew of Malta* I.i.128–38)

In the darkest regions of the Renaissance political field, Barabas presents himself as a condemned man who represents the symmetrical, inverted figure of the king. His speech drifts precisely to circumvent this grim political process.

Initially, Barabas distinguishes himself from the king ('we come not to be kings'), but by the end he insinuates himself into kingship: 'one sole daughter, whom I hold as dear / As Agamemnon did his Iphigen.' The simile is programmatic, for Marlowe refers to the event giving birth to Western tragedy, staged originally in Aeschylus's *Agamemnon* but later appropriated by Ovid in the *Metamorphoses*.[33]

Like the (Ovidian) story of Agamemnon and his children, Marlowe's 'tragedy of a Jew' is concerned with 'succession.' Barabas first places his trust in his 'one sole daughter.' Then, midway, he tells Lodowick that Abigail shall be his 'wife, and thou shalt be mine heir' (II.iii.326) – a dark strategy for robbing the Governor of Malta of his own heir. And later, after Barabas believes that Abigail has betrayed him, he adopts the slave Ithamore as his new 'heir' (III.iv.42): 'Now shalt thou see the death of Abigail, / That thou mayst freely live to be my heir' (62). Finally, towards the end of the play, when all three 'heirs' are grimly dead, Barabas is left to transact his own 'succession.' As he has surmised, however, his 'crown' has come 'urg'd by force.' Reminiscent of the Scythian shepherd Tamburlaine with King Mycetes, Barabas succeeds Ferneze as Governor.[34]

The topic of kingship alerts us to the role of tragedy in the writer's career, identifying 'the tragedy of a Jew' as a tragedy indeed, as Aristotle and the rest have devised it. 'Poets Tragicall,' writes George Puttenham, 'set forth the dolefull falles of infortunate & afflicted Princes' (rpt. in G.G. Smith, ed. 2: 27). The topic of kingship also alerts us to the political context of the portrait – that most pressing of 1590s questions: Queen Elizabeth's succession: 'crowns come either by succession, / Or urg'd by force ... / Give us a peaceful rule; make Christians kings.'[35] Finally, the topic of kingship alerts us to the problem of Marlowe's own professional 'succession': his attempt to use Ovid to succeed Spenser, for Barabas's speech on kingship centres on the resonant question that we have grounded in a genealogy tracing from Ovid to Seneca to Spenser:

> What more may heaven do for earthly man
> Than thus to pour out plenty in their laps,
> Ripping the bowels of the earth for them,
> Making the sea their servant, and the winds
> To drive their substance with successful blasts?[36]
>
> (*The Jew of Malta* I.i.106–10)

Marlowe's interlock of *generic succession*, *dynastic succession*, and *professional succession* has classical origins. According to Philip Hardie, 'the Roman imperial epic's obsession with the need for, and possibility of, [dynastic] succession reflects the historical realities of the first century A.D.; it also relates to the poet's own desire to prove himself a worthy successor to the great epic poets who lived before him, and in particular to succeed as a follower of Virgil' (*Epic Successors of Virgil* 99). Among the four imperial Roman followers of Virgil whom Hardie discusses, two follow Virgil by practising 'reverence': Statius and Silius. The other two follow Virgil by practising 'rebel[lion]': Ovid and Lucan. This professional inheritance traces to a third writer important here: Lucretius (Hardie 109–10). In *The Jew of Malta*, Marlowe relocates the interlock among generic, dynastic, and professional succession within the epic's competing genre, tragedy, in order to establish his own literary 'authority' (V.ii.28, 35, 38) in a cultural environment controversially revitalized by the recent opening of the English theatre.

In the play's second scene, we discover the rationale for the second phase of Barabas's career as described by Greenblatt: Barabas's plot of revenge against the rightful Governor of Malta. When Abigail enters, we learn that Barabas has anticipated Christian evil by laying provision aside, beneath a plank in his house: 'Rich costly jewels, and stones infinite, / Fearing the worst of this before it fell, / I closely hid' (244–6). Infinite riches under a little plank.

Still, Barabas wants his money back, and 'in extremity / We ought to make bar of no policy' (269–70). Barabas's policy takes the form we should expect – a dramatic production, by which he directs his daughter to disguise herself as a nun, so she can reenter his house, now 'turn'd … / Into a nunnery' (274–5), and recover the gold: 'Entreat 'em fair, and give them friendly speech, / And seem to them as if thy sins were great, / Till thou hast gotten to be entertain'd' (283–5). That last word appears three times within fifteen lines (277, 285, 291), underscoring the link between Barabas's play and the play the audience is watching. When Abigail agrees to 'dissemble,' Barabas delivers a programmatic statement for Marlovian art:

> As good dissemble that thou never mean'st
> As first mean truth, and then dissemble it:
> A counterfeit profession is better
> Than unseen hypocrisy.
>
> (*The Jew of Malta* I.ii.287–90)

In the first two lines, Barabas may mean '"It is quite as good to begin with a deliberate deception as to start out honestly and then lapse into trickery"'; and in the phrase 'counterfeit profession' he may mean 'the insincere vows as a nun which Abigail is about to take' (Bawcutt, ed. 92; see Siemon xxxvi). Indeed, since a 'profession' is a technical term for 'the declaration, promise, or vow made by one entering a religious order' (*OED*, Def. I.1), a 'counterfeit profession' nominally tropes religious hypocrisy. The ring of program, however, is also striking. In advocating 'deliberate deception' as the best 'policy' to 'truth,' Marlowe legitimizes metatheatre as the only truth about theatre.

The phrase 'counterfeit profession' is thus a fine oxymoron, since 'counterfeit' means *false, deceptive, concealed*, while 'profession' means *spoken audibly, acted visibly*, or *performed outwardly*. A profession that is counterfeit is a discourse self-consciously deceptive or falsified. Both words pertain to art and language: 'counterfeit' can also mean 'made to a pattern: fashioned, wrought' (*OED*, Def. A.2), with reference to 'a picture or image' (Def. A.4) and to 'writings' (Def. B.1.b); and 'profession' can mean both 'the action of declaring, acknowledging, or avowing an opinion, belief, intention, practice' (Def. II.4) and 'the occupation which one professes to be skilled in and to follow' (Def. III.6), including 'a vocation in which a professed knowledge of some department of learning or science is used in its application to the affairs of other or in the practice of an art founded upon it' (Def. III.6.a). Barabas's counterfeit profession is a counterfeit succession, veiling Marlowe's interlock of *literary career, professional rivalry*, and *counter-nationhood*.

Perhaps not so curiously for Renaissance writers in Spenser's 'Colin Clout' mould, the figure who most visibly voices this interlock is not the protagonist but his 'second self' (III.iv.15): Ithamore. '[M]yself is thine' (90), Barabas tells his 'heir,' as if to manage the succession of authorial self-presentation. Accordingly, it is Ithamore who articulates the theatrical dimension of Barabas's project most directly (Cartelli 175): 'Why, was there ever seen such villainy, / So neatly plotted, and so well perform'd? / Both held in hand, and flatly both beguil'd' (iii.1–3). Ithamore is referring to the grim deaths of Lodowick and Mathias; in explaining to Abigail that the two have killed each other, the slave transcribes a dramatic process: 'Why, the devil invented a challenge, my master writ it, and I carried it, first to Lodowick, and *imprimis* to Mathias: / And then they met, and as the story says, / In doleful wise they ended both their days' (18–21). In Act IV, scene i, when Barabas constructs a similar 'plot' (117) against the two friars, Jacomo and Bernardine, Ithamore echoes himself: ''Tis neatly done, sir' (149).

Accordingly, in the next scene Marlowe presents Ithamore quoting Marlowe:

> we will leave this paltry land,
> And sail from hence to Greece, to lovely Greece.
> I'll be thy Jason, thou my golden fleece;
> Where painted carpets o'er the meads are hurl'd,
> And Bacchus' vineyards overspread the world;
> Where woods and forests go in goodly green;
> I'll be Adonis, thou shalt be Love's Queen;
> The meads, the orchards, and the primrose-lanes,
> Instead of sedge and reed, bear sugar-canes:
> Thou in those groves, by Dis above,
> Shalt live with me and be my love.
>
> (*The Jew of Malta* IV.ii.83–93)

In that last line, critics find Marlowe parodying 'The Passionate Shepherd to His Love' (Bawcutt, ed. 162) and thus the genre of pastoral: 'Here the pastoral world is made material and common: ... the meadows require carpeting' (Rothstein 265). As with *Dido* and the *Tamburlaine* plays, here we may emphasize the significance of Marlowe's parody of his pastoral self *on the stage, in a tragedy*. The reference to 'Bacchus' vineyards' evokes the origins of tragedy in the Dionysian festivals, as does the repetition 'to Greece, to lovely Greece.' Yet Ithamore's impersonation of both 'Jason' and

'Adonis' suggests a Grecian successor, Ovid, who had retold both myths in his counter-Virgilian epic, the *Metamorphoses* (VII.1–233 and X.503–739). As with his use of his lyric voice in the first triad of plays, here Marlowe playfully *authorizes* the writing of a counter-Virgilian genre: Ovidian tragedy. Thus his heavy reliance on 'golden' poetry (C.S. Lewis, *English Literature* 64–5) measures his own countering of the 'Virgil of England.'[37] Of all the figures in the play, only Ithamore receives the author's self-reflexive *imprimatur*. 'You'd make a rich poet, sir,' the pimp Pilia-Borza tells him (115), the precise coining of which Marlowe himself appears to have had aspirations to produce.[38]

Ithamore quotes Marlowe's famous pastoral invitation to woo 'Love's Queen' – the quean Bellamira. The name, which derives from the Latin *bella* and *Mira*, 'wondrously beautiful,' gives little away, but perhaps it gives enough. The first half of the name, 'Bella,' resembles the first syllable of 'Belphoebe,' which Spenser derived to express the second of the Queen's two bodies, as he explains to Sir Walter Ralegh: 'our soveraine the Queene' in the 'person' of 'a most vertuous and beautifull Lady' is modelled on Ralegh's 'owne excellent conceipt of Cynthia' (*Letter to Ralegh*). The second half of the name, 'Mira,' also had associations with Queen Elizabeth, through Spenser himself. In fact, in Book VI of *The Faerie Queene*, we discover an Elizabeth figure who precisely reverses the name of Marlowe's Bellamira: Mirabella (vii–viii; see Hamilton's note on the etymology of her name, ed., *FQ* 671). According to Anne Shaver, 'The story of Mirabella ... refers to Elizabeth the "vertuous and beautiful lady"' (225). Shaver concludes that 'Spenser, for all his equating of courtesy with hierarchic if loving marriage, must realize that, for Queen Elizabeth, to marry at all would be to lose the self that can claim the power to rule England, and to love inappropriately could be to endanger the state. Mirabella may not be so much the bruised and punished enemy of courtesy as she is the strongest ... independent woman in Faerie Land, a whipping girl for untouchable royalty' (225).[39]

Both of Spenser's Elizabeth 'Bells' refuse to love, but Marlowe's Bellamira loves too much; she is a 'courtesan' – a word that Marlowe uses only rarely but that appears five times in *The Jew of Malta* (III.i.25, IV.iii.2, V.i.8, 34, 47). The word 'courtesan' links Bellamira with the court. In the sixteenth century, a courtesan was certainly a 'prostitute' (*OED*, 2d entry, headnote), but the *OED*'s first entry reads: 'One attached to the court of a prince' (Def. A).[40]

Throughout much of her reign, Spenser's Virgin Queen was subject to queanly castigation as 'Love's *Queen*.'[41] According to Ben Jonson, Elizabeth 'had a Membrana on her which made her uncapable of man, though for her delight she tryed many' (*Conversations with Drummond* [1619] 142). Back in 1580, Thomas Playfere rumoured that the queen had two illegitimate children by the Earl of Leicester, while in 1581 Henry Hawkins claimed the number to be 'five ... and she never goeth on progress but to be delivered.'[42] According to Louis Adrian Montrose, such examples 'manifest in what varied and casual ways the royal body – and the royal fiction – might be manipulated by the queen's subjects; and how easily such discursive manipulations might be construed by the authorities as seditious, as potentially threatening to the established order and to be punished accordingly' ('The Elizabethan Subject' 312). By subsequently relying on a theatre simile, Montrose helps us to identify the cultural working of Marlowe's Bellamira episode within 'a tragedy of a Jew': 'Like the bawdy subplot of some romantic comedy, a predominantly oral and often scurrilous counterdiscourse carnivalized the official cult of mystical royal virginity by insisting upon the physicality of the royal body, the carnal inclinations of the queen' (312). As in 'The Passionate Shepherd,' Marlowe in the Bellamira episode stages the queen-as-quean in order to carnivalize his counter-Spenserian discourse.[43]

This interpretation sheds new light on the final scene of Act IV, where Marlowe formally stages metadiscourse. As Ithamore tumbles in the quean's 'incony lap' (iv.28), Barabas enters 'with a lute, disguised' (s.d.) as a 'French musician' (29). Ordered to play, Barabas first tunes his lute, giving the courtesan time to see and request 'the posy' in his 'hat' (34). As each of the three carousers smells the flowers, Barabas speaks an aside: 'So, now I am reveng'd upon 'em all. / The scent thereof was death; I poison'd it' (41–2). As the poison works, and the victims jest over the Jew, the Jew plays a tune. At the end of the scene, Pilia-Borza suggests that they write '[o]ne letter more to the Jew' (69), while Bellamira instructs Ithamore to 'write it sharp' (70). The slave demands that they communicate 'by word of mouth' (71), and Pilia-Borza offers to carry the message himself, 'now I know the meaning' (74). Ithamore ends with a superb meta-hermeneutic line, 'The meaning has a meaning' (75).[44]

What is the meaning of the meaning? Why does Marlowe disguise Barabas as a 'French musician,' the player of a 'lute'? The dramatic context supplies a clue, for Barabas uses his disguise to infiltrate the finite riches of a little room. He is *spying*. The French musician, the lute, and the 'posy' are clearly figures for the poet and his art, but what is striking is that Marlowe employs an instrument of and a metaphor for the art of the poet as secretive vehicles for Machiavellian punishment: Barabas uses the lute and the posy to kill Ithamore, Bellamira, and Pilia-Borza.[45]

According to Charles Nicholl, 'the interesting question about Marlowe was how his position as a writer influenced his spying. Here is one answer: the writer was an ideal man to infiltrate into a household ... The poet has an *entrée*. He has a key to the door, and often to the intimate chambers, of the rich and the powerful, and it is precisely the rich and the powerful that the government is so keen to keep an eye on ... For the poet-spy, one might say, poetry itself could be used as a kind of cover, as a means of infiltration' (191–2).[46]

In the French musician scene, Marlowe appears to stage the Elizabethan 'poet-spy' – his own use of 'poetry' as 'a kind of cover, as a means of infiltration,' through which he can have access to the 'infinite chambers' of the 'rich and powerful.' Marlowe disguises Barabas as a 'French' musician in order to allude to his own work as a spy for Queen Elizabeth in Rheims, France, site of the Catholic seminary, as reported in the Privy Council minutes of a letter written on 29 June 1587 to the authorities at Cambridge: 'Christopher Morley was determined to have gone beyond the seas to Reames ... whereby he had done Her Majesty good service' (rpt. in Nicholl 92).[47]

Entertainment in the Gallery

In Act V, Marlowe stages metadrama itself, as critics demonstrate. The stage direction to scene v reads: '*Enter* [Barabas] *with a hammer, above, very busy* [*and* Carpenters].' Thus the dialogue mouths the 'little room' of the theatre: 'Leave nothing loose, all levell'd to my mind' (v.4). What Barabas and the carpenters have 'made,' Barabas subsequently informs Ferneze, is 'a dainty gallery' (35), the device by which Barabas will trap the Turks, and '[t]he floor whereof, this cable being cut, / Doth fall asunder, so that it doth sink / Into a deep pit past recovery' (36–8).

Barabas here does seem to be 'pursuing deception virtually for its own sake.' 'Say, will not this be brave?' the Jew proudly asks Ferneze (43), who replies, 'O, excellent!' (44). After Ferneze retires to set the plot in motion, Barabas delivers his last soliloquy:

> Why, is not this
> A kingly kind of trade, to purchase towns
> By treachery, and sell 'em by deceit?
> Now tell me, worldlings, underneath the sun
> If greater falsehood ever has been done.
>
> (*The Jew of Malta* V.v.49–53)

This speech is more than the final stage of a process by which we arrive at metatheatre or at Barabas's identification as Marlowe; it stages a particular 'kind' of metatheatre: the Ovidian, Senecan play of Machiavellian policy. Hence, Barabas's art is a 'kingly kind of trade' that works by 'treachery,' 'deceit,' and 'greater falsehood' in order to 'purchase' the body-politic. Marlowe contextualizes his 'Ovidian tragedy' about the Machiavellian play of policy within Spenserian discourse, for in the phrase 'Now tell me, worldlings, underneath the sun,' we can witness him entering Mammon's little room: 'God of the world and worldlings I me call, / Great Mammon, greatest god below the skye' (FQ II.vii.8).[48]

In the play's final action, then, we watch the making of theatre itself: 'How busy Barabas is there above / To entertain us in his gallery' (55–6). In the place of the stage, Barabas's position 'above' dramatizes his cultural 'authority,' for the 'traitor and unhallow'd Jew' (V.ii.13) has metamorphosed into a 'brave Jew, ... great Barabas' (20), 'Governor of Malta': 'Thus hast thou gotten, by thy policy, / No simple place, no small authority: / I now am Governor of Malta; / ... / And, since by wrong thou got'st authority, / Maintain it bravely by firm policy' (ii.27–36). Yet Marlowe raises his Renaissance artist-governor/playwright-prince to his theatrical height in order to dramatize his 'fall': 'A charge, the cable cut. A cauldron discovered [into which Barabas falls]' (s.d.). The 'tragedy of a Jew' thus nominally inscribes the orthodox Christian wisdom with which Ferneze concludes the play: 'let due praise be given, / Neither to Fate nor Fortune, but to Heaven' (125–6). Such a conclusion no doubt satisfied, or at least stifled, the Tudor and Stuart censors, but modern readers have not been duped. From Harry Levin to Thomas Cartelli, readers have found in Barabas's fall and death a 'theatrical ... triumph' (Cartelli 180; see H. Levin 76), in which Barabas's final cry is a mimesis not of unbearable physical torment ('intolerable pangs' [90]), as he sinks in a scalding cauldron, but of the exquisite pain and thundering fire of theatrical speech itself, the Marlovian tongue representing its grim suppression by orthodox Christian power and simultaneously registering its cunning resistance through its own counterfeit profession: 'Die life! Fly soul! Tongue curse thy fill, and die!' (V.v.91).

'Italian masques by night': Machiavellian Policy and Ovidian Play in *Edward II*

From the perspective of the present study, the dramatic poles of *Edward II* become two similar theatrical representations. In the opening scene, Gaveston plans to stage 'Italian masques by night' in order to 'best please his majesty' (I.i.54, 70); and, in the penultimate scene, Mortimer commissions the henchman Lightborn to stage an 'Italian' rape by night in order to best kill his majesty (V.v).[1] Both the opening and the closing 'Italian masque' are at once Machiavellian and Ovidian, the synthesis of policy and play, as both Gaveston and Mortimer are adept in the 'arts' of both *Italian plotters*. If Gaveston plans like a Machiavel to stage the Ovidian 'comed[y]' (I.i.55) of 'Actaeon peeping through the grove' (66) in order to seduce his sovereign, Mortimer schemes like a Machiavel when relying on Lightborn in order to stage an Ovidian 'tragedy' (V.v.73) of bestiality and rape so horrible in its historical reality that not even Seneca could think of it: 'was it not bravely done' (115), Lightborn asks his accomplices, Gurney and Matrevis, before they kill him. We may wish to brood over the significance of this bifold, 'Italian[ate]' structure because it provides a clue as to how we are to situate Marlowe's Machiavellian 'play of policy' within his Ovidian career.[2]

For one thing, the bifold, Italianate structure permits us to account for what may seem most curious in a play nominally about an English sovereign: Marlowe allots space to a second 'tragic' hero, as the title page to the 1594 edition advertises: 'The troublesome raigne and lamentable death of Edward the second, King of England: with the tragicall fall of proud Mortimer.' Rather than simply alerting us to a dual tragedy about the named principals, this printer's cue also reveals a dual representation of 'tragedy' in the rival 'arts' of Edward's primary favourite, Gaveston, and his primary competitor, Mortimer, as they vie for (Machiavellian and Ovidian) power over the king. Conceived in these terms, *Edward II* stages a narrative in which a Machiavellian schemer, Mortimer, uses an Ovidian plot to suppress and eliminate an Ovidian and Machiavellian schemer, Gaveston, as well as his 'successors, Spencer and Baldock' (Cartelli 131). This narrative consumes nearly the whole of the play – up until its last scene, when the Machiavellian Mortimer himself suffers a 'tragicall fall.'[3]

None the less, we need to come to terms with Marlowe's complete design. Although he emphasizes Mortimer's suppression of Gaveston, he briefly concludes with young Prince Edward's suppression of Mortimer. In this design, we can discover a model for Marlowe's poetics, including its fate, within Elizabethan culture. *Edward II* is a tragedy about 'the play of policy,' but it joins other late works – *The Jew of Malta, The Massacre at Paris, Doctor Faustus, Lucan's First Book*, and *Hero and Leander* – in emphasizing the individual's loss of *libertas*, his suppression by orthodox powers.[4]

In *Edward II*, Marlowe writes a 'tragedy' but conceals a strategy for overcoming his problem as a writer: with such heterodox views, how can he acquire authority as England's new counter-national artist? Gaveston's Ovidian art relying on Machiavellian policy, we shall see, inscribes a metatheatrical representation of Marlovian unorthodox theatre linking sex and politics; and Mortimer's Machiavellian policy relying on Ovidian play inscribes a metatheatrical representation of an orthodox art linking politics and sex that would seem to pertain to a rival or rival faction. In 1591 or 1592, who would these competitors be? Two rivals long known to Marlowe scholars suggest themselves: Spenser and Shakespeare. In the rivalry between Gaveston and Mortimer for possession of Edward, then, Marlowe may be implicating his own rivalry with his two colleagues for the ear and eye of Queen Elizabeth.

As the only play in the Marlowe canon putting an English king on the stage, *Edward II* writes nationhood more directly than *Dido*, the two *Tamburlaine* plays, or *The Jew of Malta* – plays that stage an African queen, an Eastern monarch, and a Maltese governor. 'Know,' agonizes Edward to Lightborn, 'I am a king' (V.v.88). As we saw in the introduction, Richard Helgerson argues that Shakespeare's history plays differ from those of Henslowe's playwrights: whereas 'Shakespeare's history plays are concerned above all with the consolidation and maintenance of royal power,' Henslowe's playwrights were preoccupied with 'the innocent suffering of common people' (*Forms of Nationhood* 234–5). By contrast, Spenser abandons a nationhood of 'absolute royal power' for a nationhood organized around 'aristocratic autonomy' (Helgerson 55). *Edward II* broods precisely over this tripartite structure. Our earlier glance at Gaveston's opening speech, however, revealed that Marlowe is not writing simply a nationhood of royal power, of the people's power, or of aristocratic power. Rather, he is writing a nationhood of *libertas* – in particular, free scholarship. We can trace this form of nationhood by focusing on Marlowe's metadramatic rivalry with his colleagues within the pattern of his Ovidian career.

Marlowe's strategy for managing poetic rivalry in the context of nationhood proceeds in three parts. First, he opens the play by using Gaveston to introduce the allure of his own Ovidian art. Second, he uses Mortimer to dramatize the suppression of this art by a rival faction. And third, he concludes by using Edward III to bring about the 'tragicall fall' of that faction.⁵ In *Edward II*, Marlowe registers the reception his art was receiving among (more) orthodox circles, including those of Spenser and Shakespeare; and he accurately predicts his art's cultural fate, as that metonymic event, the 1599 burning of *Ovid's Elegies* by episcopal order, records. Evidently, Marlowe's *professional* purpose in *Edward II* is to counter his rival colleagues' censoring of his works. Complexly, he uses Mortimer's grim elimination of the weaker Gaveston to simulate the triumph of Marlovian art over Spenserian and Shakespearean art. That Marlowe should choose as his principal source for this project the orthodox text of Holinshed's *Chronicles* is at once a testament to his genius and a register of the secrecy required to carry out a program securing his authority as England's counter-national poet.

This thesis reconfigures the massive scholarship on Marlowe's 'debt' to Shakespeare, as well as throw into relief the less-well-documented debt to Spenser.⁶ The sudden appearance of Shakespeare in Marlowe's representation of artistic rivalry marks a watershed event in his career; *Edward II* signals a changing of the Marlovian rival guard. As James Shapiro observes, 'in *Edward II* one can almost sense Marlowe playing at Shakespearean drama' (*Rival Playwrights* 91). This constitutes a change from the *Tamburlaine* plays, where Stephen Greenblatt and others sense Marlowe playing with Spenserian poesy. Scholars have long noted that a famous line spoken by Hamlet derives peculiarly from Mortimer – 'and as a traveller / Goes to discover countries yet unknown' (V.vi.65–6). Is it possible that in Hamlet's metaphysical discourse on '[t]he undiscover'd country, from whose bourn / No traveller returns' (*Hamlet* III.i.78–9) Shakespeare is revealing that he found himself in Marlowe's anti-Gaveston faction? And is it possible that he found in Mortimer more than a critique of himself – that is, a sympathetic homage as well? If so, we can witness a feature of Marlovian rivalry that we have not yet seen: the 'rash' playwright's attempt to pay homage to a rival he is trying to eclipse.

In *Edward II*, then, written near the close of Marlowe's (counter-Spenserian) career, we may be intrigued to discover a partially sympathetic character named 'Spencer,' and it now becomes a special challenge to discover Marlowe evoking his first great rival. 'Spencer, sweet Spencer, I adopt thee here,' cries Edward (III.ii.144). What is of particular note is the change of Marlowe's representational attitude towards Spenser. Critics typically emphasize the 'maturity' of the play, and to the usual evidence we can add the mature handling of poetic rivalry. In this play, we can detect some changes from *Tamburlaine*. First, Marlowe no longer feels the need to 'plagiarize' Spenser in order to deconstruct him; he can proceed with more subtlety, relying on what Derrida calls 'trace[s]' (26).[7] Second, as with the more famous case of Shakespeare, here Marlowe has enough confidence to pay homage to Spenser, even as he tries to eclipse him. Finally, most complex of all, Marlowe now *unfolds* his traces of Spenser into both halves of the competition for the sovereign's will – *both* Mortimer and Mortimer's victims, Spencer and Gaveston.

Along with poetic rivalry, Marlowe matures in his reading of Spenserian nationhood. From *Dido* to *The Jew*, Marlowe sees Spenser writing a nationhood of royal power; in *Edward II*, he appears to recognize Spenser's 'ambivalence concerning absolute royal power' (Helgerson, *Forms of Nationhood* 55). If Spenser does end by championing 'aristocratic independence' (57), Marlowe may have come to discern an analogue, perhaps a conjunction, between his own Lucanic- and Ovidian-based nationhood of *libertas* and Spenser's nationhood of aristocratic power.[8]

'Wanton poets': Gaveston's Marlovian Theatrics

In the first part of his strategy, Marlowe introduces Gaveston as a successful Ovidian artist relying on Machiavellian policy.[9] The opening scene, showing Gaveston alone, then in dialogue with '*three* Poor Men' (s.d.), then alone again, functions as the play's prologue, with Gaveston '[d]ramatically positioned in the role of the play's Presenter' (Cartelli 123–4). Initially, Gaveston appears '*reading on a letter that was brought him from the King*' (s.d.); this is the first instance of what Marjorie Garber calls 'the material embodiment of the concept of countertext as counterplot' ('"Here's Nothing Writ"' 301), and it occasions the opening part of Gaveston's soliloquy:

'My father is deceas'd, come Gaveston,
And share the kingdom with thy dearest friend.'
Ah, words that make me surfeit with delight!

What greater bliss can hap to Gaveston
Than live and be the favourite of a king?
Sweet prince I come; these, these thy amorous lines
Might have enforc'd me to have swum from France,
And like Leander, gasp'd upon the sand,
So thou wouldst smile and take me in thy arms.
The sight of London to my exil'd eyes
Is as Elysium to a new-come soul.

(*Edward II* I.i.1–11)

Marlowe's metadiscourse is evident in Gaveston's 'reading on a letter,' in his repetition of Edward's 'words,' and in his own phrase for his sovereign's language: 'amorous lines.' As the mention of Leander indicates, however, Marlowe contextualizes his metadiscourse in terms of his own 'Ovidian' career. Although we cannot tell whether 'Leander' refers to a *Hero and Leander* he has already written or advertises its advent, we inescapably find a self-reference.[10]

As if to emphasize the Ovidian career context of his historical tragedy, Marlowe presents his figure out of English chronicle voicing a well-known historical event (the 'decease' of Edward's 'father' and the recall of Edward's 'dearest friend') *as a revoicing of a famous Marlovian line*. Critics have long observed that Edward's quoted lines repeat with a difference the famous lines from 'The Passionate Shepherd to His Love' (Forsythe 699–700) – a repetition (or anticipation) that we have seen in *Dido*, the *Tamburlaine* plays, and *The Jew of Malta*: 'Come, Gaveston, / And share the kingdom with thy dearest friend.' Marlowe's self-imitation functions as a meta-imitation, and it inaugurates the Ovidian tragic mode, the 'amorous line,' which constitutes the political problem both in and of the play: what happens when an English sovereign *reads Marlowe*? He ceases to speak in his own regal or political voice (recorded in Holinshed); he breaks into Marlovian discourse. From the outset, the playwright contextualizes 'English history' in terms of Marlovian tragedy. The 'Edward' whom Gaveston enunciates is neither the 'historical' king who ruled between 1307 and 1327 (alas, he lies cold as stone in his grave), nor even Holinshed's 'Edward, the second of that name, the son of Edward the first' (rpt. in Thomas and Tydeman 351); rather, he is Marlowe's 'King, upon whose bosom [Gaveston wants to] ... die' (I.i.14). More technically, this sovereign is Gaveston's 'pliant King,' who '[m]ay [be] draw[n] ... which way ... [Gaveston] please[s]' (52), since Gaveston, not Edward himself, speaks Edward's words – 'words that make [Gaveston] ... surfeit with delight!' By opening the play with a character in a dramatic fiction (Gaveston) voicing the words of a sovereign (Edward), who himself imitates an English chronicle writer (Holinshed), but who in fact imitates the play's own author, Marlowe alerts his audience to the most elemental passion of his play: not early fourteenth-century English politics or sodomy, but the complex literary system of communication that can best represent the problematic conjunction of politics and sodomy in late sixteenth-century England.

When Gaveston speaks in his own words, he does not extricate himself from this system, but clarifies what Garber calls, echoing Harry Levin, 'the play's overreaching author, Christopher Marlowe' (320). Quoting 'Marlowe' even more precisely than Edward does, Gaveston reproduces the key active words that echo through 'The Passionate Shepherd,' *Dido*, the *Tamburlaine* plays, and *The Jew*; these words succinctly represent the Marlovian conversion of an Ovidian ethics (*come, live*) into an Ovidian ontology (*be*): '*live* and *be* the favourite of a king? / Sweet prince I *come*.' Syntactically, Marlowe bookends the linguistic sign of ontology with twin signs from an Ovidian ethics: *live ... be ... come*. Ontology loses its virginal *telos*, imprisoned as a hapless mediator for sexual desire. Not simply do Gaveston's words echo Edward's; his system of literary imitation reproduces Marlowe's.

If we miss this system in the first six lines, Marlowe ensures that we become alert to it in lines 7 and 8, when he refers to 'Leander.' Here we are to see not simply an analogy between Leander's love of Hero and Gaveston's love of Edward, but Marlowe's attempt to rechannel the cultural flow of sanctified desire from heterosexualism to homoeroticism. We are also to see Marlowe's attempt to reinscribe the Machiavellian policy of Gaveston's designs in Ovidian terms. Given Marlowe's initial surge of metadiscourse, we can identify Gaveston's bridging word in his Leander simile, 'like' – the formal figural trope of similitude – as itself a fine metonym for the process of literary imitation. Marlowe repeats this strategy in the remaining lines and reveals its rhetorical direction: Gaveston's heroic, and even theologically charged return to 'London' stages the return of 'the play's overreaching author.'[11]

Within this metatheatrical system, Gaveston inscribes data from another Marlowe play: *Doctor Faustus*. Again, we cannot tell whether Marlowe is referring to a play he has written or is advertising a play he plans to write, but once more we inescapably detect a self-reference. Gaveston's 'surfeit with delight' resembles Faustus's 'surfeit ... upon cursed necromancy' (Pr.25; see V.ii.37). Similarly, Gaveston's 'greater bliss' resembles Faustus's 'chiefest bliss' (Pr.27). Finally, Gaveston's comparison of London to 'Elysium' resembles Faustus's 'confound[ing] hell in Elysium' (I.iii.61).[12]

In the first half of Gaveston's opening soliloquy, then, Marlowe uses self-quotation and self-reference to *trans-scribe* what Levin calls 'the pastoral fields of Ovidian lyricism' (32) within the Holinshedian genre pertaining to English historical tragedy. What both Edward's 'amorous lines' and Gaveston's subsequent lines voice is the linguistic current that in this play must be evaporated: not simply the playwright's usurpation of generic decorum – his intrusion of the Ovidian within the Holinshedian – but the absorption of the Holinshedian by the Ovidian: the refacing of English history by Ovidian *amor*. In Marlowe's hands, Holinshed's 'lines' indeed become 'amorous': they are Ovidianized.

The last half of Gaveston's opening speech, quoted in the introduction, does not refer to or quote from the author's works, but it does strike the tenor of another prologue, spoken by the 'presenter' of *The Jew of Malta*: 'Not that I love the city or the men, ... / As for the multitude, that are but sparks / Rak'd up in embers of their poverty' (12–21). Like Machevill, Gaveston voices insolence and contempt, relies on rhetorical question and exclamation, demystifies religious orthodoxy, and even tropes the 'soul's' international migration: '*Tanti!* I'll fan first on the wind, / That glanceth at my lips and flieth away' (22–3). Whereas the first half of Gaveston's speech proceeds in the Ovidian mode, the second half proceeds in the Machiavellian. If Gaveston first uses the Ovidian to voice his intimate relation with a single individual, he next uses the Machiavellian mode to detach himself from the nation.[13]

While Gaveston's discourse identifies him as a Machiavel, we can detect a change from *The Jew of Malta*. Machiavellian policy now serves Ovidian ends. London appears to Gaveston as Elysium not because it is a place worth loving intrinsically (for 'the city or the men'), but because it 'harbours him I hold so dear.' Ovidian intimacy, not Machiavellian power over the nation, becomes the *telos* of Gaveston's appetitive imagination.

The opening soliloquy, with its elaborate system of authorial self-presentation, intensifies a revolutionary strategy that we have witnessed in embryo form in earlier plays: Marlowe dramatizes his own authorship of a medium traditionally held to be void of 'the recital of the poet himself' (Plato, *Republic* III.394b). We should not be surprised, then, when Gaveston lapses into the allure of a Machiavellian plot for a new Ovidian theatre:

I must have wanton poets, pleasant wits.
Musicians, that with touching of a string
May draw the pliant King which way I please;
Music and poetry is his delight:
Therefore I'll have Italian masques by night,
...

Sometime a lovely boy in Dian's shape,

...

Shall bathe him in a spring; and there hard by,
One like Actaeon peeping through the grove,
Shall by the angry goddess be transform'd,
By yelping hounds pull'd down, and seem to die.
Such things as these best please his majesty.

(*Edward II* I.1.50–70)

Gaveston here projects his production of a 'masque' about the Ovidian story of Diana and Actaeon as a Machiavellian strategy for wooing his sovereign.[14]

If in Gaveston's first soliloquy Marlowe uses self-reference and self-quotation to identify Gaveston as a Marlovian Ovidian poet, in this one he offers a kind of 'dumb-show' of the Marlovian Ovidian art itself (cf. Sunesen). Among the rhetorical elements of this show, a few deserve attention. The first pertains to audience and purpose. Marlowe views his art as a form of political rhetoric, designed to persuade the power structure, especially the sovereign. Within the 'play,' that sovereign is English, yet few critics have contextualized Marlowe's politics in terms of his English sovereign.[15] Yet recent political critics do see Marlowe generally 'foreground[ing] ... the idea of patronage' and 'question[ing] ... the concept of the mis-advised monarch' (Shepherd 118, 122); or they see him boldly 'represent[ing] ... the execution as well as the deposition of a monarch,' localizing Mortimer through 'topical, or Elizabethan, associations' as 'contemporary preachers' who 'attacked theatrical excess' and who criticized 'Ralegh, Essex, Hatton and the others who devoted themselves to gaining and retaining, Her Majesty's pleasure' (Sales 113, 123–4, 126). We may endorse these comments but refocus them on Marlowe's subversion of monarchical power and his topical representations of Puritan attacks on the theatre and outbursts against the Queen's favourites. In *Edward II*, Marlowe challenges a writer like Spenser who was using his art to promote himself as a servant of a wise and just queen.[16]

To discover how Marlowe uses Gaveston's 'Italian masques by night' to function as a model of his Ovidian art designed to affect Elizabeth, we can profitably turn to an arresting element in Gaveston's soliloquy: the myth of Actaeon.[17] As Leonard Barkan observes, 'the story of Actaeon is one of the paradigmatic episodes in the *Metamorphoses*.'[18]

In the famous autobiographical poem, Book II of the *Tristia*, Ovid pauses to brood over the event he does not name because it compelled Augustus to banish him: 'Why did I see anything? Why did I make my eyes guilty? Why was I so thoughtless as to harbour the knowledge of a fault? Unwitting was Actaeon when he beheld Diana unclothed; none the less he became the prey of his own hounds' (103–8). Instead of answering the questions, Ovid lapses into myth. When we desire historical event, Ovid gives us timeless mythology. And yet our foiled expectation helps us to establish our own equation: we are to see Ovid as an Actaeon who '[u]nwitting[ly]' spied a divine figure in a way that compromised that deity's privacy, and therefore his own identity as a (human) poet.

We do not know the chronological relation between Ovid's penning of the Actaeon story in the *Metamorphoses* and the Actaeon-like espial that secured his banishment; hence, we lack access to Ovid's intent in placing the story within his counter-Virgilian epic.[19] Luckily, we need not solve the question for Ovid; we need only observe what Marlowe could have *seen*. By reading the *Tristia* into the *Metamorphoses* (as modern critics themselves do), Marlowe could see a representation of Ovid's own fate in the Augustan literary system: his playful use of an amorous art that becomes subjected to political tyranny – 'the mercilessness of absolute power' (Otis 145). For Marlowe, as indeed for his own contemporaries, the Actaeon myth becomes the paradigmatic myth of Ovid's literary career.[20]

What is remarkable is not that Marlowe would appropriate the Actaeon myth to identify himself as an Ovidian poet par excellence (any astute writer could do that), but that his use of the myth in the prologue-like opening to *Edward II* should communicate so hauntingly our sense of his art near the end of his life. First, we often understand his art as an Ovidian 'comed[y]' of play redefined through the homoerotic vehicle of the Elizabethan theatre, in which 'a lovely boy in Dian's shape' works to 'hide those parts which men delight to see'; hence, under Gaveston's direction, the terribly unjust and haunting tale that Ovid tells in the *Metamorphoses* becomes the source for witty verbal play: the phrase 'By yelping hounds pull'd down, and seem to die' linguistically converts a tragedy ending in mutilation into a comic myth arriving at orgasm, as the well-noted Elizabethan pun on 'die' reveals (Deats, 'Fearful Symmetry' 246). Second, we see that Marlowe is predicting the necessarily *tragic* conclusion of such a project, as Gaveston dramatizes. By letting the second and the first conclusions collide, we can arrive at a third – a construct for Marlowe's paradigmatic representation of his art: paradoxically, he uses 'Sweet speeches, comedies, and pleasing shows' to 'peep ... through the grove.' Fusing the comic to the tragic, he uses erotic play to peer into the privacy of the Queen's political policy, making 'the goddess' *angry*. Ovidian play both masques and masks Machiavellian policy in order to fulfil Ovidian fate, not to conceal it.[21]

That Marlowe presents Gaveston as an Ovidian dramatist using an erotic art to move the sovereign may be confirmed by one subsequent 'career' image familiar from *Ovid's Elegies*, *Dido*, and the *Tamburlaine* plays: that of the chariot *cursus*. Gaveston tells Edward, 'It shall suffice me to enjoy your love, / Which whiles I have, I think myself as great / As Caesar riding in the Roman street / With captive kings at his triumphant car' (I.i.170–3). This is a bold thought, but a daring declaration, especially to a sovereign, and it situates Marlowe among contemporaries like Spenser, who were using their art to equalize themselves with their sovereign through self-presentation: the 'sovereigne of song' (*November* 25). The Ovidian origins of Marlowe's image emerge in scene iv of Act I, when Mortimer Senior quotes Ovid to refer to Gaveston's fate, '*Quam male conveniunt!*' (13: 'How ill they suit' [*Met* II.846–7]), with Warwick adding, 'Ignoble vassal, that like Phaeton / Aspir'st unto the guidance of the sun' (16–17). While Gaveston's linking of 'love' and 'car' has Ovidian origins, the image of the 'triumphant' Caesar also recalls Lucan – and so may subtly prepare for, and even trope, a Marlovian *meta* from tragedy to epic.[22]

'I see my tragedy written in thy brows': Mortimer's Counter-Marlovian Theatrics

In the second part of his dramatic strategy, Marlowe reconfigures Holinshed's depiction of Mortimer's 'tragic fall' via Machiavelli and Ovid in order to depict the counter-force to Gaveston's Ovidian comedy. In fact, the most significant change Marlowe makes to Holinshed lies in depicting Mortimer as Gaveston's enemy. To do so, Marlowe takes Holinshed's interspersed comments on Edward's revelry and makes them the topic of Mortimer's complaint against the king.[23] What is most notable is that Marlowe transfers Holinshed's 'antitheatricality' entirely to Mortimer in order to dramatize the motive for an antagonism that is itself the product of Marlowe's fancy.[24]

We can scrutinize Mortimer's indictment against Gaveston's and Edward's theatricality in terms of Marlowe's rivalry with 'the truly political animal among English sixteenth-century poets' (Crewe, *Hidden Designs* 89): Spenser.[25] The most significant borrowing for understanding Spenser's presence in the play lies in the phrase 'deads the royal vine.' Marlowe's phrase comes from the written 'message' spoken by the Herald, who has 'com'st from Mortimer and his complices' (153), and it is addressed to Edward:

> That from your princely person you remove
> This Spencer, as a putrefying branch

That deads the royal vine, whose golden leaves
Empale your princely head, your diadem,
Whose brightness such pernicious upstarts dim.

(Edward II III.ii.161–5)

The lyricism or golden imagery here – 'branch ... vine ... golden leaves ... diadem ... brightness' – has the general tenor of Spenserian discourse, but Charlton and Waller were evidently the first to alert us to an actual borrowing from Spenser.

In *The Teares of the Muses*, published in the 1591 *Complaints* volume, and thus available to Marlowe, Thalia, the Muse of Comedy, laments the defacing of English comedy by those who turn the genre to 'a laughing game' (204). She then pauses to lament the death of one individual who excelled in comedy: 'Our pleasant Willy, ah is dead of late: / With whom all joy and jolly meriment / Is also deaded, and in dolour drent' (208–10). We do not know the identity of 'pleasant Willy.'[26] What is initially striking, however, is the possibility that Marlowe is imitating a line topical in its significance: Spenser is praising a writer of comedies whom he considers to be in his own literary circle.

The 'pleasant Willy' lines are part of a larger passage in which Spenser uses Thalia to decry a group of poetasters ruining English comedy; the lines immediately following read:

In stead thereof scoffing Scurrilitie,
And scornfull Follie with Contempt is crept,
Rolling in rymes of shamles ribaudrie
Without regard, or due Decorum kept,
Each idle wit at will presumes to make,
And doth the Learneds taske upon him take.

(*The Teares of the Muses* 211–16)

As in the case of 'pleasant Willy,' we do not know here who Spenser has in mind. William Renwick can avoid the obvious inference, that Lyly and the University Wits are under attack, only by claiming that the passage was 'written about 1578–80' (209) – a conclusion rejected by recent scholars.[27] Indeed, the penultimate and final lines look to be a troping of the University Wits, with their 'Learned' art of making organized around pride in the self, wit, and ultimately will, as described by G.K. Hunter in his fine book on Lyly. The phrase 'scoffing Scurrilitie' may suggest Nashe in his debate with Spenser's friend Gabriel Harvey, which was raging in the bookstalls at precisely this time (see Moore), but the phrase also echoes contemporary descriptions of Marlowe, as in the most famous, by Robert Greene in his 1588 *Perimedes the Blacksmith*: 'such mad and *scoffing* poets, that have propheticall spirits as bold as Merlins race' (rpt. in MacLure, ed., *Marlowe* 30; emphasis added). Spenser's diagnosis that such writers are controlled by 'Contempt' anticipates Greenblatt's observation: 'For Marlowe ... the dominate mode of perceiving the world ... is *contempt*' ('Marlowe, Marx' 46; emphasis in original).

But it is in the next stanza that we may find an even more precise representation of Marlowe, when Spenser contrasts the 'pen' of 'that same gentle Spirit' (usually identified as Spenser's own [Oram et al. 277] with 'the boldnes of such base-borne men, / Which *dare their follies forth so rashlie throwe*' (217–20; emphasis added). Spenser's phrasing recalls Greene's other construction for Marlowe, 'daring God out of heaven with that Atheist Tamburlan' (rpt. MacLure, ed., *Marlowe* 29), and thus Marlowe's own construction for Tamburlaine: 'His looks do menace heaven and dare the gods' (*1 Tamb* I.ii.157). Spenser concludes by criticizing such a poet or poets for 'mockerie to sell' (222) – likely a gibe at Marlowe and the University Wits, who turned their university learning to profit by writing plays and pamphlets to suit vulgar taste.[28]

Given that Marlowe's 'vine' is 'royal,' he may also be responding to *Colin Clouts Come Home Againe* (written 1591; published 1595). Speaking of 'Cynthia' (Queen Elizabeth), Spenser writes: 'And eke to make the dead againe alive. / Her deeds were like great clusters of ripe grapes, / Which load the braunches of the fruitful vine' (599–601). Whereas Spenser tropes Elizabeth's 'deeds' as grapes loading the 'braunches of the fruitful vine,' Marlowe tropes 'Spencer's' deeds as a 'putrefying braunch' deading the 'royal vine.'[29] The vine at stake for Marlowe is certainly the traditional royal one, but as Charles Forker notes, 'the leaves that adorned the crown of Edward II ... were strawberry leaves, not vine leaves' (229). Marlowe's adjustment of the historical 'leaves' prompts us to speculate on the reason for the change.

Marlowe says that the vine Edward wears '[e]mpale[s]' his 'princely head' – 'encircle[s] ... as with a garland' (Forker 229). The image of a garland made of vine suggests Bacchus, the god of wine and tragedy, as Spenser writes in the *October* eclogue of *The Shepheardes Calender*: 'O if my temples were distain'd with wine, / And girt in girlonds of wild Yvie twine, / How I could reare the Muse on stately stage, / And teach her tread aloft in bus-kin fine' (110–13). Possibly, Marlowe's change of Edward's strawberry garland to a vine garland contributes to the well-documented metadrama of the play: Edward's empalement by his own ivy garland metonymically renders the genre of 'historical tragedy' itself. Given that the image appears to respond to Spenser within a political or 'Elizabethan' context, we may wonder what it is that Spenser is empaling here.

The larger dramatic passage in which the Spenser borrowing occurs helps us formulate a response. The earl of Arundel is informing Edward and Spenser about significant courtly news – 'for Gaveston is dead' (90) – and he uses a phrase that should alert us to the metadrama: 'Pembroke's men' (116). The Earl of Warwick, he reports, 'seiz'd' Gaveston in an 'ambush' of 'Pembroke's men,' to whom Gaveston had been 'deliver'd' (115–18). In the previous scene, Marlowe has actually staged this ambush, beginning with the stage direction to III.i: *Enter* Gaveston *mourning*, [James,] *and the Earl of Pembroke's Men.*' Warwick and '*his Company*' (s.d.) step forward to accost the procession, with the earl directing the action: 'My lord of Pembroke's men, / Strive you no longer; I will have that Gaveston' (6–7). This is splendid metadrama. For the acting 'Company' performing the ambush is named 'Pembroke's Men,' identified on the title page of the 1594 edition: 'Edward the second ... As it was sundrie times publiquely acted in the honourable citie of London, by the right honourable the Earle of Pembrooke his servants,' popularly called 'Pembroke's Men.' If we miss the identification between 'Pembroke's men' within the play and Pembroke's Men acting it, Marlowe ensures that we see it when he has the theatrically inclined Edward remark: 'In solemn triumphs and in public shows / Pembroke shall bear the sword before the King' (I.iv.349–50). Marlowe's strategy of relying on a historical family name out of the chronicles of Edward II to refer to the current Pembroke family and even his own theatrical patron, the Earl of Pembroke, also bears on the topic of Marlowe's staging of the 'Spenser' family and their relation to Edmund Spenser.[30]

Arundel's announcement of the death of Gaveston leads Edward to call immediately for 'Remembrance of revenge immortally' (140) against Warwick and Mortimer and to adopt Spenser as his new favourite: 'And in this place of honour and of trust, / Spenser, sweet Spenser, I adopt thee here' (143–4). That last line places 'Spenser' in the path of *succession*, and thus of literary imitation itself. Marlowe reiterates the phrase 'sweet Spenser' three more times in the play (IV.vi.72, 95, 110; cf. 'gentle Spenser' at III.ii.24). The phrase recalls an epithet for Edmund Spenser assigned by his own contemporaries, including Marlowe's friend and fellow street-fighter Thomas Watson, who in the 1590 'Eclogue Upon the death of ... Walsingham' had curiously used the phrase to describe Spenser as a tragedian: '*dulcis Spencere cothurno*' – sweet in the Spenser buskin – which Watson himself translated as 'sweet Spencer' (Cummings 70–1).[31]

Marlowe assigns the construction to the anti-Gaveston faction of Mortimer; thus, complexly, within a single scene we appear to find two conflicting responses to Spenser: the first calls him 'sweet' and 'adopt[s]' him 'here'; the second parodies his sweetness and disinherits him.[32]

For the most part, Marlowe's Spenserianisms come from Mortimer's enemies, especially Gaveston, Edward, and Spencer the Younger. As we have seen in the 'putrefying branch' passage, however, it is Mortimer himself who is responsible for such counter-Spenc/serian discourse. And it is Mortimer who most recurrently voices the play's metadrama – both for and against theatre.[33] Consider Mortimer's often-quoted condemnation of Gaveston at the end of Act I, uttered to his uncle, Mortimer Senior (iv.401–18): 'Midas-like he jets it in the court ... / As if that Proteus, god of shapes, appear'd' (7, 10). What makes Mortimer impatient are three traits of Gaveston's character: he is 'basely born' (402); he is extravagantly theatrical in both action and dress ('proud fantastic liveries make such show' [409]); and he scorns the theatricality of others ('flout our train, and jest at our attire' [417]).[34]

Proteus is not merely the 'god of shapes'; he is also a figure for the actor, as revealed in 'The Prologue to the Stage at the Cock-Pit' prefacing the 1633 edition of *The Jew of Malta*, which describes Edward Alleyn, 'the best of actors': 'being a man / Whom we may rank with ... / Proteus for shapes' (4–10).[35] Marlowe links the Protean Gaveston with acting not merely by using ornate dress to trope theatrical costume (the 'fantastic liver[y]' of Gaveston *is* literally the actor's costume), but also by using both the word 'show' as a transition from the description of Gaveston's dress to the Proteus simile and the word 'appear'd' to end the simile itself.

Mortimer's speech thus crafts a fine piece of metadrama; it appears to represent Marlowe's rivals' indictment of Marlowe. The competitive indictment emphasizes Marlowe's Ovidian theatre, with its rich classical mythography out of the *Metamorphoses*, its foxy Machiavellianism, its biting 'contempt,' and its homoeroticism.

As Mortimer reappears, however, he increasingly resembles the theatrical agents he is rivalling. In Act II, scene ii, for instance, he becomes a Spenserian allegorist, arriving before his sovereign with an emblematic 'device' engraved on his shield (11), as he describes it to Edward: 'A lofty cedar tree fair flourishing, / On whose top branches kingly eagles perch, / And by the bark a canker creeps me up' (16–18).[36] Alert hermeneut that he is, Edward quickly construes the allegory: 'I am that cedar; shake me not too much. / And you the eagles; soar ye ne'er so high, / I have the jesses that will pull you down, / And *Aeque tandem* shall that canker cry / Unto the proudest peer of Britainy' (38–42).

To construct Mortimer's allegory of the kingly cedar tree, the protective eagle/barons, and the canker/Gaveston, Marlowe may have collated two sonnet allegories in Spenser's 1591 *Complaints* volume. Sonnet 7 of *Visions of the Worlds Vanitie* tells how '[h]igh on a hill a goodly Cedar grewe,' until '[s]hortly within her inmost pith there bred / A litle wicked worme' (1–7). Like Mortimer's allegory, Spenser's depicts the canker worm destroying the cedar tree. To find the birds and the cedar, we may turn to a related set of allegorical sonnets, *The Visions of Bellay*: 'Upon an hill a bright flame I did see, ... / Which like incense of precious Cedar tree, ... / A Bird all white, well feathered on each wing' (11: 1–6). Although the bird emerging from the flames is not the eagle, and the 'Cedar tree' appears inside a simile, Marlowe's imagination may have ranged over this recent publication and aligned it with the cedar/canker sonnet in the previous set of poems. While in both allegories Spenser places himself in the apocalyptic tradition, Mortimer politicizes the imagery in terms of English kingship. What is noteworthy is his sudden reliance on the Spenserian allegorical mode as a Machiavellian strategy for contesting his sovereign's (Ovidian) authority.

Hence, later in the scene Mortimer ridicules Edward by lapsing into theatrical discourse: 'thy soldiers marched like players, / With garish robes, not armour; and thyself, / Bedaub'd with gold, rode laughing at the rest' (182–5). Within the drama of the play, Mortimer is accusing Edward of foolishly showing up for a war by tricking out his soldiers like 'players' in their 'garish robes.' Within the play of the drama, however, Marlowe is inscribing the theatricality of his own dramatic action, through Edward, who is 'like' an actor, and through Mortimer, who voices the theatrical simile.[37]

Not surprisingly, the critic of Edward's theatricality turns to theatricality himself. In Act IV, scene i, Mortimer enters '*disguised*' (s.d.) – doubly dressed in an actor's costume. And in Act V, scene ii, he identifies his plan to assassinate the king as 'plots and stratagems' (78). To enact the 'plot,' he devises a two-pronged Machiavellian ploy. First, he will write a death warrant with equivocation: 'And therefore will I do it cunningly. / This letter, written by a friend of ours, / Contains his death yet bids them save his life: "*Edwardum occidere nolite timere bonum est*"' (V.iv.5–7). As he put it earlier to his mistress, Queen Isabella, 'a king's name shall be underwrit' (ii.14). Second, he will direct his principal actor, Lightborn, in the supreme Ovidian act of Machiavellian play.

Critics have long focused on Lightborn, in part because he is Marlowe's splendid creation, but recently they have emphasized Marlowe's use of Lightborn to lapse into 'allegory.'[38] As Lightborn himself reports to Mortimer in an autobiography reminiscent of those by Barabas and Ithamore in *The Jew of Malta*, he seeks to enact an allegory of Machiavellian policy: 'I learn'd in Naples how to poison flowers; / To strangle with a lawn thrust through the throat; / ... / But yet I have a braver way than these' (iv.31–7). As he hints in that last claim, he is a Machiavellian plotter in the homoerotic domain.

Yet it is his acting director who links Machiavelli with Ovid most directly. As soon as Lightborn exits, Mortimer lapses into the discourse of the Machiavel by actually quoting Ovid:

The Prince I rule, the Queen do I command,

...

I seal, I cancel, I do what I will;
Fear'd am I more than lov'd: let me be fear'd,
And when I frown, make all the court look pale.

...

Mine enemies will I plague, my friends advance,
And what I list command, who dare control?
Maior sum quam cui possit fortuna nocere.

(*Edward II* V.iv.48–69)

The Ovid quotation comes from the story of Niobe, the wife of Amphion, in Book VI of the *Metamorphoses*: 'I am too great for Fortune to harm' (195) – just before Fortune strikes her down, killing her husband (Amphion commits suicide) and their seven sons. Evidently, Marlowe finds the Machiavel in Ovid, and it does not bode well for his own Ovidian Machiavel, who is using his secret affair with a queen to bring about the downfall of a king. 'Fair Isabel,' he caresses her earlier, 'now have we our desire ... / Be rul'd by me, and we will rule the realm' (ii.1–5).

Thus both the penultimate and the final scenes of the play 'underwrite' an Ovidian 'tragedy' in the Machiavellian mode. In Act V, scene v, the murder scene itself, Lightborn begins and ends with self-reflexive delight in the deception he is enacting, rehearsing the principle of theatricality articulated by Stephen Greenblatt with respect to Barabas: 'he seems to be pursuing deception virtually for its own sake' ('Marlowe, Marx' 52). Lightborn begins with a cheerful soliloquy: 'So now must I about this gear; ne'er was there any / So finely handl'd as this king shall be' (38–9). And afterwards, he exclaims to the two men about to kill him, 'Tell me sirs, was it not bravely done?' (115) – the word 'bravely' functioning as a theatrical term (Cole, *Christopher Marlowe* 118). As with Barabas, critics have identified Lightborn as a figure for the Marlovian dramatist himself, constructing savage plots.[39] We may add that Lightborn is constructing savage plots against both his sovereign and the sovereign of song. Thus the king himself sees that he is being underwritten by Lightborn's Marlovian 'tragedy': 'I see my tragedy written in thy brows' (73). It is worse than this, for Marlowe relies on Holinshed to out-Seneca Seneca: *the tragedy is written in his bowels*:[40]

they came suddenly one night into the chamber where he lay in bed fast asleep, and with heavy featherbeds or a table (as some *write*) being cast upon him, they kept him down and withal put into his fundament an *horn*, and through the same they thrust up into his body an hot spit, or (as other have) through *the pipe of a trumpet*, a plumber's instrument of iron made very hot, the which passing up into his entrails, and being rolled to and fro, burnt the same, but so as no *appearance* of any wound or hurt outwardly might be once *perceived*. (Holinshed, *Chronicles*, rpt. in Thomas and Tydeman 369; emphasis added)

'Now ... begins our tragedy':
Edward III's Counter-Marlovian Theatrics

In the play's final scene, Marlowe inscribes the final part of his strategy. He dramatizes the suppression of Mortimer by orthodox forces, represented in the new king, the young Edward III. Here Marlowe pauses to juxtapose Edward's 'tragedy' with Mortimer's, as the Queen speaks it: 'Now, Mortimer, begins our tragedy' (V.vi.23). The director of this final drama is himself self-consciously theatrical, as the young king reveals when the Lord enters '*with the head of* Mortimer' (s.d.): 'Go fetch my father's hearse, where it shall lie, / And bring my funeral robes' (V.vi.94–5). Young Edward's directive recalls Dido's directive to Aeneas at the beginning of Marlowe's dramatic career: 'Warlike Aeneas, and in these base robes! / Go fetch the garment which Sichaeus ware' (*Dido* II.i.79–80). In the later play, we may discover a metadiscursive pun on 'hearse' – as Spenser had employed it famously in his Melpomene-inspired funeral Song of Dido in the *November* eclogue: 'O heavie herse, ... O carefull verse' (60, 62). Thus we may relish the theatricality dramatized when the boy calls for his actor's 'robes.' The final utterance of the play, spoken once the new king has his hearse and wears his robes, also resounds with the Senecan ghost of Marlowe's Ovidian and Machiavellian theatre:

Sweet father here, unto thy murder'd ghost,
I offer up this wicked traitor's head;
And let these tears distilling from mine eyes
Be witness of my grief and innocency.

(*Edward II* V.vi.99–102)

Wilbur Sanders notes 'the unfinished air of the concluding lines' (128), and no modern critic has rested comfortably with them. What Frank Kermode says of Shakespeare's achievement in *Romeo and Juliet* (Introduction, *Riverside Shakespeare* 1057), we may counterfeit for Marlowe's profession in *Edward II*: that the play has a strong *professional* interest is clear; but Marlowe has now passed the stage when one could say, without too much injury to the work, precisely what that interest may have been.

'Actors in this massacre':
The Massacre at Paris and
the Orphic Guise of Metatheatre

Of all Marlowe's plays, only *The Massacre at Paris* lacks a prologue or prologue-like opening. Four of the seven plays (*Tamburlaine, Parts 1 and 2, The Jew of Malta,* and *Doctor Faustus*) have formal prologues, while the remaining two (*Dido, Queen of Carthage* and *Edward II*) have scenes that are prologue-like in their self-reflexive commentary on the action (the Jupiter/Ganymede scene and the Gaveston soliloquy). Marlowe's prologues and prologue-like openings supply us with what little information we possess about Marlowe's sense of his project. Occasionally, these openings help us understand how he authors a play within the Ovidian pattern of his career: 'I come ... / ... to present the tragedy of a Jew, / Who smiles' (28–31). By contrast, *The Massacre at Paris* opens with a 'political idyll' (Steane 244), a rather un-Marlovian marriage scene that we expect only at the end of a play (especially a comedy). In their 'nuptial rites,' Navarre and Margaret create a 'religious league' by reconciling Christian opponents, the Huguenots and the Catholics, in order to establish a political 'union' between competing families, the House of Bourbon and the House of Valois (i.3–4). What distinguishes this opening from the openings of Marlowe's other plays, however, is the staging not simply of a publicly idyllic 'solemnity' (25), but more precisely of a political, religious, and sexual action bereft of significant metatheatrical charge.[1]

The distinctive opening of *The Massacre* is worth pausing over. In the other plays, Marlowe comments on or refers to his own work; he constructs a metatheatrical lens through which we are to view his dramatic action. As he instructs us at the close of the prologue to *1 Tamburlaine*, 'View but his picture in this tragic glass, / And then applaud his fortunes as you please' (7–8). The closest that the opening to *The Massacre* comes to such metatheatre occurs in the play's fourth speech, when Charles IX, King of France, refers to 'marriage-rites perform'd' (i.18), or again in the sixth speech, when he speaks of honouring this 'solemnity' (25). If we detect metatheatre here, we have to strain to see it, and it differs in significance from that in Marlowe's other openings.[2]

It is not that *The Massacre* fails to qualify as Marlovian metatheatre; it is that in this play alone we do not witness such theatre until the *second* scene. There, the Duke of Guise, whom the title page to the undated octavo identifies as the central character in the play ('The MASSACRE AT PARIS: With the Death of the Duke of Guise'), instructs a soldier to 'play thy tragic part' (28) by 'perform[ing the Lord High Admiral's] ... death' (31). The Guise's instruction links the central action of the play – 'the massacre at Paris' – with both its literary form ('tragedy') and its theatrical agency (actors 'playing a part'). The instruction also follows the cue of the title page by identifying the Guise as both the play's principal playwright and its central actor – its primary agent of metatheatre – as Henslowe's title in his *Diary* records: 'the tragedey of the gvyes' (qtd. in Oliver xlix).[3] Thus the Guise's instruction leads quickly to the play's greatest speech, his metatheatrically significant soliloquy (more of which presently), and then to a (fragmentary) metatheatrical action for the play as a whole, centred on the Guise's rise and fall, to be countered by Navarre's fall and rise.

We cannot determine why this play alone in Marlowe's canon fails to open with significant metatheatre. More than likely, it results from the unique status of the text, which scholars identify as hopelessly mangled, perhaps the product of several actors reconstructing Marlowe's original play from memory.[4] If the play is not even Marlowe's but a team of recorders', we need to be more careful here than in other (also problematic) works in situating the play within Marlowe's literary career.[5] Accordingly, we may limit discussion to a few remarks that aim to indicate how the 'incoherent' *Massacre at Paris* appears to cohere with Marlowe's Ovidian career. Like *The Jew of Malta* and *Edward II*, *The Massacre* is one of the three 'plays of policy' emerging in 'the later part of Marlowe's short career' (Leech, *Christopher Marlowe* 157).[6] Thus we may extend the general argument made about the other two plays of policy: in *The Massacre*, Marlowe fuses Machiavellian policy to Senecan tragedy to flesh out 'Ovidian tragedy'; he does so to contest the Virgilian career of his first great rival, Spenser; and in the process he continues to write counter-nationhood.[7]

Despite the incoherent text, *The Massacre* contains a remarkable strand of metatheatre. Clifford Leech remarks that the play joins *The Jew* and *Edward II* as a 'study' of 'the relations between people, and the relations between the individual and society' – in particular, 'the aspiring mind in relation to a society that is simultaneously corrupt and powerful' (*Christopher Marlowe*

157). We may contextualize this thesis in terms of the playwright's 'aspiring mind' as it relates both to a network of literary precursors – Ovid, Seneca, Lucan, Machiavelli, Spenser – and to an Elizabethan power structure, principally the Queen. We can manage this contextualization by focusing on the figure most famous as a portrait of Marlowe. In the Guise, we discover a pattern of rise and fall similar to that of Barabas and Edward, Ithamore and Gaveston. In this pattern, Marlowe dramatizes the 'tragic' destiny of the rebel playwright, caught in the web of literary and political intrigue, which ultimately secures his fatal end.[8]

'If ever Hymen lour'd at marriage-rites': Ovid/Seneca/Lucan/Machiavelli/Spenser

Constance B. Kuriyama warns us about granting the Guise 'the exalted status of Marlovian alter ego': Marlowe remains 'ambivalent' towards the Guise, and 'the entire structure of the play not only accommodates the Guise but also works toward his rejection. It is perhaps slightly more accurate to say that Marlowe was drawn toward the history of the massacre because it dramatized some of his deepest personal concerns, and suggested some possible solutions' (85). It is possible, however, to remain sensitive to 'the intricacy of Marlowe's mind and work' by emphasizing Marlowe's complex relation with the Guise, in which he indeed expresses 'ambivalence' about 'some of his deepest personal concerns' (Kuriyama 85). These concerns are not only of a 'psychoanalytic' stripe – the 'son's' attempt 'to find a viable defense against maternal and paternal dominance' (Kuriyama 94) – but also professional: the artist's attempt to find a defence against political and literary dominance. Marlowe's 'ambivalence' towards the Guise registers his own anxiety about the cultural role of his art.[9]

In the Guise's first utterance – his grim reflection on the dark fate of the 'marriage-rites' (ii.1) solemnized in the opening scene – Marlowe imitates Ovid, tropes Seneca, follows Machiavelli, and alludes to Spenser:

> If ever Hymen lour'd at marriage-rites,
> And had his altars deck'd with dusky lights;
> If ever sun stain'd heaven with bloody clouds,
> And made it look with terror on the world;
> If ever day were turn'd to ugly night,
> And night made semblance of the hue of hell;
> This day, this hour, this fatal night,
> Shall fully show the fury of them all.
>
> (*The Massacre at Paris* ii.1–8)

The Machiavellian tenor of this speech is clear, and Una M. Ellis-Fermor could well have cited it when she termed the Guise 'the most nearly Machiavellian figure that Marlowe ever drew' (106).

Evidently, however, J.S. Bennett first glossed the opening line by comparing Marlowe's use of Hymen with Ovid's in the opening line of Book X of the *Metamorphoses*, in which Ovid's Hymen presides fatally over the marriage of the poet Orpheus to his wife Eurydice (184), and H.J. Oliver has followed suit (98): 'Thence through the boundless air Hymen, clad in a saffron mantle, departed and took his way to the country of the Ciconians, and was summoned by the voice of Orpheus, though all in vain. He was present, it is true; but he brought neither the hallowed words, nor joyous face, nor lucky omen. The torch also which he held kept sputtering and filled the eyes with smoke, nor would it catch fire for any brandishing. The outcome of the wedding was worse than the beginning; for while the bride was strolling through the grass with a group of naiads in attendance, she fell dead, smitten in the ankle by a serpent's tooth' (1–10).[10] This is the hapless event that leads 'the bard of Rhodope' to 'try the shades': 'he dared to go down to the Stygian world through the gate of Taenarus' (11–13). In other words, Ovid's Hymen ushers in the death of heterosexual marriage, one result of which is the birth of homoerotic desire: 'Orpheus had shunned all love of womankind ... He set the example for the people of Thrace of giving his love to tender boys, and enjoying the springtime and first flower of their youth' (79–85). The mention of spring and flower prompts Ovid to refer to the 'hill' with the 'wide-extending plain, green with luxuriant grass,' where Orpheus uses his lyre to call in the neighbouring trees (86–105), one of which is the cypress. Ovid then tells his first story of homoerotic desire: Apollo's love for the boy Cyparissus.

We know that both Marlowe and Spenser were interested in Ovid's retelling of the Orpheus myth in Book X of the *Metamorphoses*. Spenser imitates Ovid's famous catalogue of trees near the beginning of Book I of *The Faerie Queene* (i.5–9; see Hamilton, ed., *FQ* 32); and in canto vi he refers to Sylvanus's love for 'dearest Cyparisse, ... the lovely boy' (17; see Hamilton, ed., *FQ* 89).[11] Long ago, Douglas Bush suggested that Marlowe imitates Spenser's Cyparissus passage in *Hero and Leander* ('Marlowe and Spenser') – 'Silvanus weeping for the lovely boy / That now is turned into a cypress tree' (I.154–5) – and the borrowing has been supported by Roma Gill in her article on Marlowe in *The Spenser Encyclopedia*. Spenser and Marlowe, however, take quite different interests in the Ovidian myth. Spenser associates the myth of Orpheus, the trees, and Cyparissus with error and wandering: he imitates Ovid's Orphic catalogue of trees in order to usher the reader into the Wandering Wood of Error; and he uses Sylvanus weeping for Cyparissus to help pinpoint the limitation of the satyrs, whom Sylvanus leads, for even though they rescue Una from the lawless Sansloy, they ultimately cannot retain the fidelity of 'Truth.' Marlowe, by contrast, works from a different sexual orientation, and he appears to have been attracted precisely to the myth of the homoerotic poet.[12]

Marlowe's imitation of the Orpheus myth encourages us to view the Guise as an Orphic artist. In opposing the rites of Hymen, he constructs an Ovidian, counter-Spenserian poetics of anti-marriage in what constitutes this play's most impressive reliance on the typology of intertextuality.

Under close scrutiny, the play's opening scene, featuring the 'nuptial rites' themselves, appears to stage Spenser's representation of marriage in Book I of *The Faerie Queene*. Addressing Navarre, the Prince of Conde, and the Lord Admiral, Charles IX opens the play:

> I wish this union and religious league,
> *Knit* in these *hands*, thus join'd in nuptial rites,
> *May not dissolve till death dissolve our lives,*
> And that the *native sparks* of princely love,
> That *kindled first* this motion in our hearts,
> May still be fuell'd in our progeny.
>
> (*The Massacre at Paris* i.3–8; emphasis added)

In Spenser, another king, the King of Eden, betroths his daughter, Una, to the Redcrosse Knight:

> And to the knight his daughter deare he tyde,
> With sacred *rites* and vowes for ever to abyde.
>
> His owne two *hands* the holy knots did *knit*,
>   That *none but death for ever can devide;*
>   His owne two hands, for such a turne most fit,
>   The housling *fire* did *kindle* and provide,
>   And holy water thereon sprinckled wide;
>   At which the bushy Teade a groome did light,
>   And sacred lampe in secret chamber hide.
>
> (*The Faerie Queene* I.xii.36–7; emphasis added)

Both kings bless a marriage, decree the marriage dissolvable only in 'death,' and rely on similar tropings: the formal knitting of hands, the underlying kindling of erotic fire. While both writers may be relying on formulas for English Protestant marriages, they share a troping in Ovid's Orphic marriage; this encourages us to see Marlowe using the civic formulas as a veil for transacting poetic rivalry – a complex variation on the typology of intertextuality.[13]

The Guise is not a black magician, like Faustus, but he does indulge in a discourse imbued with magical incantation, like Tamburlaine. Marlowe may even have had Ovid's Medea in mind when the Guise calls on the sun to stain 'heaven with bloody clouds,' bidding the day to 'turn ... to ugly night' and commanding 'night' to 'ma[k]e semblance of the hue of hell.'[14] For Medea uses incantation against the elements to sabotage a marriage she opposes – that between Jason and the daughter of Creon (*Metamorphoses* VII.201–9). Yet Marlowe's most striking image, the 'bloody clouds' that 'stain' the sun, has no counterpart in Ovid's epic. To find one, we can turn to another work of Ovid's, which Marlowe translated: 'Verses deduce the hornèd bloody moon, / And call the sun's white horses back at noon' (*Ovid's Elegies* II.i.23–4). In this elegy, Ovid describes the power of 'Verses' to 'ope doors' (27: 'carminibus cessere fores') – in particular, the power of his poetry to open the door of his mistress. While in *The Massacre* it is the clouds that are 'bloody' as they stain the sun (not the moon), the *Amores* image, with its attendant metadiscourse, remains a close analogue, if not an actual origin.[15]

Marlowe may also have recalled Spenser's imitation of Ovid's Medea in his description of Arthur's magic shield in *Faerie Queene* I – in yet another instance of the typology of intertextuality:

> For so exceeding shone his glistring ray,
> That Phoebus golden face it did attaint,
> As when a cloud his beames doth over-lay;
> And silver Cynthia wexed pale and faint,
> As when her face is staynd with magicke arts constraint.[16]
>
> (*The Faerie Queene* I.vii.34)

Several words and images reappear in line three of the Guise's speech: 'cloud,' the all-important 'staynd,' and the sun. Spenser's image is of a benevolent magic (Merlin has made Arthur's magic shield [I.vii.36]) to combat evil magic, with an astral illustration enlisted and supported by two astral similes: the magic shield is so bright it 'attaint[s]' the sun; this tainting is like the sun over-lain with clouds and like the moon stained by magic. Arthur's Merlin-based magic is more powerful than either sun or moon (see

III.iii.12); it is divinely ordained. By contrast, the Guise uses magical incantation to call on the sun to stain heaven with bloody clouds – a reversal that 'attaint[s]' the Spenserian process.

While the last line in the Guise's opening speech is general, it moves the counter-Spenserian discourse from poetry to drama, elegy to tragedy, Ovid to Seneca: 'fully *show* the *fury* of them all.' Indeed, the phrase 'show the fury' is a fine metadramatic rendering of Senecan tragedy itself.[17]

The Guise's following soliloquy is certainly 'the true Marlovian violence of expression' (Oliver lxxiii) and worthy of Harry Levin's discovery of the 'stark outline' of 'Marlovian tragedy,' an 'ethos of living dangerously, between the alternatives of aspiration and sedition' (23–4). The speech relies on Machiavellian, Ovidian, Senecan, and even Lucanic discourse to imitate Spenser and so to construct a comprehensive rival poetics.[18] The lengthy speech, totalling seventy-six lines, divides roughly into four parts. In the first (ll. 34–47), the Guise identifies his huge ambition and its method of policy; in the second (ll. 48–65), he relies on the seven-times repeated anaphora, 'For this,' to amplify the particulars; in the third (ll. 66–87), he focuses on the conclusion of the second, the policy of religion, to lay out his plan against the king, relying on the 'Mother Queen' (76); and in the fourth (ll. 88–109) he considers the threat of Navarre and steels himself against it, finding precedent in Caesar's war with Pompey.

A metatheatrics of professional competition also forms the conclusion to the soliloquy: 'The plot is laid, and things shall come to pass / Where resolution strives for victory' (108–9). The word 'plot' we have seen before. Marlowe uses it in *The Jew of Malta* to draw attention to the metatheatrics of Barabas's 'villainy' against Ferneze and the Christians: 'So neatly plotted, and so well perform'd' (III.iii.1–2).[19] The word 'strives' is the most recurrent Renaissance term for rivalry, and Spenser relies on it repeatedly, as in a passage from the *August* eclogue of *The Shepheardes Calender*, where two shepherds engage in a singing contest: 'But and if in rymes with me thou dare strive, / Such fond fantsies shall soone be put to flight' (21–2; see *Teares of the Muses* 91 and 452).

In the first part of his soliloquy, the Guise identifies his goal as 'glory,' relying on resonant metaphors for a program of political ambition:

> Now, Guise, begins those deep-engender'd thoughts
> To burst abroad those never-dying flames
> Which cannot be extinguish'd but by blood.
> Oft have I levell'd, and at last have learn'd
> That peril is the chiefest way to happiness,

And resolution honour's fairest aim.
What glory is there in a common good,
That hangs for every peasant to achieve?
That like I best that *flies* beyond my reach.
Set me to scale the high Pyramides,
And thereon set the diadem of France,
I'll either rend it with my nailes to naught,
Or mount the top with my *aspiring wings*,
Although my downfall be the deepest *hell*.

(The Massacre at Paris ii.34–47; emphasis added)

What animates this speech is the Guise's willingness to share his empirically acquired wisdom with the audience ('Oft have I levell'd, and at last have learn'd'). This wisdom divides in two: (1) the individual can best find 'happiness' through 'peril' – through acting out a daring or 'tragic part'; and (2) he can best acquire 'honour' through 'resolution' – through making a daring decision in the face of grave danger. The word 'honour' alerts us to the 'aim' of this wisdom, identified in the next line: 'glory.'[20]

The Guise's speech conjoins with two passages in *The Shepheardes Calender*. The first, from *June*, anticipates both Marlowe's topic of ambition and his metaphors of height and flight, when Colin Clout withstands the temptation offered by Hobbinol to move prematurely from pastoral to epic:

I never lyst presume to Parnasse hyll,
But pyping lowe in shade of lowly grove,
I play to please my selfe, all be it ill.

Nought weigh I, who my song doth prayse or blame,
Ne strive to winne renowne, or passe the rest:
With shepheard sittes not, followe flying fame.

(June 70–75)

Colin uses a discourse of generic progression and poetic fame, the subtext for which is the myth of Pegasus. Claiming to be the pastoral poet par excellence, Colin chooses to sing only to himself 'in shade of lowly grove,' rather than 'winne renowne' on 'Parnasse hyll.' In this portrait, Spenser prepares for his own transition from lowly pastoral to high epic, shrouded oblivion to 'flying fame.'[21]

The second *Calender* passage, from *October*, also anticipates Marlowe's topic and metaphors: 'Then make thee winges of thine aspyring wit, / And, whence thou camst, flye backe to heaven apace' (83–4). Marlowe's topics – the court, religion, aspiration, the poet and his art – are all here, as is his avian metaphor for achievement. For Spenser, the poet who chooses to write poetry should use the 'winges' of his 'aspyring wit' to serve 'Princes pallace' (80); this is the 'most fitt' (81) end to which he can put his work. Only when he discovers that he can no longer serve the court should he turn away from the court and return to his ontological origin ('flye back to heaven apace').[22]

The two *Calender* passages advertise the first and the last progressions from Spenser's literary career: from pastoral to epic, and from these courtly genres to the hymn. Together, they permit us to reconfigure Levin's articulation for Marlowe: Spenser inscribes an ethos of living safely that reconciles poetic aspiration with Christian salvation.

In place of Spenser's Parnassus, the Guise climbs the Pyramides as his mountain of aspiring inspiration; and against Spenser's comedic myth of poetic fame, Pegasus, the Guise selects the tragic myth of Icarus. If Colin and the Spenserian poet are content to abide their time in the long-distant flight beyond time, the Guise likes it 'best that flies beyond [his] ... reach.' If Colin and the Spenserian poet serve the diadem of England, the Guise demands 'the diadem of France'; if they will play and sing, he will 'rend it with [his] nails to naught / Or mount the top'; if they ultimately seek 'heaven,' he is bent on sinking down to 'deepest hell.' This is a counter-Spenserian poetics of Orphic damnation.

In the second part of the soliloquy, the Guise balances two key architectural images to metadramatize his project:

> For this I wake, when others think I sleep;
> For this I wait, that scorns attendance else;
> For this, my quenchless thirst whereon I *build*,
> Hath often pleaded kindred to the King;
> ...
> For this, have I a largess from the Pope,
> A pension and dispensation too;
> And by that privilege to work upon,
> My policy hath *fram'd* religion.
>
> (*The Massacre at Paris* ii.48–65; emphasis added)

Levin terms line 50 above (with its juxtaposition of 'thirst' and 'build') 'a curious metaphor, which intermixes the acts of construction and consumption' (84). Yet our curiosity should warrant a pause. For one thing, 'the acts of construction and consumption' both pertain to the art of the writer; in a distinctly Marlovian way, they trace the process by which inspiration leads to its literary product. But the word 'build' does not simply anticipate and lead up to 'fram'd'; it also picks up the architectural term from the first part of the soliloquy, when the Guise says, 'Oft have I *levell'd*, and at last have learn'd.' Altogether, the three architectural terms support the metatheatrical close to the entire soliloquy: 'The plot is laid.' In a memorable line in the middle of the speech, the Guise articulates the full process of his plotting: 'Contrives, imagines, and fully executes, / Matters of import.' In this second part of the speech, however, the Guise emphasizes the way in which his Machiavellian 'policy' has 'fram'd religion' – a metatheatrical 'atheist' troping if ever there was one.

In the third part of the soliloquy, the Guise opens with the Machiavellian exclamation, 'Religion! *O Diabole!*' (66), discussing his plot against the king with help from the 'Mother Queen' (76), who 'works wonders for my sake, / And in my love entombs the hope of France, / *Rifling the bowels of her treasury*, / To supply my wants and necessity' (76–9; emphasis added). We have also met the italicized phrase before – but without the painful sexual contortion. In chapter 6, we examined Barabas's line 'Ripping the bowels of the earth for them' (*Jew* I.i.108), noting not merely its origins in Ovid, Seneca, and Kyd, but also in Spenser.[23] The context there was also economic and theological, as Barabas imagines 'heaven' doing the financial 'Ripping' for 'earthly man' (106), the site of the rape being, as Ovid, Seneca, and Spenser all make clear, the 'womb' of mother earth ('viscera terrae').

In *The Massacre at Paris*, Marlowe adds a sexual element to his economic and theological metaphor of rape. For now it is the male Guise imagining the female 'Mother Queen ... / Rifling the bowels of her treasury' to 'supply' his 'wants and necessity' – a contorted trope (as only Marlowe could do it) intermixing suggestions of female masturbation and male sexual prowess – all controlled through the cold exchange of currency.[24] The Guise tries to speak of the financial backing he gets from Catherine, but out slips his Oedipal complex; yet the slip also alerts us to the literariness of the line, which 'rifles' a long line of intertextuality for its 'treasury.' In the conclusion to this part of the soliloquy, the Guise reiterates the eros undermining his plot: 'All this and more, if more may be compris'd, / To bring the will of our desire to end' (86–7).[25]

In the final part to the soliloquy, the Guise identifies his culture hero and in the process permits his author to intertextualize his own plot further: 'As Caesar to his soldiers, so say I: / Those that hate me will I learn to loathe. /

Give me a look that when I bend the brows, / Pale death may walk in furrows of my face' (99–109). According to Oliver, 'This is the first of Guise's comparisons of himself to Caesar and the first of several references to Roman history in the play – perhaps both kinds of comparison being explicable by the practice of French historians or pamphleteers' (103). To this, we could add what Oliver mentions elsewhere: 'the comparison may have had special interest for Marlowe, who had translated, or was translating, Lucan's account of Caesar's civil wars' (lvii).[26] The Guise's repeated identifications with Caesar link *The Massacre at Paris* with *Lucan's First Book*. The link works in two directions. First, it identifies *The Massacre* as a transition between tragedy and epic in Marlowe's Ovidian career. Second, it identifies the Guise not simply as a Machiavellian but also as a Lucanic hero.

Critics believe that the Guise's soliloquy represents the kind of play that Marlowe originally wrote. What is remarkable is the intertextual maturity the soliloquy manoeuvres, for in it we witness the playwright carrying on a dialogue with the writers we have been examining in this study: Ovid, Seneca, Lucan, Machiavelli, and Spenser. The three classical writers and the Continental one cohere, finding their unified voice in Marlowe's criticism of Spenserian historiography: 'providence, the formal guardian of English history, is largely irrelevant. Causation has been brought down to the secular, human level, as one finds in the writings of historical theorists like Niccolò Machiavelli' (Kirk 197).

'Comment on my text'

Repeatedly, later scenes present the central action of the play in theatrical terms. The most memorable remark comes from the Guise himself, when he tells Catherine, 'They that shall be actors in this massacre / Shall wear white crosses on their burgonets, / And tie white linen scarfs about their arms' (iv.29–31). Literally, the Guise fuses the characters enacting the massacre with the actors performing it. In the same scene, Catherine tells Charles to 'make a show as if all were well' (48), and two scenes later the Duke of Anjou reveals himself to the Duke Dumaine: 'I am disguis'd, and none knows who I am' (vi.5). Even the pious Navarre cannot escape Marlowe's metadrama:

And therefore, as speedily as I can *perform*,
I'll muster up an army *secretly*,
For fear that Guise, join'd with the King of Spain,

Might *seem* to cross me in mine *enterprise*.
But God, that always doth defend the right,
Will *show* his mercy and preserve us still.
(*The Massacre at Paris* xiii.36–41; emphasis added)

That last troping is literally damning, and it is no accident that of all the characters in the Marlowe canon it is Navarre who best inverts Marlowe's 'counterfeit profession,' when he tells Pleshy at the end of this scene, 'I intend to labour for the truth, / And true profession of his [God's] holy word' (50–1).[27]

Not surprisingly, the play's most intimate scene – and one of the most remarkable – stages the act of letter writing itself. 'Go fetch me pen and ink,' the Duchess of Guise instructs her maid, 'That I may write unto my dearest lord' (xv.1, 3). After the maid delivers the instruments, the Duchess writes her own Ovidian *amores* – a poetics of adulterate desire: 'O would to God this quill that here doth write / Had late been pluck'd from out fair Cupid's wing, / That it might print these lines within his heart!' (11–13). This passage also warrants our pause.[28] In *Ovid's Elegies*, Marlowe uses the image of 'Cupid's wings' a number of times (I.ii.41, II.vii.27, ix.49, III.viii.9), but in the last, his elegy on Ovid's friend and rival Tibullus, Marlowe translates his classical precursor's unfolding of the image's vocational significance: 'Tibullus, thy work's poet, and thy fame, / Lo Cupid brings his quiver spoilèd quite, / His broken bow, his firebrand without light. / How piteously with drooping wings he stands' (5–9). In the Ovidian passage in *The Massacre*, the Duchess of Guise engages in some imaginative inscription, as she wishes that her writing 'quill' might be from 'Cupid's wing' so that her instrument could metaphysically 'print these lines' within her lover's 'heart.' Machiavellian fear prompts Ovidian eros, and it is on this cue that the Duchess's husband enters.

When the Guise wonders to whom she has been writing, the Duchess dissembles: 'To such a one, my lord, as when she reads my lines / Will laugh, I fear me, at their good array' (16–17). The exquisite rendering here of 'good array' has required some glossing. Oliver, for instance, notes that 'neither *O.E.D.* nor the Marlowe *Concordance* throws any light on this use of "array." Probably the Duchess is speaking with light-hearted irony of the lack of array – the feminine disorderliness – of her letter' (132; see Bennett 221). If so, the Duchess *dresses* her 'lines' in the costume of theatrical disguise. Her impetuous husband, however, is not duped by her laughing comedy; taking the letter from her, and spying its adulterous contents, he remarks, without self-irony,

Thou trothless and unjust, what lines are these?
Am I grown old, or is thy lust grown young,
Or hath my love been so obscur'd in thee,
That others needs to comment on my text?

                                    (*The Massacre at Paris* xv.24–7)

In the last line, Bennett finds 'a metaphor from the scholiasts,' but his further comment alerts us to the potential for some unseen intertextuality: 'The gloss or comment on the obscure text of a classical or sacred author was one of the greatest occupations of the medieval scholar' (221). The Guise thus fuses sexual with textual activity – that of the lover with that of the scholar: 'The basic idea is that of a husband's being found, like a text, insufficient, so that the services of another are needed to make up for the deficiencies' (Oliver 133). This is a tragic rendering of Marlowe's nationhood of free scholarship.

The Guise's discovery of his wife's adultery is grimly amusing, since it was he who began the play by directing 'Hymen' to 'lour' at 'marriage-rites.' That articulation, we have seen, imitates Ovid in order to respond to Spenser's poetics of marriage. In the present scene, we can detect the narrative similarity between the Guise's discovery of his wife's 'trothless' adultery and the Redcrosse Knight's similar discovery about his betrothed, Una, whose name means Truth: 'doubtfull words made that redoubted knight / Suspect her truth' (*FQ* I.i.53). Just as Archimago can barely 'restrein' the knight from killing Una as she couples with the youthful squire (ii.5), so the Duke restrains himself from killing his wife, on the grounds that she bears his heir in her womb (32–5). This Spenserian conjunction anticipates or recalls a more famous recollection of Spenser, when the Old Man snatches the dagger from Faustus – modelled on Una's rescue of Redcrosse from the Cave of Despayre (see chapter 9).

As in *Doctor Faustus*, in *The Massacre*, Marlowe stages the life of an actual scholar, and usually critics find Ramus to be a self-portrait of the playwright himself.[29] 'Alas,' Ramus tells his murderers, 'I am a scholar, how should I have gold? / All that I have is but my stipend from the King, / Which is no sooner receiv'd but it is spent' (ix.17–19). Millar MacLure once commented that these lines 'would have rung throughout the theatre'; the lines *are* theatrical, and, as MacLure wryly added, Ramus on his deathbed tries to 'defend his thesis.'[30] In the comedy of Ramus's death, we can witness Marlowe detaching himself from the scholar, and perhaps we should be reminded that it was Marlowe's enemy, Gabriel Harvey, who first brought Ramus to Cambridge.

In the one detailed analysis of the scene, however, John Ronald Glenn argues that Ramus is 'the only character capable of carrying an affirmative view of human nature ... [W]ithout him Marlowe's picture of mankind is utterly black': 'In Ramus, ... there is at least a glimpse of a hopeful Marlowe who in the most pessimistic of plays can express a guarded faith in humanity' (379). Glenn shows how 'Marlowe intended this scene to receive considerable emphasis' (369), with Ramus emerging as 'a passionate and humane individual' (376) who does not fear death (370–7) – the 'acceptable standard of humanity' by which 'all the extremists of the play [especially the Guise and Navarre] must ultimately be judged' (377).

Given these antithetical interpretations of a single figure, we may wonder whether Marlowe is varying the technique examined in chapter 5, when we discovered both Marlowe and Spenser in Tamburlaine. Thus, what Stephen Greenblatt asks with respect to the mighty opposition there (*Renaissance Self-Fashioning* 224) we may apply to Marlowe and Harvey here: what if Marlowe and Harvey are two faces of the same thing? Marlowe both critiques a nationhood of pedantic scholarship and defends a counternationhood of free scholarship: ''Tis Ramus, the King's Professor of Logic' (21).

Along similar lines, Marlowe brings on stage two writers of the Protestant cause: the great author of *Divine Weeks and Works*, whom he calls Bartus; and the author of *The Trewnesse of the Christian Religion*, whom he calls Pleshy. Wilbur Sanders is helpful in forcing Marlowe's hand on Du Bartas: 'It is a gratuitous bounty that places Du Bartas, poet and protestant, at the side of Navarre: although he was in the court, he played no such role as Marlowe gives him' (28, citing Kocher, 'Pamphlet Backgrounds ... Part Two' 316). By contrast, as Bennett says, Mornay 'served Henry of Navarre with untiring zeal and fidelity,' adding that Mornay was 'one of the stoutest leaders of the Huguenots, so much so that he was sometimes called "The Pope of the Huguenots"' (215). We may need to contextualize the function of both these characters. As Harvey himself reports, 'M. Spenser conceives the like pleasure in the fourth day of the first Weeke of Bartas. Which he esteemes as the proper profession of *Urania*' (rpt. in Cummings 49), and as Irving Ribner recalls, Mornay is the 'friend of Sir Philip Sidney' (ed., *Complete Plays* 260). In other words, in this 'most topical of Marlowe's plays' (Weil 82) the playwright conjures up two Frenchmen who were important to the Sidney–Spenser circle as writerly champions of the Protestant cause, both in service of Navarre, 'the putative hero,' in whom 'admirable qualities are conspicuously absent' (Glenn 378).

At the end of the play, it is King Henry who most visibly evokes Marlowe's metatheatre. 'I am tragicall within,' he tells his minion Epernoun (74), writing the warrant for the Guise's death. Indeed, in the play's last scene, he enacts his own tragedy during his death speech: 'Valois's line ends in my tragedy' (xxv.93) – the word 'line' being a fine metatheatrical pun.

Filling up the Room

The Massacre at Paris remains Marlowe's most ruined artefact. Yet the mangled text does occasionally glimmer with the playwright's brilliant career project. This project reveals that towards the end of his short, meteoric career Marlowe is still counterfeiting his Ovidian profession. To quote the Soldier who arrives to murder Mugeroun in the manuscript version of the scene that some think to be a holograph in Marlowe's hand, the playwright is still using 'a counterfeit key to his privy chamber' (xix.1–2 in Gill, ed., *Plays* 442). This key occasionally unlocks the Spenserian 'treasure' of royal nationhood, but luckily we need not say of Marlowe's coining what he himself has the Soldier say, when he plays on the tragically doomed Mugeroun's rifling of the Duchess of Guise's rich bowel: 'though you take out none but your own treasure, yet you put in that displeases him [the Guise], and fill up his room that he should occupy; herein sir, you forestall the market, and set up your standing where you should not' (2–6).

9

Un-script(ur)ing Christian Tragedy:
Ovidian Love, Magic, and Glory in
Doctor Faustus

In the prologue to *Doctor Faustus*, Marlowe announces a new stage to his
dramatic career:

> Not marching now in fields of Trasimene
> Where Mars did mate the Carthaginians,
> Nor sporting in the dalliance of love
> In courts of kings where state is overturned,
> Nor in the pomp of proud audacious deeds,
> Intends our muse to daunt his heavenly verse.
> Only this, gentlemen: we must perform
> The form of Faustus' fortunes, good or bad.
>
> (*Doctor Faustus* Prologue 1–8)

Marlowe here 'announces his intention of turning away from the heroic and
political themes that had occupied his attention' in previous plays (Bevington
and Rasmussen, eds., *Doctor Faustus* 106). Today, however, we cannot tell
at what point in his 'career' (Bevington and Rasmussen 1) Marlowe is
making this dramatic turn. Yet everything the present study needs to say
about *Doctor Faustus* depends on a clarification precisely of this announced
career *meta*.

The problem we face is large indeed, because the play we know as '*Doctor
Faustus*' is plagued by three sets of technical 'doubling.' First, the play exists
in two different texts: the A-text, published in 1604 (entered Stationers'
Register 7 January 1601); and the B-text, published in 1616. As David
Bevington and Eric Rasmussen write, the 'substantial differences between
the A-text and the B-text ... pose an immense problem. The B-text omits a
few short speeches or episodes totalling 36 lines in the A-text, provides new

passages totalling 676 lines, and introduces thousands of verbal changes' (eds., *Doctor Faustus* 63). The differences between the two texts are ideological as well, as Leah S. Marcus observes: 'the A text could be described as more nationalist and more Calvinist, Puritan, or ultra-Protestant, the B text as more internationalist, imperial, and Anglican, or Anglo-Catholic' ('Textual Indeterminacy' 5). Whereas earlier critics, following W.W. Greg, argued for the superiority of the B-text, more recent critics, following Fredson Bowers, argue for the superiority of the A-text. As Bevington and Rasmussen note, 'current opinion has shifted once more in favour of the A-text' (63–4).[1]

Second, the play can be assigned to two polar dates in Marlowe's career: an 'early,' 1589 date; or a 'late,' 1592 date. 'The matter,' write Bevington and Rasmussen, 'is of consequence to our view of Marlowe's career as a dramatist, for, despite their general proximity, these dates nearly span the productive career of this precocious and seemingly doomed young artist': 'Did Marlowe write *Doctor Faustus* shortly after his great success with the two parts of *Tamburlaine*, ... or is the play perhaps his last and greatest creation before his sudden death at a Deptford tavern in May of 1593?' (eds., *Doctor Faustus* 1). As with the textual problem, critics have here undergone a sea-change: where once they argued for a late date, now they argue for an early one.[2]

Third, '*Doctor Faustus*' was almost certainly written by two different authors. In his *Diary*, for instance, Philip Henslowe records that on 22 November 1602 he paid £4 to William Bird and Samuel Rowley for 'adicyones in doctor fostes' (qtd. in Bevington and Rasmussen, eds., *Doctor Faustus* 62), and critics generally agree that Marlowe's text is (and was from the start) marked by a collaborator. Bevington and Rasmussen again state the consensus: 'Scholars have long suspected that Marlowe wrote the serious and tragic portions of *Doctor Faustus*, by and large, and that a collaborator took responsibility for the comic horseplay. We support that view' (70).[3]

These three sets of technical *doubling* present a problem so enormous that we would not be unwise to replace 'the absent authorial presence we call Marlowe' with a '"Marlowe effect"' (Marcus, 'Textual Indeterminacy' 3, 5). Yet we might wish to persist a while in our folly. If there is a 'Marlowe effect,' perhaps there is (or once was) a 'Marlowe.' The prologue indicates that there was: 'our Muse.'[4] Moreover, Marlowe appears to stage the problem of authorship itself. Initially, writes Roger Sales, 'Faustus plays the playwright, cuing entrances and exits as well as ordering costume changes, whereas Mephostophilis appears to be the obedient actor. Their subsequent dialogue nevertheless reveals that Faustus' theatrical control is an illusion or shadow. Mephostophilis ... turns out to be a playwright who stages shows so that Faustus himself will be more pliant' (149).

Just as the problem of double authorship does not substantially contaminate the opening lines of the prologue quoted above, so neither does the problem of the text, for both the A- and the B-text are roughly the same here, with only one variant of significance.[5] That leaves the problem of double dating, and indeed this brings us to the critical crux with which we began. For editors who place the play early usually see lines 3–4 as referring to Marlowe's *Dido, Queen of Carthage* ('the dalliance of love / In courts of kings') and line 5 as referring to the *Tamburlaine* plays ('pomp of proud audacious deeds'). By contrast, editors who place the play late usually see lines 3–4 as referring to *Edward II* and line 5 as referring to the *Tamburlaine* plays.[6] Thus, while critics agree that Marlowe introduces *Doctor Faustus* as a new dramatic 'form,' they create two different 'career' contexts for his announcement.

We may circumvent the 'dating' problem of *Faustus* by constructing a dynamic model of authorship. Marlowe could originally have penned the play in 1589, and then, during the next three years, revised it in order to accommodate changes in his career circumstance – most notably, his rising status as a counter-laureate poet. Seen in this light, *Doctor Faustus* has a twofold function in Marlowe's career. First, it functions as a clear transition between the first and second triads, for it synthesizes the well-known network of Ovidian and Spenserian intertextuality from *Dido* and the two *Tamburlaine* plays with a portrait that dominates *The Jew of Malta*, *Edward II*, and *The Massacre at Paris*: the hero as defeated exile (Barabas, Edward, Mortimer). And second, *Doctor Faustus* functions as a transition between the second triad and (a return to the spirit of) the first triad in order to permit Marlowe to rejoin the Ovidian career path in a timely fashion; thus *Faustus* bridges tragedy and the next or epic phase of Marlowe's career, as the appearance of the Apollonian laurel bough in the epilogue intimates: 'Cut is the branch that might have grown full straight, / And burnèd is Apollo's laurel bough' (1–2). This 'laurel' passage showcasing the emblem of the national artist coheres with the laurel passage in Marlowe's *Dedicatory Epistle* of Watson's *Amintae Gaudia* to Mary Sidney, published in 1592 (see Eriksen, 'Marlowe's Petrarch'): 'the evergreen tresses of the Peneian nymph [Daphne].' The appearance of the laurel garland in two works commonly identified as dating to the penultimate year of Marlowe's life reveals priceless historical information on Marlowe's self-presentation at the close of his literary career: he is ready to present himself as an epic poet.

While acknowledging the evolving nature of the text, and its transitional function within both 'early' and 'late' career sites, we may wish to emphasize that the basic project of the play remains relatively consistent. As the prologue hints, Marlowe will not produce the kind of 'tragedy' that Aristotle had prescribed in the *Poetics* (1449b.6.I–II) and that his audience would expect from both his own practice and that of his colleagues on the newly formed Elizabethan stage: a tragedy about the fall of great and powerful national leaders. In *Doctor Faustus*, Marlowe's Muse 'intends ... to daunt his heavenly verse' in order to 'perform / The form of Faustus' fortunes, good or bad.' In addition to the change in 'subject' (from a national leader to a private individual), the playwright makes three announced changes from previous plays. First, since his muse will sing a 'heavenly verse,' he will perform a new dramatic 'form' that critics call Christian tragedy – a problematic genre if ever there was one, in which the playwright dares to confront a paradox: 'tragedy about Christianity' (Michel 422). Second, and following from the first, the playwright's Christian tragedy will trace the 'form' of his hero's 'fortunes' – transcribe the contour of his life's destiny, deal with both the agency of his being and its *telos*.[7] And third, following from the first two, the playwright's Christian tragedy will problematize the 'form' itself: the hero's fortune is evidently to be, not a singular trajectory from the Christian life to the Christian afterlife, but a curiously plural *telos* ('fortunes'), the 'form' of which is to be either 'good or bad' (we cannot tell which). As in the prologue to *1 Tamburlaine* ('applaud his fortunes as you please' [8]), the muse relies on a secretively unjudgmental poetics.[8]

Marlowe's central phrasing for his project, 'we must perform / The form of Faustus' fortunes,' is distinctly metadramatic.[9] Most generally, we shall see, Marlowe writes his new Christian tragedy in order to advance his larger dramatic phase of Ovidian tragedy, in preparation for – and in conjunction with – epic. That he chooses to situate Christian tragedy within the larger 'form' of Ovidian tragedy should alert us not simply to the paradox that Christian tragedy problematizes, but also to the play's subversive program.[10] More specifically, Marlowe's subversion is not simply theological or political, but professional as well. In *Doctor Faustus*, the playwright aims to subvert the authority of 'heavenly verse' about orthodox Protestant Christianity, represented most forcefully for him in the Protestant poetics of Spenser. Consequently, in this play Marlowe rivals England's Virgil by penning a counter-nationhood founded on the suppressed cry of Ovidian *libertas*.

What Marlowe objects to is Spenser's large-scale intellectual linkage comprised of three concepts: love, magic, and glory.[11] In Spenser's linkage, love becomes the true magic of the universe because it secures the individual's glory – both his fame within time and his grace beyond time. Spenser derives this linkage from an astute and complex fusion of concepts and archetypes from two cultural traditions: the philosophical tradition of Neoplatonism and the literary tradition of romance.[12] In Marlowe's linkage of the Spenserian concepts, love degenerates into lust, magic metamorphoses into diabolism, and glory descends to damnation. For Marlowe, eros becomes the true diabolism of the universe because it secures the individual's perdition; it does so not because eros is intrinsically evil, but because the Christian God wills it to be so. In Marlowe's ideologically dangerous universe, that which saves kills. Marlowe achieves his powerful response to Spenser principally by inserting another tradition into Spenser's equation of Neoplatonism and romance: the Ovidian, which, as we shall see, displays a tragic and naturalist commitment to eros, black magic, and earthly fame.[13] Paradoxically, however, the Ovidian matrix calls into question the received wisdom about the play: the 'pessimism of Marlowe's final tragic vision' (Gatti 111). The form of Faustus's fortunes turns out to be not simply 'good or bad,' but 'bad' *and* 'good,' for the Ovidian matrix at the close boldly asserts the author's affirmation of his own artistic power to be free from the orthodox Christian forces dangerously afoot in the universe.

Vaunting the Verse: Spenserian and Ovidian Contexts

Towards the end of *Doctor Faustus*, Marlowe's protagonist returns from a banquet with three scholars. Together, they have just completed a 'conference about fair ladies,' at which they have debated 'which was the beautifull'st in all the world' (V.i.9–11). Their selection of Helen of Troy leads the First Scholar to ask Faustus to conjure up 'that peerless dame of Greece' (14) – a request the magician grants through help from Mephistopheles. As Helen passes over the stage, the Third Scholar remarks, 'No marvel though the angry Greeks pursued / With ten years' war the rape of such a queen, / Whose heavenly beauty passeth all compare' (28–30). In the eyes of the Third Scholar, the Greeks pursued Helen not just because she was a beautiful woman, but because she was the incarnation of 'heavenly beauty.' For him, the Greeks' furious attempt to recover Helen becomes less a lustful act of folly and more a loving act of wisdom – an attempt to recover divine light. Through magic, Doctor Faustus re-creates the appearance of this idealized beauty for his colleagues, allowing them to participate momentarily in the very subject of their symposium.

This scene invites comparison with another conference on love and beauty:

that in Plato's *Symposium*. The differences between Marlowe's play and Plato's dialogue, however, are immediately apparent. First, Marlowe sees the female (not the male) as the true figure of beauty, hence as the fit object of love. And second, Marlowe sees the object of love not as a divine form in the heavenly realm, but as an earthly beloved incarnating the divine light. Leaving the obvious ironies aside for a minute, Marlowe's Neoplatonism appears to differ from the standard form developed by Marsilio Ficino in his commentary on Plato's *Symposium* (6.10: 188) and subsequently championed by Cardinal Bembo in Book IV of Castiglione's *The Courtier*: 'And thus shall [the lover] beholde no more the particular beautie of one woman, but an universall, that decketh out all bodies' (318). Marlowe's apparent rejection of this conventional Neoplatonic abstraction of the beloved suggests that he may be reflecting a special form of Neoplatonism that critics locate in the poetry of Spenser: 'In Italian courtly circles and in the language of fashion, married love and Platonic love indeed were usually contrasted ... The originality of Spenser's philosophy of love lies in the association of Platonic idealism with an acceptance of bodily union' (Ellrodt 146). For Spenser, in other words, the lover unites with the beloved, an incarnation of 'heavenly beauty,' as the most fruitful way to participate in the divine realm.[14]

Importantly for *Doctor Faustus*, Spenser in *The Faerie Queene* represents this special brand of Neoplatonic love through a traditional archetype of magic from romance, derived ultimately from the Circe/Hermes episode in Homer's *Odyssey*. In this archetype, a good magician oversees the hero's vision of a divine spirit of beauty sent from God, informs the hero of the role of love in human destiny, and arms the hero with a magic weapon that renders him invulnerable on his quest to find the incarnate form of the beloved – a quest that secures his fame and glory. In this archetype, that is, the magician becomes a figure of love linking earthly love with divine love as the central way to enter what Spenser calls the *telamond* – the perfect world.[15] Spenser's linking of love with magic traces back not merely to the *Odyssey*, but also to the *Symposium*, in which Plato portrayed Love as a magician: 'at once desirous and full of wisdom, a lifelong seeker after truth, an adept in sorcery, enchantment, and seduction' (203d). As we shall see, Plato's linking of love with magic leads Renaissance Neoplatonists like Ficino to formulate an idea that becomes important to Spenser and subsequent writers like Marlowe (including Jonson and Shakespeare): love is the true magic of the universe because it 'confirme[s]' the individual's glory (*FQ* III.iii.25). In effect, Spenser synthesizes this idea from Neoplatonism with the archetype of magic from romance in order to reveal an idea common to both Neoplatonism and romance: love is the magical power linking earth to heaven.

That Marlowe contextualizes Platonic or Neoplatonic love in terms of Spenserian love is clear from his borrowings from Spenser throughout the play.[16] The last line quoted by the Third Scholar on Helen, 'Whose heavenly beauty passeth all compare,' has been seen to originate in Spenser (see Schoeneich 98): 'Whose soveraine beautie hath no living pere' (*FQ* III.i.26) – spoken ironically by one of Malecasta's six knights. This is our first hint of Marlowe's subtle project of contextualizing his 'queen' in terms of Queen Elizabeth and Spenser's writing of nationhood.

Although *Doctor Faustus* is not specifically a love story, Marlowe's design of the Helen scene as the conclusion of a symposium on love and beauty encourages us to see the archetype of magic and its themes of love and glory as one stratum of the play's central concern with will. In the past, critics have tended to emphasize Faustus's use of will to acquire knowledge and power, so that much of the commentary has linked Faustus's magic with the concept 'knowledge is power.'[17] If Faustus's quest for knowledge is central, so is a parallel quest for love, both divine and earthly. Certainly, Faustus will be 'renowned / And more frequented for this mystery / Than heretofore the Delphian oracle' (I.i.143–5), as Cornelius promises him; but so will Faustus have spirits waiting on him, 'Sometimes like women, or unwedded maids, / Shadowing more beauty in their airy brows / Than in the white breasts of the Queen of Love' (129–31). Faustus turns to magic, at least in part, because he believes that magic will offer him both heavenly beauty in the flesh and 'renown' in the world. It should come as no surprise, then, that he thinks of magic as a personification of beauty – a figure of love: ''Tis magic, magic that hath ravished me' (112).[18]

To reconstruct Marlowe's use of the tradition linking love, magic, and glory, we need to examine the two strands of the tradition – Neoplatonic and romantic – as they reach Marlowe, in part through Spenser's synthesis of the two in *The Faerie Queene*.

In the philosophical tradition leading into the Elizabethan age, which included Neoplatonism, magic tended to be 'sympathetic magic.' The primary principle of sympathy is similarity or imitation: like produces like, an effect resembles its cause (Frazer 14; see Yeats, *Bruno* 45, 88–90). Thus, if a magician wishes to achieve a magical union with a stellar body, such as Venus, he creates a magic talisman that imitates Venus. His magical union transforms him, so that he enters an ideal state in which he can fulfil his desires. In this regard, magic becomes a power of union, an art of wish-fulfilment. Depending on whether the magician's self-created union is 'spiritual' or 'demonic,' the practice of magic could be thought of as either good or evil (see Walker). If the magician links himself with *spiritus*, he becomes a white magician, because he harnesses sympathy for the purpose of divine communion. If, on the other hand, he links himself with demons, he becomes a black magician, because he perverts sympathy for the purpose of demonic control over the universe.

In the *Oration on the Dignity of Man*, Pico della Mirandola distinguishes between 'beneficent' and black magic in precisely these terms. Beneficent magic is lawful because it works through the principle of sympathy in nature to unite the individual with God, earth with heaven: 'This beneficent magic ... does not itself work miracles so much as sedulously serve nature as she works her wonders. Scrutinizing, with greater penetration, that harmony of the universe ... and grasping the mutual affinity of things, she applies to each thing those inducements ... most suited to its nature ... As the farmer weds his elms to the vines, so the "magus" unites earth to heaven, that is, the lower orders to the endowments and the powers of the higher' (53–8). As Pico's metaphor from marriage reveals, beneficent magic is essentially a ritual of divine communion or love. In fact, he sees this magic as a specific form of the ritual of a Neoplatonic love that he discusses earlier: 'Let us be driven ... by those Socratic frenzies which lift us to such ecstasy that our intellects and our very selves are united to God ... And at last, smitten by the ineffable love as by a sting ... we shall be, no longer ourselves, but the very One who made us' (26–7). In short, beneficent magic is a means by which the individual demonstrates his love for God (58). For Pico, as for other Neoplatonic magi like Ficino, magic is not simply consistent with Christian glory; it has the power to secure it.[19]

Black magic, by contrast, is a perversion of divine love. Consisting 'wholly in the operations and powers of demons' (53), this magic, Pico says, 'alienates [the individual] from God' (58). Because black magic 'makes man a slave and pawn of evil powers' (56), it is 'the most deceitful of arts' (54). Accordingly, black magic transforms the individual into a bestial creature, giving him 'a monstrous and destructive visage' (57–8) and casting him into a lower or demonic world. In short, black magic betrays the individual's lust for control over the universe.

If post-Platonic magicians like Pico knew that beneficent magic worked as a principle and force of love, they also knew that love worked as a principle and force of magic. Plato's portrait of Love as a magician allows Plotinus to see 'the original enchanter and master of potions' as a figure for a wise and truthful love: 'How are enchantments produced,' Plotinus asks in the *Enneads*: 'through the natural concord of like principles ... The true magic is the love contained within the universe' (IV.iv.40: 114). Even more directly than Plotinus, Ficino reflects on Plato's portrait in his commentary on the *Symposium*. Why, he asks, did Plato call Love a magician: 'Because in love there is all the power of enchantment. The work of enchantment is the attraction of one thing by another because of a certain similarity of their nature ... From their common relation a common love is born, and from that love a common attraction, and this is true enchantment' (6.10: 199–200).

Ficino tries to work out the connection between the portrait of Love as a magician and the idea that love is a magical force. He thinks of Love as a magician first because love works magically ('in love there is all the power of enchantment'); and second, because magic works lovingly (the work of magic 'is the attraction of one thing by another because of a certain similarity of their nature'). Because Ficino was himself a practicing magician (like Pico, but unlike Plato and Plotinus), he was intensely interested in the traditional link between love and magic. His belief that love is the true magic is thus inseparable from his belief that magic is a form of true love. The link between love and magic is crucial, then, because it allows a magician like Ficino to see himself as a figure of love – a cosmic lover who experiences Christian grace. The idea of love as the true magic becomes important precisely because it envisions love as the saving force of the universe.

We might, then, consider how the Neoplatonic portrait of Love as a magician relates to the romance portrait of the magician as a figure of love. From Homer to the Renaissance, poets conventionally present magicians as loving intermediaries in the quest of the hero. Generally, the magician becomes an agent of divine grace or love, using his power to help the hero unite with a divinely ordained beloved. As such, magic becomes an important symbol of a love linking divine and earthly realms. According to Tasso, in *Discourses on the Heroic Poem*, 'we may regard actions performed for the sake of love as beyond all others heroic' (47). The archetype of magic, through its traditional link with love, becomes central to the presentation of the heroic lover; in fact, the hero's relation with a magician becomes part of the main framework for the hero's quest of love. Thus, in the *Gerusalemme Liberata* Rinaldo benefits from the magic power of the wise old man from Ascolona to overcome the false enchantment of Armida (Cantos XIV–XVI) in order to fulfil his divine destiny of uniting with the bridelike Jerusalem.

Renaissance commentators interpreted episodes from the romance tradition Neoplatonically. In *The Scholemaster*, Roger Ascham approaches the Circe episode in the *Odyssey* by claiming that 'Homere and Plato, have both one meanyng, looke both to one end': 'And as Homere, like a learned Poete, doth feyne, that Circes, by pleasant inchantmetes, did turne men into beastes ... even so Plato, like a true Philosopher, doth plainelie declare, that pleasure, by licentious vanitie, that sweete and perilous poyson of all youth, doth ingender in all those, that yeld up themselves to her' (226–7). Although Ascham has Plato's 'Epistles to Dionisius' in mind, not the *Symposium*, he none the less interprets Homer's enchantress in a conventional Neoplatonic way: black magic symbolizes lust, a perversion of a wise and truthful love, the true magic of the universe – which Homer presents in the other half of the archetype through Odysseus's union with Hermes and Penelope.[20]

The relation between the Neoplatonic idea of love as the true magic and the romance archetype of the magician as a figure of love is more fully clarified in Spenser, who reveals his familiarity with the Neoplatonic idea in *Fowre Hymnes*: 'Love is a celestiall harmonie, / Of likely harts composd of starres concent, / Which joyne together in sweete sympathie, / To worke ech others joy and true content' (*Hymne of Beautie* 197–200). For Spenser, as for Pico, Ficino, Plotinus, and Plato, love is the true magic, in the sense that love is a form of union between 'likely harts' drawn together by divine sanction to create a transcendent state or perfect world of fulfilled desire. The 'sweete sympathie' that exists is both between the two lovers and between earth and heaven, so that love is truly a 'celestiall harmonie.' Spenser here articulates the Neoplatonic doctrine of love that he represents in his archetype of magic from *The Faerie Queene*.

Readers have long recognized Faustus's stature as a tragic hero in the great tradition of Renaissance drama; like Macbeth, Faustus is basically a good man who is tempted by demonic powers to commit evil. Recurrently, Marlowe emphasizes Faustus's potential greatness – his success in securing earthly fame: 'none in my empire,' says the German emperor, 'nor in the whole world, can compare with thee for the rare effects of magic' (IV.i.2–4). Even Marlowe's central figure of virtue, the Old Man, sees 'an angel' hovering over Faustus's 'head, / And with a vial full of precious grace / Offers to pour the same into thy soul' (V.i.54–6). Finally, the Chorus acknowledges in the epilogue, 'Cut is the branch that might have grown full straight / ... this learnèd man' (1–3).[21] Such a portrait encourages us to see Faustus as more than merely an evil magician or a dramatization of Pico's black magic. More complexly, Faustus is a hero who becomes a black magician. This fact, together with Marlowe's repeated allusions to and borrowings from the heroic, romance tradition, encourages us to see Faustus in the great tradition of heroes. And because such heroes traditionally benefit from magic to accomplish their deeds, it is appropriate to see Faustus's magic in the light of their magic.

Spenser's use of the magician as a medium of divine love and grace in the hero's quest suggests a delicate synthesis of Pico's triumphant individualism, on the one hand, and Calvin's pessimistic fatalism, on the other. The archetype of the good magician allows him to allegorize the individual's use of his loving will in accord with the loving will of God. Although his hero does not have quite the individualism of Pico's magus, he is not as weak as Calvin's depraved will; he is somewhere in between – able to exert his influence on the world because he is the benefactor of divine grace.

Marlowe's *Doctor Faustus* deals with this central Renaissance controversy as well – 'this ebb and flow of exultant individualism and despairing fatalism' (Mahood 64). Marlowe uses the traditional metaphor to explore this problem, but he makes his hero a magus in order to deconstruct the idealism he finds in Spenser. Faustus uses magic to interfere with the working of grace as a means of creating his own perfect world, having grown impatient with theology as a potential conductor of grace.

It is within the Spenserian context of his mythos that Marlowe superimposes an Ovidian matrix: '*O lente, lente currite noctis equi!*' (V.ii.74). Not merely does Marlowe quote Ovid, but he repeatedly evokes figures from the *Metamorphoses* (Daedalus/Icarus, Paris/Oenone, Amphion, Diana/Actaeon, Semele, and Arethusa); he identifies an Ovidian origin for Faustus's magic through alluding to Medea's magic in Book VII of Ovid's epic; he builds in echoes of his own translation of the *Amores*; and he even refers to 'Ovid's flea' (II.iii.112), a medieval poem attributed to Ovid in the Renaissance.[22]

According to E.K. Rand, 'The career of Master Virgil, the Magician, has something of a counterpart in Ovid's posthumous history,' which Rand titles '*Ovidius Magus*' (*Ovid and His Influence* 138). He tells the story (138) of the two students who visited Ovid's tomb to ask his spirit which of his verses were best and which worst, with the spirit identifying the best as Helen's remark to Paris in the *Heroides* ('Virtue will even shun permitted joys'), and the worst as Phaedra's remark to Jason also in the *Heroides* ('Pleasure is truth, truth pleasure. Jove says so: / 'Tis all he knows, and all he needs to know').[23] Rand also reports what the peasants around Sulmona, Ovid's birthplace, have to say about the poet, and the report sounds remarkably like Marlowe's portrait of Faustus, complete with a mystic 'grove,' conjured building projects, magical 'change[s],' a 'chariot,' a trip to 'Rome,' and erotic 'love':

'Uiddiu,' as they call him, learned magic arts in the mystic grove of the sorceress near Lucco. In one night he put up a splendid villa, surrounded by gardens, vineyards and orchards, and watered by a spring which still is called 'The Fount of Love.' To punish the curiosity of sight-seers, he changed the men into birds, and the maidens into a long line of poplars. When the terrified inhabitants prayed his mercy, he mounted a great chariot with horses of fire, and dashed off to Rome. There he plied his profession as before, creating warriors from dragons' teeth, giving life to statues, changing a woman's hair to snakes, and her legs to fish's tail. Finally, the King's daughter fell in love with him and he with her. (Rand, *Ovid and His Influence* 139)

According to Rand, the tradition of *Ovidius Magus* results from 'a curious weaving of popular fancy about the tales of the *Metamorphoses*' (140). He concludes by recalling that during the sixteenth century 'Ovid passed, with little difficulty, from magic to alchemy,' citing Nicholas Valois's *Le Grande Olympe* (finished by Vicot), in which 'Ovid's text is made a quarry for the alchemist's pick and shovel. He strikes gold immediately and constantly ... In this fashion, the whole poem is subjected to the fatal touch of Midas' (140–1).[24]

Ovid's interest in and knowledge of magic speaks for itself. Key representations appear in his portrait of the witch Dipsas in *Amores* I.viii, which Marlowe translated; in his reliance on the language of magic to describe the seductive power of love in the *Ars amatoria* (II.99–108) and the *Remedia amoris* (249–90); in his link between magic and poetry in *Amores* II.i.17–28; in his repeated discussion of ancient rituals in the *Fasti*; and of course most famously in his portraits of magicians in the *Metamorphoses*, especially Orpheus and Medea. The last of these Marlowe echoes in *Doctor Faustus*, when the conjuror charges Mephistopheles to 'do whatever Faustus shall command, / Be it to make the moon drop from her sphere / Or the ocean to overwhelm the world' (I.iii.38–40) – an imitation of Medea's claim, 'Thee also, Luna, do I draw from the sky' (*Metamorphoses* VII.207; see Bevington and Rasmussen, eds., *Doctor Faustus* 128).[25] Marlowe's imitation of Ovid here, as well as other moments of imitation we shall examine, encourages us to read Faustus's link between love, magic, and glory in light of the Ovidian tradition. This tradition nominally emphasizes the sinister powers of magic, and thus directly opposes the possibilities that Spenser inherits from both the Neoplatonic and romance traditions. None the less, we shall see that the Ovidian tradition, as a 'counter-classical' form, subtly manages to assert its own 'affirmations' (W.R. Johnson, 'Counter-classical Sensibility').

'His waxen wings did mount above his reach': The Prologue

To understand how the Ovidian Marlowe responds to the romantic and Neoplatonic Spenser's linking of love, magic, and glory, we can profitably return to the prologue. If in the first half of the speech Marlowe introduces the play as a *meta* in his own Ovidian *cursus*, in the second half he specifies the 'form of Faustus' fortunes' that he will 'perform.' The *vita* presented for the tragic hero looks suspiciously like that of 'our muse': Faustus is 'born' of 'parents base of stock,' attends university, and 'profits in divinity.'[26] Most important to the present argument, Marlowe lends an Ovidian cast to his following description of Faustus's Christian tragedy when he selects the Ovidian myth of Icarus as his myth of the Faustian fall:

> So soon he profits in divinity,
> The fruitful plot of scholarism graced,
> That shortly he was graced with doctor's name,
> Excelling all whose sweet delight disputes
> In heavenly matters of theology;
> Till, swoll'n with cunning of a self-conceit,
> His waxen wings did mount above his reach,
> And melting heavens conspired his overthrow.
>
> (*Doctor Faustus* Prologue 15–22)

By introducing the Icarus myth as the metaphoric vehicle for Faustus's fall, Marlowe is 'perform[ing]' a distinctly Ovidian 'form' for the genre of tragedy within his Ovidian career. His use of the myth, that is, paradoxically identifies his Christian tragedy as an Ovidian tragedy.[27]

Consequently, the 'form' of Faustus's fortunes is also Ovidian. Repeatedly, the *Metamorphoses* tells stories about the gods' conspiracy against mortals – and not simply Icarus, but also such figures as Actaeon and Arachne (see chapters 7 and 11). In the passage quoted above, the key word measures the temporal transition from Faustus's achievement to his fall, his excelling in 'heavenly matters of theology' to his 'falling to a devilish exercise': 'Till.' In Marlowe's design, excellence and achievement in the 'fruitful plot of scholarism graced' *result in* diabolism and damnation: 'Excelling ... / Till, swol'n with cunning.' In line 22, we learn why excellence leads to damnation: 'heavens conspired his overthrow.'[28] In Marlowe's design, God crafts a fruitful plot for the individual by which he is doomed from the start; the reward for earthly triumph is eternal punishment. The 'sweet delights' of Faustus's intellectual brilliance produce only a dangerous appetitive condition: 'And glutted more with learning's golden gifts, / He surfeits upon cursed necromancy' (24–5). This condition compels Faustus to turn from theology to magic: 'Nothing so sweet as magic is to him, / Which he prefers before his chiefest bliss' (26–7).[29]

That last phrase, 'chiefest bliss,' is climactic, reemphasizing the idea of 'grace' mentioned twice in the polyptoton of lines 16–17: 'The fruitful plot of scholarism graced, / That shortly he was graced with doctor's name.'[30] Literally, Faustus's 'chiefest bliss' is the love and grace that Christ shows the individual in the providential working of destiny; yet Marlowe's emphasis compels us to brood over a troubling fact: Faustus 'prefers' a 'devilish exercise' to such exquisite redemption. The Ovidian basis of Marlowe's psychological insight here receives impetus from a conjunction with his own translation of the *Amores*. Bevington and Rasmussen direct us to *Ovid's Elegies* II.iv.19, where the poet says of Corinna, 'Before Callimachus one prefers me far' (eds., *Doctor Faustus* 108). Just as Corinna prefers Ovid to Callimachus, so Faustus prefers the devil to Christ. While the analogy discovers an apt equation between Ovid and the devil as subversive agencies – between Ovidian art and magic – it also alerts us to intertextual rivalry as a (concealed) topic.[31]

As we should expect, the rivalry is not merely with a dead classical writer, but also with a living English one. In the prologue, Marlowe keeps Spenser pretty well in the background, but precedent exists for discovering Spenser in the B-text's revision of 'daunt' in line 6: 'vaunt.'[32] Although we cannot attribute Marlowe's authorship of 'vaunt' with confidence, we can emphasize the central appearance of the word. It occurs right where we might expect – in the one line in which Marlowe introduces the *intention* of his 'muse' to make the *meta* from previous plays to the current one: '... Intends our muse to vaunt his heavenly verse.'

Spenser uses the word *vaunt* and its variants a total of thirty-four times, with five depicting the poet vaunting his verse, and two relying on the 'v' alliteration ('vaunt ... verse'). In the *October* eclogue of *The Shepheardes Calender*, for instance, he writes that '[t]he *vaunted verse* a vacant head demaundes' (100) – during Cuddie's speech on tragedy, where critics have found Marlovian significance (chapter 2). And in Book I of *The Faerie Queene*, Spenser reflects on his own epic art: 'famous Poetes *verse* so much doth *vaunt*' (xi.27). Although Spenser never uses the phrase 'heavenly verse,' in the 1591 *Ruines of Time* he writes a resonant line: 'Such grace the *heavens* doo to my *verses* give' (259; emphasis added). Marlowe's conjunction with Spenser helps us contextualize his turn to an Ovidian-based Christian tragedy as the next phase of his dramatic career.[33]

Making Man to Live Eternally: The Opening Monologue

Accordingly, in the play's opening monologue Marlowe makes the Spenserian linkage of love, magic, and glory something like the topic of Faustus's discourse. Alone in his study, the scholar turns to magic precisely to escape the rational world of knowledge: Aristotle's logic, Galen's medicine, Justinian's law, and Jerome's translation of the Bible (I.i.1–47). Faustus finds these forms of knowledge dissatisfying – 'Unpleasant, harsh, contemptible, and vile' (111) – because they are so antipathetic to his senses: they are agents of pain and hate, not pleasure and love. As such, they are antagonistic to the romantic spirit that seems to be surfacing in his soul. In addition, Faustus finds these forms of knowledge dissatisfying because they are finally limited: they have an 'end,' a word he uses five times in the opening monologue alone. Faustus believes he has used his 'wit' to 'attain' the 'end' of all human knowledge; he has fully encompassed the zodiac of man's mind, discovered its centre and its circumference. His quest to use knowledge to conquer the human mind, to become the commander of the little world of man, has truly come to an 'end.' In sum, Faustus rejects the rational world of knowledge both because he finds that world absent of pleasure and love and because he finds that it imprisons him within a purely mental reality: it unites him merely with the mental form of himself.

As such, the scholar's life has starved the real man in Faustus. His primary companion has been his books; the fruit of this union has been knowledge of an invisible world. The invisible or imaginative quality of this world has left him uncertain about the individual's role in the universe – about his own identity, and what he can do with his will: does the individual belong only in the study, locked in a fruitless embrace with his own soul? or does he belong out in the wide world, where he can embrace something outside himself? The world of scholarship, with theology at its centre, has isolated Faustus from the real world in which he can actually fulfil his desires, not merely imagine them.

Specifically, Faustus rejects each of the four disciplines because they do not cohere with his thirst for earthly glory. Thus we can examine his thirst within the context of Marlowe's Lucretian, Ovidian materialism. First, Faustus criticizes Aristotelian 'logic' because its 'chiefest end' is merely to 'dispute well' (8). When he asks, 'Affords this art no greater miracle' (9), he betrays the obsession on which the rest of his monologue fixates: the 'greater miracle' of glory. Second, Faustus criticizes Galenic medicine because it can only 'heap up gold' and so 'eternise' him 'for some wondrous cure' (14–15): make him famous – among men, within time, as a wealthy individual. Yet we need to pause here over Marlowe's 'eternise.'[34] Marlowe uses an Augustinian word in a Lucretian or materialist fashion, collapsing the theological concept of Christian glory into a philosophical concept of earthly fame.

As with the word 'miracle' in the passage on Aristotelian logic, the word 'eternise' here keeps the concept of Marlovian glory at the surface of Faustus's discourse. But in the remainder of this second passage Faustus articulates the ideal that drives his quest: 'Wouldst thou make man to live eternally? / Or, being dead, raise them to life again? / Then this profession were to be esteemed' (24–6). Faustus values an *esteemed profession* or famous career. Yet what form does his thirst for fame take? Roma Gill's gloss is misleading: 'Faustus craves the divine power to grant eternal life, or the power of Christ, who raised Lazarus from the dead (St. John 2: 1–44)' (ed., *Complete Works* 2: 55). While the lines do evoke Christ's raising of Lazarus, they also exhibit a subtle change. In the Bible, Christ raises Lazarus to life again 'as a "sign" [of the resurrection] in the Johannine sense' (McKenzie 501). In Marlowe, Faustus wants to raise 'men' to 'life again' only to 'make men to live eternally'; this phrasing violates the 'Johannine sense' of resurrection as a 'sign.' Marlowe's principle precisely fuses Incarnation with Resurrection. By 'live eternally,' Faustus means it; he wants to *live in the body forever.* Marlowe's principle is one of incarnational resurrection, of materialist immanence.[35]

Third, Faustus criticizes Justinian law in a way that appears to contradict the principle of materialist immanence, for this discipline 'aims at nothing but *external* trash' (35; emphasis added). By 'external,' however, Faustus means the 'pretty case of paltry legacies' (30) cited in his quotations from Justinian's *Institutes* – what he calls the 'universal body of the Church' (33). These cases raise questions of ownership and inheritance. Justinian law qualifies as 'external trash' because it cannot incarnate the resurrection.

Finally, Faustus criticizes Jerome's translation of the Bible – Scripture itself – for the reason we should expect: 'we must die an everlasting death' (48). That last phrase is a precise inversion of Faustus's beloved principle, 'liv[ing] ... eternally.' The Bible's 'doctrine' of '*Che sera, sera*' (45) eternizes the death of the body – a formulation that recalls Lucretius's great articulation: 'Death alone / Has immortality' (*De rerum natura* III.869–70; trans. Humphries). Faustus's complaint is not simply that '[t]he reward of sin is death' (41) but that the reward of life is death. That's hard.

Marlowe's opening scene is reminiscent of that in which the Spenserian hero undergoes a private visionary experience at home before setting out on his quest – a quest which has *gloriana* as its 'end.' Unlike Prince Arthur and Britomart, however, Faustus is not a youth bursting with the vigour of eros; he is a mature man dissatisfied with his present use of his will – the pursuit to create a happy or perfect world through the medium of theology, scholarship, and knowledge. To put it another way, he is dissatisfied with a world of reason, conventionally the suppressor of eros.

Not surprisingly, Faustus's turn to magic smacks of eros. 'O, this cheers my soul!' (I.i.151), Faustus tells Cornelius and Valdes after they have convinced him to turn from the rational world of the study to the more imaginative, pleasing world of magic: 'Come, show me some demonstrations magical, / That I may conjure in some lusty grove / And have these joys in full possession' (152–4). Faustus envisions practicing magic outside the study; for him, magic is a means by which he may have his wishes and dreams in 'full possession.' Magic is indeed an art of wish-fulfilment.[36]

Faustus's erotic 'end' for magic coheres with his quest for incarnational resurrection:

> These metaphysics of magicians
> And necromantic books are heavenly,
> Lines, circles, signs, letters and characters –
> Ay, these are those that Faustus most desires.
> O, what a world of profit and delight,
> Of power, of honour, of omnipotence,
> Is promised to the studious artisan!
>
> (*Doctor Faustus* I.i.51–7)

Faustus here rewrites two master concepts of Western culture: fame and glory (see Braudy). The 'metaphysics of magicians' differs from Aristotelian or a Christianized Aristotelian metaphysics in being a *physics* infused with a metaphysics. As we observed in chapter 3, Marlowe filters Christian glory back through classical fame to produce a new and striking version of the concept: *eternal life within time*. Magic is the new text that can bring about this 'greater miracle,' and in the end it is magic that reverses the art of the Neoplatonic magi, who tried to secure Christian grace. Marlowe pours Augustinian glory back into Ovidian fame. The Marlovian principle of incarnational resurrection is not of transcendence but of immanence: 'All things that move between the quiet poles / Shall be at my command ... / A sound magician is a mighty god. / Here, Faustus, try thy brains to gain a deity' (I.i.54–61).[37]

'That famous art': Materialist Immanence

With some precision, Marlowe presents the Evil Angel articulating the idea of materialist immanence within the rubric of fame:

Go forward, Faustus, in that famous art
Wherein all nature's treasury is contained.
Be thou on earth as Jove is in the sky,
Lord and commander of these elements.

(*Doctor Faustus* I.i.76–9)

The epithet for magic, 'famous art,' identifies magic as an art of immanence: the art is famous, and it makes the magician famous. Like Ovid (but unlike Virgil), Marlowe places his hero in competition with the gods. The reduction of Jove and sky to a simile, however, and the raising of man 'on earth' to full ontological status ('Be thou') clarifies the *telos* of the competition. The human 'deity' of magic makes nature eternal.

After the Evil and Good Angel depart, Faustus continues to brood over the paradox of immanence by specifying the 'desperate enterprise' he will 'Perform' (83). He will use magic to acquire a series of earthly powers (84–99); these are appetitive ('pleasant fruits and princely delicates'), economic ('gold,' 'orient pearl'), scholarly ('strange philosophy,' 'silk' for students), political ('secrets of all foreign kings'), and military ('wall all Germany with brass,' 'levy soldiers with ... coin,' 'chase the Prince of Parma from our land,' 'reign sole king,' 'invent' 'strange engines for the brunt of war').[38]

It is in Faustus's use of magic to build a brass wall that critics find a Spenserian echo of Merlin, who in Book III of *The Faerie Queene* builds a brass wall around the city of Cairmardin (iii.10) – a civic form of nationhood. Perhaps recalling his own name lodged in this famous poem, Marlowe's echo identifies Faustus as another Merlin. In fact, Marlowe seems to originate Faustus's idealized plan to use magic civically in Spenser's magico-religious idealism.

Thus Michael Hattaway sees in Faustus's later articulation of this plan a 'parod[y]' of religious 'faith' as represented in 'the powers of Fidelia in *The Faerie Queene*' (77). Through Mephistopheles, Faustus will

be great emperor of the world
And make a bridge through the moving air
To pass the ocean with a band of men;
I'll join the hills that bind the Afric shore
And make that land continent to Spain,
And both contributory to my crown.

(*Doctor Faustus* I.iii.106–11)

Hattaway is right to see a 'parod[y]' of Fidelia here: 'Sometimes great hostes of men she could dismay, / Dry-shod to passe, she parts the flouds in tway; / And eke huge mountaines from their native seat / She could commaund, themselves to beare away, / And throw in raging sea with roaring threat' (*FQ* I.x.20). As Harry Berger, Jr, notes, however, Merlin's powers 'recall the powers Spenser and God gave to Fidelia at I.x.20,' and he argues that the 'point of the echo lies in the difference between the two passages rather than in their similarity: the difference between mystical and magical power, between a theological virtue and a legendary Welsh magician, between biblical allusion and what may be a folk distortion or reduction of scripture' (*Revisionary Play* 103–4). Marlowe's two repetitions – the one of Merlin's powers, the other of Fidelia's – suggests that he understood the complex paradigm of 'similarity' and 'difference' in the two figures, but that he intended to bring them together in a single figure. He may do so in order to deconstruct the Spenserian concept of a nationally significant magico-mystical faith as an art of wish-fulfilment.[39]

Faustus's use of magic as a national art of wish-fulfilment signals an underlying drive to create a world better than that in the study. In the study, the eye saw merely words on the page, and the soul united with sterile spiritual or imaginary creatures; but in the world of magic the eye sees actual objects of beauty (or so Faustus believes) and the soul unites with them in reality. As in Spenser and the romance tradition, magic allows the hero to incarnate what once he merely imagined. In believing that his new 'dominion ... / Stretcheth as far as doth the mind of man' (i.62–3), Faustus believes that he can give a finite body to whatever object of beauty the mind can envision.

In contrast to Spenser and the romance tradition, magic in *Doctor Faustus* leads the individual away from God, to become a usurper to the cosmic throne. Magic thus leads Faustus to violate Pico's cultural – and Spenser's metaphorical – ideal, in which magic is a means of communion with God. For Faustus, magic is a means of becoming independent of God, to become God's equal. Marlowe does not say why Faustus would be led to vie with God for control of the universe, but he does provide a hint. After Faustus has turned to magic, the Good Angel tells him to abjure the demonic art and turn to God. Faustus says, 'Ay, and Faustus will turn to God again. / To God? He loves thee not' (II.i.9–10). At the heart of Faustus's problem is a problem with love; in the words of C.L. Barber, Faustus is 'unable to believe in God's love for him.' Barber refers to the Calvinists, who were particularly prone to despair: 'They had to cope with the immense distance of Calvin's God from the worshipper ... And they had to do without much of the intercession provided by the Roman Church ... Faustus' entrance into magic is grounded in despair' ("'Form'" 94, 93). Faustus turns to magic because he is lonely as a creature in the universe; theology has merely alienated him from God and the world. Hence, Faustus yearns for the kind of divine and earthly love held by the Spenserian hero.

Accordingly, in Act I, scene iii, Marlowe conjoins with Spenser when presenting Faustus using his famous art to make his first conjuration:

> Now that the gloomy shadow of the earth,
> Longing to view Orion's drizzling look,
> Leaps from th'Antarctic world unto the sky
> And dims the welkin with her pitchy breath,
> Faustus, begin thine incantations.
>
> *(Doctor Faustus* I.iii.1–5)

Editors are right to see Marlowe here imitating Spenser in Book III of *The Faerie Queene*: 'Now gan the humid vapour shed the ground / With perly deaw, and th'Earthes gloomy shade / Did dim the brightnesse of the welkin round' (x.46). What has gone unnoticed, however, is that Spenser's passage comes from the episode of Hellenore among the satyrs – Spenser's Ovidian rewriting of the Homeric and Virgilian myth of Helen of Troy.[40]

Marlowe's repetition coerces us into contextualizing Faustus's conjuration in light of Ovid and Spenser, as well as in light of the Helen myth. But this is not all, for we need to include other classical writers central to Marlowe's Ovidian, counter-Spenserian career: Lucretius, Lucan, and Virgil. In the words of Gill: 'The "pitchy breath" needs a note from Lucretius' *De rerum natura* (iv. 476 ff.), describing the vapours and fumes of the night which "fill up the sky with their blackness." Marlowe invents a new myth ... when he hints at the love of the earth's shadow for the watery star, *nimbosus* Orion. Darkness also comes quickly in *Lucan's First Book*, where Marlowe speaks of "th'earths suddaine shadow" (line 537) ... The constellation Orion appears in northern latitudes at the beginning of winter, usually heralding rain – hence the appellations *nimbosus* and *aquosus* in the *Aeneid* (i. 535 and iv. 52)' (ed., *Complete Works* 2: 63–4). Virgil, Lucan, Lucretius, Ovid, Spenser: this is a remarkable passage. What is the significance of its network of intertextuality?

As Gill observes, Marlowe is inventing a 'new myth.' Literally, Faustus reports on the coming of a cloudy night – the fit time and space for conjuration. In the process, he activates a mythologizing imagination that voices the principle of immanence. In his gender battle of the elements, a female 'gloomy shadow of the night' desires to view the male rain star

Orion, and so 'Leaps' from its ice-cold zone on earth 'unto the sky,' then suddenly strives to 'dim the welkin with her pitchy breath.'[41] The movement here is paradoxically upward, with the gloomy shadow effacing a sky light, but the effect is to eliminate the vertical progression, the shadow replacing the light as the figure of authority and power.

As the elaborate network of intertextuality indicates, Faustus's imagination is representing more than elemental usurpation; it is mythologizing literary appropriation, in which the female figure, who here resembles Marlowe's own muse ('gloomy ... Longing ... Leaps ... dims ... pitchy'), seeks to dim the brightness of her male predecessors' drizzling look. Yet not all predecessors are created equal, and we may agree with those who trace the mood and imagery to Spenser. As such, the passage qualifies as one of Marlowe's most brilliant executions of the typology of intertextuality. Here it works as a form of inspiration, replacing the traditional invocation to the muse, troping literary rivalry itself: 'Now that the gloomy shadow of the earth ... / Leaps ..., / Faustus, begin thine incantations.'[42]

Romancing the Spirit

It should come as no surprise, then, that the initial shape that Faustus's desire takes is a deity – a visible object of beauty with which he can feel a magical sympathy. When Mephistopheles appears in his true shape – an ugly devil – Faustus sends him back: 'I charge thee to return and change thy shape. / Thou art too ugly to attend on me' (I.iii.24–5). At the outset revealing his intense concern for beauty and the magical force of (Ovidian) love, Faustus desires a visible deity to love and be loved by, a 'shape' that he can actually see and be at one with. What Faustus loves about Mephistopheles is the spirit's desire to do what Faustus asks: 'How pliant is this Mephistopheles, / Full of obedience and humility! / Such is the force of magic and my spells' (30–2). Faustus's response to Mephistopheles' show of Christian virtue is a show of Christian charity: 'Had I as many souls as there be stars, / I'd give them all for Mephistopheles' (104–5).[43] Through his experience with Mephistopheles, Faustus believes magic offers the divine communion absent in the world of the study.

Marlowe's presentation of the 'sympathy' between magician and spirit reconstructs the traditional relation between national hero and deity in romance, together with its displaced form, the relation between national hero and magician. In Marlowe's play, the national hero is also the magician, and the deity a false spirit from hell, but the similarities between *Doctor Faustus* and other works in the romance tradition are clear. Just as

Mephistopheles reveals the secrets of the universe to Faustus, so Tiresias reveals the spirits of the underworld to Odysseus; the Cumaean Sibyl and Anchises, the future of the Roman race to Aeneas; Melyssa, the Este line to Bradamant; and Merlin, the English race of kings and queens to Britomart. Later, in his relations with Charles V, the German emperor, Faustus himself performs the traditional role of the magus (IV.i). Mephistopheles, though, is a mere 'semblance' of the wise and truthful spirit of beauty celebrated in romance, the magical medium of love, and Faustus has become a mere shadow of the magical hero. Faustus's sympathy with or love for Mephistopheles, then, betrays his fundamental antipathy towards God.

We can locate Spenser in passages where Marlowe works most strenuously to subvert orthodox Christian authority. In Act II, scene iii, the Good Angel pleads with Faustus to 'repent' on the grounds that 'God will [yet] pity thee' (12), while the Bad Angel argues to the contrary: 'Ay, but Faustus never shall repent' (17). Faustus himself articulates the principle of failed repentance, but now with a surge of metadiscourse:

> My heart's so hardened I cannot repent.
> Scarce can I name salvation, faith, or heaven
> But fearful echoes thunder in mine ears:
> 'Faustus, thou art damned!' Then *swords and knives,*
> *Poison, guns, halters, and envenomed steel*
> Are laid before me to dispatch myself;
> And long ere this I should have slain myself
> Had not sweet pleasure conquered deep despair.
> Have not I made blind Homer sing to me
> Of Alexander's love and Oenone's death?
> And hath not he that built the walls of Thebes
> With ravishing sound of his melodious harp
> Made music with my Mephistopheles?
>
> (*Doctor Faustus* II.iii.18–30; emphasis added)

In the literature of religious subversion, we can hardly find an utterance more damning than the opening four lines of this passage. As soon as Faustus names 'salvation, faith or heaven,' he hears 'fearful echoes thunder[ing]' in his 'ears'; these 'echoes' identify him as one of the damned – the unelected – and urge him to commit suicide in a fit of despair.[44]

What are these thundering 'echoes'? Where do they originate? The most obvious answer is the Protestant conscience, which Luther had liberated by identifying the inward faculty as the supreme authority for the individual's life. For Faustus, however, unlike for Luther, the individual's reliance on conscience to link himself with the deity 'echoes' only his eternal punishment. The innate process of Christian faith breeds religious despair. That, too, is hard.

Yet Faustus's metadiscursive surge suggests that the 'echoes' are also literary. Hence, throughout the century critics find Marlowe representing Faustus's suicidal despair through a concrete borrowing from Spenser: the Cave of Despayre in Book I of *The Faerie Queene* (canto ix).[45] The key lines from Spenser are the ones quoted by Lily B. Campbell: 'Then gan the villein him to overcraw, / And brought unto him *swords, ropes, poison*, fire / And all that might him to perdition draw' (50). When Despayre fails with these weapons, he offers the knight 'a dagger sharpe and keene' (51) – called by Una later 'the cursed knife' (52). Marlowe's catalogue of weapons may 'recreate verbally the traditional allegorical figure of Despair, carrying the instruments of self-destruction' (Snyder 573), but Campbell and others are right to alert us to a direct intersection with Spenser. Both writers are dealing with despair and suicide in a Reformation work of literature; both represent a catalogue of suicidal weapons; and both have four of the same weapons: swords, ropes, poison, and a knife.[46]

Marlowe overgoes Spenser by having Faustus cite two singers as the antidotes to despair: Homer and Amphion. Marlowe's representations of Homer and Amphion warrant a pause. We might be arrested by Faustus's claim that he has made blind Homer sing to him about Paris and Oenone, since Homer sang no such song. Evidently, Faustus imagines that he has conjured up the spirit of Homer, much as he later conjures up the spirits of Alexander and Helen, for he forces the 'blind' bard to rewrite the *Iliad* as a tragic Ovidian romance.[47] In the 1590 *The Faerie Queene*, Spenser refers to Paris and Oenone only once – and in an episode we now have reason to believe Marlowe had his eye on when composing *Doctor Faustus*: the story of Hellenore and her lover Paridell, in which Paris '[o]n faire Oenone got a lovely boy' (III.ix.36).[48]

Marlowe's Amphion is harder to account for. As with Paris, Spenser refers to Amphion only once in the poetry published before Marlowe's death – in his 1591 translation of Du Bellay, which Marlowe probably knew (see chapter 10). In *The Ruines of Rome*, Amphion joins Orpheus and Virgil as a triumvirate of great poetic builders (341–4), with the Orpheus/Amphion duo forming a 'double gesture of humanism': Orphic descent to behold the disorder of the past, and Amphionic reconstruction (Greene 233). Marlowe's pairing of Amphion with the Ovidian Homer singing of Paris subverts the humanist project: if Amphion builds the walls of Thebes, Paris brings down the walls of Troy. The conclusion to Marlowe's passage is especially damning, since again Faustus reveals that he has coerced the spirit of Amphion to do something that he has never done: 'made music with my Mephistopheles.' In other words, Faustus has coerced the great artistic builder, the hero of Spenser's and Du Bellay's humanist projects, into performing a counternational art.[49]

Not surprisingly, the central enactment of Faustus's sympathetic relation with the demonic spirit is the blood pact with Lucifer, which Mephistopheles arranges. The pact offers Faustus the promise of the sympathetic reaction: through binding his soul with Lucifer, Faustus believes he will acquire the power of Lucifer, since like produces like, an effect resembles its cause: 'And then be thou as great as Lucifer' (II.i.52). Unlike Christianity, demonic magic promises equality, not mere union, with its deity. The scene reconstructs the individual's love of the divine spirit of beauty during a private visionary experience, such as that which Arthur and Britomart undergo. Mephistopheles ends by claiming that magic will allow Faustus to 'effect all promises between us made' (94) – that is, help Faustus transform his desires of beauty and love into actuality.

As Marjorie Garber emphasizes, Faustus is 'a man enraptured by the idea of making, of poesis, of poetry – of becoming author of himself'; thus Marlowe presents Faustus not just as 'a practicing conjuror' but 'also explicitly [as] a writer, an inscriber as well as a circumscriber' ('"Here's Nothing Writ"' 310). Garber is right to note that Faustus's 'acts of [magical] writing ... are in several senses equally acts of playwrighting' (312), and nowhere do we see magic as theatre more clearly than in Marlowe's repetition of a key theatrical term: 'perform.' In his works, Marlowe uses the term twenty times; ten of them appear in *Doctor Faustus*, significantly more than in any other work (the closest competitor is *Edward II*, where it appears three times). As we have seen, the word first appears in the prologue as a theatrical term. In the play itself, however, magic does the performing: 'The miracles that magic will perform / Will make thee vow to study nothing else' (I.ii.138–9). Not simply does Marlowe link 'magic and poetry'; he also links magic and theatre. In this play, we understand theatre as the true magic of the universe, an erotic art of sympathetic union. It is the theatre of Ovid.[50]

'I will be Paris'

For this reason, soon as Faustus has used magic to link himself with a deity, he uses magic to unite with a real-world beloved. Indeed, both his first and last wishes are for a beloved. At the beginning, he asks for 'a wife, the fairest maid in Germany, for I am wanton and lascivious and cannot live without a wife' (II.i.143–5). Like Spenser's Arthur and Britomart, Faustus uses his magical power to give body to the ideal of a beloved. But Mephistopheles conjures up the parody of a wife, whom Faustus recognizes for what she is: 'a hot whore' (153). Mephistopheles denies the value of the Spenserian notion of married love when he tells Faustus, 'marriage is but a ceremonial toy. If thou lovest me, think no more of it' (154–5). Unlike the situation in Spenser, the individual here is forced to choose between deity and beloved – a grim anticipation of Adam's choice in *Paradise Lost*. As a kind of antidote to Faustus's desire for a chaste marriage, Mephistopheles offers to 'cull thee out the fairest courtesans,' whom he will bring 'ev'ry morning to thy bed' (156–7). Mephistopheles' tactic of diversion evidently works, for Faustus does not think about a beloved – until the end, when one of his colleagues asks him to conjure up Helen of Troy.

After the symposium on love and beauty, Faustus asks Mephistopheles to see Helen again. '[L]et me crave of thee,' he says to the enchanting demon, 'To glut the longing of my heart's desire' (V.i.82–3). Mephistopheles' great offering of a 'world of profit and delight' (I.i.55) – a world absent of human love – does not satisfy Faustus, for eventually he returns to the notion of romantic love: he wants '[t]hat heavenly Helen which I saw of late' to be his 'paramour' (V.i.84–5). In the B-text, Helen, a spirit conjured up through magic, arrives between two Cupids – a kind of Ovidian dramatization parodying the Neoplatonic and romantic idea of love as the true magic.

Clearly, Helen is at the heart of whatever Faustus seeks; she becomes the supreme incarnation of his desires:

> Was this the face that launched a thousand ships
> And burnt the topless towers of Ilium?
> Sweet Helen, make me immortal with a kiss.
> Her lips sucks forth my soul. See where it flies!
> Come, Helen, come, give me my soul again.
> Here will I dwell, for heaven is in these lips,
> And all is dross that is not Helena.
>
> (*Doctor Faustus* V.i.91–7)

As the metaphor from the occult tradition in the final line suggests, Helen appears to Faustus as the alchemist's elixir of life – a great symbol of his seeming success in transmuting the base metals of the imagination into the gold of an ideal reality. For Faustus, Helen appears as the incarnation of 'heaven,' the magical force of love that delivers man into a transcendent state of bliss and joy ('see where [the soul] flies!'), making man 'immortal.'[51]

In the image of Helen's kiss sucking Faustus's soul into flight, Marlowe may have his eye on the enchantment of Acrasia in Book II of *The Faerie Queene*: 'And all that while, right over him she hong, / With her false eyes fast fixed in his sight, / ... / And oft inclining downe with kisses light, ... / And through his humid eyes did sucke his spright' (xii.73). A. Bartlett Giamatti identifies Acrasia's soul-sucking kiss with *necrophilia*, the kiss of death; he sees the enchantress as a kind of vampire (*Earthly Paradise* 279; see Hamilton, ed., *FQ* 295), and usefully he records that the image is alien to the Italian poets who influenced Spenser so deeply – Tasso, Ariosto, Boiardo. The image is also alien to Homer, Virgil, Ovid, Dante, and Petrarch, as well as the Greek tragedians and Seneca.[52]

The similarities between the two kiss scenes are striking. In both scenes, a woman associated with magic performs a soul-sucking kiss on a man (Helen is a conjured demon; Acrasia, an actual enchantress). The two scenes also betray an immediate difference. The mature Faustus claims that Helen's kiss makes him 'immortal,' while Acrasia's kiss sends the young Verdant into oblivion.

In the continuation of his speech, Faustus reveals the full scope of his belief that love can magically give body to a world beyond imagination – a *telamond*:

> I will be Paris, and for love of thee
> Instead of Troy shall Wittenberg be sacked,
> And I will combat with weak Menelaus,
> And wear thy colours on my pluméd crest.
> Yea, I will wound Achilles in the heel
> And then return to Helen for a kiss.
>
> (Doctor Faustus V.i.98–103)

Through the magical power of love, Faustus believes he can refashion the old mythology, to become a second Paris, the lover of the world's greatest beauty, Helen of Troy, and the conqueror of the world's mightiest warrior, Achilles. In his own eyes, he becomes the crown of the romance tradition, the great hero as lover armed with magic power, defeating all obstacles preventing union with his beloved.

Faustus's passionate outburst – in which he sees Helen 'fairer than the evening air, / Clad in the beauty of a thousand stars' (104–5), 'More lovely than the monarch of the sky / In wanton Arethusa's azured arms' (108–9) –

betrays his intense desire for an earthly beloved and suggests the importance of Ovidian love to his own life. Helen is a powerful force because she dramatizes this desire. By associating Helen with air, stars, and gods, Faustus reveals his passion for the spirit of beauty conferring immortality in this life: the true magic of the universe.[53]

In questing for the true magic, Faustus alertly discovers his arch-hero in Paris. As indicated in the introduction, Paris is a version of the shepherd/king in the great Tamburlaine tradition: 'There have been gods who made the woods their home. And so did Paris, Prince of Troy' (Virgil, Eclogue II.60–1; see Ovid, *Heroides* V.9–32, XVI.49–59). Whereas Spenser in the Paridell/Hellenore story follows Homer and Virgil in seeing Paris as the cause of the Trojan War, Marlowe permits his hero to engage rapturously in a counter-myth, in which Paris becomes a kind of culture hero: he, alone among men, succeeded in winning the heart of heavenly Helen. In selecting Paris, rather than, say, Achilles (or Aeneas), Faustus is identifying erotic love, not honour (or *pietas*), as the basis of his identity. This identification proceeds not in a Homeric (or a Virgilian) 'vein,' but in an 'Ovidian' one, and its function is to contest the nationalist myth of England as Troynovant, championed by Spenser in *The Faerie Queene*.[54]

The nationalist, Spenserian myth suggests that we see 'queen' Helen as a figure for Spenser's heroine, Queen Eliza. The secret agent is careful here, but one of his images should catch our eye. In her earlier appearance, during the symposium on love and beauty, Helen passes over the stage, prompting the Second Scholar to remark, 'Too simple is my wit to tell her praise, / Whom all the world admires for majesty' (V.i.26–7). *Majesty* – not beauty. At least twice again Marlowe identifies Helen in terms of her majesty. Just before Helen enters, the First Scholar asks to see 'that peerless dame of Greece, whom all the world admires for majesty' (14–15). And immediately following, Faustus himself consents to the scholars' request: 'You shall behold that peerless dame of Greece / No otherways for pomp and majesty' (21–2). Marlowe follows this series of epithets with a reference to Helen's regal title: 'No marvel though the angry Greeks pursued / With ten years' war the rape of such a queen' (28–9). Within the context of the French marriage question raised in chapters 3 and 4, an Elizabethan audience may well have been reminded of their own majestic queen, whom all the world admired for majesty.[55]

Both lines in the passage quoted resemble lines in Spenser. Marlowe's 'Too simple is my wit to tell her praise' recalls Book I of *The Faerie Queene*, when Spenser pauses in his description of the New Jerusalem, 'The Citie of the great king,' to insert his own authorial voice: 'Too high a ditty for my simple song' (x.55). Marlowe's line here also recalls a line in Book II, canto x, when Spenser again pauses to insert his authorial voice, this time to praise the role of Christ's Incarnation in the construction of British nationhood: 'O too high ditty for my simple rime' (50). Similarly, Marlowe's other line, 'Whom all the world admires for majesty,' recalls Spenser's description of Queen Elizabeth in *The Teares of the Muses*, when Spenser calls his sovereign the 'myrrour of her Makers majestie' (572). Another of Spenser's epithets for the Queen in this poem may also underlie Marlowe's iterated reference to Helen as a 'peerless dame,' for Spenser similarly reiterates Elizabeth as '[m]ost peereles Prince, most peereles Poetresse' (577).[56] In any case, Marlowe's *Helenic* discourse is decidedly *Elizabethan*.

In effect, then, Faustus uses magic to stage a perfect nationhood founded on the cult of a Virgin Queen. The idealization of Helen and its political matrix resemble Marlowe's invitation to Elizabeth in 'The Passionate Shepherd to His Love': he sues for her patronage, with a hint of eroticism; dangerously, he participates in Elizabeth's politics of mirth. In re-creating the nation's romance mythology as a means of entering a perfect world, he thus reveals his drive to usurp the throne of the poet, the creator of that world: 'Have not I made blind Homer sing to me'? Faustus indeed becomes 'conjurer laureate' – an Ovidian counter-laureate. The attempt rounds out his earlier drive to re-create Christian mythology, in which he attempts to usurp the throne of Christ: '*Consummatum est*,' he has said (II.i.74). Through magic, Faustus seeks to become creator and creature, poet and hero, a principal actor in his own divine comedy, embracing the object of his desire. He uses magic to raise himself above God and Homer, to incarnate the poetic Word. Whereas the 'books' of both God and Homer create a spiritual or imaginative world within the mind, the 'books' of magic seem to create a real world outside the mind. Faustus believes that magic is the power of love literalizing religion and poetry. He thinks it enables him to conjure up a literal deity (Mephistopheles–Lucifer) and to lift up, as it were, poetic beloveds such as Helen of Troy from the printed page, to make them real, and then to unite with them in the *telamond*.

In other words, the tremendously inviting energy of the Helen scene entreats us to discover beneath the grim surface of impending damnation a normative, authorizing festivity of carnival liberty. Nowhere is this clearer than in its final manifestation.

'O lente, lente': The Final Monologue

Within a carnival, counter-Spenserian context, we can profitably understand Faustus's surge of Ovidian discourse in his final monologue. The surge, often understood to be incongruent with the horror of Faustus's immanent damnation, compels us to witness at the end a powerful un-script(ur)ing of Christian tragedy itself. Four Ovidian moments rupture the surface of the orthodox scene, revealing Marlowe's attempt to encode his authority as an Ovidian artist.[57]

Faustus's famous cry, '*O lente, lente currite noctis equi!*' (V.ii.74), bor-rowed from Ovid's *Amores*, becomes gleefully appropriate: he is the great Ovidian writer, the cosmic poet-lover.[58] Jonathan Bate calls this borrowing 'perhaps the most extraordinary Ovidian allusion in Elizabethan drama': 'The introduction of this pagan and erotic line in a sequence of the play in which one would expect attention to be wholly focused on Christian matter – the possibility of last-minute salvation, the descent into hell – is one of Marlowe's boldest strokes' (45). Yet critics have not penetrated the bold-ness.[59]

We may take a cue supplied by Lee T. Pearcy, who discovers a 'Pythago-rean' structure organizing Marlowe's ten-poem edition of *Ovid's Elegies* (21–36).[60] The key to this structure, Pearcy argues, are the two poems at the numerical centre (25): I.xv, the great paean to poetic fame, which empha-sizes the poet's power over 'kings' (32–3); and I.xiii, the magnificent poem to morning, which contains the line 'lente currite, noctis equi.' From this structure, Pearcy concludes that the 'symmetrical arrangement of poems around 1.15 and 1.13 revealed the poet in 1.15 triumphant over the powers of this earth and even, through his power to immortalize in verse, over death. The placing of 1.13 ... suggests that the poet's powers may go even farther [over even Jove and the gods]' (33). Thus the morning aubade draws an 'analogy' between the poet's 'creative intellect' and 'the divine creative intellect' represented by 'Apollo' (33): 'By placing Ovid's aubade sixth in his selection of ten translations, after the central emphasis on the power of poetry and the association of the poet with Apollo, Marlowe transforms the poet's request to the dawn from a mere conceit into a command [to control nature] that might be obeyed' (33).

By quoting this particular Ovid poem and line at the end of *Doctor Faustus*, Marlowe identifies his tragic hero as an Ovidian erotic poet con-testing the authority of kings, gods, and other poets, like Spenser.[61] The reappearance of Ovid's image for the literary career, that of the chariot (see *Amores* III.xv), has both generic and career significance, alerting us to the Ovidian cast of Marlowe's deconstructed Christian tragedy. While the Ovidian line may be 'incommensurate with the context of the theological *agon*' (Birringer, *Marlowe's 'Dr Faustus's and 'Tamburlaine'* 213), it is precisely commensurate with the context of Marlowe's Ovidian *agon* with Spenser. Marlowe's strategy is to conceal beneath Faustus's desperate plea for the impossible (to make the horses of night run slowly so that he can postpone damnation) a powerful participation in the poetic eternal.

This pattern re-emerges in Faustus's subsequent remark, 'O, I'll leap up to my God! Who pulls me down?' (77). As J.B. Steane alertly notes (282), Faustus echoes another passage from the *Amores* – and precisely the one articulating the poet's power over kings: Elegy I.xv. More specifically, Steane shows, Faustus echoes Marlowe's own rewriting of Ovid's conclusion to this powerful testament to poetic immortality: 'Then though death rakes my bones in funeral fire, / I'll live, and as he pulls me down mount higher' (41–2: 'ergo etiam cum me supremus adederit ignis, / vivam, parsque mei multa superstes erit' ['I, too, when the final fires have eaten up my frame, shall still live on, / and the great part of me survive my death' (Loeb trans.)]). Long ago, Harry Levin noted Marlowe's change of Ovid here: 'Ovid, speaking for the poet in his *Amores*, boasts that he will survive; Marlowe caps this, in his *Elegies*, by promising to "mount higher"' (22). By echoing this powerful intertextual moment about the immortality of the poet during Faustus's grimmest moment, Marlowe again encodes an astonishing comedic conclusion to his Ovidian tragedy. Simultaneous with Faustus's impotence – his wish to leap up to God, followed by the devils pulling him down – Marlowe asserts his own power as a writer to triumph over the deity himself: 'mount higher.'[62]

Not surprisingly, the pattern appears a third time with specific reference to Ovidian metamorphosis and Pythagorean transmigration. At the end, Faustus wishes that the Ovidian idea of magical transformation were true, 'and I be changed / Unto some brutish beast' (V.ii.108–9), and he specifically wishes that 'Pythagoras' *metempsychosis*' were 'true' (107). In the context of the present argument, Marlowe is referring not simply to the transmigration of souls, but also to two related Ovidian concepts in the fifteenth book of the *Metamorphoses*: 'the translation of one poet into another' (J. Bate 3); and a 'version of epic succession' (Hardie, *Epic Successors of Virgil* 103).[63] At the end of *Doctor Faustus*, Marlowe brilliantly records his own contestation of damnation as a *telos* by engaging in an Ovidian career utterance. This utterance counters the orthodoxy of England's Virgilian poet of royal nationhood by announcing Marlowe's 'succession' as national artist (cf. Snow 95, 97).

Finally, just before the clock strikes midnight, Faustus refers to his origins: 'Curst be the parents that engendered me!' (113). This curse loosely translates a line in Book II of Ovid's *Tristia* – the great autobiography: 'cur me docuere parentes' (343: 'why did my parents teach me [learning]'). Ovid's utterance is not strictly about genealogy but also about scholarship. Consequently, we can read the conclusion to Marlowe's soliloquy doubly: 'I'll burn my books. Ah, Mephistopheles!' (123). Faustus may offer to burn his books, but the four brilliant encodings of Ovidian poetic fame into the final monologue compel us to see, here at the horrible close, an Ovidian *author* joyfully presenting his own *book*. No matter how repeatedly editors and critics have sought to censor the very last words of the A-text (see Marcus, 'Textual Indeterminacy' 1–2), the text will not be burned: '*Terminant hor diem; terminant author opus*' ('The hour ends the day; the author ends his work').

In Faustus's last utterance, 'Ah, Mephistopheles' (123), we can thus discover not simply a final resignation to a grim fate, but simultaneously an ultimate expression of artistic satisfaction.[64]

Marlowe's Ovidian Faustus represents a powerful deconstruction of the Spenserian ideal of love as the true magic, the national vehicle for Christian glory, and an equally powerful cry for Ovidian counter-nationhood founded on the burning books of free scholarship itself.

PART III

TRUMPETS AND DRUMS: EPIC

Finally, Marlowe contributes to Western poetics by situating the genre of epic in the oscillating pattern of his counter-Spenserian, Ovidian *cursus*.

In 1592–3, Marlowe seizes an institutional opportunity, afforded when the theatres close because of plague, to complement his work in tragedy with new work in epic. As if he knew the end were coming, he begins fully to circumscribe the Ovidian *meta* to the *area maior*.

The institutional evidence of this *meta* appears in the Stationers' Register, which, on 28 September 1593, almost exactly four months after Marlowe's death, enters *Lucan's First Book* and *Hero and Leander* into the historical record together. *Lucan's First Book* is a translation from a ten-book, counter-Virgilian epic, the *Pharsalia*; *Hero and Leander*, an epyllion or minor epic derived from a fifteen-book, counter-Virgilian epic, the *Metamorphoses*. The co-appearance of these two works in the counter-Virgilian genre at the end of Marlowe's life provides evidence for re-evaluating the (premature) close of his literary career. This evidence initially compels us to witness Marlowe turning to the genre of epic – specifically, counter-epic – in order to fulfil the prediction made back in *Ovid's Elegies*. The evidence then encourages us to contextualize Marlowe's turn to counter-epic in terms of his rivalry with England's Virgil, and thus to witness his strange writing of nationhood.

Marlowe's two experiments in counter-epic are both brief and fragmentary. *Lucan's First Book* is a translation of only one of ten books in a long poem, while *Hero and Leander* is an 818-line poem that does not complete the classical myth it sets in motion. In both cases, we cannot tell whether Marlowe finished his experiment or left it unfinished at his death. Not having access to his intentions, we lack certainty about the drift of his epic phase. The drift falters when we acknowledge that we do not know when

Marlowe composed either work; critics have proposed early and late dates for both. As we saw in the introduction, however, critics are nearly unanimous in dating *Hero and Leander* at the end of Marlowe's life, and increasingly they are dating *Lucan* late as well. What remains to be done is to speculate on the significance of Marlowe's writing of two counter-Virgilian epics near the end of his life.

For an Elizabethan poet, translation could function as preparation for the real thing. Perhaps not by coincidence, Spenser serves as an important precedent. As is well known, England's New Poet prepared for his Petrarchan sonnet sequence, *Amoretti*, by translating both Petrarch and Du Bellay (*A Theatre for Worldlings*, *The Ruines of Rome*, *The Visions of Petrarch*, *The Visions of Bellay*). The case of Chapman suggests another alternative: the translator could *make* his translation his epic, as the 1616 volume *Whole Works of Homer* reveals (Helgerson, *Self-Crowned Laureates* 38–9, 255). Thus not all poets who translated epic – Surrey is another example – went on to write their own epic. Whether following Spenser or Surrey, or anticipating Chapman, we need to acknowledge that a twenty-eight-year-old writer of so much original composition could have been translating Lucan as part of his own project to mine the counter-imperialist vein.

Similarly, the minor epic *Hero and Leander* has a natural link with major epic. Clark Hulse argues that the two genres are intimately linked: 'The minor epic was, in effect, the proving ground for ... epic ... By ... its identity as a "mixed" genre (combining ... high and low genres), the minor epic was the medium by which the poet could transform himself from ephebe to high priest. It was a genre for young poets ceasing to be young, a form somewhere above the pastoral or sonnet and below the epic, the transition between the two in the *gradus Vergilianus*' (11–12). Just *where* Hulse discusses the 'relationship of minor epic to epic' (11) is crucial here. In his chapter 'Spenser's Ovidian Epics,' he argues for an intimate relation between Spenser's minor epic, *Muiopotmos*, and part of his major epic, Book III of *The Faerie Queene* (262). However, Hulse does not argue what his discussion makes available: that Spenser's minor epic of play *required* a serious major epic response. Nor in his chapter on Marlowe does he situate *Hero and Leander* in the pattern of the poet's career. Yet the 'transitional' role Hulse assigns to the minor epic in the Elizabethan literary system confirms what we may infer: in *Hero and Leander*, Marlowe is experimenting with epic.[1]

We may thus like to apply to Marlowe a career structure that Hulse applies only to Shakespeare: 'The two poems [*Venus and Adonis* and *The Rape of Lucrece*] stand at the watershed between his apprenticeship and early maturity as a dramatic writer' (12). Later, Hulse shows how Shakespeare managed this career transition: 'In the progress from *Venus and Adonis* to *Lucrece*, Shakespeare travels the Vergilian path, beginning in a middle style akin to sonnet, pastoral, and comedy, and ending in the regions of epic and tragedy' (175). In chapter 11, we shall see that *Hero and Leander* itself manages a brilliant move along the 'Vergilian path,' beginning in the 'middle style' of 'sonnet, pastoral, and comedy,' and ending in the 'regions of epic and tragedy.'[2]

Corroborating evidence emerges in the *Dedicatory Epistle* of Thomas Watson's *Amintae Gaudia*. Watson's work was entered in the Stationers' Register on 10 November 1592 – a few months after Watson's death. Marlowe was a good friend of Watson's, and thus he may have 'acted as editor for his friend's unpublished work' (Eriksen, 'Marlowe's Petrarch' 21). In his dedication to Mary Sidney, Marlowe asks 'Delia' to adopt 'this posthumous Amyntas' as her 'son,' but in the process he communicates less information about Watson than he does about himself. Most important for the present argument, in 1592 Marlowe refers to his past poetry and projects future poetry.

Near the beginning of the dedication, he asks the Countess to 'imbue' his 'yet unripe quill with the spirit of a lofty rage': 'by whose aid, wretch as I am, I believe that I can achieve more than my unripe natural talents are accustomed to bring forth.' Marlowe's troping of pastoral ('rudi calamo') and epic ('elati furoris') reveals the terms by which he sues for the Countess's patronage: he is promising to move from immature pastimes to the higher vein of a national art.[3] Then, at the end of the dedication he makes a specific generic prophecy: 'So shall I, whose scanty riches are but the shore-myrtle of Venus and the evergreen tresses of the Peneian nymph [Daphne], call you to my aid on the first page of every poem, as mistress of the Muses. In short, your virtue, which surpasses virtue itself, will likewise surpass eternity itself.' Roy T. Eriksen believes that the 'shore-myrtle of Venus' refers to Marlowe's translation of the *Amores* (which recurrently refers to the Venerean myrtle [I.i.34, I.ii.23, I.xv.37, III.i.34]), while the 'evergreen tresses of the Peneian nymph' refers to some lost Petrarchan sonnets.[4] We may add three points. First, Marlowe is identifying these erotic works as the 'scanty riches' of his youth ('opes tenuissimae'). Second, he is projecting a career *meta* ('So *shall I ... call* you ... *on the first page* of *every [future] poem*') to mature works of the highest cultural calling – those which, as the Countess's Protestant leanings suggest, can function as a means of Christian glory ('*will* likewise *surpass eternity* itself'). And third, he is identifying himself as occupying a transition zone between youth and maturity, between lyric and epic phases of his career (hence the recurrent future tense: 'shall ... will').[5]

What might arrest us here is Marlowe's apparent abandonment of his Ovidian *cursus* for a Virgilian one, including his adoption of the Christianized *telos* of salvation that Spenser was just then championing ('ipsam quoque aeternitatem superabit'). Conspicuously absent is any mention of the theatre – of tragedy – with its less ambitious worldly aims of 'pleasing' an audience. This is even more arresting if we recall that the Countess's husband, the Earl of Pembroke, had recently been staging Marlowe's tragedies, including *Doctor Faustus* (see Empson, *Censor* 41). What is Marlowe up to here?

One answer is supplied by recalling what we observed in the introduction: throughout his canon, Marlowe inhabits the deep Virgilian structure of Spenser's career in order to counter the authority of England's New Poet. Further confirmation is supplied by a hitherto undetected repetition of Spenser. In *The Teares of the Muses*, published the previous year in *Complaints* (1591), Spenser relies on another Ovidian myth to decry the state of poetry in England: the myth of Philomela – a myth Ralegh alertly reads into Marlowe's Virgilian paradigm in 'The Passionate Shepherd to His Love' (chapter 3). Euterpe, the muse of pastoral poetry, 'whose joy was earst with Spirit full / To teach the warbling pipe to sound aloft' (289–90), likens herself and her sister muses to 'Faire Philomele,' because they, like that 'dearling of the Summers pryde,' have just lost the 'goodly fields' to 'winters stormie wrath' (235–7). Euterpe means that she and the Muses have been 'oppressed' by 'Ignorance' (288). The 'tears' of the Muses result from this oppression. As Thalia, the muse of Comedy, puts it in the preceding complaint, 'ugly Barbarisme, / And brutish Ignorance' are 'ycrept of late / Out of dredd darknes of the deep Abysme' (187–9).

Marlowe entertains Spenser when he represents Delia as 'assailed by the blows of *barbarism* and *ignorance*,' and as having 'taken refuge, as once Philomela* from the Thracian tyrant' ('barbariei et ignorantiae impetu violata, ut olim a Thricio tyranno Philomela'). Just as Philomela has been raped by Tereus, so 'barbarism and ignorance' have 'assailed' Delia.[6] Evidently, Marlowe is advertising himself as a solution to this problem – a saviour to the oppressed maiden. He is re-sounding the famed poet of the Sidney circle in part to ingratiate himself to the Countess; in part, to identify himself as Spenser's *superior*: a poet of high calling who can solve the cultural abuse against learning that Spenser (only impotently) 'complains' about. At this point, we can observe the Marlovian twist to his troping of poetic fame. He does not say that his verse will make the Countess eternal; he says that his verse will make her 'surpass eternity itself' – overgo it. Only Marlowe would, while seeking patronage from a devout Protestant, dare to rely on the Spenserian terms of Christian glory to trope Lucretian 'atheism.' This is not the tears of the muses so much as *a smile of the muse*.

Marlowe's ambiguous or indeterminate troping of 'eternity' in the dedication coheres with his strategy in staging damnation in *Doctor Faustus*. Evidently perplexed, Eriksen observes, 'It is certainly remarkable that the opening address of Marlowe's Latin dedication should contain images which call to mind *the branch* and Apollo's *Lawrell bough* employed to characterize learned Faustus' ('Marlowe's Petrarch' 22). Yet the repetition of laurel imagery in the two seemingly unrelated works provides historically significant information about Marlowe's project during the penultimate year of his life.

In the epilogue to *Doctor Faustus*, the Chorus concludes, 'Cut is the branch that might have grown full straight, / And burnèd is Apollo's laurel bough / That sometime grew within this learnèd man' (1–3). Eriksen argues that Marlowe is imitating Song 269 from the *Rime sparse*, in which Petrarch laments the deaths of Cardinal Colonna and Laura: '"Broken are the high Column and the green Laurel ..."' (qtd. in Eriksen, 'Marlowe's Petrarch' 14). He speculates that the recurrence of the laurel image in the Sidney dedication connects Sir Philip Sidney and Faustus, or at least, that 'Marlowe somehow aligned the deaths of these men of state [Sidney and Colonna], for the imagery which the Latin epistle and the Epilogue have in common suggests some such connection' (22).

The repetition of the laurel garland in the play and the dedication, however, could lead us to speculate in another direction. In the dedication, as Eriksen does observe, Marlowe is 'clever[ly]' trying to establish 'a poetic kinship' among himself, the Countess, and her brother. If at the beginning he identifies Delia as 'sprung from a laurel-crowned race' ('Laurigera stirpe prognata') – as 'true sister of Sidney the bard of Apollo' ('Sidonaei vatis Apollineri genuina sorer') – at the end he insinuates himself into this company by identifying himself as the author of 'the evergreen tresses of the Peneian nymph.' With the subtle (and characteristically grim Marlovian) hint of incest between brother and sister (Apollo and Daphne), Marlowe is risking a lot, including his real goal in linking the two laurel images at beginning and end: to promote his earlier (immature) Petrarchan verse as part of his larger (counter-)*laureate* program. Not merely is Marlowe posing as a *vatis Apollinei* prophesying a (counter-)laureate art of a divine or religious nature; he is defending his youthful poetry as part of that art, and citing the Countess's famous brother as a precedent.

In short, Marlowe *is* linking his dedication to the Countess of Pembroke and his play written for her husband's Men. Superficially, Marlowe is posing as a laureate poet who is moving on to a mature Christian art. Beneath the surface, however, the former Matthew Parker scholar remains unrepentant.

10

Counter-Epic of Empire:
Lucan's First Book

Read Lucan. You must read Lucan. His poem breaks rules, inflicts pain and suffering. Don't bother to reclaim *this* classic in the name of a 'literature': this text screams a curse on its readers and upon itself – not at every moment in its duration, or you may begin to lose the edge of its imprecation, but in a press of destabilising counter-creation.

John Henderson, 'Lucan/The Word at War' 123

In translating the first book of Lucan's *Pharsalia*, Marlowe constructs Elizabethan England's first – and last – counter-epic of empire in order to attack and resist the great Virgilian epic of empire, *The Faerie Queene*.

The historical significance of *Lucan's First Book* has long escaped critics, but it is not hard to understand why. Only within the last few decades have classicists launched a Lucan revival, and only within the last few years have Renaissance scholars joined in. Perhaps few readers would share the exuberance of Statius, who judged Lucan superior to Virgil as Rome's true poet of epic (*Silvae* II.vii). Most medieval and Renaissance writers, however, would probably agree with Dante, who placed Lucan in the company of Homer, Virgil, Horace, Ovid, and (of course) himself (*Inferno* IV.88–90). Chaucer was even more explicit, writing of '[t]he grete poete, daun Lucan': 'Of yren wroght ful sternely, ... / And on hys shuldres bar up than, / As high as that y myghte see, / The fame of Julius and Pompe' (*House of Fame* 1498–1502) – a quite impressive troping of 'the poet of iron, the stern Stoic who writes of weapons.'[1] In sixteenth-century England, Lucan formed a final phase of the grammar-school curriculum, recommended by both Elyot and Erasmus, and in the 1590s the author of the *Pharsalia* experienced a remarkable renaissance. In addition to Marlowe's ground-breaking translation, Daniel published his *Civil Wars* in 1595, Drayton printed his *Mortimeriados* in 1596, and Shakespeare played *Julius Caesar* in 1599: works all indebted to the example of Lucan – and probably more directly to the example of Marlowe's Lucan.[2]

Given that Renaissance critics are now resurrecting Lucan's 'importance,' it is hardly surprising that they should have neglected the historical significance of Marlowe's translation. Of all Marlowe's works, *Lucan's First Book* has proved the most impermeable to criticism. We possess only three article-length studies, one note, and several short overviews in books.[3]

It is not that *Lucan's First Book* has lacked admirers, although until quite recently even the admirers have been trapped by their own ambivalence. In 1908, for instance, Swinburne remarks that Marlowe's 'translation of the first book of Lucan alternately rises above the original and falls short of it; ... Its terseness, vigour, and purity of style would in any case have been praiseworthy, but are nothing less than admirable, if not wonderful, when we consider how close the translator has on the whole (in spite of occasional slips into inaccuracy) kept himself to the most rigid limit of literal representation.'[4] In 1954, C.S. Lewis crowned this tradition of ambivalence by remarking that *Lucan's First Book* 'is of very great merit': 'If it were ever reasonable to reject a contemporary ascription on purely internal evidence, I should be tempted to deny this work to Marlowe' (*English Literature* 486). Recent classicists, however, praise Marlowe's translation with enthusiasm, and Charles Martindale is pristine: *Lucan's First Book* is 'arguably one of the underrated masterpieces of Elizabethan literature' (*Redeeming the Text* 71).[5]

Criticism on *Lucan's First Book* emphasizes an array of topics: the dating of the translation; its textual history; Marlowe's kinship with Lucan; the accuracy of Marlowe's translation, including the changes he makes; and attempts to formulate the literary significance of his document.[6] The time may then be ripe for a reading of *Lucan's First Book* within a neglected historical context: the structure of Marlowe's Ovidian career, his rivalry with England's Virgil, and his writing of counter-nationhood.

Let us begin with a historical fact: Marlowe's translation of Lucan is the very first published in English.[7] From this fact, we can begin to glean something of the significance of Marlowe's document. He alone among his contemporaries succeeded in voicing 'this outrageous, sour, impossible poem' with its 'obscure, frightening evocation of strange gods, of nameless powers whose spheres of action and whose relationships with the human world are unknown and indeed unknowable but whose capacity for intervening in human affairs is as fearful as it is manifest' (W.R. Johnson, *Momentary*

Monsters 1, 4). To enter fully the strangeness of Lucan's poem, however, you 'must read' John Henderson, who calls Lucan 'the boy-wonder' (122) and who brilliantly voices Lucan's own brilliantly sane derangement, as the epigraph for this chapter attempts to reveal. It is Marlowe, Elizabethan England's boy wonder, who *reads Lucan*, screams the curse, walks the edge of imprecation, and translates the press of destabilizing counter-creation. It is Marlowe who boldly dares to raise the spirit that had defied, rather than deified, the two powers that be: the emperor and the emperor's poet – both Nero and Virgil – in order to pen an 'anti-imperial politics' (Quint 134) and a counter-Virgilian poetics.[8]

Lucan's First Book qualifies as a counter-epic of empire, and Marlowe inscribes this strange national poem to inaugurate epic within his Ovidian *cursus*. As we shall see, he intends this phase to rival and contest the literary/political authority of Spenser's epic of empire, *The Faerie Queene*.[9]

'Trumpets and drums like deadly threat'ning other'

Marlowe's use of Lucan to begin his phase of Ovidian epic only appears to be a paradox. Among critics, Harry Levin best enters that paradox: Marlowe 'could not have selected two Roman exemplars more unlike each other than Lucan, the clangorous laureate of civil war, and Ovid, the mellifluous singer of the loves of the gods. His own strain would modulate back and forth between those two registers, lyric seduction and epic conquest, between the respective modes of Venus and Mars' (10). For classicists, however, Lucan's role as Ovid's successor in the writing of a counter-Virgilian epic of empire is a commonplace.[10] Nowhere is the succession of Ovid and Lucan in Marlowe's career glimpsed more formally than in the Stationers' Register, where *Lucan's First Book* and the Ovidian *Hero and Leander* show up together, under the same date, back to back: two sides of the same counterfeit coin.

In *Lucan's First Book*, Marlowe occasionally lets Ovid – more accurately, his own translation of Ovid – infiltrate his translation. Millar MacLure notes three such instances, the first and third both reflective of a single line in *Ovid's Elegies*:

- That rampires fallen down, huge heaps of stone.   (*Lucan's First Book* 25)
  Such rampired gates besiegéd cities aid.   (*Ovid's Elegies* I.vi.29)

- The grounds which Cirius and Camillus till'd.   (*Lucan's First Book* 170)
  We touched the walls, Camilus, won by thee.   (*Ovid's Elegies* III.xii.2)

- And sudden rampire rais'd of turf snatch'd up.   (*Lucan's First Book* 515)
  Such rampired gates besiegéd cities aid.   (*Ovid's Elegies* I.vi.29)

While none of these versions of Marlowe's famous self-quotation is particularly significant, together they suggest that Marlowe read Lucan as classicists read him today: through the lens of Ovid.

Critics also include Spenser in their commentaries. In the self-reflexive proem to the work, J.B. Steane calls line 2 'a technical or Spenserian felicity,' even though he adds that Marlowe 'probably learnt [it] from Chaucer' (269). Clifford Leech attributes Marlowe's stylistic failure with blank verse to Spenser's success with rhyme, implying that Marlowe might have chosen his medium in direct response to Spenser: 'He did not succeed here in establishing his medium, as he did in the drama, for only occasional and nugatory examples of nondramatic blank verse are to be found between his Lucan and Milton's epics. Here, in fact, Milton was the successful, Marlowe the unsuccessful, pioneer. Probably in the late sixteenth and early seventeenth centuries the prestige of Spenser was too strong – too strong perhaps for even Marlowe himself, who adopted the more sensuous couplet for *Hero and Leander*' (*Christopher Marlowe* 33). Finally, Clifford J. Ronan offers a remark during his review of Lucan's interest for Renaissance writers, the repercussions of which have not yet been pursued: 'no other ancient work is so often quoted in Du Bellay's *Antiquitez de Rome*, which Spenser retitled *The Ruines of Rome* in his translation widely circulated in 1591' (305).

As with Marlowe's Ovid, with Marlowe's Lucan recent editors occasionally gloss phrasing with Spenser, although usually the glosses are simple comparisons. L.C. Martin supplies three comparisons, but only the third is significant. To Marlowe's rendering of the Bacchic matron's hymn to Phoebus in lines 676–80 ('whither am I haled? where shall I fall, / Thus borne aloft ...'), he compares Spenser's 'Ah whither, Love, wilt thou now carrie mee?' in the hymn to Love in the *Hymne of Beautie* (294; see 276, 293). MacLure repeats the first two of Martin's glosses (ed., *Poems* 236 and 653), but not the last. Finally, Roma Gill gives us our second significant reference when she glosses Marlowe's 'wreak' in line 32 ('These plagues arise from wreak of civil power'): 'In the *Ruines of Rome: by Bellay*, Spenser invites the reader's contemplation of Rome' (ed., *Complete Works* 1: 248).

While such comments and comparisons remain slender, they none the less tantalize us to examine the poem more deeply. In the programmatic proem to *Lucan's First Book*, Marlowe finely Englishes Lucan's imitation of the opening of the *Aeneid*, but even more complexly he overgoes Lucan through precise generic indicators:

> Wars worse than civil on Thessalian plains,
> And outrage strangling law, and people strong
> We sing, whose conquering swords their own breasts launched,
> Armies allied, the kingdom's league uprooted,
> Th' affrighted world's force bent on public spoil,
> Trumpets and drums like deadly threat'ning other,
> Eagles alike displayed, darts answering darts.[11]
>
> (*Lucan's First Book* 1–7)

We have already noted that Steane finds line 2 here displaying 'a technical or Spenserian felicity'; it is Levin, however, who alertly catches Marlowe in the act of appropriation: Marlowe went 'out of his way to insert the phrase, "conquering swords," into the invocation as a kind of signature,' and he 'replaced *signis* a few lines later with "trumpets, and drums"' (10). Presumably, Levin is referring to Marlowe's use of the phrase 'conquering sword' in the prologue to *1 Tamburlaine*: 'you shall hear the Scythian Tamburlaine / Threat'ning the world with high astounding terms, / And scourging kingdoms with his conquering sword' (4–7).[12] Similarly, Gill helps us see that Marlowe's stubbornly pluralized 'We sing,' unnecessary as a translation of Lucan's 'canimus,' may render Marlowe's joint authorship with Lucan here.[13] To these comments, we may add two. First, by inserting 'trumpets and drums,' Marlowe is quoting himself a second time; for in *2 Tamburlaine* he has Techelles say, in a splendid moment of theatricality, 'Trumpets and drums, alarum presently! / And, soldiers, play the men!' (III.iii.62–3), while again in another theatrical display from *Edward II*, the king himself exclaims, 'Sound drums and trumpets! March with me, my friends; / Edward this day hath crown'd him king anew' (III.iii.75–6).[14] Second, in the very line within which he quotes himself, Marlowe uses a word that more than any other functions as a Marlovian signature: 'Threat'ning' (see *1 Tamb* Prologue 5; chapter 5).

Viewed in this light, that sixth line, 'Trumpets and drums like deadly threat'ning other,' looks to be a remarkable programmatic statement – not simply of poetic selfhood, but more complexly of poetic rivalry. This idea continues into the last line: 'Eagles alike displayed, darts answering darts.' Marlowe's rivalry is with Lucan, as well as with Virgil, but we may also see a glimmering of his rivalry with Spenser. The trumpet is the musical instrument that Spenser had singled out as a synecdoche for his Virgilian epic in *his* Proem to *his* national epic – in a passage and line we know Marlowe had his eye on in *1 Tamburlaine* (I.ii.34–43): 'For trumpets sterne to chaunge mine Oaten reeds' (*FQ* I.Pr.1). Both the 'drums' and the doubling of instruments are Marlowe's inventions; they recall Spenser's pastoral prophecies of his turn to epic in *The Shepheardes Calender*. In *June*, for example, Hobbinol says of Colin Clout: 'I sawe Calliope wyth Muses moe, / Soone as thy oaten pype began to sound, / Theyr Yvory Luyts and Tamburins forgoe' (57–9). The 'Tamburins' are 'tabors, small drums' (Oram et al. 111) – another instrument of epic (Cheney, *Spenser's Famous Flight* 95, 120–1, and 275, nn. 13–14). Marlowe's phrase for military competition, 'Eagles alike dis*played*,' has a theatrical ring, but the 'darts' look suspicious, and indeed Spenser uses the word and its variants about seventy times.[15]

Marlowe's career rivalry with Spenser proceeds along the lines of nationhood. Lucan indicts Virgil and a Virgilian-led Rome for its canons of self-slaughter – 'whose conquering swords their own breasts launched.' Romans display the standard of empire, the eagles, but they do so 'alike' – against each other, 'darts answering darts.' Marlowe repeats Lucan's 'outrage' but redirects it towards his own historical circumstances, in which the imperial poet of England repeats the Virgilian hegemony of empire only to bring the country closer to civil war.[16] Marlowe translates Lucan – and Lucan's rivalry with Virgil in the context of Roman imperialism – but simultaneously he 'displays' himself and his own rivalry with Spenser in the context of English nationhood.

If Marlowe opens *Lucan's First Book* in this way, he closes it in a similar one, as Martin's gloss on the hymn to Phoebus by the Bacchic Roman matron helps us see:

'Paean [= Apollo], *whither* am I haled? where shall I fall,
Thus borne *aloft*? I see Pangaeus' hill
With hoary top, and under Haemus' mount
Philippi plains. Phoebus, what *rage* is this?
Why grapples Rome, and makes war, having no foes?
Whither turn I now? ...
See, impious war defiles the Senate-house,
New factions rise; now through the world again
I go; O Phoebus, show me Neptune's shore,
And other regions, I have seen Philippi.'
This said, being tired with *fury* she sunk down.
                    (*Lucan's First Book* 677–94; emphasis added)

The opening stanza of Spenser's *Hymne of Beautie* reads:

Ah *whither*, Love, wilt thou now carrie mee?
What wontlesse *fury* dost thou now inspire
Into my feeble breast, too full of thee?
Whylest seeking to aslake thy *raging* fyre,
Thou in me kindlest much more great desyre,
And up *aloft* above my strength doest rayse
The wondrous matter of my fyre to prayse.

(Hymne of Beautie 1–7; emphasis added)

In the next chapter, on *Hero and Leander*, we shall have occasion to think that Marlowe had seen Spenser's first two *Hymnes* – the *Hymne of Love* and the *Hymne of Beautie* – in manuscript (pub. 1596), which Spenser says he composed during 'the greener times of ... [his] youth' (*Dedicatory Epistle*). That two Marlowe works entered in the Stationers' Register on the same day both conjoin with these same two *Hymnes*, probably composed in the early 1590s, suggests internal evidence for dating both *Hero and Leander* and *Lucan's First Book* late in Marlowe's career.

As Martin recognizes, Spenser and Marlowe rely on the same rhetorical construction, signalled by their similar use of the rhythmic word 'wither.' They use a similar vocabulary: 'whither'/'whither'; 'rage'/'raging'; 'aloft'/ 'aloft'; 'fury'/'fury.' And they both use the first-person 'I' in a hymnic prayer to a deity: Marlowe's matron addresses Apollo; Spenser's narrator, Love. Moreover, lines 678–9 have a distinctly Spenserian ring: 'I see Pangaeus' hill / *With hoary top*, and *under* Haemus' *mount*.' Spenser uses the words 'hoary' and 'mount' often, and twice during Marlowe's lifetime he brings the two words together. In Book I, canto iii, of *The Faerie Queene*, he describes the locale of Una's meeting with Abessa, itself echoing Moses's meeting with God on Mount Sinai (Hamilton, ed., *FQ* 57): '*Under* the steepe foot of a *mount*aine *hore*' (10). And in *Colin Clouts Come Home Againe* (orig. written 1591; pub. 1595) he describes the locale in which Colin meets the Shepherd of the Ocean, a well-recognized allegory for Spenser's original meeting with Sir Walter Ralegh: '*Under* the foote of Mole that *mount*aine *hore*' (57). One other time, in a description of the Homeric Sirens during Guyon's Odyssean voyage to the Bower of Bliss in Book II of *The Faerie Queene*, Spenser supplies similar phrasing: '*With* the brode shadow of an *hoarie hill*' (xii.30; emphasis added) – a passage that refers to the 'Theatre' and tropes poetic competition in its reference to the Muses' singing contest with the Sirens (31).

Lucan is concluding his opening book with a Bacchic prophecy of the battle at Pharsalus and an Apollonian prayer to head off the coming 'civil broils' (671).[17] According to Philip Hardie, 'recent criticism has dragged into the light the shadow of the epic poet Lucan lurking behind characters engaged in acts of prophecy,' and he cites 'the frenzied matron whose apocalyptic visions close the first book of the *Bellum Civile* ... inspired by Apollo, and compared to a Maenad filled with the god Bacchus, two gods considered (before being rejected) as sources of poetic inspiration by Lucan in the prologue of book I': 'The *furor* that gives her no rest (I.681) is scarcely to be distinguished from the *furor* which impels the citizens of Rome to destroy themselves in civil war (I.8) and which also drives Lucan to compose the epic of that civil war ... In th[is] passage ... we may see aspects of Lucan's own poetic nature and inspiration scattered in fragments over the several actors involved' (*Epic Successors of Virgil* 107–8; see Feeney 275). Hardie concludes with a Lucanic/Ovidian intertextuality: 'there is a contrast between the enormous resources of power and knowledge hinted at, and the exiguous amount of information actually revealed ... [T]he Pythia ... ha[s] ... a complete grasp of history and time, a kind of ideal model of the universal epic and particularly close to the Ovidian version of that model' (108; see n. 35 for details). Thus Hardie helps us see how Lucan crossdresses himself within his own epic, uses that cross-dressing to counter Virgil with an 'Ovidian ... model' of the 'universal epic,' and unifies the structure of Book I, so that the first and last passages echo each other. Marlowe, we can assume, joyfully participates in Lucan's cross-dressing of his muse, in his countering of Virgilian epic via an 'Ovidian model,' and in his unifying of his own translation. Additionally, he contextualizes his repetition of Lucan in terms of his own rivalry with Spenser and the epic writing of English nationhood.

By contrast, Spenser opens his hymn with an Orphic prayer to Love, the source of his poetic inspiration. He is writing in the non-epic genre, the religious hymn. Thereby, he largely absents himself from the writing of English nationhood. If Marlowe is superimposing Spenser's hopeful hymn to Love onto the Lucanian matron's frenzied prayer to Apollo, he would seem less to be firing his own verse with Spenser than firing Spenser's verse with Lucan. To read the Spenserian hymn in light of Marlowe's translation is to force a rereading of Spenser – to reveal the volcanic Lucanian *furor* concealed beneath the artifice of Spenserian gentility. Marlowe contaminates Spenserian inspiration.

The Ruins of Rome

If Marlowe both opens and closes his work with intimations of his great rival, we might also expect him to disrupt his translation with Spenserian fissures.

The one fissure identified by Gill and Ronan turns out to be productive, for it leads us to speculate that in *Lucan's First Book* Marlowe is critiquing more than Spenser's Virgilian progression to epic in *The Faerie Queene* or his theory of erotic inspiration from the first two *Hymnes*; he might also be critiquing another imperial poem of nationhood available to Marlowe in print after 1591 and one that exerted a strong influence on Marlowe's second great rival when he wrote his *Sonnets: The Ruines of Rome*.[18]

As we have seen, Gill glosses 'wreak' in line 32 ('These plagues arise from wreak of civil power') with lines 33–5 of Spenser's translation of Du Bellay's 1558 *Antiquitez de Rome*: 'Behold what wreake, what ruine, and what wast, / And how that she [Rome], which with her mightie powre / Tam'd all the world, hath tam'd herselfe at last' (*Ruines of Rome* 33–5). As Gill recognizes, 'wreake' is another Spenserian word; the New Poet uses it and its variants a total of fifty-one times. Steane's comment on Marlowe's line can lead us to speculate that the translator of Lucan may have had his eye on the translator of Du Bellay: 'The poem begins with the phrase "Wars worse then civill" and its first section ends with the line: ["]These plagues arise from wreake of civill power ... ["] The Latin here reads *alta sedent civilis vulnera dextrae*, literally "wounds caused by hands raised in civil conflict are deep and permanent." ... This is different from Marlowe's "wreake of civill power," which is something very Elizabethan and akin to Ulysses' "order" [in Shakespeare's *Troilus and Cressida*]: a picture of what happens "when Degree is shak'd"' (251). Marlowe changes Lucan, evoking the fracturing of the 'Elizabethan World Picture' (Steane's topic). As Gill helps us see, Marlowe changes Lucan via Spenser, who is translating Du Bellay.

The plot thickens, because, as Frank Mcminn Chambers reveals, Du Bellay is himself imitating Lucan, albeit a few lines earlier than the passage under discussion.[19] To grasp the magnitude of what is happening here, we need to recall one of Chambers's alert observations: Du Bellay's borrowings from Lucan 'are restricted almost entirely to the first book of Lucan, ... likely because only the first book suited his purpose' (937) – which is, to complain against the ruins of Rome.

Lucan's first book is a complaint against the ruins of Rome.

Lucan's First Book is a complaint against *The Ruines of Rome*.[20]

'French Bardi'

Critics have long observed one of Marlowe's most curious changes: he expands Lucan's 'Bards' to 'French Bardi' in the only self-reflexive passage on poetic fame in Book I – a passage, moreover, within which critics find yet another Marlovian signature from *Tamburlaine*:

And you, French Bardi, whose immortal pens
Renown the valiant souls slain in your wars,
Sit safe at home and chant sweet poesy.

(*Lucan's First Book* 443–5)

L.C. Martin (283) and MacLure (ed., *Poems* 243) gloss 'French' as 'Marlowe's addition'; by contrast, Gill appears to solve the mystery: 'Sulpitius provided the nationality for Lucan's *Bardi: poetae, qui lingua Gallica cantores significant*' (ed., *Complete Works* 1: 260). Yet other critics have asked some interesting questions – Boas, for instance: 'And in three lines whose music is in an exceptionally soft key (443–5) ... may we not find a source and seed of the glorious rhapsody in *Tamburlaine*, Part I, v. ii, beginning: "If all the pens that ever poets held"' (*Christopher Marlowe* 48). Conversely, Steane wondered: 'are we wrong if we think that the lines about French poets are not as innocent as they look ... The "immortal pens" are not under suspicion; but "sit safe at home" has a familiar, cosy sound, to be played off against the romantic literary "chaunt sweet Poesie," and the lines are ... amusingly placed, picturing this secure pacific body in the procession of militants' (276).

As Boas permits us to observe, Marlowe appears once again to be engaging in self-quotation, with 'immortal pens' consolidating Tamburlaine's 'ivory pen' (V.ii.82) and 'immortal flowers of poesy' (103), with that last word re-emerging in 'chant sweet poesy,' and with 'sweet' originating in Tamburlaine's 'sweetness that inspir'd their [the poets'] hearts' (100). Like the nationality of the poets, their instrument is Marlowe's addition. Moreover, as Steane observes, so is 'Sit safe at home.' Marlowe is clearly criticizing the 'French Bardi,' who hypocritically sit at home to chant sweet poesy about valiant souls slain in wars while the valiant souls themselves had no such luxury.

This leads us to a final question: Is Marlowe critiquing two French Bardi in particular – Du Bellay, who appropriated Lucan for a Christian cause, a complaint against the ruin of time; and Spenser, who repeated Du Bellay's appropriation through his own translation? Marlowe's use of the word 'Renown' in line 444 encourages us to answer in the affirmative, for critics have long identified the word as one of Marlowe's recurrent repetitions of his Virgilian rival.[21] The trope of *chanting* sweet poesy is elsewhere alien to Marlowe, but it recurs in Spenser in contexts that are metaphorically vocational: 'birds ... / Do chaunt sweet musick' (*Faerie Queene* I.vii.3). Marlowe's portrait of the French Bardi especially recalls Spenser's self-portrait opening *Colin Clouts Come Home Againe*: 'The shepheards boy ... / Sate (as his custome was) upon a day, / Charming his oaten pipe unto his peres' (1–5). If, as D.C. Feeney observes, Lucan's passage is 'a wicked parody of Vergilian language' (277), Marlowe's translation of Lucan may well be a wicked parody of the Virgilian Spenser's language.²²

While we cannot determine the case with certainty, it does seem likely that Marlowe found in Lucan's first book a counter-Spenserian 'ruines of Rome' – a complaint not just against the fall and decadence of Rome but also against those 'French Bardi' who had sung her complaint. By enclosing his own complaint against a contemporary rival within a counter-epic of civil war, Marlowe breaks ground in the epic genre, and so prepares for a new phase of his Ovidian career. Whether he would have continued his translation to precede Chapman in counterfeiting another poet's epic profession as his own, thus producing a historical epic as his alternative to the mythological epics of Virgil and Spenser; or whether he would have followed through with the intimations we shall next see signalled in *Hero and Leander* in order to produce a counter-Virgilian, counter-Spenserian mythological epic in the Ovidian vein, we cannot tell.

> Thus, in ambiguous terms
> Involving all, did Arruns darkly sing.
>
> (*Lucan's First Book* 636–7)

Read *Lucan*.
You must read *Lucan*.
Marlowe's text screams a curse on Spenser and upon itself – in a press of destabilizing counter-creation.

11

Marlowe, Chapman, and the Rewriting of Spenser's England in *Hero and Leander*

Recent criticism on *Hero and Leander* raises a challenge for the present study. Is it possible that Marlowe the epicist is the product not of Marlowe but of George Chapman?

The question exists because, as with *Doctor Faustus*, we possess two texts of *Hero and Leander*, both published in 1598. The first was published early in the year by Edward Blount, who printed Marlowe's name on the title page and supplied a dedication to Marlowe's patron at the time of his death, Sir Thomas Walsingham. This text, which survives in only one copy, is printed without the division into 'sestiads' and concludes with the editorial gloss '*Desunt nonnulla*' ('Some sections are missing'). The second text was published later in the year by Paul Linley with a new authorship line: 'Begun by Christopher Marloe; and finished by George Chapman.' This text, which survives in several copies and was republished eight times by the mid-seventeenth century, bears the indelible hand of Chapman, who supplied a new dedication, addressed to Lady Walsingham; divided Marlowe's 818 lines into two 'sestiads'; supplied a verse 'Argument' for each; erased '*Desunt nonnulla*'; and wrote four new sestiads. As Chapman reveals, he turned Marlowe's comedic fragment into the full tragic myth: 'New light gives new directions, fortunes new, ... / More harsh (at least more hard) more grave and high / Our subject runs, and our stern muse must fly; / Love's edge is taken off, and that light flame, ... / Must now grow staid, and censure the delights, / That being enjoyed ask judgement' (III.1–9).[1]

Until recently, critics were largely content to abide by Chapman's authority. Most editions of Marlowe's poem concluded with Chapman's continuation, and commentary naturally focused on the relation between the two poets and their radically different handling of the same myth.[2]

Recently, however, critics have followed up on hints by Muriel Bradbrook and Richard Neuse to side with Louis L. Martz, who in 1972 published a facsimile edition of the first or earlier text, free of George Chapman. Martz also supplied an introduction that aimed to 'persuade all admirers of this poem to avoid speaking of Marlowe's "fragment" and Chapman's "continuation"' (1): 'this is a finished comedy, celebrating the joys of physical love' (13). Then, in 1984 Marion Campbell argued that 'what we read as "Marlowe's *Hero and Leander*" is in fact a construct designed by Chapman to validate his own poem, and that to read the two pieces as parts of a single whole is to obscure the shape and significance of Marlowe's poem' (241). Specifically, Campbell argued that 'Chapman intends the completed poem to be read as a minor epic,' for which the 'translator of Homer' coined the term 'sestiad' on 'the analogy of "Iliad"' in order to place Marlowe's poem in the tradition of 'the epics of Virgil and Homer' (250) via the 'moralized Ovidian tradition' of the *Metamorphoses* (251): 'Chapman's poem, then, represents a reactionary attempt to moralize the erotic epyllion and to reaffirm the true epic status of this version of the Hero and Leander story' (262). Consequently, 'only by extricating *Hero and Leander* from Chapman's construction of it can we hope to do justice to the poem Marlowe wrote' (267). Finally, in her 1987 Oxford edition, Roma Gill virtually institutionalized this line of criticism by eliminating Chapman's continuation altogether: 'I can see no justification for including Chapman's work in a modern edition of Marlowe's poem' (ed., *Complete Works* 1: 185). The critical line from Martz to Campbell to Gill suggests that Chapman is responsible for packaging Marlowe as an epicist.

This line is persuasive, but it has one unfortunate consequence; it closes off the likelihood that we will discover the original context within which Marlowe wrote his poem: his attempt to fulfil the generic pattern of his Ovidian *cursus* predicted in *Ovid's Elegies*, in rivalry with England's Virgil, to pen a poetics of counter-nationhood.

As we shall see, the second or Chapman text, with its advertised binary authorship, encodes a disagreement about the merits of Spenser and his writing of England, especially with respect to England's queen and her erotic cult of chastity. We must not forget what Raymond B. Waddington articulates: 'Chapman is Spenser's successor' ('Chapman, George'). While we do not need Chapman's continuation to discover Marlowe's contestation of Spenser – it is deeply embedded in the 818 lines of *Hero and Leander* – we can benefit from Chapman's continuation because Chapman is the first to clarify the original context of Marlowe's composition. As the translator of the Homeric corpus, he appears to have been presenting himself as a 'laureate' pursuing a Homeric *cursus*.[3] Surely, then, Chapman understood what Nashe observed in 1592 when he called Spenser the 'Virgil of England' (*Pierce Penilesse* in McKerrow 1: 299): that Spenser was pursuing a Virgilian *cursus*. Is it unreasonable also to suppose that Chapman understood Marlowe as an Ovidian laureate – a counter-Virgilian and counter-Homeric poet – pursuing an Ovidian *cursus*? As one who himself chose to pen the erotic epyllion, he presumably understood the origins of Marlowe's poem to lie in the epic *Metamorphoses*. In other words, he likely understood that Marlowe's 'minor epic was, in effect, the proving ground for ... epic' (Hulse 12). Chapman's 'epic' packaging of *Hero and Leander* is thus consistent with Marlowe's decision to mine the generic vein. Indeed, Chapman demonstrates an alert attempt to clarify Marlowe's *meta* within his *Ovidian cursus*. The 'epicist' alterations that Chapman makes do not simply 'validate his own poem'; they simultaneously validate Marlowe's Ovidian career. This does not mean that Chapman approved of Marlowe's project; his attempt to purify *Hero and Leander* indicates that he did not, or at the least that he felt the need to counter Marlowe's Ovidian program with his own 'Homeric' one. If so, Chapman understood the danger of Marlowe's subversion for late sixteenth-century England; he discovered what was at stake both professionally and culturally: just how England was going to judge its great national poet as a writer of nationhood.

'Witnesse Leander, in the Euxine waves'

Unanimously, critics identify *Hero and Leander* as an Ovidian narrative poem. While the Elizabethan genre derives from the *Metamorphoses*, Marlowe derives his epyllion from Ovid's two verse letters on Hero and Leander in the *Heroides* (XVIII and XIX), as well as from the eroticism of the *Amores*.[4] Similarly, critics repeatedly find Marlowe responding to Spenser. Most famously, Muriel Bradbrook calls *Hero and Leander* 'a Hymn to Earthly Love and Beauty, an anti-Spenserian manifesto.'[5] By looking at Marlowe's use of Spenser to contextualize Ovid, we can see concretely how the 'minor epic' *Hero and Leander* endangers the erotic cult at the centre of Elizabethan nationhood.

Marlowe could have found Virgilian/Homeric epic, the Hero and Leander myth, Ovidian *amor*, and Spenserian nationhood where Bradbrook directs us. The true lover, Spenser writes in the *Hymne of Love*, manoeuvres '[t]hrough seas, through flames, through thousand swords and speares' (228):

Witnesse Leander, in the Euxine waves,
And stout Aeneas in the Troiane fyre,
Achilles passing through the Phrygian glaives,
And Orpheus daring to provoke the yre
Of damned fiends, to get his love retyre.

(Hymne of Love 231–5)

Spenser's reference to the classical quartet of heroic lovers identifies four classical poets of heroic love: Musaeus writing of Leander in *Hero and Leander*; Virgil writing of Aeneas in the *Aeneid*; Homer writing of Achilles in the *Iliad*; and (we may posit) Ovid writing of Orpheus in the *Metamorphoses* (Books X-XI).[6] If Spenser grants epic status both to Ovid's myth of Orpheus and to Musaeus's myth of Hero and Leander, Marlowe turns the 'epic' myth to counter-Spenserian purposes.[7]

Critics emphasize Marlowe's critique of Spenser's poetics of married love. Spenser centres this poetics on the intersection of three principal relations: the mutual heterosexual relation between a man and a woman within the institution of marriage; the cosmic relation between the married couple and God in the workings of a benevolent providence securing the couple's salvation; and the political relation between the divinely sanctioned couple and culture in the performance of virtue – especially as man and woman subject themselves to a virgin queen's cult of chastity. For Spenser, the individual's sexual desire originates in God, finds its object in the gendered other, and expresses itself through service to the sovereign and her state (*FQ* III.iii.1). To the sexual, theological, and political dimensions of this poetics, we can add a poetic or vocational one. As Spenser reveals in the *Letter to Ralegh*, the 'generall end' of *The Faerie Queene* is 'to fashion a gentleman or noble person in vertuous and gentle discipline' (3: 485). Spenser's complex poetics of married love ultimately tracks a comedic contour.[8]

'Guilty of true love's blood': The Prologue

In the opening lines of *Hero and Leander*, Marlowe uses Ovid to respond to Spenser: 'On Hellespont, guilty of true love's blood, / In view and opposite two cities stood, / Sea-borderers, disjoined by Neptune's might: / The one Abydos, the other Sestos hight' (I.1–4). Marlowe introduces the central principle of his Ovidian-based poetics of desire: separation – rendered here in physiological, political, theological, and metadiscursive forms.

In the opening line, he introduces the physiology of separation by identifying 'Hellespont' as 'guilty of true love's blood' – a phrase which could serve as a motto for Marlowe's entire poetics.[9] While literally 'Hellespont' is 'guilty' because it houses the deaths of Hero and Leander, Marlowe is careful to construct the paradox that drives the poem: 'true love' originates in 'blood' that is inherently 'guilty.' Hero and Leander are doomed from the start, and not simply by geography, but by nature – the nature of things, identified as the red stream of life flowing within the human frame. The oxymoronic pairing of *truth* with *guilt* is a Marlovian miniature at its most refined. What is true is what ruins; what we are born with annihilates us. Love destroys; blood kills.

In the second line, Marlowe identifies a political origin for the separation: 'In view and opposite two cities stood.' Yet it is Chapman in his section called 'Of Abydus and Sestus' prefacing his 1616 translation of Musaeus's *Hero and Leander* who clarifies the imperialistic politics of Marlowe's geography: 'Abydus and Sestus were two ancient Towns; one in Europe, another in Asia; East and West, opposites' (Chapman, ed. Shepherd 2: 94).[10] Like Barabas, who sets up shop where 'East met West' (H. Levin 65), or like Tamburlaine, who will 'write' empire 'from the East unto the furthest West' (*1 Tamb* III.iii.245–6), Marlowe situates his poem right where Europe and Asia wed, East and West marry. As we shall see, it is not simply the nature of human 'blood' that in this poem moves Marlowe to 'rage' but also 'the established social and moral order' (M. Turner 414).

In the third line, Marlowe identifies a theological origin for the lovers' separation: 'disjoined by Neptune's might.' In addition to our blood and our culture – our very nature and our own institutions – the gods (our creators) conspire to form our human tragedy. In the myth of Hero and Leander, the sea, Neptune, drowns Leander and motivates Hero's suicide; a deity 'disjoins' the lovers. Neptune is, as Joanne Altieri remarks, 'the poem's reigning god' (157).

Finally, the opening lines metadiscursively render separation as the centre of Marlowe's poetics. The virtuoso use of parallelism and balance weaving antithesis together, especially in the splendid 'In view *and opposite two* cities stood,' shows Marlovian verbal play at its height: 'The one Abydos, the other Sestos hight.' Only perhaps in that last word may we detect a formal Spenserism.[11] Marlowe's poetics of tragic desire is 'opposite' to, 'disjoined' from, Spenser's comedic poetics of married love. Perhaps, too, Marlowe understood what Chapman again reveals in notes prefacing his translation of Musaeus: Englishman called the Hellespont 'the Arm of Saint George' (Shepherd, ed. 2: 94–5). As we shall see, this is not the only time Marlowe writes the body of St George into his poem.

This analysis encourages us to resist a mainstream conclusion: that in *Hero and Leander* Marlowe is writing a 'comedy,' and thus that the 'poem ends in glorious and harmonious fulfillment – the apotheosis of comedy' (Gill, ed., *Complete Works* 1: 185).[12] Rather, Marlowe chose the Hero and Leander myth because it permitted him, in a decidedly Ovidian manner, to tell a 'tragedy' within an 'epic' form, and perhaps even to make a transition from tragedy to epic.[13] By calling *Hero and Leander* a tragedy within the epic form, we need not deny its 'comic tone' nor argue for its fragmentary state. An 'Ovidian tragedy,' like an Ovidian epic, can only be Ovidian, and it is certain that the poem we possess seeks to transform the traditional genre. Like the stage tragedies, *Hero and Leander* is 'play on the brink of an abyss, *absolute* play' (Greenblatt, *Renaissance Self-Fashioning* 220).

'Buskins of shells': Hero

The opening portraits of Hero and Leander represent the Marlovian mode of Ovidian play on the brink of an Ovidian abyss. The portrait of Hero looks to represent Ovidian tragedy itself: 'Buskins of shells all silvered usèd she' (I.31). The word 'buskin' has pastoral connotation, becoming part of the iconography of Diana, as repeatedly in Spenser: 'Her silver buskins from her nimble thigh' (*FQ* III.vi.18). According to A.C. Hamilton, Spenser here 'imitates Ovid, *Met*. iii 173–90, which describes the grotto in which Actaeon surprises Diana' (ed., *FQ* 358), and it seems significant that Golding translates Ovid's *vincla* (III.168: 'sandal') with 'buskins' (III.197). By dressing 'Venus' nun' (I.45) in the boots of Diana, Marlowe literally attires Hero in the paradox of the female that his portrait foregrounds (see Keach, '"Venus' Nun"'). But the paradox opens up a second definition of 'buskin' during the period – one Golding alertly recognizes as well suited to the myth of Diana and Actaeon: 'The high thick-soled boot (*cothurnus*) worn by the actors in ancient Athenian tragedy' (*OED*, Def. 2). All five of Marlowe's other uses of 'buskin' come from *Ovid's Elegies* – and all represent Ovidian tragedy (II.xviii.15, 18; III.i.14, 31, 63). For Marlowe, as for Spenser, the word has a deep connection with Ovid.

Not surprisingly, in portraying Hero Marlowe has his eye on Spenser, and in particular on Spenser's 'most extended portrait' in *The Faerie Queene* (Hamilton, ed., *FQ* 195): the chaste virgin huntress Belphoebe, who mythically derives from Diana but who allegorically refers to Queen Elizabeth.[14] Thus Spenser describes Belphoebe's 'streight legs' as 'most bravely ... embayld / In gilden buskins of costly Cordwaine' (II.iii.27). Marlowe evokes Spenser's portrait of Elizabeth in her private person in order to offer a deep probe of the 'cult of the Virgin Queen' (the phrase is Levin's) and a critique of the national poet who was then expressing sympathy for that cult.

Marlowe's portrait of Hero intersects other Spenserian texts. Gill, for instance, glosses the description of Hero's veil with both *Faerie Queene* II.xii.61 and Ovid's *Metamorphoses*, 'the description of Arachne's web' (ed., *Complete Works* 1: 291). Gill mistakenly cites Book V of the *Metamorphoses*; but L.C. Martin is more accurate, citing VI.128–9: 'ultima pars telae, tenui circumdate limbo, / nexilibus flores hederis habet intertextos' (127–8 in the Loeb: 'The edge of the web with its narrow border is filled with flowers and clinging ivy intertwined'). As Nancy K. Miller reveals in another context, this is not just any passage, but one that contains – ends with – the word 'intertextos,' *interweave*, from which 'intertextuality' derives (82, 96). Marlowe writes, 'Upon her head she ware a myrtle wreath, / From whence her veil reached to the ground beneath. / Her veil was artificial flowers and leaves, / Whose workmanship both man and beast deceives' (17–20). Marlowe may have recalled Golding's translation of the Arachnean web: 'Round about the utmost Verdge was set / A narrow Traile of pretie *flowers* with *leaves* of Ivie fret' (VI.159–60; emphasis added). The myth of Arachne is among the most – if not *the* most – subversive in the entire *Metamorphoses*, for Arachne defeats Athena in the spinning contest, only to be punished by the revengeful goddess. Like the Actaeon myth, it forms an analogue to Ovid's own relation with Augustus (see chapter 7).[15]

Just as Ovid veils his subversion of the Emperor, so Spenser veils his Arachne-figure, Acrasia. The passage Gill cites describes the fountain in the middle of the Bower of Bliss: 'And over all, of purest gold was spred, / A trayle of yvie in his native hew' (61). Unannotated in modern critical editions, this passage glances at the very lines of Ovid in the Golding translation of Arachne's web, as the repetition of 'trayle' and 'yvie' reveals. Yet to get from an image of inanimate artifice that deceives to the image of the deceiving female artist, we need to glance at Acrasia herself, whom Spenser depicts 'arayd, or rather disarayd': 'All in a vele of silke and silver thin, / That hid no whit her alablaster skin, / ... / More subtile web Arachne cannot spin' (77). Acrasia's Arachnean veil, when combined with the fountain imagery cited by Gill, best glosses the veil of Hero.

Traditionally, the veil is a trope for allegory itself (*FQ* II.Pr.5). Thus, in Hero's veil we find signs of metadiscourse; 'artificial' and 'workmanship' speak for themselves, but the 'flowers' that are 'artificial' and that work to 'deceive' the beholder also suggest the 'flowers of Poetrie' in 'Apollos Garden' (Sidney, *Defence of Poesy* in G.G. Smith, ed. 1: 152). Hero's 'leaves,' however, are likely from the ivy vine of Bacchus, as Marlowe's glance at both Golding's Ovid and Spenser reveal. If so, 'flowers and leaves' function as a synecdoche for the 'artifice' of the *area maior* of epic and tragedy. That Marlowe is situating both genres within the Ovidian mode is clear from Hero's 'myrtle wreath.'[16] In short, Marlowe's metadiscourse tropes the female Hero as a form of Ovidian art – amorous, epic, tragic: a kind of Ovidian career typology all in one.

The art of Hero is tragic for the reason Marlowe reveals in describing her 'garments' (9): 'Her wide sleeves green, and bordered with a grove, / Where Venus in her naked glory strove / To please the careless and disdainful eyes / Of proud Adonis that before her lies. / Her kirtle blue, whereon was many a stain, / Made with the blood of wretched lovers slain' (11–16). Unlike Spenser's heroines in *The Faerie Queene* (Belphoebe), but like his lascivious dames (Acrasia), Hero is trapped by her own desire. Marlowe is intrigued with a paradox: the female is created in the image of God, with a body so stunning she attracts erotic desire ('both men and beasts'); yet the female is trained in a code of chastity, underwritten by religion, law, and ethics, which prohibits her from responding sensitively to her desire. She is, as only Marlowe could put it, 'Venus' nun,' and in the end it is Hero's counterfeit profession that will lead to her guilt, shame, anguish, and (in Chapman's continuation) death.

Curious Dints: Leander

In the homoerotic portrait of Leander, Marlowe's Ovidian rivalry with Spenser intensifies:

> *I could tell ye*
> How smooth his breast was, and how white his belly,
> And whose immortal fingers did imprint
> That heavenly path with *many a curious dint*
> That runs along his back, but *my rude pen*
> Can hardly *blazon* forth the *loves of men*,
> Much less of powerful gods: let it suffice
> That *my slack muse* sings of Leander's eyes.
>
> (*Hero and Leander* I.65–72; emphasis added)

As in the case of Tamburlaine, Marlowe's blason of the other conjoins with Spenser's epic self-presentation of the shepherd who becomes a king:

Me, all too *meane*, the *sacred Muse* areeds
To *blazon* broad emongst her learned throng:
Fierce warres and *faithfull loves* shall moralize my song.
...
O helpe thou *my weake wit*, and sharpen *my dull tong*.
                              (*The Faerie Queene* I.Pr.1–2)

Both Spenser and Marlowe rely on the inability topos to present themselves;
they use a similar vocabulary; and they both write of 'love.' Yet Marlowe's
self-presentation reads like a parody of Spenser's, and indeed it should, for
Marlowe's Ovidian-based 'slack muse,' derived from the *cursus* of chariot-
racing, underwrites Spenser's Virgilian-based 'sacred Muse.'[17] We know
that Marlowe read this opening stanza of *The Faerie Queene* carefully,
because he 'plagiarized' it in *1 Tamburlaine*, and it is not surprising to find
him returning to it here, when he makes another career *meta*: to his own
epic.

Moreover, the 'immortal fingers' that 'imprint / That heavenly path with
many a curious dint' along Leander's 'back' are only superficially the work
of the Christian God; more literally, they are either those of the homoerotic
Neptune or the 'slack muse' himself. To arrive at this image of (pagan)
incarnation, Marlowe may have recalled Spenser's opening description of
the Redcrosse Knight's Christian armour: 'Wherein old dints of deepe
wounds did remaine, / The cruell markes of many' a bloudy fielde' (I.i.1).
The youth and innocence of Leander's spine contrast with the age and
experience of St George's inherited armour, and the contrast offsets a poetics grounded in homoeroticism ('loves of men') from a poetics of heterosexual marriage ('faithful loves'). Marlowe's 'I could tell ye' reads like an
answer to one of the questions echoing throughout *The Faerie Queene*: 'O
who can tell' (I.ii.10, II.iii.44, II.ix.46) – a question Marlowe actually
plagiarizes later: 'O who can tell' (II.23).

The political dimension of the Leander blason emerges in one line: 'Fair
Cynthia wished his arms might be her sphere' (59). This line subtly equates
Hero with Queen Elizabeth, and Leander with a certain suitor. We do not
have to look far to discover who this suitor might be; he is the lover of 'Fair
Cynthia,' Sir Walter Ralegh. Thus, in another Ovidian narrative poem,
Ocean to Cynthia, Ralegh identifies Elizabeth as Hero and himself as Leander:

on Sestus shore, Leanders late resorte
Hero hath left no lampe to Guyde her love
Thow lookest for light in vayne, and stormes arise

Shee sleaps thy death that erst thy danger syth-ed
Strive then no more bow down thy weery eyes.[18]

(*Ocean to Cynthia* 487–91)

Perhaps, as Abraham Fraunce said in 1592, 'Leander and Heroes love is in every mans mouth' (rpt. in MacLure, ed., *Poems* xxvi); but the conjunction of the myth in two colleagues at about the same time once more compels us to consider that Marlowe's Cynthia conceit may read Ralegh politically: Cynthia/Elizabeth wishes Leander/Ralegh's arms to be her 'sphere.'[19]

That Marlowe is quite literally troping Ralegh's own conceit of Cynthia is at least possible. In 'Praisd Be Dianas Faire and Harmles Light,' a poem attributed to Ralegh in *The Phoenix's Nest* (1593), we find the following line: 'In heaven Queene she is among the spheares' (9).[20] Yet it is in *Ocean to Cynthia* that Ralegh uses the same conceit as Marlowe – and in a line that again suggests a conjunction between Marlowe and Spenser: 'Bellphebes course is now observde no more / That faire resemblance weareth out of date' (271–2). Borrowing Spenser's name for the Queen in her private person, yet responding to Spenser's encomia for the chaste moon goddess, Ralegh images Elizabeth veering from her 'course' – her orbit, her 'sphere' – in what forms the center of 'the poem's most compelling image of fragmentation' (Cousins 93).[21] While *Hero and Leander* is not an 'allegory of Ralegh and Elizabeth,' as Spenser's story of Timias and Belphoebe is in *The Faerie Queene* (III.v, IV.vii–viii), Marlowe appears to evoke a politically erotic relation of great concern to the nation.[22] Specifically, he is trying to advance the powerful courtier's claim to power, at the same time that he is assailing the sanctity of the Queen's palisade of chastity: 'Ne'er king more sought to keep his diadem, / Than Hero this inestimable gem' (II.77–8). Marlowe's subtle cross-dressing of Hero ('king') catches the Virgin Elizabeth in the process of losing her 'inestimable gem,' on which she founded her cult.[23]

Venus's Glass

Marlowe situates his 'Ovidian' critique of the Queen's cult in Venus's Church, and here it becomes clearer that he is critiquing not just the Elizabethan cult, but Spenser's Elizabethan cult. Indeed, critics recurrently catch Spenser lurking in Marlowe's Church – usually the Spenser of the Ovidian House of Busirane. But Marlowe also appears to have had his eye on the Bower of Bliss, as his opening lines reveal: 'The walls were of discoloured jasper stone, / Wherein was Proteus carvéd' (I.136–7).[24] During the voyage to the Bower, Guyon and the Palmer pass 'the quicksand of Unthriftyhed,' which they can 'descry' by 'the sea discoloured' (II.xii.18). As Marlowe's reference to Proteus reveals, he, too, has the sea in mind; but his 'discoloured' image of 'jasper stone' may derive from a later Spenser image, at which we have already glanced – the description of Acrasia's fountain: 'a fountaine stood, ... / And over all, of purest gold was spred, / A trayle of yvie in his native hew: / For the rich mettall was so *coloured*, ... / That through the waves one might the bottom see, / All *pav'd beneath* with *Jaspar* shining bright' (II.xii.60–2; emphasis added). All three words italicized in the last line recur in Marlowe's description: in the 'pavement' that is 'of crystal shining fair' (cf. Spenser's 'drops of Christall' at 61: 9); in the mythological depictions that are 'underneath this radiant floor'; and of course in the 'jasper stone' of the walls. Spenser himself is parodying St John's description of the New Jerusalem, which Marlowe re-parodies by relocating the jasper from Spenser's submarine pavement back to the original 'wall' of an above-ground edifice: 'And the buylding of the wall of it was of Jasper ...: And ... the first fundacion was Jasper' (Rev 21: 18–19; see 4: 3, 21: 11). The Geneva gloss is pertinent – 'Ever grene & florishing' – for it identifies the jasper stone as an analogue of the poet's laurel tree, which Spenser mentions in the next stanza (63). Thus Marlowe's two-storey Church structure has an origin in Acrasia's two-layered fountain.[25]

What Spenser exiles to a distant island paradise of intemperance, Marlowe locates in downtown Sestos, 'in the midst' (157) of culture, at the very centre of society's laws, codes, and institutions: 'There might you see the gods in sundry shapes, / Committing heady riots, incest, rapes' (I.143–4). Yet Marlowe displays not simply 'a remarkable microcosm of the human condition' (Neuse 430), but a poetics of that microcosm. The architecture of the Church is the most enigmatic expression of this poetics, and the enigma centres on the 'crystal ... pavement' (141), or 'radiant floor' (145), of what 'the town of Sestos' calls 'Venus' glass' (142). This 'glass' is the mirror of Venus.[26]

Marlowe's 'Venus' glass' is not just a 'Lewis Carroll mirror' figuring the enigmatic reflections of 'the human imagination.' It is also an Edmund Spenser mirror figuring the enigmatic reflections of an Ovidian poetics. Thus, in Book III of *The Faerie Queene* Spenser offers perhaps his clearest metaphor for his own poem and art, and in the opening canto he terms it 'Venus looking glas' (i.8). In canto ii, he reveals that the maker of this glass is 'The great Magitian Merlin' (18), who in part allegorizes the great poet Spenser: 'It vertue had, to shew in perfect sight, / What ever thing was in the world contaynd ... / It was a famous Present for a Prince, / And worthy worke of infinite reward, ... / Happie this Realme, had it remained ever since' (19–21). Marlowe would likely have been interested in this episode, because, as Robert Greene knew, Marlowe went under the name 'Merlin' at Cambridge.[27] We are to understand 'Venus' glas' – and Venus's Church as a whole – as a 'competing' 'world of glas' representing the relation 'betwixt the lowest earth and heavens hight' (*FQ* III.ii.19, 20). Whereas Spenser's magic mirror shows a providential poetics of a wise and just married love (III.iii.1–2), Marlowe's shows a materialist poetics of unrestrained desire threatening both individual and state: 'Love kindling fire, to burn such towns as Troy' (I.153).[28]

'Will in us is overruled by fate'

Marlowe's subsequent description of Hero and Leander falling in love at first ill-fated sight remains embroiled in his 'competition' with Spenser:

> It lies not in our power to love or hate,
> For will in us is overruled by fate.
> When two are stripped, long ere the course begin
> We wish that one should lose, the other win;
> And one especially do we affect
> Of two gold ingots like in each respect.
> The reason no man knows: let it suffice,
> What we behold is censured by our eyes.
> Where both deliberate, the love is slight;
> Who ever loved, that loved not at first sight?
>
> (*Hero and Leander* I.167–76)

Critics are troubled by those first two lines, because they are 'seemingly un-Marlovian': 'This is fate conceived of as accident' (M. Turner 404).[29] We can help clear up the trouble by contextualizing the passage in terms of the author's own professional environment.

William Keach helps us begin the process: 'The narrator of *Hero and Leander* is as distanced from Marlowe as the speaker of the *Amores* is from Ovid; he is usually as distanced from the story he tells as the speaker of the *Ars Amatoria* is from his subject. He shares with both Ovidian voices a sophisticated, often cynical erotic expertise. Above all, he calls attention to his own presence in a way which constantly reminds us that a cunningly created and projected persona is guiding our experience of the narrative' (*Elizabethan Erotic Narratives* 88).[30] Marlowe's narrator, we may add, inscribes a form of deterministic fate to indict Elizabethan culture for its destructive Calvinist, Spenserian ideology, voiced in *The Faerie Queene* by 'Merlin' in his address to Britomart/Elizabeth: 'It was not ... thy wandring eye, / Glauncing unwares in charmed looking glas, / But the streight course of heavenly destiny, / Led with eternall providence ... / Therefore submit thy wayes unto his will, / And do by all dew meanes thy destiny fulfill' (III.iii.24). Rather than articulating his own personal view of the relation between 'will' and 'fate' – love and destiny – Marlowe inscribes the tyranny of the Spenserian dynamic ordering that relation. In Marlowe's Ovidian-based, materialistic poetics, as in Spenser's Calvinist-based Christian poetics, 'eternall providence' does guide our 'glaunce'; but in Marlowe, unlike in Spenser, this glance is what kills us. As both Ovid and Lucan knew, the gods exist; they exist to annihilate us.

Marlowe's two metaphors for a counter-Spenserian poetics of will and fate trope the enigma of human choice. The first, that of the running race, is a metaphor of competition, and it alludes to the Ovidian myth of Atalanta and Hippomenes in Book X of the *Metamorphoses* (560–739), which interrupts the story of Venus and Adonis (Mills 301). Yet it is not Venus who tells the Atalanta story, but Orpheus, who has lost his wife, Eurydice, turned to the love of boys (X.64–85), and thereby moved from an epic Gigantomachy to elegy (150–4; see chapter 1). The Ovidian Atalanta story, in other words, is self-reflexivity par excellence (see Otis 166–230), and at its centre lies the idea of competition (Mills 302). For Renaissance mythographers and poets, the Atalanta myth is a classical version of the fall, in which the apples that Hippomenes throws down to distract and so defeat and finally marry his rival beloved function as 'the golden apples of worldly pleasure and profit, which Hippomenes the Devil flings in our way' (Alexander Ross, qtd. in Hamilton, ed., *FQ* 234). Hence, Spenser includes the myth in his Garden of Proserpina in the Mammon episode in *Faerie Queene* II (vii.54) when he catalogues stories about 'treacherous apples, bringing discord' (K. Williams 60). In *Amoretti* 77, he daringly rewrites the myth of the Edenic fall by identifying Elizabeth Boyle's breasts with the 'twoo golden apples of unvalewd price: / far passing ... / ... those which Atalanta did entice' (6–8). Marlowe is bolder even than Spenser, for he relocates paradise in the female womb itself: the 'new Elysium' (I.411). Unlike Spenser, however, Marlowe rewrites the myth of the fall to tragic ends.

The second metaphor also contains an undetected conjunction with Spenser; the 'two gold ingots alike in each respect' recall Spenser's description of Mammon's gold: 'And round about him lay on every side / Great heapes of gold, that never could be spent: ... / Some others were new driven, and distent / Into great Ingoes, and to wedges square' (II.vii.5). As the *OED* reveals, the word 'ingot' is rare in English, with Spenser's usage, spelled 'Ingowes' in the 1590 *Faerie Queene*, requiring special comment as 'either a misprinting or a mistaken archaism' (headnote), since it is revised for the 1596 *Faerie Queene* as 'Ingoes' (Def. 2). In chapter 6, we found Marlowe brooding over this passage in *The Jew of Malta*, and he may have retained Spenser's image and its 'g'-sound alliteration here. That both the 'running' and the ingot metaphor should have their locus in this episode is not surprising, since Mammon is not merely the god of gold but, as 'God of the world and worldings' (8), a figure for a materialist conception of the cosmos, and therefore for human fate (11).

The summarizing line that follows the metaphors of racing and ingots produces a three-word quotation from Spenser. Why is it that we like one runner over the other 'long ere the course begin,' or that we 'affect' two ingots of gold 'like in each respect': 'The reason *no man knows*.' The quotation comes from the episode preceding the Mammon episode – that of the Lucretian hedonist songster, Phaedria, during her lily song, which parodies the 'lilies of the field' from Matthew 6: 25–34 (Hamilton, ed., *FQ* 216). How, Phaedria asks, do the 'flowres, the fields ... pleasant growe': 'no man knowes, / They spring, ... / And deck the world with their rich pompous showes' (*FQ* II.vi.15). Phaedria's phrase 'no man knowes,' as Spenser's brilliant emphasis and cadence reveals (reproduced by Marlowe), is a materialist troping of providence or fate, artfully crafted to contest the providential design of Christ's sermon: we do not know why the flowers grow – they spring. For Marlowe's narrator, 'no man knows' why we choose one runner or ingot over another, for will in us is overruled by fate.

L.C. Martin was evidently the first – and last – to locate the conclusion to the 'will'/'fate' passage – 'Who ever loved, that loved not at first sight?' – in 'Spenser's "Hymn in honour of Beautie," 208–10' (37): 'For all that like the beautie which they see, / Streight do not love: for love is not so slight, / As streight to burne at first beholders sight.' While Spenser did not publish *Fowre Hymnes* until 1596, he 'composed these former two Hymnes in the praise of Love and Beautie' in 'the greener times of ... [his] youth' (*Dedicatory Epistle*), and critics now believe that a possible date of composition is 'somewhat earlier than 1592' (Ellrodt 18).[31] If this chronology is at all accurate, we may witness Marlowe here rejecting Spenser's refined Neoplatonism in favour of a more compulsive Ovidian *amor*.

An additional conjunction with Spenser's first two hymns has surfaced, revealing *Hero and Leander* to be indeed a Hymn to Earthly Love and Beauty, an anti-Spenserian manifesto. Marlowe tropes the relation between Love, Chaos, and Fate during the inset tale of Mercury:

> Cupid for his [Mercury's] sake,
> To be revenged on Jove did undertake,
> And those on whom heaven, earth, and hell relies,
> I mean the adamantine Destinies,
> He wounds with love, and forced them equally
> To dote upon deceitful Mercury.
> They offered him the deadly fatal knife
> That shears the slender threads of human life;
> At his fair feathered feet the engines laid,
> Which th' earth from ugly Chaos' den upweighed.
> These he regarded not.
>
> (*Hero and Leander* I.441–51)

According to A.R. Braunmuller, Marlowe introduces an 'alternate tradition' (58) that derives the genealogy of the Fates from 'Demogorgon and/or Chaos' (59): 'the Destinies' engines' have actively 'drawn the earth up from Chaos' den' (57). Braunmuller glosses Marlowe with Spenser, first with *Faerie Queene* IV.ii.47 in order to show the 'Fates' descent from Chaos' (59), and then with *Hymne of Love* 61–3 and 76–7 (60, n. 3) in order to make 'the Fates and Love roughly equivalent – the first bring order from Chaos, the other causes them to submit their powers to Mercury' (60).

Spenser's lines on the three cosmic forces in his first earthly hymn suggest that 'ere' the 'world' crept out of 'Chaos ugly prison,' 'Love' was awakened by 'Clotho' from 'Venus lap'; and that then he makes 'his way' to the 'world,' which he 'make[s]' by 'order[ing]' disparate 'parts' in the links of 'Adamantine chaines' (57–89). Both Spenser's and Marlowe's myths of origin bring the three cosmic forces into alignment; both see the Fates descending from Chaos; and both identify the Fates with Love. But whereas Spenser uses his myth to represent the origin of creation, Marlowe uses his to represent the origin of destruction. Spenser explains how love creates a providentially harmonious universe; Marlowe, how love fates the individual to annihilation. Both myths also consolidate an aetiology of artistic production, as Spenser's metadiscourse confirms (Cheney, *Spenser's Famous Flight* 214 and 288–9, n. 22), and as Marlowe reveals through his concluding references to the outcome of the cosmic battle on 'Learning' (465), 'every scholar poor' (471), and 'the Muses' sons' (476).[32]

Kingly Neptune

Given the different sexual orientation of Spenser and Marlowe, we may find resonance in Marlowe's gaze at Spenser during the homoerotic Neptune passage. When 'the sapphire-visaged god' mistakes the youth for 'Ganymede,' Leander 'strived, the waves ... / ... pulled him to the bottom, where the ground / Was strewed with pearl': 'and in low coral groves / Sweet singing mermaids sported with their loves / On heaps of heavy gold, and took great pleasure / To spurn in careless sort the shipwrack treasure' (II.155–64). This mermaid-site is where 'the stately azure palace stood / Where kingly Neptune and his train abode' (165–6). According to A.B. Taylor, Marlowe 'has his eyes upon a work in which love is treated rather differently, Book III of *The Faerie Queene*' (224). Having overthrown Marinell on the Rich Strond, Britomart abstains from the loot her competitor has protected: 'pearles and pretious stones of great assay, / And all the gravell mixt with golden owre' (iv.18). Immediately following, Marinell's mother, Cymoent, convinces Neptune to let Marinell preside over the Rich Strond: 'Eftsoones his heaped waves he did commaund, / Out of their hollow bosome forth to throw / All the huge threasure' (22). According to Taylor, Spenser's incident shows that 'chaste love is above thoughts of material wealth. As Leander swims towards Hero's tower and sexual fulfillment, Marlowe has paused to parody Spenser's rather heavily made point with his gesturing mermaids: the traditional figures for sensuality are just as deliberately scornful of material wealth. Sensual love, he seems to maintain, with his tongue firmly in his cheek, is just as highly principled and devoted to duty' (225).[33]

We can contextualize Marlowe's gaze at Spenser here, for one effect of the imitation is to identify Leander as a Marinell figure. For Spenser, Marinell is a figure for Ralegh (see J.B. Morris), so that Britomart's defeat of the knight and rejection of his 'huge threasure' (22) allegorizes the Queen's resistance to Ralegh's New World project, as Marlowe's phrase 'shipwrack treasure' indicates. In effect, Marlowe critiques Spenser's critique of Ralegh. The appearance of Marlowe's rivalry with Spenser over Ralegh in the homoerotic Neptune passage betrays a counter-'Elizabethan' sexuality that we witnessed surfacing in 'The Passionate Shepherd to His Love' (chapter 3).

Night's 'Loathsome Carriage'

Perhaps not surprisingly, the final scene of Marlowe's poem begins with a description of Hero's body that looks like the New World: 'Much like a globe (a globe may I term this, / By which love sails to regions full of bliss)' (II.275–6). Such a depiction leads to the conclusion of the poem, with its masculine colonization of Hero's body, and what David L. Miller terms the masculine 'erasure of her subjectivity' ('Death of the Modern' 776): 'Love is not full of pity (as men say) / But deaf and cruel where he means to prey' (287–8). The following avian simile captures the paradox of a sweet violence that Marlowe finds as the motivating animus of male mastery: 'Even as a bird, which in our hands we wring, / Forth plungeth, and oft flutters with her wing, / She trembling strove' (289–91). Miller speculates that the unnamed species here 'must be a nightingale – specifically, Philomel ... [r]avished in voice as well as body,' and he quotes Ralegh from 'The Nymph's Reply': 'Philomel becometh dumb' (775). Such 'strife,' Marlowe adds in a bold stroke of biblical parody, is 'like that / Which made the world,' for it 'another world begat / Of unknown joy' (291–3). But it is in the next metaphor that we discover Marlowe's New World mapping of the heroic joys of sexual violence: 'Leander now, like Theban Hercules, / Entered the orchard of th' Hesperides, / Whose fruit none rightly can describe but he / That pulls or shakes it from the golden tree' (297–300). The effect of the male's Herculean shaking of the female fruit is striking: it separates the couple immediately. For her part, Hero feels regret (303–9), and she recoils instinctively (310–11), 'Leaving Leander in the bed alone' (312).

Hero's instinct exposes her to shame, for 'as her naked feet were whipping out, / He on the sudden clinged her so about / That mermaid-like unto the floor she slid; / One half appeared, the other half was hid. / Thus near the bed she blushing stood upright' (313–17). Marlowe exposes more than Hero here; he exposes Spenser, who had hypocritically indulged in shameless eroticism when describing the two wrestling damsels in the pool at the Bower of Bliss, with its jasper-paved fountain that 'did sayle upright' (II.xii.62): 'Then th'one her selfe low ducked in the flood, / Abasht, that her a straunger did a vise: / But th'other rather higher did arise, / And her two lilly paps aloft displayd' (II.xii.66). And just as Spenser likens the damsels emerging from the water to 'that faire Starre, the messenger of morne' rearing '[h]is deawy face out of the sea' (65), so Marlowe likens Hero to the coming of day: 'A kind of twilight break, which through the hair, / As from an orient cloud, glimpse here and there. / And round about the chamber this false morn / Brought forth the day before the day was born' (319–22).

The female's attempt to extricate herself from the grasp of the male compromises her dignity and prepares for a corresponding masculine effect: 'So Hero's ruddy cheek Hero betrayed, / And her all naked to his sight displayed, / Whence his admiring eyes more pleasure took / Than Dis on heaps of gold fixing his look' (323–6). Female shame produces male voyeurism; the male reduces the female's living flesh to the cold fixity of hard cash. That last line contains another quotation from Spenser, which we have seen in our analysis of *The Jew of Malta*; it is Mammon, whom Spenser repeatedly associates with Dis or Pluto, god of the underworld (II.vii.3, 21, 24): 'Great heapes of gold' (*FQ* II.vii.5). Marlowe critiques Spenser's visionary poetics, with its optimism about the 'look' that men and woman cast on each other. For Marlowe, beauty and love lead to separation: the female is exposed in her shame – to the bliss of the male voyeur 'feed[ing] his eye' (*FQ* II.vii.4) with dead currency.

By ending in sexual separation, female shame, and male voyeurism, *Hero and Leander* makes a self-conscious journey down 'the Vergilian path,' which Clark Hulse locates only in Shakespeare – 'in the progress from *Venus and Adonis* to *Lucrece*': from 'a middle style akin to sonnet, pastoral, and comedy' to 'the regions of epic and tragedy' (175):

By this Apollo's golden harp began
To sound forth music to the Ocean,
Which watchful Hesperus no sooner heard,
But he the day's bright-bearing car prepared,
And ran before, as harbinger of light,
And with his flaring beams mocked ugly Night,
Till she, o'ercome with anguish, shame and rage,
Danged down to hell her loathsome carriage.

(*Hero and Leander* II.327–34)

Marlowe depicts the *meta* from night to day as a cosmic competition between the masculine Apollo and the feminine Night. Apollo appears as both a musician and a charioteer, and his appearance at the end of the poem recalls the opening, where 'Apollo courted [Hero] for her hair' (I.6). Henry Petowe noticed Marlowe's privileging of Apollo, for he opens his continuation of *Hero and Leander* with the sun-god, repeatedly refers to him, gives the Delphic oracle a role in the action, writes an allegory of Apollo and Mercury, identifies Marlowe with Apollo, and even discovers a fine opportunity for a rhyme in their names: 'Quick-sighted spirits, this supposed Apollo, / Conceit no other but th'admired Marlowe' (57–8 in Orgel ed.). Petowe clearly sees Marlowe's Apollo as a Marlovian super-hero: 'And with his flaring beams mocked ugly Night.' Apollo's mockery of Dame Night extends from earth to heaven the betrayal that Hero experiences, to the extent that, as Miller puts it, we read 'Hero as Night' (781): 'she, o'ercome with anguish, shame, and rage, / Danged down to hell her loathsome carriage.'

Marlowe may allude here to Duessa's descent to the underworld in the carriage of Dame Night in Book I of *The Faerie Queene* (v.19–45) – when these two demonic women use a car to rescue the fallen knight Sansjoy: 'Descends to hell' (31). Like Marlowe, Spenser emphasizes the competition between Apollo and Night, with the dark female subjected to the bright male: 'Where griesly Night, with visage deadly sad, / That Phoebus chearefull face durst never vew' (20; see 24–5, 44). And both dark women drive carriages – Spenser's terms are 'charet' (20) and 'wagon' (28; see 30, 32, 44).[34]

Marlowe's appropriation of Spenser's 'charet' for the final word of his poem sustains professional significance. In the poem's final image, with 'ugly Night' overcome with anguish, shame, and rage, and danging down to hell her 'loathsome carriage' – the victim of the mighty god who drives 'the day's bright-bearing car' – we discover a literal *cursus* from comedy to tragedy within the minor epic.

Marlowe, Chapman, and Spenser

It is precisely the need to turn from comedy to tragedy within epic that Chapman emphasizes; his turn responds cohesively to the conclusion of Marlowe's poem. This is not to say that Marlowe planned to continue his own epyllion. What might interest us, however, are two features of Chapman's continuation: his decision to dress Marlowe's 818–line poem as a minor epic in the Homeric and Virgilian vein; and his use of Spenser to do so.

Just as critics identify Chapman's attempt to convert *Hero and Leander* into an epic, so they identify his imitations of Spenser during his continuation.[35] We may extend this line of criticism by contextualizing the 1598 text(s) in terms of Chapman's dispute with Marlowe over the merits of Spenser and the late-Elizabethan penning of national subjects 'grave and high.'

We do not know why Chapman chose to finish Marlowe's poem. Twentieth-century examination disputes the notion that Marlowe asked Chapman to finish his poem on his deathbed, for we now believe that Marlowe died 'suddenly' in that little room in Deptford (Bakeless 2: 113). Chapman himself supplies only two brief, tantalizing phrases on why he acted on Marlowe's behalf. The first (often neglected) appears in his *Dedicatory Epistle* to Lady Walsingham: 'being *drawn by strange instigation* to employ some of my serious time in so trifling a subject' (Orgel 41; emphasis added). All three key words here are evocative. The word 'drawn' means 'moved by traction; dragged' (*OED*, Def. 1). The word 'strange' is more complicated, with the *OED* citing sixteen definitions, the most applicable being 'Unfamiliar, abnormal, or exceptional to a degree that excites wonder or astonishment' (Def. 10); overwhelmingly, however, the word connotes something foreign or alien, as the first seven definitions reveal: 'Of a place or locality: Other than one's own' (Def. 2). The third word, 'instigation,' is the most important, as well as the least complicated, with only one definition offered: 'The action of instigating or goading; an urging, spurring, or setting on; incitement, stimulation' (*OED*). All of the examples of *instigation* listed before 1598 identify or emphasize a person as an instigator of the action, and one looks pertinent here, since it forms part of the discourse of prefatory material: 'Here begynneth the hystory of the noble Helyas knyght of the swanne newly translated out of frensshe into englysshe at thynstygacyon of the puyssaunt & illustryouse prynce lorde Edwarde duke of Buckyngham' (Wynkyn de Worde, *Helyas* 1512). The words 'drawn' and 'strange,' then, both pertain to the idea of an independent, personal inspiration, but all three words also pertain to an agent who does the drawing and strange instigating. The sense of the phrase may thus be that Chapman is identifying *another person* as the agent of his own motivation; whether this person was Lady Walsingham, her husband (Sir Thomas), Marlowe himself, or someone else, we cannot determine.

The second phrase (well known) appears near the midpoint of the Third Sestiad: 'how much his late desires I tender' (195). As Keach observes, 'it is difficult to say exactly what Chapman means' (*Elizabethan Erotic Narratives* 116). Yet John Bakeless's speculation is still reasonable: 'It remains possible that Marlowe, knowing the extreme personal danger in which he stood in the last few months of his life, may have suggested something of the sort to Chapman, with whom he was probably acquainted ... [I]t is quite possible that ... Marlowe actually did ask him, as a friend, to finish the poem in the event of his own sudden death' (2: 113–14). Chapman's key word, 'tender,' has two primary senses: 'respect' (L.C. Martin 79, citing *OED*, whose Def. 3 for its 5th entry reads: 'To feel or act tenderly toward; to regard or treat with tenderness'); or '*Law.* A formal offer duly made by one party to another' (2d entry, Def. 1). Whether Chapman is merely respecting 'desires' he assumes Marlowe had or acting on an actual request, 'who can tell'?

In this second phrase, however, we can again detect ambiguity, with the two alternatives for each phrase clearly traceable: Chapman is either acting out 'desires' Marlowe tendered to him or acting on his own, drawn perhaps by his sense of what his colleague had in mind. In either case, we have to grant Chapman his 'judgement': he is doing what he believes his colleague desired.

Within the rubric of these desires, Chapman responds vigorously to his dead colleague's work. What he responds to is Marlowe's 'naturalism,' his 'atheism,' his 'joy graven in sense' (III.35) – and (we may add) Marlowe's critique of Spenser.

Chapman's deity presiding over the marriage of Hero and Leander, Ceremony, has been found to have Spenserian origins, with much of the poem after 'the exquisite Epithalamion Teratos' to be 'Edmund Spenser reborn' (Spivack 43). According to Waddington, 'If Chapman can be twinned with any of his contemporaries, a far better case could be made for Edmund Spenser than for John Donne' (*Mind's Empire* 2–3): 'Chapman's true poetic peers are Spenser and Milton, both vatic, public, ceremonious poets as conscious of form and genre as Chapman' (13). Specifically, Waddington finds the origin of such features of the poem as Chapman's number symbolism to lie in *Epithalamion* (196).[36]

What Chapman restores to the Hero and Leander myth is a Spenserian vision of love and marriage within the epic context of English nationhood – what he calls 'virtuous love' (IV.202). The Fifth Sestiad reads like a meta-allegory of sanctified Spenserian desire: the episode in which Hero oversees the marriage of Almane and Mya; 'The Tale of Teras' about Hymen's love for and eventual marriage to Eucharis ('So Hymen looked, that even the chastest mind / He moved to join in joys of sacred kind' [113–14]), in which the god of marriage heroically rescues his beloved from thieves and then exquisitely presides over his wife's loss of virginity ('And yet eternized Hymen's tender bride / To suffer it dissolved so sweetly cried' [395–6]); and finally Teras' formal singing of '*Epithalamion Teratos*' itself: these features all celebrate Spenser's great national achievement in the erotic domain.

We may discover Chapman's pro-Spenser project epitomized in his own Spenserian manifesto, *The Tears of Peace*, the title of which echoes a Spenserian text we have had occasion to mention (*The Teares of the Muses*), when 'Spenser's successor' observes that 'th' effect / Proper to perfect Learning' is 'to direct Reason in such an art as that it can / Turn blood to soul, and make both one calm man; / So making peace with God' (Chapman, ed. Shepherd 2: 118).

Turn blood to soul. In *Hero and Leander*, Marlowe uses his counter-Spenserian learning and art to direct the English nation to *turn soul to blood.* He makes no man calm (nor woman neither), and so makes war with God.

Afterword:
Counterfeiting the Profession

In 1678, Milton's nephew, Edward Phillips, introduces the critical lens that the present study, in its broadest scope, seeks to reconstruct:

Christopher Marlow, a kind of second Shakesphear (whose contemporary he was) not only because like him he rose from an actor to be a maker of plays, though inferior both in fame, and merit; but also because in his begun poem of "Hero and Leander," he seems to have a resemblance of that clean, and unsophisticated Wit. (Phillips, *Theatrum Poetarum Anglicanorum*, rpt. in MacLure, ed., *Marlowe* 51)

Less than a century after Marlowe's death, commentators are viewing his canon through a Shakespearean lens. Marlowe is 'a kind of second Shakesphear' because he shadows the Bard in penning the two kinds of works that in fact Shakespeare pens: 'plays' and 'poem[s].' The two kinds are not created equal, for Marlowe, 'like' Shakespeare, was primarily 'an actor' and a 'maker of plays' ('because ... he rose'); secondarily ('but also because'), he was a poet, having 'begun' a poem, '"Hero and Leander,"' that 'resembl[es]' (we may infer) Shakespeare's Ovidian narrative poems, *Venus and Adonis* and *The Rape of Lucrece*. According to the Shakespearean lens, then, Marlowe was principally a playwright who *happened* to turn to poetry when Shakespeare primarily did, during 1592–3, when the theatres closed because of plague. Like Shakespeare as well, Marlowe understood himself to be – or Phillips understood Marlowe to be – a *dramatist* on the new Elizabethan stage.

The Shakespearean lens is supported almost immediately by William Winstanley in 1687: 'Christopher Marlow was ... not only contemporary with William Shakespear, but also, like him, rose from a Actor, to be a maker of Comedies and Tragedies, yet was he much inferior to Shakespear, not only in the number of his Plays, but also in the elegancy of his Style. His pen was chiefly employed in Tragedies ... He also began a Poem of "Hero and Leander"' (rpt. in MacLure, ed., *Marlowe* 52). In 1691, George Langbaine repeats the information but emphasizes Marlowe's role as an actor – 'One who trod the Stage with Applause both from Queen Elisabeth, and King James' (rpt. in MacLure 53). Towards the end of the eighteenth century, Thomas Warton is still repeating the information (rpt. in MacLure 57), although he is the first to complicate it. In the nineteenth century, from Lamb at the beginning to Dyce in the middle to Shaw at the end, critics are still viewing Marlowe as 'a kind of second Shakesphear,' although that century is also notable for its complication of the Phillips portrait.[1] Yet even the Marlowe commemoration at Canterbury in 1891 shows signs of succumbing to the trend: 'Marlowe ... was the first, the only, herald of SHAKESPEARE. He was the father of the great family of English dramatic poets, and a lyrical poet of the first order among Elizabethans' (rpt. in MacLure 185).

Rather than reconstructing the primary lens for viewing Marlowe, twentieth-century commentators intensify the Shakespearean lens in yet more complicated ways.[2] In 1986, for instance, Simon Shepherd advocated a 'study of the critical construction of Marlowe-who-isn't-Shakespeare' (xiv). Then, in 1991 Thomas Cartelli 'pursue[d] such a study' but 'without assembling another trap in which the Marlowe-who-isn't-Shakespeare plays the subversive antagonist in a dramatic competition devoted to the decanonization of the Shakespeare-who-isn't-Marlowe' (1). While Cartelli and others work to extricate Marlowe from the shadow of Shakespeare, we have not succeeded in extricating Marlowe from a discourse that is foundationally Shakespearean. More accurately, we have not situated Marlowe's relation with Shakespeare along the continuum of his 'intellectual biography.' This has been the most general goal of the present project.[3]

The Shakespearean lens is suspect from its inception. Not merely do we lack evidence of Marlowe's career as an 'Actor,' but we possess other evidence, more tangible and compelling, for which the Shakespearean paradigm – First a Dramatist, Second a Poet – cannot account.[4] Marlowe's career includes two *other* kinds of works that Shakespeare does not bequeath to us: a scholarly edition of a colleague's Latin poetry, prefaced with a Latin *Dedicatory Epistle* to a well-known female patron; and translations of classical Latin poems. One of these translations, *Lucan's First Book*, inscribes another genre Shakespeare does not pen: epic. Although joining Marlowe in writing in the minor epic, Shakespeare alone reserved 'epic' only for the stage – principally in the Henriad (see *Riverside Shakespeare* 934). To these differences, we can add one more: Marlowe penned an epigram in Latin on the death of a contemporary jurist (Sir Roger Manwood). All these works betray the Shakespearean paradigm, suggesting the need for a new one, which we might call a paradigm of *artistic scholarship*. Not surprisingly, Jonson criticizes Shakespeare precisely along this line: he had 'small Latine, and lesse Greeke' ('To the memory of my beloved, The Author,' rpt. in *The Riverside Shakespeare* 65).

Jonson's memorial poem is a testament of professional insight; among other things, he sees the need to distinguish Shakespeare from his great national predecessors: 'The applause! delight! the wonder of our Stage! / My Shakespeare, rise; I will not lodge thee by / Chaucer, or Spenser.' Jonson cannot 'lodge' Shakespeare 'by' either the Old or the New Poet precisely because he, not they, is 'the wonder of our Stage.' In this context, we can profitably view Jonson's famous remark about Marlowe: 'how farre thou didst our Lily out-shine, / Or sporting Kid, or Marlowes mighty line.' Jonson's Shakespeare is the one we still see today: Shakespeare is a dramatist, as Jonson's roll call of famous classical and contemporary comedians and tragedians confirms (the classical list includes Aristophanes, Aeschylus, Sophocles, Euripides, and Seneca). By referring to Marlowe's 'mighty line,' Jonson only appears to be inaugurating the tradition tracing to Phillips. In fact, he is contextualizing Marlovian drama (as well as the drama of Lyly and Kyd) in terms of a judgment that turns out to be prophetic: Shakespeare's legacy is to be fundamentally dramatic. In other words, Jonson is not reducing Marlowe to his theatrical achievement; he is accommodating that part of Marlowe's canon that coheres with his judgment of Shakespeare as the wonder of England's stage. Here in Marlowe's theatrical presence we may discover an absence that is historically accurate.

The first to understand the absent Marlowe was curiously enough one of Marlowe's most famous detractors. In 1597, within four years of Marlowe's death, Thomas Beard foregrounds the paradigm of artistic scholarship, but quickly complements it with the elements of drama and poetry from the Shakespearean paradigm – gleefully exempt of Shakespeare himself: '... one of our own nation, of fresh and late memory, called Marlin, by profession a scholler, brought up from his youth in the Universitie of Cambridge, but by practise a playmaker, and a Poet of scurrilitie'[5] (rpt. in MacLure, ed., *Marlowe* 41).

By profession a scholar. The phrase is intriguing because it suggests that Marlowe *was* a scholar and that he openly *professed* himself to be such. The inference is confirmed by Robert Sidney's description to Lord Burleigh: 'Christofer Marly, by his profession a scholar ... The scholar says himself to be very well known both to the Earl of Northumberland and my Lord Strange' (rpt. in Nicholl 235). *The scholar says.* Beard, not Phillips, has gotten it right: Marlowe *was* a scholar, a playwright, and a poet – not a playwright and then a poet. Marlowe *was* 'by profession a scholler,' trained at Cambridge, and 'by practice a playmaker, and a Poet.' Marlowe was also 'one of our own nation' – an English writer – and so absorbed in and concerned with the problem of being a writer in the England of Queen Elizabeth.

Beard is also right to observe that Marlowe's death could not kill him – or kill his writings – for at the end of the 1590s Marlowe's 'memory' is still 'fresh.' Beyond the grave, Marlowe's profession as a scholar and his practice as a playmaker and a poet have made him famous. This happens to be the source of Beard's conjuration of Marlowe's perturbed spirit, which he hopes once and for all to lay to unsettled rest (Beard's wording is 'smothered and kept under'), as his phrase 'of scurrilitie' hints and as both his earlier indictment of Marlowe's 'Atheisme & impiety' and his later criticism of 'all Atheists in this realme' confirm (rpt. in MacLure 41–2).

Marlowe's translations of Ovid and Lucan, his seven plays, and his Ovidian verse testify to the validity of Beard's threefold paradigm. But it will take nearly two centuries before Warton will mention *Ovid's Elegies* and *Lucan's First Book* (MacLure 57, 58) – evidently the first in the record to do so. Between Warton and the post–Second World War era, few critics pause to account for Marlowe's commitment to scholarship as an underlying – self-professed – cultural formation for English nationhood.[6]

This book has sought remediation against the dominant critical tradition that still views Marlowe through a 'Shakespearean' or 'dramatic' lens. The Marlowe presented here is a translator, a playwright, and a poet – not principally one, but all three.[7]

Historically speaking, Marlowe's paradigm is not Shakespearean but 'Spenserian.' For Spenser was also a translator, a poet, and a writer of *Nine Comedies*, as well as a contributor to the Elizabethan discourse on the English theatre: on tragedy (*October* 98–114) and on tragedy and comedy (*Teares of the Muses* 115–234). Indeed, Marlowe may have initially found a model for his 'scholarly' activities in Spenser, a recent fellow alumnus from Cambridge University.

This hypothesis receives support from Marlowe's debt to Spenser throughout his career – a debt the present study has only begun to trace. We have seen that Spenser was Marlowe's first great rival and that Shakespeare was his second. This evolution more accurately historicizes Marlowe within his immediate literary environment than does the current industry of Marlowe studies, which Shepherd, Cartelli, and others acknowledge to be founded on the Shakespearean paradigm. Thus we might study more carefully those moments in the Marlowe canon where we witness the simultaneity of Spenser and Shakespeare: in *Edward II*, for instance, especially in the figure of Mortimer (chapter 7), but also in *The Massacre at Paris*, such as in the opening marriage solemnity (chapter 8). The advantage to this approach would be that we formally avoid the 'trap,' more satisfactorily than done here, of constructing a 'Marlowe-who-isn't Spenser.' We would try to track Marlowe along his *cursus* in terms of his penchant for rivalry as it changes through his career.

The present study has argued only that Marlowe responds to Spenser's Virgilian career and its Renaissance version, the progression from pastoral to epic, with an Ovidian career modelled on the paradoxically oscillating pattern of three fixed genres: amatory poetry, tragedy, and epic. What is most vital in the competition between Marlowe and Spenser, we have seen, is the writing of English nationhood. Marlowe responds to Spenser's nationhood of royal power with a counter-nationhood founded on individual power, or *libertas*, especially as it expresses the freedom of scholarship itself – the fruit of the university as a cultural institution. Marlowe's Ovidian career of counter-nationhood inhabits Spenser's deep structures in order to deconstruct his Virgilian career of English nationhood. This is *my* counterfeit profession.[8]

Initially, the present study suggests that we adjust the way we think about Marlowe's literary career. For Marlowe qualifies as a 'prophetic' poet in the tradition of the national poet.[9] Like the laureates he counters, Marlowe is a poet who advertises a career pattern and then attempts to fulfil it. Marlowe's translation of the *Amores*, which takes many creative liberties, functions as a document for his career prophecy, and his movement into tragedy and epic functions as the beginning of his career fulfilment. Thus the Ovidian *cursus* constructs a critical lens that Marlowe himself appears to have sanctioned for viewing his project – a lens that permits us to see such diverse works as *Ovid's Elegies*, *Tamburlaine*, *Lucan*, and *Hero and Leander* as part of a disorienting but still intelligible career idea. As a result, the *cursus* suggests an alternative for structuring future biographies and studies of Marlowe, which hitherto have uniformly followed the popular model (based on Shakespeare) discussed in the introduction.

Additionally, the study suggests that we adjust the way we think and write about professional rivalry during the Elizabethan period. For Marlowe tends to transact his intrasystemic rivalry with Spenser through the agency of an intersystemic rivalry with classical or Continental authors.[10] Marlowe's rivalry with Spenser is not strictly intersystemic, but intrasystemic, the product of synchronic, not just diachronic, workings. Thus we can locate at the centre of at least some Elizabethan rivalry a typological relation between the two literary systems (inter-/intra-) and their temporal dimensions (diachronic/synchronic). We may need to come to terms with this intriguing veil of secrecy.

Finally, the study suggests that we adjust the way we understand nationhood, especially as we formulate the relation between the poets and scholars who were producing books in the older but still evolving Elizabethan print culture, and the playwrights writing for the new Elizabethan theatre. For the most part, English Renaissance critics today divide into drama critics and poetry critics, with the division affording little interchange between the two. Steven Mullaney, for instance, has made famous a liminal 'place of the stage' for the Elizabethan theatre, with playwrights such as Marlowe and Shakespeare functioning on society's margins. For Mullaney and others, the playwrights form a breed apart, radically subversive of hierarchical power structures. Sixteenth-century authorial practice, however, belies twentieth-century critical practice, for playwrights like Marlowe wrote both plays and poetry (and both original verse and verse translation), while poets like Spenser contributed to the discourse on the English theatre.[11] Marlowe's inscription of an Ovidian *cursus* of free counter-nationhood contesting Spenser's Virgilian *cursus* of English nationhood reveals that Marlowe participated in a larger literary system still controlled by hierarchical power structures. Marlowe's genius lay not simply in subverting hierarchy, but in moving shrewdly through it. He professed a counterfeit form of nationhood, but still he professed a form of nationhood. Marlowe's form countered the patriotism that ordered other English forms by writing the poet as the true nation. The present study, then, may also help revise the way we think and write about nationhood as it was transacted through the competition between drama and poetry/translation, stage and printshop, within Elizabethan culture.

Notes

Introduction: Marlowe's Ovidian Career, Spenser, and the Writing of
Counter-Nationhood

1 The last comprehensive reading was Leech's *Christopher Marlowe: Poet for the Stage*, which was published posthumously in 1986 – nine years after my great teacher's death. In a preface, Anne Lancashire says that Professor Leech had asked her as early as 1973 'to see to his Marlowe if his health should prevent him from completing the work himself,' and she indicates that he had accounted for Marlowe criticism only through 1969 (vii) – nearly thirty years ago.

2 On the 'new Poete,' see E.K., *Dedicatory Epistle* to *SC* 19. For the commonplace that Marlowe criticizes past drama, see Leech, *Christopher Marlowe* 42; and Helgerson, *Forms of Nationhood* 199–200, 225. For Marlowe's imitation of the *October* passage, see Bakeless 1: 208. On the role of the *October* prediction in Spenser's literary career, see Cheney, *Spenser's Famous Flight* 27–38.

3 In 'Counter-classical Sensibility,' W.R. Johnson distinguishes between Spenser and Ovid: 'where classical poetry attempts affirmations of man's capacities ..., counter-classical poetry attempts to stress man's ... limitations' (126). For Johnson, Ovid is the great hero of counter-classicism (137–48) and the *Metamorphoses* the most powerful counter-classical text: 'the *Metamorphoses* is an attack on Augustus' efforts to reform society ... [S]o far from being merely another indication of Ovidian shallowness, [the *Metamorphoses*] constitutes a bold and powerful defense of human ... individuality in the face of ferocious and arbitrary attempts to control human nature' (147). On Ovid's response to Virgil here, see Johnson 138–9, 144–5. Johnson has 'chosen "counter-classical" ... because the term ... is essentially positive: its renunciations exist only for the sake of new affirmations' (124, n. 3). Healy calls Ovid a 'powerful model' for

Marlowe because 'He found in the Roman author a host of examples of how to *counter* a literary establishment' (35; emphasis added). Our primary taxonomy of nationhood remains Helgerson's *Forms of Nationhood*, which identifies Spenser's and Marlowe's forms of nationhood as equally subversive (more of which later).

4 Letter to the Lord Keeper, Sir John Puckering (1593), rpt. in MacLure, ed., *Marlowe* 33. Kyd's claim was produced under pressure; as Nicholl acknowledges, however, 'For all this, Kyd's words are troubling,' and he cites the cruelty in Marlowe's plays (169–70). See H. Levin on Marlowe's 'incendiary genius' (5); and Greenblatt on Marlowe's 'potent self-destructiveness' ('Marlowe, Marx' 54).

5 I owe this phrase to David Riggs, who is writing his own 'biography' of Marlowe (personal communication, March 1994). Lipking traces the intellectual biography to Johnson's *Lives of the Poets* (1779–81), and he identifies his own approach, which intersects 'life and poetry' (x), as the first of an alternative kind (193). Marlowe's 'greatness' has been a topic of commentary for two centuries, but traditionally most critics have responded in the affirmative; see (as cited in MacLure's Critical Heritage volume): Bradley 131; Symonds 132–4; Lowell 161–2; Saintsbury 164; and Swinburne 178–80, 184. To these, we may add Eliot, who wrote of Marlowe's 'indubitably great poetry' (65–6). For disagreement, see Sanders. On the nineteenth-century invention of the Marlowe we read today, see Dabbs.

6 Versions of the popular model of Marlowe's literary career appear in Ellis-Fermor 22–3, 131–2; Boas, *Christopher Marlowe* 49; Bakeless 2: 99–101; Kocher, *Christopher Marlowe* 18, 300–21, esp. 316 and 320; Poirier viii–ix, 78–80; H. Levin 160–1; Steane 339, 357; Rowse 35, 37–49, 186; Wraight and Stern 86–7, 243; and Knoll 26–40. Leech, *Christopher Marlowe*, maps the popular model in detail (23–5) and thereby crowns a tradition that stretches across the twentieth century. For the virtual institutionalization of this model, see Gill, ed., *Complete Works* 1: xi–xv. Books on the plays include those by Cole; Sanders; Masinton; Cutts; Godshalk; Summers; Pinciss; Weil; Kuriyama; and Brandt. Books on a single play include those by Battenhouse (*Tamburlaine*); Howe (*Tamburlaine*); M.E. Smith (*Dido*); Empson (*Faustus*); and McAlindon (*Faustus*). And books on two plays include that by Birringer (*Tamburlaine, Faustus*). The most recent books, by Shepherd, Barber, Sales, Cartelli, Bartels, and Healy, show little interest in a model of Marlowe's literary career, with only Bartels relying on a chronological chapter structure, and with all five focusing on the plays. I return to Levin's model later, since it is the only one that anticipates my argument. I am grateful, however, to the studies by Boas, Steane, and Leech for discussing *Ovid's Elegies* and *Lucan* in

praiseworthy detail. [After completing this study, I reviewed three publications for *Renaissance Quarterly* and so have not incorporated them systematically here: Cole's *Christopher Marlowe*; Proser's *Gift of Fire*; and Gill's Oxford edition of *The Jew of Malta*.]

7 For a review of such problems, see Leech, *Christopher Marlowe* 13–25. On individual works, see the Revels Plays editions. On the Sidney *Dedication*, see Eccles 162–71 and Urry 81. For pointing out to me the scantness of Marlowe's use of the first person, I am again indebted to David Riggs.

8 Dowden first understood that Marlowe had a career worth shaping (rpt. in MacLure, ed., *Marlowe* 100), but see Collier (rpt. in MacLure 82). Traditionally, critics have said what Bloom articulates: 'Nor can anyone prophesy usefully how Marlowe might have developed if he had lived another quarter century' (ed. 1). None the less, see Danson: 'Marlowe did know what he was doing,' and 'the problems we encounter are often part of his artistic method' (3). For this view as the recent trend, see Duane 51.

9 No one has written even an article on Marlowe's 'literary career.' By contrast, Spenser studies has produced three books on the topic – by Bernard; Rambuss; and Cheney – as well as several seminal essays (Helgerson, 'Spenser's Idea of a Literary Career'; D.L. Miller, 'Spenser's Career'; DeNeef; Loewenstein; and Alpers, 'Spenser's Late Pastorals').

10 On Marlowe's imitation of *FQ* I.Pr.1 here, see Crawford 204. On the 'theatricality' of Spenser's 'maske,' see Crewe, *Hidden Designs* 93.

11 Ovid himself may be deauthorizing Virgil, for the conjunction *dum* (while) subtly restricts, and even playfully *ends*, the temporal *telos* of Rome's triumph (see Braudy 136 on Ovid's view of Rome in the *Metamorphoses*). McKeown observes that Ovid here 'is echoing Verg. *Aen* 9.446ff.' (1: 45), where Virgil uses *dum* (IX.448). On *Amores* I.xv, see Vessey; on the Virgilian distich, see Barsby, ed. 161.

12 Jonson joins Marlowe in minimizing Virgilian fame and in neutering the principals; this may be in keeping with his critique of Spenser. Jonson includes his translation in *The Poetaster* (I.i.43–84). On Jonson's detached attitude towards Virgil, see Helgerson, *Self-Crowned Laureates* 113–16; towards Ovid, see 111–12; towards Spenser, see 110–22. Marlowe may have 'ousted' georgic in keeping with Renaissance practice (Fowler, *Kinds of Literature* 31) – as Spenser did – but his scrambling of the sacred Virgilian order looks suspicious, and appropriately Jonson restores it (MacLure, ed., *Poems* 140).

13 The oppositions between Ovid and Virgil, and between Lucan and Virgil, are commonplaces. See esp. Hardie, *Epic Successors of Virgil*. On Ovid as an anti-Virgilian poet, see Hardie, 'Anti-*Aeneid*.'" On Lucan as an anti-Virgilian poet, see Quint 4–9, 131–57. Critics emphasize Seneca's praise of Virgil (C. Segal,

Seneca's 'Phaedra' 3, 7, 47, 77, 105); but for Seneca's response to Virgil's anti-imperialism, see Hardie, *Epic Successors of Virgil* 72.

14 Aristotle, *Poetics* 26.1461b.27, 1462a.14–18, 1462b.1–15 (see Herrick 3). All of Marlowe's plays, *Lucan*, and *Hero and Leander* are in the 'tragic' mode. In writing that 'Marlowe was by temperament a tragedian,' H. Levin (159) crowns a long tradition tracing to Meres ([1598] rpt. in MacLure, ed., *Marlowe* 46) and the *Parnassus* plays ([1601] rpt. in MacLure 46). Critics, however, deny that certain of Marlowe's plays are 'tragedies' (e.g., Eliot on *The Jew* [63]); they find *Hero and Leander* to be a 'comedy' (Leech, *Christopher Marlowe* 24); and they write widely on 'Marlowe's humour' (Kocher, *Christopher Marlowe* 267–99). On Marlowe's 'generically unstable plays,' see Birringer, *Marlowe's 'Dr Faustus' and 'Tamburlaine'* 11. On Jonson and Marlowe, see Eliot 71, 73–76, 79–81; Kernan vii, xii–xiii; Riddell; Shapiro, '"Lucan"' and *Rival Playwrights*; and Levine 89–107.

15 Critics understand Marlowe's relation with each of these classical writers to be special. On Marlowe as 'an Ovidian poet,' see Bloom, ed. 1; see also Keach, *Elizabethan Erotic Narratives* 85–116; Braden, *Classics* 55–153; Hulse 93–140; Pearcy 1–36; and J. Bate 38. On Marlowe's primary role in bringing Seneca to the stage, see R.A. Martin, 'Fate, Seneca,' and Braden, *Renaissance Tragedy* 182–97. On Marlowe as England's first translator of Lucan, see Steane 249–79; Gill, 'Sulpitius'; and Shapiro, '"Lucan."' Finally, on Marlowe as 'the Lucretius of the English language,' see Ellis-Fermor xi; see also H. Levin 3, 16, 38, 117, 164–5; and Hadzsits 279 (including n. 33).

16 See Kenney: 'The phrase *area maior* suggests the major genres of tragedy and epic' ('Ovid' 2: 421). Marlowe translates the phrase as the 'greater ground' (*Ovid's Elegies* III.xiv[xv].18).

17 Long ago, H. Levin introduced three phases of Marlowe's literary career that approximate this pattern. Levin fuses a psychoanalytic-based *appetitive* model, structured on 'the triad of basic urges,' and a triadic *generic* model of literary 'modes,' derived from Roman authors: 'the lyric plea for *libido sentiendi*, the epic vaunt for *libido dominandi*, and the tragic lament for *libido sciendi* ... If Marlowe learned the lyric mode from Ovid and the epic mode from Lucan, it may well have been Lucretius who schooled him in tragic discernment of the nature of things' (160–1, 165). None the less, Levin neglects to mention that Marlowe could have found this career model in Ovid, that the model functions as an alternative to the Virgilian model, and that in 'taking' the 'course' (32) from the lower to higher genres Marlowe is contesting the Virgilian course taken by a famous rival. While supporting Levin's linkages between Ovid and early lyric and between Lucan and epic, I alter his model by placing *Lucan's First Book* late in Marlowe's career (more of which presently). Then I overcome

his identification of Lucretius, a writer of 'epic,' as the generic father of Marlowe's plays, by substituting Seneca. Finally, I place the entire *cursus* under an 'Ovidian' rubric and reidentify Lucretius as its animating genius.

18 This line invokes the metaphor of the *cursus*; see Braudy: 'Although the Latin *cursus* remains most obviously in the English *course*, it shares a more intriguing metaphorical relation with *career*: Both are words that first applied to horse races and later to the stages of professional development' (61, n. 4). On *Dido* and the two *Tamburlaine* plays as 'generally accepted as the first and second of Marlowe's plays,' see Bartels 182, n. 61. On the three 'plays of policy' as coming after the first triad, I am following a well-established tradition that stretches from 1927 to 1991, dates that belong to the major publications of Ellis-Fermor (88–122) and Cartelli (121–3), respectively. On *Doctor Faustus* as forming its own group, see, e.g., Bevington and Rasmussen, eds., *Doctor Faustus* 1; Snow offers the most powerful justification for this structure: 'whatever the actual chronology of Marlowe's plays, no work of art ... communicates more powerfully the *sense* of a "last work" than does *Doctor Faustus*' (78).

19 See Bawcutt, who shows how sixteenth-century writers contextualize Machiavelli in terms of both Seneca and Lucan (23). I would add that Machiavelli both constructs and enters a professional pattern approximating the Virgilian pattern from pastoral to epic. As he says to Lorenzo de' Medici in his *Dedicatory Epistle*, 'I hope it will not be thought presumptuous if a man of low social rank undertakes to discuss the rule of princes' (Adams 3), and in *The Prince* itself he discusses the pattern of a 'private citizen' becoming a 'prince' (15; see 27).

20 We do not know what Marlowe planned to do with *Lucan*, but see chapter 10 for my speculations. In chapter 11, I follow Hulse in seeing *Hero and Leander* as a 'minor epic' (93–140) and in understanding this genre as 'the proving ground for ... epic' (11).

21 We confront deep problems if we base our understanding of Marlowe's literary career on the dating of his works. Thus the topic of 'Marlowe's canon' is fraught with controversy. Cf. Brooke, 'Canon'; R. Taylor; Muir; Godshalk 18–28; Leech, *Christopher Marlowe* 13–25; and Healy 21–30, esp. 29.

22 Marcus, 'Textual Indeterminacy,' replaces 'the absent authorial presence we call Marlowe' with simply a '"Marlowe effect"' (3, 5). By contrast, I apply to Marlowe the principle that Helgerson articulates for Shakespeare: 'He helped make the world that made him' (*Forms of Nationhood* 215). See also Keefer, ed. xvi–xxii, for a vigorous defence of such a principle: the 'historical traces he left are sufficiently distinct and strange to make his authorship ... of *Doctor Faustus* an important fact' (xxii).

23 The tradition begins with Robert Greene, who inaugurated Marlowe criticism

by identifying the author of *Tamburlaine* with its lead character: a 'Gentle-m[a]n Poet ... daring God out of heaven with that Atheist Tamburlan' (rpt. in MacLure, ed., *Marlowe* 29). In 1870, Dowden remarks that Marlowe 'seems to have lived in and for his art. His poetry was no episode in his life, but his very life itself' (rpt. in MacLure 102). See also Symmonds (rpt. in MacLure 134). For recent versions, see Greenblatt, 'Marlowe, Marx' 51–3; Bloom, ed. 2; and Cartelli 131–3.

24 My point focuses Hardison: 'To say that it [the "mighty line" of *Tamburlaine*] is "Marlovian" is to say that the poet's voice frequently overrides the voices of the characters' (269). On Marlowe's self-quotation, see Bakeless 2: 153. On Marlovian metadrama, see Crewe, 'Theatre,' esp. 322–3, 331–3. Maus suggests that, 'in Marlowe's plays, persuasion or a simulacrum of persuasion converts to violence': 'Marlowe's plays reflect some of the dilemmas that arise from Renaissance conceptions of personal inwardness, and from the questionable inquisitorial methods developed for ... modifying that inward domain from the outside' (72, 74). Marlowe's inward theatrical violence is often self-inflicted, for repeatedly the playwright stages a rivalry between two characters often identified as authorial figures (e.g., Barabas kills Ithamore; Lightborn, Edward II). Thus Marlovian sadism often takes the form of masochism; Marlovian authorship keeps strange inward bedfellows. On subjectivity, see Barker; and Belsey, *Subject of Tragedy*. While both Barker (31, 36–7, 58) and Belsey (33–54) argue that 'the unified subject of liberal humanism is a product of the second half of the seventeenth century' (Belsey 33), Maus disagrees (2–3, 26–34), relying on the concept of 'inwardness.' Marlowe's dramatic strategy for revealing authorship through lyric *self*-quotation is allied with the project of 'inwardness displayed' that Maus eloquently articulates (32).

25 Most criticism has been on Marlowe's *second* rival, Shakespeare (e.g., Charney; Shapiro, *Rival Playwrights*; and Cartelli). I return to this topic in the afterword to my study.

26 Like Lucan, Marlowe is 'post-Ovidian': 'Ovid in the *Metamorphoses* had flaunted his collapse of epic decorum into an Ego-trip for the artiste-narrator, had treated World History as a "perpetual" flow of poems pouring bodies into the path of his "self-perpetuating" mind, had pronounced his *own* fame as the bequest of his metamorphic writing ... [,] collapsing as the goal of his narrative "the Age of Augustus" ... into "the Brain of Ovid." ... Lucan shifts narration away from slighting insouciance to defiling disfigurement. His epic defaces his city's walls, unmakes its foundation and its history, implodes its traditions and ideologies along with the documents which bear them' (J. Henderson 143). Marlowe's challenge to Elizabeth differs from what Montrose sees as Spenser's relation with the Queen: a 'reciprocal' process of 'self-fashioning' ('Elizabethan Subject' 303, 308). If anything, Marlowe's

challenge resembles Ovid's relation with Augustus, especially after the Emperor exiled him, as defined by Kenney and others: a process of guerrilla warfare. As we shall see, especially in chapter 2, Marlowe is not 'post-Ovidian' in his commitment to homoerotic relations.

27 Jerome reports that in 55 B.C. Lucretius committed suicide after taking a love potion (cf. Dalzell 2: 213). In A.D. 8, Augustus banished Ovid, and in A.D. 65 Nero ordered both Seneca and Lucan to commit suicide for plotting against the Empire.

28 On Spenser's Christianizing of the Virgilian progression, see Cheney, *Spenser's Famous Flight* 3–22, 23–76. On Virgilian poetic fame and Christian glory in Spenser, see Cheney xi, 7–10, and 248–9, n. 7. For Spenser's reconstruction of the Augustan Empire in England, see *October* 55–78. And for Spenser's gender dynamics, see Oram et al. 589–91. On Marlowe's anti-imperialism, see Bartels. On Elizabeth and her male poets, see S. Frye 97–47; Berry 134–65; and Montrose, 'Elizabethan Subject.' Critics have neglected Marlowe's relation with the Queen (see esp. chapter 4).

29 See also Eliot 60–2; Bush, 'Marlowe and Spenser'; Battenhouse 178–92; Bakeless 1: 204–9; Jump, 'Spenser and Marlowe'; A.B. Taylor; Coe; Greenblatt, *Renaissance Self-Fashioning* 222–4; and Cheney, 'Love and Magic.' In 1844, Hunt was the first to compare Marlowe with Spenser (rpt. in MacLure, ed., *Marlowe* 91; see chapter 5). For other nineteenth-century comparisons, see MacLure's Critical Heritage volume: Bradley (130); Lowell (157–8); and Swinburne (175, 176, 177).

30 That is to say, no one has ever come to terms with this compelling topic. In this study, I focus on Marlowe's response to Spenser, because Spenser's response to Marlowe is a topic in its own right (and the subject of my Spenser Society paper at the 1995 MLA: 'Compassing the Weighty Prize: The Rival Poetics of Spenser and Marlowe'). Occasionally, I do refer to the interchange, and the critical record does supply evidence of one (Gill, 'Marlowe'). Even though emphasizing Marlowe's response, I have hardly exhausted the topic (e.g., I have cut a section on Marlowe's motivation in pursuing Spenser). For readers tempted to think that Marlowe might be complimenting Spenser, consider that his borrowings almost always occur in significant contexts, mouthed by Tamburlaine, Zenocrate, and Bajazeth, not the King of Argier, Capolin, or Anippe. Moreover, Marlowe's borrowings typically display a contextual contortion and wry sadism. Memorably, yet programmatically, Marlowe takes the speeches of Una, the distressed female figure of Truth (*FQ* I.vii.22–3), and locates them in the mouth of the abject pagan male Bajazeth (*1 Tamb* V.ii.195, 226–7, 238–40; see Crawford 204). Spenser shows Una's distress as part of the providential plan for faith; Marlowe presents Bajazeth's Unian speech of despair as the verbal vehicle of suicide.

31 In chapter 7, I suggest that *Edward II* esp. shows some softening of the Marlovian heart – a softening that may have intensified had Marlowe fully survived what Bloom calls the ephebe stage (*Anxiety of Influence*).

32 On Donne and Spenser, see Hollander, 'Donne.' On Jonson and Spenser, see Barton. Riddell and Stewart argue that Jonson shared with Spenser a view of the 'poet laureate' as 'a heroic defender of the nation' (71); thus we need to discriminate carefully among Spenser, Jonson, and Marlowe.

33 I am more interested in the strategic definition of deconstruction articulated here than one that may be more familiar, which emphasizes play and open-endedness. For giving me confidence to do so, I am indebted to my colleague Jeffrey T. Nealon, a specialist in Derrida and deconstruction who has also contributed significantly to my understanding of imitation and intertextuality. What is astonishing is how recurrently Marlowe's habitation of Spenser's structures privileges the underprivileged half of Spenser's binary oppositions.

34 See also Bloom's first two of six 'revisionary ratios,' *clinamen* and *tessera* (*Anxiety of Influence* 14); and Greene's first three of 'four types of strategies of humanist imitation,' *reproductive* or *sacramental*, *eclectic* or *exploitive*, and *heuristic* (38–43). Occasionally, these critics do touch on the synchronic dimension (e.g., Bloom, *Anxiety of Influence* 11–12; Hutcheon 31).

35 Two other recent books bear on my study: Marcus's *Puzzling Shakespeare* and Shapiro's *Rival Playwrights*. Like Helgerson, both are interested in the legitimacy of the 'author function' (Foucault, 'What Is an Author?,' rpt. in *The Foucault Reader* 101–20), and they are vocal about their interest in 'intentionality' (Shapiro 6; Marcus 19, 42, 68–70). Both, however, focus exclusively on the genre of drama, and only Shapiro fuses 'imitation' theory with New Historicism, although he does little theorizing on his own: 'The model of influence that informs this book is ... eclectic' (viii).

36 The closest I have seen to this principle is what classicists call 'double allusion'; see McKeown 1: 37–45, who notes that the technique 'seems not to be widely recognised as a standard technique in Latin poetry' (37), and who defines it as 'the simultaneous allusion to two antecedents, one of which is based on the other' (37; see also R.F. Thomas). McKeown supplies the alternative name 'by-passing technique,' because 'the immediate model ... is by-passed' in favour of a less immediate one (43–4), as when 'Ovid by-passes Tibullus to exploit Callimachus' (40). I see Marlowe reversing this process: he uses an obvious classical text to exploit the less obvious text of a (living) colleague. My typology functions as an alternative to Culler's principle for mediating the extremes of Bloom's simplistic theory of influence – in which an author is influenced by a single precursor (*Anxiety of Influence*) – and Barthes' impractical theory of intertextuality – in which a text encodes an indeterminate number of anony-

mous intertexts ('Theory of the Text'). For Culler, 'intertextuality is less a name for a work's relation to particular prior texts than an assertion of a work's participation in a discursive space and its relation to the codes which are the potential formalizations of that space' (1382). Moreover, for licence in letting *intertextuality*, a traditionally text- or reader-centred term (Kristeva), cohere with *imitation*, an author-centred term (W.J. Bate), I follow such practitioner-theorists as Greene, and even Riffaterre (115–63) and N.K. Miller, as well as work within current definitions of *intertextuality*: Hebel 1–19; Still and Worton 1–44; Clayton and Rothstein 3–36; and Harris 175–8. In particular, I follow Butler in 'reformulat[ing]' *agency* 'as a question of how signification and resignification work' (144), so that, in S. Frye's extrapolation, '"agency" describes ... conscious and unconscious participation in the practice of signification' (7). We need this definition of agency, as well as a fusion of *influence* and *intertextuality*, to get at the conjunction of discourse in the writings of Marlowe and Spenser, the history of which we cannot reconstruct via *imitation* or *intertextuality* alone.

37 Long after *The Shepheardes Calender* Spenser presents himself as Colin Clout – esp. *Colin Clouts Come Home Againe* and Book VI, canto x, of *The Faerie Queene* (see also *Ruines of Time* 225; and *Daphnaida* 229). Thus his contemporaries usually refer to him as 'Colin' (see Wells 30–1).

38 Only *The Massacre at Paris* seems exempt from the pastoral-epic grid, although it does contain an 'epic' dimension through its intertextuality with the epics of Ovid and Spenser. For quite different interpretations of Marlowe's persona as a 'shepherd,' see Levine 90–1 and Hopkins.

39 For other studies of the Elizabethan literary nation, see P. Edwards; W. Cohen; and Hadfield. Hadfield observes that 'the problem of national identity required urgent attention in the sixteenth century' (9). For historical studies of nationalism and English nationalism, see Hurstfield, *Elizabethan Nation*; Kohn; B. Anderson; Habermas; Kedouri; P. Anderson; Giddens; A.D. Smith; Hobsbawm; and Gellner. For theoretical and practical criticism on 'nation and narration,' see Bhabha, ed., esp. essays by Bhabha, Renan, and Brennan.

40 On Lucan as Ovid's heir, see W.R. Johnson, *Momentary Monsters* 58, n. 25 and 60; on Lucan as the champion of *libertas*, see 30, and passim. According to Johnson, Lucan writes the *Pharsalia* as 'an eternal contest between freedom and slavery ... freedom versus Caesar' (30). Lucan decides that 'freedom is incompatible with empire,' and 'this underground thought ... haunts the poem' (88). Habermas's definition of '"the public sphere"' so important to Hadfield depends on the concept of freedom (which Hadfield neglects): 'Citizens behave as a public body when they confer in an unrestricted fashion – that is, with the guarantee of freedom of assembly and association and the freedom to express

and publish their opinions – about matters of general interest' (49). Helgerson, too, mentions freedom (13). But it is P. Anderson's work on the Absolutist State that most helps us contextualize Marlowe's project of freedom: 'In the course of the 16th century, the Absolutist State emerged in the West ... The result was a reinforced apparatus of royal power, whose permanent political function was the repression of the peasant and plebeian masses at the foot of the social hierarchy' (15, 19). Unlike literary historians, historians often emphasize the relation between 'nationalism and freedom.' See, Kohn 16–29: 'The first full manifestation of modern nationalism occurred in seventeenth century England ... English nationalism became identified, to a degree unknown anywhere else, with the concept of individual liberty' (16). See also B. Anderson: 'nations dream of being free' (16). Finally, see Kedouri, who follows Kant in identifying 'autonomy' as 'the essential end of politics:' 'A good man is an autonomous man, and for him to realize his autonomy, he must be free' (22; see 12–23, 30–1, 39–40).

41 On *libertas*, see Lewis and Short, Def. II.D, '*Freedom of speech or thought,*' citing the pseudo-Ovidian *Heroides* XV.68, the self-reflexive letter from Sappho to Phaon: 'As for me, because I often warned him well and faithfully, he hates me; this has my candour brought me, this my duteous tongue.' Ovid uses the word *libertas* eight times, most notably in the last elegy of the *Amores* (III.xv.8–10). For Lucan, *libertas* means most often the freedom of the Republic – '*Civil freedom, liberty*' (Lewis and Short, Def. II.A), '*Political freedom, liberty, or independence* of a people not under monarchical rule' (Def. II.B). Lucan's freedom is different from modern American freedom in that it is fundamentally an aristocratic condition dependent, in part, on a slave system. On freedom in the English Renaissance, see Hurstfield, *Freedom*; and esp. Woods (to whom I am indebted for guidance and conversation): 'Freedom and Tyranny' and 'Politics, Poetics.' Woods suggests that 'Freedom for the Elizabethan was largely the citizen's right to participate, under the law, in affirming and maintaining public order'; however, she argues that for Sidney, 'freedom is knowledgeable choice,' and she observes that 'the right of free speech' is 'a beloved notion' of the 'writers' ('Freedom and Tyranny' 166, 170, 168). Marlowe uses *freedom* and its variants forty-six times, and *liberty* and its variants sixteen, bringing the total to sixty-two. See, e.g., Tamburlaine's 'I love to live at liberty' (*1 Tamb* I.ii.26).

42 Nowhere is this idea more powerfully displayed than in Lucan, for whom 'the gods are not indifferent to us because they are powerless over us [as Epicurus thought]; they are not indifferent and they are very powerful ... [Similarly,] the gods, though very much concerned with mortals, do not want to lead us to happiness [as the Stoic Zeno thought], they want us annihilated. *Gods, nature,*

fate, fortune – these are words, words that dimly and inaccurately signify an inscrutable, omnipotent malevolence at the heart of history, of human experience' (W.R. Johnson, *Momentary Monsters* 11).

43 Giddens defines 'organization' as a 'collectivity' (12), but if, as we shall see, Marlowe follows Ovid in writing a (counter-)nationhood of one – himself as poet – he appears to reject '"political" organization' (Giddens 19–20) altogether. Yet, for an organization of poetic values for the new Marlovian nation, see the end of chapter 3 in the present study.

44 See Birringer, *Marlowe's 'Dr Faustus' and 'Tamburlaine'*: 'God's and the devil's faces become one' (174; on the '"fallibility" of freedom' see 29). On Lucifer as a 'Renaissance prince,' see Sales 151. For testimonials of Marlowe's deep urge to free himself from constraint, see P. Edwards 55; Garber, 'Closure' 6; Summers, 'Sex, Politics' 231; Voss 518; and McAlindon, *Renaissance Tragedy* 83–4. Brandt, *Christopher Marlowe*, discusses the 'metaphysical' problem of free will in the plays.

45 It is as a 'scholar' that Marlowe appears to have presented himself or to have been known to his contemporaries: 'Christofer Marly, by his profession a scholar ... The scholar says himself to be very well known ...' (Letter from R. Sidney to Burleigh, 26 January 1592). See also Beard (1597): 'Marlin, by profession a scholler, brought up from his youth in the Universitie of Cambridge' (rpt. in MacLure, ed., *Marlowe* 41). Finally, see the Canterbury native and Cambridge graduate Simon Aldrich, who reported to Henry Oxiden that 'Marloe ... was a rare scholar and made excellent verses in Latin' (qtd. in Wraight and Stern 86). For relevant definitions of *scholar*, see *OED*, Defs. 2b and 3. The idea that Marlowe presents himself as a 'scholar' may help clarify his leadership role as a 'University Wit.' This idea also helps to contextualize Marlowe and the University Wits in terms of a broad historical narrative that anticipates, prefigures, or leads to the achievements, in late eighteenth- and early nineteenth-century Germany, of what Kedouri calls the 'post-Kantian philosophers' (34) – 'Fichte, Schleiermacher, and their fellow-writers,' including Herder and Schiller – who 'belonged to a caste which was relatively low on the social scale': 'they were ... the sons of pastors, artisans, or small farmers. They somehow managed to become university students, most often in the faculty of theology ... When they graduated they found that their knowledge opened no doors ... These students and ex-students felt in them the ability to do great things' (35–6). According to Kedouri, these scholar-writers' 'exaltation of the state also exalts the philosopher, the academic': '"the Scholar is the *Guide* of the human race"' (Fichte, qtd. in Kedouri 42). These scholars are histoically important because they construct a nationhood organized around 'the claim ... that the state should be the creator

of man's freedom not in an external and material sense, but in an internal and spiritual sense' (39–40).

46 Marlowe's repeated quotation of classical writers in his plays is one form his persona as a 'scholar' takes. I count a total of about twenty-seven such lines: eight from *Dido*; one from *The Jew*; four from *Edward II*; and fourteen from *Doctor Faustus*. The lines come principally from Virgil, Ovid, Seneca, and Aristotle. These statistics do not include Marlowe's recurrent use of Latin tags or quotations from other languages, such as Spanish in *The Jew of Malta*.

47 See Helgerson's distinction between 'the state' and 'the nation' (*Forms of Nationhood* 2): the state is the Tudor state ruled by Queen Elizabeth; the nation is a broader formation, England, not necessarily tied to the Tudor state (see also Gellner 3–5). On 'nation' as 'a problematic though widely used term,' see Helgerson 8. Most of Helgerson's writers choose to serve the nation rather than the state. Thus, despite subversion, they remain patriotic. The same can be said of Hadfield's men (Skelton, Bale, Sidney, Spenser, Baldwin, the Earl of Surrey), but Hadfield is alone in self-advertising his project as flattening out the writing of English nationhood: 'What all the texts analysed in this book have in common is their desire to help constitute and participate within a national public sphere' (5).

48 See Watt: Faustus is 'loyal to his emperor, revered by his students, generous to his servant; but there is no suggestion of any wish to serve others, or to sacrifice anything for them' (43). Garber's citation of 'Tamburlaine's definition of kingship' ('Closure' 8) is esp. sobering, reminding us of the grim restrictions of Marlovian freedom: 'Keeping in iron cages emperors' (*2 Tamb* I.iii.49).

49 Cf. K. Cunningham: Marlowe 'was not a political reformer ... His first allegiance ... is to the theater'; Marlowe 'reveals that theatricality is a point of view ... [, c]ountering the claims of absolute rulers with his shows of alternativity' (219–20). I extend Marlowe's alternativity beyond the theatre.

Part I: Sea-Bank Myrtle Sprays: Amatory Poetry

1 See Braudy on the 'the stately procession through public offices that the Romans called the *cursus honorum* (race-track of honors)' (61), 'the official Roman pattern for a political career' (65), which Virgil and Horace accommodated to the Roman literary career (see 128–9, 131), and which St. Augustine accommodated to 'a course of Christian development, a spiritual journey' (161–4).

2 The anonymously printed *ALL OVIDS ELEGIES: 3. Bookes By C.M. Epigrams by J.D*, which prints the whole of Marlowe's translation, purports to come out of Middlebourgh, Holland, and was printed either in the latter half of

the 1590s or early in the seventeenth century – but in England, for the Middlebourgh location is generally agreed to be spurious. Yet two separate editions of the translation with ten selected poems also survive, one titled *EPIGRAMMES and ELEGIES. [By I.D. and C.M]* and the other *CERTAINE OF OVIDS ELEGIES. By C Marlow*. At least one of these editions was banned and burned in 1599; however, the primary target appears to have been Davies's poem (Gill, ed., *Complete Works* 1: 7). On the Bishops' ban, see McCabe. On the publication history, see L.C. Martin 14–17; MacLure, ed., *Poems* xxxi–xxxiii; Gill and Krueger; Bowers, 'Early Editions'; and Gill, ed., *Complete Works* 1: 6–12. Nosworthy argues for a '1595' publication date ('Marlowe's *Elegies*' 261), and he suggests that Jonson may have overseen the volume's production, since the first complete edition (the Mason text) prints his translation of *Amores* I.xv alongside Marlowe's ('Marlowe's *Ovid*').

3 On the date, see MacLure, ed., *Poems* xxxii; and Gill, ed., *Complete Works* 1: xi. On manuscript circulation, see Boas, *Christopher Marlowe* 30; and Bakeless 2: 172, 209 – both of whom note that Nashe quotes two lines from the translation (II.iii.3–4) in *The Unfortunate Traveller* (1593; see McKerrow 2: 238), and that Shakespeare might have quoted a single line (I.xiii.43) in *The Merchant of Venice* (1596–7; V.i.109). For further evidence that Marlowe's contemporaries took an interest in his translation, see Dent, who cites four passages reproduced in *The Insatiate Countesse* (1613).

4 See Gill and Krueger 247; Gill, ed., *Complete Works* 1: 7, 10–11; and Pearcy 21–51.

5 My colleague Robert R. Edwards suggests that here the poet is displacing the idea of 'freedom' (line 9: *libertas*) from the national centre, 'Rome,' to his own ancestral home: 'Peligny's *nation*' (personal communication 1995).

Chapter 1: Ovid's Counter-Virgilian *Cursus* in the *Amores*

1 On the two editions of the *Amores*, see Cameron, 'First Edition'; and McKeown 1: 74–89.

2 Otis inscribes the view of Ovid's career to which I respond: 'The *Metamorphoses* represented a radical break in Ovid's poetical career. He had been an elegist: he then turned to epic' (4). For commentary anticipating my map, see Kenney, 'Ovid' 2: 420; Barsby, ed. 6; and Booth 86. In emphasizing what Marlowe could have found in Ovid, I am offering a concrete instance of the reception methodology articulated by Martindale in *Redeeming the Text*: 'it is hardly surprising if my reading of Marlowe should have affected my reading of Ovid' (73). Martindale explains: 'If ... the account of reading offered in the first chapter is accepted ['*Meaning ... is always realized at the point of reception*' (3)],

it sets both "Ovid" and "Marlowe" in motion, and also means that their
relationship is always already interlinked in various ways, since "Marlowe" has
been part of the process of the construction of "Ovid", and *vice versa*, and so
on (*ad infinitum*); moreover the reader is herself entrammelled within the
discourses which constitute both. *We read from within a tradition, or a
discourse, or a set of reading practices, or we do not read at all'* (73; emphasis in
original).

3 Typically, critics devote only a passage to these poems, as do Du Quesnay,
'*Amores*' 5–6; and Kenney, 'Ovid' 2: 420–2. Cahoon writes 'Program for
Betrayal' on the programmatic poems opening the three books, but she does
not include the other two or relate the three to Ovid's subsequent career. C.
Martin examines the programmatic poems (17–33), but these are not his
principal topic.

4 When Davis discusses the programmatic poems, he emphasizes their dramatic,
not their programmatic, quality.

5 Ovid critics have long debated the seriousness of the *Amores*, and in arguing
for its major and 'serious' significance I am indebted to Fränkel; Kenney,
'Ovid'; W.R. Johnson, 'Counter-classical Sensibility'; Conner; D. Parker;
Fyler, '*Omnia Vincit Amor*'; Elliott; Cahoon, 'Raping the Rose'; and Farrell,
'Dialogue of Genres.'

6 Secondary evidence includes those passages evoking epic (e.g., I.ii.9–12, 49–57,
82–3; I.ix.1, 33–40; I.x.1–2, 56; II.xvii.14–22; and III.xi.13–16, 21–44).

7 See also Putnam 196–8; and Clausen 174–5. More recently, see Cameron,
Callimachus 454–83: Callimachus in his *Aetia* fragment (i.fr.I.21–4, discovered
in 1927) does not 'denounce epic' (455), but Virgil does (460), even though
'Vergil was indeed faced with a vogue for epic' (459).

8 On this 'topos of inability or affected modesty' as 'an indirect tactic of self-
assertion,' through which Spenser predicts 'Colin's transformation into a poet
of epic,' see Oram, et al. 107–8.

9 For other uses of the *recusatio* along Horace's counter-Virgilian line, see
Propertius, *Elegies* III.iii.1–26; and Tibullus, *Elegies* II.iv.13–20 (see also
I.i.53–6, I.x.27–32). Sannazaro appears to have read the Virgil passage the way I
am suggesting Spenser does; see *Arcadia*, ch. 7, pp. 74–5, and ch. 10, pp. 104–5,
as well as Nash's comments, trans. 14 and 104–5. See also W.L. in his 1628
translation of the *Eclogues* for a reading of the *Georgics* and *Aeneid* into the
pastoral (e.g., 31, 36, 37).

10 In Elegy II.xxxiv.61–84, Propertius inscribes the Virgilian *cursus*, but he puts
the *Aeneid* first, the *Eclogues* second, and the *Georgics* third, and he does not
place the triad in the context of either Rome or fame. Vessey thinks that 'Ovid
may well have had Propertius II. 34 in mind' (613). We think Propertius wrote

his poem around 26 or 25 B.C.; Cameron states that Ovid wrote 'the first book of the first edition of the *Amores* c. 25 B.C.' ('First Edition' 326); he remarks that 'there is no particular reason to suppose that the general character of the first edition was significantly different from the second' (325); and he thinks that 'I.15 may well have been ... included ... in the first edition' (333).

11 Cf. C. Martin 18–19 for the insight that Virgil expands but Ovid attenuates; his conclusion, however, that Ovid presents himself as a compromised figure, is misleading, since it is subject to the traditional view of Ovid as a non-serious writer caught in his own play.

12 On Ovid's opening imitation of the opening of the *Aeneid*, see McKeown 2: 11–12. On Ovid's debt to Callimachus, see Lateiner.

13 Barsby (ed. 41) and Cahoon ('Program for Betrayal' 31) identify the Gigantomachy with epic. In 'Ovid's Gigantomachia' (ed. 63–81), Owen argues that Ovid *did* write a Gigantomachy in his youth (63), that the poem was an 'epic' (64), that fragments of it remain (66–8), and that Ovid abandoned the poem (65, 79). Innes rejects Owen's theory (165, 167), but Sharrock appears willing to entertain it (116 and n. 46; see 114–17, 134–5, 137–8, 168). Ghisalberti notes (36) that one medieval rendition of the Ovidian canon includes the Gigantomachy (see 36, n. 4, for details); he adds that 'this was taken up later by Polenton' (36), who 'believes that the poem was begun and left half finished' (36, n. 4).

14 On the *Metamorphoses* as Ovid's epic, see Otis. I have seen little commentary linking the two Gigantomachy passages, but see Owen: 'The sketch in the Metamorphoses [*sic*] may be a compression of the fuller earlier version contained in the Gigantomachia of Ovid's youth' (ed. 78).

15 Owen emphasizes the 'political significance' of the Gigantomachy for the Romans (ed. 73, 75), with 'the parallel ... often drawn between Jupiter and Augustus' (76). The key text is Horace, *Odes* III.iv.37–64. Sharrock remarks that 'Gigantomachy is the theme which above all others epitomizes martial epic, which is the most daring of literary exploits and exactly that attempted by Virgil. Gigantomachy epitomizes the ultimate in poetic audacity, the most quintessentially epic of epics, the polar opposite of Callimacheanism' (115). See also *Ex Ponto* II.ii.9–14 and IV.59–60.

16 On Ovid's ability 'to see everything with the eyes of the woman,' see Fränkel 22. For rejections of this line, see Gamel; and Cahoon, 'June's Chaste Festival,' 'The Parrot and the Poet,' 'Raping the Rose,' and 'The Bed as Battlefield.' For a counter-critique, see C. Martin 15.

17 I am indebted to Booth: 'After professed attempts at both epic (5–12) and tragedy (13–18), Ovid has returned to love-elegy' (86). By inserting a programmatic poem in the penultimate position of a book, Ovid has baffled his modern

editors (see Booth 11, 87). Ovid, however, is playfully violating his own
pattern of beginning and ending each book of the *Amores* with a programmatic
poem (see C. Martin 30–1). None the less, says Martin, 'to grasp its full
significance, we must understand 2.18 as the central moment in a three-poem
sequence ending the central book' (31). I disagree with Martin's conclusion:
'*Amores* 2.18 pivots, finally, upon the idea of resignation to genres best suiting
one's talents and temperament, rather than struggling against the odds' (31–2).
In line 14, as well as in III.i.25–30, Ovid identifies his best talent and temperament to lie in the genre of tragedy; this judgment is confirmed by Quintilian
and Tacitus (more of whom later).

18 Many critics take Ovid's announcement here seriously: Wilkinson 115–16;
Fränkel 46; Cameron, 'First Edition' 331–3; Newman 183, n. 3, and 186; and
Kenney, 'Ovid' 2: 421.

19 Luck comments: Ovid 'refuses to have anything to do with a life of action
himself. He loves Rome, the city; Rome, not Corinna, is in a sense the real
protagonist of the *Amores*' (142). On Ovid's well-known resistance to the
Augustan regime, see esp. Braudy 135.

20 On Ovid and fame in the *Amores*, see Kenney, 'Ovid': 'the poet's passion for
fame is vital and sincere' (2: 421). On Ovid and fame generally, see Braudy
134–43.

21 On typology in the Virgilian progression from pastoral to georgic to epic, see
Coolidge 11, 20.

22 Many critics examine the relation between Ovid and Virgil, but almost always
with respect to a single genre or contrasting set of works (e.g., the *Metamorphoses* as an 'anti-*Aeneid*'). See Curran; Hardie, *Epic Successors of Virgil*;
Javitch, 'Ovid's Revision of the *Aeneid*'; and Myers 5–15, 95–113.

23 I owe this idea to my colleague Robert R. Edwards (personal communication,
April 1994).

24 Cf. Kenney, 'Ovid': 'It appears that Ovid had already embarked on the single
letters [the *Heroides*], and probably the *Ars amatoria* as well, before completing the final revision of the *Amores*. Thus, before the ink was dry on his initial
tour de force, he was already carrying the congenial theme of love into one new
literary field after another' (2: 421). Cf. also Booth 86.

25 Critics usually see 'profitemur Amoris' as a reference to the *Ars* (see McKeown
1: 86–8), but Cameron argues that the phrase refers to the *Amores* itself ('First
Edition' 331–2).

26 Ovid critics debate whether this reference to the *Heroides* indicates that Ovid
had written all or part of his letters by the time he wrote this elegy (McKeown
1: 86–8).

27 Jonson's mentioning of the *Medea* in *The Poetaster* (I.ii.12) postdates Marlowe

by over a decade. For a reference predating Marlowe, see Poliziano's poem on Ovid, including his reference to *Medea* (10; trans. Sandys, *Metamorphoses*, 1626 ed., and marginal note). Poliziano was familiar to E.K., Spenser's glossarist in *The Shepheardes Calender* (*March* 170–3). Sandys follows with a unit he calls 'Ovid Defended,' which extracts quotations from great classical and Christian figures who defend Ovid against 'fastidious censures' (sig. b3ᵛ), including Seneca, whom Sandys declares to be '[a] constant Imitor of his [Ovid's], through all his Philosophie; but especially in his Tragedies. Wherupon, some have conjectred that Seneca's Medea belongeth to Ovid' (sig. b4ʳ). He also quotes Quintilian on 'Ovid's Medea' (sig. b3ᵛ), as well as Tacitus (b4ʳ).

28 See *Amores* III.xiii, where Ovid writes of his wife in the past tense, since (obviously) he had already married her: 'Cum mihi pomiferis coniunx foret orta Faliscis ...' (1). Marlowe was unmarried, and here is his translation: 'When fruit-filled Tuscia *should* a wife give me' (*Ovid's Elegies* III.xii.1).

29 See Fyler, '*Omnia Vincit Amor*' 198, 203. Hinds is also instructive on Ovid's manipulation of genre boundaries; see '*Arma* in Ovid's *Fasti*: Part 1' and 'Part 2.' For Ovid on generic mixing, see *Tristia* II.371–420 and 533–8 – esp. the phrase 'the loves of tragedy' (407: 'tragicos ... ignes').

30 For a chronology accepted as canonical in medieval biographies of Ovid, see Ghisalberti 36–7. On the 'overall shape of Ovid's tragic career, from the playful games of the *Ars amatoria* to the bitter exile of the *Tristia* and the *Ex Ponto*,' see Calabrese, esp. 5.

31 On the incomplete status of the *Fasti* and the *Metamorphoses*, see *Tristia* II.549–52 and 555–6. The *Fasti*, Ovid claims, was dedicated to Augustus, and in the most recent (and book-length) analysis of the poem Herbert-Brown calls the *Fasti* an 'elegiac epic' (30). On 'elegy and epic' in the *Fasti* and the *Metamorphoses*, see Hinds, *Metamorphoses of Persephone* 99–134.

32 Cf. Davisson, who concludes that in the *Tristia* and *Ex Ponto* Ovid uses the parent–child metaphor to emphasize 'the fraternal relationship between past and present poems' (113).

33 See also *Tristia* II.445–66 on the line of Gallus, Tibullus, and Propertius: 'I was their successor' (466); and V.ix.31 on his muse as Thalia. Finally, see *Ex Ponto* III.iii.79–82.

34 See Currie; and Tarrant. Cf. Nikolaidis. On the *Medea* in medieval biographies of Ovid, see Ghisalberti 25. In 'The Life, Works, and Approof of Ovid' prefacing his 1640 translation of the *Fasti*, Gower thinks that Ovid wrote more than one tragedy: 'He penned also some Tragedies: Of which *Medea* is highly approved by Quintilianus and Corn. Tacitus, and not without desert; for in it he hath shewn the very vigour and quintessence of wit' (sig. Bʳ).

35 Cf. Hinds, '*Arma* in Ovid's *Fasti*: Part 1' 87. Hinds is the only critic I have read

to note this career linkage. But see Sharrock on the two turning posts *within* the structure of the *Ars amatoria*: the 'meta' at both I.40 and II.727 (20).

Chapter 2: Marlowe's New Renaissance Ovid: '*Area maior*' in *Ovid's Elegies*

1 See Striar: 'what is particularly remarkable about Marlowe's translation of Ovid's *Amores* is that it is the very first translation of this work into any vernacular' (187), citing Jacobsen 156 and Bolgar 530–3 (189, n. 2). Jacobsen precedes Striar in his enthusiasm for 'the nature and extent of ... [Marlowe's] originality' (157). By contrast, Lerner voices the received wisdom: 'Everyone knows Francis Meres's claim in 1598 that "the sweet witty soul of Ovid lives in mellifluous and honey-tongued Shakespeare", and the same compliment was paid to Daniel, Drayton and even Chapman' (122). To this, Lerner adds: 'But for the true English imitation of the sweet (or sour) and witty Ovid, we should turn to Donne's *Elegies*' (125). Lerner mentions *Ovid's Elegies* largely to criticize it (124, 125). In Marlowe, we may discern a more alert reader of Ovid than in any contemporary, including Shakespeare and Donne.
2 See Jacobsen 152–6, who adds that, despite the conspiracy, 'we have ... overwhelming evidence that people privately read, enjoyed, and imitated the *Amores* at all times' (154). When Marlowe translated the poem, all of Ovid's other major poems had been translated not simply into Continental languages but into English (Bolgar 530–3).
3 I use the terms of McCanles in his analysis of the 'document and monument' of Spenser's *Shepheardes Calender*. The terms come from Foucault, *The Archaeology of Knowledge* 7, 138–9. The documents include Golding's 1567 translation of the *Metamorphoses*; Turbervile's 1569 translation of the *Heroides*; Underdowne's 1577 translation of the *Ibis*; Churchyard's 1578 translation of the *Tristia*; F.L.'s 1600 translation of the *Remedia amoris*; Sandys's 1626 and 1632 translations of the *Metamorphoses*; Catlin's 1639 translation of the *Tristia*; Saltonstall's 1639 translation of the *Heroides*; Gower's 1640 translation of the *Fasti*; Saltonstall's 1640 translation of the *Ex Ponto*; Saltonstall's 1672 translation of the *Tristia*; and Dryden's edition of the 1680 translation of the *Heroides*.
4 See J. Bate: [William] Webbe's emphasis on Golding's service to his country reminds us that the Elizabethan translation movement in which Golding was prominent was a significant part of a post-Reformation project to establish England as a Protestant nation with its own high culture' (30). On this generational project of writing nationhood (Helgerson, *Forms of Nationhood*), see *A Discourse of English Poetrie* (1586), rpt. in G.G. Smith, ed. 1: 243, 262. For similar praise of Golding, see Nashe in his Preface to Greene's *Menaphon*

(1589), rpt. in Smith 1: 315; Puttenham, *The Arte of English Poesie* (1589), rpt. in Smith 2: 63, 65; Harington, *A Briefe Apologie of Poetrie* (1591), rpt. in Smith 2: 196; and Meres, *Palladis Tamia* (1598), rpt. in Smith 2: 322.

5 According to Lewis and Short, the Latin word *area* in Ovid's phrase 'area maior' means '*An open space for games, an open play-ground … Also, a race-ground*' (Def. II.B). For Virgil's use of the chariot as a trope for his poetry, see esp. *Georgics* II.541–2, III.16–39, and, for resonant commentary, Hardie, *Epic Successors of Virgil* 100–1. On Ovid's use of the chariot for his own poetry, see Kenney, 'Nequitiae Poeta' 206. On Marlowe's use of the chariot, see MacLure, ed., *Poems* 216.

6 Bate continues: 'This broad shift does not, however, mean either that moral and allegorical readings disappeared in the Elizabethan period … or that moralization was the only medieval approach to Ovid' (25). Bate cites Fyler, *Chaucer and Ovid*; and Barkan, *Gods Made Flesh*. On the medieval Ovid, see Ghisalberti; Rand, *Ovid and His Influence* 112–49; Wilkinson 366–98; Robathan; and Cahoon, 'Raping the Rose.' On the Renaissance Ovid, see Cooper; Bush, *Mythology* 73, 78; Boas, 'Ovid and the Elizabethans'; H. Smith 64–130; Doran; Rand, *Ovid and His Influence* 150–65; Staton; Wilkinson 399–438; Ogilvie 1–33; Jameson; Keach, *Elizabethan Erotic Narratives* 3–35; Orlandi; Javitch, 'Rescuing Ovid' and 'Ovid's Revision'; Hulse; Lerner; Holahan; Burrow; P.A. Miller; Enterline; and Shuger 167–91. (Stapleton's *Harmful Eloquence* appeared after I completed my study; since he focuses on the figure of the 'desultor amoris,' he does not often cross the tracks of my argument.)

7 In *The House of Fame*, 'Chaucer is professedly Ovid's pupil in the art of love, and he deeply understands the master's teaching' (Rand, *Ovid and His Influence* 146). On the way in which Chaucer molds his own biographical pattern in imitation of the accessus tradition with Ovid, see Calabrese. On the role of the dream visions in Chaucer's career, I am indebted to R.R. Edwards. At V.1786, Chaucer calls *Troilus and Chrisyede* 'litel myn tragedye.' On *The Canterbury Tales* as an epic, see Rand, *Ovid and His Influence* 146–8. With Chaucer, as with Ovid (see Farrell, 'Dialogue of Genres'), single-genre designations like 'epic' remain problematic, but generic integrity and generic mixing are not at odds, as R. Cohen explains: 'Since genres … were interrelated, it is self-evident that each genre had a specific identity' (50). I would add that the career idea I am emphasizing suggests that as much as a poet may play with generic boundaries he necessarily depends on generic integrity. Such play is entirely within keeping of what we know about Ovid – and heirs like Chaucer. On the consonance between Ovid and later Christian culture, see Braudy 135.

8 W. Cohen writes that the 'permanent, public, commercial theaters ... opened in both countries [England and Spain] in the late 1570s' (17; see 264). The *Encyclopaedia Britannica* (15th ed.) says that the 'permanent theatres were established in Seville, Valencia, and Madrid, where two of the first were the Corall de la Cruz (1579) and the Corral del Principe (1582)' (28: 538).

9 By neglecting the 'career' dimension of Ovid's *Amores*, critics misgauge Marlowe's motive in translating the poem for late sixteenth-century culture. Keach articulates the received wisdom: 'it was not just Ovid's own wit and eroticism which aroused the interest of Marlowe and his friends, but the status of the *Amores* in the minds of conservative sixteenth-century readers ... The *Amores* ... remained forbidden fruit ... Marlowe would have looked upon the *Amores* not only as a challenge to his skill as a poet, but also as an opportunity to flout and subvert the established approach to Ovid's poetry' (*Elizabethan Erotic Narratives* 29). This last motive identifies Marlowe as a transitional figure in the turn from the 'medieval' to the 'Renaissance' Ovid emphasized by Bush, H. Smith, Barkan, and J. Bate (already mentioned), as well as by Ellis-Fermor 11; Boas, *Christopher Marlowe* 31; Steane 300; and Leech, *Christopher Marlowe* 32. Even though the motives Keach articulates likely played a role in Marlowe's translation, each forms a cornerstone to a popularized Ovid and a popularized Marlowe.

10 See Martindale, *Redeeming the Text* 75–100: 'The translated text is already an interpretation' (13). On Marlowe's appropriation of Ovid, see Pearcy 4–6, 18–19; and Gill, 'Art of Translation' 329–30 and '"Snakes."' Most commentary emphasizes Marlowe's accuracy (from Ellis-Fermor 10–14 to Leech, *Christopher Marlowe* 26–32). Pearcy is more direct than Steane: 'The paradoxical effect of Marlowe's special kind of literalness is to deny the original the importance it usually has in literal translation and to place the imprint of his choice of words on every line' (6). Pearcy asks, 'Why did Marlowe ... produce this ... version of the *Amores*? Line-for-line translation of a work one-quarter the length of the *Aeneid* does not seem ... [a] lightly undertaken pastime' (20). See also Gill and Krueger 247.

11 Other advertisements in sixteenth-century translations of Ovid include the following: 'The. xv. Bookes of P.Ouidius Naso, entytuled Metamorphosis, translated oute of Latin into English meeter, by Arthur Golding Gentleman'; '*Ovid: Heroyall epistles* tr. George Turbervile'; '*The Three First Bookes of Ovids de Tristibus* translated into English by Thomas Churchyard'; *Ovid His Invective against Ibis* Tr. Thomas Underdowne.' The title page of *Ovid's Elegies* even differs significantly from the title page of Marlowe's other translation: 'LUCANS FIRST BOOKE TRANSLATED LINE FOR LINE BY CHR. MARLOW.'

12 Gill writes of this last elegy: 'Marlowe is less confident of vocation [than Ovid] in his mistranslation' of line 18, where 'Ovid's mighty steeds are carthorses to Marlowe' ('"Snakes"' 139, nn. 7 and 8). Marlowe's translation may be weak, but the horses are more georgic than Gill allows, as Marlowe's tilling metaphor reveals. Is there, then, a Virgilian/Spenserian dimension to his translation (see, e.g., *Amoretti* 80: 5–8)?

13 Among modern editors, the only exception appears in a gloss on I.i.34, where Gill compares Marlowe's use of 'shine' with Spenser's in *FQ* IV.iii.3 (ed., *Complete Works* 1: 223).

14 Hamilton's gloss supports this conjecture: '"mountaines in Scythia, where as is continuall wynter, and snow with huge wyndes" (Cooper)' (ed., *FQ* 376).

15 For the metadiscursive significance of *wax*, see *Metamorphoses* X.283–6; and Enterline 126. I discuss the Petrarchan basis of the imagery in 'Two Florimells' 330–3.

16 On Florimell as Elizabeth, see also Hadfield 193, 196. In another context, S. Frye cites a 1601 speech to Parliament in which Elizabeth chastely presents herself as 'a tapere of trewe virgin waxe' (114); Frye also cites a 1592/3 entertainment at Theobolds where Robert Cecil presented Elizabeth with a 'candle of virgin's wax, meete for a Virgin Queene' (185, n. 43).

17 Cf. Segal, *Orpheus*, who agrees with Otis (67) but adds a qualification: 'The happiness of such love [as that between Orpheus and Eurydice] has no place in the real world' (69).

18 Cf. *Amores* I.i.19–20. On the '"homosexual" element' in Roman elegy, see D. Kennedy 26–30, 39–43; and Keach, *Elizabethan Erotic Narratives* 18–19.

19 On the 'familial Ovid,' see Martindale, introduction, *Ovid Renewed* 8–9.

20 Thus, Marlowe differs from Sidney, Spenser, Shakespeare, Jonson, Donne, and Milton, all of whom married; produced children; left fairly substantial records of their families behind; and, in the case of Spenser, Donne, and Milton, wrote stunning poems on their wives.

21 The only other bedfellows in the Marlowe record are that hapless betrayer of male friendship, Kyd, and, of course, Baines (on the latter, see Kendall 533).

22 See Snow; Kuriyama; Barber, *Creating Elizabethan Tragedy* 45–86; and Donaldson. Barber extends and qualifies Kuriyama's Oedipal reading of Marlowe in his chapter on *Tamburlaine*: 'its hero is shaped by a latent family constellation' (52). On Marlowe's relation with his father and mother, see Barber 73. Along this line, Proser's *Gift of Fire* is the most recent, detailed analysis.

23 See Boas, *Christopher Marlowe* 1–6; Bakeless 1: 3–30; and esp. Urry 25–39.

24 On Ovid's detachment from Roman religion, see Barsby, 'Ovid' 25–6. On Marlowe's 'atheism,' I am especially indebted to Riggs.

25 See Fränkel on Ovid as '[h]umorous ... by nature' (127; see 265).
26 On Marlowe's 'Death's-head jesting,' see Kocher, *Christopher Marlowe* 292.
27 This thesis revises my argument about *October* in Spenser's *Famous Flight* (27–38), which itself sought to revise the received wisdom on the eclogue.
28 Cheney, Spenser's *Famous Flight* 27–38. At lines 55–60, Spenser refers to the generic triad of 'the Romish Tityrus' (55), and in lines 196–9 E.K. glosses the reference.
29 Maclean and Prescott 529, n. 5; Renwick, rpt. in *Variorum Edition* 7: 394. The *Variorum Edition* glosses ll. 100–1 of *October* with *Ars amatoria* III.549–50. Cf. Herman: 'After illustrating ... the dubiousness of a *public* role for poetry, Cuddie affirms poetry as a *private* endeavor, poetry as Catullan lyric expression rather than as a Vergilian instrument of political reform' (22).
30 Coolidge points out that Ovid uses the phrase at *Metamorphoses* V.416–17 (2, n. 3). Ovid first uses the phrase, however, at *Amores* II.xvii.14, where he turns it to his own counter-Virgilian advantage in a defence of his amatory indulgence: 'Small things with greater may be copulate' ('aptari magnis inferiora licet'). The wonderful 'copulate' is Marlowe's addition.
31 See J. Goldberg, *Voice-Terminal Echo* 63–5; and L.S. Johnson 84.
32 On the extent to which we are encouraged to identify the New Poet with Cuddie, see Cheney, Spenser's *Famous Flight* 31–2.
33 On 'the bombastic style that is the mainstay of Senecan tragedy,' see Braden, *Renaissance Tragedy* 38, quoting *Medea* 530–8; and B. Smith 19–20, 28, 34. For Senecan *furor*, see *Medea* 406–14. On the Senecan *thunder*, see *Phaedra* (*Hippolytus*) 681–3. On 'the expanding circle of intimidation' and for the thought that 'Senecan dramatic rhetoric is at its strongest a rhetoric of intimidation,' see Braden 53. For potential origins of Spenser's line in Heywood's translation of *Thyestes*, see I.96, 100, II.116, and V.iv.62.
34 On wine and meat in Heywood's translation, see I.65; 1 Chorus 27–9, 48; IV.ii.158–9; V.i.15, 28, 29–33; V.iii.4, 66. Classical writers think of the Thyestes myth as programmatic for tragedy (Horace, *Ars poetica* 91); Spenser, as programmatic for Senecan tragedy (see E.K.'s gloss on Melpomene's call to the 'grieslie ghostes' in *November* [53–5]: 'The maner of Tragicall Poets, to call for helpe of Furies and damned ghostes: so is Hecuba of Euripides, and Tantalus brought in of Seneca' [234–6]).
35 Heywood uses 'rage' nine times in his translation. On Heywood and Spenser, see the Daalder ed. xlv.
36 E.K. mentions the 'Tragicall poets' – the Greek tragedians and Seneca – in *Julye* (336–8), *October* (262–6), and *November* (234–6).
37 Critics find the coming of Marlowe in Spenser's passage. J. Goldberg notes that 'we might take Tamburlaine's progress from shepherd to king as the tragic

counterpart to the Virgilian pattern of ascent; it is perhaps to be attached to the paradigm as it is articulated in *October*, and especially in Cuddie's theatrical aspirations' (*Voice-Terminal Echo* 173, n. 21). In 1906, Greg saw a 'charter of the new age of England's song' and found a 'prophecy of Marlowe and mighty music to come' (rpt. in *Variorum Edition* 7: 390). In the *October* passage, I suggest, Marlowe found a prophecy of Marlowe.

38 Helgerson identifies both Drayton and Daniel as laureate poets (*Self-Crowned Laureates* 16, 30–4, 48). See also *Spenser's Famous Flight* 39–41, 43–5.

39 Propertius, *Elegies* II.x.7, which reads in the Loeb ed. 'aetas prima canat Veneres, extrema tumultus'; Daniel, title page to *Delia* in the *Complete Works*, ed. Grosart 1: 20. See Hulse 59. It is not the one-genre Propertius, however, but the multigenre Ovid who anticipates Daniel's *cursus*. Thus, Daniel in his *Dedicatory Epistle* to Mary Sidney prefacing his 1602 *Works* identifies his move from amatory poetry to tragedy; the Countess '[c]all'd up my spirits from out their low repose, / To sing of State, and tragicke notes to frame' (7–8): 'I ... Made musique to my self that pleasd me best, / And onelie told of *Delia* ... : Madam, had not thy well grac'd *Antony* ... / Requir'd his *Cleopatras* company' (9–16). Generously, Spenser recognizes Daniel's alternative career model in *Colin Clouts Come Home Againe*, when he encourages Daniel to move beyond 'loves soft laies and looser thoughts delight' to 'Tragick plaints and passionate mischance' (423–7). See Cheney, *Spenser's Famous Flight* 44. Oram glosses 'Tragick plaints' here with Daniel's *Cleopatra* (Oram et al. 542). On Daniel's 'Senecan tragedies,' see Hulse 12. On Daniel's *Civil Wars* as modelled on Lucan's *Pharsalia*, see McCoy 103–26 and Quint 204–5. Two Elizabethan texts approximate the contours of the 'Ovidian' *cursus*. First, in *The Scholemaster*, Ascham describes 'Poeticum' according to genre, and he lists four: 'Comicum,' 'Tragicum,' 'Epicum,' and 'Melicum' (comedy, tragedy, epic, and lyric, represented for him by Terence, Seneca, Virgil, and Horace [rpt. in G.G. Smith, ed. 1:23]). Second, in *Virgidemiae*, Hall writes that the Virgilian poet can prepare for '*Arma Virum*' not merely through pastoral ('The sheepe-cote'), but also through amatory poetry ('in Venus Chamber train'd' [VI.268–77]). Other writers varied the pattern, but the topic needs further research. See, e.g., *The choise of valentines*, in which Nashe tells Lord Strange that he will move from 'a wanton Elegie' to 'better lynes' (dedicatory poem 4, 14), and specifically from 'Ovids wanton Muse' to 'Apollo's ... purifide word's [*sic*], and hallowed verse' (concluding poem 4, 2–10). This latter phrasing suggests a *meta* from Ovidian elegy to epic, divine poetry, and/or encomium. Even though Nashe appears to have his eye on *Amores* III.xv, he does not mention tragedy; none the less, he is careful to call his poem a 'plaie' (316). On Nashe's 'theatre' here, see Crewe, *Unredeemed Rhetoric* 49. Crewe sees Nashe 'stag[ing]' a 'shift' from

'pastoral' to the 'city' (48); if so, we can witness another Elizabethan who overwrites the Virgilian career pattern with an Ovidian one (Crewe observes that 'generic uncertainties are never resolved' [53]).

40 I am indebted to David Riggs for this point (personal communication, April 1994).

41 Unlike Marlowe, Daniel was not a counter-national poet, but, as Helgerson says, a 'laureate.' See also *Forms of Nationhood*, esp. 59–62.

42 In *The Elizabethan Prodigals*, Helgerson writes chapters on Gascoigne, Lyly, Greene, Lodge, and Sidney; again, he mentions Ovid only in passing (31, 38, 61, 76, 97, 107). In both of his first two books, as in *Forms of Nationhood* (1, 197, 199–200, 204, 242, 243), Helgerson lets Marlowe slip through the classification crack. Perhaps this is so because Marlowe does not fit the classification; he is not a prodigal, an amateur, a professional, a laureate, or a patriotic writer of nationhood.

43 Swinburne was the first to see the need to discriminate carefully between Marlowe and the University Wits (7, 16, 17).

44 The closest Marlowe comes to repentance is in *Doctor Faustus*, but this representation requires special analysis, and accordingly I defer it until chapter 9. For now, I note simply that Marlowe's third-person representation of Faustus's cry for repentance does not resemble the representations that Helgerson finds in the amateurs. Moreover, Helgerson appears to misunderstand Ovidian repentance. While Ovid does repent (see *Tristia* II.313–16, V.5–10; *Ex Ponto* I.i.59–60), he repents only of his 'carmen et error' – that is, of his penning of the *Ars amatoria*, not of poetry in general, nor even of his other poetry. What is astonishing about Ovid is that, unlike the Elizabethan amateurs, he writes until the very end of his life – at the ripe old age of fifty-nine or sixty. In other words, he writes as long as Virgil and Horace, or Spenser, Jonson, and Milton.

Chapter 3: Career Rivalry, Counter-Nationhood, and Philomela in 'The Passionate Shepherd to His Love'

1 Bakeless 2: 149–50. The Walton quotation comes from *The Compleat Angler* (1653, 1655), qtd. by Thomas Warton in his 1781 'History of English Poetry,' rpt. in MacLure, ed., *Marlowe* 60. Swinburne calls the poem '[o]ne of the most faultless lyrics ... in the whole range of descriptive and fanciful poetry' (rpt. in MacLure 183). Forsythe observes that 'The Passionate Shepherd' has 'exercised ... upon English poetry an influence ... which is equalled by that of few poems' (742). And MacLure identifies the poem as 'the most popular of all Elizabethan lyrics' (ed., *Poems* xxxvii).

2 We possess little information on the circumstances of composition and publication of 'The Passionate Shepherd.' In 1599, *The Passionate Pilgrim* printed four stanzas by an anonymous poet; then, in 1600, *England's Helicon* printed the longer version, attributed it to Marlowe, and added replies by Ralegh ('The Nymph's Reply') and an anonymous poet ('Another of the Same Nature, Made Since'). On the MS history and dating, see Bowers, ed. 2: 519–33; and Woods, 'Transmission.' The accepted composition date remains 1588; see Forsythe 701 and Bruster 62. Critics agree with Forsythe that the 'ultimate source' of the poem is Theocritus's Idyll XI on Polyphemus's wooing of Galatea (694), but that the 'immediate classical source' (695) is Ovid's version of the myth in the *Metamorphoses* (XIII.789–897). See also Sternfeld and Chan 180, 183. Gill cites Theocritus but overlooks Ovid (ed., *Complete Works* 1: 212). Bakeless (2: 157) and Gill (ed., *Complete Works* 1: 212) cite Virgil's Eclogue II. Among Renaissance sources, I single out Spenser (Forsythe 696), whom I discuss later. On Marlowe's use of the poem in his plays, see Forsythe, who finds 'fourteen passages ... in which "The Passionate Shepherd" is suggested, in material, in purpose and, at times, in metre' (701), with four of these in *Tamburlaine* being 'advance hints' (697–9) and the rest 'echoes' (699–701). See also D. Henderson 120–66. For a detailed list of imitations of Marlowe, see Forsythe 702–42; but see also Sternfeld 175–82. On the poem as a 'cosmopolitan sort of pastoral,' see Heninger 69. On 'Marlowe's Epicureanism,' see H. Levin 70. Finally, on the 'political aspects,' see Bruster 50.

3 Cf. Bruster, who finds Ovid's myth, which ends when Polyphemus crushes his rival, Acis, as a forerunner to the 'violence' in the 'Renaissance treatment of the invitation/denial scenario' (50–1).

4 See Mack 35–40. On the politics in the Virgilian section of the *Metamorphoses*, see Galinsky 210–61. In approaching Ovid's subversion, Galinsky is more cautious than most critics, who usually see Ovid carrying out a 'campaign of psychological warfare – for it was nothing less – against Augustus' (Kenney, introduction to '*Tristia*,' trans. Melville xix). On the Polyphemus–Galatea myth in its political context, see Galinsky 230–3. Kenney calls the myth 'burlesque of a high poetic order,' and he cites it as an 'example' and 'the strongest possible testimony to Ovid's importance ... as mediator between the old world and the new' ('Ovid' 2: 437). Farrell relies on Bakhtin to see the myth as a dialogic 'crossroads of several distinct poetic traditions – primarily the genres of pastoral, erotic elegy, and heroic epos' ('Dialogue of Genres' 240).

5 On the 'overlap' of 'homosexual and heterosexual desire' in the *Idylls*, see Burton 84 (on the overlap in Idyll VI, see 85); on patronage, see Burton 125–49; and on 'Theocritus highlight[ing] ... gender and gender relations in his urban mimes that approach royal patrons,' see Burton 126.

6 Servius identifies the homoerotic singer Corydon with Virgil himself (Rieu, trans. 129–30). In his 1589 translation, Fleming says 'by Corydon is meant Virgill' (sig. D2). Kenney remarks that 'as early as the first century A.D. we find it taken for granted that Corydon in *Eclogue* 2 was Virgil himself,' adding that 'the poem ... reflects in an immediate way the poet's own experience of thwarted love' ('Elegiac Sensibility' 44).

7 On Eclogue II, see Putnam 82–119; Du Quesnay, 'From Polyphemus to Corydon'; and Clausen 61–85. On Eclogue VII, see Leach 196–201; Fantazzi and Querbach; and Clausen 210–32. Du Quesnay emphasizes that, whereas in both of his idylls Theocritus depicts a male singing about a female, Virgil depicts a male singing about a male (52–3).

8 Ralegh was the first to have found Ovid in 'The Passionate Shepherd'; but Donne was the second. See Low, who sees 'The Bait' responding to 'an undercurrent of Ovidian sexuality' in Marlowe (8); and Cunnar, who sees Donne in line 2 alluding to 'the opening lines of *Amores* 2.11' in order to 'undermine ... Marlowe's smooth pastoralism' (87). On the 'mannerist' context of all three 'pastoral' poems, see Mirollo 160–78: 'poems in the mannerist mode ... insist that ... art ... is first of all art' (178).

9 On the origins of the *Aprill* trope in Theocritus and Marot, see the *Variorum Edition* 7: 279. On the origin of the *June* trope in Virgil, see the *Variorum Edition* 7: 311. Critics usually link these two tropes (*Variorum Edition* 7: 279), but neglect the ones in *August* and *December*. Recently, Cain supplies no glosses (Oram et al.); but Brooks-Davies glosses *Aprill* with both Theocritus and *June* (67).

10 And because of Marlowe, we can add his imitators: Ralegh, 'The Nymph's Reply' 7; Anonymous, 'Another of the Same Nature, Made Since' 9–12; and Donne, 'The Bait,' who totally absorbs the water metaphor. In his edition of Marlowe's poems, Orgel reprints all three imitations, together with a mid-seventeenth-century imitation, by J. Paulin, which does not include the water trope. On Spenser's waterfall trope, see Knapp 90 and 284, n. 59; but esp. Hollander, *Melodious Guile* 173–6. Like the *Variorum* editors, Hollander calls Spenser's trope 'a kind of colophon or signature to be acknowledged' (176), and he supplies an extended list of imitations, to which he appends Drayton, Browne, and George Wither. In a note on these three, he adds, with hesitation: 'We may even consider, I think, Marlowe's lines from "The Passionate Shepherd to His Love" ... as another instance' (252, n. 16).

11 Among the imitations of Marlowe reprinted in Orgel's edition, the following include the avian with the water trope: Ralegh, 'The Nymph's Reply' 6–7; and Anonymous, 'Another of the Same Nature' 9–22. Neither of these, however, reproduces the precise trope of the birds responding to the waterfall.

12 Heninger notes that Ralegh's Nymph 'abruptly recalls the shocking tragedy of

Philomela' (66), adding: 'The pastoralist, of all poets, is most painfully aware of reality; and pricked by this thorn, like Philomela, he therefore sings most sweetly' (70). On Philomela, pastoral, and the preparation for epic, see Cheney, *Spenser's Famous Flight* 77–110, esp. 82–3, 86. D.L. Miller, 'Death of the Modern,' reads the nightingale into the 'bird' whose neck Marlowe 'wring[s]' in *Hero and Leander* (II.289–90), and he quotes Ralegh's nightingale line from 'The Nymph's Reply' (775).

13 See also Martial, Epigram I.53.10; Sannazaro, *Arcadia*, Eclogue 1.22–4; and Ronsard, 'Elegie,' in *Les Poemes*, Book 2 (15), in *Oeuvres complètes* vol. 17.

14 Aristophanes, *Birds*, ed. Hadas, trans. Webb 255. On Ovid's Philomela, see Barkan, *Gods Made Flesh* 59–63: 'The tale ... is based upon a tension between the order posited by a rigid system of familial and social ties and the disorder wrought by the passions of the individual' (59). Barkan later emphasizes the discursive dimension of Ovid's myth (247), seeing Philomela in *Titus Andronicus* as 'a metonym for the whole history of the book in which Shakespeare found her story' (247; see 243–8). On Philomela and fame, see Cheney, *Spenser's Famous Flight* 26, 83–5. On vocational, gender, and political dimensions of the myth, see Lamb 194–228; and Hinson.

15 On Spenser's influence on Ralegh's poetry after the publication of the *Calender*, see the Latham ed. xxxiii. In his second *Commendatory Verse* to the 1590 *Faerie Queene*, Ralegh also employs the nightingale myth (2: 1–2).

16 For an early comment on the remarkable influence of the Marlowe lines on 'generations ... [of] men's hearts,' see MacLure, ed., *Marlowe* 141.

17 On the importance of depth in Spenser's water imagery, see Comito, 'Fountains' and 'Wells.'

18 Leiter reads Marlowe's 'falls' metaphorically (446). And Heninger (68) notes Ralegh's punning response to Marlowe's 'falls': 'fancy's spring' is 'sorrow's fall' ('Nymph's Reply' 11).

19 On the biographical relation between Marlowe and Ralegh, see Nicholl 45, and passim. Belsey, 'Desire's Excess,' reminds us that Ralegh wrote a poem called 'Would I were chang'd into that golden showre' (99, n. 9, citing the Latham ed. 81–2). Belsey also discusses the Danae 'tradition of representing the beautiful captive as a courtesan,' which *Edward II* 'evokes' at III.i.266–8 (88).

20 Marcus, *Politics of Mirth*; on Bakhtin, see 7; on the 'Roman Floralia' 151–2, 159, and 170. On the carnivalesque in Renaissance drama, see Bristol; and Helgerson, *Forms of Nationhood* 215–28.

21 See Heninger: Shakespeare sang Marlowe's song 'to the Queen's taste' (63). Bruster cites both Greene and Peele, who imitate Marlowe and 'see the invitation framed in terms bearing a specific relationship with Elizabethan imperialism and oriental fantasy' (62).

22 Cain compares the spelling with the more familiar 'gall' at *FQ* IV.x.1 (Oram et

al. 62). Brooks-Davies develops this idea in terms applicable to Marlowe: the emblem 'invite[s] the reader to interpret *March* as a warning against marriage to Alençon' (55; see 30). On the background of this marriage, see McLane 13–26; and Bednarz. Marlowe mentions Alençon twice in *The Massacre at Paris* (xiv.65, xxii.105).

23 Since Alençon had died in 1584 – four years before the conventional dating for 'The Passionate Shepherd' – we confront a curious circumstance, and I see three potential explanations: (1) we need to abandon the lead I take from Heninger (there is no French marriage connection here); (2) we need to push the dating of the poem back to the Cambridge years, perhaps to around 1584–5; or (3) we need to link Marlowe's strategy with the one I introduce in my next chapter, on *Dido*, which *other* critics have recurrently linked with the Alençon marriage: Marlowe is not targeting Alençon so much as those writers opposing the French marriage, like Spenser. Of these three explanations, the last seems the most plausible, but I remain intrigued with the second, esp. since critics typically date Marlowe's original composition of *Dido* around 1585 – that is to say, also *after* Alençon's death. In another context, P. Roberts remarks that as late as 1592 Marlowe was cautiously evoking Alençon before the gaze of Elizabeth (434–5).

24 On Marlowe's self-repetition in *Dido* (esp. I.i.1), see Forsythe 700–1. On *Tamburlaine*, see Bruster 58–60. On *The Jew of Malta* (IV.ii.93), see Gill, ed., *Complete Works* 1: 212. On *Edward II* (esp. I.i.1–5), see H. Levin 93.

25 See Braudy 134–43 (on Ovid) and 167 (on Augustine). In *Spenser's Famous Flight*, I emphasize Spenser's attempt to fuse Virgilian poetic fame with Augustinian glory. On 'Marlowe's ... "post-Christian" vision,' see Snow 78.

26 See Neuse 427 on Lucretian materialism and Ovidian *amor*. For Lucretian moments in the *Amores*, and Marlowe's translation, see *Ovid's Elegies* I.xv.23–4, III.iii.1, 23–5, III.viii.17–20, 35–8.

27 Berger, *Second World, Green World* 11. Berger distinguishes between the 'second world' and what he calls the 'green world,' which is the poem or artefact using 'the second world *as* a fiction' (13–14). In what looks to be a modern replay of the debate between Ralegh and Marlowe, Berger responds to N. Frye, who mistakenly 'refers to the green world *as* a second world' (13). Berger argues that 'it is ... the dynamic and shimmering interplay between these two possibilities that makes the embodiments of Renaissance imagination so fascinating' (14). The dialogue between Ralegh and Marlowe bears his thesis out.

28 On Ralegh's interest in 'inwardness,' see Maus 4, 7–8.

29 For the Elizabethan pun on posies/poesies, see Fowler, 'Spenser's *Prothalamion*' 65, n. 21.

30 On the difference between masculine 'achievement' and feminine 'affiliation,' an 'ethic of justice' and an 'ethic of care,' and the corresponding images,

'hierarchy' and 'web,' see esp. Gilligan 62–3. Heninger alertly discovers the Nymph's reliance on (masculine) abstractions – 'such weighty concepts as "truth," "time," "care," "folly," and "reason,"' which 'identify her as a [male] philosopher' (68).

31 Bakeless supports the citation (2: 158). Renwick glosses the *Januarye* passage with Eclogue II (rpt. in *Variorum Edition* 7: 250).

32 On E.K. as Spenser, see Starnes; Schleiner; and Waldman. On the homoeroticism of Spenser and Harvey here, see J. Goldberg, 'Colin to Hobbinol.'

33 On Marlowe's homoeroticism in his plays, see esp. J. Goldberg, *Sodometries* 105–43.

Part II: Sceptres and High Buskins: Tragedy

1 Harvey mentions the *Nine Comedies* (Letter III in G.G. Smith, ed. 1: 115). Oruch remarks that it is 'possible that few of the "lost" works ever existed except as ideas,' adding: 'The range is almost that of Spenser's age with the most notable omissions being tragedy and prose fiction. The most surprising item is the nine comedies, for no drama by Spenser exists' (738). In *Spenser's Famous Flight*, I suggest that Spenser relocates dramatic tragedy within the lyric complaint (258, n. 18).

2 Def. A.7 in the *OED* reads: 'Pertaining to the state or body politic.' The first instance given is from Milton in 1641, but this is not the first time we have occasion to move an *OED* date back a bit.

3 I say 'appears' because, as we shall see, Marlowe's genius is to fuse Machiavelli with Ovid.

4 According to Sandys, however, 'some have conjectred that Seneca's Medea belongeth to Ovid' (sig. b4ʳ).

5 But see Currie's 'Ovid and the Roman Stage': 'Whatever the truth about [the stage history of] his "Medea", the fact of its composition alone argues that Ovid had some interest in drama' (2704). Periodically, Currie isolates elements that would have appealed to Ovid in previous drama: 'elements of danger, bloodshed, or suffering' (2709); 'didacticism consonant with *gravitas*' (2710); certain 'metrical effects' (2712); the 'aesthetic level' – a 'regular preoccupation with fine details of language and thought and with the exploration of ideas for their own sakes' (2720); a 'rationalising spirit' (2722); a 'delight … in sadism' and the evasion of 'moral concerns' (2724); and 'violent plots, … flamboyant characterisation, and … forceful rhetoric' (2728). See also Frank 562–4; and Tarrant.

6 Fränkel says that the phrase '*cura nostra tragoedia crevit* means that a tragedy had begun to take shape … Furthermore, the future participle in line 4,

ausurus grandia, indicates that the drama was no more than a project when Amor interfered with Ovid's work on it' (195, n. 3).

7 Currie explains Ovid's denial of writing for the stage in this way: 'perhaps the poet is implying that the theatrical representations of his work at Rome (with dance and music) have taken place without his collaboration and prior knowledge or permission, the "Medea" belonging to a quite separate category. Or maybe Ovid has the "Medea" in mind as well in the sense that it was possibly written by him to be read (a "closet drama") and not to be produced. And maybe it always had a literary existence only ... Who knows?' (2702–3; for similar uncertainty, see Tarrant 260). Clearly, we are on our own here.

8 The Loeb editor explains: 'The words do not appear in our texts of Virgil,' but one critic 'suggests that they originally came in the description of the Sibyl in *Aen.* 6.45 *seq.*' (2: 542–3, n. 2).

9 Cf. Dante, whose Virgil calls the *Aeneid* 'l'alta mia tragedia' (*Inferno* XX.113). On the *Aeneid* and tragedy, see Hardie, *Epic Successors of Virgil* 23, 36, 68, 71–3.

10 See Currie: 'The poet himself announces the play [*Medea*] at Am. 3.1.29: "*nunc habeam per te, Romana Tragoedia, nomen*"' (2703).

11 Tarrant adds that 'Seneca's poetic style is heavily indebted to Virgil, Horace, and above all Ovid' (261): Ovid 'provided Seneca with models not only of diction and expression but also of characterization and thematic ideas' (262); 'Seneca's Clytemnestra in *Agamemnon*, for example, is clearly based in part on a passage in the *Ars amatoria*, and his Phaedra on Ovid's sketch of that character in the *Heroides*' (262). After citing a third example, Seneca's debt in *Thyestes* to Ovid's myth of Philomela in the *Metamorphoses*, Tarrant remarks: 'Seneca's originality as a poet and dramatist can only be grasped in an Ovidian context' (263; see 262–3). Tarrant cheerfully concludes: 'I could gladly part with the *Hercules Oetaeus* ... in return for Ovid's *Medea*' (263).

12 The Heywood excerpts below come from Gilbert 552–64.

13 The three passages on tragedy and the stage come, respectively, from the *Remedia amoris* 375; the *Ars amatoria* III.405–6; and the *Ars* III.411 (see Gilbert 554–5).

14 In the remainder of his discourse on tragedy, Heywood quotes Ovid a number of times (see Gilbert 556, 557 [twice], 558, 562). Heywood appears to consider Ovid's *Ibis* a tragedy; at the least, he includes it under a 'tragic' rubric, within the mode of tragedy.

Chapter 4: *Dido, Queen of Carthage* and the Coining of '"Eliza"'

1 On 'topical reading,' see Marcus, *Puzzling Shakespeare*, who sees 'localization'

as 'a deliberate strategy' (68), emphasizing the Elizabethan 'passion for topical decoding' (69). However, Marcus confines her principle to three political contexts: 'Elizabeth,' 'James,' 'London' (chapter titles). Brooks-Davies reports that '"Dido" was a familiar cult name for Elizabeth' (172).

2 In the *Republic*, Plato had set the cast for Western tragedy as a literary form: 'there is one kind of poetry and taletelling which works wholly through imitation, ... tragedy and comedy, and another which employs the recital of the poet himself, best exemplified, I presume, in the dithyramb, and there is again that which employs both, in epic poetry' (III.394c). Perhaps Marlowe found a precedent for staging his own authoring of tragedy in the *Octavia*, where Seneca (we now think a pseudo-Seneca) presents the character 'Seneca' within the context of the Neronian Empire.

3 On the play as ''prentice work' see Bakeless 2: 41. On *Dido* in Marlowe's career, see Leech, *Christopher Marlowe* 26, 35, 41. On *Dido* as 'the only play in which Marlowe has made sexual love the real centre,' see Brooke, ed., *Life ... and 'Dido'* 123. On love and honour, see Rogers; and Pinciss 111–24. On destructive love, see Godshalk 38–58; and Stilling. On destiny and empire, see Brandt, *Christopher Marlowe* 15–49; and Bartels 29–52. On race and nation, see Hendricks. On the limits of human power, see Summers, *Christopher Marlowe* 39–40; and on the 'fatal danger of divine love,' see Kelsall 34. See also H. Levin on 'the mood of enticement that predominates' (17); Gibbons, on 'the inner complexities of the sublime and the heroic' (46); Cutts, *Left Hand of God*, on Marlowe's critique of religion and heroism (1–28); Cole, on love, violence, and suffering (*Suffering and Evil* 75–86); and W.C. Turner on 'the triviality of the gods' and 'the folly of unreasonable passion' (5). These themes say differently what Proser identifies as Marlowe's 'central plot concern': 'the conflict between Dido's imperious passion for Aeneas and the Trojan's divinely appointed obligations and ambitions' ('Dramatic Style' 86). On Marlowe's 'rhetoric,' see Rousseau. On Marlowe and Virgil, see Gill, 'Marlowe's Virgil'; and R.A. Martin, 'Fate, Seneca.' On Marlowe's *Dido* and the Dido tradition, see D.C. Allen; and Roberts-Baytop 98–103. On the medieval Dido, see Rudd, 'Chaucer and Virgil'; and Desmond. On Virgil's Dido, see Hexter; and J. Watkins.

4 Leech, *Christopher Marlowe* 41. The twin poles of this question are represented by Steane, who sees the play as a high tragedy along Virgilian lines 'glorying in romantic love' (29); and Leech himself, who sees the play as a comedy displaying a good deal of 'humor' (40).

5 I am not heedless of *Dido*'s deep textual problems. First, we are ignorant about the date of composition; arguments range from 1581 to 1592, with most scholars settling on 1585–6 (see Gill, ed., *Complete Works* 1: 115, 120). Second, we do not know whether the play is of Marlowe's authorship or whether Nashe collabo-

rated (1594 title page); most scholars believe that Marlowe wrote the play and that Nashe functioned as an editor (Bowers, ed. 1: 3–4). Third, we do not know whether the play underwent revision, and, if it did, whether Marlowe, Nashe, or someone else made the changes; critics have reached no real consensus, although revision seems likely (see Brooke, ed., *Life ... and 'Dido'* 387–9; and M.E. Smith 163–5). Finally, we cannot be certain about the stage history, although scholars abide by the title page, believing that Marlowe originally wrote for boy actors performing before Elizabeth (Oliver xxx–xxxiii).

6 The closest anyone has come is D. Henderson 165, n. 33, published after the present study was completed.

7 In the *Dedicatory Epistle* to the volume titled *AMORETTI and Epithalamion*, the publisher, William Ponsonby, states that Spenser wrote his two marriage poems in 'Ireland.' From Ponsonby's information, we believe that Spenser sent his manuscript to England in September 1594 – several months after the publication of *Dido*. *Epithalamion* was not entered in the Stationers' Register until the next autumn, 19 November 1594; and it was not published until the next year (1595; title page). On this textual history, see Oram et al. 585, 595–6, and 598.

8 On 'humour,' see Kocher, *Christopher Marlowe* 268–70. Gill finds Marlowe converting 'tragedy into comedy' when he 'dispatches' Dido, Iarbus, and Anna 'in fifteen lines' ('Marlowe's Virgil' 146).

9 Critics who find the play using Dido's relation with her suitors to evoke Elizabeth's relation with her suitors include Gibbons 29; Godshalk 57; and Roberts-Baytop 102. The Duc Alençon had left England in 1581 and had died in 1584. I return to this topic.

10 See Weil 17; Brooke, ed., *Life ... and 'Dido*,' who glosses twenty-two passages with citations from Ovid; Bono, *Literary Transvaluation* 136; and J. Bate, who summarizes: '*Dido* contaminates Virgil with Ovid' (39).

11 On Ovid's Dido and Virgil's Dido, see Jacobson, esp. 93; Desmond 33–45; and Healy 37–43. R.A. Martin anticipates my argument, but he permits us to include Seneca ('Fate, Seneca'). Martin brings the three Roman authors into a clear equation, but my 'Ovidian' career context leads me to make three alterations. First, Marlowe's diachronic literary base here is not Seneca (the Seneca who uses Ovid to rewrite Virgil), but Ovid (the Ovid who mediates Virgil and Seneca). Second, Marlowe relies on this diachronic literary equation not as an end in itself, but as a means for transacting a goal that is finally synchronic in its workings. And, third, the synchronic context includes both the political and the literary; if I am reading Marlowe's metatheatre aright, he subsumes the political under the literary. Virgil and Augustus are dead; England's Virgil and England's 'queen' are not.

12 See Gibbons 29; and Archer, who sees Marlowe's plays as 'an implicit challenge to Elizabeth's politics of heterosexual courtship,' quoting the '"Eliza"' passage (88). Hendricks argues that Marlowe emerges as a 'dependent' of '"English-ness"' – especially of England's 'glorious "past"' (166) – and she sees Marlowe joining Spenser in this patriotic project (185). I am indebted to the English Honors Thesis of Jessica K. Nassau: 'Chastity, Desire, and Imperialism: The Cult of Elizabeth and Marlowe's *Dido, Queen of Carthage*' (University Park: Pennsylvania State University, 1995).

13 McLane follows Parmenter to popularize the identification of 'Elizabeth as Dido' (chapter title; 47–60). This argument has proved controversial, but it has been accepted by W.J. Kennedy 102; Bono, 'Dido' 218; Brooks-Davies 172–3; and, to an extent, Montrose, '"The perfecte paterne"' 50–1.

14 Recall Brooke on Marlowe's and Spenser's 'Eliza' line. But Brooke also glosses Marlowe's I.i.191–2 – a translation of Virgil's 'quam te memorem virgo' and 'o dea certe – with the following gloss: these lines 'served Spenser as concluding emblem for the April eclogue of the *Shepherds' Calendar* [sic]' (ed., *Life … and 'Dido'* 141). Similarly, in Spenser studies McLane follows McKerrow in finding Elizabethan precedent for the link between Dido, Elissa, and Eliza (52), but he adds 'Marlowe's *Tragedy of Dido*' (53).

15 See also Poirier 82; Gill, 'Marlowe's Virgil' 150; and Bush, 'Marlowe and Spenser.'

16 Advertisements for Spenser's Virgilian epic had begun in the *Calender*, and they had continued in the 1580 Spenser–Harvey letters (Letter III in G.G. Smith, ed. 1: 100; Letter IV in Smith 1: 115–16). Moreover, in 1588 Fraunce quotes *FQ* II.iv.35 in his *Arcadian Rhetorike*, and it is likely that the manuscript was circulating earlier – perhaps when Marlowe was composing *Dido*. As Hamilton observes, Marlowe beat Fraunce to the punch with his 1587–8 *Tamburlaine* (*FQ*, ed. x). It is not improbable that Marlowe had access to Spenser's manuscript when he (first) composed *Dido*.

17 Boas (*Christopher Marlowe* 52–3) and Gibbons (36) cite Chambers's stage division; and Oliver adds to it (xxx–xxxi). R.A. Martin refers to the play's 'pastoral setting' ('Fate, Seneca' 54).

18 On the piscatorial eclogue, see Marinelli, who traces it from Theocritus's Idyll XXI to Sannazaro's *Piscatorial Eclogues* to Fletcher's *Piscatorie Eclogs* (29–30). Marinelli is discussing Donne's imitation of Marlowe's 'Passionate Shepherd' in 'The Bait,' in which 'Donne cunningly transfers the setting from a pastoral to a piscatorial setting' (29; see also Low; and Cunnar). According to Bruster, 'the piscatorial tradition is already embedded in the invitational process of Marlowe's lyric' (70, n. 10). Like *Dido*, 'The Passionate Shepherd' broods over the Spenserian paradigm of Virgilian pastoral and epic but mediates that paradigm

through the Ovidian *cursus* of amatory poetry, tragedy, and epic. On Drayton's piscatorial eclogues, see Ettin 2. On Fletcher's, see Piepho; and Bouchard.

19 On Ovid's *Halieutica*, see Owen, 'Notes' 267–71. In *Heroides* VII, Ovid has Dido imitate the Virgilian lines in question (89–90).

20 Marlowe's metaphors are of class, but Gibbons speculates that 'when Aeneas first enters he is dressed "like a Fisher swaine"' (34).

21 See J. Goldberg, *Sodometries*, for some good thoughts on 'the construction of gender in its relationship to theater and to the imperial project' in *Dido* (137).

22 Cf. D. Goldberg, who sees Marlowe in *Dido* and the *Tamburlaine* plays 'undermin[ing] ... the concept of special providence' (570); on *Dido* as a 'satire of providentialism,' see 578–81.

23 See Fairclough (Loeb): 'thy children's *fates* abide *unmoved*'; Day Lewis: 'Your people's *destiny* is *unaltered*'; Knight: 'You have your people's *destiny still*'; and Fitzgerald: 'Your children's *destiny* / has not been *changed*.'

24 Marlowe's strategy anticipates what Bakhtin calls 'dialogism,' in which a text's single utterance constructs a dialogue between two competing voices of authority (*Dialogic Imagination* 7, 272–3, 279).

25 Marlowe's word 'billows' is a favourite of Spenser's, and Marlowe's phrase 'heave him up to heaven' is as well: 'heaved up on high' (*FQ* I.viii.14; repeated with variations eight times). Cf. also Marlowe's 'Proteus, raising hills of floods on high' (*Dido* I.i.76) and Spenser's 'her bowre / Is built of hollow billowes heaped hye' (*FQ* III.iv.43), which also deals with 'Proteus' (37).

26 On this reading of *Januarye*, see Cheney, *Spenser's Famous Flight* 90–2. On the summarizing role of Iarbas's prayer, see Brandt, *Christopher Marlowe* 48–9.

27 Cf. Archer: 'That the echo of the name [Eliza] is "hideous" here may signal the play's subtle critique of Elizabeth's courtly reign' (88).

Chapter 5: 'Thondring words of threate': Spenser in *Tamburlaine, Parts 1 and 2*

1 On authorship, see J.S. Cunningham 6–9; on staging in 1587 and print in 1590 (Stationers' Register, 14 August 1590), see 20–31; on the texts, see 85–94. Questions of authorship, dating, and text are not in serious dispute here; see Bevington and Rasmussen, eds., *Christopher Marlowe* ix–x, xxvi; they observe that 'the Latinate act and scene headings along with the unusually formal conclusion of Part I ... suggest a manuscript prepared in the study rather than the playhouse' (xxvi).

2 See *Thyestes* 1–121. J.S. Cunningham glosses 'triple moat' with *Aeneid* VI.548–51 (253), and 'Fatal Sisters' with earlier references to *Tamburlaine*; one of them, *1 Tamb* I.ii.159–60 (his ed.), he glosses with 'Ovid, *Metam.*, vii.409ff., or iv.450–1' (130).

3 Schoeneich (28–9) sees Marlowe at *2 Tamb* V.iii.229–35 – 'Clymene's brainsicke son' – imitating *FQ* III.xi.38: 'The sonne of Climene ... / ... bold to guide the charet of the Sunne.'

4 Harper 7. Similarly, in his gloss on 'jigging,' J.S. Cunningham finds Marlowe referring only to conventions of the Elizabethan stage (113). On 'the kinds of drama' to which Marlowe refers, see Leech, *Christopher Marlowe* 42–67.

5 See Bakeless 1: 208. Benston refers to the Virgilian origins of Marlowe's prologue, but he neglects the Spenserian origin: Marlowe puts 'the major premises of contemporary "high" drama into doubt by courting pious formal assumptions,' one of which is that 'the Virgilian progression from pastoral to epic will place the hero in a romantic context of fulfilled national mission' (215).

6 On word and sword, see Reiss 105–9; and Thurn, 'Sights' 6–7 and n. 7. H. Levin glosses Marlowe's 'threatening' with a Gascoigne phrase from *The Steele Glas*: 'In rymeless verse, which thundreth mighty threates' (qtd. in *The Overreacher* 11).

7 Cf. Weil on Marlowe's 'ironic [Erasmian] style' (2, 9, passim): 'Marlowe's tragic glass is ... enigmatic' (106). She does not link this glass with Spenser, but see 185, n. 46.

8 See also III.Pr.5, ii.18–21; K. Williams xvii; and Grabes.

9 Marlowe's poetic is notorious for being unjudgmental. As Hulse puts it: 'There is no way to pin down a single ... meaning, either orthodox or heretical' (117). See also Altman 7; and Bartels 18–23. The first to note this poetic was Chapman, in his 'continuation' of *Hero and Leander*: 'New light gives new directions, ... / That being enjoyed ask judgement' (III.1, 9, in the Orgel ed.). Marlowe may have learned this technique from Ovid and Lucan. On Ovid's unjudgmental poetics, see Keach, *Elizabethan Erotic Narratives* xvi; on Lucan's, see Toohey 178, 184.

10 Bloom helps me see how Tamburlaine qualifies as a portrait of the ephebe, the young poet as literary rival: 'For every poet begins ... by rebelling ... against the consciousness of death's necessity ... The ... ephebe ... is already the anti-natural or antithetical man, and from his start as a poet he quests for an impossible object, as his precursor quested before him' (*Anxiety of Influence* 10). See Bloom also on 'the greatest of all human illusions, the vision of immortality' (9).

11 Hunter, 'Beginnings' 46. See also Barber, *Creating Elizabethan Tragedy* 61; and McAlindon, *English Tragedy* 85–6. Thurn helps explain how Marlowe could identify with a tragic protagonist who ultimately succumbs to death ('Sights' 4–6). Both R. Levin ('Contemporary Perception') and Berek emphasize that contemporary references and allusions to *Tamburlaine* reveal that Marlowe did not condemn his hero. Cf. Howe.

12 R. Levin notes that Greene and Harvey 'equat[e] ... Marlowe with the play-
wright's protagonist' ('Contemporary Perception' 65). Nicholl denies that
Harvey targets Marlowe here (60-4); but Harvey's criticism of Marlowe as
Tamburlaine is part of the historical record. For instance, Harvey refers to
'Marlowes bravados' and calls atheism 'no Religion, but precise Marlowisme'
(qtd. in Moore 341). For two astute analyses of Marlowe as Tamburlaine, see
Kuriyama 1–52; and Proser, 'Art of Destruction.'

13 Battenhouse 239. See R. Levin's overview of the 'ironic' critics ('Contemporary
Perception,' esp. 51 and 66–7, n. 1); they include Cole, *Suffering and Evil*
86–120; Cutts, *Left Hand of God* 29–107; Godshalk 102–68; and Masinton 14–55.

14 Greenblatt writes: 'All of the signals of the tragic are produced, but the play
stubbornly, radically, refuses to become a tragedy' (*Renaissance Self-Fashioning* 202). For versions of this third camp, see Hawkins 24; Schuman 33; Berek
56; Hardin 225; Birringer, 'Marlowe's Violent Stage' 231–2; Brandt,
Christopher Marlowe 69–80; Duane; and Sinfield, *Faultlines* 240.

15 Marlowe's strategy varies Virgil's dismembering of himself in the *Eclogues*
through Tityrus and others (see Patterson, *Pastoral and Ideology* 28–40).
Hardie, *Epic Successors of Virgil*, sees Lucan employing this strategy for himself
in Book I of the *Pharsalia* (107–8), which Marlowe translated. Indeed, Marlowe
may have borrowed his description of Tamburlaine from Spenser (Schoeneich
70-1): Tamburlaine's 'stature tall' (*1 Tamb* II.i.7) echoes Spenser's golden man,
Disdayne, who is of 'stature tall' (*FQ* II.vii.41), as well as his effeminate man,
Ease, 'of stature tall' (II.xii.46). Tamburlaine's 'So large of limbs, his joints so
strongly knit' (*1 Tamb* II.i.9) echoes both Sansfoy, 'full large of limbe and
every joint / He was' (I.ii.12), and Maleger, 'Full large he was of limbe'
(II.xi.20); and Tamburlaine's eyes, 'his piercing instruments of sight' (*1 Tamb*
II.i.14), echo Una's description of her own eyes, 'Ye dreary instruments of
dolefull sight' (I.vii.22). The collage effect, plus the gender crossover, is
intriguing. On Marlowe's stature as 'tall,' see Nicholl 7.

16 In 'Compassing the Weighty Prize: The Rival Poetics of Spenser and Marlowe,'
a paper delivered before the Spenser Society of America (December 1994), I
asked why Marlowe would pursue Spenser so vociferously. I suggested that
Marlowe kept finding himself encoded in Spenser's allegory, disguised in
hypocrisy, citing Spenser's description of Archimago at *FQ* I.i.37.

17 Critics note other borrowings from the Orgoglio episode; see Schoeneich 20.

18 See J.S. Cunningham 145–6, citing Wills and adding Warren on Shakespeare.
The 'aspen-leaf' image is not in Ovid.

19 Neither Schoeneich nor Crawford notes a Marlovian borrowing from Spenser
here. And the following editions of Spenser lack a note: Maclean and Prescott;
Hamilton; Roche; Kellogg and Steele; and the *Variorum Edition*.

20 Schoeneich (84) cites *FQ* I.ii.33: 'Where Boreas doth blow full bitter bleake.'

21 Critics have long noted that Marlowe has his eye on this passage in *Doctor Faustus*, when Mephistopheles hands the dagger to Faustus, only to be checked by the Old Man (see chapter 9).

22 We should not simply universalize a passage like this, as Daiches does in finding 'symbols for the undefinable ambitions of the unfettered human imagination' (85). Marlowe's line is another instance of the typology of intertextuality. As J.S. Cunningham notes, 'here, Marlowe is close to Golding's translation of the story of Baucis and Philemon, who welcome Jove and Mercury to their cottage' in *Metamorphoses* VIII (20). This typology becomes doubly self-reflexive if Weil is correct that Marlowe uses the Ovidian allusion to suggest that 'the poet, like the hero, competes with God' (133).

23 On *translatio imperii*, see Kerrigan and Braden 5–7. On Marlowe and empire/imperialism in *Tamburlaine*, see Friedenreich, 'Fall of the Empire'; Mead; Bartels 53–81; and R. Wilson.

24 On marriage in sixteenth-century England, see Dubrow 1–41.

25 On Spenser's Neoplatonic 'mirrhor' (derived from Plato, *Phaedrus* 255d), see Ellrodt 32–4. On Neoplatonism in Tamburlaine's soliloquy, see M.J.B. Allen. On the 'neo-platonic element' in the *Tamburlaine* plays, see J.S. Cunningham 41–2.

26 On Baldwin's change of 'march' in line 187 to 'mask,' see 175–6; and J.S. Cunningham 202.

27 Hope argues that the soliloquy identifies 'sovereignty and beauty as the two supreme human aspirations' in which 'beauty has a power to subdue sovereignty' (51). He does not recall that the Arguments of Arms and Beauty – 'fierce warres and faithful loves' – are the twin topics that will 'moralize' Spenser's 'song' in *The Faerie Queene* (I.Pr.1). See also Benston on 'Beauty's essential antagonism to both heroic self-conception and its expression' (223); and Shepard's wonderful argument that 'Marlowe's play itself does not endorse the unilateral hegemony of men over women' (746). Spenser's program, esp. in *FQ* III, sees beauty and love as inspiration for heroic behaviour (iii.1–2).

28 Marlowe critics neglect fame, but see Burnett, 'Renaissance Concept of Honour.' On poetic fame and Christian glory in Spenser, see Cheney, *Spenser's Famous Flight* xi–xii, 14–15, 248–9, n. 7.

29 H. Levin reminds us that Clemen 'located Marlowe's "upward thrust" more concretely in his inclination toward such verbs as "mount," "climb," "soar," and "rise"' (22).

30 Cf. Burnett, 'Elizabethan Vagabond,' on Marlowe's reinvention of Tamburlaine as a 'vagabond' – particularly in his role as 'thief' (*1 Tamb* I.i.36). At II.v.49–54, Tamburlaine steals one of his most famous lines, spoken

originally by Meander (49): 'And ride in triumph through Persepolis' (54).
Schoeneich (78) allows us to see Marlowe *stealing* Spenser's description of theft
in order to describe Tamburlaine as a thief, comparing *1 Tamb* I.i.36, 'that
sturdy Scythian thief,' with *FQ* I.iii.17, 'a stout and sturdie thiefe.'

31 On Erycina, see Ovid, *Amores* II.x.11, III.ix.45, *Ars amatoria* II.420, *Met*
    V.363; and Baldwin, 'Genesis [I]' 158–62. On Ovid's use of double allusion in
    the Erycina trope (first to Virgil, and then to Catullus), see O'Hara. Marlowe's
    insertion of the Ovidian trope – which is itself a Virgilian and a Catullan trope
    – into his rivalry with Spenser is a rather complex instance of the typology of
    intertextuality.

32 *Hamlet* III.ii.275. I'm grateful to Professor Robert R. Edwards for reminding
    me of the *plume* as a poet's *quill* (personal communication, April 1994).

33 R. Levin, 'Identity of the Rival Poet'; Charney, 'Jessica's Turquoise Ring' and
    talks at the MLA Convention in New York, 1992, and the Third International
    Conference on Marlowe in Cambridge, England, 1993; Shapiro, *Rival Play-
    wrights*; and Cartelli.

Chapter 6: Machiavelli and the Play of Policy in *The Jew of Malta*

1 In the most recent account of Machiavellianism, Kahn does not discuss
   Marlowe in any detail (see 89), but she argues that the popular Elizabethan
   view of Machiavelli represented in the stage figure of the Machiavel was not an
   ignorant reading of the real politics of Machiavelli (esp. 87–92).

2 Conventionally, critics locate this shift in *The Jew of Malta*, and in the
   following way by Ellis-Fermor: this play is 'less passionate and less lyrical than
   its predecessors' (95–7). Later, Ellis-Fermor refers to 'that rich descriptive
   power which so *strangely* fell into abeyance in [the plays of policy]' (103;
   emphasis added). Unlike H. Morris, she does not attribute Marlowe's 'lyricism'
   to Spenser (or Ovid).

3 These issues correspond to well-known problems in *Jew of Malta* criticism: 'date
   and chronology'; 'genre'; 'theme'; and 'sources.' See Van Fossen xii–xxv;
   Bawcutt, ed. 1–37; and Craik vii–xviii. Craik is representative: 'The date of *The
   Jew of Malta* is uncertain,' although 'the play can be assigned with reasonable
   confidence to 1589 or 1590. The chronology of Marlowe's plays being controversial, *The Jew of Malta* cannot be given a certain place in it, but the play is
   known to be later than *Tamburlaine* and earlier than *Edward II*, and is usually
   placed before *Doctor Faustus*' (viii); 'This critical detachment, and the promi-
   nence of comedy throughout the play, do not prevent its being a "tragedy"'
   (xviii); 'Is ... ['the theme of the play'] Barabas's villainous career or is it universal
   machiavellism' (xi); and 'This violent story has no known source ... Marlowe has

drawn mainly on his imagination, supplemented by his casual reading in recent works of history and geography' (ix). Henslowe in his *Diary* 'records a total of thirty-six performances, mostly at the Rose theatre, and given by various companies, between February 1592 and June 1596' (Bawcutt, ed. 1).

4 Our textual source for the play is Heywood's 1633 edition, and we are not sure whether Heywood (or someone else) altered Marlowe's original (Van Fossen vii–xiv, xxvi–xxviii; Bawcutt, ed. 37–49; and Craik xiv–x). Critics once believed that Marlowe wrote only Acts I and II, but in his 1992 edition Craik welcomes the old argument of Maxwell: 'it is hard to see these early scenes as pointing forward to anything substantially different from what we actually have' (qtd. in Craik ix). Today, *The Jew* holds a high place in English Renaissance drama (Greenblatt, 'Marlowe, Marx'). Bloom calls Barabas 'Marlowe's grandest character' and *The Jew* 'certainly Marlowe's most vital and original play' (ed. 2). Bawcutt notes that *The Jew* affected contemporary audiences considerably between about 1590–1610 (ed. 2).

5 As H. Levin observes, Marlowe uses the word 'policy' thirteen times (61). Cf. Ellis-Fermor: the prologue 'introduces a new phase of Marlowe's work and is the brief epitome of a philosophy of life and statecraft that he was to consider and re-consider and upon which his next ... plays were to furnish forth comments' (88). Critics have focused on three prologue topics: Marlowe's deviation from the political philosophy of Machiavelli (see Ribner, 'Marlowe and Machiavelli'; Praz; Babb; Bawcutt; Minshull; and Scott); Barabas's deviation from the political philosophy of the 'Machevill' of the prologue (see esp. Cartelli 161–80); and what both Machevill and Barabas serve, the genre of the play: Eliot first used the label 'farce' (63), and most critics have followed suit. The results are three conclusions: in 'Machevill,' Marlowe invents his own stage figure, which neither is nor tries to be faithful to the real Machiavelli; in Barabas, Marlowe creates a Machiavellian villain who eventually gets out-Machiavelled by Ferneze, 'the master Machiavellian' (Cartelli 171; cf. McAdam 62–4); and in *The Jew* Marlowe creates a new genre, whether 'farce' or not. On how *The Jew* 'repeatedly suggests alternative forms of tragedy,' see Siemon's new edition (xxi; and xix–xxxix).

6 See Steane: 'It is best to regard the play as *sui generis*' (166).

7 Critics have long written on what Cartelli calls 'the theatrical orientation of the play' (164); see H. Levin 73; Harbage 56, 58; Goldman 31–4; Greenblatt, 'Marlowe, Marx' 51–3; Danson 5; Bloom, ed. 2–3; Shepherd 176; Mullaney 58; Jones 79–98; Freer, esp. 145, 148; Cartelli 173, 179, 180; Bartels 98–108; and Healy 61–7. Only Deats and Starks have taken metadrama as a primary topic, though their analysis is not exhaustive.

8 Cf. E. Segal, who thinks Marlowe is representing a *spiritual* process akin to

'Pythagorean metempsychosis' (129). See also Bawcutt 36; and Jones 69. Yet Steane is right to call Machevill's discourse 'dramatic doublethink' (173). I find a hitherto undetected analogue and potential origin for Marlowe's process in a document he began translating, Lucan's *Pharsalia* (IX.1–18). On the consonance of Lucan and Machiavelli, see Palmer, 'Marlowe's Naturalism' 161–2.

9 Boitani reminds us that 'fame is language' (72).

10 Rebhorn helps me see that Marlowe is reading Machiavelli astutely here, for Rebhorn's 'primary' thesis is that 'Machiavelli saw the world through the lens of literature ... Machiavelli's political vision is mediated by literature' (ix).

11 Machiavelli was obsessed by the idea of fame; see *The Prince*, ed. and trans. Adams 21, 25, 37, and 42.

12 H. Levin notes that on Malta, 'if anywhere, East met West' (65); Bartels sees political significance in the meeting of East and West (88); and Hunter sees theological significance ('Theology' 202–3).

13 On our 'complicity' in Barabas's crimes, see H. Levin 73; and Greenblatt, 'Marlowe, Marx' 51.

14 See also Harbage 56, 58; Greenblatt, 'Marlowe, Marx 51–3; and Danson 5. On Barabas as equated with the play's spirit, see Cartelli 173.

15 In her new edition, Gill makes this the single topic of her introduction (*Complete Works* 4: ix–xv). The character traces to the Barabbas of Scripture, and so does not escape 'history.' Still, 'Barabas' does not *represent* Barabbas the way 'Machiavel' represents Machiavelli.

16 Critics regularly emphasize Marlowe's 'caricatured *personae*' (Steane 186).

17 Machiavelli writes to Vettori that one of the books he carries in his pocket is 'Ovid' (ed. and trans. Adams 127). On Ovid and Machiavelli in Marlowe, see Palmer, 'Marlowe's Naturalism' 157. Bawcutt cites six passages in *The Jew* indebted to Ovid (ed. 65, 96, 97, 99, 139, 188). Of course, I am situating Marlowe's Ovid and Machiavelli within Senecan tragedy (see Ribner, 'Marlowe and Machiavelli' 349–50).

18 On the first two stages, see Summers, *Christopher Marlowe* 106–7. On the move from the first to the third, see Godshalk 206; and Steane 196, 203. For a critique of 'Greenblatt's Marlowe,' see Felperin.

19 See Foucault, 'What is Enlightenment' in *The Foucault Reader*, ed. Rabinow 45–6; 'Truth and Power' in *The Foucault Reader* 51–75, 56 and 58–9; 'What Is an Author?' in *The Foucault Reader* 101–20, esp. 119; and *The Archaeology of Knowledge* 28, 49, 55, 111–13, 117. Foucault insists that the 'positivities ... must not be understood as a set of determinations imposed from the outside on the thought of individuals, or inhabiting it from the inside, in advance as it were; they constitute rather the set of conditions in accordance with which a practice is exercised' (*Archaeology of Knowledge* 208).

20 On the way in which 'money is equated only with policy' here, see E. Segal 130.

21 In his epigram on Machiavelli in *Gratulationum Valdinensium*, Gabriel Harvey has Machiavelli identify himself as 'The King of all Kings' (rpt. in Thomas and Tydeman 335).

22 For other Shakespearean renderings of Marlowe's famous line, see *Henry V* Prologue 15–16, II.Chorus 17, and, of course, *As You Like It* III.iii.15.

23 In another context, Eccles quotes a 1597 phrase from the Acts of the Privy Council: 'stages, gallories, and roomes' (17). For 'galleries' as a theatrical term, see V.v.35. An analogue to the usage of *room* emerges in Marlowe's use of 'Truce' at V.i.83. Even though the word appears in the 1633 edition, editors emend it variously, but Van Fossen retains the original word (99), and Simmons argues that 'Truce' also means *truss*: Marlowe offers a 'photograph ... structure ... of [the] playhouse' (96–7). On the theatricality of Barabas's rising from the wall, see Mullaney 58; and Kermode 220–1.

24 Shakespeare's 'great reckoning in a little room' in *As You Like It* also occurs in an Ovidian context (see 'Ovid' in line 7 of III.iii). Other words in Barabas's soliloquy that the *OED* permits a metadramatic meaning to include 'return,' 'made,' 'venture,' and 'summ'd.' On riches as a trope for poetic fame, see Cheney, *Spenser's Famous Flight* 142–4.

25 Gill usefully glosses 'Samnites' with Lucan, *Pharsalia* II.137 (ed., *Complete Works* 4: 96).

26 Dowden first linked Barabas with the 'Mammon' of Scripture (rpt. in MacLure, ed., *Marlowe* 108); but Godshalk finds an 'interesting analogue to Marlowe's Barabas' in 'Spenser's Mammon, who concentrates infinite riches in his cave and tempts Guyon with his beautiful daughter, Philotime' (202, n. 31). Thomas and Tydeman do not include Spenser as a source.

27 Of course, this fact alone does not constitute evidence of direct borrowing, but it does open up the possibility of one, especially if more concrete evidence emerges.

28 Weil notes: 'The idea that Heaven so obligingly rips earth represents a complete inversion of the values implied when Guyon describes covetousness to Mammon in *The Faerie Queene* (1590),' quoting this passage, and adding, 'More to the point ... is the fact that the "pathetic" rhetorical question asked by Barabas almost persuades us of his assumptions; we tend to agree that Heaven is indeed generous before noting that his question is premised on the most outrageous materialism' (34).

29 See Abigail as Proserpina at I.ii.374–5 (Bawcutt cites Ovid, *Metamorphoses* V.385–96 [ed. 96]): 'The sweetest flower in Cytherea's field, / Cropp'd from the pleasures of the fruitful earth.' Compare Spenser's phrasing for the Garden of

Proserpina: 'Not such, as earth out of her fruitfull woomb / Throwes forth to men, sweet and well savoured' (*FQ* II.vii.51).

30 We may recall that Marlowe appears to have had his eye on Disdayne when creating Tamburlaine (see chapter 5, n. 15).

31 Giamatti is commenting on *FQ* IV.xi.17. Evidently, Godshalk finds 'the basic image of *The Faerie Queene*' in the Mammon episode, and he deploys Marlowe's language to describe it: 'Spenser's Mammon … concentrates infinite riches in his cave.' For a classical origin pertinent here, see Lucretius, *De rerum natura* IV.159: 'So many images in such little room' (trans. Humphries).

32 Three other conjunctions are worth citing: (1) Marlowe's rare use of 'worldings' at V.v.49 and Spenser's equally rare use of 'worldings' at *FQ* II.vii.39 and 81 (to be discussed later); (2) Marlowe's 'Laden with riches' at I.i.85 and Spenser's 'laden with rich fee' at *FQ* II.vii.56; and (3) Marlowe's 'exceeding store' also at I.i.85 and 'exceeding store' at *FQ* II.vii.31. Schoeneich compares *1 Tamb* I.i.121 ('Lading their ships with gold and precious stone') with *FQ* II.xii.19 ('Laden from far with precious merchandize') (78). He also cites two additional *Jew of Malta* echoes from elsewhere in *The Faerie Queene*: (1) 'walls of brass' (*Jew of Malta* I.ii.381; cf. *Faustus* I.i.86) and 'brazen wall' (*FQ* II.iii.10) (91–2); and (2) 'let the brightsome heavens be dim' (II.iii.328) and 'Dimmed her former beauties shining ray' (*FQ* I.i.38) (98–9). To this list, we may add one more: Marlowe's 'sin or want of faith' (I.ii.320) and Spenser's 'want of faith or guilt of sin' (*FQ* I.vii.45: 8).

33 See Gill, who cites 'Ovid in *Metamorphoses*, xii. 29ff.' (ed., *Complete Works* 4: 99).

34 What Hunter says of Barabas's earlier speech on kingship I would apply here: the 'only king that Barabas will rescue is himself' ('Theology' 198).

35 See de Grazia on the 1590s as a '"time of crisis,"' with 'the queen herself aging … a particular cause for anxiety when succession was contested by twelve claimants, exposing England to the possibility of both internecine strife and foreign invasion' (40). De Grazia's interest lies in using the 1590s to plot 'an important turning point in three coordinate histories (of early capitalism, subjectivity [Joel Fineman], and authorial genius [Dowden's map of 'authorial development, from "apprentice" to "master-dramatist"'])' (44). She locates the turning-points for the last two, subjectivity and authorial genius, in Shakespeare (41–4); they may appear first, however, in Marlowe.

36 For Marlowe's '*pour* out plenty in their *laps*,' see Spenser's '*poure* into his Lemans lap' (*FQ* I.i.6).

37 We may extend to Marlowe's self-quotation in *The Jew* what H. Morris says of 'The Passionate Shepherd' itself: 'the pastoral influence … comes to him from Spenser' (137). Morris adds: 'the surer clue to Spenser's influence is the

adjective ... the "brave" adjective; it is compounded of color, especially gold and silver, of rare gems, rare stones, rare metals, of charged emotion' (138).

38 See Nicholl on Marlowe's Corpus Christi portrait: 'It shows him as a young man with money to spend – not just the doublet, which even second-hand would have cost him thirty shillings or more; not just the rows of golden buttons like so many counterfeit coins; but the very fact of the portrait. It was not everyone who could afford the services of a good "limner". The portrait itself is a luxury' (5). See also Hammer 24: 'making money for himself was an important, even central, part of the poet's motivation.' Critics 'neglect' Ithamore, as Priest observes (86), but 'Ithamore's role may serve as a dramatic paradigm for what happens to the Jew and ultimately to the reductive world of the play itself, as it drifts from apparent sophistication to near-burlesque' (86–7). Priest concludes, however, that Ithamore is 'a ludicrous fool ... a version of the ... "zany" figure, ... who mocks through parodic antics the ... machinations of a primary character' (90). Freer sees Marlowe's 'self-parody' stretching beyond Ithamore: 'The different poetic modes that Marlowe employs in this play constitute something close to an index of self-parody' (152); for Ithamore on the 'edge of parody,' see 156.

39 Spenser does not publish the Mirabella story until 1596, although we cannot rule out the possibility that Marlowe had access to Spenser's manuscript or that a version of the Mirabella story existed by 1589–90, the usual dates assigned to *The Jew of Malta*.

40 Gill glosses IV.ii.94 ('running banquet ... rags') as follows: 'Bellamira now imitates the Queen in Marlowe's *Dido Queen of Carthage* (Act II scene i), where Dido entertains Aeneas at her banquet and expresses horror at his "base robes"' (ed., *Complete Works* 4: 119). Thus Bellamira imitates a figure who imitates Elizabeth (see chapter 4).

41 Should we be surprised that in Spenser's only use of the phrase Colin Clout repeats the Shepherd of the Ocean's 'undersong' in his 'lamentable lay' to Queen Cynthia (*Colin Clouts Come Home Againe* 169, 164) – a clear allegory for Ralegh's love of Elizabeth: 'Ah my *loves queene*, and goddess of my life, / Who shall me pittie, when thou doest me wrong?' (170–1). Spenser had written *Colin Clout* by 1591, although he did not publish it until 1595.

42 Qtd. in Montrose, 'The Elizabethan Subject' 311. Montrose is discussing those individuals who 'contested' the 'authorized version of the queen' as the Virgin (esp. 307–12).

43 Is, then, 'Pilia-Borza' (Italian for 'pickpocket' [Bawcutt, ed. 126]) an anagram for Burleigh, Elizabeth's chief adviser? Or perhaps Sir Francis Walsingham, head of the secret service under Elizabeth, the relative of Marlowe's patron, Sir Thomas Walsingham, and Marlowe's own boss? On Walsingham's role in the

intelligence service, see Nicholl 102–13, 172–4; on Marlowe's association with
Sir Francis, see 102, 133, 169, 219, 220.

44   In 'The Language of Faith,' Ricoeur speaks of 'language' and 'double-meaning'
when he refers to 'the meaning of the meaning' (234). He has just been
discussing Shakespeare and the theatre (231). To use Ricoeur's terms, Marlowe
is troping 'symbolic language.'

45   Cf. Priest: 'Poison, of course, is the standard Machiavellian "policy"' (91). And
Scott: 'indifference to the commonweal ... is the hallmark of the Machiavellian
rebel' (167). Marlowe's scene may evoke the Babington Plot against Elizabeth
in 1586, which Nicholl discusses at length (147–65), finding Robert Poley, one
of Marlowe's murderers, deeply involved. The Babington Plot derived from
'heads filled with wine, with dreams of Catholic rebellion, with an overheated,
cultish devotion to the imprisoned Queen Mary,' but Nicholl emphasizes that
'what shape it [the plot] had in terms of real action was largely provided by the
government itself, whose agents infiltrated the conspiracy not so much to
destroy it, as to encourage it' (147). Mary, of course, was 'Queen of France.'
Nicholl observes that the 'real animus' of the plot was John Ballard, 'a mission-
ary Catholic from Rheims' (148). The project involved a France-based 'invasion
of England' (149).

46   For literal spying in *The Jew*, see V.i.66–7.

47   See Nicholl on Rheims: 'in the 1580s going to Rheims meant one thing and one
thing only. It meant turning your back on Queen and Country, and enlisting
in the Catholic struggle against the established church and government' (92).
Rothstein sees the political matrix of Catholicism in the play (267), with
Barabas as a French Catholic in disguise (268). Minshull provides an equally
rare political context for *The Jew* (51–3).

48   In the Argument to canto vii, Spenser presents Mammon 'Sunning his
threasure hore' (2).

Chapter 7: 'Italian masques by night': Machiavellian Policy and Ovidian Play in *Edward II*

1   Cf. Deats, 'Fearful Symmetry': 'the play opens and closes with two similar
rituals, the funeral of an older Edward and the assumption of royal power by
an heir of the same name' (241). My approach differs from this and other
structural approaches (Fricker; Waith, 'Shadow of Action'; McCloskey; Thurn,
'Sovereignty, Disorder'; see Forker's review [66–82]). Kocher, *Christopher
Marlowe*, notes Marlowe's 'poetic realizations of the schemes of Mortimer and
Gaveston' (205; see 291; Cutts, *Left Hand of God* 200–1; Brandt, *Christopher
Marlowe* 156–9; and Deats, 'Fearful Symmetry' 255), but no one has isolated
this rivalry in terms of Marlowe's Ovidian career.

2 Things have not changed much since Bakeless: 'All critics are generally agreed that this is the maturest of Marlowe's plays and ... the latest' (2: 4). On dating, which most assign to 1591–2, see Merchant xi–xii; Forker 14–17; and Rowland xiv–xv. Critics usually identify *Edward II* as a 'Machiavellian play of policy,' and they find a number of Machiavellian plotters, especially Gaveston and Mortimer (Cartelli 121–3, 128–33), but also Queen Isabella (Summers, *Christopher Marlowe* 172–4). Less often, critics mention Ovid (F.P. Wilson 133; Zucker 170–3; and Deats, 'Myth and Metamorphosis' 309, 311, 314, 316); but we need to take Marlowe's cues more seriously: Gaveston's Ovidianism; the recurrent references to myths from the *Metamorphoses* (I.iv.16,172–3, 178–80, 407, II.ii.53–4, III.iii.82–3, etc.); and two lines quoted from Ovid's epic (I.iv.13 from *Met* II.846–7; and V.iv.69 from *Met* VI.195). As J. Bate remarks, '*Edward II* sometimes seems to require an extremely detailed recall of Ovid's Latin' (44). Of course, Marlowe mediates his synthesis of Machiavelli and Ovid with Seneca, as his quotation from *Thyestes* hints (IV.vi.53–4 from *Thy* 613–14; see H. Levin 99, 101).

3 Marlowe invents the rivalry between Gaveston and Mortimer. In Holinshed, Mortimer does not appear until after Gaveston is dead, when the Earl of Lancaster is 'the chief occasioner of his death' (rpt. in Thomas and Tydeman 360). See Fricker: 'for the first time in Marlowe's plays the hero [Edward] is confronted with an enemy of equal stature, namely Mortimer' (206). Critics debate the question of genre; Ribner's phrase, 'Historical Tragedy,' fuses the elements usually identified. See Clemen, '*Edward II*' 138; Bevington and Shapiro 263; and Forker's review (85, 86–91).

4 Cf. McCloskey on *Edward II* as 'the odd play out' (35). I do agree that 'Edward's story illustrates ... how circumstances in the world constrain human action and conspire to destroy human agents' (36). McCloskey identifies the loss of 'freedom' as 'the pattern of experience central to his play's meaning' (43), although she does not contextualize that 'story.'

5 See McCloskey, who examines the play's 'divided structure' (37), with 'the play break[ing] ... radically at Gaveston's death' (37, n. 3). On Edward III in the play, see Tyler 61–2.

6 On Marlowe's debt to Shakespeare in *Edward II*, see Forker's review (17–41). Although a few critics supply clues for Marlowe's debt to Spenser, no one has examined the topic.

7 For this thought, I am indebted to Chad G. Hayton, in an unpublished essay, 'Spenser, Marlowe, and the Dangerous Supplement': 'It should not come as a surprise that the traces of Spenser's influence on Marlowe become less visible as he matures as a poet. It would be a mistake, however, to assume that because Spenser's influence is less obvious it is less profound. Rather, we should take more pains to uncover the evidence of Spenser's influence' (3).

8 Lucan's obsession with *libertas* traces to his nostalgic desire to return Rome to the days of the Republic, where the correlate of the Elizabethan aristocracy, the Roman nobility, reigned sovereign.

9 See Forker: '*Edward II* becomes more than usually significant as a piece of evidence in the ongoing study of Marlowe's perennially discussed but puzzlingly obscure psyche' (86). Greenblatt discusses 'Marlowe's implication in the lives of his protagonists' (*Renaissance Self-Fashioning* 221). In addition to Gaveston (Cartelli 127, 131), critics find Marlowe in Edward (Poirier 185), Baldock (H. Levin 104), the French spy Levune (Archer 80), and Lightborn (Cartelli 133–3).

10 Martindale observes: '*Meaning ... is always realized at the point of reception*; if so, we cannot assume that an "intention" is effectively communicated within any text' (*Redeeming the Text* 3). I aim to contextualize Garber's deconstructive model, in which 'the act of writing or signing conveys ... a struggle for mastery of stage and text between the playwright and his inscribed characters' (301). Like Garber, I isolate 'the trope of writing and unwriting' (318), but I veer from her conclusion: that Mortimer is 'ultimately cancelled or slain by [his] own hands: ... by writing against the hand of the playwright' (320). Marlowe's use of written documents may derive from Holinshed, but the playwright alters the chronicler in representing the most important document – the letter containing the Bishop of Hereford's 'sophistical form of words' issuing Edward's murder, which Marlowe assigns to Mortimer: '*Edwardum occidere nolite timere bonum est*' (rpt. in Thomas and Tydeman 368–9; *Ed II* V.iv.11)

11 On Gaveston as intersecting Marlovian 'desire' and 'theatricality,' see Belsey, 'Desire's Excess' 88–9. Bullen long ago noted Marlowe's 'admirably drawn' portrait of Gaveston (rpt. in MacLure, ed., *Marlowe* 139); and Bullen's anonymous reviewer added, '"Edward the Second" might have been called "The Tragedie of Piers Gaveston"' (rpt. in MacLure 145).

12 Two of these conjunctions come from the prologue to *Faustus*, confirming the idea that the Gaveston scene functions as a prologue. Moreover, the *Faustus* prologue also includes an itinerary of works, including *Edward II* (see chapter 9). I respond to Cutts: 'Edward's missive to him [Gaveston] may sound like "Come live with mee ...," but it is not a Jupiter calling for a Ganymede to dangle on his knee. Gaveston likens himself to a Leander swimming across the English Channel of a Hellespont ..., but unlike Marlowe's own Leander, Gaveston *gasps* upon the sand ... Gaveston confounds London in Elysium, however, every bit as much as Faustus confounds Hell in Elysium' (*Left Hand of God* 203).

13 As Emily C. Bartels observes, the effect is to tie the discourse even more to issues of the state (personal communication, April 1996).

14 On this soliloquy, see Cartelli 123–7; and Bartels 167–70. I disagree with Tyler:

'Gaveston ... has elaborate plans for frivolous entertainments to keep "the pliant king" under his influence' (57).

15 For pertinent comments not pertaining to Elizabeth, see Ribner, 'Historical Tragedy' 146–7; Viswanathan 82–3, 89 (n. 6), 92; and Summers, *Christopher Marlowe* 155. Tyler best represents the tendency: 'The structure of *Edward II* ... is a double demonstration of how sexual motives enter the political scene, subvert its proper order, and engender a reaction designed to reassert that order' (64; see also 64–5).

16 See Ashby in his note on Warton's observations: 'It seems somewhat remarkable that Marlow, in describing the pleasures which Gaveston contrived to debauch the infatuated Edward, should exactly employ those which were exhibited before the sage Elizabeth' (rpt. in MacLure, ed., *Marlowe* 65). For a rare comment on the 'parallel between Edward and Elizabeth,' see Archer 77. See also Zunder 53.

17 Many critics comment on the Ovidian origin of this myth in the *Metamorphoses* without recognizing its localizing significance for both Ovid and Marlowe (Weil 161–2, 164; Zucker 170-1; and J. Bate 38–9, who none the less refers to 'the Renaissance reading of the myth as an emblem of the fate of those who peer into the sacred cabinets of princes' [39]).

18 Barkan, *Gods Made Flesh* 46. Barkan explains: 'transformation always succeeds in capturing the human essence of the subject and at the same time in filling us with uncomprehending wonder at the immanence and intimacy of otherwordly powers' (46). For other commentary on the Actaeon myth in the Renaissance, see esp. Vickers; Couliani 72–80; and Enterline.

19 Otis is cautious: 'There is no overt criticism of Augustus and his court (even Actaeon's *error* has probably nothing to do with the *error* that led to Ovid's banishment), but there is certainly an implicit criticism of Augustan ideology and practice' (145). Otis observes that the 'mention of Actaeon in *Tristia* II, 105 as an analogue of Ovid's own crime (*imprudenti cognita cupa*, 104) is of course suggestive'; he cites M. Pohlenz on the suggestion that Ovid gave to lines 142–3 of the story a 'personal nuance'; then he backs off: 'But the chronology is uncertain: Ovid could have thought of Actaeon as he did without a personal reason' (145, n. 1). In *Redeeming the Text*, Martindale takes Ovid's use of the myth in the narration of his *carmen et error* seriously (60-2).

20 So Renaissance translators of Ovid thought. Although Ovid in the Exile Poetry relies on several myths to represent his predicament, the translators latched onto the first one Ovid uses: that of Actaeon. See Gower's translation of the *Fasti* (sig. A3^r); Sandys in his 'Life of Ovid' prefacing his translation of the *Metamorphoses* (sig. b1^v); and Catlin's 'To the Courteous Reader' prefacing his translation of the *Tristia* (sig. A3^r).

21 The record includes the comedic version of this construction: the 1587 letter
from the Privy Council rescuing Marlowe's MA degree, on the grounds that 'it
was not Her Majesty's pleasure that anyone employed, as he had been, in
matters touching the benefit of his country, should be defamed by those that
are ignorant in th'affairs he went about' (qtd. in Nicholl 92). Riggs reminds us
that the record also includes the tragic version: in a letter of August 1593, Sir
Thomas Drury wrote to Anthony Bacon that 'the notablest and vildest articles
of atheism [written by Marlowe] ... were delivered to Her Highness, and
command given by herself to prosecute it to the full' (rpt. in Nicholl 304;
Riggs, 'Marlowe Learns to Write,' MLA Convention, 1995). Nicholl's conclusion to *The Reckoning* resonates with the Actaeon myth: 'the cause of
Marlowe's death was a perception – perhaps a momentary perception of
political necessity. He died in the hands of political agents: a victim, though not
an innocent victim, of the court intrigues that flourished in this "queasy time"
of change and succession' (329).

22 In their editions, W.D. Briggs (114), Charlton and Waller (78), and Forker
(152) all cite Peele's *Edward I*, while Rowland cites *The Massacre at Paris* and
Tamburlaine (94). Yet Marlowe's linking of Phaethon with Caesar constitutes a
virtual signature for the translator of Ovid and Lucan.

23 See Sanders 123. Thrice Holinshed describes Edward's behaviour in theatrical
terms: Edward 'counterfeited a kind of gravity ... ; forthwith he began to play
divers wanton and light parts'; 'the king might spend both days and nights in
jesting, playing, banqueting'; and his revenging army is 'more seemly for a
triumph' (rpt. in Thomas and Tydeman 351, 352, 356).

24 On Mortimer's theatricality, see Leech, *Christopher Marlowe* 127; and Cartelli
133–4.

25 In his detailed list of Marlowe's borrowings from his colleagues, Bakeless
excludes Spenser (2: 27–40). None the less, criticism has turned up several
borrowings (citations from the play differ from editor to editor; I cite Gill, ed.,
Plays, but give page numbers for other editions). Schoeneich identifies seven
borrowings (99–101), although only the first four look like probable echoes,
and only the second of real significance: (1) *FQ* I.vi.2 for Edward's 'wander to
... Inde' at I.iv.50; (2) *Mother Hubberds Tale* 487–99 for Spencer's courtly
advice to Baldock at II.i.31–43; (3) *FQ* II.i.10 for Edward's 'earth ... mother' at
III.ii.128; (4) *FQ* III.ix.35 for Isabella's 'channel overflow with blood' at
IV.iv.12; (5) *FQ* II.ix.48 for Edward's 'famous nursery of arts' at IV.vi.17–19;
(6) *FQ* III.ii.15 for Edward's 'gentle words might comfort me' at V.i.5–6; and
(7) *FQ* II.i.13 for Isabella's 'wrings his hands' at V.vi.18. Steane glosses two
passages with 'the Spenser of *The Shepheardes Calender*' (208): II.iv.25–6 and
II.ii.61–2. Both Godshalk (62) and Zucker (169) find Acrasia, the Bower of

Bliss, and Spenser's idea of bestial transformation in Gaveston's dream of staging the Actaeon myth for Edward. And G. Roberts compares Spenser's use of Circe/Duessa at *FQ* I.viii.14 with Marlowe's use of Circe/Isabella at I.iv.170–4 (433–4). Among editors, W.D. Briggs accepts the first four of Schoeneich's seven borrowings (122–3, 134–5, 158–9, 171), cites Schoeneich 77 on the Spenserian origin of 'Renowmed' at II.v.41 (151), mentions one incidental comparison (144), and introduces one substantial borrowing: *FQ* I.v.28 for 'iron car' at IV.iii.42–3 (171). Charlton and Waller accept the borrowings of 'Inde' (89), 'Renowmed' (134), and 'iron car' (160-1), add one incidental comparison with *Mother Hubberds Tale* (136), a potential borrowing of *FQ* III.i.39 for 'Whilom' at IV.vi.13, and another of *March* 76 and *FQ* I.i.3 for 'earns' at IV.vi.70 (173), but then introduce one borrowing of great significance: *Teares of the Muses* 210 for 'deads the royal vine' at III.ii.163 (146). Forker mentions Spenser twice, citing Charlton and Waller on *Teares* 209–10 for 'deads' at III.ii.163; and Briggs on *FQ* I.v.28 for 'iron car' at IV.iii.42–3. Finally, Rowland adds three Spenser origins: *FQ* IV.x.27 and III.xii.7 for 'Hylas' at I.i.43 (94); *Virgils Gnat* 339–44 on 'Tisiphon' at V.i.45 (119); and *FQ* I.x.57 on 'youngling' at V.ii.109 (122). All told, Marlowe critics have turned up around twenty potential borrowings from Spenser, with several significant indeed. These figures are not definitive; Chad G. Hayton discovers two more significant ones: *FQ* I.x.63:1–5 for IV.vi.17–23; and *FQ* I.xi.55: 8–9 for IV.vi.19–22. These figures indicate that at the end of his dramatic career, as at the beginning, Marlowe is contending with his first great precursor.

26 Speculation includes, in the 1928 words of Renwick, 'the names of Shakespeare, T. Wilson, Alabaster, and Sidney,' as well as 'Richard Tarlton,' though Renwick rules out all of these, because none is 'a writer of comedies'; he introduces the possibility of George Gascoigne, who first translated Ariosto's comedy *Suppositi* (210). More recently, Oram sees Willy as Sidney (Oram et al. 277), while Maclean sees a more 'plausible' allusion to Lyly (182).

27 Oram thinks a later date likely – in the early '1590s' (Oram et al. 263, 277n), and Maclean cites 'Thalia's lament and that of Euterpe' as evidence of 'at least' some late revision (182–3).

28 Rowland glosses Marlowe's 'deads' also by referring to 'Marivell's "lively spirits deaded quite" (*Faerie Queene* IV. iii. 20)' (111). He means Marinell, and the line comes from canto xii. He could also have cited VI.vii.25. The peculiar usage appears to have been a favourite of Spenser's.

29 On the textual problem of Spenser's 'braunches,' see Smith and de Sélincourt 1: 520.

30 Thomson sees this principle working in 'Shakespeare's English history plays': 'Among the courtiers who watched these in performance would have been

many descendants of the Knights and Earls who made up the *dramatis personae*' (28).

31 Spenser's contemporaries used several epithets to describe him and his poetry, but 'sweet' is especially recurrent. Citations with dates in the following catalogue come from Cummings's Critical Heritage volume: 'sweete Faery Queene' (Gabriel Harvey [1592] 53); 'sweete Poet' (Harvey [1593] 55); 'saith most sweetely' (William Webbe [1586] 56); 'sweete brest' (H.B. [1590] 64); 'sweet hunnie vaine' (Watson [1590] 70); 'saith most sweetly' (Francis Meres [1598] 96); 'Sweete Spenser' (John Weever [1600] 101); 'A sweeter swan ... sweetly of his Faiery Queene he song' (anon., *The Returne from Parnassus* [1606] 116, 117); 'sweet singer' (Richard Niccols [1610] 124); and 'sweet Spencer' (William Browne [1616] 134). Among the list, Robert Salter's note 'Mr. Edmund Spenser' (1626) is historically perhaps the most important, since he transfers the epithet from Spenser's poetry to his person: 'The great contentment I sometimes enjoyed by his Sweete society, suffereth not this to passe me, without Respective mention of so trew a friend' (Cummings 146, n.). In his edition of *Edward II*, Merchant reminds us that the 1594 edition spells the name 'Spencer' as 'Spenser': 'There are some curious features in the speech-prefixes of the texts on which the present edition is based ... SPENCER is spelt Spenser' (5).

32 As noted, Schoeneich and others find Marlowe borrowing from Spenser just a few lines before the 'deads' passage, when Edward speaks of 'earth, the common mother of us all' (128); cf. *FQ* II.i.10: 'earth, great mother of us all.' Thus, within thirty-seven lines – between the 'earth' and 'deads' passages (128–65) – we can detect four borrowings or allusions to Spenser, to which I shall add two more, bringing the total to six, supplying overwhelming evidence that Marlowe is concerned with Spenser in the 'Spencer' scene. As we shall see in chapter 9, critics find Marlowe imitating the third Spenser passage in *Doctor Faustus*. Further evidence emerges in Schoeneich's discovery that Spencer's advice to Baldock to 'cast the scholar off, / And learn to court it like a gentle-man' (II.i.31–2) borrows from *Mother Hubberds Tale*, when the Priest teaches the Fox deception (488–99). Marlowe's lines 'making low legs to a nobleman, / Or looking downward, with your eyelids close' (38–9) resemble Spenser's lines 'look[ing] ... lowly on the ground, / And unto everie one doo curtesie meeke' (498–9). See also Bredbeck: Marlowe's Spencer 'works through the channels of orthodox monarchical power' (73). In this light, Spencer looks to be a photo-graph of the Spenser who privileges a nationhood of royal power. To compli-cate things further, I observe that Marlowe's portrait of the theatrical Gaveston appears to be indebted to Spenser's description of the first two masquers in

Busirane's Masque of Cupid in *FQ* III.xii.7–8: 'Fancy, like a lovely boy' and 'amorous Desyre, / Who seemd of riper years, then th'other Swaine.' As we have seen, Rowland cites the Hylas reference here for Marlowe's Hylas, and it is not hard to understand Marlowe's attraction to this homoerotic passage. Elsewhere, Sir John of Hainhalt's comment on the game of bidding base, 'We will find comfort, money, men and friends / Ere long, to bid the English King a base' (IV.ii.66–7), may have an origin in the *October* eclogue, when Piers refers to Cuddie's poetic art: 'In rymes, in ridles, and in bydding base' (5). Spenser and Marlowe are referring to the game of Prisoner's base, 'in which a player was safe only so long as he remained at his base' (Merchant 71; on Spenser, see Oram et al. 171). Finally, it seems striking that Marlowe should twice refer anachronistically to the St George legend: 'St. George for England' (III.iii.33, 35). Forker explains the 'anachronism': 'St. George was not adopted as the patron saint of England until the reign of Edward III' (233); as Merchant puts it, 'This is Marlowe's addition' (65).

33 On Mortimer as a figure for the poet, see esp. McElroy 216, 218, 219.

34 Cf. Tyler: Mortimer's 'principal objection is that Gaveston is low-born (a point stressed by Marlowe but not by his sources)' (57). Voss suggests that 'Gaveston, and later Spencer, come to represent a challenge to the traditional hierarchy of birth which is the basis of the peers' social position and the backbone of the entire English state' (520), but he does not recall that Edmund Spenser repeatedly supports this hierarchy in *The Faerie Queene*.

35 See Sales on Proteus and acting (125–6). On Mortimer's speech, see Summers, *Christopher Marlowe* 166–7. Spenser had linked Proteus with the theater through his portrait of the enchanter Archimago (*FQ* I.ii.10).

36 Poirier links this allegory with vogues in Elizabethan literature but specifically to the one created by Lyly: 'when he [Mortimer] describes the *imprese* chosen by the noblemen, he refers to the custom of his own time and conforms to the vogue of euphuism' (187).

37 In this part of the scene, Mortimer repeatedly accuses Edward of subjecting himself to literariness; see ll. 156–9, 176–7, and 187–94.

38 Thurn sees 'a perverse allegory of homosexual rape' ('Sovereignty, Disorder' 136); Bartels notes that Lightborn 'smacks of allegory' (158); and Forker links Lightborn with the 'emblematic figure' of 'good and evil' (88). H. Levin originally suggested that 'Lightborn's name reveals ... "Lucifer"' (101).

39 See Cartelli 133–4. Kocher, *Christopher Marlowe*, remarks: 'the humor of the play ... is summed up and made incarnate in Lightborn' (291).

40 See Bredbeck: the spit 'can be seen as an attempt to "write" onto him the homoeroticism constantly ascribed to him' (76).

Chapter 8: 'Actors in this massacre': *The Massacre at Paris* and the Orphic Guise of Metatheatre

1 On Marlowe's prologues, see Brinker, who defines the form as a 'speech rendered by a single neutral figure – standing apart from the realm of dramatic illusion of the play – the so-called Presenter' (1). Brinker's definition of the induction, which Marlowe 'never really uses' (11), describes the Jupiter scene opening *Dido*: 'a short independent scene laid in the theater just before the action begins' (11). On this scene as an induction, see Greenfield xv, 146, who denies that the Machevill scene in *The Jew* is a prologue (xv). On Gaveston in *Edward II* as 'the play's Presenter,' see Cartelli 123–4.

2 Cf. Cutts, *Left Hand of God*, who terms the opening scene 'an induction' because it prepares for the Guise's 'ruminat[ion]' on the marriage (170). Eriksen, 'Construction,' recalls that Marlowe opens the play with a wedding in imitation of Shakespeare in *Henry the VI, Part Two* (42). As in *Edward II*, we begin to see signs of Marlowe's second great rival.

3 See Sales: 'The Guise in *The Massacre at Paris* choreographs the theatre of violence, making sure that the "actors in this massacre" (4.28) perform the parts that he has written for them' (125).

4 See Bennett 170-5; and Oliver lii–lxi. The play totals 1,250 lines – half of a typical play. Critical appraisals range from many scathing indictments to a few defences. For the most famous indictment, see Sanders: the play is a 'nasty piece of journalistic bombast' (22) in which 'Marlowe has sold out to the basest elements in himself and his audience' (28). As early as 1940, however, Boas was claiming that the play 'has a more important place in the canon ... than his editors have been willing to allow' (*Christopher Marlowe* 153). More recently, Kuriyama remarks, 'the *Massacre* is one of the most illuminating of Marlowe's plays' (94). It is Weil, however, who claims 'a central position' for the play (84): 'enough of Marlowe's art has survived to hint that his irony could have been a response to the contradictions of religious warfare, a defence against pain, and an attack upon the very sources of political disorder' (85). Similarly, J. Briggs recalls that the 'play was one of the earliest to present recent historical and contemporary political events on the English stage' (257). Finally, Kirk discovers in 'Marlowe's disfigured portrait of contemporary French history' a powerful 'recontain[ment] ... under the auspices of Queen Elizabeth's authority' (193).

5 See Kuriyama: 'we seem to be left with the skeletal remains of what was probably never a very good play' (76). Sanders remarks, 'The alarming thing about the play ... is ... that it is so thoroughly Marlovian ... And, as a result, it raises most pressingly the question of Marlowe's real stature' (36).

6 Weil emphasizes the important relation between *The Massacre*, *The Jew*, and *Edward II* (84); as does Poirier (163). We do not know when Marlowe composed the play, although Bakeless remains authoritative: 'between 1590 and 1593' (2: 72). In his *Diary*, Henslowe records that the play was first performed in January 1593. Our authority for the text comes from an undated octavo, published in 'London' (title page) and 'perhaps printed in the early years of the seventeenth century' (Gill, ed., *Plays* 402). We do possess a single manuscript page, which gives us a different version of scene xix, and which may (or may not) be in Marlowe's own handwriting (Oliver lviii–lix).

7 Cole calls *The Massacre at Paris* a 'history play,' but he stresses its independence from the genre (*Suffering and Evil* 155). Weil argues that *The Massacre* is 'a satire on the inhuman worldliness of Christian rulers' – 'an inverted *speculum principis*' (102) or a 'historical satire' (104). Eriksen remarks that the play is 'no tragedy' but does convey 'an essentially tragic view of history' ('Construction' 52).

8 Critics emphasize Marlowe's representation of 'the historical conflict between Protestantism and Catholicism, as seen from the contemporary English Protestant viewpoint' (Cole, *Suffering and Evil* 150). Cole argues for a 'black vs. white antagonism' among the Catholic villain, the Guise, and the Protestant hero, Navarre: 'The general framework is thus completely orthodox' (150). Critics disagree about how to respond to the antagonism. Those who argue that '"Marlowe perversely admires this paragon of evil" (the Guise)' (Cole 151–2, n. 31) include Kocher, 'Pamphlet Backgrounds ... Part Two' 314 (see 'François Hotman' and 'Pamphlet Backgrounds'); and esp. J. Briggs, who offers the most persuasive evidence. Critics who disagree, finding Marlowe's sympathy to lie with the Protestants, include Godshalk 84, 86–7; and Summers, *Christopher Marlowe* 149–54. A few critics emphasize Marlowe's 'ambivalence' towards the Guise (Sanders 35; and Kuriyama 85); and a few see Marlowe criticizing Navarre (Glenn 378–9; J. Briggs 272–3; and Brandt, *Christopher Marlowe* 134–9). Today, critics remain divided: whereas Healy argues that the 'play presents a good case for viewing Marlowe as a Protestant dramatist' (71) in the tradition of 'Spenser' (69), Kirk argues that the play 'merg[es]' the 'ostensible Protestant hero Navarre with Guise,' thereby 'foreclos[ing]' the 'experience, absorbing it in the image of English power' (208). Marlowe's art, or the mangled text, is complex, but the complexity does not rule out what critics emphasize: Marlowe's 'fascination with a figure who was as much eulogized as reviled in the sources available to him' (P. Roberts 435).

9 Earlier critics resisted the conclusion that the play has a 'social or political *context*' (Sanders 32 – emphasis in original; see Cole, *Suffering and Evil* 156). Critics interested in Elizabethan politics (Shepherd, Bartels) have little to say

about *The Massacre*; for a rare remark in earlier criticism, see Weil 101. Recently, Healy emphasizes that the play raises 'fears about a Catholic assassination of Elizabeth' and 'the possibility of a joint Anglo-French alliance against the Pope' (68–9; see 71). Finally, Kirk finds the English agent at the end 'perhaps a reflection of Marlowe' (193) – or of 'Elizabeth symbolically present' (208).

10 Cutts supplies a rare comment: 'The extended application of this analogy ... seems to have escaped attention ... The Guise makes himself the serpent inflicting death on the bride's mother by poisoning her through the perfumed gloves ... [T]he overriding symmetry of the classical analogy of the serpent in the Orpheus and Eurydice context is more significant, especially in view of his long exposition of his motivations delivered in almost the next breath' (*Left Hand of God* 172).

11 Spenser uses the Orpheus myth as a model for the poet's career in *October* (25–9). In *Epithalamion*, he invokes Orpheus to sing a marriage song to another Elizabeth (17–18), and Lotspeich cites Ovid, *Metamorphoses* X.1–3 as an origin (rpt. in the *Variorum Edition* 8: 460). Thus both Spenser and Marlowe had their eye on the same Ovidian lines.

12 See Kuriyama: 'Certainly this tendency to represent the Guise as a mother's boy [to the Queen-Mother, Catherine] does not enhance his credibility as a Marlovian superman' (88). I suggest that Marlowe imitates Ovid to identify the Guise as an Orphic figure – but with some trappings that Ovid merely hints at – and I would add that we need Seneca and Machiavelli in order to see these trappings. Bennett supplies four Spenser glosses for the play (191, 227, 244, 252), but none is particularly significant. Oliver does not repeat any of them, nor does he add any of his own.

13 See *FQ* I.ii.19:1–2 for 'the sleeping *spark* / Of *native* vertue'; and ii.35:1–3: 'when corage hot / The fire of love and joy of chevalree / *First kindled* in my brest' (emphasis added). Marlowe's language in the opening speech is Spenserian. What is equally intriguing is Marlowe's intertextual linkage here with *both* his great rivals within a single scene, as the Shakespearean origins noted earlier suggest.

14 Cutts notes an analogy between the Guise and Ovid's Alecto and Megaera in the *Metamorphoses* (*Left Hand of God* 173), and he sees another analogy between the Guise and Tantalus in their 'quenchless thirst' (*Massacre* ii.50), paving the way for a Senecan allusion, for Megaera is the Fury presiding over the House of Tantalus in Seneca's *Thyestes*. Shakespeare's use of Ovid's Medea speech in *The Tempest* is well known (see *Riverside Shakespeare* 1608).

15 See also *Ovid's Elegies* I.viii.11–12; and *Heroides* XVI.207–8.

16 On Spenser's imitation of Ovid's Medea passage, see Hamilton, ed., *FQ* 103.

17 In *Renaissance Tragedy*, Braden identifies 'the all-consuming subject of Senecan tragedy' as the 'voice of a style' that he terms 'rage' (2). The Guise resembles the Fury in the opening scene of *Thyestes*. The mixture of Ovid and Seneca in the Guise's speech receives support from Bennett, who concludes his gloss on the Ovidian Hymen line with this note: 'The whole passage is much in the Senecan style, with its parallel of sentences and meteorological references' (184). Perhaps more than the style is Senecan; see the speech of the Ghost of Agrippina in *Octavia* (593–600).

18 On the complexity of seeing the Guise as a Machiavel in the Machiavellian tradition, see Cole, *Suffering and Evil* 144, 152, 157. Kocher first argued that 'there could have been little room for Machiavellian influence on the dramatist' because Marlowe's sources, the contemporary pamphlets on the massacre at Paris, excoriated the Guise on their own ('Pamphlet Backgrounds ... Part Two' 314).

19 See Summers, *Christopher Marlowe*: 'What Marlowe does in this play is to present Guise initially as more like Tamburlaine than Barabas, then gradually to reveal him as becoming more ... like the anti-Machiavellian caricature' (136). I suggest that Marlowe metamorphoses the Guise from Machiavellian hero-villain into a caricature in order to represent the Guise's theatricality – a technique we have witnessed in *The Jew*. Is it possible that this metamorphosis is also Marlowe's way of closing off the Machiavellian phase of his career? Cole emphasizes the link between the two plays (*Suffering and Evil* 144–5), calling the Guise and Barabas 'two monsters of iniquity' (158; see Weil 86).

20 Cf. Cole, *Suffering and Evil*: 'The Guise's soliloquy ... reveals his ultimate goal, the crown of France' (151). As Weil remarks, however, 'We tend to lose sight here of the French diadem, his ostensible aim' (86). The Guise's use of 'learned' indicates that he has been reading Seneca, whose Atreus also repeatedly steels himself against weakness (e.g., l. 324).

21 See Cheney, *Spenser's Famous Flight* 95–6. The phrase 'flying fame' refers to the myth of Pegasus, as E.K. reveals elsewhere (*April* 211–16). On the importance of the Pegasus myth to Spenser, see *Spenser's Famous Flight* 72–4. H. Levin discovers the primary subtext of Marlowe's 'ethos of living dangerously' in the tragic Ovidian myth of the high-flying Icarus (23–4, 159–61). He notes that 'in *Tamburlaine* the emblem of tragic pride is Phaëthon ... In *Doctor Faustus* it is Icarus ... In each instance it is a question of flying too high' (112). On Icarus and Marlowe's 'preoccupation with unfettered soaring,' see Levin 134. Critics regularly discuss Marlowe's preoccupation with '[Icarian] soaring' in *Tamburlaine* (Daiches 80, 82; Benston 211, 225–6, 227), yet no one links Marlowe's flight imagery with the idea of fame or contextualizes it in terms of Spenser.

22 For the Augustinian basis of this passage, especially its reliance on flight to represent the ambition for salvation within the hymn, see Cheney, *Spenser's Famous Flight* 29, 199–200, and 254, n. 2.

23 Weil notes that the Guise and Barabas 'favour the bowel metaphor in describing the sources of their income' (86). Marlowe varies the line later, when the Guise remarks that he will 'rip the golden bowels of America' (xx.34). Moreover, when King Henry vaunts, 'I'll fire his crazed buildings' (xxiv.63), Marlowe may echo Spenser's description of the razing of Acrasia's Bower of Bliss in *The Faerie Queene*: 'Their banket houses burn, their buildings race' (II.xii.83). Marlowe's word 'crazed' echoes *acrasia*; Oliver notes that Marlowe's line appears in *Edward II* (I.iv.100 [161]).

24 On the Oedipal connection between the Guise and the 'Mother Queen,' see Kuriyama 82–9.

25 Accordingly, Catherine imitates the Guise, in a related exchange later about the royal treasury: 'All this and more hath Henry with his crown,' which prompts this echo from the Cardinal: 'And long may Henry enjoy all this, and more' (xiv.9–10).

26 Oliver is discussing the link with *Julius Caesar*. Critics writing on the 'sources' of *The Massacre* do not include Lucan's *Pharsalia*. Thomas and Tydeman, who mention Lucan (258–9), do not include him in their list of eight sources (251–92). On 'the conqueror-villain-hero of the *Pharsalia*,' see Blissett. Weil quips: 'One doubts that the historical Caesar ever said anything of the kind' (87).

27 Weil emphasizes Marlowe's ironic repetition of the word *truth* to undercut Navarre's claim (90).

28 Cf. Poirier: 'what has the Duchess of Guise's adultery to do with the clash between the two religions' (167). On the historical confusion of this event, see Oliver 131–2.

29 See H. Levin 104–5. Kuriyama notes, 'the unconventional or rebellious actions ascribed to Ramus (sexual, religious, and intellectual) are similar to those associated with Marlowe' (85–6).

30 MacLure, personal communication (Marlowe seminar, University of Toronto, 1975). Weil argues that 'the King's professor of logic ... is foolishly illogical' (102).

Chapter 9: Un-script(ur)ing Christian Tragedy: Ovidian Love, Magic, and Glory in *Doctor Faustus*

1 Greg, ed. 15–97; Bowers, ed. 2: 123–55. For recent reviews of the textual problem, see Bevington and Rasmussen, eds., *Doctor Faustus* 62–70; Gill, ed., *Complete Works* 2: xv–xxi; Empson, *Faustus and the Censor*; and Keefer, 'Verbal Magic' and ed. lx–lxix. All privilege the A-text as 'both aesthetically

preferable to the B-version and more authentic, in the sense of being closer to what Marlowe actually wrote' (Keefer, 'Verbal Magic' 324).

2 For recent reviews of the dating, see Bevington and Rasmussen, eds., *Doctor Faustus* 1–3; Gill, ed., *Complete Works* 2: xii; and Keefer, ed. lv–lx.

3 We do not know who Marlowe's collaborator was. Bevington and Rasmussen remark that Rowley and another candidate, Thomas Dekker, were both too young; they cite Kocher's argument for Marlowe's friend Thomas Nashe; but they suggest Henry Porter, 'Marlowe's contemporary at Cambridge and a dramatist for the Admiral's Men at the time Marlowe was writing *Tamburlaine* and *Doctor Faustus*' (eds., *Doctor Faustus* 71–2). By contrast, Gill argues for Nashe (ed., *Complete Works* 2: xviii–xxi).

4 Cutts argues against Greg, who saw the phrase as 'an indication either of "common authorship" or "community of authorship"' ('Marlowe Canon' 72; Greg, ed. 295): 'The expression might equally well refer to Marlowe himself. The "royal" we is used by Marlowe in the opening lines of the *Tamburlaine* prologue ... Surely there can now be no doubt that "*Our Muse*" is Marlowe's Muse' (72). Bevington and Rasmussen gloss the phrase as 'our poet, one under the guidance of a Muse ... ; a standard Renaissance metonymy,' and they follow modern consensus in granting authorship to Marlowe: 'Marlowe announces his intention ...' (eds., *Doctor Faustus* 106).

5 The B-text prints 'vaunt' for 'daunt' in line 6 (more of which presently). See Cutts, 'Marlowe Canon': 'From the collation it is at once obvious that nothing of the basic pattern of thought in the 1604Q (A) has been changed in the 1616Q (B)' (71).

6 See Cutts, 'Marlowe Canon' 73. The following editions, all based on the B-text, gloss lines 3–5 as Marlowe's references to *Edward II* and the *Tamburlaine* plays: Jump, ed. 4; Gill, 1965 (New Mermaids), ed. 4; Steane, ed. 590; and Barnet, 23. In her later New Mermaids edition of the 1604 text, Gill reduces her annotation to *Edward II* (ed. 5), but in her recent Oxford edition she exchanges her gloss of *Edward II* for *Dido* (ed., *Complete Works* 2: 49). Bevington and Rasmussen cite '*Dido* and *Tamburlaine*' (eds., *Doctor Faustus* 106). Keefer cites *Dido* and *Edward II* for ll. 3–4 and *Tamburlaine* for l. 5 (ed. 3). Critics agree that we are not sure whether Marlowe is referring to his own plays or to plays by his acting company. For instance, we do not know of a play that fits the description of the opening two lines on Hannibal's victory over the Carthaginians at Lake Thrasimene. But Cutts argues vigorously that Marlowe is referring to his own plays and that the Hannibal lines refer to 'an unknown play by Marlowe' ('Marlowe Canon' 72). This seems to me likely, for Hannibal is not simply a precursor of the Marlovian superman (Machiavelli calls him a type of 'inhuman cruelty' [*The Prince*, ed. and trans. Adams 46–7]);

he is also the subject of Silius Italicus's post-Virgilian epic, the *Punica* (see Quint 135). Although Silius remains reverential towards Virgil (Hardie, *Epic Successors of Virgil* 110), his Hannibal is a proto-Faustian/Tamburlaine figure; Hardie calls him 'Hellish Hannibal' (60): 'Hannibal is a hero in the mould of Lucan's Caesar' (64); he is 'a fairly close relative also of Milton's Satan' (80), because he claims to be '"made equal with the gods" [IV.810]' (96). Silius was part of the 1580 curriculum at St Paul's in London (Martindale, *Redeeming the Text* 26). An intriguing essay could be written on this topic.

7 Long ago, Kierkegaard remarked, 'one has always been ashamed to call the life of Christ a tragedy' (rpt. in Corrigan 356). On the topic of 'Christian tragedy,' see especially Michel, who traces the topic to Sewell (403), but who concludes that no such genre can exist: 'there is a basic incompatibility between the tragic and the Christian view. And nothing has yet come forth which can be called, without cavil, both Christian and Tragedy at the same time' (428). I believe that it is precisely this 'incompatibility' that Marlowe opens up, the fissure that he enters (see Michel 424 for a one-sentence dismissal of *Faustus* as a Christian tragedy). On *Faustus* and Christian tragedy, see Stroup; Waswo; and Bevington and Rasmussen, eds., *Doctor Faustus* 35–8. Waswo rejects Michel's thesis, and Sewell himself is eloquent on the play as a 'Christian Tragedy' (50-6, 57–67). For other generically inclined essays, see Gardiner; McAlindon, 'Christian Tradition'; and Deats, 'Chapbook to Tragedy.'

8 Cf. Snow, who speaks of Marlowe's poetics as 'nonjudgmental' (75).

9 Cf. Langer's metadramatic definition of tragedy as a genre, in which 'everything in it is poesis' (rpt. in Corrigan 123): 'Fate in tragedy is the created form' (119). Bevington and Rasmussen note that the 'verbal repetition' of 'perform / The form' is 'characteristic of Marlowe' (eds., *Doctor Faustus* 106). On theatricality in *Doctor Faustus*, see esp. Traci; Greenblatt, *Renaissance Self-Fashioning* 214–21; Shepherd 91–108; Kott 1–27; Sales 133–60; McAlindon, '*Doctor Faustus*' 62–84; Healy 57–61; and Hammill, esp. 321, 332.

10 For recent, influential, or astute readings of Marlowe's subversion, see Greenblatt, *Renaissance Self-Fashioning*, esp. 196–200, 209–14; Dollimore 109–19; Marcus, 'Textual Indeterminacy'; and Bartels 111–42. Dollimore sets the pace: '*Dr. Faustus* is best understood as ... not an affirmation of Divine Law, or conversely of Renaissance Man, but an exploration of subversion through transgression' (109). Marcus emphasizes the '"Marlowe effect"' (5): 'a theatrical event balanced on the nervous razor edge between transcendent heroism and dangerous blasphemy – transgression not only against God but also against cherished national goals and institutions' (4).

11 Cf. Watt on 'the three basic themes of the Faust myth': 'earthly beauty,' 'the excitement of knowledge,' and 'spiritual damnation' (29).

12 I follow N. Frye's definition of 'romance' in *The Secular Scripture* (3–31). In 'Language of Romance,' R.A. Martin follows Frye (see *Secular Scripture* 67) to view the *Tamburlaine* plays as a romance, and we may do the same for *Doctor Faustus*, which has the narrative and imagistic patterns that Frye discusses. On *The Faerie Queene* as a 'romance,' see P.A. Parker, *Inescapable Romance* 54–113, and 'Romance.' The 'romances' I consider are all versions of 'Virgilian epic.'

13 On damnation, see Greg, 'Damnation'; Gardiner; and Brockbank. The most detailed study of 'Eros and Magic in the Renaissance' comes from Couliano.

14 See Cheney, 'Two Florimells.' On Spenser's Neoplatonism, see also Bieman, *Plato Baptized*; and Quitslund.

15 The word *telamond* comes from the title page to Book IV of *The Faerie Queene*: 'The Legend of Cambel and Telamond.' On 'telamond' as 'perfect world,' see Roche 16–17. In my dissertation on magic in *The Faerie Queene*, I examine this archetype; see also 'Spenser's Completion,' '"Secret Powre Unseene,"' and 'Two Florimells.'

16 Schoeneich identifies a number of comparisons, but I find only four likely borrowings or echoes: (1) I.i.90 ('I'll have them wall all Germany with brass') from *FQ* III.iii.10 (91); (2) II.iii.21–3 ('Poison, guns, halters, and envenomed steel') from *FQ* I.ix.50 (93–4); (3) III.i.18 ('threates the stars with her aspiring top') from *The Ruines of Rome* 43 (96); and (4) IV.1.27 ('thousand furies wait' [B-text]) from *FQ* II.ii.30 (97). Gill in her 1990 Oxford edition cites only the first borrowing (50), but she cites the *OED* and *FQ* III.ii.6 as justification for changing 'daunt' to 'vaunt' in line 6 of the prologue (50); and she cites *FQ* I.viii.42 as a gloss on 'influence' at V.ii.90 (87). In his edition, Keefer introduces two new glosses: I.i.43–7 with *FQ* I.ix.53 (7); and I.i.73 with *FQ* I.ix.46 (9); he also cites the 'brass' wall passage (9) and the dagger scene of V.1 (80). In their edition, Bevington and Rasmussen also support the borrowings at I.i.90 from *FQ* III.iii.10 (116); and they gloss I.iii.1–4 ('Now that the gloomy shadow of the earth') with *FQ* III.x.46, following Jump, 'Marlowe and Spenser' (125). To these, I would add one new borrowing from the B-text: III.Chorus 18–19 ('mounted then upon a dragon's back, / That with his wings did part the subtle air,' spoken of Faustus), which may derive from *FQ* I.ii.3: 2–3 ('spread / A seeming body of the subtile aire,' spoken of another demonic magician, Archimago).

17 H. Levin 108; see also Sewell 64; Barber, 'Form'; Snow; and Greenblatt, whose Marlowe chapter in *Renaissance Self-Fashioning* is titled 'Marlowe and the Will to Absolute Play' (193–221). For Faustus's use of magic to acquire knowledge and power, see Kocher, 'Witchcraft Basis'; West; Blackburn; Yates, *Occult Philosophy* 115–25; and Mebane 113–36. In 'Magic and Poetry,' Palmer sees 'magic' as the 'subject' of the play (200).

18 In 1884, Symmonds identified the 'leading motive' pervading Marlowe's work as '*L'Amour de l'Impossible*' (rpt. in MacLure, ed., *Marlowe* 135). More recently, see McAlindon, '*Doctor Faustus*' 41–2. On 'Marlowe and the histrionics of ravishment,' see Goldman.

19 This point forms one of the cornerstones of Reformation attacks on Roman Catholicism (Calvin, 'Prefatory Address,' *Institutes* 16–18). See also K. Thomas 51–77, esp. 75–6.

20 Pico also interprets Circe Neoplatonically; see Hughes 388.

21 See Snyder, whose title is 'Marlowe's *Doctor Faustus* as an Inverted Saint's Life.'

22 In their edition of *Faustus*, Bevington and Rasmussen include eleven Ovid glosses under the A-text (ed. 107–8, 108, 114–15, 118, 128, 151 [two glosses], 156, 175, 191, 195), not including (curiously) Marlowe's reference to Arethusa (V.i.109). They add no new Ovid glosses to the B-text.

23 Regrettably, Rand does not supply a source for this story; needless to say, the translations are his.

24 Rand notes, 'This sort of interpretation must have something of a history before Valois and Vicot; one of their authorities was Arnaldus de Villa Nova, who was as learned in alchemy as we have found him in medicine' (141). On 'Virgil the Necromancer,' see Spargo's book by that name. Marlowe refers to this latter, more well-known, tradition at III.i.13–15.

25 On 'the magical associations of erotic and poetic seduction' in Ovid's poetry, see Sharrock 50–86. In a section subtitled 'Love, Poetry, and Magic' (53–61), she remarks, 'The metaphorical connection between love and magic, and actual pharmacological practice in erotic matters, constitute a well-developed, though elusive, tradition in literature when they are appropriated by Roman elegy' (53). For the history of 'Enchantment, Eros, and Elegy' coming out of Homer and Plato's *Symposium*, see her section by this title (61–7).

26 Ellis-Fermor remarks that the prologue is 'rich in autobiographical suggestion' (70–1). See also Wraight and Stern 322; and Barber, *Creating Elizabethan Tragedy* 49. On Marlowe as 'an *anima naturaliter Faustiana* himself,' see Watt 29–31.

27 The most famous remarks on the Icarus myth come from H. Levin (159–61), but for Ovidian annotation see Bevington and Rasmussen, eds., *Doctor Faustus* 107–8; and Gill, ed. *Complete Works* 2: 51. Cf. Gatti, who sees Marlowe following Bruno here (81–9, 112). On the Icarus myth in Ovid, see Wise; Carubba; and Ahearn. On the Renaissance Icarus myth, see Ashton. For a survey of the myth from classical Rome through the present day, see the two-essay sequence by Rudd 21–53.

28 As McAlindon recently remarks, the word 'conspire' has provoked a good deal

of comment. He himself rejects the 'predestinarian interpretation,' which sees the passage rehearsing a clear Calvinist process, arguing that Marlowe 'chose the word simply because it was metrically right' (*'Doctor Faustus'* 108–9). Both his and the Calvinist reading, however, neglect the Ovidian point I am making about human excellence as the *cause* of divine conspiracy.

29 What Feeney says of Lucan I would say of Faustus: 'He has not abandoned the gods, they have abandoned him' (285; see Martindale, *Redeeming the Text* 70–1).

30 Gill explains *polyptoton* as 'one of Marlowe's favourite rhetorical devices': 'Scholarship was adorned (*OED grace* 4) by Faustus, just as he was honoured (*OED grace* 5) by the conferment of the doctor's degree' (ed., *Complete Works* 2: 50). She adds: 'Marlowe is thinking in familiar terms of the official "grace" which permitted a candidate to proceed to his degree at the University of Cambridge. Marlowe's own name was entered in the Grace Book in 1584 and 1587' (2: 51). Marlowe's self-conscious device here is further evidence of the way in which the playwright *authors* his tragic hero.

31 See Birringer, *Marlowe's 'Dr Faustus' and 'Tamburlaine'* 68–70 on the consonance here between Marlowe's poetics and Ovid's in the *Amores*.

32 See Gill, who cites *FQ* III.ii.16 (ed., *Complete Works* 2: 50).

33 Marlowe's phrase evokes Spenser's role as a Protestant poet celebrating the virtue of 'holiness,' culminating in his role as divine poet. One of the recurrent epithets given to Spenser by his contemporaries is 'divine.' Most important among them, Marlowe's friend Nashe refers to 'divine Master Spencer' (rpt. in Cummings 60), and he calls the New Poet 'heavenlie Spencer' (rpt. in Cummings 60). Marlowe's manoeuvre here is also consistent with his imitation of Spenser in the *Dedicatory Epistle* to Watson's *Amintae Gaudia*, where he projects for Mary Sidney's benefit his turn to *higher* kinds of writing within the context of Christian glory (see introduction to Part III).

34 See Gill: 'Although sense 3 of *eternize* (= to immortalize, make perpetually famous) is not recorded until 1610 in *OED*, it was a favourite form with Marlowe' (ed., *Complete Works* 2: 54). The first *OED* usage is the one we need to recall: 'To make eternal, i.e. everlasting or endless,' with a key example from a 1610 translation of St Augustine's *City of God*, 'His [God's] holy will ... can eternise creations' (Def. 1).

35 Bevington and Rasmussen participate in the confusion when they note that Faustus 'blasphemously equates himself with Christ,' citing Storm (eds., *Doctor Faustus* 16; see 41). My point is that Faustus does not equate himself with Christ, but *rewrites* Christ by solving humankind's most haunting problem: the fact of death. Ingram states the idea clearly: 'what he lusts after is eternal living rather than the life-eternal' (75). The origin of Marlowe's principle may lie in Lucan's great witch, Erichtho, who 'is not content to call up ghosts, but

instead brings the corpse itself back to life' (Hardie, *Epic Successors of Virgil* 108). Michel says that 'the question of immortality' is 'the key to all problems' in both tragedy and religion (418). On 'the theme of immortality' in the opening soliloquy, see Storm 43. McAlindon remarks that '*Doctor Faustus* ... attaches an importance to death that is exceptional, if not unique, in tragedy' ('*Doctor Faustus*' 96). Traci sees 'the theme of the artist,' as well as poetic fame, contained in both 'eternise' and 'make man to live eternally' (5). Snow sees the 'act of translation' as 'itself a central motif of the soliloquy' (75), and he understands perfectly the problem Marlowe confronts: 'Faustus is time, and time Faustus' (104).

36 See Couliano: 'At its greatest degree of development, reached in the work of Giordano Bruno, magic is a means of control over the individual and the masses based on deep knowledge of personal and collective erotic impulses ... Magic is merely eroticism applied, directed, and aroused by its performer' (xviii). On Marlowe's relation with Bruno, see Gatti 74–113.

37 Perhaps the earliest attempt to formulate the Marlovian principle comes in 1875 from Swinburne, that ardent admirer of Marlowe: 'In Marlowe the passion of ideal love for the ultimate idea of beauty in art or nature found its perfect and supreme expression, faultless and unforced ... No poet ever came nearer than Marlowe to the expression of this inexpressible beauty, to the incarnation in actual form of ideal perfection, to the embodiment in mortal music of immortal harmony' (rpt. in MacLure, ed. *Marlowe* 175, 176). In his prologue to *Doctor Faustus* for William Poel's 1896 play, Swinburne rhapsodizes the principle this way: 'Incarnate man, fast found as earth and sea / Spake, when his pride would fain set Faustus free. / Eternal beauty, strong as day and night, / Shone, when his word bade Helen back to sight' (rpt. in MacLure 177).

38 In Act I, scene ii, Wagner's conversation with the two scholars wittily inscribes the philosophical basis of the paradigm of immanence in reference to what Gill calls 'the current academic definition of the subject-matter of physics': the phrase from Aristotle, '*corpus naturale seu mobile*' or 'a natural body and [therefore] capable of movement' (ed., *Complete Works* 2: 62). See also Bevington and Rasmussen for a fine explanation of Wagner's use of the concept (eds., *Doctor Faustus* 123).

39 Cf. Waswo, who sees Faustus's flights of fancy as 'ludicrous and absurd,' a 'school boy fantasy of what fun it would be to play God' (84). The repetition of Spenser complicates the comedy.

40 For analyses of the Hellenore episode, see Berger, *Revisionary Play* 154–71; Brill (who remarks that 'Renaissance readers were likely to regard Helen less as "the face that launch'd a thousand ships" (Marlowe *Dr Faustus* 18.99) than as the epitome of a faithless wife' [352]); Suzuki 159–73; and Krier 176–86. Critics

agree that Spenser is rewriting both Homer and Virgil via Ovid; as Krier puts it, 'The marks of Ovid's elegies are everywhere,' with specific allusions to the 'coy game with spilled wine, drawn from *Amores* 2.5 and *Heroides* 17' and to Ovid's mating with Corinna 'nine times' in one night from *Amores* III.vii (180). Krier calls the event closing the episode, Malbecco's metamorphosis into the monster Jealousy (III.x.57), 'Spenser's darkest interpretation of Ovid's work' (181). She also calls the scene of Hellenore's coupling with the satyrs, which Marlowe is imitating, 'the Ovidian woods, latent with erotic energy' (184). Berger concludes that the episode is 'Spenser's judgment on Helen and the centuries of male worship which have elevated her into a heroic institution. Hellenore is Helen *deglamorized* and returned to her proper place' (163).

41 As Gill notes, in line 1 the A-text prints 'shadow of the earth,' which she retains in her 1990 Oxford edition, but the B-text prints 'shadow of the night,' following the anonymous author of *The Taming of A Shrew* (1594) (ed., *Complete Works* 2: 63).

42 The metadiscourse here joins with other images to identify Faustus as a Marlovian poet: 'sweet Musaeus' (I.i.118); 'conjurer laureate' (I.iii.33). Not surprisingly, criticism finds Spenser entangled in Faustus's Latin conjuration itself: 'Sint mihi dei Acherontis propitii … Demogorgon' (I.iii.16–18). Hamilton glosses Spenser's reference to another conjuror's incantation, Archimago's call to 'Great Gorgon, Prince of darknesse and dead night' (I.i.37), by noting that 'in Marlowe's *Faustus* I iii, he [Gorgon] is one of the infernal trinity invoked with Lucifer and Beelzebub' (ed., *FQ* 39).

43 According to H. Levin, 'The man has an extraordinary affection for the spirit, the spirit a mysterious attraction to the man'; Levin calls their relationship a 'profound sympathy' (116–17).

44 Cf. Snow on the 'experiences of grace' in *Doctor Faustus*: 'one can in fact observe their potential affirmation being systematically converted into terror and "despair"' (104).

45 Crawford first saw a direct borrowing (203). For early commentary, see Mahood 109; and Barber, '"Form"' 180–1. See also Campbell 235; Cole, *Suffering and Evil* 199; Sachs 635, 645; Waswo 82–3; Birringer, *Marlowe's 'Dr Faustus' and 'Tamburlaine'* 191–2; and Keefer, ed. xlix–l.

46 In her list of iconographical examples of despair, Snyder includes 'Book I of *The Faerie Queene*' (573, n. 15).

47 Bevington and Rasmussen cite 'post-Homeric continuations of the Troy story,' including 'Ovid's *Heroides* v,' commenting, 'Marlowe here imagines in an Ovidian vein the death of the heartbroken woman' (eds., *Doctor Faustus* 151).

48 Marlowe also had his eye on the phrase 'lovely boy' at *Faerie Queene* I.vi.17, for he echoes it in *Hero and Leander* (Bush, 'Marlowe and Spenser').

49 Virgil refers to the Amphion myth in an eclogue we know Marlowe penetrated with great interest: Eclogue II (23–4), the homoerotic eclogue featuring Corydon and Alexis, the last of whom, says Kyd, Marlowe aligned with the homoerotic Christ (rpt. in MacLure, ed., *Marlowe* 35).

50 On the theatricality of 'perform,' see Kott 8. Usefully, Sales links the site of Faustus's magical performance, the solitary grove, with the 'public theatres, in the Liberties of London' (141).

51 Brandt traces Marlowe's image of Helen kissing Faustus through the tradition of 'the soul-in-the-kiss conceit,' which 'was widespread in the ancient world, but with the coming of Christianity,' the conceit acquired a 'new meaning,' including the 'liturgical kiss of peace,' the '*mors osculi*' or 'kiss between soul and Deity,' which signifies 'salvation and eternal bliss,' and the 'Neoplatonic' kiss represented in Castiglione's *Book of the Courtier*, which leads to the 'intermingling of souls' in the 'ascent up the Neoplatonic ladder' ('Marlowe's Helen' 119). According to Brandt, Marlowe parodies this multifaceted conceit in order to 'confirm' Faustus 'on his path to damnation' (119).

52 The image is indeed rare; the closest I have seen comes from Spenser's own *Astrophel*, when Stella kisses the dying hero (163–6). This scene, however, contains no magic. In the context of the Marlowe/Spenser relation, Hammill's discovery of 'sodomy' concealed in the sucking-forth conceit of 'Faustus' and 'succubus' (331) is, if nothing else, full of intrigue.

53 McAlindon, 'Classical Mythology,' sees Faustus's conjuration of Helen as the supreme example of his attempt to use magic and mythology as replacements for theology. On the topic of 'Heavenly Helen,' see also Forsyth. More recently, Healy cites the Paris passage as an example of what he calls 'the Marlowe effect,' formed through a strategy of 'extravagance,' which is 'Marlowe's tool for an intellectual exploration of humanity's inability to live content in this world' (1). In the Paris passage, 'Hellish illusion becomes more attractive and desirable than Christian certainties ... [Marlowe] is dramatically forcing the suspension of certain norms which governed an Elizabethan construction of the satanic and Christian, the hellish and heavenly' – what he calls 'Faustus's creation of a heroic theater in which he casts himself in a major role' (7).

54 See V.i.23–4, where Faustus tells the three Scholars that they shall see Helen 'when Sir Paris crossed the seas with her, / And brought the spoils to rich Dardania.' For excellent commentary on Paris as the 'archetype of the shepherd,' see H. Smith 6 (see also 3–9). Smith goes on to relate the shepherd to the prince, pastoral to epic: 'Paris, the son of Priam, King of Troy, was the most famous of all classical shepherds because from his action sprang the whole epic narrative of the siege of Troy' (3–4; for a similar paradigm with reference to

Spenser, see 6–7). Marlowe's Faustian interest in Paris confirms this 'plot' as 'surely one of the great achievements of the Western imagination' (4). For Paris as a figure in a *cursus* ('a course of life'), see 5.

55 Bradbrook sees Faustus's rapture over Helen 'beginning in the remoteness of a Cynthia empyrean,' observing of the Helen speech: 'This is a development from the method of [Ralegh's] *Cynthia*' (*School of Night* 105–6).

56 See also *Aprill* 150 for 'dame Eliza'; and *FQ* III.ii.3 for 'rimes too rude and rugged.' Finally, see *FQ* I.Pr.2 for Spenser's 'O helpe thou my weake wit' and for Elizabeth as '[m]irrour of grace and Majestie divine.' On Marlowe's presentation of Lucifer as a 'Renaissance prince' in the Machiavellian mode, see Sales 145, 151, and esp. 160.

57 Cf. Keefer, who articulates the received wisdom: '*Doctor Faustus* does not invite its audience to imagine any secure alternative to the [Calvinist] orthodoxy which it questions. Indeed, it seems unlikely that Marlowe possessed such an alternative himself ... A Calvinistic orthodoxy [of 'predestined damnation to eternal torment'] may appear to win out at the end of this play, but it does so at the cost of being exposed, in the moment of triumph, as intolerable' (ed. xiv). I suggest that Marlowe superimposes onto this interrogation an 'Ovidian' alternative that proceeds with some triumph. In his discussion of the carnivalesque in *Doctor Faustus* (150–5), Bristol overlooks this Ovidian dimension of Marlovian festivity, including its contribution to the play's dialogism, concentrating instead on 'clowning and devilment' (150) as they enter into dialogue with 'the story of Faustus's fatal and apocalyptic contract with Lucifer' (152). Hammill allows us to see an extension of the Ovidian dimension in the B-text's final scene: 'The ripping apart of Faustus' own body repeats another version of the Actaeon story' as told by Ovid in the *Metamorphoses* (322).

58 On the *Amores* elegy, see esp. Elliott; D. Parker 80–3; and Gransden. In *The Shadow of Night*, Chapman identifies the horses of morning as Pegasus – the poet's horse of fame (Chapman, ed. Shepherd 2: 6; see 2: 9).

59 Perhaps this is because they consider the boldness to be Faustus's rather than Marlowe's. The best commentary remains that by Snow (77–8), but I disagree with his conclusion: 'Marlowe is too self-critically implicated in his protagonist ... to bestow upon his character a creaturely grace predicated upon authorial transcendence' (104).

60 The edition reorders the poems in the following sequence: I.i, I.iii, I.v, III.xiii, I.xv, I.xiii, II.iv, II.x, III.vi, and I.ii.

61 Pearcy contextualizes Marlowe's practice in terms of the numerology of both *Epithalamion* (26–7) and *The Teares of the Muses* (30), but he does not suggest that Marlowe might be *responding* to Spenser.

62 Cf. Garber, 'Closure,' who sees here merely a 'despairing cry ... a moment of aspiration' that 'comes too little, too late' (5). Later, however, she notes that the line contains what she calls the '"aspiring foot"': 'we can count not ten but eleven syllables; at the very moment that he aspires most fervently to escape damnation, his language aspires to escape the formal strictures of language' (20). I would say 'does escape' – an idea Garber anticipates in her subsequent remark: 'the answer to Faustus' question is clear: ... it is the author who succeeds in enclosing' (20).

63 Bate cites Dryden on the Spenser/Chaucer relation (n. 4 [see *FQ* IV.ii.32–4]), but he could have cited the process Spenser calls 'traduction' in *FQ* IV.iii.13 in the story of the three sons of Agape (see Cheney, 'Spenser's Completion' and 'Triamond'). W.R. Johnson links the Ovid and Marlowe accounts ('Counterclassical Sensibility' 139). In his *Dedicatory Epistle* 'To the Reader' prefacing his translation of the *Odyssey*, Chapman uses both 'transmigration' and 'traduction' to speak of the art of literary translation (2: 242). Finally, see Greene: 'The image that propelled the humanist Renaissance and that still determines our perception of it, was the archaeological, necromantic metaphor of disinterment, a digging up that was also a resuscitation or a reincarnation or a rebirth' (92; see 30–3). Greene sees 'the humanist necromancer-scholar' epitomized in Petrarch (92).

64 Cf. Greenblatt, *Renaissance Self-Fashioning*, who organizes his essay on Marlowe to emphasize Marlowe's 'haunting sense of unsatisfied longing' (221). None the less, Proser remarks that 'aggression in Marlowe's works has a sexual dimension, so that the satisfactions of revenge for the characters, the cruel punishments or blood deaths, come to stand for orgasmic release' (*Gift of Fire* 198). Long ago, Empson observed (as Frank Romany kindly points out to me [personal communication, June 1996]), 'the main meaning is a shuddering acceptance ... But behind this there is also a demand for the final intellectual curiosity, at whatever cost, to be satisfied' (*Seven Types* 233; see *Censor* 162–3). See also Snow 83, who cites Barber's seminal essay ('Form') on 'triumph' in *Doctor Faustus* (Snow 108–9, n. 15)

Part III: Trumpets and Drums: Epic

1 In addition to Spenser, other laureates – Daniel in *The Complaint of Rosamond*, Drayton in *Endimion and Phoebe*, and Chapman in his continuation of *Hero and Leander* – wrote minor epics.

2 Evidently, Hulse situates Shakespeare's minor epics, but not Marlowe's, within the career model moving from apprenticeship to maturity because only Shakespeare lived long enough to make the move. I observe, however, that the

role Hulse assigns the minor epic in the model indicates that Marlowe *was precisely in the process of making the move.*

3 Marlowe's self-deprecating remarks may look un-Marlovian, but Marlowe himself can be un-Marlovian. See *Hero and Leander* for his reliance on the topoi of inability and modesty (I.69–72).

4 This topic warrants a pause. In 1850, for instance, a short entry appeared in *Notes and Queries* signed simply 'm,' who mentioned a manuscript containing one eclogue and sixteen sonnets written by 'Ch.M.' This manuscript remained 'lost' to Marlowe scholars, but by 1942 Bakeless concluded: 'Marlowe's lost sonnets may have been genuine' (2: 161; see also 2: 290). Bakeless found the probability increased because of the technical mastery that he and Brooke thought Marlowe displayed in the handling of the ottava rima stanza in some verses printed in *England's Parnassus* (1600), titled 'Description of Seas, Waters, Rivers, &c' (2: 161; see also 2: 290). Three years later, Kocher discovered a sonnet embedded in *1 Tamburlaine* (V.i.160–73), which Marlowe adapted to the blank verse line ('A Marlowe Sonnet'). Then, in 1979 Ranson identified Marlowe as the 'Phaeton' who authored a commendatory sonnet, 'Phaeton to His Friend Florio,' in John Florio's *Second Frutes*. Finally, in 1986 Eriksen argued that Marlowe 'took particular interest in the sonnets [of Petrarch] entitled *"In Morte di Madonna Laura"*, two of which must be considered as sources for the Epilogue of *Doctor Faustus*,' and he proposed a *second* sonnet embedded in the blank verse of *Tamburlaine* ('Marlowe's Petrarch' 14, 20): at *2 Tamburlaine* II.iv.1–14. Thus we may have at least *three* Marlovian sonnets. Furthermore, Eriksen argued that Marlowe's *Dedicatory Epistle* to Mary Sidney 'refers to some of his own poems ... as *Nymphaeque Peneiae semper virens coma ...*, a reference that must point to a group of sonnets in view of the inevitable association of Daphne and the laurel with Petrarch's sonnets to Laura' (13). Eriksen astutely observed that Marlowe addresses Mary Sidney by her Petrarchan sonnet persona, 'Delia,' given to her by Daniel, and that Marlowe 'mentions the author of *Astrophil and Stella*' (13). Finally, Eriksen speculated that the sonnets to which the dedication refer might be the lost set of sixteen mentioned in *Notes and Queries*. In 1988, however, Chaudhuri printed the 'lost' manuscript, finding no evidence that *our* Christopher Marlowe is the author, assigning the poems rather to Christopher Morley, a Fellow of Trinity College, Cambridge, who died in 1596. Thus, if Chaudhuri is correct about the authorship of these poems, we are forced to abandon Eriksen's enticing supposition about Marlowe's actual reference to his Petrarchan poetry. Even so, Eriksen's reading of the laurel passage in the 'Delia' dedication does identify Marlowe as an author in the Petrarchan genre, and I think we need to take his reading seriously.

5 Marlowe's phrasing here participates in a broad European discourse imitating or interpreting Virgil's *Eclogues*, represented by Sannazaro, *Arcadia*: 'he by nature having a genius disposed to higher things, and not contenting himself with so humble a strain, took in exchange that reed that now you see there, larger and newer than the others, to be the better able to sing of greater things' (ch. 10, pp. 104–5; see ch. 7, pp. 74–5; and chapter 2 of the present study).

6 Spenser's use of the Philomela myth to decry the state of poetry is relatively rare, if not original. The only other instance I can cite is this one by Marlowe. D.L. Miller, 'Death of the Modern,' sees a parallel between Marlowe's Philomela image and Spenser's 'mute[ness]' at the end of *The Teares of the Muses* (778), but he does not cite Spenser's own Philomela image. He usefully sees the consonance between the Mary Sidney *Dedication* and *Hero and Leander*: the 'erasure of [woman's] ... subjectivity' (776), 'the theft of her voice' (778).

Chapter 10: Counter-Epic of Empire: *Lucan's First Book*

1 Dilke 84. See also *Troilus and Criseyde* V.1792, *The Monk's Tale* 3909–10, and *The Man of Law's Tale* 400–3. According to Dilke, 'Lydgate, in his *Fall of Princes*, derives much of his historical material on the fall of Pompey indirectly from Lucan, by way of ... Boccaccio's *De Casibus Virorum Illustrium*' (84); Skelton mentions Lucan in his *Garland of Laurel* (85); and Thomas Hughes in his 1588 tragedy, *The Misfortunes of Arthur*, 'purloined whole sections from Seneca's tragedies and Lucan' (85). In her new translation of the *Pharsalia*, Joyce observes that 'Lucan's epic is the only poem from the classical era included among the *editiones principes*, classical texts printed between 1465 and 1469, the first five years of the printing press' (xvi).

2 In classical studies, critics have been carrying out what W.R. Johnson calls 'the task of freeing Lucan from his long near oblivion' (*Momentary Monsters* 2) – among them, Ahl, *Lucan*; J. Henderson; Feeney; and Martindale, *Redeeming the Text*. No one is more eloquent on the 'greatness' of Lucan and his poem than Johnson himself: 'Undistracted by its possible flaws, we can begin to see something of its greatness, can begin to experience something of the energy, the violent beauty, and the strong craving for truth that made Dante admire it and prompted Marlowe to begin its translation' (*Momentary Monsters* 3). In Renaissance studies, Hulse (199–205, 210–14, 279), McCoy 103–26, and esp. Quint (5–10, 131–60) have joined classicists in reviving Lucan from oblivion. Quint tries 'to establish a political genealogy of the [epic] tradition itself' (13), and heroically he makes 'claims for the importance of Lucan's *Pharsalia* and its alternative tradition in the history of epic' (16). Granting Lucan something

close to equal status with Virgil in the twin creation of 'two rival traditions of epic' – 'epics of the imperial victors and epics of the defeated' (8) – Quint speaks of 'the genius of Lucan' (131) as the inaugurator of 'a rival, anti-Virgilian tradition of epic whose major poems – the *Pharsalia* itself, *La Araucana* of Alonso de Ercilla, and *Les Tragiques* of Agrippa d'Aubigné – embrace the cause of the politically defeated' (133). On Lucan in the Middle Ages and the Renaissance, see (in addition to Dilke 83–102) Crosland; Blissett, esp. 554–6; Ronan 305 and n. 1; Shapiro, '"Lucan"' 316–17; and G.M. Maclean 26–44. Subsequent to Marlowe, great admirers of Lucan include Montaigne, Dr Johnson, and Shelley (see Joyce xvi–vii).

3 The three article-length studies are by Steane 249–79; Gill, 'Sulpitius'; and Shapiro, '"Lucan."' The one note is by Ronan. The short overviews are by Ellis-Fermor 14–17; Boas, *Christopher Marlowe* 42–8; Bakeless 2: 163–6; Blissett 262–6; Knoll 29–32; and Leech, *Christopher Marlowe* 32–5. To this list, I would add the series of illuminating remarks by H. Levin (10, 17, 21, 32, 48, 53, 100, 165).

4 Swinburne, rpt. in MacLure, ed., *Marlowe* 183 – the first substantive comment. MacLure reprints brief reports by Thomas Warton in 1781 (58); Bradley in 1880 (129); and Saintsbury in 1887 (163).

5 For other praise, see W.R. Johnson, *Momentary Monsters* xii, 3, 14–16, 57, n. 23, 75; and Joyce, who calls *Lucan's First Book* a 'splendid translation' (xvi). For other critical comments through the 1960s, see 'The Poems and Their Reputation' in MacLure, ed. *Poems* xxxix–xliv.

6 We are not sure when Marlowe made his translation, but most critics select either the Cambridge years (around 1585 [Gill, ed., *Complete Works* 1: 88]) or 1592–3, when the theatres close (Lewis, *English Literature* 486; Shapiro, '"Lucan"' 323–4). Nor are we sure when *Lucan* was first published. With *Hero and Leander*, the work was entered to John Wolf in the Stationers' Register on 28 September 1593, but we know of no publication until seven years later, when Peter Short prints it for Thomas Thorpe. On the complexities of this printing history, see esp. Brooke, ed., *Works* 643; and Gill, ed., *Complete Works* 1: 90–2. As to be expected, critics have spent most of their space examining the accuracy of Marlowe's translation, but Steane articulates the most important conclusion here: 'The voice is distinctively and forcefully Marlowe's. Individuality emerges in every passage ... [T]he translation is ... as essentially Marlovian as anything he did ... Marlowe's Lucan is in fact an English poem' (254, 261, 270; see also Leech, *Christopher Marlowe* 34–5; and Gill, 'Sulpitius' 403–4). On Marlowe's kinship with Lucan, critics have turned up varying but not contradictory lists of affinities; for instance, H. Levin emphasizes a 'temperamental kinship' (10); and Steane singles out 'their violent

and early deaths' (254), their reputations as 'bold, independent mind[s], given to strong antipathies and enthusiasms, with an irreverent and ironical streak which courted danger' (255), their 'partisan' works hopelessly backing the defeated (255–6), their commitment to 'hyperbole' (257), their 'unorthodoxies in artistic and religious matters' (257), and what Steane identifies as 'the most striking affinity,' their 'sadis[m]' (258). Finally, critics have assigned significance differently, although most would agree with Hardison: 'the only sustained sixteenth-century heroic poem in blank verse after Surrey is Marlowe's translation of the first book of Lucan's *Pharsalia*' (265). Occasionally, critics contextualize the translation briefly in terms of 'the Elizabethan preoccupation with the evils of civil war' (Steane 251), but we have not gotten beyond this generality.

7 See Bolgar 530–1; and MacLure, ed., *Poems* xxxv. Before Marlowe, both Turbervile and Googe tried to translate the *Pharsalia* but failed (Shapiro, '"Lucan"' 316–17). After Marlowe, Gorges (1614) and May (1627) both succeeded (Steane 266–71).

8 See Quint: 'the poems of Lucan's tradition criticize a Virgilian ideology that couples emperor-king and imperial conquest' (11).

9 H. Levin calls *Lucan* 'a glance in the direction of the epic' (10; see 17, 32) – with this conclusion: 'Marlowe learned ... the epic mode from Lucan' (165). See Gill: Marlowe 'made out of the first book of the *Pharsalia* the beginning of an epic poem worthy of notice in itself' ('Sulpitius' 406). My argument complements that of Quint, who overlooks Marlowe's translation, thus missing a historically priceless contribution to the project of 'trying to establish a political genealogy of the [epic] tradition itself.' Quint also curiously neglects Lucan's crucial relation with Ovid, whom Johnson terms Lucan's 'master' (58, n. 25). Quint does not mention Ovid until p. 76, when he compares the *Metamorphoses* with the *Aeneid*, and only on p. 141 does he observe in passing that 'Lucan indeed learned from Ovid, and the episodicity by which the *Pharsalia* departs from and resists classical form also finds a corollary thematic reflection in its depiction of the body.' I emphasize both the Marlovian and the Ovidian contributions to the Lucanic epic tradition that Quint discusses. Unfortunately, we are not privy to Marlowe's intentions in translating Book I: did he plan to finish his translation, as Chapman would shortly do with his published excerpt of the *Iliad*? or did he plan to let the book stand on its own, as many critics believe (Shapiro, '"Lucan"' 323; and MacLure, ed., *Poems* xxxiv–xxxv). In either case, *Lucan's First Book* catches Marlowe in the act of writing epic, and I remain intrigued by the remark of L.C. Martin: 'The work is chiefly interesting ... as a fore-shadowing of what Marlowe might himself have achieved if he had later attempted an original narrative poem in that form' (19).

10 See Hardie, *Epic Successors of Virgil* 7, 60–2, 94–5, 105–1; Johnson, *Momentary Monsters* 58 (n. 25), 60, 64, 65–6; and Martindale, *Redeeming the Text* 55–74. Marlowe critics do see the poetic succession; Leech calls Ovid and Lucan 'dissident Roman poets' (*Christopher Marlowe* 26). Some, like Healy, amplify on the writers' similarities: both write 'classical texts which deal with deception, civil disorder, and ungovernable emotions both in private and civic life' (18). Still others, like Blissett, locate the succession in Marlowe, whose 'verse is ... an alloy of Ovidian copper and Lucanic iron' (555–6).

11 See Feeney: 'Unlike the poems of Homer, Vergil, even Apollonius, this epic has nothing to say about the wishes or designs of any deity in its proem ... There is no Muse' (272–3, 275).

12 MacLure calls 'trumpets and drums' Marlowe's 'lively elaboration of "signa", standards' (ed., *Poems* 223). See also Gill, ed., *Complete Works* 1: 247. In his translation, Gorges writes 'conquering hand' and 'ensignes,' while May writes 'victorious swords' and 'Ensignes' (qtd. in Steane 266–7).

13 Gill, ed., *Complete Works* 1: 247: 'Thus Marlowe translates Lucan's *canimus*, disregarding the fact, pointed out by Sulpitius, that the Roman poet's plural form (instead of the more usual *cano*) was probably dictated by the metre: *Metrice eloquimur*.' For Marlowe's debt to Sulpitius' commentary on the *Pharsalia*, see Gill, 'Sulpitius.'

14 In fact, the phrase 'trumpets and drums' is a recurrent stage direction in *2 Tamburlaine*.

15 See Gill, ed., *Complete Works* 1: 247: 'With "darts" Marlowe offers an acceptable Elizabethan equivalent for Lucan's *pila*' or javelin. Spenser also uses the word in the Proem to *his* epic (*FQ* I.Pr.3).

16 Cf. Orgel 253: 'to the Elizabethans, this classic study of the horrors of civil war had a special relevance ... Lucan's concerns were the substance of modern history ... [I]n such circumstances Lucan should have been regarded more as a model for the treatment of recent events [the English Civil War]).' And Gill: 'Some of the best writing in *Lucan's First Booke* speaks directly to the Elizabethans, warning of the horror of civil war'; the translation thus has a 'grim topicality,' esp. in light of the Babington Plot (ed., *Complete Works* 1: 89). Probably, we should reread *Lucan* in light of Ahl: 'In book 1 ... Lucan has taken some pains to make his criticism [of Caesarism] oblique by attributing these words [ll. 668–72] to one of his characters ... [T]he *Pharsalia* is hostile to Caesarism ... [In t]he invocation of Nero in 1.33–66 ... every element admits of double entendre ... At the opening of the epic, the work's final nature is not manifest; the reader does not yet know that this is to be an epic without gods, in defiance of tradition. Thus only the more playful aspects of the satire would be noticeable ... [T]here is no compelling reason to assume ... that the *Pharsalia*

is favorable to *princeps* and principate. But there is much to suggest the opposite. Even if one does not concede the satirical nature of the apotheosis [of Nero] in book 1, we ought to bear in mind that dedications to kings and emperors are part and parcel not only of Roman, but of Elizabethan and Jacobean poetry. To renounce one's emperor in the opening book of an epic would be ill-advised, possibly even fatal to both poet and poem' (*Lucan* 44, 46, 47, 48, 49, 54).

17 On this prophecy, see Feeney 286–7; and Makowski, who emphasizes Lucan's rejection of Virgilian prophecy: 'The only certitude about the future is death' (195).

18 On Shakespeare's use of *The Ruines of Rome* in *The Sonnets*, see Hieatt. On Spenser's reading of Du Bellay, see Prescott, 'Spenser (Re)Reading du Bellay.' And on Du Bellay in Renaissance England, see Prescott, '*Translatio Lupae*' and 'Du Bellay in Renaissance England.'

19 Chambers quotes *Pharsalia* I.21–3 as the source of Du Bellay's III.34–5 (the last two lines of the Spenser passage quoted). Chambers's argument is that 'du Bellay had Lucan in mind, or actually before him, when he wrote the *Antiquitez*' (937), and he assembles fourteen passages to prove it. Spenser's recent editors neglect the Lucan/Du Bellay connection, observing instead that 'Virgil is preeminent here' (Oram et al. 381), although they do gloss a number of lines with passages from the *Pharsalia* (397, 398, 399, 401, 403). *The Spenser Encyclopedia* contains no article on Lucan.

20 Back in 1901, Crawford observed that 'Spenser's "Ruines of Rome"... [is] a poem that was evidently a favorite of Marlowe's, who has taken suggestions from it for several of the speeches on "Tamburlaine"' (63). He compares *Ruines of Rome*, stanzas 20–2 and 26 with *1 Tamb* II.vi.1–4 and V.1.512–13, and *Ruines*, stanza 10, with *1 Tamb* II.ii.47–56. Following Chambers's lead, we might reconfigure a commonplace of Marlowe criticism about the translator of Ovid and Lucan: 'At a still earlier age and before writing anything original, Spenser had similarly translated Petrarch and Du Bellay into English verse. Both poets were thus following Horace's precept, which had but lately been recalled by Sidney: if one is born a poet, it is nevertheless only through imitation and practice that one can hope to scale the height of Parnassus' (78). While I do not accept an early date for *Lucan*, and observe that only Spenser's *Visions of Bellay*, not his translation of *Antiquitez de Rome*, qualifies as 'juvenilia' (see Oram et al. 217), we may wonder whether Marlowe found in Spenser's translation of Du Bellay more than a convenient comparison.

21 Schoeneich (77), W. D. Briggs (151), and Charlton and Waller (134) all accept Marlowe's 'Renowmed' at *Edward II* II.v.41 as Spenserian in origin. On Du Bellay and Spenser's 'overtly Christian recoil from Rome's seductive

allurements,' see Oram et al. 382; and Ferguson 29. I am struck by the similarity of Marlowe's description of the French Bardi and a recent description of Spenser: 'The diminutive, distinctively unsoldierlike Spenser, weak in health, at once timid and incautious, was no man to drag about on [Lord] Grey's skirmishes and coercions, which Spenser did not witness' (Bruce 356).

22 Throughout, Feeney emphasizes Lucan's attack on 'Stoic Providence' (see 283–4).

Chapter 11: Marlowe, Chapman, and the Rewriting of Spenser's England in *Hero and Leander*

1 On the two editions, see Greg, 'Copyright.' We do not know when Marlowe composed *Hero and Leander*, but critics agree that he wrote it either 'early,' during his Cambridge years, or 'late,' during the 1592–3 closing of the theatres, with the majority opting for a late date. See L.C. Martin 3–4; MacLure, ed., *Poems* xxv; and Gill, ed., *Complete Works* 1: 179.

2 For the editions, see L.C. Martin; MacLure; Orgel; and Bowers. For critics who find Marlowe's poem in need of Chapman's completion, see Kostic; Bakeless 2: 99–101; Bush, *Classical Mythology* 121–36; Zocca 232–47; C.S. Lewis, *English Literature* 486–9; B. Morris; Bieman, 'Comic Rhyme'; Keach, *Elizabethan Erotic Narratives* 85–116; and Braden, *Classics* 55–153.

3 In 'The occasion of this Impos'd Crowne,' prefacing vol. 2 of *The Whole Workes of Homer*, Chapman clarifies the structure of the Homeric *cursus*, in three [Virgilian-like] phases: (1) Epic, divided into the tragedic *Iliad* and the comedic *Odyssey*; (2) Mock-Epic, represented by the *Batrachomyomachia*; and (3) Hymns and Epigrams, represented by the *Homeric Hymns* and *Epigrams*. Chapman sees Homer's literary career as having a tragic trajectory: the Gods 'envy' Homer, so that he 'liv'd unhonord and needie till his death,' even though in the end he comedically acquires poetic fame.

4 Braden notes that the *Heroides* are the first extant version of the myth (*Classics* 56); he adds that 'Marlowe's only firmly established ancillary sources of any importance are Ovidian: the *Heroides* ..., and the *Amores*' (125). On Ovid in the epyllion, see Donno, ed. 1–20; Donno, 'Epyllion'; Keach, *Elizabethan Erotic Narratives* xv–xviii, 3–35, 219–32; and Hulse 16–34. On Ovid in *Hero and Leander*, see Keach, *Elizabethan Erotic Narratives* 85–116; and Hulse 93–140. Yet Marlowe's direct source is Musaeus, whose *Hero and Leander* Marlowe imitates (Braden, *Classics* 55–153). On Marlowe's use of Ovid to rewrite Musaeus, see Keach, *Elizabethan Erotic Narratives* 87. To Ovid and Musaeus, Marlowe adds elements of Petrarchism, Neoplatonism, and Lucretian materialism (Neuse 424–5). On the opposition between Ovidian and

Petrarchan/Neoplatonic elements, see Walsh 38–46; and Royston 33, 36. On Neoplatonism, see Braunmuller; Labriola; and Chapman himself, who in *Ovid's Banquet of Sense* (1595) reverses the Ovidian/Platonic opposition (Waddington, 'Chapman' 139). On Lucretius in *Hero and Leander*, see Neuse 427; Altieri 154, 162; and M. Turner 397, 403.

5 Bradbrook, *Shakespeare and Elizabethan Poetry* 59. Evidently, Bradley first inserted Spenser into criticism on *Hero and Leander* (rpt. in MacLure, ed., *Marlowe* 130). See also Courthope (qtd. in Bakeless 2: 146); Bush, *Mythology* 116, 135; Tuve 173, 175; H. Levin 19; C.S. Lewis, *English Literature* 487; M.T. Williams 227–30; B. Morris 130; Poirier 199; Collins 118; Walsh 39, n. 12; M. Turner, 400–1; Braunmuller 59; Labriola 17; Braden, *Classics* 140; Kelsall 24–5; Hulse 98; and Zunder 78. Two recent critics emphasize the significance of the mighty opposition: Keach, *Elizabethan Erotic Narratives*, who argues that the epyllion poets, including Marlowe, 'challenge Spenser's vision of the "glorious fire" of love ideally realized in the creative chastity of marriage' (232); and Altieri, who contextualizes the 'poetically essential anti-Platonism in Marlowe's poetic procedures' (151) in terms of 'the Petrarchism of both Sidney and Spenser' (152), but especially the latter. Like Keach, Altieri offers no specific intertextuality.

6 On 'Ovid's Orpheus' as 'a persona for Ovidian poetics,' see C. Segal, *Orpheus* 93, including two superb chapters (54–94) which emphasize Ovid's 'revolt' (55) against the Virgilian Orpheus.

7 I take up the problem of chronology later. Jortin was the first to see Spenser's peculiar scholarship here: 'Not the Euxine waves, but the Hellespont' (rpt. in *Variorum Edition* 7: 519; see also Brooks-Davies, who cites both Musaeus and Ovid's *Heroides* and refers to the 'Marlowe/Chapman poem' (336). The Euxine sea, of course, is the Black Sea, and it rolls up on Tomis, the site of Ovid's exile (*Tristia* III.xiii.27–8). It is as if Spenser is *Ovidianizing* the myth, perhaps unconsciously.

8 See Cheney, '"Secret Powre Unseene"'; 'Two Florimells'; and *Spenser's Famous Flight* 149–94, 195–224, and 225–45. On *The Faerie Queene* as a 'divine comedy,' see King 221–6.

9 Braden remarks: 'The first line is Marlowe's own, but the next three work almost entirely from [Musaeus]' (*Classics* 125). He adds that 'disjoined by Neptune's might' is 'Marlowe's one substantial addition to Mousaios here' (126), attributing it to Marlowe's 'pervasive concern with power' (126–7).

10 Critics often neglect this dimension, as Bartels does by excluding *Hero and Leander* from her wonderful analysis of Marlowe's anti-imperialist project.

11 Spenser had no monopoly on the term, but he uses 'hight' more than 160 times!

12 See also B. Morris, 'Comedy'; Bieman, 'Comic Rhyme'; and M. Campbell 263. For resistance, see Walsh 54; M. Turner 397; and esp. D.L. Miller, 'Death of the Modern.'

13 Elsewhere, Gill calls *Hero and Leander* 'an epic poem' (ed., 1989 *Doctor Faustus* xii). On the transition from *Faustus* to *Hero and Leander*, see Ellis-Fermor 78–9. And on 'the theatrical aspects of the epyllia,' see Royston 31. Marlowe writes that 'divine Musaeus' has 'sung' Leander's 'tragedy' (I.52); and in his *Dedicatory Epistle* Blount refers to 'this unfinished tragedy.'

14 For Belphoebe as Diana, see *FQ* II.iii.3; and for Elizabeth as Belphoebe/Diana, modelled on Ralegh's Cynthia, see the *Letter to Ralegh* (3: 486) On Spenser's use of 'Ovid and Queen Elizabeth' to intersect the Virgilian dimension of the Belphoebe story, see Krier 67–79. On Belphoebe in *Hero and Leander*, see M. Turner 400-1. Altieri sees the False Florimell (152).

15 On how 'Arachne is Ovid's artistic double,' see Ahl, *Metaformations*: 'The kinds of motifs she represents are very similar to ... the heavenly tales Ovid himself tells. And she, like Ovid, suffers for her outspoken criticism' (227).

16 See Gill, ed., *Complete Works* 1: 291, who cites *Amores* III.i.34.

17 Editors neglect the self-quotation of Marlowe's 'slack muse' from the counter-Virgilian opening of *Ovid's Elegies*: 'Love slacked my muse, and made my numbers soft' (I.i.22). Three more of Marlowe's ten uses of *slack* appear in *Ovid's Elegies* (I.ii.12, III.ii.11, III.iv.15), the last two inscribing the *cursus*.

18 Most recent critics would agree with May: 'the available evidence has Ralegh devising the Cynthia/moon conceit by 1588 and incorporating it into one or more poems in praise of the queen before 1590. Spenser read this work in 1589' (44), but revised his own 1591 representation of Ralegh's poem in *Colin Clout* after Ralegh's 1592 disgrace and banishment over the Elizabeth Throckmorton affair, which in large part motivated the composition of *Ocean to Cynthia* (43-4).

19 On Ralegh's revision of the myth, by which 'Hero ... is the cause of Leander's death,' and through which Ralegh depicts 'a situation underlying the whole poem,' see Duncan-Jones 150-2. On the epyllion and the cult of Elizabeth, see Berry 137-9.

20 In her edition, Latham identifies this poem as 'doubtful' (ed. 191-3), but she concludes that it 'seems ... to be ... in Ralegh's manner' (ed. 194). Ralegh and Marlowe do use 'sphere' differently.

21 Ralegh's argument in *Ocean to Cynthia* (he is making an argument) emerges in the final line: 'her love hath end. My woe must ever last' (522). He alone is constant; Cynthia changes. Space prohibits analysis of similar political lines: 'A brow for love to banquet royally' (I.86). This line, evocative of the Queen, may conflate two images from Spenser, both pertaining to 'Elizabeth': *FQ* II.iii.24;

and *Amoretti* 77: 1–4. See also *HL* I.225–36, which reads like an allegoresis of the *Ocean to Cynthia* and Ralegh's New World project, and I.259–60, II.162–4, and II.271–6.

22 See Altieri on differences between Spenserian allegory and Marlovian metaphor (156–7, 160–1). For Marlowe, unlike for Spenser, 'things decidedly are things' (157).

23 Within this context, we can profitably read Leander's critique of 'Virginity, albeit some highly prize it' (I.262) and 'foolishly do call it virtuous' (277): 'And know that some have wronged Diana's name?' (284) – 'some vile tongues' (286). The leading candidate for this foolishly vile tongue is surely Spenser.

24 L.C. Martin glosses 'discoloured' by comparing 'Spenser, *Epithalamion* 51' (35).

25 See Gill, who sees Marlowe 'enter[ing] into competition with the mythological displays of the Temple of the Sun (*Metamorphoses*, ii), Arachne's web (*Metamorphoses*, vi), and the House of Busyrane (*The Faerie Queene*, III. xi. 28–46' (ed., *Complete Works* 1: 294). She also notes the general repetition of Marlowe's catalogue of Jovian metamorphoses in Busirane's tapestries (2: 294–5). For a specific textual repetition, see Danae's 'brazen tower' (*HL* I.145; *FQ* III.xi.31). Similarly, Bush believes that Marlowe's lines on the Cyparissus myth here (I.154–6) imitate *FQ* I.vi.17 ('Marlowe and Spenser').

26 Neuse asks, 'Why is the mythological pantheon and its "haddie ryots, incest, rapes" represented in the pavement mirror?' And answers: 'First, the pavement reflects what is above man in the form of myths that fix the cosmic bacchanalia ... Indeed, by treading on the floor where the gods are imaged, the Sestians may feel that they have mastered their collective intuition of the riotous way of the world ... In the second perspective – ... of the Marlovian narrator – the mirror functions to suggest the Epicurean conception or reduction of the gods as a preconception of the human mind ... [T]he point of the pavement in the temple [is precisely this:]: it is a Lewis Caroll mirror, and those walking on it actually see in it their own ... fantasies in "divine" form' (431–32). Neuse goes on to emphasize the 'presence of just the two gods Proteus and Bacchus *above* the pavement in the temple' (433). Identifying Proteus as a Piconian summation of 'that oceanic multiplicity of forms which in the human imagination – the pavement mirror – becomes the "sundrie shapes" of the gods,' and Bacchus as an Epicurean '"ape god,"' a 'hieroglyph of man as he [Marlowe] conceives him' (432), Neuse ventures this question: 'is Marlowe not hinting at a metaphoric wedding of the Piconian god-man with the Epicurean ape-become god?' (433). In 'Two Florimells,' I link Pico's Proteus with Spenser's Proteus (335–6).

27 Greene speaks of 'such mad and scoffing poets, that have propheticall spirits as bold as Merlins race' (rpt. in MacLure, ed., *Marlowe* 30). Bakeless writes: 'The

allusion to "Merlin's race" – the *e* being pronounced as *a*' suggests that Greene 'play[s] ... on the name of the magician, Merlin' (1: 96).

28 Marlowe goes on to write: 'And in the midst *a silver* altar stood' (I.157). The lines may echo *FQ* II.vii.53: '*And in the midst* thereof *a silver* seat.' On the centralizing significance of 'in the midst' for Spenser, see Baybak, Delany, Hieatt.

29 Whereas Boas emphasizes *will* as 'amorous desire ... primal impulse' (*Christopher Marlowe* 230), Neuse emphasizes *fate* as '"nature," "natural urge," or "inclination"' (427). Neuse argues that the opening couplet has an 'epic resonance' but that the remaining lines show 'a characteristic switch to trivial examples,' so that the 'total effect ... is mocking and debunking.' He singles out the two metaphors that I examine: 'To divorce love from reason is a defensible move, but to put it (even by way of a simile) on a par with the choice between runners in a race and between *identical* gold ingots is to cast a very ironic glance on it' (426).

30 Keach adds: 'It is this conspicuous, intrusive, self-dramatizing persona ... which most clearly differentiates Marlowe's epyllionic technique from Shakespeare's' (88). On the narrator, see Cubeta.

31 See also the *Variorum Edition* 7: 657–62; Oram et al. 683–4; and Brooks-Davies 320-1. Jayne thinks that the origins of the first two hymns trace to 'about 1579,' and he finds Spenser competing with Chapman in the genre of the hymn (5–6).

32 See D.L. Miller, 'Death of the Modern,' on how Marlowe's myth leads 'to the poet himself ... to a scene of rivalry, the site from which Marlowe utters his own protest' (776–7): 'Marlowe's complaint says ... that the social order treats poets as women,' citing *Teares of the Muses* (778). For other conjunctions, compare *Hero and Leander* I.274 with *Hymne of Beautie* 132–3; *Hero and Leander* I.273 and II.29–32 with *Hymne of Beautie* 197–100; and *Hero and Leander* I.444 and *Hymne of Love* 89.

33 See Poirier: 'The picture of the submarine dwelling of Neptune may have been inspired by Cymoent's watery chambers in *The Faerie Queene*' (199).

34 On the origins of Spenser's representation of Night, see Lotspeich 91, where Spenser draws on Comes, *Mythologiae*, with help from Ovid, *Metamorphoses* XIV.403–5, and Virgil, *Aeneid* V.721.

35 C.S. Lewis says that 'the line' which Chapman takes on 'marriage' is 'the same as Spenser's' ('*Hero and Leander*' 240). Leech writes, 'To find in the 1590's an approach to this account of a woman alone with her anguish, we should have to turn to Book V of *The Faerie Queene* ... Perhaps Chapman was influenced by Spenser' ('Venus and Her Nun' 267). M. Campbell says that Ceremony's 'presentation is reminiscent of some of the allegorical figures of Spenser's

Faerie Queene, like Lucifera, or Mercilla, or Dame Nature, and her introduction so early in the poem alerts us to Chapman's literary allegiances' (260). As we shall see, the critic who examines the subject in most detail is Waddington.

36 For other borrowings, see Waddington, *Mind's Empire* 163, 166, 168–9, 171, 175, 180.

Afterword: Counterfeiting the Profession

1 On Lamb, Dyce, and Shaw, see MacLure, ed., *Marlowe* 69, 93, and 199–200. In 1820, J.P. Collier first speaks of Marlowe's canon in terms of a *cursus*: 'The other dramatic productions in which Marlow was alone concerned are five in number, and as we have before alluded to the gradual change he occasioned from rhyme to blank verse, from low comedy to stately tragedy, and subsequently from inflated bombast to a more refined and chastened style, it is comparatively easy to trace the *course and progress* of his muse' (rpt. in MacLure 82; emphasis added). Writing towards the end of the century, Dowden is instrumental in forging this 'developmental' view, even though he fully participates in the Shakespearean paradigm (rpt. in MacLure 99–109): 'A more important thing to recognise is that up to the last Marlowe's great powers were ripening, while his judgment was becoming sane, and his taste purer' (109).

2 The three most recent critics to tackle the Marlowe–Shakespeare connection are Charney, Shapiro, and Cartelli. Charney is writing a book on the topic, and Shapiro and Cartelli constitute about one-half of the book-publishing done on Marlowe in the last few years. [Like the introduction, this afterword was written in 1995.]

3 Recently, I peered into the General Catalogue at the British Library in London, finding Marlowe classified under the following heading: 'Marlowe (Christopher) the Dramatist.' Earlier, I had encountered this paradigm when I visited a distinguished bookstore in Marlowe's own university town, finding 'Marlowe' shelved in the 'Drama' section. (I remember mentioning my observation to the sales person, and when I returned to Heffers in the spring of 1996 I discovered that 'Marlowe' had been taken out of the 'Drama' section and relocated in the regular 'Literature' section.) The practice at both Heffers and the BL appears institutionalized in countless editions and studies of Marlowe's works. The five most recent books on Marlowe (Shapiro, Cartelli, Sales, Bartels, Healy), all important, confine themselves to the plays, with the last appearing as late as 1994, advertised paradoxically as an overview in a 'new series of writers and their work' (back cover): 'This is a book about Marlowe's drama' (Healy vii).

4 Bradley says that an 'old ballad tells us' that Marlowe 'acted at the Curtain
   Theatre in Shoreditch and "brake his leg in one rude scene, When in his early
   age"' (rpt. in MacLure, ed., *Marlowe* 126). Leech's influential paradigm, 'poet
   for the stage,' remains unsatisfactory because it is not quite accurate; it is still
   under the influence of 'Shakespeare' and 'drama.' Mullaney's recently influential paradigm, which cordons drama off from poetry, is equally unsatisfactory.
   Mullaney laments that drama critics have been trained 'to regard plays as
   poems, and drama as primarily (if not entirely) a literary phenomenon' (6–7).
   On Shakespeare as a 'playwright and occasional poet,' see Thomson 100; this
   paradigm has now been virtually institutionalized in the new *Riverside
   Shakespeare* (Boston: Houghton, 1997), where Heather Dubrow's fine essay,
   'Twentieth-Century Shakespeare Criticism' (27–54), reproduces the pattern:
   her first sentence mentions Shakespeare's 'plays and poems,' but quickly,
   decisively she turns to the plays. Thus her opening twenty-page discussion of
   criticism on the plays need not bear the heading 'The Plays' the way her final
   six-page section bears the title 'The Poems.'
5 In 1618, Edmunde Rudierde casts the paradigm in similar terms: Marlowe was
   a 'Cambridge scholar who was a Poet, and a filthy Play-maker' (qtd. in '*A Poet
   and a filthy Play-maker*' ix).
6 Warton says he has 'considered' Marlowe 'as a translator, and otherwise being
   generally ranked only as a dramatic poet' (rpt. in MacLure, ed., *Marlowe* 59).
   In MacLure's Critical Heritage volume, the next to mention Marlowe's
   translations – and only *Ovid's Elegies* – is Dyce in 1850 (95); then Bradley in
   1880, who mentions both *Ovid's Elegies* and *Lucan* (129); next Saintsbury in
   1887, who also mentions both (163); and, finally, Swinburne in 1908, who
   mentions both again (183). The three hundred years of commentary traced in
   MacLure's volume produce only a handful of isolated sentences (noted by
   MacLure 24). For the limited but improved commentary in the twentieth
   century, see the introduction and chapters 2 and 10.
7 Early on, both Peele and Drayton emphasize Marlowe the writer of verse.
   Peele calls Marlowe 'the Muses darling for thy verse' (1593, rpt. in MacLure,
   ed., *Marlowe* 39); and Drayton calls him one of the 'first Poets,' singling out his
   'verses cleere': 'For that fine madnes still he did retaine, / Which rightly should
   possesse a Poets braine' (1627, rpt. in MacLure 47). Chapman, who 'continues'
   Hero and Leander, certainly understood Marlowe's achievements as a poet. So
   did Heywood, who calls Marlowe 'the best of poets in that age,' referring to
   both *Tamburlaine* and *Hero and Leander* ('Prologue to the Stage' 2–6).
   According to Gill, Heywood 'seems to think that the narrative poem *Hero and
   Leander* gave more prestige to Marlowe than his plays' (ed., *Complete Works* 3:
   124).

8 See Tucker, who contextualizes a series of '1993' British works on Marlowe in terms of the 'ethical and ideological values we admire' today (124, n. 18) – what he calls 'the contemporary Marlowe mythos ... of Marlowe as intellectual challenger' (122).

9 I respond here to work done on Marlowe as a prophetic poet by Weil; Hulse 93–140; and Barber, *Creating Elizabethan Tragedy* 79–86. On Spenser as a prophetic poet, see Cheney, *Spenser's Famous Flight*, esp. 32, 48, 110, and 255, n. 5.

10 My 'typology of intertextuality' responds to commentary on Marlovian 'imitation' represented most recently by Healy in his chapter by that title (35–43). Healy opens and closes with Marlowe's rejection of Spenser's and Sidney's 'didactic' use of literature (31, 43). In between, he examines Marlowe's use of Ovid in *Dido* to critique Virgil (37–43); and he even sees Marlowe developing his critique of the literature promoted by Spenser and Sidney (43). But he does not see Marlowe using Ovid to critique England's Virgil.

11 Bloom summarizes the received wisdom: 'What the common reader finds in Marlowe is precisely what his contemporaries found: impiety, audacity, worship of power, ambiguous sexuality, occult aspirations, defiance of moral order ... [Marlowe's] originality [lies in his] defiance of all moral and religious convention' (ed. 1–2). Recently, both Cartelli (163, 174, 175) and Bartels (xv, 26) have emphasized Marlovian defiance through what Sinfield terms 'dissi-dent' writing (*Faultlines*). By contrast, see Summers, 'Sex, Politics': 'For all his radical iconoclasm and brutal honesty, the playwright places himself in a venerable humanist tradition' (237): 'Marlowe discovers value in the frustrating quest for individual wholeness' (236). The argument I present here represents yet another position. I am grateful to Emily C. Bartels for generously prompt-ing – and at times voicing – these professions.

Works Cited

Aeschylus. *Agamemnon. Greek Tragedies*. Trans. Richmond Lattimore. Ed. David Grene and Richmond Lattimore. Chicago: U of Chicago P, 1991. 1: 1–60.

Ahern, Charles F., Jr. 'Daedalus and Icarus in the *Ars Amatoria*.' *Harvard Studies in Classical Philology* 92 (1989): 273–96.

Ahl, Frederick M. *Lucan: An Introduction*. Ithaca: Cornell UP, 1976.

– *Metaformations: Soundplay and Wordplay in Ovid and Other Classical Poets*. Ithaca: Cornell UP, 1985.

Allen, Don Cameron. 'Marlowe's *Dido* and the Tradition.' *Essays on Shakespeare and Elizabethan Drama in Honor of Hardin Craig*. Ed. Richard Hosley. Columbia: U of Missouri P, 1962. 55–62.

Allen, Michael J.B. 'Tamburlaine and Plato: A Colon, A Crux.' *Research Opportunities in Renaissance Drama* 23 (1980): 21–31.

Alpers, Paul J. 'Spenser's Late Pastorals.' *ELH* 56 (1989): 797–817.

– 'Style.' *The Spenser Encyclopedia*. 674–6.

Altieri, Joanne. '*Hero and Leander*: Sensible Myth and Lyric Subjectivity.' *John Donne Journal* 8 (1989): 151–66.

Altman, Joel B. *The Tudor Play of Mind: Rhetorical Inquiry and the Development of Elizabethan Drama*. Berkeley: U of California P, 1978.

Anderson, Benedict. *Imagined Communities: Reflections on the Origins and Spread of Nationalism*. London: Verso, 1983.

Anderson, Perry. *Lineages of the Absolutist State*. London: NLB; Atlantic Highlands: Humanities P, 1974.

Archer, John Michael. *Sovereignty and Intelligence: Spying and Court Culture in the English Renaissance*. Stanford: Stanford UP, 1993.

Aristophanes. *The Birds. The Complete Plays of Aristophanes*. Trans. R.H. Webb. Ed. Moses Hadas. New York: Bantam, 1924. 229–86.

Aristotle. *The Basic Works of Aristotle*. Ed. Richard McKeon. New York: Random, 1941.

Ascham, Roger. *The Scholemaster. English Works of Roger Ascham.* Ed. William Aldis Wright. Cambridge: Cambridge UP, 1904.

Ashton, J.W. 'The Fall of Icarus.' *Renaissance Studies in Honour of Hardin Craig.* Stanford: Stanford UP, 1941. 153–9.

Austin, R.G. '*Ille Ego Qui Quondam* ...' *Classical Quarterly* 18 (1968): 107–15.

Babb, Howard S. 'Policy in Marlowe's *The Jew of Malta.*' *ELH* 24 (1957): 85–94.

Baines, Barbara J. 'Sexual Polarity in the Plays of Christopher Marlowe.' *Ball State University Forum* 23 (1982): 3–17.

Bakeless, John. *The Tragicall History of Christopher Marlowe.* 2 vols. 1942; Hamden, CT: Archon, 1964.

Bakhtin, M.M. *The Dialogic Imagination: Four Essays.* Trans. Caryl Emerson and Michael Holquist. Ed. Michael Holquist. Austin: U of Texas P, 1981.

Baldwin, T.W. 'The Genesis of Some Passages Which Spenser Borrowed from Marlowe [I].' *ELH* 9 (1942): 157–87 .

– 'The Genesis of Some Passages Which Spenser Borrowed from Marlowe [II].' *ELH* 12 (1945): 165.

Barber, C.L. *Creating Elizabethan Tragedy: The Theater of Marlowe and Kyd.* Ed. Richard P. Wheeler. Chicago: U of Chicago P, 1988.

– '"The Form of Faustus' Fortunes Good or Bad." '*Doctor Faustus*,' ed. Ribner. 173–99. Orig. pub. *Tulane Drama Review* 8 (1964): 92–119.

Barkan, Leonard. *The Gods Made Flesh: Metamorphosis and the Pursuit of Paganism.* New Haven: Yale UP, 1986.

Barker, Francis. *The Tremulous Private Body: Essays on Subjection.* New York: Methuen, 1984.

Barnet, Sylvan, ed. '*Doctor Faustus.*' New York: Signet, 1969.

Barsby, John. *Ovid.* Oxford: Clarendon, 1978.

– ed. and trans. *Ovid 'Amores' I.* Bristol: Bristol Classical P, 1979.

Bartels, Emily C. *Spectacles of Strangeness: Imperialism, Alienation, and Marlowe.* Philadelphia: U of Pennsylvania P, 1993.

Barthes, Roland. 'Theory of the Text.' *Untying the Text: A Post-Structuralist Reader.* Ed. Robert Young. London: Routledge, 1981. 31–47.

Barton, Anne. 'Jonson, Ben.' *The Spenser Encyclopedia.* 411–12.

Bate, Jonathan. *Shakespeare and Ovid.* Oxford: Clarendon, 1993.

Bate, W. Jackson. *The Burden of the Past and the English Poet.* Cambridge, MA: Harvard UP, 1970.

Battenhouse, Roy W. *Marlowe's 'Tamburlaine': A Study in Renaissance Moral Philosophy.* Nashville: Vanderbilt UP, 1941.

Bawcutt, N.W., ed. '*The Jew of Malta': Christopher Marlowe.* Manchester: Manchester UP, 1978.

– 'Machiavelli and Marlowe's *The Jew of Malta.*' *Renaissance Drama* 3 (1970): 3–49.

Baybak, Michael, Paul Delaney, and A. Kent Hieatt. 'Placement "In the Middest" in *The Faerie Queene.*' *Papers on Language and Literature* 5 (1969): 227–34.

Bednarz, James P. 'Alençon.' *The Spenser Encyclopedia.* 14–15.

Bellamy, Elizabeth J. *Translations of Power: Narcissus and the Unconscious in Epic History.* Ithaca: Cornell UP, 1992.

Belsey, Catherine. 'Desire's Excess and the English Renaissance Theatre: *Edward II, Troilus and Cressida, Othello.*' *Desire on the Renaissance Stage.* Ed. Susan Zimmerman. New York: Routledge, 1992. 84–102.

– *The Subject of Tragedy: Identity and Difference in Renaissance Drama.* New York: Methuen, 1985.

Bennett, H.S., ed. *'The Jew of Malta' and 'The Massacre at Paris.'* New York: Dial, 1931.

Benston, Kimberly. 'Beauty's Just Applause: Dramatic Form and the Tamburlanian Sublime.' *Christopher Marlowe*, ed. Bloom. 207–27.

Berek, Peter. '*Tamburlaine*'s Weak Sons: Imitation as Interpretation before 1593.' *Renaissance Drama* 13 (1982): 55–82.

Berger, Harry, Jr. 'The Renaissance Imagination: Second World and Green World.' *Second World and Green World: Studies in Renaissance Fiction-Making.* Ed. John Patrick Lynch. Berkeley: U of California P, 1988. 3–40.

– *Revisionary Play: Studies in the Spenserian Dynamics.* Berkeley: U of California P, 1988.

– 'Spenser's *Prothalamion*: An Interpretation.' *Essential Articles*, ed. Hamilton. 509–23. Orig. pub. *Essays in Criticism* 15 (1965): 363–79.

Bernard, John D. *Ceremonies of Innocence: Pastoralism in the Poetry of Edmund Spenser.* Cambridge: Cambridge UP, 1989.

Berry, Philippa. *Of Chastity and Power: Elizabethan Literature and the Unmarried Queen.* London: Routledge, 1989.

Bevington, David, and Eric Rasmussen, eds. *Christopher Marlowe: 'Tamburlaine, Parts I and II,' 'Doctor Faustus,' A- and B-Texts, 'The Jew of Malta,' 'Edward II.'* Oxford: Clarendon, 1995.

– '*Doctor Faustus*': A- and B-texts (*1604, 1616*). The Revels Plays. Manchester: Manchester UP, 1993.

Bevington, David, and James Shapiro. '"What are kings, when regiment is gone?": The Decay of Ceremony in *Edward II.*' *'A Poet and a filthy Play-maker,'* ed. Friedenreich, Gill, and Kuriyama. 263–78.

Bhabha, Homi K. Introduction. *Nation and Narration*, ed. Bhabha. 1–7.

– ed. *Nation and Narration.* New York: Routledge, 1990.

Bieman, Elizabeth. 'Comic Rhyme in Marlowe's *Hero and Leander.*' *English Literary Renaissance* 9 (1979): 69–77.

– *Plato Baptized: Towards the Interpretation of Spenser's Mimetic Fictions.* Toronto: U of Toronto P, 1988.

Binns, J.W., ed. *Ovid*. London: Routledge, 1973.

Birringer, Johannes H. *Marlowe's 'Dr Faustus' and 'Tamburlaine': Theological and Theatrical Perspectives*. Frankfurt: Verlag Peter Lang, 1984.

– 'Marlowe's Violent Stage: "Mirrors" of Honor in *Tamburlaine*.' *ELH* 51 (1984): 219–39.

Blackburn, William. '"Heavenly Words": Marlowe's Faustus as a Renaissance Magician.' *English Studies in Canada* 4 (1978): 1–14.

Blissett, William. 'Lucan's Caesar and the Elizabethan Villain.' *Studies in Philology* 53 (1956): 553–75.

Bloom, Harold. *The Anxiety of Influence*. London: Oxford UP, 1973.

– ed. *Christopher Marlowe*. New York: Chelsea, 1986.

Boas, Frederick S. *Christopher Marlowe: A Biographical and Critical Study*. Oxford: Clarendon, 1940.

– *Ovid and the Elizabethans*. London: The English Association, 1947.

Boitani, Piero. *Chaucer and the Imaginary World of Fame*. Cambridge: D.S. Brewer; Totowa, NJ: Barnes, 1984.

Bolgar, R.R. *The Classical Heritage and Its Beneficiaries*. Cambridge: Cambridge UP, 1954.

Bono, Barbara J. 'Dido.' *The Spenser Encyclopedia*. 218–19.

– *Literary Transvaluation: From Vergilian Epic to Shakespearean Tragicomedy*. Berkeley: U of California P, 1984.

Booth, Joan, ed. *Ovid: The Second Book of 'Amores.'* Warminster, England: Aris, 1991.

Bouchard, Gary M. 'Phineas Fletcher: The Piscatory Link between Spenserian and Miltonic Pastoral.' *Studies in Philology* 89 (1992): 232–43.

Bowers, Fredson, ed. *The Complete Works of Christopher Marlowe*. 2d ed. Cambridge: Cambridge UP, 1981.

– 'The Early Editions of Marlowe's *Ovid's Elegies*.' *Studies in Bibliography* 25 (1972): 149–72.

Bradbrook, Muriel C. *The School of Night: Studies in the Literary Relationships of Sir Walter Raleigh*. Cambridge: Cambridge UP, 1936.

– *Shakespeare and Elizabethan Poetry*. London: Chatto, 1961.

– *Themes and Conventions of Elizabethan Tragedy*. Cambridge: Cambridge UP, 1980.

Braden, Gordon. *The Classics and English Renaissance Poetry*. New Haven: Yale UP, 1978.

– *Renaissance Tragedy and the Senecan Tradition: Anger's Privilege*. New Haven: Yale UP, 1985.

Brandt, Bruce Edwin. *Christopher Marlowe and the Metaphysical Problem Play*. Salzburg, Austria: Insitut Für Anglistik Und Amerikanistik Universität Salzburg, 1985.

– 'Marlowe's Helen and the Soul-in-the-Kiss Conceit.' *Philological Quarterly* 64 (1985): 118–21.

Braudy, Leo. *The Frenzy of Renown: Fame and Its History.* New York: Oxford UP, 1986.

Braunmuller, A.R. 'Marlowe's Amorous Fates in *Hero and Leander.*' *Review of English Studies* 29 (1978): 56–61.

Bredbeck, Gregory W. *Sodomy and Interpretation: Marlowe to Milton.* Ithaca: Cornell UP, 1991.

Brennan, Timothy. 'The National Longing for Form.' *Nation and Narration*, ed. Bhabha. 44–70.

Briggs, Julia. 'Marlowe's *Massacre at Paris*: A Reconsideration.' *Review of English Studies* 34 (1983): 257–78.

Briggs, William Dinsmore, ed. *Marlowe's 'Edward II.'* London: Nutt, 1914.

Brill, Lesley. 'Hellenore.' *The Spenser Encyclopedia.* 352.

Brinker, Ludger. 'The Art of Marlowe's Prologues: Subtle Innovations within Traditional Patterns.' *Cahiers Elisabethains* 42 (1992): 1–15.

Bristol, Michael D. *Carnival and Theater: Plebeian Culture and the Structure of Authority in Renaissance England.* New York: Methuen, 1985.

Brockbank, J.P. *Marlowe: 'Dr. Faustus.'* London: Arnold, 1962.

Brooke, C.F. Tucker, ed. *The Life of Marlowe and 'The Tragedy of Dido Queen of Carthage.'* London: Methuen, 1930.

– 'The Marlowe Canon.' *PMLA* 37 (1922): 367–417.

– ed. *The Works of Christopher Marlowe.* Oxford: Clarendon, 1910.

Brooks-Davies, Douglas, ed. *Edmund Spenser: Selected Shorter Poems.* London: Longman, 1995.

Brown, John Russell, ed. *Marlowe: 'Tamburlaine the Great,' 'Edward the Second' and 'The Jew of Malta.'* London: Macmillan, 1982.

Bruce, Donald. 'Spenser's Irenius and the Nature of Dialogue.' *Notes and Queries* (1992): 355–6.

Bruster, Douglas. '"Come to the Tent Again": "The Passionate Shepherd," Dramatic Rape and Lyric Time.' *Criticism* 33 (1991): 49–72.

Bullen, A.H., ed. *The Works of Christopher Marlowe.* 3 vols. London: Nimmo, 1885.

Burnett, Mark Thornton. '*Tamburlaine* and the Renaissance Concept of Honour.' *Studia Neophilologica* 59 (1987): 201–6.

– 'Tamburlaine: An Elizabethan Vagabond.' *Studies in Philology* 84 (1987): 308–23.

Burrow, Colin. 'Original Fictions: Metamorphoses in *The Faerie Queene.*' *Ovid Renewed*, ed. Martindale. 99–119.

Burton, Joan B. *Theocritus's Urban Mimes: Mobility, Gender, and Patronage.* Berkeley: U of California P, 1995.

Bush, Douglas. 'Marlowe and Spenser.' *Times Literary Supplement* (1 Jan, 1938): 12.

– *Mythology and the Renaissance Tradition in English Poetry.* New York: Norton, 1963.

Butler, Judith. *Gender Trouble: Feminism and the Subversion of Identity.* New York: Routledge, 1990.

Cahoon, Leslie. 'The Bed as Battlefield: Erotic Conquest and Military Metaphor in Ovid's *Amores.' TAPA* 118 (1988): 293–307.

– 'Juno's Chaste Festival and Ovid's Wanton Loves: *Amores* 3.13.' *Classical Antiquity* 2 (1983): 1–8.

– 'The Parrot and the Poet: The Function of Ovid's Funeral Elegies.' *Classical Journal* 80 (1984): 27–35.

– 'A Program for Betrayal: Ovidian *Nequitia* in *Amores* 1.1, 2.1, and 3.1.' *Helios* ns 12 (1985): 29–39.

– 'Raping the Rose: Jean de Meun's Reading of Ovid's *Amores.' Classical and Modern Literature* 6 (1986): 261–85.

Cain, Thomas H. *Praise in 'The Faerie Queene.'* Lincoln: U of Nebraska P, 1978.

Calabrese, Michael A. *Chaucer's Ovidian Arts of Love.* Gainesville: UP of Florida, 1994.

Callimachus. *Callimachus: 'Hymns' and 'Epigrams'; Lycophron; Aratus.* Trans. G.R. Mair. Cambridge, MA: Harvard UP; London: Heinemann, 1955.

Calvin, John. *The Institutes of the Christian Religion.* Trans. Ford Lewis Battles. Ed. John T. McNeill. 2 vols. Philadelphia: Westminster, 1960.

Cameron, Alan. *Callimachus and His Critics.* Princeton: Princeton UP, 1995.

– 'The First Edition of Ovid's *Amores.' Classical Quarterly* ns 18 (1968): 320–33.

Campbell, Lily B. '*Doctor Faustus*: A Case of Conscience.' *PMLA* 67 (1952): 219–39.

Campbell, Marion. '"Desunt Nonnulla": The Construction of Marlowe's *Hero and Leander* as an Unfinished Poem.' *ELH* 51 (1984): 241–68.

Carrubba, Robert W. 'The White Swan and Daedalian Icarus.' *Eranos* 80 (1982): 145–9.

Cartelli, Thomas. *Marlowe, Shakespeare, and the Economy of Theatrical Experience.* Philadelphia: U of Pennsylvania P, 1991.

Castiglione, Baldassare. *The Book of the Courtier.* Trans. Sir Thomas Hoby. London: Dent, 1974.

Catlin, Zachary, trans. *Publ. Ovid. De Tristibus: or Mournefull Elegies, in Five Bookes.* London, 1639.

Chambers, E.K. *The Elizabethan Stage.* 4 vols. Oxford: Clarendon, 1923.

Chambers, Frank Mcminn. 'Lucan and the *Antiquitez de Rome.' PMLA* 60 (1945): 937–48.

Chapman, George. *The Works of George Chapman: Plays.* Ed. Richard Herne Shepherd. 3 vols. London: Chatto, 1911–24.

– trans. *Whole Works of Homer.* London, 1616.

Charlton, H.B., and R.D. Waller, eds. *'Edward II.'* London: Methuen, 1933.

Charney, Maurice. 'Jessica's Turquoise Ring and Abigail's Poisoned Porridge: Shakespeare and Marlowe as Rivals and Imitators.' *Renaissance Drama* 10 (1979): 33–44.

Chaucer, Geoffrey. *The Riverside Chaucer.* Ed. Larry D. Benson et al. Boston: Houghton, 1987. Based on *The Works of Geoffrey Chaucer,* ed. F.N. Robinson. 2d ed. Boston: Houghton, 1957.

Chaudhuri, Sukanta. 'Marlowe, Madrigals, and a New Elizabethan Poet.' *Review of English Studies* 39 (1988): 199–216.

Cheney, Patrick. '"And Doubted Her to Deeme an Earthly Wight": Male Neoplatonic "Magic" and the Problem of Female Identity in Spenser's Allegory of the Two Florimells.' *Studies in Philology* 86 (1989): 310–40.

– 'Love and Magic in *Doctor Faustus*: Marlowe's Indictment of Spenserian Idealism.' *Mosaic* 17 (1984): 93–109.

– 'Magic in *The Faerie Queene.*' Diss. University of Toronto, 1979.

– '"Secret Powre Unseene": Good Magic in Spenser's Legend of Britomart.' *Studies in Philology* 85 (1988): 1–28.

– 'Spenser's Completion of *The Squire's Tale*: Love, Magic, and Heroic Action in the Legend of Cambell and Triamond.' *Journal of Medieval and Renaissance Studies* 15 (1985): 135–55.

– *Spenser's Famous Flight: A Renaissance Idea of a Literary Career.* Toronto: U of Toronto P, 1993.

– 'Triamond.' *The Spenser Encyclopedia.* 698–9.

Churchyard, Thomas, trans. *The Three First Bookes of Ovids 'de Tristibus' Translated into English* (1578). London: Shakespeare, 1816.

Clausen, Wendell, ed. *A Commentary on Virgil: 'Eclogues.'* Oxford: Clarendon, 1994.

Clayton, Jay, and Eric Rothstein, 'Figures in the Corpus: Theories of Influence and Intertextuality.' *Influence and Intertextuality in Literary History.* Madison: U of Wisconsin P, 1992. 3–36.

Clemen, Wolfgang. *'Edward II.' Marlowe,* ed. Leech. 138–43.

Coe, David Wright. 'Arthur and Tamburlaine's Cosmological Dispute: A Clash of Realities in the Works of Spenser and Marlowe.' Diss. U of Texas at Austin, 1980.

Cohen, Ralph. 'On the Interrelations of Eighteenth-Century Literary Forms.' In *New Approaches to Eighteenth-Century Literature.* Ed. Philip Harth. Selected Papers from the English Institute. New York: Columbia UP, 1974. 33–78.

Cohen, Walter. *Drama of a Nation*. Ithaca: Cornell UP, 1985.

Cole, Douglas. *Christopher Marlowe and the Renaissance of Tragedy*. Lives of the Theatre. Contributions in Drama and Theatre Studies 63. Westport, CT: Greenwood, 1995.

‒ *Suffering and Evil in the Plays of Christopher Marlowe*. Princeton: Princeton UP, 1962.

Collins, S. Ann. 'Sundrie Shapes, Committing Headdie Ryots, Incest, Rapes: Functions of Myth in Determining Narrative and Tone in Marlowe's *Hero and Leander*.' *Mosaic* 4 (1970): 107‒22.

Comito, Terry. 'Fountains.' *The Spenser Encyclopedia*. 314‒15.

‒ 'Wells.' *The Spenser Encyclopedia*. 728.

Connor, Peter J. 'His Dupes and Accomplices: A Study of Ovid the Illusionist in the Amores.' *Ramus* 3 (1974): 18‒40.

Conte, Gian Biagio. *The Rhetoric of Imitation: Genre and Poetic Memory in Virgil and Other Latin Poets*. Trans. and ed. Charles Segal. Ithaca: Cornell UP, 1986.

Coolidge, John S. 'Great Things and Small: The Virgilian Progression.' *Comparative Literature* 17 (1965): 1‒23.

Cooper, Clyde Barnes. *Some Elizabethan Opinions of the Poetry and Character of Ovid*. Menasha, WI: The Collegiate P-George Banta, 1914.

Cope, Jackson I. *Dramaturgy of the Daemonic*. Baltimore: Johns Hopkins UP, 1984.

Corrigan, Robert W., ed. *Tragedy: Vision and Form*. 2d ed. New York: Harper, 1982.

Couliano, Ioan P. *Eros and Magic in the Renaissance*. Trans. Margaret Cook. Chicago: U of Chicago P, 1987.

Cousins, A.D. 'The Coming of Mannerism: The Later Ralegh and the Early Donne.' *English Literary Renaissance* 9 (1979): 86‒107.

Craik, T.W., ed. *Christopher Marlowe: 'The Jew of Malta.'* New York: Norton, 1992.

Crawford, Charles. 'Edmund Spenser, "Locrine," and "Selimus."' *Notes and Queries* 9th ser. 7 (1901): 61‒3, 101‒3, 142‒4, 203‒5, 261‒3, 324‒5, 384‒6.

Crewe, Jonathan. *Hidden Designs: The Critical Profession and Renaissance Literature*. New York: Methuen, 1986.

‒ 'The Theatre of the Idols: Marlowe, Rankins, and Theatrical Images.' *Theatre Journal* 36 (1984): 321‒33.

‒ *Unredeemed Rhetoric: Thomas Nashe and the Scandal of Authorship*. Baltimore: Johns Hopkins UP, 1982.

Crosland, Jessie. 'Lucan in the Middle Ages.' *Modern Language Review* 25 (1930): 32‒51.

Cubeta, Paul M. 'Marlowe's Poet in *Hero and Leander*.' *College English* 26 (1965): 500‒5.

Culler, Jonathan. 'Presupposition and Intertextuality.' *MLN* 91 (1976): 1380–96.

Cummings, R.M., ed. *Spenser: The Critical Heritage*. New York: Barnes, 1971.

Cunnar, Eugene R. 'Donne's Witty Theory of Atonement in "The Baite."' *Studies in English Literature, 1500–1900* 29 (1989): 77–98.

Cunningham, J.S., ed. *'Tamburlaine the Great': Christopher Marlowe*. The Revels Plays. Manchester: Manchester UP; Baltimore: Johns Hopkins UP, 1981.

Cunningham, Karen. 'Renaissance Execution and Marlovian Elocution: The Drama of Death.' *PMLA* 105 (1990): 209–22.

Curran, Leo C. 'Transformation and Anti-Augustanism in Ovid's *Metamorphoses*.' *Arethusa* 5 (1972): 71–91.

Currie, H. MacL. 'Ovid and the Roman Stage.' *Aufstieg und Niedergang der römischen Welt* 31 (1981): 2701–42.

Cutts, John P. *The Left Hand of God*. Haddonfield, NJ: Haddonfield House, 1973.

– 'The Marlowe Canon.' *Notes and Queries* ns 6 204 (1959): 71–4.

Dabbs, Thomas. *Reforming Marlowe: The Nineteenth-Century Canonization of a Renaissance Dramatist*. London: Associated UP, 1991.

Daiches, David. 'Language and Action in Marlowe's *Tamburlaine*.' *Christopher Marlowe*, ed. Bloom. 77–96.

Dalzell, Alexander. 'Lucretius.' *Cambridge History of Classical Literature*, ed. Kenney. 2: 207–29.

Daniel, Samuel. *Complete Works in Verse and Prose*. Ed. Alexander Grosart. 5 vols. London, 1885–96.

– *The Works of Samuel Daniel, Newly Augmented*. London, 1602.

Danson, Lawrence. 'Christopher Marlowe: The Questioner.' *English Literary Renaissance* 12 (1981): 3–29.

Dante Alighieri. *The Divine Comedy*. Trans. Charles S. Singleton. 3 vols. in 6. Princeton: Princeton UP, 1970–5.

Davis, John T. *'Fictus Adulter': Poet as Actor in the 'Amores'*. Amsterdam: Gieben, 1989.

Davisson, Mary H.T. 'Parents and Children in Ovid's Poems from Exile.' *Classical World* 78 (1984): 111–14.

Day Lewis, C., trans. *The 'Aeneid' of Virgil*. Garden City, NY: Doubleday-Anchor, 1952.

Deats, Sara Munson. '*Doctor Faustus*: From Chapbook to Tragedy.' *Essays in Literature* 3 (1976): 3–16.

– 'Marlowe's Fearful Symmetry in *Edward II*.' *'A Poet and a filthy Play-maker,'* eds. Friedenreich, Gill, and Kuriyama. 241–62.

– 'Myth and Metamorphosis in Marlowe's *Edward II*.' *Texas Studies in Literature and Language* 22 (1980): 304–21.

Deats, Sara Munson, and Lisa S. Starks. '"So neatly plotted, and so well perform'd": Villain as Playwright in Marlowe's *The Jew of Malta*.' *Theatre Journal* 44 (1992): 375–89.

De Grazia, Margreta. 'Fin de Siècle Renaissance England.' *Fins de Siècle: English Poetry in 1590, 1690, 1790, 1890, 1990*. Ed. Elaine Scarry. Parallax: Re-visions of Culture and Society. Baltimore: Johns Hopkins UP, 1995. 37–63.

DeNeef, A. Leigh. 'Ploughing Virgilian Furrows: The Genres of *Faerie Queene* VI.' *John Donne Journal* 1 (1982): 151–68.

Dent, R.W. 'Ovid, Marlowe, and "The Insatiate Countess."' *Notes and Queries* 208 (1963): 334–5.

Derrida, Jacques. *Of Grammatology*. Trans. Gayatri Chakravorty Spivak. Baltimore: Johns Hopkins UP, 1974, 1976.

Desmond, Marilynn. *Reading Dido*. Minneapolis: U of Minnesota P, 1994.

Dilke, O.A.W. 'Lucan and English Literature.' *Neronians and Flavians: Silver Latin I*. Ed. D.R. Dudley. London: Routledge, 1972. 83–112.

Dollimore, Jonathan. *Radical Tragedy: Religion, Ideology and Power in the Drama of Shakespeare and His Contemporaries*. Chicago: U of Chicago P, 1984.

Donaldson, Peter S. 'Conflict and Coherence: Narcissism and Tragic Structure in Marlowe.' *Narcissism and the Text: Studies in Literature and the Psychology of Self*. Ed. Lynne Layton and Barbara Ann Schapiro. New York: New York UP, 1986. 36–63.

Donne, John. *The Poems of John Donne*. Ed. Herbert J.C. Grierson. 2 vols. Oxford: Clarendon, 1912.

Donno, Elizabeth Story, ed. *Elizabethan Minor Epics*. New York: Columbia UP; London: Routledge, 1963.

– 'The Epyllion.' *English Poetry and Prose, 1540–1674*. Ed. Christopher Ricks. London: Sphere, 1970. 82–95.

Doran, Madeleine. 'Some Renaissance "Ovids."' *Literature and Society*. Ed. Bernice Slote. Lincoln: U of Nebraska P, 1964. 44–62.

Drayton, Michael. *The Works of Michael Drayton*. Ed. J. William Hebel. 5 vols. Oxford: Blackwell, 1931–41.

Dryden, John, trans. *Virgil's 'Aeneid.'* New York: Airmont, 1970.

Du Quesnay, M. Le M. 'The *Amores*.' *Ovid*, ed. Binns. 1–48.

– 'From Polyphemus to Corydon: Virgil, *Eclogue* 2 and the *Idylls* of *Theocritus*.' *Creative Imitation and Latin Literature*, ed. West and Woodman. 35–69.

Duane, Carol Leventen. 'Marlowe's Mixed Messages: A Model for Shakespeare?' *Medieval and Renaissance Drama in England* 3 (1986): 51–67.

Dubrow, Heather. *A Happier Eden: The Politics of Marriage in the Stuart Epithalamium*. Ithaca: Cornell UP, 1990.

Duncan-Jones, Katherine. 'The Date of Raleigh's "21th: And Last Booke of the Ocean to Scinthia."' *Review of English Studies* 21 (1970): 143–50.

Eccles, Mark. *Christopher Marlowe in London*. Cambridge, MA: Harvard UP, 1934.

Edwards, Philip. *Threshold of a Nation: A Study in English and Irish Drama*. Cambridge: Cambridge UP, 1979.

Edwards, Robert R. *The Dream of Chaucer: Representation and Reflection in the Early Narratives*. Durham: Duke UP, 1989.

Eliot, T.S. *Elizabethan Dramatists*. London: Faber, 1963.

Elliott, Alison G. '*Amores* 1.13: Ovid's Art.' *Classical Journal* 69 (1973): 127–32.

Ellis-Fermor, U.M. *Christopher Marlowe*. Hamden, CT: Archon, 1967.

Ellrodt, Robert. *Neoplatonism in the Poetry of Spenser*. Geneva: Librarie E. Droz, 1960.

Empson, William. *Faustus and the Censor: The English Faust-book and Marlowe's 'Doctor Faustus.'* Oxford: Blackwell, 1987.

– *Seven Types of Ambiguity*. New York: Meridian, 1955.

Enterline, Lynn. 'Embodied Voices: Petrarch Reading (Himself Reading) Ovid.' *Desire in the Renaissance*, ed. Finucci and Schwartz. 120–45.

Eriksen, Roy T. 'Construction in Marlowe's *The Massacre at Paris*.' *Papers from the First Nordic Conference for English Studies*. Ed. Stig Johansson and Bjorn Tysdahl. Oslo: Institute of English Studies, University of Oslo, 1981. 41–54.

– 'Marlowe's Petrarch: *In Morte di Madonna Laura*.' *Cahiers Elisabethains* 29 (1986): 13–25.

Ettin, Andrew V. *Literature and the Pastoral*. New Haven: Yale UP, 1984.

Evans, Maurice. *Spenser's Anatomy of Heroism: A Commentary on 'The Faerie Queene*.' Cambridge: Cambridge UP, 1970.

Fantazzi, Charles, and Carl W. Querbach. 'Sound and Substance: A Reading of Virgil's Seventh Eclogue.' *Phoenix* 39 (1985): 355–67.

Farrell, Joseph. 'Dialogue of Genres in Ovid's "Lovesong of Polyphemus" (*Metamorphoses* 13.719–897).' *American Journal of Philology* 113 (1992): 235–68.

– *Virgil's 'Georgics' and the Traditions of Ancient Epic: The Art of Allusion in Literary History*. New York: Oxford UP, 1991.

Feeney, D.C. *The Gods in Epic: Poets and Critics of the Classical Tradition*. Oxford: Clarendon, 1991.

Felperin, Howard. 'Marlowe our Contemporary.' *The Uses of the Canon: Elizabethan Literature and Contemporary Theory*. Oxford: Clarendon, 1990. 100–21.

Ferguson, Margaret W. '"The Afflatus of Ruin": Meditations on Rome by Du Bellay, Spenser, and Stevens.' *Roman Images*. Ed. Annabel Patterson. Baltimore: Johns Hopkins UP, 1984. 23–50.

Ficino, Marsilio. *Marsilio Ficino's Commentary on Plato's 'Symposium': The Text and a Translation, with an Introduction*. Trans. Sears Reynolds Jayne. Columbia: U of Missouri P, 1944.

Finucci, Valerie, and Regina Schwartz, eds. *Desire in the Renaissance: Psychoanalysis and Literature*. Princeton: Princeton UP, 1994.

Fitzgerald, Robert, trans. *'The Aeneid': Virgil*. New York: Random Vintage, 1990.

F.L., trans. *Ovidius Naso His Remedie of Love. Translated and Intituled to the Youth of England*. London, 1600.

Fleming, Abraham. *The Bucoliks of Publius Virgilius Maro ... Together with his Georgiks ...* London, 1589.

Fletcher, Angus. *The Prophetic Moment: An Essay on Spenser*. Chicago: U of Chicago P, 1971.

Fletcher, Phineas. *Giles and Phineas Fletcher: Poetical Works*. Ed. Frederick S. Boas. 2 vols. Cambridge: Cambridge UP, 1908.

Forker, Charles R., ed. *'Edward the Second': Christopher Marlowe*. The Revels Plays. Manchester: Manchester UP, 1994.

Forsyth, Neil. 'Heavenly Helen.' *Etudes de Lettres* 4 (1987): 11–21.

Forsythe, R.S. 'The Passionate Shepherd; and English Poetry.' *PMLA* 40 (1925): 692–742.

Foucault, Michel. *The Archaeology of Knowledge*. Trans. A.M. Sheridan. New York: Pantheon, 1972.

– *The Foucault Reader*. Ed. Paul Rabinow. New York: Pantheon, 1984.

Fowler, Alastair. *Kinds of Literature: An Introduction to the Theory of Genres and Modes*. Cambridge, MA: Harvard UP, 1982.

– 'Spenser's *Prothalamion*.' *Conceitful Thought: The Interpretation of English Renaissance Poems*. Edinburgh: U of Edinburgh P, 1975. 59–86.

Frank, Tenney. 'Horace on Contemporary Poetry.' *Classical Journal* 13 (1917–18): 550–64.

Fränkel, Hermann. *Ovid: A Poet between Two Worlds*. Berkeley: U of California P, 1945.

Frazer, Sir James George. *The Golden Bough*. London: Macmillan, 1922.

Freer, Coburn. 'Lies and Lying in *The Jew of Malta*.' *'A Poet and a filthy Play-maker,'* ed. Friedenreich, Gill, and Kuriyama. 143–65.

Fricker, Robert. 'The Dramatic Structure of *Edward II*.' *English Studies* 34 (1953): 204–17.

Friedenreich, Kenneth. '"Huge Greatnesse" Overthrown': The Fall of the Empire in Marlowe's *Tamburlaine* Plays.' *ClioW* 1 (1972): 37–48.

Friedenreich, Kenneth, Roma Gill, and Constance B. Kuriyama, eds. *'A Poet and a filthy Play-maker': New Essays on Christopher Marlowe*. New York: AMS, 1988.

Friedman, Alan Warren. 'The Shackling of Accidents in Marlowe's *Jew of Malta*.' *Texas Studies in Literature and Language* 8 (1966): 155–67.

Frye, Northrop. *The Secular Scripture: A Study of the Structure of Romance.* Cambridge, MA: Harvard UP, 1976.

Frye, Susan. *Elizabeth I: The Competition for Representation.* New York: Oxford UP, 1993.

Fyler, John M. *Chaucer and Ovid.* New Haven: Yale UP, 1979.

– '*Omnia Vincit Amor*: Incongruity and the Limitations of Structure in Ovid's Elegiac Poetry.' *Classical Journal* 66 (1971): 196–203.

Galinsky, G. Karl. *Ovid's 'Metamorphoses': An Introduction to the Basic Aspects.* Berkeley: U of California P, 1975.

Gamel, Mary-Kay. '*Non Sine Caede*: Abortion Politics and Poetics in Ovid's *Amores.*' *Helios* 16 (1989): 183–206.

Garber, Marjorie. '"Here's Nothing Writ": Scribe, Script, and Circumspection in Marlowe's Plays.' *Theatre Journal* 36 (1984): 301–20.

– '"Infinite Riches in a Little Room": Closure and Enclosure in Marlowe.' *Two Renaissance Mythmakers*, ed. Kernan. 3–21.

Gardner, Helen. 'Milton's "Satan" and the Theme of Damnation in Elizabethan Tragedy.' *English Studies* 1 (1948): 46–66.

Gatti, Hilary. *The Renaissance Drama of Knowledge: Giordano Bruno in England.* London: Routledge, 1989.

Gellner, Ernst. *Nations and Nationalism.* Ithaca: Cornell UP, 1983.

The Geneva Bible: A Facsimile Edition. Ed. Lloyd E. Berry. Madison: U of Wisconsin P, 1969.

Ghisalberti, Fausto. 'Mediaeval Biographies of Ovid.' *Journal of the Warburg and Courtauld Institute* 9 (1946): 10–59.

Giamatti, A. Bartlett. *The Earthly Paradise and the Renaissance Epic.* Princeton: Princeton UP, 1966.

– *Play of Double Senses: Spenser's 'Faerie Queene.'* Englewood Cliffs: Prentice, 1975.

Gibbons, Brian. 'Unstable Proteus: Marlowe's *The Tragedy of Dido Queen of Carthage.*' *Christopher Marlowe*, ed. B. Morris. 27–46.

Giddens, Anthony. *The Nation-State and Violence: Volume Two of 'A Contemporary Critique of Historical Materialism.'* Berkeley: U of California P, 1985.

Gilbert, Allan H., ed. *Literary Criticism: Plato to Dryden.* Detroit: Wayne State UP, 1962, 1967.

Gill, Roma, ed. *The Complete Works of Christopher Marlowe.* 4 vols. Oxford: Clarendon, 1987–.

– ed. '*Doctor Faustus.*' New Mermaids. London: Black; New York: Norton, 1965.

– ed. '*Doctor Faustus.*' New Mermaids. New York: Norton, 1985.

– ed. '*The Jew of Malta.*' Oxford: Clarendon, 1995. Vol. 4 of *The Complete Works*, ed. Gill.

– 'Marlowe, Christopher.' *The Spenser Encyclopedia.* 453–4.

– 'Marlowe and the Art of Translation.' *'A Poet and a filthy Play-maker,'* ed. Friedenreich, Gill, and Kuriyama. 327–41.

– 'Marlowe, Lucan, and Sulpitius.' *Review of English Studies* 24 (1973): 401–13.

– 'Marlowe's Virgil: *Dido Queene of Carthage.*' *Review of English Studies* 28 (1977): 141–55.

– ed. *The Plays of Christopher Marlowe.* London: Oxford UP, 1971.

– ed. *Poems, Translations and 'Dido, Queen of Carthage.'* Oxford: Clarendon, 1987. Vol. 1 of *The Complete Works,* ed. Gill.

– 'Snakes Leape by Verse.' *Christopher Marlowe,* ed. B. Morris. 135–50.

Gill, Roma, and Robert Krueger. 'The Early Editions of Marlowe's Elegies and Davies's Epigrams: Sequence and Authority.' *The Library* 5th ser. 26 (1971): 243–9.

Gilligan, Carol. *In a Different Voice: Psychological Theory and Women's Development.* Cambridge, MA: Harvard UP, 1982.

Glenn, John Ronald. 'The Martyrdom of Ramus in Marlowe's *The Massacre at Paris.*' *Papers on Language and Literature* 9 (1973): 365–79.

Godshalk, W.L. *The Marlovian World Picture.* The Hague: Mouton, 1974.

Goldberg, Dena. 'Whose God's on First? Special Providence in the Plays of Christopher Marlowe.' *ELH* 60 (1993): 569–87.

Goldberg, Jonathan. 'Colin to Hobbinol: Spenser's Familiar Letters.' *South Atlantic Quarterly* 88 (1989): 107–26.

– *Sodometries: Renaissance Texts and Modern Sexuality.* Stanford: Stanford UP, 1992.

– *Voice Terminal Echo: Postmodernism and English Renaissance Texts.* New York: Methuen, 1986.

Golding, Arthur, trans. *The. xv Bookes of P. Ovidius Naso, entytuled Metamorphosis.* London, 1567.

Goldman, Michael. 'Marlowe and the Histrionics of Ravishment.' *Two Renaissance Mythmakers,* ed. Kernan. 22–40.

Gower, John, trans. *Ovids Festivalls, or Roman Calendar.* Cambridge, 1640.

Grabes, Herbert. 'Mirrors.' *The Spenser Encyclopedia.* 477–8.

Gransden, K.W. 'Lente Currite, Noctis Equi.' *Creative Imitation and Latin Literature,* ed. West and Woodman. 157–71.

Greenblatt, Stephen. 'Marlowe, Marx, and Anti-Semitism.' *Learning to Curse: Essays in Early Modern Culture.* New York: Routledge, 1990. 40–58.

– *Renaissance Self-Fashioning: From More to Shakespeare.* Chicago: U of Chicago P, 1980.

– *Sir Walter Ralegh: The Renaissance Man and His Roles.* New Haven: Yale UP, 1973.

Greene, Thomas M. *The Light in Troy: Imitation and Discovery in Renaissance Poetry.* New Haven: Yale UP, 1982.

Greenfield, Thelma N. *The Induction in Elizabethan Drama.* Eugene: U of Oregon P, 1969.

Greg, W.W. 'The Copyright of *Hero and Leander. The Library* 4th ser., 24 (1944): 165–74.

– 'The Damnation of Faustus.' *Modern Language Review* 41 (1946): 97–107.

– ed. *Marlowe's 'Doctor Faustus,' 1604–1616: Parallel Texts.* Oxford: Clarendon, 1950.

Habermas, Jürgen. 'The Public Sphere: An Encyclopedia Article (1964).' *New German Critique* 3 (1974): 49–55.

Hadfield, Andrew. *Literature, Politics and National Identity: Reformation to Renaissance.* Cambridge: Cambridge UP, 1994.

Hadzsits, George Depue. *Lucretius and His Influence.* New York: Cooper Square, 1963.

Hall, Joseph. *Virgidemiae. The Collected Poems of Joseph Hall.* Ed. A. Davenport. Liverpool: Liverpool UP, 1949. 5–99.

Halperin, David M. *Before Pastoral: Theocritus and the Ancient Tradition of Bucolic Poetry.* New Haven: Yale UP, 1983.

Hamilton, A.C., ed. *Edmund Spenser: 'The Faerie Queene.'* London: Longman, 1977.

– ed. *Essential Articles for the Study of Edmund Spenser.* Hamden, CT: Archon, 1972.

Hammer, Paul E.J. 'A Reckoning Reframed: The "Murder" of Christopher Marlowe Revisited.' *English Literary Renaissance* 26 (1996): 225–42.

Hammill, Graham. 'Faustus's Fortunes: Commodification, Exchange, and the Form of Literary Subjectivity.' *ELH* 63 (1996): 309–36.

Harbage, Alfred. 'Innocent Barabas.' *Tulane Drama Review* 8 (1964): 47–58.

Hardie, Philip. *The Epic Successors of Virgil.* Cambridge: Cambridge UP, 1993.

– 'Ovid's Theban History: The First "Anti-*Aeneid*"?' *Classical Quarterly* 40 (1990): 224–35.

Hardin, Richard F. 'Irony and Privilege in Marlowe.' *Centennial Review* 33 (1989): 207–27.

Hardison, O.B., Jr. 'Blank Verse before Milton.' *Studies in Philology* 81 (1984): 253–74.

Harper, J.W., ed. *'Tamburlaine': Christopher Marlowe.* London: Benn, 1971.

Harris, Wendell V. 'Intertextuality.' *Dictionary of Concepts in Literary Criticism and Theory.* New York: Greenwood, 1992. 175–8.

Hattaway, Michael. 'The Theology of Marlowe's *Doctor Faustus.' Renaissance Drama* 3 (1970): 51–78.

Hawkins, Harriett. 'The Morality of Elizabethan Drama: Some Footnotes to Plato.' *English Renaissance Studies Presented to Dame Helen Gardner in Honour of Her Seventieth Birthday.* Oxford: Clarendon, 1980. 12–32.

Healy, Thomas. *Christopher Marlowe*. Plymouth, England: Northcote House in Association with the British Council, 1994.

Hebel, Udo J., ed. *Intertextuality, Allusion, and Quotation: An International Bibliography of Critical Studies*. New York: Greenwood, 1989.

Helgerson, Richard. *The Elizabethan Prodigals*. Berkeley: U of California P, 1976.

– *Forms of Nationhood: The Elizabethan Writing of England*. Chicago: U of Chicago P, 1992.

– 'The New Poet Presents Himself: Spenser and the Idea of a Literary Career.' *PMLA* 93 (1978): 893–911.

– *Self-Crowned Laureates: Spenser, Jonson, Milton, and the Literary System*. Berkeley: U of California P, 1983.

Henderson, Diana E. *Passion Made Public: Elizabethan Lyric, Gender, and Performance*. Urbana: U of Illinois P, 1995.

Henderson, John. 'Lucan/the word at war.' *The Imperial Muse: Ramus Essays in Roman Literature of the Empire to Juvenal through Ovid*. Ed. A.J. Boyle. Victoria: U of British Columbia P, 1988. 122–64.

Hendricks, Margo. 'Managing the Barbarian: *The Tragedy of Dido, Queen of Carthage*.' *Renaissance Drama* 22 (1992): 165–88.

Heninger, S.K., Jr. 'The Passionate Shepherd and the Philosophical Nymph.' *Renaissance Papers* (1962): 63–70.

Herbert-Brown, Geraldine. *Ovid and the 'Fasti.'* Oxford: Clarendon, 1994.

Herman, Peter C. '*The Shepheardes Calender* and Renaissance Antipoetic Sentiment.' *Studies in English Literature, 1500–1900* 32 (1992): 15–33.

Herrick, Marvin Theodore. *The 'Poetics' of Aristotle in England*. New Haven: Yale UP, 1930.

Hexter, Ralph. 'Sidonian Dido.' *Innovations of Antiquity*. Ed. Ralph Hexter and Daniel Selden. New York: Routledge, 1992. 332–84.

Hieatt, A. Kent. 'The Genesis of Shakespeare's *Sonnets*: Spenser's *Ruines of Rome: by Bellay*.' *PMLA* 98 (1983): 800–14.

Hinds, Stephen. '*Arma* in Ovid's *Fasti* Part 1: Genre and Mannerism.' *Arethusa* 25 (1992): 81–112.

– '*Arma* in Ovid's *Fasti* Part 2: Genre, Romulean Rome and Augustan Ideology.' *Arethusa* 25 (1992): 113–53.

– *The Metamorphosis of Persephone: Ovid and the Self-Conscious Muse*. Cambridge: Cambridge UP, 1987.

Hinson, Cheryl L. 'Sidney's Enticing Song: Rewriting the Philomela Myth and the *Arcadia*.' Diss. Pennsylvania State University, 1995.

Hobsbawm, E.J. *Nations and Nationalism since 1780: Programme, Myth, Reality*. Cambridge: Cambridge UP, 1990.

Holahan, Michael. 'Ovid.' *The Spenser Encyclopedia*. 520–2.

Hollander, John. 'Donne, John.' *The Spenser Encyclopedia*. 221–2.
- *Melodious Guile: Fictive Pattern in Poetic Language*. New Haven: Yale UP, 1988.
Homer. *The 'Iliad' of Homer*. Trans. Richmond Lattimore. 1951; Chicago: Phoenix–U of Chicago P, 1967.
- *The 'Odyssey' of Homer*. Trans. Richmond Lattimore. 1965, 1967; New York: Harper Torchbooks–Harper and Row, 1968.
Hope, A.D. '*Tamburlaine*: The Argument of Arms.' *Christopher Marlowe*, ed. Bloom. 45–54.
Hopkins, Lisa. '"Dead Shepherd, now I find thy saw of might": *Tamburlaine* and Pastoral.' *Research Opportunities in Renaissance Drama* 35 (1996): 1–16.
Horace. *Horace: The 'Odes' and 'Epodes.'* Trans. C.C. Bennett. Loeb Classical Library. 1935; Cambridge, MA: Harvard UP; London: Heinemann, 1967.
- *Horace's 'Satires' and 'Epistles.'* Trans. Jacob Fuchs. New York: Norton, 1977.
Howe, James Robinson. *Marlowe, Tamburlaine, and Magic*. Athens: Ohio UP, 1976.
Hughes, Merritt Y. 'Spenser's Acrasia and the Circe of the Renaissance.' *Journal of the History of Ideas* 4 (1943): 381–99.
Hulse, Clark. *Metamorphic Verse: The Elizabethan Minor Epic*. Princeton: Princeton UP, 1981.
Hunter, G.K. 'The Beginnings of Elizabethan Drama: Revolution and Continuity.' *Renaissance Drama* 17 (1986): 29–52.
- *John Lyly: The Humanist as Courtier*. London: Routledge, 1962.
- 'The Theology of Marlowe's *The Jew of Malta.*' *Christopher Marlowe's 'The Jew of Malta.'* Ed. Irving Ribner. New York: Odyssey, 1970. 179–218. Orig. pub. *Journal of the Warburg and Courtauld Institute* 27 (1964).
Hurstfield, Joel. *The Elizabethan Nation*. New York: Harper, 1964.
- *Freedom, Corruption and Government in Elizabethan England*. Cambridge, MA: Harvard UP, 1973.
Hutcheon, Linda. *A Theory of Parody: The Teachings of Twentieth-Century Art Forms*. New York: Routledge, 1985.
Ingram, R.W. '"Pride in Learning goeth before a fall": Dr. Faustus' Opening Soliloquy.' *Mosaic* 13 (1979): 73–80.
Innes, D.C. 'Gigantomachy and Natural Philosophy.' *Classical Quarterly* 29 (1979): 165–71.
Jacobsen, Eric. *Translation: A Traditional Craft*. Copenhagen: Gyldendanske Boghandel–Nordisk Forlag, 1958.
Jacobson, Howard. *Ovid's 'Heroides.'* Princeton: Princeton UP, 1974.
Jameson, Caroline. 'Ovid in the Sixteenth Century.' *Ovid*, ed. Binns. 210–42.
Javitch, Daniel. 'The *Orlando Furioso* and Ovid's Revision of the *Aeneid.*' *Modern Language Notes* 99 (1984): 1023–36.

– 'Rescuing Ovid from the Allegorizers.' *Comparative Literature* 30 (1978): 97–107.

Jayne, Sears. 'Attending to Genre: Spenser's *Hymnes*.' *The Spenser Newsletter* 3 (1972): 5–6.

Johnson, Lynn Staley. *'The Shepheardes Calender': An Introduction*. University Park: Pennsylvania State UP, 1990.

Johnson, W.R. *Momentary Monsters: Lucan and His Heroes*. Ithaca: Cornell UP, 1987.

– 'The Problem of the Counter-classical Sensibility and Its Critics.' *California Studies in Classical Antiquity* 3 (1970): 123–51.

Jones, Robert C. *Engagement with Knavery: Point of View in 'Richard III,' 'The Jew of Malta,' 'Volpone,' and 'The Revenger's Tragedy.'* Durham: Duke UP, 1986.

Jonson, Ben. *Ben Jonson*. Ed. C.H. Herford and Percy and Evelyn Simpson. 11 vols. Oxford: Clarendon, 1925–52.

Joyce, Jane Wilson, trans. *Lucan: 'Pharsalia.'* Ithaca: Cornell UP, 1993.

Jump, John, ed. *Marlowe: 'Doctor Faustus.'* The Revels Plays. London: Macmillan, 1969.

– 'Spenser and Marlowe.' *Notes and Queries* 209 (1964): 261–2.

Kahn, Victoria. *Machiavellian Rhetoric from the Counter-Reformation to Milton*. Princeton: Princeton UP, 1994.

Keach, William. *Elizabethan Erotic Narratives: Irony and Pathos in the Ovidian Poetry of Shakespeare, Marlowe and Their Contemporaries*. New Brunswick: Rutgers UP, 1977.

– 'Marlowe's Hero as "Venus' Nun."' *English Literary Renaissance* 2 (1972): 307–20.

Kedouri, Elie. *Nationalism*. 4th ed. Oxford: Blackwell, 1993.

Keefer, Michael, ed. *Christopher Marlowe's 'Doctor Faustus': A 1604-Version Edition*. Peterborough, ON: Broadview, 1991.

– 'Verbal Magic and the Problem of the A and B Texts of *Doctor Faustus*.' *Journal of English and Germanic Philology* 82 (1983): 324–46.

Kellogg, Robert, and Oliver Steele, eds. *Edmund Spenser: Books I and II of 'The Faerie Queene.'* Indianapolis: Odyssey, 1965.

Kelsall, Malcolm. *Christopher Marlowe*. Leiden: Brill, 1981.

Kendall, Roy. 'Richard Baines and Christopher Marlowe's Milieu.' *English Literary Renaissance* 24 (1994): 507–52.

Kennedy, Duncan F. *The Arts of Love: Five Studies in the Discourse of Roman Love Elegy*. Roman Literature and Its Contexts. Cambridge: Cambridge UP, 1993.

Kennedy, William J. 'The Virgilian Legacies of Petrarch's *Bucolicum Carmen* and Spenser's *Shepheardes Calender*.' *The Early Renaissance: Virgil and the Classical*

Tradition. Ed. Anthony L. Pellegrini. Binghamton, NY: Center for Medieval and Early Renaissance Studies, 1985. 79–106.

Kenney, E.J., ed. *Latin Literature.* Cambridge: Cambridge UP, 1982. Vol. 2 of *The Cambridge History of Classical Literature.* 2 vols. 1982–5.

– 'Nequitiae Poeta.' *Ovidiana.* Ed. Niculae I. Herescu. Paris: Les Belles Lettres, 1958. 201–9.

– 'Virgil and the Elegiac Sensibility.' *Illinois Classical Studies* 8 (1983): 44–59.

Kermode, Lloyd Edward. '"Marlowe's Second City": The Jew as Critic at the Rose in 1592.' *Studies in English Literature, 1500–1900* 35 (1995): 215–29.

Kernan, Alvin, ed. *Two Renaissance Mythmakers: Christopher Marlowe and Ben Jonson.* Baltimore: Johns Hopkins UP, 1977.

Kerrigan, William, and Gordon Braden. *The Idea of the Renaissance.* Baltimore: Johns Hopkins UP, 1989.

Kierkegaard, Soren. 'The Ancient Tragical Motif as Reflected in the Modern.' *Tragedy,* ed. Corrigan. 350–65.

King, John N. *Spenser and the Reformation Tradition.* Princeton: Princeton UP, 1990.

Kirk, Andrew M. 'Marlowe and the Disordered Face of French History.' *Studies in English Literature, 1500–1900* 35 (1995): 193–213.

Knapp, Jeffrey. *Empire from Nowhere: England, America, and Literature from 'Utopia' to 'The Tempest.'* Berkeley: U of California P, 1992.

Knight, W.F. Jackson, trans. *Virgil: 'The Aeneid.'* Harmondsworth: Penguin, 1956.

Knoll, Robert E. *Christopher Marlowe.* New York: Twayne, 1969.

Kocher, Paul H. *Christopher Marlowe: A Study of His Thought, Learning, and Character.* New York: Russell, 1962.

– 'Contemporary Pamphlet Backgrounds for Marlowe's *The Massacre at Paris.*' *Modern Language Quarterly* 8 (1947): 151–73.

– 'Contemporary Pamphlet Backgrounds for Marlowe's *The Massacre at Paris,* Part Two.' *Modern Language Quarterly* 8 (1947): 309–18.

– 'François Hotman and Marlowe's *The Massacre at Paris.*' *PMLA* 56 (1941): 349–68.

– 'A Marlowe Sonnet.' *Philological Quarterly* 24 (1945): 39–45.

– 'The Witchcraft Basis in Marlowe's *Faustus.*' *Modern Philology* 38 (1940): 9–36.

Kohn, Hans. *The Idea of Nationalism: A Study in Its Origins and Background.* 1944; New York: Macmillan, 1946.

Kostic, Veselin. 'Marlowe's *Hero and Leander* and Chapman's Continuation.' *Renaissance and Modern Essays Presented to Vivian de Sola Pinto in Celebration of His Seventieth Birthday.* Ed. G.R. Hibbard. New York: Barnes, 1966. 25–34.

Kott, Jan. *The Bottom Translation: Marlowe and Shakespeare and the Carnival*

Tradition. Trans. Daniela Miedzyrzecka and Lillian Vallee. Evanston: Northwestern UP, 1987.

Krier, Theresa M. *Gazing on Secret Sights: Spenser, Classical Imitation, and the Decorums of Vision*. Ithaca: Cornell UP, 1990.

Kristeva, Julia. 'Word, Dialogue, and Novel.' Trans. Alice Jardine, Thomas Gora, and Leon S. Roudiez. *The Kristeva Reader*. Trans. Alice Jardine, Thomas Gora, and Leon S. Roudiez. Ed. Toril Moi. New York: Columbia UP, 1986. 35–61.

Kuriyama, Constance Brown. *Hammer or Anvil: Psychological Patterns in Christopher Marlowe's Plays*. New Brunswick: Rutgers UP, 1980.

Labriola, Albert C. 'Perspective and Illusion in *Hero and Leander*.' *English Language Notes* 16 (1978): 14–18.

Lamb, Mary Ellen. *Gender and Authority in the Sidney Circle*. Madison: U of Wisconsin P, 1990.

Langer, Suzanne. 'The Tragic Rhythm.' *Tragedy*, ed. Corrigan. 113–23.

Lateiner, Donald. 'Ovid's Homage to Callimachus and Alexandrian Poetic Theory.' *Hermes* 106 (1978): 188–96.

Leach, Eleanor Winsor. *Vergil's 'Eclogues': Landscapes of Experience*. Ithaca: Cornell UP, 1974.

Leech, Clifford. *Christopher Marlowe: Poet for the Stage*. Ed. Anne Lancashire. New York: AMS, 1986.

– ed. *Marlowe: A Collection of Critical Essays*. Englewood Cliffs: Prentice, 1964.

– 'Power and Suffering.' *Marlowe*, ed. Brown. 148–68.

– 'Venus and Her Nun: Portraits of Women in Love by Shakespeare and Marlowe.' *Studies in English Literature, 1500–1900* 5 (1965): 247–68.

Leishman, J.B. ed. *The Three Parnassus Plays (1598–1601)*. London: Nicholson, 1949.

Leiter, Louis H. 'Deification through Love: Marlowe's "The Passionate Shepherd to His Love."' *College English* 27 (1966): 444–9.

Lerner, Laurence. 'Ovid and the Elizabethans.' *Ovid Renewed*, ed. Martindale. 121–35.

Levin, Harry. *The Overreacher: A Study of Christopher Marlowe*. Cambridge, MA: Harvard UP, 1952.

Levin, Richard. 'Another Possible Clue to the Identity of the Rival Poet.' *Shakespeare Quarterly* 36 (1985): 213–14.

– 'The Contemporary Perception of Marlowe's Tamburlaine.' *Medieval and Renaissance Drama in England* 1 (1984): 51–70.

Levine, Laura. *Men in Women's Clothing: Anti-theatricality and Effeminization, 1579–1642*. Cambridge: Cambridge UP, 1994.

Lewis, C.S. *English Literature in the Sixteenth Century Excluding Drama*. 1954; London: Oxford UP, 1973.

- 'Hero and Leander.' *Elizabethan Poetry: Modern Essays in Criticism*. Ed. Paul J. Alpers. London: Oxford UP, 1967. 235–50.

Lewis, Charlton T., and Charles Short. *A Latin Dictionary*. 1879; Oxford: Clarendon, 1987.

Lipking, Lawrence. *The Life of the Poet: Beginning and Ending Poetic Careers*. Chicago: U of Chicago P, 1981.

Loewenstein, Joseph. 'Echo's Ring: Orpheus and Spenser's Career.' *English Literary Renaissance* 16 (1986): 287–302.

Lotspeich, Henry Gibbons. *Classical Mythology in the Poetry of Edmund Spenser*. Princeton: Princeton UP, 1932.

Low, Anthony. 'The Compleat Angler's "Baite"; or, The Subverter Subverted.' *John Donne Journal* 4 (1985): 1–12.

Lucan. *Lucan: 'The Civil War.'* Trans. J.D. Duff. Loeb Classical Library. 2 vols. Cambridge, MA: Harvard UP; London: Heinemann, 1928.

Luck, Georg. *The Latin Love Elegy*. London: Methuen, 1959.

Lucretius. *'De Rerum Natura.'* 3d ed. Trans. W.H.D. Rouse; rev. Martin Ferguson Smith. Loeb Classical Library. Cambridge, MA: Harvard UP; London: Heinemann, 1975.

- *The Way Things Are*. Trans. Rolfe Humphries. 1968; Bloomington: Indiana UP, 1969.

Machiavelli, Niccolò. *Niccolò Machiavelli: 'The Prince.'* 2d ed. Ed. and trans. Robert M. Adams. New York: Norton, 1992.

Mack, Sara. *Ovid*. New Haven: Yale UP, 1988.

Maclean, Hugh. 'The Teares of the Muses.' *The Spenser Encyclopedia*. 182–3.

Maclean, Hugh, and Anne Lake Prescott, eds. *Edmund Spenser's Poetry: Authoritative Texts and Criticism*. 3d ed. New York: Norton, 1993.

MacLean, Gerald M. 'The Debate over Lucan's *Pharsalia*.' *Time's Witness: Historical Representation in English Poetry, 1603–1660*. Madison: U of Wisconsin P, 1990. 26–44.

MacLure, Millar, ed. *Marlowe: The Critical Heritage, 1588–1896*. London: Routledge, 1979.

- ed. *The Poems: Christopher Marlowe*. London: Methuen, 1968.

Mahood, M.A. *Poetry and Humanism*. London: Cape, 1950.

Makowski, John F. *'Oracula Mortis* in the *Pharsalia.'* *Classical Philology* 72 (1977): 193–202.

Marcus, Leah S. *The Politics of Mirth: Jonson, Herrick, Milton, Marvel, and the Defense of Old Holiday Pastimes*. Chicago: U of Chicago P, 1986.

- *Puzzling Shakespeare: Local Reading and Its Discontents*. Berkeley: U of California P, 1988.

- 'Textual Indeterminacy and Ideological Difference: The Case of *Dr. Faustus*.' *Renaissance Drama* 20 (1989): 1–29.

Marinelli, Peter. *Pastoral*. London: Methuen, 1971.

Marlowe, Christopher. *Epigrammes and Elegies [By I.D. and C.M.]*. Middleborugh, n.d.

– *LUCANS FIRST BOOKE TRANSLATED LINE FOR LINE, BY CHR. MARLOW*. London, 1600.

Marot, Clément. *Lamentation for Madame Louise of Savoy. The Pastoral Elegy*. Trans. Thomas Perrin Harrison. New York: Octagon, 1968. 134–45.

Martial. *Epigrams*. Trans. Walter C.A. Ker. Loeb Classical Library. 2 vols. Cambridge, MA: Harvard UP; London: Heinemann, 1919.

Martin, Christopher. *Policy in Love: Lyric and Public in Ovid, Petrarch and Shakespeare*. Pittsburgh: Duquesne UP, 1994.

Martin, L.C., ed. *Marlowe's Poems*. New York: Dial, 1931.

Martin, Richard A. 'Fate, Seneca, and Marlowe's *Dido, Queen of Carthage*.' *Renaissance Drama* 11 (1980): 45–66.

– 'Marlowe's Tamburlaine and the Language of Romance.' *PMLA* 93 (1978): 248–64.

Martindale, Charles, ed. *Ovid Renewed: Ovidian Influences on Literature and Art from the Middle Ages to the Twentieth Century*. Cambridge: Cambridge UP, 1988.

– *Redeeming the Text: Latin Poetry and the Hermeneutics of Reception*. Cambridge: Cambridge UP, 1993.

Martz, Louis L., ed. *'Hero and Leander' by Christopher Marlowe: A Facsimile of the First Edition, London 1598*. New York: Johnson Reprint, 1972.

Masinton, Charles G. *Christopher Marlowe's Tragic Vision*. Athens: Ohio UP, 1972.

Maus, Katharine Eisaman. *Inwardness and Theater in the English Renaissance*. Chicago: U of Chicago P, 1995.

May, Steven W. *Sir Walter Raleigh*. Boston: Twayne, 1989.

McAdam, Ian. 'Carnal Identity in *The Jew of Malta*.' *English Literary Renaissance* 26 (1996): 46–74.

McAlindon, T. 'Classical Mythology and Christian Tradition in Marlowe's *Doctor Faustus*.' *PMLA* 81 (1966): 214–23.

– *'Doctor Faustus': Divine in Show*. New York: Twayne, 1994.

– *English Renaissance Tragedy*. Vancouver: U of British Columbia P, 1986.

McCabe, Richard A. 'Elizabethan Satire and the Bishops' Ban of 1599.' *Yearbook of English Studies* 11 (1981): 188–93.

McCanles, Michael. '*The Shepheardes Calender* as Document and Monument.' *Studies in English Literature, 1500–1900* 22 (1982): 5–19.

McCloskey, Susan. 'The Worlds of *Edward II*.' *Renaissance Drama* 16 (1985): 35–48.

McCoy, Richard C. *The Rites of Knighthood: The Literature and Politics of Elizabethan Chivalry*. Berkeley: U of California P, 1989.

McElroy, John F. 'Repetition, Contrariety, and Individualization in *Edward II*.' *Studies in English Literature, 1500–1900* 24 (1984): 205–24.

McKenzie, John L. *Dictionary of the Bible*. New York: Macmillan; London: Collier Macmillan, 1965.

McKeown, J.C., ed. *Ovid: 'Amores': Text, Prolegomena and Commentary*. 4 vols. London: Cairns, 1987–.

McKerrow, Ronald B., ed. *The Works of Thomas Nashe*. Ed. F.P. Wilson. 5 vols. Oxford: Blackwell, 1958.

McLane, Paul E. *Spenser's 'Shepheardes Calender': A Study in Elizabethan Allegory*. Notre Dame: U of Notre Dame P, 1961.

Mead, Stephen X. 'Marlowe's *Tamburlaine* and the Idea of Empire.' *Works and Days* 7 (1989): 91–103.

Mebane, John S. *Renaissance Magic and the Return of the Golden Age*. Lincoln: U of Nebraska P, 1989.

Melville, A. D., trans. *Ovid, Sorrows of an Exile: 'Tristia'*. Intro. E.J. Kenney. Oxford: Clarendon, 1992.

Merchant, W. Moelwyn, ed. *'Edward the Second'*. New Mermaids. London: Black; New York: Norton, 1967.

Michel, Laurence. 'The Possibility of a Christian Tragedy.' *Thought* 31 (1956): 403–28.

Miller, David L. 'The Death of the Modern: Gender and Desire in Marlowe's *Hero and Leander*.' *South Atlantic Quarterly* 88 (1989): 757–87.

– 'Spenser's Vocation, Spenser's Career.' *ELH* 50 (1983): 197–231.

Miller, Nancy K. 'Arachnologies: The Woman, the Text, and the Critic.' *Subject to Change: Reading Feminist Writing*. Ed. Nancy K. Miller. New York: Columbia UP, 1988. 77–101.

Miller, Paul Allen. 'Sidney, Petrarch, and Ovid, or Imitation as Subversion.' *ELH* 58 (1991): 499–522.

Mills, John. 'The Courtship Ritual of Hero and Leander.' *English Literary Renaissance* 2 (1972): 298–306.

Minshull, Catherine. 'Marlowe's "Sound Machevill."' *Renaissance Drama* 13 (1982): 35–53.

Mirandola, Giovanni Pico della. *Oration on the Dignity of Man*. Trans. A. Robert Caponigri. Chicago: Regnery, 1956.

Mirollo, James V. *Mannerism and Renaissance Poetry: Concept, Mode, Inner Design*. New Haven: Yale UP, 1984.

Montrose, Louis Adrian. '"Eliza, Queene of shepheardes," and the Pastoral of Power.' *English Literary Renaissance* 10 (1980): 153–82.

– 'The Elizabethan Subject and the Spenserian Text.' *Literary Theory / Renaissance Texts*, ed. Parker and Quint. 303–40.

- '"The perfecte paterne of a Poete": The Poetics of Courtship in *The Shepheardes Calender.*' *Texas Studies in Literature and Language* 21 (1979): 34–67.
Moore, Hale. 'Gabriel Harvey's References to Marlowe.' *Studies in Philology* 23 (1926): 337–57.
Morris, Brian, ed. *Christopher Marlowe.* New York: Hill, 1968.
- 'Comic Method in Marlowe's *Hero and Leander.*' *Christopher Marlowe,* ed. B. Morris. 115–31.
Morris, Harry. 'Marlowe's Poetry.' *Tulane Drama Review* 8 (1963): 134–54.
Morris, Jeffrey B. 'Poetic Counsels: The Poet/Patron Relation between Spenser and Ralegh.' Diss. Pennsylvania State University, 1993.
Muir, Kenneth. 'The Chronology of Marlowe's Plays.' *Proceedings of the Leeds Philosophical and Literary Society* 5 (1943): 345–56.
Mullaney, Steven. *The Place of the Stage: License, Play, and Power in Renaissance England.* Chicago: U of Chicago P, 1988.
Mulvihill, James D. 'Jonson's *Poetaster* and the Ovidian Debate.' *Studies in English Literature, 1500–1900* 22 (1982): 239–55.
Myers, K. Sara. *Ovid's Causes: Cosmogony and Aetiology in the 'Metamorphoses.'* Ann Arbor: U of Michigan P, 1994.
Neuse, Richard. 'Atheism and Some Functions of Myth in Marlowe's *Hero and Leander.*' *Modern Language Quarterly* 31 (1970): 424–39.
Newman, J.K. *Augustus and the New Poetry.* Bruxelles-Berchem: Latomus Revue D'études Latines, 1967. Vol. 88 of *Collection Latomus.*
Nicholl, Charles. *The Reckoning: The Murder of Christopher Marlowe.* New York: Harcourt, 1992.
Nikolaidis, A.G. 'Some Observations on Ovid's Lost *Medea.*' *Latomus* 44 (1985): 383–7.
Nosworthy, J.M. 'Marlowe's Ovid and Davies's Epigrams – A Postscript.' *Review of English Studies* 15 (1964): 397–8.
- 'The Publication of Marlowe's Elegies and Davies's Epigrams.' *Review of English Studies* 4 (1953): 260–1.
Ogilvie, R.M. 'Ovid and the Seventeenth Century.' *Latin and Greek: A History of the Influence of the Classics on English Life from 1600 to 1918.* Hamden, CT: Archon, 1969. 1–33.
O'Hara, James J. 'The Significance of Vergil's *Acidalia Mater* and *Venus Erycina* in Catullus and Ovid.' *Harvard Studies in Classical Philology* 93 (1990): 335–42.
Oliver, H.J., ed. *'Dido Queen of Carthage' and 'The Massacre at Paris': Christopher Marlowe.* The Revels Plays. Cambridge, MA: Harvard UP, 1968.
Oram, William et al., eds. *The Yale Edition of the Shorter Poems of Edmund Spenser.* New Haven: Yale UP, 1989.
Orgel, Stephen, ed. *Christopher Marlowe: The Complete Poems and Translations.* Baltimore: Penguin, 1971.

Orlandi, Mary-Kay Gamel. 'Ovid True and False in Renaissance Poetry.' *Pacific Coast Philology* 13 (1978): 60–70.

Oruch, Jack B. 'Works, Lost.' *The Spenser Encyclopedia*. 737–8.

Otis, Brooks. *Ovid as an Epic Poet*. 2d ed. Cambridge: Cambridge UP, 1970.

Ovid. *'Metamorphoses.' Shakespeare's Ovid*. Ed. W.H.D. Rouse. Trans. Arthur Golding. New York: Norton, 1966.

– Ovid. 2d ed. Trans. Frank Justus Miller; rev. G.P. Goold. Loeb Classical Library. 6 vols. Cambridge, MA: Harvard UP; London: Heinemann, 1984.

– *Ovid's Epistles, Translated by Several Hands*. Ed. John Dryden. London, 1680.

Owen, S.G., ed. and trans. 'Notes on Ovid's *Ibis, Ex Ponto Libri*, and *Halieutica*.' *Classical Quarterly* 8 (1914): 254–71.

– *P. Ovidi Nasonis: 'Tristium' Liber Secundus*. Amsterdam: Hakkert, 1967.

Palmer, D.J. 'Magic and Poetry in *Doctor Faustus*.' *'Doctor Faustus*,' ed. Ribner. 201–14.

– 'Marlowe's Naturalism.' *Christopher Marlowe*, ed. B. Morris. 151–75.

Parker, Douglass. 'The Ovidian Coda.' *Arion* 8 (1969): 80–97.

Parker, Patricia A. *Inescapable Romance: Studies in the Poetics of a Mode*. Princeton: Princeton UP, 1979.

– 'Romance.' *The Spenser Encyclopedia*. 609–18.

Parker, Patricia, and David Quint, eds. *Literary Theory / Renaissance Texts*. Baltimore: Johns Hopkins UP, 1986.

Patterson, Annabel. *Pastoral and Ideology: Virgil to Valéry*. Berkeley: U of California P, 1987.

Pearcy, Lee T. *The Mediated Muse: English Translations of Ovid, 1560–1700*. Hamden, CT: Archon, 1984.

Pendry, E.D., ed. *Christopher Marlowe: Complete Plays and Poems*. London: Dent, 1976.

Phaer, Thomas, trans. *The Aeneid of Virgil*. Completed by Thomas Twyne. London, 1573.

Piepho, Lee. 'The Latin and English Eclogues of Phineas Fletcher: Sannazaro's *Piscatoria* among the Britons.' *Studies in Philology* 81 (1984): 461–72.

Pinciss, Gerald. *Christopher Marlowe*. New York: Ungar, 1975.

Plato. *The Collected Dialogues of Plato*. Ed. Edith Hamilton and Huntington Cairns. Princeton: Princeton UP, 1961.

Plotinus. *Enneads. Select Passages Illustrating Neoplatonism*. Trans. E.R. Dodds. New York: Macmillan, 1923.

Poirier, Michel. *Christopher Marlowe*. London: Chatto, 1968.

Praz, Mario. 'Machiavelli and the Elizabethans.' *Proceedings of the British Academy* 14 (1928): 49–97.

Prescott, Anne Lake. 'Du Bellay in Renaissance England: Recent Work on Translation and Response.' *Euvres et Critiques* 20 (1995): 121–8.

– 'Spenser (Re)Reading du Bellay: Chronology and Literary Response. *Spenser's Life and the Subject of Biography*. Ed. Judith H. Anderson, Donald Cheney, and David R. Richardson. Amherst: U of Massachusetts P, 1996. 131–45.

– '*Translatio Lupae*: Du Bellay's Roman Whore Goes North.' *Renaissance Quarterly* 42 (1989): 397–419.

Priest, Dale G. 'Knave or Fool? Ithamore as Dramatic Paradigm in *The Jew of Malta*.' *Explorations in Renaissance Culture* 8–9 (1982–3): 85–96.

Propertius. *The Elegies*. Trans. G.P. Goold. Loeb Classical Library. Cambridge, MA: Harvard UP; London: Heinemann, 1990.

Proser, Matthew N. '*Dido Queene of Carthage* and the Evolution of Marlowe's Dramatic Style.' '*A Poet and a filthy Play-maker*,' ed. Friedenreich, Gill, and Kuriyama. 83–97.

– *The Gift of Fire: Aggression and the Plays of Christopher Marlowe*. Renaissance and Baroque Studies and Texts 12. New York: Lang, 1995.

– '*Tamburlaine* and the Art of Destruction.' *University of Hartford Studies in Literature* 20 (1988): 37–51.

Putnam, Michael C.J. *Virgil's Pastoral Art*. Princeton: Princeton UP, 1970.

Querbach, Carl W. 'Sound and Substance: A Reading of Virgil's Seventh Eclogue.' *Phoenix* 39 (1985): 355–67.

Quint, David. *Epic and Empire: Politics and Generic Form from Virgil to Milton*. Princeton: Princeton UP, 1993.

Quintilian. *The 'Institutio Oratoria' of Quintilian*. Trans. H.E. Butler. Loeb Classical Library. 4 vols. Cambridge, MA: Harvard UP; London: Heinemann, 1969.

Quitslund, Jon A. 'Platonism.' *The Spenser Encyclopedia*. 546–8.

Ralegh, Sir Walter. *The Poems of Sir Walter Ralegh*. Ed. Agnes M.C. Latham. Cambridge, MA: Harvard UP, 1951.

Rambuss, Richard. *Spenser's Secret Career*. Cambridge: Cambridge UP, 1993.

Rand, E.K. 'The Chronology of Ovid's Early Works.' *American Journal of Philology* 18 (1907): 287–96.

– *Ovid and His Influence*. 1925; New York: Cooper Square, 1963.

Ranson, Nicholas. 'A Marlowe Sonnet?' *Arkansas Philological Association* 5 (1979): 8.

Rebhorn, Wayne A. *Foxes and Lions: Machiavelli's Confidence Men*. Ithaca: Cornell UP, 1988.

Reiss, Timothy J. *Tragedy and Truth: Studies in the Development of a Renaissance and Neoclassical Discourse*. New Haven: Yale UP, 1980.

Renan, Ernest. 'What Is a Nation?' *Nation and Narration*, ed. Bhabha. 8–22.

Renwick, W.L., ed. '*Complaints*': *Edmund Spenser*. London: Scholartis, 1928.

Ribner, Irving, ed. *Christopher Marlowe's 'Doctor Faustus': Text and Major Criticism*. New York: Odyssey, 1966.

– ed. *The Complete Plays of Christopher Marlowe*. New York: Odyssey, 1963.

– '*Edward II* as a Historical Tragedy.' *Marlowe*, ed. Brown. 140–8.

– 'Marlowe and Machiavelli.' *Comparative Literature* 6 (1954): 348–56.

Ricoeur, Paul. *The Philosophy of Paul Ricoeur: An Anthology of his Work*. Ed. Charles E. Reagan and David Stewart. Boston: Beacon, 1978.

Riddell, James A. 'Ben Jonson and "Marlowes mighty line."' '*A Poet and a filthy Play-maker*,' ed. Friedenreich, Gill, and Kuriyama. 37–48.

Riddell, James A., and Stanley Stewart. *Jonson's Spenser: Evidence and Historical Criticism*. Pittsburgh: Duquesne UP, 1995.

Riffaterre, Michael. *Semiotics of Poetry*. Bloomington: Indiana UP, 1978.

Riggs, David. 'Persuading Men to Atheism: Marlowe's Quarrel with God.' Third International Marlowe Conference, Cambridge, England, 1993.

Robathan, Dorothy M. 'Ovid in the Middle Ages.' *Ovid*, ed. Binns. 191–209.

Roberts, Gareth. 'Three Notes on Uses of Circe by Spenser, Marlowe and Milton.' *Notes and Queries* 223 (1978): 433–5.

Roberts, Penny. 'Marlowe's *The Massacre at Paris*: A Historical Perspective.' *Renaissance Studies* 9 (1995): 430–41.

Roberts-Baytop. *Dido, Queen of Infinite Literary Variety: The English Renaissance Borrowings and Influences*. Salzburg: Institut Für Englische Sprache und Literatur, 1974.

Roche, Thomas P., Jr, ed. '*The Faerie Queene*.' 1978; New Haven: Yale UP, 1981.

– *The Kindly Flame: A Study of the Third and Fourth Books of Spenser's 'Faerie Queene*.' Princeton: Princeton UP, 1964.

Rogers, David M. 'Love and Honor in Marlowe's *Dido, Queen of Carthage*.' *Greyfriar* 6 (1963): 3–7.

Ronan, Clifford J. '*Pharsalia* 1.373–378: Roman Parricide and Marlowe's Editors.' *Classical and Modern Literature* 6 (1986): 305–9.

Ronsard, Pierre de. *Oeuvres complètes*. Ed. Paul Laumonier. Rev. and completed by Isidore Silver and Raymond Lebègue. 20 vols. Paris: Hachette, 1914–75.

Rothstein, Eric. 'Structure as Meaning in *The Jew of Malta*.' *Journal of English and Germanic Philology* 65 (1966): 260–73.

Rousseau, G.S. 'Marlowe's "Dido" and a Rhetoric of Love.' *English Miscellany* 19 (1968): 25–49.

Rowland, Richard, ed. '*Edward II*.' Oxford: Clarendon, 1994. Vol. 3 of *The Complete Works*, ed. Gill.

Rowse, A.L. *Christopher Marlowe: His Life and Work*. New York: Harper, 1964.

Royston, Pamela. '*Hero and Leander* and the Eavesdropping Reader.' *John Donne Journal* 2 (1983): 31–53.

Rudd, Niall. 'Chaucer and Virgil: Two Portraits. Dido.' *The Classical Tradition in Operation*. Toronto: U of Toronto P, 1994. 3–31.

– 'Daedalus and Icarus (ii) From the Renaissance to the Present Day.' *Ovid Renewed*, ed. Martindale. 37–53.

– 'Daedalus and Icarus (i) From Rome to the End of the Middle Ages.' *Ovid Renewed*, ed. Martindale. 21–35.

Sachs, Arieh. 'The Religious Despair of Doctor Faustus.' *Journal of English and Germanic Philology* 63 (1964): 625–47.

Sales, Roger. *Christopher Marlowe*. New York: St Martin's, 1991.

Saltonstall, Wye, trans. *Ovid's Heroical Epistles*. London, 1639.

– trans. *Ovid De Ponto*. 2d ed. London, 1640.

– trans. *Ovid's Tristia containing Five Books of mournful Elegies*. 4th ed. London, 1672.

Sanders, Wilbur. *The Dramatist and the Received Idea: Studies in the Plays of Marlowe and Shakespeare*. Cambridge: Cambridge UP, 1968.

Sandys, George, trans. *Ovid's Metamorphosis Englished*. London, 1626.

– *Ovid's Metamorphosis Englished, Mythologiz'd, and Represented in Figures. An Essay to the Translation of Virgil's Aeneis*. Oxford, 1632.

Sannazaro, Jacopo. *'Arcadia' and 'Piscatorial Eclogues.'* Trans. Ralph Nash. Detroit: Wayne State UP, 1966.

Schleiner, Louise. 'Spenser's "E.K." as Edmund Kent (Kenned / of Kent): Kyth (Couth), Kissed, and Kunning-Conning.' *English Literary Renaissance* 20 (1990): 374–407.

Schoeneich, Georg. *Der Litterarische Einfluss Spensers auf Marlowe*. Halle: Buchdruckerei Hohmann, 1907.

Schuman, Samuel. 'Minor Characters and the Thematic Structure of Marlowe's *Tamburlaine: II.' Modern Language Studies* 8 (1978): 27–33.

Scott, Margaret. 'Machiavelli and the Machiavel.' *Renaissance Drama* 15 (1984): 147–74.

Segal, Charles. *Language and Desire in Seneca's 'Phaedra.'* Princeton: Princeton UP, 1986.

– *Orpheus: The Myth of the Poet*. Baltimore: Johns Hopkins UP, 1989.

Segal, Erich. 'Marlowe's *Schadenfreude*: Barabas as Comic Hero.' *Christopher Marlowe*, ed. Bloom. 121–36.

Seneca. *Seneca*. Trans. E.F. Watling. Harmondsworth: Penguin, 1966.

– *Seneca's Tragedies*. Trans. Frank Justus Miller. Loeb Classical Library. 2 vols. Cambridge, MA: Harvard UP; London: Heinemann, 1929.

– *Thyestes: Lucius Annaeus Seneca*. Trans. Jasper Heywood (1560). Ed. Joseph Daalder. London: Benn; New York: Norton, 1982.

Seneca the Elder. *The Elder Seneca: Declamations*. Trans. Michael Winterbottom. Loeb Classical Library. Cambridge, MA: Harvard UP; London: Heinemann, 1974.

Sewell, Robert B. *The Vision of Tragedy.* New Haven: Yale UP, 1980.

Shakespeare, William. *The Riverside Shakespeare.* Ed. G. Blakemore Evans et al. Boston: Houghton, 1974.

Shapiro, James. '"Metre meete to furnish Lucans style': Reconsidering Marlowe's *Lucan.' 'A Poet and a filthy Play-maker,'* ed. Friedenreich, Gill, and Kuriyama. 315–25.

– *Rival Playwrights: Marlowe, Jonson, Shakespeare.* New York: Columbia UP, 1991.

Sharrock, Alison. *Seduction and Repetition in Ovid's 'Ars Amatoria' 2.* Oxford: Clarendon, 1994.

Shaver, Anne. 'Rereading Mirabella.' *Spenser Studies: A Renaissance Poetry Annual* 9 (1991): 211–26.

Shepard, Alan. 'Endless Sacks: Soldiers' Desire in *Tamburlaine.' Renaissance Quarterly* 46 (1993): 734–53.

Shepherd, Simon. *Marlowe and the Politics of Elizabethan Theatre.* New York: St Martin's, 1986.

Shore, David R. 'Colin Clout.' *The Spenser Encyclopedia.* 172–3.

Shuger, Debora Kuller. *The Renaissance Bible: Scholarship, Sacrifice, and Subjectivity.* Berkeley: U of California P, 1994.

Shulman, Jeff. '*Te Quoque Falle Tamen*: Ovid's Anti-Lucretian Didactics.' *Classical Journal* 76 (1981): 242–53.

Sidney, Sir Philip. *The Defence of Poesy (An Apologie for Poetrie).' Elizabethan Critical Essays,* ed. G.G. Smith. 1: 148–207.

– *The Poems of Sir Philip Sidney.* Ed. William A. Ringler, Jr. Oxford: Clarendon, 1962.

– *Sir Philip Sidney: 'The Countess of Pembroke's Arcadia' ('The Old Arcadia').* Ed. Jean Robertson. Oxford: Clarendon, 1973.

Sidney, Sir Robert. *Letter to Lord Burleigh. State Papers 84/44, F.60.* From Flushing on the Netherlands, 26 January 1592.

Siemon, James R., ed. *'The Jew of Malta.'* New Mermaids. 2d ed. London: Black; New York: Norton, 1994.

Simmons, J.L. 'Elizabethan Stage Practice and Marlowe's *The Jew of Malta.' Renaissance Quarterly* 4 (1971): 93–104.

Sinfield, Alan. *Faultlines: Cultural Materialism and the Politics of Dissident Reading.* Berkeley: U of California P, 1992.

Smith, Anthony D. *Theories of Nationalism.* 2d ed. New York: Holmes, 1983.

Smith, Bruce R. 'Toward the Rediscovery of Tragedy: Productions of Seneca's Plays on the English Renaissance Stage.' *Renaissance Drama* 9 (1978): 3–37.

Smith, G. Gregory, ed. *Elizabethan Critical Essays.* 2 vols. London: Oxford UP, 1904.

Smith, Hallett Darius. *Elizabethan Poetry: A Study in Conventions, Meaning, and Expression.* 1952; Cambridge, MA: Harvard UP, 1966.

Smith, Mary Elizabeth. *'Love Kindling Fire': A Study of Christopher Marlowe's 'The Tragedy of Dido Queen of Carthage.'* Salzburg: Institut Für Englische Sprache und Literatur, 1977.

Snow, Edward A. 'Marlowe's *Doctor Faustus* and the Ends of Desire.' *Two Renaissance Mythmakers*, ed. Kernan. 70–110.

Snyder, Susan. 'Marlowe's *Doctor Faustus* as an Inverted Saint's Life.' *Studies in Philology* 63 (1966): 565–77.

Spargo, John Webster. *Virgil the Necromancer: Studies in Virgilian Legends.* Cambridge, MA: Harvard UP, 1934.

Spenser, Edmund. *The Poetical Works of Edmund Spenser.* Ed. J.C. Smith and Ernest de Sèlincourt. 3 vols. Oxford: Clarendon, 1909–10.

– *The Works of Edmund Spenser: A Variorum Edition.* Ed. Edwin Greenlaw et al. 11 vols. Baltimore: Johns Hopkins UP, 1932–57.

The Spenser Encyclopedia. Ed. A.C. Hamilton et al. Toronto: U of Toronto P, 1990.

Spenser, Edmund, and Gabriel Harvey. *Spenser–Harvey Correspondence. Elizabethan Critical Essays*, ed. G.G. Smith. 1: 87–126.

Spivack, Charlotte. *George Chapman.* New York: Twayne, 1967.

Stanyhurst, Richard, trans. *Thee First Foure Bookes of Virgil His Aeneis.* Leiden, 1582.

Stapleton, M.L. *Harmful Eloquence: Ovid's 'Amores' from Antiquity to Shakespeare.* Ann Arbor: U of Michigan P, 1996.

Starnes, D.T. 'Spenser and E.K.' *Studies in Philology* 41 (1944): 181–200.

Statius. *Statius.* Ed. J.H. Mozley. Loeb Classical Library. 2 vols. Cambridge, MA: Harvard UP; London: Heinemann, 1961.

Staton, Walter F., Jr. 'The Influence of Thomas Watson on Elizabethan Ovidian Poetry.' *Studies in the Renaissance* 6 (1959): 243–50.

Steane, J.B., ed. *Christopher Marlowe: The Complete Plays.* New York: Penguin, 1969.

– *Marlowe: A Critical Study.* Cambridge: Cambridge UP, 1964.

Sternfeld, Frederick W. 'Come Live with Me and Be My Love.' *The Hidden Harmony: Essays in Honor of Philip Wheelwright.* New York: Odyssey, 1966. 173–92.

Sternfeld, Frederick W., and Mary Joiner Chan. '"Come live with me And be my love."' *Comparative Literature* 22 (1970): 173–87.

Still, Judith, and Michael Worton. Introduction. *Intertextuality: Theories and Practices.* Ed. Michael Worton and Judith Still. Manchester: Manchester UP, 1990. 1–44.

Stilling, Roger. *Love and Death in Renaissance Tragedy*. Baton Rouge: Louisiana State UP, 1976.

Storm, Melvin. 'Faustus' First Soliloquy: The End of Every Art.' *Massachusetts Studies in English* 8 (1982): 40–9.

Striar, Brian Jay. 'Theories and Practices of Renaissance Verse Translation.' Diss. Claremont Graduate School, 1984.

Stroup, Thomas B. '*Doctor Faustus* and *Hamlet*: Contrasting Kinds of Christian Tragedy.' *Comparative Drama* 5 (1971–2): 243–53.

Summers, Claude J. *Christopher Marlowe and the Politics of Power*. Salzburg: Institut Für Englische Sprache und Literatur, 1974.

– 'Sex, Politics, and Self-Realization in *Edward II*.' '*A Poet and a filthy Playmaker*,' ed. Friedenreich, Gill, and Kuriyama. 221–40.

Sunesen, Brent. 'Marlowe and the Dumb Show.' *English Studies* 35 (1954): 241–53.

Suzuki, Mihoko. *Metamorphoses of Helen: Authority and Difference in Homer, Virgil, Spenser, and Shakespeare*. Ithaca: Cornell UP, 1989.

Swinburne, Algernon Charles. *Christopher Marlowe in Relation to Greene, Peele and Lodge*. London: Wise, 1914.

Tacitus. *Tacitus: 'Dialogus,' 'Agricola,' 'Germania.'* Trans. William Peterson. Loeb Classical Library. Cambridge, MA: Harvard UP; London: Heinemann, 1963.

Tarrant, R.J. 'Senecan Drama and Its Antecedents.' *Harvard Studies in Classical Philology* 82 (1978): 213–63.

Tasso, Torquato. *Discourses on the Heroic Poem*. Ed. Mariella Cavalchini and Irene Samuel. Oxford: Clarendon, 1973.

– *Jerusalem Delivered*. Trans. Edward Fairfax. Ed. John Charles Nelson. New York: Capricorn–Putnam, 1963.

Taylor, A.B. 'Britomart and the Mermaids: A Note on Marlowe and Spenser.' *Notes and Queries* 216 (1971): 224–5.

Taylor, Rupert. 'A Tentative Chronology of Marlowe's and Some Other Elizabethan Plays.' *PMLA* 51 (1936): 643–88.

Theocritus. *The Poems and the Fragments. The Greek Bucolic Poets*. Trans. J. M. Edmonds. Loeb Classical Library. Cambridge, MA: Harvard UP; London: Heinemann, 1928.

Thomas, Vivien, and William Tydeman, eds. *Christopher Marlowe: The Plays and Their Sources*. London: Routledge, 1994.

Thomas, Keith. *Religion and the Decline of Magic*. New York: Scribner's, 1971.

Thomas, R.F. 'Virgil's *Georgics* and the Art of Reference.' *HSCP* 90 (1986): 171–98.

Thomson, Peter. *Shakespeare's Professional Career*. Cambridge: Cambridge UP, 1992.

Thurn, David H. 'Sights of Power in *Tamburlaine*.' *English Literary Renaissance* 19 (1989): 3–21.

- 'Sovereignty, Disorder, and Fetishism in Marlowe's *Edward II*.' *Renaissance Quarterly* 21 (1990): 115–41.

Toohey, Peter. *Reading Epic*. London: Routledge, 1992.

Traci, Philip J. 'Marlowe's Faustus as Artist: A Suggestion about a Theme in the Play.' *Renaissance Papers* (1967): 3–9.

Tucker, Kenneth. 'Dead Men in Deptford: Recent Lives and Deaths of Christopher Marlowe.' *Research Opportunities in Renaissance Drama* 34 (1995): 111–24.

Turbervile, George, trans. *Ovid: Heroical epsitles*. London, 1569.

Turner, Myron. 'Pastoral and Hermaphrodite: A Study in the Naturalism of Marlowe's *Hero and Leander*.' *Texas Studies in Language and Literature* 17 (1975): 397–414.

Turner, W. Craig. 'Love and the Queen of Carthage: A Look at Marlowe's *Dido*.' *Essays in Literature* 11 (1984): 3–9.

Tuve, Rosemond. *Elizabethan and Metaphysical Imagery: Renaissance Poetic and Twentieth-Century Critics*. Chicago: U of Chicago P, 1947.

Tyler, Sharon. 'Bedfellows Make Strange Politics: Christopher Marlowe's *Edward II*.' *Drama, Sex and Politics*. Ed. James Redmond. Cambridge: Cambridge UP, 1985. 55–68.

Underdowne, Thomas, trans. *Ovid his Invective against Ibis*. London, 1577.

Urry, William. *Christopher Marlowe and Canterbury*. Ed. Andrew Butcher. London: Faber, 1988.

Van Fossen, Richard W., ed. *Christopher Marlowe: 'The Jew of Malta'*. Lincoln: U of Nebraska P, 1964.

Vessey, D.W.T. 'Elegy Eternal: Ovid, *Amores*, 1.15.' *Latomus* 40 (1969): 80–97.

Vickers, Nancy J. 'Diana Described: Scattered Woman and Scattered Rhyme.' *Critical Inquiry* 8 (1981–2): 265–79.

Virgil. *The Pastoral Poems*. Trans. E.V. Rieu. 1949; Harmondsworth: Penguin, 1954.

- *Virgil*. Trans. H. Rushton Fairclough. 2 vols. Cambridge, MA: Harvard UP; London: Heinemann, 1935.

Viswanathan, S. 'King Edward II's "Two Bodies": A Perspective on Marlowe's Play.' *The Literary Criterion* 16 (1981): 76–93.

Voss, James. '*Edward II*: Marlowe's Historical Tragedy.' *English Studies* 63 (1982): 517–30.

Waddington, Raymond B. 'Chapman, George.' *The Spenser Encyclopedia*. 139–40.

- *The Mind's Empire: Myth and Form in George Chapman's Narrative Poems*. Baltimore: Johns Hopkins UP, 1974.

Waith, Eugene M. '*Edward II*: The Shadow of Action.' *Tulane Drama Review* 8 (1964): 59–76.

– *The Herculean Hero in Marlowe, Chapman, Shakespeare and Dryden.* New York: Columbia UP, 1962.

Waldman, Louis. 'Spenser's Pseudonym "E.K." and Humanist Self-Naming.' *Spenser Studies: A Renaissance Poetry Annual* 9 (1991): 21–31.

Walker, D.P. *Spiritual and Demonic Magic: From Ficino to Campanella.* 1958; Notre Dame: U of Notre Dame P, 1975.

Walsh, William P. 'Sexual Discovery and Renaissance Morality in Marlowe's *Hero and Leander.' Studies in English Literature, 1500–1900* 12 (1972): 33–54.

Warren, Roger. 'Trembling Aspen Leaves in *Titus Andronicus* and Golding's Ovid.' *Notes and Queries* 227 (1982): 112.

Waswo, Richard. 'Damnation, Protestant Style: Macbeth, Faustus, and Christian Tragedy.' *Journal of Medieval and Renaissance Studies* 4 (1974): 63–99.

Watkins, John. *The Specter of Dido: Spenser and Virgilian Epic.* New Haven: Yale UP, 1995.

Watkins, W.B.C. 'The Plagiarist: Spenser or Marlowe?' *ELH* 11 (1944): 249–65.

Watt, Ian. *Myths of Modern Individualism: Faust, Don Quixote, Don Juan, Robinson Crusoe.* Cambridge: Cambridge UP, 1996.

Webb, Wm. Stanford. 'Vergil in Spenser's Epic Theory.' *Critical Essays on Spenser from 'ELH.'* Baltimore: Johns Hopkins UP, 1970. 1–23. Orig. pub. *ELH* 4 (1937): 62–84.

Weil, Judith. *Christopher Marlowe: Merlin's Prophet.* Cambridge: Cambridge UP, 1977.

Wells, William, ed. *Spenser Allusions in the Sixteenth and Seventeenth Centuries.* Studies in Philology 68. Durham: U of North Carolina P, 1971.

West, David, and Tony Woodman, eds. *Creative Imitation and Latin Literature.* Cambridge: Cambridge UP, 1979.

West, Robert H. 'The Impatient Magic of Dr. Faustus.' *English Literary Renaissance* 4 (1974): 218–40.

Wilkinson, L. P. *Ovid Recalled.* Cambridge: Cambridge UP, 1955.

Williams, Gordon. *Tradition and Originality in Roman Poetry.* Oxford: Clarendon, 1968.

Williams, Kathleen. *Spenser's World of Glass: A Reading of 'The Faerie Queene.'* Berkeley: U of California P, 1966.

Williams, Martin T. 'The Temptations in Marlowe's *Hero and Leander.' Modern Language Quarterly* 16 (1955): 226–31.

Wills, Mary W. 'Marlowe's Role in Borrowed Lines.' *PMLA* 52 (1937): 902–5.

Wilson, F.P. '*The Massacre at Paris* and *Edward II.' Marlowe,* ed. Leech. 128–37.

Wilson, Richard. 'Visible Bullets: Tamburlaine the Great and Ivan the Terrible.' *ELH* 62 (1995): 47–68.

Wise, Valerie Merriam. 'Flight Myths in Ovid's *Metamorphoses*: An Interpretation of Phaethon and Daedalus.' *Ramus* 6 (1977): 44–59.

Woods, Susanne. 'Elective Poetics and Milton's Prose: *A Treatise of Civil Power* and *Considerations Touching the Likeliest Means to Remove Hirelings Out of the Church*.' *Politics, Poetics, and Hermeneutics in Milton's Prose.* Ed. David Loewenstein and James Grantham Turner. Cambridge: Cambridge UP, 1990. 193–211.

– 'Freedom and Tyranny in Sidney's *Arcadia*.' *Sir Philip Sidney's Achievements.* Ed. M.J.B. Allen, Dominic Baker-Smith, Arthur F. Kinney, with Margeret M. Sullivan. New York: AMS, 1990. 165–75.

– '"The Passionate Shepherd" and "The Nimphs Reply": A Study of Transmission.' *Huntington Library Quarterly* 34 (1970): 25–33.

Wraight, A.D., and Virginia F. Stern. *In Search of Christopher Marlowe: A Pictorial Biography.* 1965; Chichester, Sussex, England: Hart, 1993.

Yates, Frances A. *Giordano Bruno and the Hermetic Tradition.* 1964; New York: Random–Vintage, 1969.

– *The Occult Philosophy in the Elizabethan Age.* London: Routledge, 1979.

Zitner, S.P. 'Gosson, Ovid, and the Elizabethan Audience.' *Shakespeare Quarterly* 9 (1958): 206–8.

Zocca, Louis R. 'Marlowe and His Imitators.' *Elizabethan Narrative Poetry.* New Brunswick: Rutgers UP, 1950. 232–47.

Zucker, David Hard. 'Images of Royal Richness and Private Pleasure.' *Marlowe*, ed. Brown. 168–77.

Zundar, William. *Elizabethan Marlowe: Writing and Culture in the English Renaissance.* Cottingham, Hull, England: Unity, 1994.

Index